The Origins of the World War
BEFORE SARAJEVO

SIDNEY BRADSHAW FAY

BEFORE SARAJEVO

The Origins

of the

World War

VOLUME I

Second Edition, Revised

THE FREE PRESS, *New York*
COLLIER-MACMILLAN LIMITED, *London*

INTRODUCTION TO THE
PAPERBACK EDITION

TODAY, looking back on more than half a century of study, I am more than ever impressed by the tremendous impact the World War of 1914–18 has had upon world developments of the next fifty years. The war ushered in a period of international political and social change unequaled in history. At the same time enormous innovations in electronic and genetic sciences occurred and the speed of transportation was enormously increased with the use of the automobile and the airplane.

The World War also opened a new age of violence that contrasted greatly with the era of comparative peace that had preceded it. In this earlier period, from 1815 to 1914, peace generally prevailed in Europe except for some "local" wars that were fought with traditional weapons, were comparatively short-lived, and wreaked small destruction. Most of Asia and of Africa were still tolerably quiescent under the colonialism imposed by European imperialist powers. Diplomatic relations were strictly secret and were conducted unhurriedly by trained officials who kept in touch with their home governments by means of couriers and coded letters rather than by telegraph. After 1914, however, the "little" wars exploded into global conflicts that raged for several years and were fought with new weapons like submarines, tanks and air missiles that caused terrific losses of life and property. At the same time, in Asia and Africa, the yellow and dark-skinned populations, no longer quiescent, began a struggle to end all European colonial domination and to establish their own independence and power. In the conduct of international relations the wisdom and caution of experienced ambassadors was often undermined by special envoys who lacked sufficient international knowledge and by the increasing tendency of top authorities to make statements by radio to the whole world, thereby disturbing the secrecy of diplomatic negotiations.

During the turbulent half-century that began in 1914, the causes of the war and the responsibility for its outbreak have remained problems of high historical interest and of deep political importance. The subject has given rise to a great mass of controversial literature, which may be said to fall into three periods in each of which the scope and value of the work was more or less dependent on the evidence available to the writers.

In the first period, 1914–19, persons writing on the immediate causes of the war were largely dependent on *apologiae* made by men who had held responsible political positions at the outbreak of war, and on the so-called "color books," small and highly selective collections of diplomatic documents that were issued by each of the principal governments involved. These writings were intended to prove the wisdom and honesty of the conduct of each and throw on others the blame for starting the war. Much of this literature of the first period was also badly warped by wartime hatred, prejudice, and political propaganda. The assertions put forth by writers on the side of the ultimate victors were summed up by the Versailles Treaty, which implied that the war was caused solely by the aggression of Germany and her allies.

The second period, 1920–30, was notable for the publication of astonishingly full and reliable collections of diplomatic documents relating both to the crisis of July 1914 and to the events of the preceding forty years. The unprecedented and extensive public revelation of secrets from the archives was begun by the German Republic. Other governments soon followed her example. The German and French collections each eventually comprised some forty volumes and dealt with international relations as far back as the Franco-Prussian War.

After long and careful study of as much of this valuable material as had already appeared in print, I published in

1928 the present two-volume work, *The Origins of the World War*. The first volume is devoted to the underlying causes of the war during several decades, and the second volume to the hectic diplomatic crisis which precipitated its outbreak in 1914. I tried to maintain as fairminded and scholarly attitude of mind as possible, leaving aside earlier controversial literature and basing my account entirely on the new documentary evidence. The result was highly gratifying. Reviewers generally praised it as an important and interesting historical survey of the much-disputed question of responsibility for the war. It consequently had a large sale and was published in German, French, and Russian translations. A noted Soviet historian (V. Chvostov in *Istorik Marksist*, Vol. 18–19, 209–216, 1930) castigated me as a decadent bourgeois historian, probably paid by Wall Street, who completely failed to understand that the true cause of the war was "finance capitalism." To prove his point he quoted parallel passages from Lenin's writings and from my book, but he concluded his long review more favorably, saying that it was the best book in any language, that it ought to be used in all Russian schools and universities. The Soviet government printed an edition of 50,000 copies.

I published a revised two-volume-in-one edition of my book in 1930. This edition took note of the documentary and other material that had appeared since the first edition two years earlier.

During the third period, since 1930, the French and the British have completed their invaluable documentary collections, the Russians have extended theirs, the Austrians have published nine volumes of diplomatic material for the years 1908 to 1914, and the Italians have issued the first volume of a series. The total amount of this new evidence revealed since 1930 is perhaps equal to that of the preceding period, but its fresh importance to the historian is much less. That is to say, it has added relatively little to the account which I gave in my revised edition of 1930 or which Professor Bernadotte E. Schmitt gave in his valuable two-volume work, *The Coming of the War, 1914* also published in 1930.

His work is more severe in its judgment of Germany than mine, and it deals mainly with the outbreak of the war in 1914, rather than with the earlier underlying causes. But the general picture that emerges from both books is not likely to be much modified by later archival revelations, biographies or monographs, though some minute details may be added to the picture and obscure points may be clarified.

The intense scholarly and popular interest in the causes of war in 1914 naturally abated somewhat as attention became absorbed in the second war. But during the past decade it appears to have revived, judging from the increased sales of my book and the publication of many new ones on the subject. Two of these are notable. Luigi Albertini, *The Origins of the War of 1914* (London, 1952–57), translated from the Italian, deals mainly with the immediate origins and is the most detailed and probably the most authoritative account so far written, but its three large volumes, averaging nearly 700 pages each, are somewhat repetitious and sometimes prejudiced. Fritz Fisher, *Griff nach der Weltmacht* (Hamburg, 1961), deals severely with Germany and tends to assume that Germany's undoubted annexationist policies after war broke out are evidence of her policies prior to the war.

It had been my intention eventually to completely rework my revised edition of 1930. This would have enabled me to cut out passages in which I had expatiated at length to establish certain views that have been generally accepted by historians and no longer need such explanation. Such, for instance, is the chapter on the Potsdam Council in which I definitely demolished the widely accepted myth that the Kaiser had deliberately plotted the war at a meeting with his top officials at Potsdam. The space thus saved I hoped to use for a fuller discussion of such causes as economic factors, the influence of the press, the psychology of certain officials, and, of course, the inclusion of the results of new documentary revelations and the researches of other historical scholars. But the press of other work caused me to postpone this intended revision until declining eyesight made it impossible.

Therefore, when The Free Press proposed reprinting the 1930 edition as a paperback, I readily assented. The edition is fairly broad in outlook, surveying mounting international frictions many years before the war, and describes in detail the fatal diplomatic crisis of 1914. Yet it is so condensed that the whole account is not unduly long. It is based on strictly contemporary evidence, is as rigidly objective as possible, and avoids polemics and lengthy disputes about "guilt" and responsibility for the war. On the basis of such new light as has appeared since 1930, historians no doubt will long continue to differ as to the exact effect of this or that action and as to the precise responsibility of each nation in causing the war. My book, I hope, will prove a convenient spring-board for a deeper plunge into the controversies.

SIDNEY B. FAY

Cambridge, Mass.
1966

PREFACE TO THE SECOND EDITION
REVISED

Since the publication of the first edition nearly two years ago, the stream of new documentary material on the origins of the war has continued to flow very freely. Dr. G. P. Gooch and Professor H. W. Temperley have pushed forward with energy their admirable collection of *British Documents,* so that the sixth volume carries the story of Anglo-German relations through the failure of the Haldane Mission in 1912. Austrian scholars took everyone by surprise last Christmas by presenting the world with eight closely packed volumes on *Oesterreich-Ungarns Aussenpolitik,* containing nearly 12,000 documents from their archives covering the years 1908 to 1914. This collection runs parallel to the German *Die Grosse Politik,* and is of especial value for the additional light that it throws on Balkan problems in general and on Austro-Serbian relations in particular. The French Government has published three initial volumes of *Documents Diplomatiques Français,* a monumental series which will eventually illuminate French foreign policy from 1871 to 1914 in the same detail as has been done for German policy in the same period by *Die Grosse Politik.*

In addition to these official publications there have also appeared many valuable private publications containing important new documents or based on unpublished first-hand material. Dr. Bogitchevitch's unofficial collection, *Die Auswärtige Politik Serbiens 1903-1914,* partly compensates for the Serbian Government's persistent failure to follow the example of other states in disclosing fully and

x

frankly their secret pre-war archives. Interesting light on leading English personalities and their psychology is contained in charming biographies, like Lord Newton's *Lord Lansdowne*, Mr. Harold Nicolson's *Lord Carnock* (better known as Sir Arthur Nicolson), and in Lord Morley's remarkable *Memorandum on Resignation*. In *La Politique Russe d'avant Guerre* Baron Taube has stated in no uncertain terms what he knew of Izvolski and certain episodes in Russia's pre-war policy. The present writer has also been privileged to read the advance pages of the first volume of Professor B. E. Schmitt's scholarly and detailed forthcoming work, *The Coming of the War, 1914*.

These and many other recent publications of source material, as well as innumerable secondary monographic studies, can usefully be drawn upon to add an infinite amount of new detail to the story of the main outline of the origins of the war which I have tried to give within the compass of two volumes. But I do not find that they so essentially modify the chief thread of my narrative or my general conclusions that it is necessary in a revised edition to recast the whole form of the book. I have therefore mainly confined the revision to rewriting several passages, to calling attention in the footnotes to important new material, and to adding a few supplementary notes at the end of the first volume. This has made possible the retention of the paging of the first edition, which it is hoped will be a convenience to students. Many of these revisions have already been made in the German and French editions.

SIDNEY B. FAY

Harvard University,
June 28, 1930

PREFACE

WHEN the World War suddenly set Europe aflame and American public opinion, soon under the influence of propaganda and war prejudice, began to denounce Germany and the Kaiser as being guilty of causing it, the present writer refused to join in the chorus. His historical sense told him that in this present case, as in the past, no one country or no one man was solely, or probably even mainly, to blame. A little study of the documents in the Blue, Yellow and Orange Books which were early issued by the English, French and Russian Governments quickly convinced him that these documentary publications were by no means so complete and reliable (though more so than the White and Red Books, issued by Germany and Austria) that one could safely base sound and final conclusions upon them, as seemed to be believed by the millions of men and women who read such facile and superficial arguments as those of Mr. James M. Beck, and others who followed his cue. Therefore the present writer during the War remained silent, except for his discussions of the subject in college class rooms.

When, however, the new socialist governments of Germany and Austria published in 1919 a very complete collection of documents from the secret archives relating to the diplomatic crisis of July, 1914, this seemed to provide material for reaching at last some tentative opinion about the immediate causes of the War. These the present writer ventured to express in "New Light on the Origins of the War" published in the American Historical Review in

1920-1921. This called to the attention of scholars in this country the desirability of reconsidering opinions formed during the heat of the battle as to the immediate responsibility of causing it. With the publication of more documents, especially from the Russian sources, and with the refusal of the French and British Governments to issue any such convincingly complete documentary record of their conduct in July, 1914, there soon arose a group of writers who demanded a "revision" of that clause in the Treaty of Versailles declaring that Germany and her allies were solely responsible. With some of these writers— especially with some of the anti-Poincaré revisionists in France—the pendulum of opinion has been in danger of swinging nearly as far away from the golden mean of historical truth as in the case of those who formerly followed in the propagandist path of Mr. Beck.

The present writer is no more inclined to accept the arguments of the former than of the latter. In the pages which follow he has no political motive, either to justify the Treaty of Versailles or to demand its revision but simply to carry out what a great master has defined as the proper task of the historian—to tell how it really came about. He has written, he hopes, *sine ira ac studio*. If he has made infrequent citations from the mass of controversial literature which has grown up in regard to the origin of the war, this is not because he has not read a very considerable part of it, but because he wishes to avoid controversy and reach his conclusions as far as possible from documentary evidence. The mass of documentary and autobiographical material is now so great that it affords either of two possibilities. On the one hand, a writer by centering attention on the acts of any one man or country, and by picking out passages in the documents to support his contention, can easily make a seemingly convincing argument for the uninitiated, that this or that man or country was altogether angelic or devilish in motives and methods. On the other hand, a writer may conscientiously try to look fairly at all sides of the question, explain acts from the point of view of the actors themselves instead of from that of their champions or enemies, and try to reach an unbiassed judgment. Needless to say it is the latter possibility which is attempted in the present volume. With what success, the reader must judge.

In the troublesome matter of transliterating Slavic proper names the best practice of American libraries has been followed, so far as is possible, without the use of diacritical marks. But in the case of some Russian names of German origin, like Schilling for Shilling, and in a few Serbo-Croat names, such as Princip for Printsip, popular usage has been allowed to prevail over proper practice.

Quotations from the documents and foreign works are usually made from direct translations from the original, rather than from translations into English which have been made by others. This is because the latter are sometimes abridged, or because the present writer made his translation prior to the publication of other translations, or because he prefers his own rendering to that of others. If the quotations from the documents are often tediously long, it is because he wishes to avoid as far as possible picking out phrases or sentences which might give a *suggestio falsi* or *suppressio veri*. In some cases, for the sake of brevity, prolix phrases and titles have been curtailed or omitted; "Austria," for instance, has been commonly used in place of "Austria-Hungary."

No formal bibliography is included in these volumes, because reference to all the more important recent literature of the subject has been made either in the List of Abbreviations, in the text, or in the numerous bibliographical footnotes in connection with each topic in the text; most of those which contain several titles are cited in the Index under "Bibliography."

Among the various bibliographies which include references to the less recent literature, the most helpful are the following: G. W. Prothero, *Subject Index of the Books relating to the European War, 1914-1918, acquired by the British Museum, 1914-1920* (London, 1922); A. von Wegerer, *Literatur zur Kriegsschuldfrage* (Berlin, 1923, new ed., 1926); J. L. Kunz, *Bibliographie der Kriegsliteratur* (Berlin, 1920); *Die Kriegsschuldfrage: Ein Verzeichnis der Literatur des In- und Auslandes*, hrsg. *vom Börsenverein der Deutschen Buchhändler* (Leipzig, 1925); A. Lumbroso, *Bibliografia ragionata della guerra delle nazioni* (Roma, 1920); H. H. B. Meyer, *Check List of the Literature and Other Material in the Library of Congress on the European War* (Washington, 1918); and the valuable *Catalogues Méthodiques* (Paris, 1921 ff.), issued by the *Bibliothèque et Musée de la Guerre*, and edited by J. Dubois, C. Appuhn, C. Bloch, and others.

For keeping abreast with current literature on the origins of the War there are two excellent periodicals largely devoted to the subject: *Die Kriegsschuldfrage*, edited by A. von Wegerer (Berlin, 1923 ff.); and *Revue d'Histoire de la Guerre Mondiale* (Paris, 1923 ff.). Articles, critical reviews, and titles of new books may be found in the various historical and political journals, such as the *American Historical Review, English Historial Review, Slavonic Review, Historische Zeitschrift, Revue Historique, Krasnyi Arkhiv, Foreign Affairs*, the New York Times *Current History, Political Science Quarterly, European Economic and Political Survey, Archiv für Politik und Geschichte, Europäische Gespräche, L'Europe Nouvelle, Evolution*, the *Bulletin of the Central Commission for Neutral Investigation of the Causes of the World War*, and many others.

To those who have kindly permitted the reproduction of

many of the illustrations the writer wishes to express his gratitude—to Mr. Hamilton Fish Armstrong for the portrait of M. Pashitch and the facsimile of the Austrian Declaration of War; to Mr. R. H. Lutz of the Hoover War Library for the Minutes of the Russian Council of Ministers; to the editors of *Current History* for the portraits of MM. Sazonov and Sukhomlinov; to the Frederick A. Stokes Company for the portraits of MM. Benckendorff, Cambon, Metternich, and Lichnowsky, which appeared in Viscount Grey's *Twenty-Five Years;* and to Herr A. von Wegerer for several of the German and Austrian portraits and for the material for the maps which appeared in *Die Kriegsschuldfrage.*

Finally, the author takes pleasure in acknowledging his indebtedness to Professor J. F. Jameson and the late Professor Coolidge, who first encouraged him to undertake this study; to Professor B. E. Schmitt, who read parts of the manuscript; and to Professors W. L. Langer and L. B. Packard, who read the proofs. But they are in no way responsible for the errors or the views expressed.

S. B. F.

July 28, 1928.
Northampton, Mass.

ABBREVIATIONS

Citations from collections in which the documents antedate July, 1914 (like "Affaires Balkaniques," "G.P.," "Siebert-Schreiner," and "Stieve") are by *volume and page*, because the documents are often long despatches extending over many pages, and a page reference is therefore more precise. But documents of July, 1914 (like those in "A.R.B.," "B.D.," etc.) are mostly short telegrams, and are cited by *serial number* of the publication in which they appear.

Affaires Balkaniques: Ministère des Affaires Étrangères, Les Affaires Balkaniques, 1912-1914, 3 vols., Paris, 1922.

A.R.B.: [Austrian Red Book of 1919] Diplomatische Aktenstücke zur Vorgeschichte des Krieges, 1914, 3 vols., Wien, 1919. (Eng. trans., 1920.)

B.B.B.: [British Blue Book] Great Britain and the European Crisis, Correspondence, and Statements in Parliament, together with an Introductory Narrative of Events. London, 1914. (Cd. 7467).

B.D.: British Documents on the Origins of the War, 1898-1914. Edited by G. P. Gooch and Harold Temperley. Vols. I-VI, XI. London, 1926-1930. (Vol. XI, Foreign Office Documents, June 28th-August 4th, 1914, cited merely as "B.D." and by serial number).

Bogitchevitch: M. Boghitschewitsch, Kriegsursachen. Zurich, 1919. (Eng. trans., 1919; 2nd ed. in French, 1925.)

Bourgeois et Pagès: E. Bourgeois et G. Pagès, Les Origines et les Responsabilités de la Grande Guerre. Paris, 1921.

Brandenburg: E. Brandenburg, Von Bismarck zum Welkriege, Berlin, 1924. (Eng. trans. of 2nd ed., 1927.)

Conrad: Feldmarschall Conrad von Hötzendorf, Aus meiner Dienstzeit. 5 vols., Wien, 1921-25.

D.D.F.: Ministère des Affaires Étrangères, Documents Diplomatiques Français, 1871-1914. Paris, 1929 ff.

Deutschland Schuldig?: Deutsches Weissbuch über die Verantwortlichkeit der Urheber des Krieges. 3rd ed., Berlin, 1919. (Eng. trans., 1924.)

Dirr: Dr. P. Dirr, Bayerische Dokumente zum Kriegsausbruch und zum Versailler Schuldspruch. Dritte erweiterte Auflage. Munich and Berlin, 1925.

Dobrorolski: S. Dobrorolski, Die Mobilmachung der russischen Armee, 1914. Berlin, 1921.

Frantz: Gunther Frantz, Russlands Eintritt in den Weltkrieg. Berlin, 1924.

F.Y.B.: [French Yellow Book] Ministère des Affaires Étrangères, La Guerre Européenne, 1914. Paris, 1914.

Gooss: Dr. Roderich Gooss, Das Wiener Kabinette und die Entstehung des Weltkrieges, Wien, 1919.

G.P.: Die Grosse Politik der Europäischen Kabinette 1871-1914, Sammlung der Akten des Deutschen Auswärtigen Amts, 40 vols. Berlin, 1922-27.

Grey: Viscount Grey of Fallodon, Twenty-five Years, 1892-1916, 2 vols. New York, 1925.

Investigating Commission: Die Deutsch Nationalversammlung: Beilagen. . . . über die Oeffentliche Verhandlungen des [ersten] Untersuchungsausschusses; Heft I, Zur Vorgeschichte des Weltkrieges; Heft II, Militärische Rüstungen und Mobilmachungen. Berlin, 1920-21 (Eng. trans. of Heft I, 1923.)

Jevtitch: B. Jevtitch, Sarajevski Atentat. Sarajevo, 1922.

K.A.: Kasnyi Arkhiv, 34 vols. Moskva, 1923-30.

K.D.: [Kautsky Documents] Die deutschen Dokumente zum Kriegsausbruch, edited by Karl Kautsky, Graf Max Montgelas and Prof. Walter Schücking, 4 vols. Berlin, 1919; new enlarged edition, 1927. (Eng. trans., 1924.)

KSF.: Die Kriegsschuldfrage: Berliner Monatshefte für internationale Aufklärung, hrsg. von der Zentralstelle für Erforschung der Kriegsursachen; ed. by Alfred von Wegerer. 8 vols. Berlin, 1923 ff.

L.N.: Un Livre Noir: Diplomatie d'avant-Guerre d'après les Documents des Archives Russes, 1910-1914, ed. R. Marchand, 2 vols. Paris, 1922-23.

Montgelas, Leitfaden: Graf Max Montgelas, Leitfaden zur Kriegsschuldfrage, Berlin and Leipzig, 1923. (Eng. trans., 1925.)

M.F.R.: [Materials for the History of Franco-Russian Relations] Materialy po Istorii Franko-Russkikh Otnoshenii za 1910-1914. Moskva, 1922.

Nicolson: Harold Nicolson, Sir Arthur Nicolson, Bart., First Lord Carnock. London, 1930.

Oe.-U.A.: Oesterreich-Ungarns Aussenpolitik von der Bosnischen Krise 1908 bis zum Kriegsausbruch 1914. Edited by L. Bittner, A. F. Pribram, H. Srbik and H. Uebersberger. 9 vols. Vienna and Leipzig, 1930.

Paléologue: M. Paléologue, La Russie des Tsars pendant la Grande Guerre, 3 vols. Paris, 1922. (Eng. trans., 1924-1925.)

Pharos: Professor Pharos [pseud.], Der Prozess gegen die Attentäter von Sarajewo. Berlin, 1918.

Poincaré: R. Poincaré, Au Service de la France, 5 vols. Paris, 1926-28. (Abridged Eng. trans., 1927 f).

Pribram: A. F. Pribram, Die politischen Geheimverträge Oesterreich-Ungarns 1879-1914. Wien, 1920. (Eng. trans., 1920.)

Renouvin: P. Renouvin, Les Origines Immédiates de la Guerre. 2nd ed. Paris, 1927. (Eng. trans., 1928.)

R.O.B.: [Russian Orange Book] Ministère des Affaires Étrangères: Recueil des Documents Diplomatiques, Négociations ayant précédé la Guerre, 10/23 Juillet-24 Juillet/6 Aout 1914. Petrograde, 1914.

Romberg: G. von Romberg, Falsifications of the Russian Orange Book. New York, 1923.

Schilling's Diary: How the War Began in 1914: Being the Diary of the Russian Foreign Office . . . of July, 1914; translated from the original Russian by Major W. Cyprian Bridge. London, 1925.

Schwertfeger: Zur Europäischen Politik: Unveröffentlichte [Belgische] Dokumente, herausgegeben unter Leitung von Bernhard Schwertfeger, 5 vols. Berlin, 1919; 2nd ed., 6 vols., 1925.

Seton-Watson: R. W. Seton-Watson, Sarajevo: A study in the Origins of the Great War. London, 1925.

Siebert-Schreiner: G. A. Schreiner, Entente Diplomacy and the World. New York, 1921. (Eng. trans., re-arranged with annotations of Diplomatische Akten-stücke zur Geschichte der Ententepolitik der Vor-kriegsjahre, hrsg. B. von Siebert. Berlin and Leipzig, 1921. New enlarged ed., 3 vols. Berlin and Leipzig, 1928.)

S.B.B.: [Serbian Blue Book] Les Pourparlers Diplo-matiques 16/29 Juin-3/16 Aout. Paris, 1914.

Stieve: F. Stieve, Der Diplomatische Schriftwechsel Is-wolskis, 1911-1914, 4 vols. Berlin, 1924.

Taube: Baron M. de Taube, La Politique Russe d'Avant-Guerre et la Fin de l'Empire des Tsars, 1904-1917. Paris, 1928. (Enlarged German edition, Berlin, 1929.)

CONTENTS

CHAPTER I

INTRODUCTION:
IMMEDIATE AND UNDERLYING CAUSES

THE Greek historian Thucydides, in his history of that catastrophe to ancient civilization when Spartan militarism triumphed over Athenian democracy, makes the distinction between the more remote or underlying, and the immediate, causes of war. It is the distinction between the gradual accumulation of inflammable material which has been heaped up through a long period of years and the final spark which starts the conflagration. The distinction is a good one. It is equally applicable to the World War. Failure to observe it has often led to confusion of thought in regard to responsibility for the War, since responsibility for the underlying causes does not always coincide with responsibility for the immediate causes. One country may for years have been much to blame for creating a general situation dangerous to peace, but may have had relatively little to do with the final outbreak of war—or *vice versa*.

The question of the causes of the War may be said to have passed through three phases during the past dozen years, each phase being determined to some extent by the material available for judging the question. During the first two phases the discussion centered largely around the question of the immediate causes, that is, the rapid train of events from the assassination of the Austrian Archduke at Sarajevo on June 28, to the outbreak of war between Germany and England on August 4. In the third phase,

1

however, scholars have begun to explore more fully and justly the remoter causes of the War. In each of these phases there has been a change in the angle from which the question has been approached. At first, during the War, writers sought to fix the "guilt" for having caused this un- paralleled "crime" upon a few single individuals—chiefly the Kaiser, the Pan-Germanists, and the Austrian and German militarists. Then, with the publication of more complete documents which began in 1919, it was seen that the Entente thesis of the sole responsibility of Germany and her allies was no longer tenable, and writers who de- manded a "revision" of the Treaty of Versailles tended to go to the other extreme of fixing the "guilt" upon Entente leaders—MM. Izvolski, Poincaré, Sazonov, and even upon Sir Edward Grey. Finally, with the growing realization that all the Powers were more or less responsible, and with the increased attention which came to be given to the under- lying causes of the War, more judiciously and historically minded persons were less inclined to accept the easy solution of explaining the War on the scapegoat or personal devil theory—that is, of the "guilt" of this or that individual.[1] They fell back on the truer explanation that the War was caused by the system of international anarchy involved in alliances, armaments, and secret diplomacy.[2]   But, after all, the "system" was worked by individuals; their personal acts built it up and caused it to explode in 1914.   In the discussion of the future, it will be the work of the historian to explain the political, economic, and psychological mo- tives which caused these individuals to act as they did. He will also cease to talk about "war guilt," since no person in authority was guilty of deliberately working to bring about

[1] *Cf.* M. H. Cochran, "New Phase of War Guilt Controversy," in *Current History*, XXVI, 71-76, April, 1927.

[2] Mr. G. Lowes Dickinson gives a scholarly, effective, and charmingly written exposition of this view: *The International Anarchy, 1904-1914,* London, 1926.

a general European War. But he will still continue to discuss the "responsibility" which each statesman must bear for acts which ultimately contributed to the catastrophe.[3] For this reason the present writer has always preferred the term "war responsibility" to "war guilt." The German phrase, *Kriegsschuldfrage,* is open to either interpretation.

Let us now look briefly at the various phases through which the discussion has passed, as determined to some extent by the material upon which it has been based.

1. THE DISCUSSION OF "RESPONSIBILITY," 1914-1919

During the War and the Versailles Peace Conference, the discussion concerning responsibility for the immediate outbreak of the War, so far as it rested on anything more than national prejudice, war hatred, and deliberate propagandist misrepresentation, was based on the public statements of leading officials, and on the collections of diplomatic documents published by each government soon after July, 1914. The first of these was the "Preliminary Memoir and Documents Concerning the Outbreak of War," commonly known as the *German White Book*. It was laid before the Reichstag on August 3, having been, in the words of the German Chancellor, "put together under the pressure of overwhelming events." Its purpose was to prove to the German people that Germany was fighting a war of self-defense against Russian aggression. It was a plausible statement. It was supported by 27 telegrams and letters which were neatly fitted into the argument, but were not given in their proper chronological sequence. To the German people, to whom the book was primarily addressed, the argument was

---

[3] *Cf.* G. P. Gooch, *Recent Revelations of European Diplomacy* (London, 1927), pp. 206-214. This volume, which he describes as "a *causerie,* not a bibliography", is an admirably fairminded and well informed summary review of some three hundred of the most important documentary publications and other first-hand material appearing since the outbreak of the War and dealing with the period 1890-1919.

convincing. They went through the War, honestly believing that they were fighting a war of self-defense forced upon them by Russia. Outside of Germany, however, the *White Book* made the worst possible impression. It was quickly noted that among the 27 telegrams there was not a single despatch between Berlin and Vienna; and yet everyone knew that during the July crisis there must have been a very active interchange of telegrams between the two Central Powers. Germany had asserted that she tried to exert pressure upon Austria to accept negotiations to preserve peace, but there was not a document in the *White Book* to prove the assertion. People naturally concluded that Germany did not dare to publish the truth. They distrusted the specious argument by which the German Chancellor persuaded the Reichstag to vote the war credits. In fact, the *White Book,* instead of convincing persons outside Germany of her innocence, had exactly the opposite effect. As we now know, however, the *German White Book* contained a great deal of truth, but not the whole truth. One reason for the inclusion of so few documents was the physical impossibility of printing within a few hours the great mass of telegrams which had been exchanged during the preceding weeks. Even could they have been published in time to be laid before the Reichstag, it would have been impossible to read and digest their contents in a short time. The Chancellor evidently had to make a selection, and he selected those few letters and telegrams which were of greatest significance and which supported his arguments. He also omitted so far as possible matters which would have offended England and France, with whom Germany was still at peace at the time the *White Book* was compiled —a fact often overlooked in judging it later.[4]

In contrast to the *German White Book* was the *British*

[4] *Cf.* A. Bach, "Das erste deutsche Weissbuch," in *Die Kriegsschuldfrage,* III, 768-776, Nov., 1925.

Blue Book, which was laid before Parliament on August 6, 1914. This contained 159 documents.[5] They were arranged in strict chronological order and left to tell their own story. Compared with the German publication, the British book seemed to be fairly complete, candid and convincing. At first sight it appeared that all documents of any importance were included. They gave the impression that Sir Edward Grey had striven honestly for the preservation of peace, but that he had been thwarted in his efforts by Germany's rejection of all peace proposals, and by Austria's precipitate action against Serbia. Outside Germany, therefore, a host of writers hastily jumped to the conclusion that Germany and Austria had deliberately plotted the War and were solely responsible for it. This conclusion was strengthened by the documentary publications put forth by the other Governments in the following months.

A *Russian Orange Book,* published August 7, with 79 documents emphasized Russia's efforts for peace. By falsification and suppression of documents (as we now know) it concealed the truth about Russia's mobilization and placed the war guilt on the Central Powers. In October, a *Belgian Gray Book,* with 79 numbers, gave the details of Germany's flagrant violation of international law in disregarding the neutrality of Belgium. The *Serbian Blue Book* of November 18, 1914, recounted in 52 documents what this little country had had to suffer at the hands of Austrian oppression. It gave no hint of Serbia's guilty responsibility for the Sarajevo assassination which has recently been revealed. On the contrary, it asserted Serbia's innocence and regret. It pointed out the criminal deceit by which the Austrian Government at first assured Europe of its moderation, then suddenly issued an ultimatum impos-

[5] Two other documents, Nos. 160 and 161, were added in a later edition. *Cf.,* B.D., pp. vi-xiii. Further bibliographical details concerning this, and the other documentary publications mentioned below, may be found in the list of abbreviations above.

sible of acceptance, and finally made a general conflagration inevitable by declaring war on Serbia.

Finally, on December 1, 1914, the French Government, after ample time for compiling a collection of documents, published its *Yellow Book*. This differed from the collections hitherto published in that it contained a selection of alleged telegrams dating back several months prior to the Archduke's murder. These set forth all Germany's bellicose tendencies and military preparations, and easily convinced readers, who had been hearing exaggerated stories of German atrocities in Belgium and France, that William II "had come to think that war with France was inevitable," and "believed in the crushing superiority of the German army and in its certain success." The rest of the *French Yellow Book,* like the *English Blue Book,* appeared to be a fairly complete, candid, and convincing set of documents chronologically arranged; they are full of suspicions of German and Austrian duplicity and warlike intentions, in contrast to assertions of French desire for peace, as evidenced, for instance, by the order for the withdrawal of French troops ten kilometres behind the frontier. It was not till many years later that it became evident that the *French Yellow Book* was neither so complete nor candid after all, since some important telegrams had been suppressed altogether and others had been altered.[6]

An *Austrian Red Book,* published on February 3, 1915, as a reply to the *Serbian Blue Book,* contained 69 documents, but the most important of these had already appeared in the daily press, and the remainder threw but little light on the secret relations between Berlin and Vienna in connection with Austria's ultimatum to Serbia and the

[6] The most complete and severe criticism of it is by G. Demartial, *L'Évangile du Quai D'Orsay,* Paris, 1926. The German edition, *Das französische Gelbbuch von 1914,* Berlin, 1926, prints conveniently such French documents as have been made public since 1914, and contains valuable footnotes on others.

failure of all peace proposals. The *Austrian Red Book* evidently had suppressed a large number of essential documents. By persons outside Austria and Germany, therefore, it was generally thought to be as unreliable and self-incriminatory as the *German White Book* itself.

As the life and death struggle of the nations went on from month to month and became ever more grim and bitter, war hatred, national prejudice, and poisonous propaganda wrought such devastating results that few persons cared, or were able, to study carefully and critically even such documentary evidence as was now at hand. Leading officials in all countries had made war speeches asserting the innocence of their own acts, and throwing the responsibility upon the enemy. The result was that, at the close of the War, a "Commission on the Responsibility of the Authors of the War," presided over by Mr. Lansing, solemnly reported to the Peace Conference:

> The War was premeditated by the Central Powers together with their allies, Turkey and Bulgaria, and was the result of acts deliberately committed in order to make it unavoidable. Germany, in agreement with Austria-Hungary, deliberately worked to defeat all the many conciliatory proposals made by the Entente Powers.

In the deliberations of this Commission, as one of its members, Mr. J. B. Scott, tardily recognized five years later, "Unfortunately no Germans were allowed to take part." A German delegation, to be sure, was officially allowed to present a *German White Book Concerning the Responsibility of the Authors of the War*,[7] drawn up by Professor Hans Delbrück, the well-known historian, Professor Mendelssohn-Bartholdy, Count Montgelas, and Dr. Max Weber.

[7] *Deutschland schuldig? Deutsches Weissbuch über die Verantwortlichkeit der Urheber des Krieges*, Berlin, 1919. (Eng. trans. published by the Carnegie Endowment for International Peace, 1924).

"It is an official document whose importance can neither be overlooked nor minimized," as Mr. Scott correctly observes in the English translation published by the Carnegie Endowment for International Peace in 1924. It contained valuable new evidence tending to prove that the accusation formulated by the Commission was historically incorrect, and morally unjustifiable. In spite of this, the Commission paid virtually no attention to it, and Germany was forced to accept the dictum of the victors in Article 231 of the Treaty of Versailles:

> The Allied and Associated Governments affirm, and Germany accepts, the responsibility of Germany and her allies for causing all the loss and damage to which the Allied and Associated Governments and their nationals have been subjected as a consequence of the war imposed upon them by the aggression of Germany and her allies.

2. THE DISCUSSION OF "RESPONSIBILITY" AFTER 1919

(a) New Documents on the Immediate Causes

A second phase of the question of the immediate causes of the War began with the publication of the *Kautsky Documents*. These, and other new documents and memoirs to be mentioned below, made it clear that Germany had not plotted or wanted a European war. Scholars in all countries gradually came to agree that, though Germany was responsible for having at first foolishly encouraged Austria to take action against Serbia, Germany supposed (wrongly, as it turned out) that the conflict could be "localized"; but when it began to appear that "localization" was doubtful and that Russia might intervene, Germany tried to restrain Austria and made genuine efforts to prevent the Austro-Serbian conflict from developing into a World War. What are these new documents and memoirs upon which this revised view rests?

The *Kautsky Documents,*[8] published in December, 1919, were a consequence of the German revolution at the close of the War. The new German republic made the veteran Socialist leader, Karl Kautsky, Assistant Secretary of State for Foreign Affairs. He was authorized to edit all the documents in the German Foreign Office which might throw light on the origins of the World War. He and his assistants carefully copied, arranged, and annotated a mass of papers in eighteen volumes in the archives containing the diplomatic correspondence during the July crisis of 1914. In contrast with the meager *German White Book* of 1914, with its 27 documents, the Kautsky publication comprises 1123 documents, of which 937 are given *in extenso* and the remainder in a sufficiently full summary. The letters and telegrams are arranged in strict chronological order, and allowed to speak for themselves. The editors have merely added convenient cross references, indexes, and data as to the exact day, hour and minute when each despatch was sent and received. This extraordinarily precise and unprecedentedly complete compilation, containing detailed information which was unfortunately lacking in documentary publications issued early in the War, now made it possible to determine with considerable nicety just how much a German official knew when he took any action. It enabled one for the first time to judge with knowledge and fairness of the motives, the honesty, and the ability of the men guiding the German ship of state in 1914. It laid the basis for the beginning of a scholarly study of the immediate responsibility for the War. It showed scholars that during the critical days before the War, Germany had made real efforts to avert it, but that she had been guilty of blunders

8 *Die deutschen Dokumente zum Kriegsausbruch*, ed. by Karl Kautsky, Graf Max Montgelas and Prof. Walter Schücking, 4 vols., Charlottenburg, 1919, new enlarged edition, 1927; Eng. ed., *Outbreak of the World War, German Documents Collected by Karl Kautsky*, New York, 1924 (Carnegie Endowment for International Peace).

and mistakes in judgment which contributed to set fire to the inflammable material heaped up in the course of years. It showed, moreover, that the notion that Germany had deliberately plotted the World War was a pure myth.

In Vienna, Dr. Roderich Gooss did for the Austrian Foreign Office what Kautsky had done for the German. In contrast with the 69 documents of the original *Austrian Red Book,* Dr. Gooss's three-volume *Austrian Red Book of 1919,*[9] contained 352 documents. They revealed the reckless diplomacy by which Austria dragged Germany into a World War which Austria did not want, but which she was willing to risk in her determination to put an end to the danger which menaced her from the side of Serbia.

In Moscow the Bolshevists had already taken advantage of their advent to power to publish in their newspaper, *Pravda,* in the winter of 1917-1918, a series of secret treaties and other papers which revealed the imperialist and militarist aims of the fallen Tsarist régime between 1881 and 1917.[10] To these the Soviet Government added in 1922 a massive and invaluable collection of *Materials for the History of Franco-Russian Relations from 1910 to 1914.* This contained, among other things, the complete exchange of telegrams between the Russian Foreign Office and the Russian Embassy in Paris between July 24 and August 2, 1914.[11] Baron von Romberg took this series of telegrams and printed them in conjunction with the telegrams between Paris and St. Petersburg which had appeared in the *Russian Orange Book* of 1914. By using red ink for the former and black ink for the latter, his *Falsifications of the Russian*

[9] *Diplomatische Aktenstücke zur Vorgeschichte des Krieges 1914: Ergänzungen und Nachträge zum Österreichisch-Ungarischen Rotbuch,* 3 vols., Vienna, 1919 (Eng. trans. 1920).

[10] Rearranged and translated, in *Dokumente aus den russischen Geheimarchiven soweit sie bis zum Juli 1918 eingegangen sind,* Berlin, 1918.

[11] *Materialy po Istorii Franko-Russkikh Otnoshenii za 1910-1914,* Moskva, 1922, pp. 513-526.

Orange Book [12] gave striking proof of the deceptions by which the Russian Government had sought in 1914 to hide its responsibility for the War. Not only had it completely suppressed half of the telegrams actually exchanged between Paris and St. Petersburg, including some of great importance, but, even in the telegrams which were published, important passages were omitted, and in some cases deliberately forged words were added. These Russian revelations began to shake the confidence of scholars in the completeness and reliability of the other Entente documentary publications which had been accepted outside the Central Powers as good evidence of Entente innocence and German guilt.

The incompleteness and unreliability of the Tsarist *Russian Orange Book* was further evidenced in 1922 by the publication in the Bolshevist historical journal, *Red Archives,* [13] of all the despatches exchanged between St. Petersburg and the Russian Embassy in Berlin during July, 1914. Accompanying these is a long memoir which Bronevski, the Russian Chargé d'Affaires at Berlin, wrote immediately upon his return to Russia at the outbreak of War, in which he recounted in detail the events of his last days in Berlin.

In 1923 Baron Schilling's *Diary of the Former Ministry of Foreign Affairs,* which had lain hidden away in a cupboard, was discovered and published by the Bolshevists. [14] It gave a new and vivid account of the doings and conversations of the Russian Foreign Minister, M. Sazonov, between July 16 and August 1, 1914. The diary is especially valuable because Schilling was M. Sazonov's confidential assistant (*Chef de Cabinet*) at the Foreign Office, and sum-

---

[12] G. von Romberg, *Die Fälschungen des russischen Orangebuches, Der wahre Telegrammwechsel Paris-Petersburg bei Kriegsausbruch,* Berlin and Leipzig, 1922 (Eng. trans., 1923).

[13] *Krasnyi Arkhiv,* I, 163 ff.

[14] "Nachalo Voiny 1914: Podennaia Zapis b. Ministerstva Inostrannykh Del," in *Krasnyi Arkhiv,* IV, 1-62.

marized on the spot conversations which his chief reported to him, but of which no other Russian record exists. Baron Schilling also pasted into the diary the text or summaries of important telegrams which passed in and out of the Foreign Office, but which were suppressed from the *Russian Orange Book*, and had hitherto remained unknown. In the introduction to Major Bridge's English translation of the diary, Baron Schilling, who has been living in London, confirms its authenticity and high historical importance, and gives interesting details of the manner in which it was composed.[15]

From these various Bolshevist publications we now have a fairly complete record of the Russian diplomatic correspondence for the July crisis. It consists of more than 200 telegrams, instead of the misleading and partly falsified 79 documents in the *Russian Orange Book of 1914*.[16]

Some Entente sympathizers, like Grelling, Romieu, and Ex-President Poincaré, have sought to throw suspicion and doubt on the honesty and reliability of these new revelations from the German, Austrian and Russian archives.[17] This is

[15] Major W. Cyprian Bridge, *How the War Began in 1914, Being the Diary of the Russian Foreign Office* (London, 1925), pp. 11-17; cited hereafter as "Schilling's Diary," but the present writer does not always follow the wording of the English translation which is sometimes inaccurate; for instance telegrams Nos. 1504-1509 (p. 36·f.) belong under July "26" instead of "25."

[16] A convenient German edition of them has been published by A. von Wegerer, *Das Russische Orangebuch von 1914*, Berlin, 1925. There appear to be still lacking some of the despatches exchanged by the Russian Minister of Foreign Affairs with Russia's representatives in London, Vienna and the Balkan States; for his despatches to his representatives in Turkey, Bulgaria, Rumania, and Italy from July, 1914, until the entrance of these states into the war, see *Das Russische Orangebuch ueber den Kriegsausbruch mit der Türkei*, ed. F. Stieve (Berlin, 1926); and *Das Zaristische Russland im Weltkriege*, ed. M. Pokrovski (Berlin, 1927).

[17] R. Grelling, *La Campagne "Innocentiste" en Allemagne et le Traité de Versailles*, Paris, 1925; J. Romieu, *The Bolshevist Publications and French Policy*, Paris, 1922; R. Poincaré, "The Responsibility for the War" in *Foreign Affairs* (N.Y.), October, 1925, pp. 10-11; *Au service de la France*, I, 186 f., 308, 310, 360, 374; II, 336; III, 92 ff.

because these new documents have led scholars to believe that Germany was much less responsible, and that Russia and France were much more to blame, than was at first supposed. But no one has ever satisfactorily proved that the documents just described are in any way fictitious or falsified. On the contrary, all the new material fits together like a mosaic, and one part confirms another. Furthermore, one of the best reasons for believing that these documents are genuine and fairly complete, and that the Socialist editors have made no effort to exculpate Germany, Austria, and Russia, is to be found in the fact that the editors have each tried to place the war guilt upon his own former government. It is curious to see how they have written pamphlets, based on the documents in their own archives, tending to prove that their own former imperialist rulers were mainly to blame for the World War.[18]   According to Kautsky, Germany deliberately and willingly pushed a hesitating Austria into action against Serbia and so into a World War. According to Gooss, the unsuspecting Emperor William was the sacrificial lamb offered up on the altar of Berchtold's reckless perfidy and obstinacy. While according to Pokrovski, the Director of the Archives in Soviet Russia—who is much nearer the truth—the causes of the War are to be found in the century-old Russian imperialist ambition for the control of Constantinople, the influence of Grand Dukes and militarists, the desire of Izvolski for revenge on Austria, and the support to these malign influences which the Tsarist régime felt encouraged to expect from the capitalist governments of France and England. While the historian may take such partisan conceptions

[18] K. Kautsky, *Wie der Weltkrieg entstand,* Berlin, 1919; R. Gooss, *Das Wiener Kabinett und die Entstehung des Weltkrieges,* Wien, 1919; M. N. Pokrovski, *Drei Konferenzen,* Hamburg, 1920; and Pokrovski's articles in various Russian periodicals which are summarized by A. von Wegerer, "Aus Russischen Quellen." in *Die Kriegsschuldfrage,* III, 159-177, March, 1925.

with a grain of salt, he may at least be sure that none of these editors have consciously suppressed documents which would incriminate their former rulers, or have concocted material which would exculpate them.

On the basis of this new documentary evidence, no serious historians any longer accept the dictum of the Allied victors of 1919 that Germany and her allies were solely responsible. They are all agreed that the responsibility is a divided one; they differ merely as to the relative responsibility of each of the Great Powers. Some writers, indeed, not alone in Germany but in other countries, especially in France,[19] have been inclined to push the pendulum to the other extreme. For various reasons, they tend to relieve Germany and Austria of a large part of the responsibility, and place an increasing amount of the blame upon Russia, Serbia, France, and even England. One reason for this is that Serbia and France have never made the same complete and frank publication of archive material as Germany, Austria and Russia; and England did not do so until December 1, 1926.

Finally, however, the British Government, realizing the undesirability of preserving further silence, and yielding to the request of distinguished historians, has at last, after a dozen years, issued an admirable collection of all its diplomatic documents relating to the July crisis of 1914.[20] It

---

[19] *E.g.*, Pevet, Demartial, Dupin, Morhardt, Victor Margueritte, Lazare, and others; and in America, Judge Bausman, Mr. J. S. Ewart, and Mr. H. E. Barnes.

[20] *Foreign Office Documents, June 28th-August 4th, 1914,* collected and arranged with introduction and notes by J. W. Headlam-Morley, London, 1926 (forming vol. XI of *British Documents on the Origins of the War, 1898-1914,* edited by G. P. Gooch and Harold Temperley). Among the numerous criticisms and reviews of these British Documents the following are especially noteworthy: H. Lutz, *Lord Grey und der Weltkrieg* (Berlin, 1927), pp. 171-261, 346-408 (Eng. trans., 1928); Count Montgelas, in KSF, 97-140, 443-448 (Feb.-Mar., 1927); Count Montgelas, *British Foreign Policy under Sir Edward Grey* (N. Y., 1928); H. Delbrück, in *Zeitschrift f. Politik,* XVI, 561-570 (May, 1927); H. E. Barnes, in (N. Y.) *Nation,* CXXV, 161-163 (Aug. 17, 1927); B. E. Schmitt, in

contains some 500 new documents and many important passages which were omitted from the *British Blue Book* of 1914. These suppressed passages relate largely to England's relations with France and Russia, who were soon to become her allies, and show the close solidarity of the Triple Entente Powers. The addition of private letters of Sir Edward Grey, Sir Arthur Nicolson, and Sir Eyre Crowe, of the British Foreign Office, and their marginal "minutes" upon the documents, enables one to trace with the same accuracy the development of events in London, as was made possible by the *Kautsky Documents* for Germany.

(b) MEMOIRS AND RECOLLECTIONS

In addition to these diplomatic documents, there has come a flood of apologetic memoirs and pamphlets from the men who played a prominent part in 1914. Some of these deal only with the diplomatic crisis immediately preceding the War; most of them also reach back and touch upon the remoter underlying causes as well. As was to be expected, the stream began to flow from the defeated side. After the German collapse of 1918, just as after the French *débâcle* of 1871, the ex-Kaiser's former officials sought to throw the blame for the War on the late enemy or upon fellow officials. Austrian leaders soon followed German example. And more recently the stream has been swollen by Russians in exile, Frenchmen on the defensive, injudicious Serbians, and even by hitherto reticent Englishmen. A full account of this autobiographical material may be found in Mr. G. P. Gooch's *Recent Revelations of European Diplomacy,* pubished in 1927, with *Supplements,* 1928-29. A few of the more important names may be mentioned at this point.

Current History, XXV, 844-851 (Mar. 1927); and other American scholars in *The Saturday Review of Literature,* III, 729 f., 750 f., 781 f. (April 16-30, 1927). Vols. I-VI of these *British Documents,* covering the years 1898 to 1912 in part, and the new *Documents Diplomatiques Français* (3 vols., Paris, 1929-30) will form, when completed, together with the new Austrian Documents (9 vols., 1930), invaluable counterparts to *Die Grosse Politik* mentioned below in notes 63-64.

The *Reflections on the World War* [21] by the late German Chancellor, Herr von Bethmann-Hollweg, deserve more serious attention than they have received; but they were written before peace was signed, under the terrible strain of war, by a man already broken in spirit and health. Without the new documentary material at his disposal, Bethmann still clung to the misconception which overtook him early in the War, that England was chiefly to blame. Herr von Jagow, the German Secretary of State for Foreign Affairs, in his *Causes and Outbreak of the World War*,[22] does not produce an impression of equal sincerity, but is illuminating in regard to the attitude of the German Foreign Office. Count Pourtalès, the German Ambassador in St. Petersburg, gives a very straightforward and reliable account of his last days in the Russian capital, and of his honest efforts to carry out the instructions of his Government to keep Russia quiet and thus preserve the peace of Europe. His narrative, *At the Parting of the Ways*,[23] has the advantage of being based on notes which he made on his journey home in August, 1914, while the facts were still fresh in his mind, and on the Embassy telegrams which he appears to have taken with him. Baron von Schoen, as German Secretary of State from 1907-1910 and Ambassador at Paris from 1910-1914, has left *Memoirs* [24] which are distinguished for their frankness and breadth of view; he is one of the few German diplomats of whom M. Poincaré speaks with cordiality and praise. These writers defend and justify the policy of the German Foreign Office.

In contrast to them are other Germans who are wise

[21] Th. v. Bethmann-Hollweg, *Betrachtungen zum Weltkriege*, 2 vols., Berlin, 1919-20 (Eng. trans., 1920).

[22] G. v. Jagow, *Ursachen und Ausbruch des Weltkrieges*, Berlin, 1919.

[23] Graf Pourtalès, *Am Scheidewege zwischen Krieg und Frieden*, Berlin, 1922. This is amplified in his more recent volume, *Meine letzten Verhandlungen in St. Petersburg Ende Juli 1914*, Berlin, 1927.

[24] Freiherr von Schoen, *Erlebtes: Beiträge zur politischen Geschichte der neuesten Zeit*, Berlin, 1921 (Eng. trans., 1922).

after the event. Admiral von Tirpitz,[25] in *My Memoirs* and in his more recent and valuable *Political Documents,* takes Bethmann severely to task for his optimism in hoping for a friendly understanding with England during the years before the War, and for his diplomatic bungling in the final crisis of 1914. Prince Lichnowsky's bitter pamphlet, *My London Mission,*[26] which was written during the War under a feeling of failure and the fire of criticism at home, is often unjust in its criticism of the German Government and not always well informed. It has been relied on outside Germany to an extent far beyond what it deserves. The *Memoirs* [27] of the ex-Kaiser at Doorn, which ungenerously attempt to lay the blame on everyone else but himself, are full of inaccuracies and misconceptions. They are of little historical value except for the psychological light they throw upon their author, and tend to obscure rather than elucidate the truth as to the causes of the War. General von Moltke's posthumous *Recollections* [28] consist largely of letters to his wife covering the thirty years before the War. The brief chapter on the July Crisis, written after the Battle of the Marne and his removal from active com-

[25] A. v. Tirpitz, *Erinnerungen,* Leipzig, 1919 (Eng. trans., 1921); also *Politische Dokumente: Der Aufbau der deutschen Weltmacht; Deutsche Ohnmachts-politik im Weltkriege,* 2 vols., Hamburg and Berlin, 1924-26.

[26] Prince Lichnowsky, *Meine Londoner Mission, 1912-1914,* Eng. trans. edited with notes by Amer. Assoc., for International Conciliation, No. 127, June, 1917, pp. 227-404. For criticisms of Lichnowsky, see G. von Jagow, *Remarks, ibid.,* pp. 352-367; and M. Ritter, *Der Ausbruch des Weltkrieges nach den Behauptungen Lichnowskys und nach dem Zeugnis der Akten,* Munich and Berlin, 1918. Of much greater value is Prince Lichnowsky's large, more recent work, *Auf dem Wege zum Abgrund,* 2 vols., Dresden, 1927, covering the whole period of his London mission and containing unpublished documents (Eng. trans., *Heading for the Abyss,* 1928).

[27] Wilhelm II, *Ereignisse und Gestalten, 1878-1918,* Berlin, 1922 (Eng. trans., 1922). Equally unreliable are his "Comparative Tables," which were neatly dissected by Ch. Appuhn and P. Renouvin, *Introduction aux Tableaux d'Histoire de Guillaume II,* Paris, 1923. Much more trustworthy and informing is his most recent volume, *My Early Years,* London, 1926.

[28] Helmuth v. Moltke, *Erinnerungen, Briefe, Dokumente, 1887-1916.* Stuttgart, 1922.

mand, reflects his consternation at England's entrance into
the War, and his despair at the Kaiser's delay in deciding
for War, which the German militarists believed "inevitable,"
but which Bethmann and the Kaiser hoped to avert.

The Austrians, and with very good reason, have made
relatively little effort to exculpate themselves. Count
Berchtold, who more than anyone else was responsible for
the World War, has long kept silent, except for a few short
and tardy exculpatory articles, but his memoirs are now announced for early publication. Count Czernin, Austrian
Minister to Rumania in 1914, and Austrian Foreign Minister during the War, wrote an interesting volume, *In the
World War*.[29] Though dealing mainly with diplomacy
during the War, he gave an excellent picture of the Archduke Franz Ferdinand's character and views, and expressed
the opinion that the German Ambassador at Vienna,
Tschirschky, used his personal influence to encourage
Austria in her action against Serbia. Dr. Fraknói [30] has
told us something of Count Tisza's initial opposition to an
Austrian war against Serbia, not explaining altogether satisfactorily why the powerful Hungarian Premier changed his
attitude in the middle of July, 1914. Count Tisza himself,
had he lived, might have been able to tell the truth fear-
lessly, but he lies in a bloody grave, assassinated on his own
doorstep at the close of the War; his lips were sealed forever, and the recent edition of his papers by the Hungarian
Academy contains virtually nothing on the immediate
causes of the War. Baron Musulin, who drew up the text
of the Austrian ultimatum to Serbia, has published a delightful volume covering the experiences of his diplomatic
life and his activity at the Austrian Foreign Office.[31] He

29 Ottokar Czernin, *Im Weltkriege,* Berlin and Vienna, 1919 (Eng.
trans., 1919).

30 W. Fraknói, *Die ungarische Regierung und die Entstehung des
Weltkrieges,* Vienna, 1919.

31 Freiherr von Musulin, *Das Haus am Ballplatz,* Munich, 1924.

is convincing everywhere except precisely in those chapters which deal with his share in the events which precipitated the World War. Here he minimizes his own share of responsibility, and his narrative, perhaps through faulty memory, is often contradicted by the contemporary records.

Count Bilinski, whose position as Austro-Hungarian Joint Finance Minister from 1912 to 1914 gave him direct charge of the civil administration of Bosnia and Herzegovina, has much to say in his Polish *Recollections and Documents* [32] concerning his efforts to ameliorate conditions in these troubled and restless provinces. But concerning the preparations of the Archduke's journey thither, and the lack of police precautions at Sarajevo, the alleged "warning" from Serbia, and the preparation of the ultimatum, he tells less than one might have hoped. These were tragic matters in connection with which he has been severely criticized, and over which in later years he preferred to draw the veil of silence. A Galician Pole by birth, he joined the Polish cause during the War, and is often regarded as a traitor to his former fatherland, which—in retrospect—he holds largely responsible for the War. More generous in tone and more readable in form is the volume by his predecessor as Joint Finance Minister, Count Burián, *Austria in Dissolution*.[33] Count Burián, who also became Austrian Foreign Minister during the War, makes no effort to shift the blame for the War to other shoulders, but gives an admirable account of the desperate situation in which Austria-Hungary found herself, because of the growing restlessness of her subject nationalities.

The only Austrian diplomatic representatives abroad in 1914, beside Count Czernin, who have left memoirs of importance, were Baron Szilassy at Athens and Baron Giesl

[32] Leon Bilinski, *Wspomnienia i Dokumenty, 1846-1922,* 2 vols., Warsaw, 1924-1925.

[33] Stephan Graf Burián, *Drei Jahre aus der Zeit meiner Amtsführung im Kriege,* Berlin, 1923 (Eng. trans., 1925).

at Belgrade. A broad-minded and intelligent Magyar, with French and English sympathies, whose horizon had been further enlarged in subordinate diplomatic positions in Tokio, St. Petersburg, Constantinople and elsewhere, Szilassy gives the impression in his *Fall of the Danubian Monarchy* [34] that the appointment of Count Berchtold as Austrian Foreign Minister was a colossal blunder—it gave minor officials in the Foreign Office, and militarists in the General Staff, the chance to seize upon the Archduke's assassination as the pretext for the "inevitable" war with Serbia. Baron Giesl, the Austrian Minister at Belgrade in 1914 and formerly at Cettinje, was well acquainted with the Turkish and Slavic languages; his Memoirs throw interesting light on Balkan conditions before the War and add some details concerning the final diplomatic rupture between Austria and Serbia.[34a]

The most valuable to the historian of all the Austro-Hungarian memoirs is the voluminous work of the Austrian Chief of Staff, Baron Conrad von Hötzendorf.[35] It consists in large part of an undigested mass of important documents of all sorts, copies of which he evidently took from the official files and published in chronological order, with a commentary of his own. It also includes conversations in dialogue form which appear to be taken from a diary kept from day to day. With extraordinary frankness, he recounts the repeated efforts he made to have Austria make war on Italy or Serbia on what he regarded as numerous favorable occasions between 1906 and 1914. In July, 1914, it was probably he, more than anyone else, who galvanized the incompetent and hesitating Berchtold into an active advocate of war against Serbia. Conrad is the best—that

[34] Baron von Szilassy, *Der Untergang der Donaumonarchie: Diplomatische Erinnerungen,* Berlin, 1921.

[34a] Baron Wladimir Giesl, *Zwei Jahrzehnte im nahen Orient,* Berlin, 1927.

[35] *Aus meiner Dienstzeit,* 5 vols., Vienna, 1921-25.

is, the worst—example of the militarist mind, which believes that war is "inevitable," is ever eager to wage a "preventive" war, and throws all its weight in favor of hasty mobilization in a time of diplomatic crisis. Conrad's views have been severely criticized by two of his generals.[36]

Another Austrian writer, who was not in an official position, yet who deserves mention because of his caustic criticism of the civilian and military officials whom he observed at close range in Vienna, is Herr Heinrich Kanner,[37] formerly editor of the Vienna Socialist daily, *Die Zeit*.

The Russian autobiographical material is almost wholly from hands which had been more accustomed to wield the sword than the diplomatic pen. Sazonov's Memoirs, written in exile more than ten years after the events, without notes and documents at hand, have been riddled by the reviewers as wholly unreliable.[37a] Few Russian diplomatic representatives abroad, except Baron Rosen,[38] have left their record of the immediate causes of the War. But many Russian military officers have left important recollections. General Dobrorolski, who was Chief of the Mobilization Section of the Russian General Staff in 1914, has revealed in a very frank and reliable pamphlet,[39] how the Russian militarists, upon hearing of the Austrian ultimatum, at once jumped to the conclusion that war was "inevitable," began

[36] A. Krauss, *Die Ursachen unserer Niederlage*, Vienna, 1920; Auffenberg-Komarów, *Aus Oesterreichs Höhe und Niedergang*, Munich, 1924.

[37] Heinrich Kanner, *Kaiserliche Katastrophenpolitik*, Vienna, 1922; also *Der Schlüssel zur Kriegsschuldfrage*, Münich, 1926.

[37a] S. D. Sazonov, *Fateful Years* (N. Y., 1928), has been confuted in numberless passages by F. Stieve and M. Montgelas, *Russland und der Weltkonflikt* (Berlin, 1927), and by others in *Rings um Sazonoff* (Berlin, 1928).

[38] Baron Rosen, *Forty Years of Diplomacy*, 2 vols., N.Y., 1922. His memoirs deal more with the period preceding July, 1914, as do also: A. Nekludoff, *Diplomatic Reminiscences* (1920), and A. Savinsky, *Recollections of a Russian Diplomat* (1927).

[39] S. Dobrorolski, *Die Mobilmachung der russischen Armee, 1914.* Berlin, 1921.

secret military preparations, and urged "general mobilization" at as early a date as possible. From Dobrorolski's account, it is also clear that "partial mobilization" against Austria was a mere diplomatic "bluff" by the threat of which Sazonov hoped to make Austria back down in her demands on Serbia; but the Russian military authorities had made no technical preparations for such a "partial mobilization," and were therefore absolutely opposed to it and insistently urged "general mobilization." Dobrorolski thus helps to establish the true facts in regard to the final orders for Russian mobilization, and corrects the falsehoods which were told so freely by General Sukhomlinov, who was Russian Minister of War in 1914, and by others, at the famous Sukhomlinov trial in 1917. Sukhomlinov's *Recollections*,[40] which were published in German in 1924, reveal a man full of loyalty to the Tsar, but very cloudy in his mind as to his own share in the fatal events of July, 1914. His volume, however, as well as General Polivanov's *Diaries*,[41] and the first part of General Danilov's *Russia in the World War*,[42] describe authoritatively and fairly satisfactorily the great efforts for the reorganization and increase of the Russian army which they made with a view to an "inevitable" war with Germany and Austria. Perhaps the most reliable and accurate sources for precise information concerning the Russian military preparations actually made in July, 1914, are the Russian military telegrams which were sent out by the Russian General Staff. More than a hundred of these were later captured by the Germans in the course of the War, and were published in 1919 in Robert Hoeniger's *Russia's Preparation for the World War*.[43] Five years

40 W. A. Suchomlinow, *Erinnerungen*, Berlin, 1924.
41 Gunther Frantz, *Russland auf dem Wege zur Katastrophe: Tagebücher des Grossfürsten Andrej und des Kriegsministers Poliwanow; Briefe der Grossfürsten an den Zaren*, Berlin, 1926.
42 J. Daniloff, *Russland im Weltkriege, 1914-1915*, Jena, 1925.
43 R. Hoeniger, *Russlands Vorbereitung zum Weltkrieg*, Berlin, 1919.

later, the telegrams were edited in more complete form and with a more adequate commentary by Gunther Frantz, *Russia's Entry into the World War*.[44] Though primarily a technical study of secret military measures, this excellent volume helps to clear away the legends and misstatements which have long passed current as a result of the Franco-Russian suppression of the truth in 1914 and the false assertions at the Sukhomlinov trial in 1917.

Foremost among French *apologias* is ex-President Poincaré's *Origins of the War*,[45] containing six lectures delivered at the Sorbonne in 1921. This is a skilful lawyer's statement of the case for France and a personal defense of his own policy. By centering attention largely upon Austria and Germany, and by concealing much of the activity of France and Russia, M. Poincaré gives plausible support to the official Entente thesis of German war guilt as embodied in the Versailles Treaty. In a notable article four years later on "The Responsibility for the War," in *Foreign Affairs* (N. Y., Oct., 1925), he abandons, to be sure, some of the legends concerning German guilt which have been proved to be wholly without foundation. But in spite of these concessions to a truer view of history, his later article is open to much the same criticism as his Sorbonne lectures. It is doubtful whether his plausible arguments convinced others than those who need no convincing.[46] Far more valuable is his magisterial defense of his foreign and domestic policy in the first four volumes of his memoirs which have so far appeared.[47] These describe minutely, almost day by day, his activities from the beginning of 1912 to August 3, 1914. Thus they throw light on both the un-

---

[44] G. Frantz, *Russlands Eintritt in den Weltkrieg*, Berlin, 1924.

[45] R. Poincaré, *Les Origines de la Guerre*, Paris, 1921.

[46] *Cf.* the present writer's article, "M. Poincaré and War Responsibility," in *The New Republic*, Oct. 14, 1925.

[47] R. Poincaré, *Au Service de la France*, 4 vols., Paris, 1926-27, (abridged Eng. trans. of vols. I and II, 1926).

derlying and the immediate causes of the War. M. Poincaré writes with lawyer-like vigor and perfect confidence in
the wisdom and righteousness of all his acts. He quotes
at length from his innumerable speeches in defense of the
power and dignity of France, her love of peace and her
loyalty to Russia and England. He uses much unpublished
material from the French archives, which makes his volumes
of great value to the historian. But he frequently turns
aside, with sarcasm and with overwhelming minutiae of
detail, in attempts to confute his critics; this often makes
his work an acrid polemic rather than a calm historical
retrospect.

M. Poincaré's most severe critics have been his own
countrymen—Pevet, Judet, Fabre-Luce, Converset, Morhardt, Victor Margueritte, Lazare, and a host of lesser
lights. They have charged him with getting rid of cautious
ambassadors like M. Georges Louis in St. Petersburg and
M. Crozier in Vienna to make way for a chauvinist like
M. Delcassé or puppets like M. Paléologue and M. Dumaine,
in order that he might be more free to work with Izvolski
in bringing about a war which should recover Alsace-
Lorraine for France and secure Constantinople and the
Straits for Russia. Many of his replies to their criticisms
are sound. He manages to explain away some of the in-
criminating remarks that Izvolski attributes to him. But
in many other cases he seems to take refuge in the practice
of throwing dust in the reader's eye by diverting attention
from the main point to minor matters.

On the general question of war responsibility, M. Poincaré tries to prove that as Premier and President he in no
way deviated from the pacific policy of his predecessors.
He attempts to show that he and M. Georges Louis were
in complete agreement as to the nature and interpretation
of the Franco-Russian alliance. To one who has read all
the available documents, his arguments are not always con-

vincing. There was a distinct change during 1912, when he was Premier and Minister of Foreign Affairs, in the direction of tightening the alliance and extending French support to Russian ambitions in the Balkans. This was not, however, as many of his critics assert, with the aim of bringing about a war by which France should recover Alsace-Lorraine. It was to establish greater solidarity in the Triple Entente. In so doing he tended to divide the Powers more and more into two armed and opposing camps, so that the Triple Entente could impose its will on the Triple Alliance; or, if a diplomatic crisis should arise, the former could safely defy the latter, and willingly risk war with superior forces rather than accept a diplomatic defeat. This is exactly what happened in 1914. He believed a European war "inevitable"; in tightening the Entente and in making promises to Russia he did in fact tend to make it inevitable. Herein lies his responsibility.

After M. Delcassé had occupied the French Embassy at St. Petersburg for a few weeks in 1913, it was handed over to one of President Poincaré's old school friends and most devoted followers, M. Maurice Paléologue. In the opening pages of *An Ambassador's Memoirs*,[48] M. Paléologue describes vividly the gala events and chauvinistic enthusiasm accompanying President Poincaré's visit to the Tsar, and the situation in Russia on the eve of the War. Though the facts related by the French Ambassador do not always have the accuracy and definiteness which one would expect if his charmingly written book were really based on a diary written day by day, it is, nevertheless, of much value to the historian. It reproduces with fidelity the exultant war spirit inspired in Russian ruling circles by President Poincaré's presence and speeches. It describes dramatically, for instance, the gala banquet of July 22 at which the two

[48] M. Paléologue, *La Russie des Tsars pendant la Grande Guerre*, 3 vols., Paris, 1922 (Eng. trans., 1924-26).

Montenegrin princesses (one of whom was the wife of the Grand Duke Nicholas) joyously told Paléologue how their father had written them that there would be war within a month. It pictures their ecstasy at the prospect of the ruin of Austria, the French reconquest of Alsace-Lorraine, and the defeat and destruction of Germany. Three days later, before it was known that Austria had rejected the Serbian reply as unsatisfactory, Paléologue tells how he went to the railway station to speed M. Izvolski on his return to France: "It is very lively on the platform; the trains are crowded with officers and soldiers. This suggested mobilization already. We exchanged rapidly our impressions and came to the same conclusion: *Cette fois, c'est la guerre.*" [49] The impression that he sympathized with the war spirit in Russia, and encouraged it by his repeated assurances that France would stand firm in the support of her ally, is confirmed by passages suppressed from the *British Blue Book* of 1914, but now printed in the new edition of British Documents.

Drab in comparison with Paléologue's vividness is the colorless picture presented by his colleague, M. Dumaine, the French Ambassador in Vienna.[50] For a man in ambassadorial position, M. Dumaine seems to have been surprisingly lacking in information and influence. From that trio of most able French Ambassadors, M. Paul Cambon at London, his brother, M. Jules Cambon at Berlin, and M. Barrère at Rome, we have unfortunately no full memoirs. However, an enterprising French journalist, M. Raymond Recouly, had the happy idea of interviewing them, and others, while their memories were relatively fresh, and has recorded these interviews in an excellent volume.[51]

49 M. Paléologue, *La Russie des Tsars pendant la Grande Guerre,* I, 27.

50 Alfred Dumaine, *La Dernière Ambassade de France en Autriche,* Paris, 1921.

51 Raymond Recouly, *Les Heures Tragiques d'Avant-Guerre,* Paris, 1923.

The Serbian Government always denied that it was in any way directly responsible for the assassination of the Austrian Archduke.   But the celebration of the tenth anniversary of his assassination and the outbreak of the War, which resulted in the creation of the united nation of which Serbian Nationalists had dreamed, inspired some interesting reminiscences which cast doubt on the official Serbian attitude.   Ljuba Jovanovitch, who was Minister of Education in the Pashitch Cabinet of 1914, without perhaps quite realizing the importance of his words, let the cat out of the bag in 1924.   In the *Blood of Slavdom*,[52] he describes in a vivid but simple way how some of the Pashitch Cabinet were aware of the Sarajevo plot for nearly a month; and yet, in spite of this guilty knowledge, took no effective steps to arrest the conspirators or to warn the Austrian authorities of the impending danger.   This amazing admission on the part of a leading Serbian official has given rise to other Serbian revelations and denials concerning the part in the Sarajevo plot taken by the secret Serbian military organization commonly known as the "Black Hand," and especially by Col. Dragutin Dimitrijevitch.   This reckless, generous, idolized, childish hero, who seems to belong to the spirit of the sixteenth rather than of the twentieth century, was the head of the espionage department of the Serbian General Staff.   As the founder and dominating figure in the Serbian "Black Hand," he was the most influential military officer in Serbia.   These Serbian revelations place the Austro-Serbian conflict in a new light and, if true, greatly increase the burden of Serbia's share of responsibility.   They tend to confirm what Austrian officials suspected, but could not prove, in 1914.   They help to explain, though they do not justify, Austria's determination to deal energetically with what was regarded as the Serbian

---

[52] Ljuba Jovanovitch, "After Vidov-Dan, 1914," in *Krv Slovenstva,* Belgrade, 1924.

menace to the very existence of the Hapsburg Monarchy.[53]

With characteristic regard for what Mr. Asquith calls the
British tradition of being "scrupulously niggardly in im-
parting information as to the proceedings in the Cabinet,"
British officials have long been relatively chary of revealing
the part they played. However, Lord Haldane's *Before the
War* (1920) described with dignity and authority the failure
of his efforts to secure a better understanding with Germany
in 1912, and his activity in preparing an English army to
fight on the Continent. Lord Loreburn, in *How the War
Came* (1920), charged Sir Edward Grey with grave responsibility for the War, because of the secret engagements
which he had made with France and which virtually committed England to support France and Russia in a European
war. These commitments, he thinks, encouraged France
and Russia in aggressive ambitions, but were long kept
secret from the British Cabinet, contrary to English constitutional practice. Mr. Asquith's *Genesis of the War* (1924)
tells us little of the true origin of the War. The ex-Prime
Minister was still content to write in 1924 as if we knew no
more about the causes of the War after a decade than we did
in 1914. To him Germany is still solely responsible. He
writes as a politician making a case, not as a statesman
seeking to reveal the truth. In certain chapters, however,
he gives an illuminating account of the splendid preparations for war made by the Committee for Imperial Defense. He quotes the significant statement which Sir
Edward Grey made behind closed doors to the Dominion
Premiers in May, 1911: "What really determines the foreign policy of this country is the question of sea power."
This dictum is amply confirmed in *The World Crisis, 1911-
1914* (1923) by Mr. Winston Churchill, First Lord of the

[53] Some of these Serbian revelations were discussed by the present
writer in *Current History*, Oct., Nov., 1925.

Admiralty during this period.   Mr. Churchill gives us much valuable new information as to his strengthening and increasing of the British navy after Germany's folly in refusing British proposals for the limitation of naval armaments.

The memoirs of Sir George Buchanan, British Ambassador to Russia, add little to our knowledge of the immediate causes of the War beyond what can be learned from the *British Blue Book*.   But when he says that, with one exception, this "recorded all the communications which passed between me and that Department [the British Foreign Office] during those critical days," [54] he is guilty of serious misrepresentation; the new *British Documents* contain more than a score of such communications not printed in 1914, not even counting the important passages omitted from several telegrams and letters.   Lord Bertie's *Diary*, though mainly concerned with events after the outbreak of the War, contains some significant passages on the pacific attitude of the French people until they were stirred up by their newspapers, and by Izvolski.   Of the latter he writes, July 27: "Izvolski is expected back here today or tomorrow, and he is not an element of peace."   And on July 28: "Izvolski told Granville that war is inevitable. . . . He will do a good deal of mischief in fomenting a war spirit here."   And later, on November 10: "What a fool Izvolski is! . . . At the beginning of the war he claimed to be its author:—'*C'est ma guerre!*'" [55]   This attitude is confirmed by several passages now printed for the first time in the new *British Documents*, in which we learn that Bertie told the French that "public opinion in England would not sanction a war in support of Russia if she, as protector of Slavs, picked a quarrel with Austria over Austro-Serbian

[54] Sir George Buchanan, *My Mission to Russia and other Diplomatic Memories* (2 vols., London, 1923), I, 211.

[55] *The Diary of Lord Bertie of Thame, 1914-1918* (2 vols., London, 1924), I, 2, 3, 66.

difficulty." He also at first denounced "the absurd and ob-solete attitude of Russia being the protectress of all Slav States, whatever their conduct." [56]

Most valuable of all the recent memoirs is Viscount Grey's *Twenty-five Years, 1892-1916* (1925). By charm of style and absence of bitterness, by transparent honesty of intention and nobility of tone, and by the sweet reason-ableness of his retrospective reflections, Grey's *apologia* is unique. Though writing ten years or more after the events, he appears to have a remarkably clear memory. Further-more, he has had his friend, Mr. Spender, search the For-eign Office records to refresh his mind on all points where he feared his memory might play him tricks. His book is thus, in a sense, a history based on the archives; yet the clear flow of his narrative is unclogged by quotations and footnotes. Admitting, however, Sir Edward Grey's abso-lute sincerity in attempting to preserve the peace of Europe and his unquestionable honesty of intent in his memoirs, serious criticisms remain to be made of his conduct of British foreign policy to which we shall return in a later chapter. At this point it may be merely noted that his great fault was what has been regarded as the great virtue of British constitutional leaders—the preference for practical compromise for the present instead of theoretical perfec-tion for the future. He did not look far ahead, work out a logical policy, and study all its possible consequences. He was content in foreign affairs, as the British have always been content in dealing with their constitutional develop-ment, to meet situations as they arose and deal with them according to the most practical and common sense needs of the moment. As Grey himself says, when alleging that Great Britain never pursued a "Balance of Power" policy: "I suppose that in this, as in most investigations of British foreign policy. the true reason is not to be found in far-

[56] B.D. 129. 192.

sighted views or large conceptions or great schemes. . . . If all secrets were known it would probably be found that British Foreign Ministers have been guided by what seemed to them to be the immediate interest of this country without making elaborate calculations for the future." [57] The result of this hand-to-mouth procedure of *solvitur ambulando* was that he became more and more enmeshed in his secret understandings with France, until he was morally bound by them in 1914. Though he had always been careful to state to the French that his hands were to remain free, and that it would always be for Parliament to decide whether England would support France in a European war, he had, nevertheless, become gradually so committed that, as he twice admits, he would have felt bound to resign his office if he had been unable to persuade the Cabinet and Parliament to enter the war against Germany.[58]

In his retrospect, Viscount Grey rightly has much to say of the poisonous effect of suspicion as a cause of war, but he also reveals in several passages his own deep-rooted suspicion of Germany. "It seemed at the time (1914), and still seems true to me, that the military power in Germany chose the time and precipitated the War." [59] He seems to have believed that the German militarists even selected the month as well as the year for making war, choosing July in 1914 as they had chosen July in 1870 and were ready to choose July in 1905 and 1911 had it not been that France yielded in the first Morocco crisis, and that England assumed a very firm tone after Agadir.[60] Though Germany's actions gave much ground for suspicion, as we shall see, this

[57] Grey, I, 6.   [58] Grey, I, 303, 316.   [59] Grey, I, 90.

[60] "Had the [Agadir] crisis led to war, this would have come at the very season that we know was favoured for the purpose by German military leaders in 1870, and that was selected for the menace to France in 1905, and that we believe was decided by the military authorities for war in 1914." Grey, I, 231. For other passages indicating Grey's suspicion that the German militarists had fixed upon war for 1914, see I, 313-314; II, 23-31, 56, 144, 278.

particular suspicion of Sir Edward Grey's was wholly incorrect. But the fact that he harbored it must be accounted one of the immediate causes of the War, because it contributed to the failure of Germany's eleventh hour efforts to prevent a general European conflagration. To be sure, Viscount Grey generously and correctly acquits the German civil authorities of planning or desiring war in 1914, but he thinks that Bethmann and Jagow were powerless in the face of the militarists.

Thus, there is at present a wealth of documentary and memoir material, unprecedented in quantity and quality, at the disposal of historians seeking to find the immediate causes of the War. Never before in history have archives been so quickly and freely thrown open by so many Great Powers; never before have so many statesmen hastened to tell at such length the part they played. In this respect, as in so many others, the World War has outstripped all precedents and surpassed all expectations. In the case of former wars, at least a generation or two passed before satisfactory accounts of their causes could be written. Today, only fourteen years after the outbreak of the War, it may safely be said that the materials are now at hand on which to base a fairly exact statement of the course of events between the murder of the Archduke at Sarajevo on June 28, and the advent of war between England and Germany on August 4. This is the main subject of my second volume.

3. THE UNDERLYING CAUSES OF THE WAR

Though it is now possible, in a single volume, to treat in detail and somewhat definitively the immediate causes of the War, this is by no means true in the case of the underlying causes. These are so complex and reach so far back into the past that any attempt to describe them adequately would involve nothing less than the writing of the whole diplomatic history of Europe since 1870, or rather from

1789; some questions go back to the age of Louis XIV, and even to that of Charlemagne. It would also involve the difficult technical study of the military and naval forces of the various countries, their plans of campaign, the relation of the military to the civilian authorities in each country, the psychology of fear, and all the other factors which go to make up the somewhat vague conceptions of "militarism" and "navalism" as causes of war. No less important would be the analysis of that complex force which first began to be a powerful, disruptive agency during the French Revolution, and which steadily gathered strength for a century and a quarter, which we call "nationalism." This in turn is closely bound up with psychological and political questions of race, religion, democracy, education, and popular prejudice. Still more important, in many minds, as underlying causes of the War are the intricate political and economic problems which have arisen from the transformation of society during the past hundred years by the modern industrial system which began in England and subsequently penetrated more or less all the great countries of the world— problems of excess population, food supply, foreign markets and raw materials, colonial possessions, and the accumulation of capital seeking investment abroad. Finally, the influence of the newspaper press is a factor much greater than commonly supposed in causing the World War. For decades it fed the constant undercurrents of irritation of one country against another, and by its clamor and misrepresentations often made difficult or impossible the peaceful settlement of sources of conflict. How far government officials controlled newspaper opinion, and how far they themselves were hampered in their freedom of action by it, is a subject which greatly needs further careful historical investigation. Obviously, no single volume can hope to deal thoroughly with all these complex and interrelated factors which constitute the underlying causes of the World War. They may be conveniently grouped under five heads: (a) the system of secret alliances; (b) militarism; (c) nationalism; (d) economic imperialism; and (e) the newspaper press.

(a) THE SYSTEM OF SECRET ALLIANCES

The greatest single underlying cause of the War was the system of secret alliances which developed after the Franco-Prussian War. It gradually divided Europe into two hostile groups of Powers who were increasingly suspicious of one another and who steadily built up greater and greater armies and navies. Though this system of alliances in one sense tended to preserve peace, inasmuch as the members within one group often held their friends or allies in restraint for fear of becoming involved in war themselves, the system also made it inevitable that if war did come, it would involve all the Great Powers of Europe. The members of each group felt bound to support each other, even in matters where they had no direct interest, because failure to give support would have weakened the solidarity of the group. Thus, Germany often felt bound to back up Austria-Hungary in her Balkan policies, because otherwise Germany feared to lose her only thoroughly dependable ally. Similarly, France had no direct political (only financial) interests in the Balkans, but felt bound to back up Russia, because otherwise the existence of the Dual Alliance would have been threatened, the balance of power destroyed, and the best guarantee of French safety from a German attack would have been lost. Likewise, the officials of the British Foreign Office became increasingly convinced that England must support France and Russia in order to preserve the solidarity of the Triple Entente as a check to the Triple Alliance. In the crisis of July, 1914, it was not merely a question of Austria, Serbia and the Balkans; it was a question of the solidarity and prestige of the two groups of Powers into which Europe had become divided.

As one reads the new *British Documents,* one is struck by
the emphasis on this necessity of preserving the solidarity
of the Triple Entente. As Sir Eyre Crowe noted in a
"minute" early in the crisis: "It is clear that France and
Russia are decided to accept the challenge thrown out to
them. Whatever we may think of the merits of the Austrian charges against Servia, France and Russia consider
that these are the pretexts, and that the bigger cause of
Triple Alliance versus Triple Entente is definitely engaged. I think it would be impolitic, not to say dangerous,
for England to attempt to controvert this opinion, or to
endeavour to obscure the plain issue, by any representation
at St. Petersburg and Paris. . . . Our interests are tied up
with those of France and Russia in this struggle, which is
not for the possession of Servia, but one between Germany
aiming at a political dictatorship in Europe and the Powers
who desire to retain individual freedom." [61] It was stated
more bluntly by Herr Zimmermann to the British Ambassador in Berlin on August 1, when he saw with excited regret that Germany, France, and perhaps England, would be
drawn into a war which none of them wanted: "It all came
from this d——d system of alliances, which was the curse
of modern times." [62]

In view of the fatal consequences of this system of secret
alliances in 1914, and of the fact that there has recently
appeared much new material throwing light upon it, an
attempt to sketch in outline its development will be made
in the three following chapters. As indicated above, many
of the documents and memoirs dealing with the immediate
causes of the War contain also material on the earlier period.
But the most important single contribution to our fuller
knowledge of the growth of the system of secret alliances
is the great set of new German diplomatic documents cover-

[61] B.D., 101.
[62] B.D., 510.

ing the years from 1871 to 1914.[63] This consists of the most
secret instructions sent by Bismarck and his successors to
the German Ambassadors abroad, their reports to the German Foreign Office, and the secret papers exchanged between the German Emperor and his Foreign Office officials.
It includes exceedingly interesting marginal notes on documents from the hand of Bismarck, and later from that of
William II. Bismarck's notes reveal the Iron Chancellor's
innermost thoughts on foreign policy. They formed the
basis of instructions sent by the German Foreign Office to
the ambassadors abroad. William II's marginal notes,
which are more numerous, more emotional, and often
merely indicative of the mood of the moment, are interesting as a study of the psychology of the imperial mind, but
exercised somewhat less directive influence upon the German Foreign Office than did Bismarck's masterly notes.
From this collection of documents one sees that the German
Foreign Office did not always completely inform William II
on all matters and often made its will prevail over his
preferences. So far as one can judge, *Die Grosse Politik* is
fairly complete within the limits set by the editors, and
aims at giving the basis for an honest and detailed picture
of German foreign policy from the Franco-Prussian War
to the World War.[64] But we still lack any equally compre-

[63] *Die Grosse Politik der Europäischen Kabinette, 1871-1914: Samm-
lung der Diplomatischen Akten des Auswärtigen Amtes,* edited by Johannes
Lepsius, Albrecht Mendelssohn-Bartholdy and Friedrich Thimme, 40 vols.,
Berlin, 1922-27; cited hereafter as "G.P."

[64] A further account of *Die Grosse Politik* is given by the present
writer in the *Amer. Hist. Rev.,* XXVIII, 543-548; XXX, 136-141; XXXI,
130-133; XXXIII, 126-134. *Cf.* also the appreciations by various scholars
in KSF, IV, 900-946. Dec., 1926; the criticisms of M. Lhéritier in *Rev.
d'Hist. de la Guerre Mondiale,* IV, 97-116, April, 1926, and of E. Bourgeois, in *Revue Historique,* CLV, 39-56, May-June, 1927; and the replies
to these criticisms by Albrecht Mendelssohn-Bartholdy and by F. Thimme
in *Europäische Gespräche,* IV, 377-390, July, 1926, and V, 461-479. Sept.,
1927.

A French translation of *Die Grosse Politik,* under the editorship of
A. Aulard, in which the documents are arranged chronologically instead

hensive publication from the archives of France, Russia, and the other countries, which may be used to check and balance these German documents. Very recently, however, similar admirable collections of documents have been, or are being, officially issued: *Austria-Hungary's Foreign Policy, 1908-1914; British Documents on the Origins of the War, 1898-1914;* and the *French Diplomatic Documents, 1871-1914.*[64a]

Professor Pribram's invaluable edition of *The Secret Treaties of Austria-Hungary, 1879-1914,*[65] made possible for the first time a satisfactory study of the Triple Alliance treaties and their evolution from a purely defensive system into one which was used for aggressive purposes by Italy and Austria.

The Bolshevist *Materials for the History of Franco-Russian Relations from 1910 to 1914,* mentioned above, contains much of the correspondence between the Russian Foreign Office and the Russian Embassy in Paris during the four years before the War. It enables one to see how Izvolski and Poincaré were transforming the Franco-Russian alliance from its originally defensive character into a potentially aggressive combination to support Russian ambitions in the Balkans. Much of this material has been made easily accessible to Western readers in René Marchand's *Livre Noir.*[66] It has been further completed by some five hundred additional letters and telegrams of Izvolski's correspondence, which have been published in

---

of topically and in which the German editorial notes are omitted. is now being published, and is discussed by F. Thimme in KSF, V, 897-907, Sept., 1927.

[64a] For the full titles of these recent documentary publications, see "Oe.—U.A.," "B.D." and "D.D.F." in the List of Abbreviations above.

[65] A. F. Pribram, *Die politischen Geheimverträge Oesterreich-Ungarns,* 1879-1914, Vienna and Leipzig, 1920 (Eng. trans., ed. by A. C. Coolidge, 2 vols., Cambridge, Mass., 1920-22).

[66] *Un Livre Noir: Diplomatie d'Avant-Guerre d'Après les Documents des Archives Russes,* ed. by R. Marchand, 2 vols., Paris, 1922-23.

German translation by Friedrich Stieve.[67]   Parallel to this
Paris-St. Petersburg correspondence, supplementing and
confirming it, is the London-St. Petersburg correspondence
of Count Benckendorff for the years 1908-1914.   His letters
and other secret papers were clandestinely copied by B. von
Siebert, a counsellor in the Russian Embassy at London.
They were apparently sold or conveyed to German authorities, and published by von Siebert in a German edition in
1921.[68]   They have been conveniently rearranged and published in English translation by G. A. Schreiner, *Entente
Diplomacy and the World* (1921).   They show the efforts
of Russia and France to strengthen the friendship with
England and to tighten the bonds of the Triple Entente
into a combination which should be firm and powerful
enough to defy the Triple Alliance, if necessary.

From the French archives, a few documents were published by Professors Bourgeois and Pagès, as a French
Senate Report on *Les Origines et Les Responsabilités de la
Grande Guerre*.[69]   But these French documents are few and
meager as compared with the German, Austrian and Russian publications, and are selected to prove a case, rather
than to furnish historians with material for study.   More
valuable are the French *Yellow Books* containing documents
on such special subjects as the *Franco-Russian Alliance*
and *Balkan Affairs, 1912-1914,* though these are clearly far
from complete.

(b) MILITARISM

A second underlying cause of the War, closely connected
with the system of secret alliances, was militarism.   The
word is often used vaguely.   But usually it includes at least

---

[67] F. Stieve, *Der Diplomatische Schriftwechsel Iswolskis, 1911-
1914,* 4 vols., Berlin, 1924.

[68] B. von Siebert, *Diplomatische Aktenstücke zur Geschichte der Ententepolitik der Vorkriegsjahre,* Berlin and Leipzig, 1921.

[69] Published in the *Journal officiel,* Jan. 9, 1921; republished, in book
form, with some material from the Kautsky Documents, Paris, 1921.

two definite conceptions. First, the dangerous and burdensome mechanism of great standing armies and large navies, with the attendant evils of espionage, suspicion, fear, and hatred. Second, the existence of a powerful class of military and naval officers, headed by the General Staff, who tend to dominate, especially at a time of political crisis, over the civilian authorities.

The system of great armies, embracing the larger part of the male population capable of bearing arms, began with the French during the Revolution and under Napoleon. It was extended and efficiently developed by the Prussians in the War of Liberation. As a result of its success in the victories of Moltke and Bismarck in the Wars of 1864, '66 and '70, it came to be esteemed and imitated in the rest of Continental Europe. From the Franco-Prussian War onwards the military and naval armaments of all the Great Powers tended to grow larger and larger, and the financial burden became heavier and heavier. Armaments were alleged to be for defense and in the interests of peace, according to the fallacious maxim, *si vis pacem, para bellum.* They were intended to produce a sense of security. That was the argument used in getting from legislatures the necessary grants of money. What they really did produce was universal suspicion, fear, and hatred between nations. If one country increased its army, built strategic railways, and constructed new battleships, its fearful neighbors were straightway frightened into doing likewise. So the mad competition in armaments went on in a vicious circle. This was especially the case during and after the Balkan Wars of 1912-1913, when it seemed that the Great Powers might be involved. It was also accentuated by the system of alliances. Germany and Austria, uncertain of Italy's loyalty, believed they must increase their armaments to secure their own safety. France urged Russia to increase her army and build strategic railways against Germany, and readily

loaned her half a billion francs on condition that it be spent
for these purposes. Russia urged France to extend the
term of French military service from two to three years.
"Russia is ready; France must be also," declared the Russian Minister of War in an alarming newspaper article early
in 1914. So armaments were increased, not only to give
security to an individual country, but also to strengthen
the alliance to which it belonged.

Militarism implied also the existence of an influential
body of military and naval officers, whose whole psychological outlook was naturally colored by the possibility, if not
the "inevitability," of an early war. To these professional
fighters war held out the prospect of quick promotion and
great distinction. It would, however, be a grave injustice
to them to imply that they urged war for selfish motives of
personal advancement. Nevertheless, the opportunity to
put into practice the results of the work of preparation for
war to which their lives were devoted cannot have failed
to have its psychological effect. Quite aside from any personal motives, the military officers in all countries had a
high sense of national honor and patriotic duty, as they
understood it. It was their supreme duty to be ready at
any moment to protect the state by force of arms. It was
the constant preoccupation, day and night, of the General
Staff in every country to be ready to make or meet an attack
in the shortest possible time. To this end every General
Staff drew up or revised every year the most minute and
complete plans for mobilization and march to the frontier
to satisfy all possible contingent situations. Military officers generally held to the theory that it was advantageous
to take the offensive. This meant striking the foe before
his mobilization was complete—at the moment, therefore,
when the enemy country was in the most vulnerable process
of transforming itself from a peace to a war footing. It
meant also that the war, with all its frightful economic

devastation and demoralizing political and psychological effects, would be carried on in the enemy's country instead of within one's own frontiers. In a political crisis, therefore, the military leaders were always quick to conclude that war was "inevitable," and exerted all their influence to persuade the ruling civilian authorities to consent to an order for general mobilization at the earliest possible moment, in order to gain the advantage of the offensive. But a general mobilization, according to prevailing military opinion, actually did make war inevitable. It was a process virtually impossible to halt when once begun. This was one of the greatest evils of militarism. It is always at a crisis, precisely when it is most difficult for diplomats to keep their heads clear and their hands free, that militarist leaders exert their influence to hasten decisions for war, or get the upper hand altogether.

Another evil of militarism was the fact that the plans of the General Staff were technical and were worked out and guarded in such absolute secrecy. Not only were they unknown to Parliament and the public; they were often not even known to the Minister of Foreign Affairs, or at least their details and significance were not grasped by him. Sir Edward Grey says that between 1906 and 1911 he knew nothing of the plans which the English and French military authorities were working out for Anglo-French military cooperation in Northern France. As to the negotiations between the Anglo-Russian naval authorities in the spring of 1914, he likewise writes: "I never enquired at the Admiralty afterwards, but I imagine the practical result of the consultations between the two naval authorities was not great. . . . [In the Siebert documents they] are constantly referred to as 'conventions.' How the military and naval authorities themselves described them, I do not know." [70] Similarly, in Russia, it is clear that M. Sazonov did not at

[70] Grey, I, 91, 274-277.

first grasp the fact that the plans of the militarists made a
"partial mobilization" against Austria a piece of folly, if
not a downright impossibility. And in Germany Herr von
Bethmann-Hollweg never envisaged clearly the implications
of the Schlieffen-Moltke plan to attack France through
Belgium, although he was probably aware of it, according
to Ludendorff, as early as 1912.

This then was another evil of militarism. The General
Staffs worked out in absolute secrecy the plans which they
calculated to be best adapted to bring military victory,
regardless of the political implications which they might
thereby impose on the civilian authorities. And when war
became "inevitable," there was tremendous pressure upon
the civilians to accept the arrangements which the militarists had long planned in secret. The militarist mind was
much the same in all the countries, but there was a difference as to the extent to which the military and civilian
authorities exercised control. General Joffre, in 1912, precisely like the German strategists, urged the strategic necessity of disregarding Belgian neutrality; but while Moltke
was allowed to build his whole plan of campaign upon this
violation of a treaty which Bethmann was helpless to avert
if war came, M. Poincaré was strong enough and shrewd
enough to veto General Joffre's views. He realized the bad
effect it would have on public opinion in England, and the
danger that it might cause the British Government to make
use of its stipulated freedom to withhold armed aid.

Closely akin to this influence of military and naval officers was the pressure exerted on civilian authorities by
munition makers and "big business."

Some militarists believed in "preventive" war—the
waging of a war upon a neighbor while he was still weak,
in order to prevent him growing stronger later on. So it is
often alleged that Germany wanted war in 1914, in order to

have a final reckoning with Slavdom before Russia should have completed her "Great Program" of military reorganization in 1916 or 1917. M. Poincaré and his associates are alleged to have wanted war in 1914 before Germany grew any stronger by reason of her rapidly increasing population, wealth, and naval force, and also before French Socialists, revolting against the burden of French military expenditure, should repeal the recently voted three-year term of service. For the same reasons Russian militarists are said to have wanted war sooner rather than later. England even is often said to have been glad of the opportunity to crush the growing German navy before it should become a greater menace to that of England. Though here and there some individual military and naval officers in most countries may have held such views, the present writer does not think that the militarist doctrine of preventive war was a decisive factor in causing the World War. Only in Austria-Hungary did it exercise a strong influence on state policy; here it was generally felt that a conflict with Serbia must come sooner or later, and, as Baron Conrad repeatedly urged, the sooner the better. The murder of the Heir to the Throne was eagerly seized upon as a good excuse for trampling upon the Greater Serbia danger.

Nor is there any more substantial truth in the common assertion that the German authorities welcomed war as a means of crushing the rising tide of socialism, than there is in the similar assertion that Russia welcomed war as a good way of putting an end to workingmen's strikes and revolutionary unrest.

Generally speaking, it may be said that this aspect of militarism—the influence of the military upon the civilian authorities—was a serious matter in the three eastern monarchies of Germany, Austria, and Russia. It was much less in France, and virtually non-existent in England, where civilian ministers were ordinarily in charge of the army and navy.[71]

We shall have something more to say about militarism and navalism in connection with the system of alliances.

(c) NATIONALISM

Nationalism, whose essence and development have recently been so admirably analyzed by a distinguished American historian,[72] must be accounted one of the major underlying causes of the War. In its chronic form of Pan-Germanism, Pan-Slavism and *revanche*, it nourished hatred between Germany and her two neighbors on the East and West. It worked in curious and devious ways. It had contributed happily to the unification of Germany and Italy. On the other hand, it had disrupted the Ottoman Empire and threatened to disrupt the Hapsburg Monarchy. In its virulent form, it had contributed for a century to a series of wars for national liberation and unity in the Balkans. It was such an important factor in the Balkan situation and led so directly to the immediate occasion of the World War that some account of it in this corner of Europe will be given below in the chapter on Balkan Problems.

(d) ECONOMIC IMPERIALISM

Economic imperialism embraces a series of international rivalries which resulted in large part from the Industrial Revolution in England and its subsequent introduction into the other great countries of the world.[73] It led to quantity

[71] On these aspects of militarism, *cf.* H. N. Brailsford, *The War of Steel and Gold,* London, 1914; Karl Liebknecht, *Militarism,* New York, 1917; Munroe Smith, *Militarism and Statecraft,* New York, 1918; [F. C. Endres], *Die Tragödie Deutschlands,* 3rd ed., with abundant bibliographies, Stuttgart, 1924; and the admirable volume of G. L. Dickinson, *The International Anarchy, 1904-1914,* London, 1926.

[72] C. J. H. Hayes, *Essays on Nationalism,* New York, 1926; and "Contributions of Herder to the Doctrine of Nationalism," in *Am. Hist. Rev.,* XXXII, 719-736 (July, 1927).

[73] For an excellent recent discussion of this whole subject, see Parker

production of goods which in turn involved the struggle for new markets and new sources of raw materials. It resulted in a great increase of population, part of which sought to emigrate to the still unoccupied regions of the world, thereby sharpening the colonial rivalry of the Great Powers. It brought about the accumulation of capital which sought investment abroad, thus leading to economic exploitation and political competition. In consequence of these and other factors, the Great Powers began to partition Africa among themselves, to secure territory or exclusive spheres of influence in China, and to build railroads in Turkey and elsewhere. This struggle for markets, raw materials, and colonies became more acute during the last quarter of the nineteenth and the beginning of the twentieth century, owing to the fact that Germany and Italy entered the competition. Hitherto politically weak and divided, they had now secured national unity and wished to come forward to share with the other Powers in the partitioning of the world. It can hardly be said that any one of the Great Powers was more responsible than another for the international jealousies and friction which arose out of this economic imperialism. By 1914, all the Great European Powers had secured slices of Africa. In China, Italy only had failed to gain something for herself. In the matter of railway construction, which was one of the most important forms of economic imperialism because it involved political as well as economic interests, one sees the English building the Cape-to-Cairo railway, the Russians the Trans-Siberian, and the Germans the so-called Bagdad Railway. The first of these came into conflict with German, Belgian and French ambitions; the second was partly responsible for the Russo-Japanese War; the third caused endless sus-

T. Moon, *Imperialism and World Politics*, New York, 1926; and A. Lumbroso, *Le origini economichi e diplomatichi della guerra mondiale*, Milano 1927.

picions and friction between Germany and the Triple Entente.

Protective tariffs which usually accompanied the modern industrial system, except in England, were another form of economic imperialism. "Tariff wars" and retaliatory measures caused irritation between countries, especially in the mind of the man in the street and in newspaper discussion. There was always the danger that great merchants and industrialists would use official government support to secure economic advantages for themselves. This tended to bring governments into conflict with one another.

Generally speaking, however, this economic imperialism is usually exaggerated as one of the underlying causes of the War. It is often said, for instance, that the industrial development of Germany, and the jealousy with which it was regarded by England, made a war between these two countries "inevitable" sooner or later. This, however, is an unsound view. It arises from the fact that economic rivalry tends to become exaggerated in the mind of the public, because it is a subject which touches the pockets of wide classes, and is more generally discussed and perhaps understood than other questions like secret treaties, militarism, or nationalism. It often happens that great merchants or industrialists own or control newspapers which are selfishly interested in contributing to the exaggeration of these economic questions. But if one reads the diplomatic correspondence of the years before the War, one is struck by the relatively slight importance which is given to these economic rivalries which haunt so largely the mind of the average business man and newspaper editor. It is not so much questions of economic rivalry as those of prestige, boundaries, armies and navies, the Balance of Power, and possible shiftings in the system of alliances, which provoke reams of diplomatic correspondence and raise the temperature in Foreign Offices to the danger point.

(e) THE NEWSPAPER PRESS

Another underlying cause of the War was the poisoning of public opinion by the newspaper press in all of the great countries. This is a subject which is only beginning to receive the careful investigation which it deserves.[74]

Too often newspapers in all lands were inclined to inflame nationalistic feelings, misrepresent the situation in foreign countries, and suppress factors in favor of peace. In the diplomatic correspondence of the forty years before the War there were innumerable cases in which Governments were eager to establish better relations and secure friendly arrangements, but were hampered by the jingoistic attitude of the newspapers in their respective countries. Ambassadors and Cabinet Ministers frequently admitted the senseless attitude of the leading newspapers in their own country, apologized for it and promised to exert themselves to restrain it, if only the other Government would do the same toward its press. These were often quite genuine efforts and may frequently be seen in Anglo-German relations in the quarter of a century before the War. At other times, however, Ministers sought to score an advantage or to defend their attitude by alleging that their freedom of action was restricted because of the press and public opinion—that if they yielded the point under dispute there would be such a howl from the newspapers and the public that they would be turned out of office. Such allegations are sometimes true, but more often they are not, particularly in the countries of Central and Eastern Europe, where

74 *Cf.* E. M. Carroll, "French Public Opinion in the War of 1870," in *Amer. Hist. Rev.*, XXXI, 679-700, July, 1926; J. F. Scott, *Five Weeks: a Study of the Surge of Public Opinion on the Eve of the Great War*, New York, 1927; I. C. Willis, *How We Went into the War*, London, 1918; L. M. Salmon, *The Newspaper and Authority* (N. Y., 1923), chs. xii-xiv; F. R. Flournoy, *Parliament and War—The Relation of the British Parliament to the Administration of Foreign Policy in Connection with the Initiation of War*, London, 1927.

the Government was generally able to exercise a greater control over the press than in England. It is, nevertheless, true that the newspapers of two countries often took up some point of dispute, exaggerated it, and made attacks and counter-attacks, until a regular newspaper war was engendered, which thoroughly poisoned public opinion, and so offered a fertile soil in which the seeds of real war might easily germinate. A particularly good example of this is to be seen in the press feud carried on between Austria and Serbia in the weeks following the murder of the Archduke Ferdinand. Here was a case in which the Governments of both countries, instead of apologizing for their press or trying to restrain it, deliberately allowed the newspapers to incite public opinion and fire it to an indignation and enthusiasm for war. It would, perhaps, be too much to say that, had it not been for this Austro-Serbian newspaper feud, the War might have been averted. But it is true that the violence of the Serbian press was one of the determining factors which led Count Tisza to change his opinion and to accept war with Serbia, whereas at first he had been stubbornly opposed to it; and without his consent Count Berchtold and the militarists could not have made war on Serbia.

There is a vast literature on freedom of the press, censorship of the press, slander and libel, and the professional aspects of journalism, but there is very little sound writing on the relations of the press to governmental control and on its influence in fomenting national hatreds and war. Yet there is abundant material for the study of this in the newspapers themselves; in *Die Grosse Politik*, and other diplomatic documents; and in the writings and biographies of men like W. T. Stead, Wickham Steed, Spender, and Northcliffe; of Busch, Hammann, and Theodor Wolff; of Lauzanne, Gauvin, and Tardieu; of Blowitz and Suvorin; and of Godkin, Ogden, Villard, and Lippmann. It is to be hoped that some careful scholars will turn their attention to this problem of the influence of the newspaper press as one of the underlying causes of the War. Bismarck's oft-quoted remark is even more true for the generation immediately preceding the World War than for his own: "Every country is held at some time to account for the windows broken by its press; the bill is presented, some day or other, in the shape of hostile sentiment in the other country."

CHAPTER II

THE SYSTEM OF SECRET ALLIANCES, 1871-1890: DOMINATION OF THE EASTERN EMPIRES

THE CONSEQUENCES OF THE FRANCO-PRUSSIAN WAR

THE Franco-Prussian War reversed a situation which had existed for two hundred years. After the Thirty Years' War in the seventeenth century Germany remained weak. Economically she had been exhausted by that terrible conflict in which all Europe trampled on her soil. Politically she was weak by her division into an incongruous multitude of states differing in size and character, and by the increasing rivalry for leadership between the decaying power of the Hapsburgs and the growing vigor of the Hohenzollerns. Consequently she was continually subject to the French policy of Richelieu and Mazarin, which aimed to keep her weak and divided. Occasionally, also, she was subject to actual invasion and dismemberment by French armies, as in the time of Louis XIV and Napoleon. Early in the nineteenth century, to be sure, in a time of great danger and humiliation, Prussia and Austria had temporarily sunk their mutual rivalry; with English and Russian assistance they had united in the War of Liberation to expel and dethrone Napoleon. But Waterloo did not end Germany's internal weaknesses. The loose Confederation of 1815 and the continued jealousy of Austria and Prussia left Germany still comparatively impotent and unimportant as an international power. Finally, in the 1850's at the Frankfort Diet, Bismarck became convinced that Germany's weakness could only be cured by a fratricidal war in which

50

Austria should be forcibly expelled from the German body politic. At Paris and at Biarritz, he learned to gauge the weakness and ambition of Napoleon III which could be turned to Germany's advantage. So he annexed Schleswig-Holstein, expelled Austria by the Prussian victory at Sadowa, and established the North German Federation under Prussian leadership. In 1870-1871, by Sedan and Versailles, he at last transformed Germany into a strong unified Empire. The situation between France and Germany was now reversed: it was no longer Germany, but France, which was weak and in danger from an attack from across the Rhine.

Bismarck's unification of Germany was hailed at the time as a desirable, even glorious, accomplishment of the spirit of nationalism. But it was accompanied by the annexation of Alsace-Lorraine. The French have always regarded this as a crime—"the brutal dismemberment of a nation," "the tearing of children from their mother." History shows that it was worse than a crime, it was a blunder.

In Bismarck's defense it has been said that he was only "liberating" territory which had been wrested from Germany by Louis XIV at a time when Germany was weak and divided against herself. Victors had always seized territory from the vanquished if they could, and if it suited their purposes. Moltke and the Prussian military authorities insisted that the provinces between the Vosges and the Rhine must be in German hands to prevent a possible attack by a revengeful France upon the South German States, which were none too enthusiastically or securely incorporated into the new German Empire. Bismarck, it is argued, could not come back to Berlin and face a Reichstag and the popular German demand for French territory without laying himself open to the charge of having been weakly generous to the successors of Louis XIV and Napoleon. Moreover, the majority of the population in the annexed districts spoke German. There is some truth in this point of view.

On the other hand, there is much more truth in another point of view. There was a vast difference between the French annexations in the seventeenth century and Bismarck's annexation in 1871. Between these two periods lay the French Revolution and the forces to which it had given rise. Louis XIV in seizing the Alsatian districts did not dismember Germany, because there was at that time no united German body politic—nothing but a conglomeration of mutually jealous German territories. The so-called Holy Roman Empire was neither Holy, nor Roman, nor an Empire, but "an irregular sort of a body like a monster," [1] incapable of feeling a wound. The French Revolution, however, had swept away provincial boundaries in France, and created a new self-conscious nation, "one and indivisible." France, including the annexed districts of Alsace and Lorraine, had become one body, powerfully conscious of its unity and nationality; if one of its members suffered, all suffered together. Bismarck had mutilated a living body and the wound would not heal; it was to remain an awful open sore threatening the peace of Europe for forty years. Nor was Alsace-Lorraine necessary to Germany's safety from a military point of view; the Rhine was as good a boundary as the Vosges. And though the majority of the million and a half people in Alsace and Lorraine were German speaking, that did not mean that they were German thinking; on the contrary, the great majority were bitterly opposed to separation from France and protested vigorously, but in vain. Could Bismarck have peered into the future and seen how French pride and French bitterness over the loss of Alsace-Lorraine was to vitiate every effort

---

[1] "Irregulare aliquod corpus et monstro simile," wrote "Severin de Monzambano" [Pufendorf] in his famous tract, *De Statu Imperii Germanici* (1667), cap. VI, sec. 9.

at permanently satisfactory relations between Germany and France—could he have foreseen how, by its direct and still more its indirect consequences, it was to be one of the main underlying causes of the World War, perhaps then he would have acted otherwise in 1871. But though he was possessed of unusual political foresight, he can scarcely have expected that the French would never become reconciled to their loss; that, on the contrary, the desire for *revanche,* unspoken perhaps, but fixed in the heart, would persist and even grow in intensity in later years. In fact, Bismarck's policy in the decade 1875-1885 seems to indicate that he had hopes of winning the French to something like frank friendship and an acceptance of the *fait accompli.*[2] Nevertheless, whatever he may have hoped as to the future, he had no illusions about the present. He knew that for the years immediately following the war, French resentment would run high. He must therefore protect the new German Empire, the child of his creation, by making it strong of itself—strong by holding France weak and isolated, and strong by the establishment of close relations with the two other Great Powers bordering on Germany on the east and south, that is, with Russia and Austria.

THE LEAGUE OF THE THREE EMPERORS, 1872-1878

Between Russia and Prussia there had existed traditional bonds of friendship ever since their armies had fought side by side for the overthrow of Napoleon. These bonds had been further strengthened during the Crimean War and the Polish uprising of 1863. Both Powers had a common interest in preventing the reëstablishment of Polish independence, which would have deprived them of the spoils of the partitions of Poland. During the Franco-Prussian

---

[2] "Je désire en arriver à ce que vous pardonniez Sedan comme vous avez pardonné Waterloo," Bismarck said to the French ambassador in December, 1884; Bourgeois et Pagès, *Les Origines et les Responsabilités de la Grande Guerre,* Paris, 1921, p. 307.

War, Russia had done Bismarck the great service of main
taining an attitude of benevolent neutrality and of tending
to restrain Austria from joining France and seeking *revanche* for Sadowa. The long months during the siege of
Paris were for Bismarck a critical and difficult period, and
Russia might, if she had chosen, have greatly embarrassed
him. Bismarck therefore at once frankly recognized the
service which Russia had done him in 1870-1871 by assent-
ing to the Tsar's abrogation of the humiliating Black Sea
Clauses, imposed on Russia after the Crimean War. A still
stronger bond between the two countries was the close personal tie between old Emperor William and his nephew,
Alexander II, a tie which was renewed by the visit which the
Tsar paid to Berlin in the month following the signature of
peace between Germany and France.

With Austria, Bismarck was especially anxious to establish firm and friendly relations. Having accomplished
his purpose of establishing German unity under Prussian
leadership, he believed that the natural relation of the two
countries which contained such large German elements and
which for centuries had formed part of the same Holy
Roman Empire should be one of friendship. After Sadowa
he had purposely refrained from humiliating Austria further by annexing Austrian territory or by allowing the victorious German army to enter the Austrian capital. He
had also maintained close relations with the powerful
Magyar elements in Hungary who had used Prussian victories to secure for themselves from Francis Joseph the
favorable constitutional Compromise of 1867. Austria, on
her part, was ready to recognize 1866 as a *fait accompli* and
to give up any hope of changing the arrangements which
Bismarck had established. Accordingly, Bismarck was able
to bring about friendly personal meetings between Emperor
William and Francis Joseph in the summer of 1871 on
Austrian soil. In November, 1871, the good relations be-

tween the two Powers were greatly strengthened through
a change in the Foreign Office at Vienna: Count Beust, a
Saxon who had never liked Bismarck and was inclined to
the side of France, was replaced by Count Julius Andrássy,
a Magyar and an old friend of Bismarck's.

In April, 1872, Count Andrássy suggested that Emperor
Francis Joseph should pay a return visit to Emperor William at Berlin.   When Tsar Alexander II heard of the intended visit he asked the German Ambassador in St.
Petersburg, "Have they not written to ask you whether
they would like to have me there at the same time with the
Emperor of Austria?" [3]

Alexander did not want to be left out in the cold while
his two brother monarchs were conferring together.   He
suggested that such a meeting of the three Eastern monarchs would be the strongest guarantee for the peace of
Europe and would strike a blow at the French desire for
revanche which was the most permanent menace to this
peace.   But his suggestion was a little embarrassing to
Bismarck.   He did not quite know how Francis Joseph
would take it.   When, however, the Austrian Emperor's
consent had been secured, it was finally arranged that the
three monarchs, accompanied by their Foreign Ministers,
should visit Berlin together in the second week of September, 1872.   This interview of the three Emperors, accompanied by extraordinary gala festivities meant to impress
the world, resulted in a still closer understanding between
the three Eastern Powers.   Though no written agreement
was signed, and though the Foreign Ministers conferred in
pairs and not all together, there was established a close
"understanding" or *"Entente à trois,"*—the basis for the
"League of the Three Emperors" a few months later.   In
a sense, this Entente was a renewal of the old Holy Alliance
of 1815; as in the days of Alexander I and Metternich the

[3] G.P., I, 197.

three Eastern Powers had stood together in defense of con-
servatism and the *status quo,* so now they were to stand together in defense of monarchical solidarity against the rising
danger of international socialism, and for the preservation
of the peace and *status quo* of Europe against possible
moves of France or others to disturb it. On the whole, the
meeting was a triumph for Bismarck, though he was not
without irritation at the Russian minister, Gorchakov,
whose vanity and suspected intrigues were ever a trial to
his nerves. Gorchakov, for instance, on this occasion had
greatly embarrassed Emperor William by remarking to him
in the presence of the French Ambassador, "Well, I have
just been at Prince Bismarck's to discuss with him the
points on which we are agreed, but nothing has been put in
writing; promises suffice between sovereigns and ministers."[4] For the suspicion which this remark may easily
have aroused in the mind of the French Ambassador there
was absolutely no ground. Alexander had no thought of
participating in any aggressive policy toward France.

The Entente of the Three Emperors was further
strengthened in the following year when Emperor William,
accompanied by Bismarck and Moltke, visited St. Petersburg. A secret military convention was soon signed by
which Russia and Germany promised to each other the
assistance of two hundred thousand men in case either was
attacked by a European Power.[5] A few weeks later, when
Tsar Alexander journeyed to Austria to attend the Vienna
Exhibition of 1873, he and Francis Joseph signed an agreement that they would consult one another on any questions
in which they might have divergent interests; in case of any
aggression by a third Power menacing the peace of Europe,
they promised to come to an understanding with one another, without seeking or contracting new alliances, in order
to reach a common line of conduct; and if, as a result of this

4 G.P., I, 202.   5 G.P., I, 203.

understanding, military action should become necessary, it
should be arranged for by a special military convention.
This agreement was communicated to Emperor William
who gave his adhesion to it on October 22, 1873. In this
way came into being the so-called League of the Three
Emperors.[6]

Germany, as a result of her recent victories and her large
army, was the strongest of the three Powers. And of the
three ministers—Gorchakov, Andrássy and Bismarck—
the last was by far the ablest in grasping the European
situation as a whole, in seeing what the political interests of
his neighbors were, and in being willing to recognize and
bargain on the basis of these interests. The natural result
was that the guiding spirit of the League was the German
Chancellor. He used its influence to preserve the peace
of Europe, and incidentally to prevent France from forming any coalition or seeking revenge against Germany. This
at first was not difficult. Italy followed the lead of the three
Emperors. England was still holding to her traditional
policy of splendid isolation. France was too exhausted and
too occupied with domestic political problems to think of
disturbing the peace.

But in 1875, the harmony of the League was seriously
ruffled. Gorchakov's vanity made it difficult for him to
play second fiddle to Bismarck. With personal inclinations
toward France, which were not shared by the Tsar, he
listened to anti-German reports of his representatives at
Berlin, Belgrade and Constantinople. He came into conflict with Bismarck over a Montenegrin affair and over the
question of the rank to be enjoyed by Rosen, the German
Consul General at Belgrade. Bismarck feared, with reason,
that Gorchakov might influence the Tsar against Germany
and thus weaken the League of the Three Emperors. He
therefore sent Radowitz to St. Petersburg to take the

[6] G.P., I, 206-209.

place of the German Ambassador who was on indefinite sick leave. Radowitz was to represent Bismarck's views to Gorchakov energetically, and he did so successfully. But Gorchakov then circulated rumors which grew into the French legend that Radowitz had been sent to bribe Russia to give Germany a free hand against France in return for Germany's giving Russia a free hand in the Orient. This alarmed France and England and contributed to the so-called "war-scare of 1875." Bismarck was unjustly suspected of contemplating a "preventive war" against France. Whether Bismarck had any hand in inspiring the German newspaper articles which added to the scare, or whether they started with the irresponsible communications of a newspaper reporter in Vienna, as now seems likely, is not wholly clear. At any rate, it is quite probable that he was willing to make use of it as a means of frightening France out of completing her proposed army reorganization, and there is no doubt that the French felt they were menaced. The French Foreign Minister appealed to Tsar Alexander and Queen Victoria to use their influence to prevent Germany from any aggressive action. Gorchakov easily persuaded the Tsar, on his visit to Berlin, to make it clear that Russia could not allow France to be crushed.[7] Gorchakov's pompous announcement from Berlin, "Now peace is assured," flattered his own vanity, but made Bismarck very angry, because Gorchakov seemed to have implied that Germany had really intended a preventive war and that Russia had averted it—an implication the truth of which Bismarck always energetically denied, and for which he

---

[7] *Cf.* J. V. Fuller. "The War Scare of 1875," in *Amer. Hist. Rev.*, XXIV, 196-226 (Jan., 1919). The current French version of the war-scare of 1875 needs correction in the light of *Die Grosse Politik*, I, 245-300; Radowitz, *Aufzeichnungen und Erinnerungen*, Stuttgart, 1925, I, 302 ff.; Hajo Holborn, *Bismarck's Europäische Politik zu Beginn der siebziger Jahre und die Mission Radowitz*, Berlin, 1925; and K. Klingenfuss, "Beust und Andrássy und die Kriegsgefahr von 1875," in *Archiv. f. Pol. u. Gesch.*, IV., 616-643 (1926).

never forgave the Russian foreign minister.[8] The incident
led to cooler relations between Berlin and St. Petersburg,
but cannot be said to have really destroyed the League of
the Three Emperors, since Alexander II and William I still
remained close personal friends.

THE NEAR EASTERN CRISIS, 1875-1878

Another event in 1875 which threatened the harmony of
the League of the Three Emperors was the outbreak of a
new and prolonged crisis in the Balkans. The progressive
dissolution of the Sick Man of Europe and the outrages
committed by his savage soldiers on his long-suffering Christian subjects led Russia again to consider the possibility of
his demise. In Herzegovina the cruelty of the land-owning
aristocracy, a large part of whom were of Serb blood but
who had become converted to Mohammedanism in order to
live on better terms with the Turkish rulers, caused an uprising of the unhappy Christian peasantry in July, 1875.
The uprising spread rapidly into Bosnia. It awoke the
fanatical sympathy of Serb brethren in Austria-Hungary
and the neighboring principality of Serbia. On account
of the mountainous nature of the region and the inefficiency
of the Sultan's government, the Turks seemed powerless to
suppress the revolt. Russia and Austria were at once brought
face to face again in their old rivalry over Balkan interests.
Bismarck now had the difficult task during the next fifteen
years of preventing this rivalry from causing a rupture
between the two Powers whom he wished to have as friends

---

[8] *Cf.* Bismarck, *Reflections and Reminiscences*, ch. xxvi: "I reproached Prince Gorchakov sharply. It was not, I said, a friendly part
suddenly and unexpectedly to jump on the back of a trustful and unsuspecting friend, and get up a circus performance at his cost; proceedings of
this kind between us, who were the directing ministers, could only injure
the two monarchies and states. If he was anxious to be applauded in
Paris, he need not on that account injure our relations with Russia; I
was quite ready to assist him and have five-franc pieces struck at Berlin,
with the inscription *Gorchakov protège la France.*"

and whom he wished to prevent from gravitating toward France.

Russia's ambitions in the Balkans were of long standing. With the remarkable rise and consolidation of the Russian state at Moscow, the Slav Empire had begun to push steadily southward toward the Black Sea and the Dardanelles. Peter the Great, in wars with Turkey, had acquired for a short time at Azov his coveted "window" on the Black Sea, and given that impetus to Russian progress toward the south which his successors came to regard as Russia's historic mission. Catherine the Great, taking up anew the war with Turkey, had secured the Crimea and the whole northern shore of the Black Sea. Conveniently for Russia's ambitions, the spirit of nationalism awakened by the French Revolution had stimulated in Greeks and Slavs of the Balkans the desire to throw off the Turkish yoke. Russia was ready, as usual, to support their desire in order to fish in troubled waters herself. Already she had waged eight wars against Turkey, either for her own territorial expansion or for the ostensible purpose of assisting the subject nationalities of Slavic blood and Orthodox Greek faith. In the last of these wars—the Crimean—she had been checked by England and France and by the hostile attitude which Austria had assumed. This attitude of Austria, during the war and at the Congress of Paris, had contributed to Russia's loss of part of Bessarabia and caused great bitterness in Russia. It was felt to be an unpardonable act of Hapsburg ingratitude, coming, as it did, so soon after Nicholas I had sent a Russian army to help the Hapsburgs crush the Hungarian revolt of 1849. Russia's bitterness of feeling had subsided after the establishment of the League of the Three Emperors, but now there was danger that it might revive. Russia was anxious to win back the part of Bessarabia lost in 1856 and was inclined to support a new revolt like that in Bosnia and Herzegovina, which promised further to break up the Turkish Empire. Though Gorchakov had at first been opposed to Austria's annexing Bosnia and Herzegovina,[9] he gradually came round to accept such an arrangement, provided Russia in turn could secure adequate compensations for herself.

Austria, on the other hand, had no ostensible ties of religion and blood with the oppressed Christian nationalities in the Balkans and no desire to see them achieve independence as clients of Russia. Austria-Hungary—especially Hungary—already included more Slav peoples than could be easily assimilated. With the growing spirit of nationalism, these Slav subjects were becoming more and more difficult to govern. The Austrian Minister of Foreign Affairs, Andrássy, a Magyar, was therefore at first opposed to the acquisition of Bosnia and Herzegovina, which he feared would aggravate the internal problem of the Dual Monarchy of ruling over a large number of Slavs.[10] He preferred to have the Great Powers act jointly by way of a Conference and enforce reforms upon Turkey for the benefit of the peasantry in Bosnia and Herzegovina, but he did not desire to begin the partition of the Ottoman Empire. His desire found expression in the "Andrássy Note" of December 30, 1875, which demanded an armistice, a series of reforms, and the appointment of a mixed Christian and Mohammedan commission to look after the carrying out of the reforms. The Turks, as usual, made a pretense of accepting the demands; but the insurgent Bosnians, fired with enthusiasm by their successes and by their hope of support from their brother Serbs in Serbia and Montenegro, refused to abide by the terms of the Andrássy Note. The crisis became more serious.

Bismarck's chief concern in the whole Eastern Question was to prevent it from disturbing the peace of Europe and

9 Wertheimer, *Graf Julius Andrássy*, II, 118.
10 Wertheimer, *Graf Julius Andrássy*, II, 259 ff.

the satisfactory relations between Austria and Russia which had been established by the League of the Three Emperors. In a conversation with Gorchakov at Berlin in December, 1875, he had already emphasized this.[11] Germany herself, as he repeatedly declared, had no selfish interests of her own in the Balkans. "The whole Eastern question was not worth the bones of a Pomeranian grenadier." [12] But the danger of a split between Russia and Austria, or of the formation of a European coalition in connection with the Bosnian crisis, were very serious matters to him. Andrássy's idea of a conference of the Powers he did not look upon with favor, because he feared that Austria would naturally side with England and that Russia consequently might draw closer to France. Gorchakov, he suspected, would not be averse to flirting with France. But such a division of Europe into an Anglo-Austrian and Franco-Russian grouping would place Germany in a delicate and dangerous position: she would have the thankless task either of acting as arbitrator between the two groups, or she would have to cast in her vote on the Anglo-Austrian side, thus laying Germany open to hostile Powers on two fronts. Such a grouping would also endanger the League of the Three Emperors and its safeguarding of the peace of Europe.[13]

Meanwhile, however, Tsar Alexander and Emperor Francis Joseph, accompanied by their Ministers, had come together at Reichstadt and on July 8, 1876, reached a secret but somewhat hazy "agreement" without Bismarck's knowledge. They agreed to refrain from intervention in Turkey for the present. But for the future, if the Turks should regain the upper hand over the insurgents, Russia and Austria would protect the Serbs from excessive violence and insist upon real reforms. If, on the other hand, the insur-

11 G.P., I, 207.
12 Bismarck's Reichstag speech of December 7, 1876.
13 G.P., II, 31 ff.

gents continued their successful resistance and the Ottoman Empire in Europe should crumble to pieces, Austria was to annex part of Bosnia, Russia was to regain the part of Bessarabia lost in 1856 and territories on the eastern shore of the Black Sea [in which Austria had no interest]; Bulgaria and Rumelia were to be autonomous; additions of territory were to be given to Serbia, Montenegro and Greece; and Constantinople was to be erected into a free city.[14]

By this Reichstadt Agreement Gorchakov had secured Austria's agreement in principle to the partition of Turkey. The terms, as Andrássy conceived them, were exceedingly favorable for Austria. The agreement contemplated the development of a number of small, weak states in the Balkans, but expressly excluded the creation of a large, strong Slav state, whether Serbian or Bulgarian, which would have naturally affiliated itself with Russia on racial and religious grounds and have been a menace to Austria. Moreover, by the stipulation that Austria might annex Bosnia and Herzegovina, Austria would assure the safety of her outlying Dalmatian possessions, would check the danger from the growing nationalist aspirations of the Serbs, and would acquire territory which might be regarded as compensation for the loss of Venetia in 1866. Andrássy, who had originally been opposed to the break-up of the

[14] Reichstadt "agreement" is a misnomer, since there was a misunderstanding from the outset. No formal document was drawn up, "agreed upon," and signed at Reichstadt. After the meeting, the Austrian and Russian ministers each dictated his own recollection of the substance of the views exchanged. This explains many marked differences between the Austrian and Russian versions of the "agreement" as printed respectively by Wertheimer (*Graf Julius Andrássy*, II, 322 ff.) and by the Bolsheviks in *Krasnyi Arkhiv* (Moscow, 1922), I, 36. According to the Russian version, for instance, Montenegro was to annex Herzegovina, and Austria was merely to take Turkish Croatia and a small adjacent part of Bosnia contiguous to the Austrian frontier. According to Andrássy's version, Austria was to annex all of Bosnia and Herzegovina except certain "extensions" allotted to Serbia and Montenegro "to round them off." Cf. G. H. Rupp, "The Reichstadt Agreement," in *Amer. Hist. Rev.* XXX, 503-510 (April, 1925); and G.P., II, 34-37.

Ottoman Empire, was now well content with the agreement. The failure of his efforts to secure reforms in the region from the Turks during the past months had convinced him of the futility of attempting to preserve the *status quo* or to secure any permanent satisfactory settlement for the Christian peasantry so long as they remained under Turkish misgovernment. And if Austria was to annex Bosnia and Herzegovina it was much better to do it in friendly agreement with Russia than in opposition to her.

But the fortunes of war in the Balkans during the following weeks did not bear out the probable expectation of Gorchakov and Andrássy that Turkey was on the point of collapsing. On the contrary, the Turks showed an extraordinary revival of energy. They defeated the insurgents in one encounter after another, until finally on August 29, Prince Milan of Serbia called for help. Gorchakov and the Russian Pan-Slavs were not deaf to the call. They felt that they must intervene on behalf of the oppressed Orthodox Slav peasantry, in spite of the principle of non-intervention for the present, which had formed the first clause of the Reichstadt Agreement. This at once renewed the old hostility between Russia and Austria over Balkan affairs and led to a tense situation between the two Great Powers. Both accordingly turned to Bismarck.

On September 13, 1876, Andrássy informed the German Ambassador in Vienna of the Reichstadt Agreement, which hitherto, at Gorchakov's request, had been concealed from Bismarck.[15] Gorchakov on his part resorted to a stratagem which aroused Bismarck's indignation. Instead of communicating in the proper official way through the Russian Ambassador at Berlin, he was suspected by Bismarck of instigating the Tsar to make use of Baron Werder, Emperor William's personal representative to the Tsar. Werder, who was staying with Alexander at Livadia in the Crimea

15 G.P., II, 45-47.

was suddenly asked the blunt question whether in case of war between Russia and Austria, Germany would observe benevolent neutrality as Russia had done in 1870. Werder telegraphed the embarrassing and indiscreet question to Berlin. But Bismarck evaded giving any answer to it, and would have recalled Werder except for Emperor William's fear that it would hurt the Tsar's feelings. But a few days later, employing the correct channel of communications by instructions to the German Ambassador at St. Petersburg, Bismarck again emphasized his aim of preserving peace in Europe and harmony in the League of the Three Emperors. If Russia decided to intervene and make war on Turkey, Bismarck would use his influence to prevent Austria from attacking Russia, and he hoped he could succeed in this. If not, and if war broke out between Russia and Austria in spite of all his efforts, Germany would not necessarily abandon neutrality. He would make no promises beforehand, but he would say that German interests could not allow a coalition of all Europe permanently to weaken Russia's position as a Great Power; nor could he, on the other hand, permit Austria to be endangered in her position as a European Power or in her independence, and so cease to be one of the factors on which Germany could reckon in the European balance· of power.[16] "We could endure that our friends should lose or win battles against each other, but not that one of the two should be so severely wounded and injured that its position as an independent Great Power, taking its part in the councils of Europe, would be endangered." [17]

Bismarck's refusal to give Russia a free hand against Austria caused Gorchakov to moderate his attitude. It was arranged that the representatives of the Christian Powers should meet in conference at Constantinople and convince

[16] G.P., II, 72-79; cf. also II, 108, and VI, 356 f.
[17] Bismarck, *Reflections and Reminiscences*, II, 234.

Abdul Hamid of the need of making real reforms. But convincing the Turk was about as easy a matter as making a donkey gallop. Abdul Hamid thwarted the conference by a clever pretense of proclaiming a constitution for Turkey and by promising even more wide-reaching reforms than the Powers themselves had demanded. Gorchakov, however, rightly had no confidence in the honesty of the Sultan's promises. He therefore prevailed upon Austria to sign a new secret Budapest Convention of January 15, 1877, providing for the war which Russia contemplated waging against Turkey. Austria agreed not to threaten the Russian flank upon its advance south of the Danube, and in return Russia approved the idea of Austria's annexation of Bosnia and Herzegovina and the other provisions which Andrássy understood had been agreed upon at Reichstadt.[18]

In April, 1877, as soon as weather conditions permitted, Russia opened against Turkey the war which she had long desired. Though checked for months at Plevna, she eventually won a series of victories which brought her armies to the outskirts of Constantinople and forced Turkey to accept the Treaty of San Stefano on March 3, 1878. This provided for the creation of a great Bulgarian State, more or less comprising the predominantly Bulgarian parts of Turkey and embracing an extensive sea coast on the Aegean. The Treaty met with objections on every side: by Greece, Serbia, and Rumania because this "Greater Bulgaria" was to be so much more powerful than any one of themselves. It was objected to by Austria and England who feared the greatly enlarged Bulgaria would be virtually a vassal state under Russian control; Austria did not like to see such an increase of Russia's power near her border, and England feared for the safety of the Suez Canal. Both these Powers therefore insisted on a Congress for the revision of the Treaty of San Stefano. Bismarck at first had no great

18 G.P., II, 111-115.

liking for this proposal, but finally consented to act as "Honest Broker," and invited the Powers to the Congress of Berlin.

In the various preliminary negotiations which settled almost all the essential points before the Congress met, so that the Congress merely had to register decisions which had already been arranged by Bismarck, the German Chancellor strove hard to satisfy both Austrian and Russian interests. In the end, Austria was again accorded by the Treaty of Berlin the right to occupy and administer Bosnia and Herzegovina and also, if military necessity required, to occupy the tongue of territory between Serbia and Montenegro known as the Sanjak of Novibazar. Russia acquired the part of Bessarabia lost in 1856 and valuable territories between the Black and Caspian Seas. These were important gains for Russia, but to Gorchakov they seemed but slight rewards after all Russia's military efforts and successes. He left the Congress with bitter feelings against Bismarck. He felt that Bismarck had betrayed Russian interests and been guilty of unpardonable ingratitude in view of Russia's benevolent neutrality during the Franco-Prussian War. In Russia there was a violent outburst in the Pan-Slav press against Germany which Bismarck regarded as altogether unjustifiable. Though he had supported Austria and England on many points, he had also done Russia a real service, getting far more for her at the Congress than she could have gotten for herself. He thought Russia ought to look with satisfaction at the real gains that she had made, instead of comparing the Treaty of Berlin with what she would have gained by the Treaty of San Stefano. The result of this personal bitterness between the two Ministers and of the violent newspaper attacks of one country against the other put an end for the time being to that harmony and coöperation which had been the object of the League of the Three Emperors.

THE AUSTRO-GERMAN ALLIANCE OF 1879

The hostility between Russia and Germany was not confined merely to personal bitterness between the Ministers or to the recriminations of newspapers. In the commissions established for executing the terms of the Treaty of Berlin, the German delegates sided regularly with Austria against Russia. In reply, Russia undertook a vigorous increase in armaments and pushed her troops westward into Poland toward the German frontier. "Russia must prepare for War," declared General Miliutin, and his declaration was reiterated by the Pan-Slavs. At last, in the summer of 1879, even Alexander himself, unable longer to restrain his feelings, poured out his grievances to the German Ambassador in St. Petersburg, and wrote a letter to Emperor William complaining of Bismarck's policy and warning him of "the disastrous consequences which might follow." [19]

At about the same time Bismarck heard that his friend Andrássy was soon to resign and was likely to be replaced by Baron Haymerle, on whose friendship he did not feel sure that he could count. In view of the danger from Russia he decided to seek at once a defensive alliance with Austria while Andrássy was still in office. He accordingly drew up with him the Treaty of October 7, 1879, which established the Austro-German Alliance. He would have liked a treaty in which Austria and Germany would promise to support each other in case either were attacked by a third Power, whether Russia, France, or Italy. But Austria was unwilling to expose her eastern frontier to a Russian attack by promising unconditionally to assist Germany in the West in case the French should undertake a war of revenge. Austria was mainly concerned with the danger from the side of Russia. Therefore the treaty provided that should Austria or Germany be attacked by Russia, the

[19] G.P., III, 16.

two Contracting Parties were bound to come to the assistance one of the other with their whole war strength; should either be àttacked by a Power other than Russia [such as France or Italy], the other Contracting Party bound itself to observe a benevolent neutrality; should, however, the attacking Power be supported by Russia, then the other Contracting Party would come to the assistance of her ally with her whole strength. The treaty was to be for five years and renewable. It was also to be secret, though if the armaments of Russia really proved menacing, the Contracting Powers would consider it a duty of loyalty to let the Tsar know, at least confidentially, that they would consider an attack on either as an attack on both.[20]

The Austro-German Alliance consolidated the Central Empires and became henceforth, until their collapse in November, 1918, the very foundation rock of German policy. It indicated a political course from which neither Bismarck nor his successors ever seriously swerved. In its origin, and as long as Bismarck remained at the helm, it was essentially defensive in purpose and fact. Germany and Austria mutually protected each other against the rising tide of Pan-Slavism; and Germany, if attacked by an outbreak of French *revanche*, could count upon Austria's neutrality, just as Austria could count on that of Germany in case of an outbreak of Italian Irredentism.

Contemporary opinion regarded Bismarck's establishment of this Alliance as a master stroke. In the words of the French Ambassador at Berlin: "From the point of view of his prestige in Europe and of his popularity in Germany, Bismarck has never accomplished a work so considerable as that of the Alliance with Austria. . . . He has realized without wars, without conquests dearly bought, without

[20] Pribram, I, 6-9. For the detailed negotiations by which Bismarck arranged this treaty and overcame his own sovereign's strong objections to it, see G.P., III, 1-136.

burdensome or enfeebling annexations, the German political
dream of union of all the States where the German race
dominates in a common political system and a powerful
solidarity." [21] This contemporary opinion has for the most
part been endorsed by posterity.[22] Only here and there
before the World War were there those who criticized it.
But after 1914, when German support of Austria became
one of the causes which involved all Europe in war, many
voices, even in Germany, questioned Bismarck's wisdom.
They alleged that Bismarck, by further alienating Russia
through alliance with Austria, made inevitable the Franco-
Russian Alliance; and that by taking sides with Austria
against Russia in the Balkans, he prepared the way for the
clash which came in 1914.

Such critics, however, are wrong in thinking that Russia
was permanently alienated from Germany after 1879. They
did not know of the very secret treaty which Bismarck made
with Russia within two years (June 18, 1881) and which he
renewed (with modifications) and kept effective as long as
he remained in power. They are wrong in thinking that it
made the Franco-Russian alliance inevitable. This was
perhaps "inevitable" anyway, in view of the growth of Pan-
Slavism in Russia and the persistence of Alsatian memories
in France. And they are wrong in thinking that Bismarck's
alliance of 1879 necessarily involved an Austro-Russian
clash in the Balkans. True to the defensive aims with which
he had established the Austro-German Alliance, Bismarck
continually warned Austria in the following years that Germany would not fight to support Austrian expansion or
aggression in the Balkans. He repeatedly took occasion to
remind her that the alliance was defensive, not offensive.[23]
In 1885, for instance, with prophetic vision, he warned

---

21 St. Vallier to Freycinet, March 22, 1880; Bourgeois et Pagès, p. 370
22 *Cf.* C. Grant Robertson, *Bismarck*, p. 363 f.
23 G.P., IV, 338; V, 8, 26 ff., 35 f., 136 ff., 149 ff., 194 f.

Austria that in supporting Serbia too strongly she might so arouse Serbian ambitions that Serbia would some day "turn against Austria and talk of a Serbia Irredenta in the Banat" of Hungary.[24] It was not until many years after Bismarck's dismissal that Austria began to pursue the more aggressive and independent policy, which tended to pervert the Austro-German Alliance from one which was defensive in form to one which became offensive in fact. Criticism should not be directed against Bismarck, but against his later successors—especially Bülow and Bethmann—who failed to follow sufficiently closely his conservative policy of holding Austria in check.

It is also a mistake to imply, as so many writers do, that Bismarck's choice of Austria in preference to Russia in 1879 was final, and that the wire between Berlin and St. Petersburg was permanently broken down. It was not. Bismarck was only waiting for an opportunity to repair it. He had by no means permanently turned his back upon Russia. In allying with Austria he was only taking a step which prudence for the moment counselled, but this did not preclude another step later in the direction of Russia. The opportunity for this soon came.

THE ALLIANCE OF THE THREE EMPERORS, 1881-1887

Among Russia's diplomats there were two who did not allow themselves to be blinded by indignation against Bismarck over the outcome of the Congress of Berlin. One of these was Giers, who soon assumed virtual charge of Russian foreign affairs in place of Gorchakov. The other was Peter Saburov, who foresaw the probability of an Austro-German alliance even before it was signed.[25] In January, 1880, Saburov came as Ambassador to Berlin, where he had many

24 G.P., V, 11 f.
25 Cf. his interesting and friendly conversations with Bismarck at Kissingen in July, 1879, in *Krasnyi Arkhiv*, I, 68-84.

intimate interviews with Bismarck with a view to reknitting
the close personal relations between Tsar Alexander II and
Emperor William I, thus reviving the League of the Three
Emperors.[26]

Saburov, like all Russian diplomats, always had one eye
out for Russian control or influence at Constantinople. He
had realized in 1878 how easy it was for an English fleet
to threaten the Turkish capital and he feared for the future.
He therefore laid before Bismarck his view of Russia's
danger in a memorandum to the following effect. In 1833
Russia had aided Turkey against the victorious army of
Mehemet Ali, and was rewarded for this service by the
Treaty of Unkiar Skelessi, in which Turkey undertook to
close the Dardanelles to all enemy fleets which sought to
penetrate to the Black Sea. This stipulation, negotiated
exclusively for Russia's benefit, protected her southern
shores from hostile attack; but this stipulation was modified to her detriment by the Treaty of London of 1840 and
the Straits Convention of 1841, in which the principle of
the closure of the Straits, hitherto applied to entry into the
Black Sea, was equally extended to exit from it. Russia
was thus shut off from sending her navy into the Mediterranean. These principles were confirmed in the Treaty of
Paris in 1856 which in addition forbade Russia and Turkey
to have ships of war on the Black Sea; this treaty remained
in force until the Treaty of London of 1871. The London
agreement, resulting from Russia's attempt to abrogate the
Black Sea Clauses while France and Germany had their
hands tied by the Franco-Prussian War, annulled the provision of 1856 forbidding Russian or Turkish war vessels
on the Black Sea, but admitted for the first time the principle that foreign navies might enter the Straits if the Sultan

26 G.P., III, 139-179. J. Y. Simpson, "Russo-German Relations and
the Sabouroff Memoirs," in *The Nineteenth Century*, LXXXII, 1111-1123;
LXXXIII, 60-75 (Dec., 1917; Jan., 1918).

judged it necessary for the safeguarding of the other clauses of the Treaty of Paris. This reversed completely to Russia's disadvantage the principle of the closure of the Straits, which in its origin had been intended to provide Russia with a lock and chain at the Dardanelles for the protection of her shores and her influence over Turkey. At the Congress of Berlin, England had declared that "her obligations, concerning the closure of the Straits, were limited to an engagement to the Sultan to respect in this matter only the *independent* decisions of the Sultan"; in other words, England was not obliged to respect the decision of the Sultan if the latter tried to close the Straits at Russia's demand, for such a decision would not be "independent." England, Saburov concluded, was reserving the right to enter the Straits and threaten Russian interests whenever she pleased. Russia's lock and chain were valueless therefore, unless she could get the support of Germany and Austria.[27] This is what Saburov wanted and what Bismarck was willing to give, in return for the restoration of friendly relations with Russia. A friendly agreement with Russia would mean a renewal of the League of the Three Emperors, and tend to guarantee the peace of Europe. Saburov had also been duly impressed by the Austro-German Alliance and began to realize Russia's diplomatic isolation. Russia was anxious again for German and Austrian support.

Bismarck, on his side, in spite of his relatively friendly relations at this time with France, could never wholly rid

[27] Russian Aide-Mémoire of Feb. 5, 1880, given by Saburov to Bismarck; G.P., III, 144f. For an excellent historical sketch of the Straits question to 1878, see J. T. Shotwell, "A Short History of Question of Constantinople and the Straits" in *International Conciliation*, No. 180, Nov., 1922, pp. 463-527; see also S. M. Goriainov, *Le Bosphore et les Dardanelles*, Paris, 1910; P. H. Mishev, *La mer noire et les détroits de Constantinople*, Paris, 1899; E. Driault, *La Question d'Orient*, Paris, 1905; N. Dascovici, *La Question du Bosphore et des Dardanelles*, Genève, 1915; N. E. Buxton and C. Phillipson, *The Question of the Bosphorus and the Dardanelles*, London, 1917; and below, ch. v. especially note 11.

himself of the nightmare that the French might make a coalition with Russia against him. To diminish the likelihood of this, he believed it would be highly desirable to restore the old harmony between the three Eastern Emperors, which had existed before the Congress of Berlin. Austria also would derive advantage from such a renewal of good relations with both her neighbors, because it would tend to safeguard the new position which she had acquired in Bosnia and Herzegovina, and would make more certain that any future changes in the *status quo* in the Balkans— which was still very unstable—would not be made single-handed by Russia to the sole benefit of the Slavs and to the detriment of Austria; such changes would only be made on the basis of a mutual understanding between the three Eastern Empires.

In view of the advantages to each of the three Powers, it was not difficult to reach the very secret agreement which was signed by Bismarck, Saburov, and Szechenyi on June 18, 1881. It was regarded as so secret that Bismarck did not entrust the drawing up of documents in regard to it to the chancery secretaries, but wrote them out with his own hand; and the diplomatic correspondence dealing with it was marked with special numbers and reserved for the eye of as few initiates as possible. The secret was so well preserved that the world knew nothing of it until part of it was published by Professor Goriainov in 1918.[28] It provided among other things (Art. I) that "in case one of the High Contracting Parties should find itself at war with a fourth Great Power, the other two will preserve a benevolent neutrality toward it and will devote their efforts to the localizing of the conflict." In other words, if Germany should be at war with France, or Austria at war with Italy,

[28] S. Goriainov, "The End of the Alliance of the Emperors," *Amer. Hist. Rev.*, XXIII, 325 (Jan., 1918). The full text is printed by Pribram, p. 11, and, with the negotiations leading up to it, in G.P. III, 139-179.

or Russia at war with Turkey, the country at war need have no fear of an attack on its rear by either of the other two Eastern Empires. Austria's interest in the Balkans was safeguarded by the provision that this first clause in Art. I should apply to a war between Russia and Turkey, "but only in case a previous agreement has been reached between the three Courts relative to the results of that war."

In Art. II the three Signatory Powers agreed to respect the rights acquired by Austria in Bosnia and Herzegovina by the Treaty of Berlin, and to make no changes in the territorial *status quo* of "Turkey in Europe" except by common consent. By tacit implication this meant that Russia could still pursue her forward policy in the Caucasus where Austria and Germany were not particularly interested.

Saburov's fears of an English fleet in the Straits were quieted by Art. III:

> "The three Courts recognize the European and mutually obligatory character of the principle of the closure of the Straits of the Bosphorus and of the Dardanelles. . . . They will take care jointly that Turkey shall make no exception to this rule in favor of the interests of any Government whatsoever by lending to warlike operations of a belligerent Power the portion of its Empire constituted by the Straits. In case of infringement, or to prevent it if such infringement should be in prospect, the three Courts will inform Turkey that they would regard her, in that event, as putting herself in a state of war towards the injured Party, and as having deprived herself thenceforth of the benefits of the security assured to her territorial *status quo* by the Treaty of Berlin."

A supplementary protocol provided for friendly coöperation between the consular and other agents of the Signatory Powers in the Balkans, and for the possible reunion of Bulgaria and East Rumelia. Russia's concessions to Austria in the Reichstadt Agreement and Budapest Convention were reaffirmed by a clause agreeing that:

"Austria reserves the right to annex the provinces of Bosnia and Herzegovina [already occupied in 1878] at whatever moment she shall deem opportune."

This treaty of 1881, which revived the League of the Three Emperors and converted it into an alliance, served Bismarck's great purpose of preserving peace in Europe, and especially of preventing a conflict between Russia and Austria in the Near East. It established by tacit consent a kind of line of demarcation between the two. Russia was to have unhampered and dominant influence in Bulgaria and the Eastern Balkans such as Austria was to have in Serbia and the Western Balkans. The establishment of the frontier between Bulgaria and Serbia as the demarcation line dividing Russian and Austrian interests, Bismarck rightly believed, was the surest and best way to avoid dangerous rivalries and suspicions in the Balkans. He was quite ready to use Germany's decisive influence in the balance to force each of his allies to keep behind the line of demarcation in their proper spheres. In contrast to the policy of his successors, he was ready to restrain Austria by timely warnings and pressure from taking aggressive action in the Balkans which would arouse dangerous Russian opposition. He did not care who ruled in Bulgaria nor what took place there. That was Russia's sphere and she could do as she liked in it. Russia had originally established Alexander of Battenberg as Prince of Bulgaria; but if Russia wanted to turn him out when he no longer proved the pliant tool which the Pan-Slavs had expected, that was Russia's affair and Austria ought not object. He warned Austria that she must keep hands off in Bulgaria, and that he would not allow anyone to throw a noose about his neck in this matter which would embroil Germany with Russia. His wise advice to Austria was: "The Eastern Question is a game of patience; he wins who waits." [29]

[29] G.P. V, 195.

Bismarck's policy of a demarcation of interests between Austria and Russia, and the pressure he put upon each, helped to preserve the peace of Europe even during the violent Balkan crisis that arose through the union of the two Bulgarias in September, 1885. Austria did nevertheless so encourage the Serbians against the Bulgarians that Alexander III refused to renew the Alliance of the Three Emperors when the Treaty ran out in 1887.

The Tsar had an ineradicable distrust of Austria. He had inherited it from his grandfather at the time of Austria's "astonishing ingratitude" during the Crimean War. It had been fostered and nourished by his tutors and advisers, who belonged to the Pan-Slav group represented by Miliutin and Katkov, and it had taken a deep hold on him during the long Bosnian crisis which ended so unsatisfactorily for Russia in the Congress of Berlin. Bismarck worked hard to bring about the renewal of the tripartite agreement of 1881. He did not want to see it "thrown behind the stove." [30] But when he found that the Tsar was unshakeable in his distrust of Austria, he had no mind to forfeit Russia's friendship because of Austria's unnecessarily aggressive support of Serbians against Bulgarians. Moreover, his relations with France had grown very much worse during recent months as Boulanger had come into prominence, and he had heard rumors in September, 1886, and in the spring of 1887, of secret negotiations for a Franco-Russian coalition.[31]

THE RUSSO-GERMAN "RE-INSURANCE TREATY," 1887-1890

Bismarck therefore accepted with alacrity a Russian proposal that in place of the existing tripartite agreement, Russia and Germany should make a defensive treaty of their own without Austria. With a characteristic directness of action, Bismarck drew out of his portfolio the text of the

[30] Instruction of Dec. 21, 1886; G.P., V, 211.   [31] G. P., VI. 89 ff.

Alliance of 1879 and read it to Schuvalov, declaring that he sincerely regretted that Russia's attitude at that time had compelled Germany to protect herself by means of this treaty. Nevertheless it existed; Germany must and would remain loyal to its terms and to Austria, and therefore this fact must be taken into consideration in framing any treaty between Russia and Germany. After the discussion of a number of alternatives, this difficulty was finally overcome by the wording agreed upon in Art. I: "If one of the High Contracting Parties shall find itself at war with a third Great Power, the other will maintain towards it a benevolent neutrality and will devote its efforts to the localization of the conflict. This provision shall not apply to a war against Austria or France resulting from an attack made upon one of these two powers by one of the Contracting Parties." [32] This defensive arrangement was perfectly satisfactory to Bismarck as he had no intention of attacking France; and in case France should attack Germany he had been insured since 1879 against danger on his Southern frontier by Austria's promise of benevolent neutrality. Now, by the new treaty with Russia, he was re-insured against any danger on his Eastern frontier. Furthermore, if Russia should attack Austria, the new "Re-insurance Treaty" in no way conflicted with his obligation to protect Austria, in accordance with the Austro-German Alliance.

With his characteristic willingness to consider the aims and ambitions of other Powers and to bargain on the basis of them, Bismarck then further recognized Russia's Balkan interests and Saburov's desire to secure a Russian lock and chain against the English in the Straits. The Re-insurance Treaty accordingly recognized (Art. II) "the rights historically acquired by Russia in the Balkan Peninsula and particularly the legitimacy of a preponderating and decisive influence on her part in Bulgaria and East Rumelia"; and

[32] G.P., V, 253; Pribram, p. 305.

Art. III reaffirmed the principle already agreed upon in 1881 that Russia and Germany should support each other in putting pressure on the Sultan to keep the Bosphorus and the Dardanelles closed to the warships of foreign Powers. They also pledged themselves to permit no modification of the *status quo* in the Balkan Peninsula except by a previous mutual agreement. In a supplementary protocol Bismarck went even further in recognizing the Russian point of view by agreeing that "in case Russia finds it necessary to undertake herself the task of defending the entrance into the Black Sea in order to safeguard the interests of Russia, Germany engages to lend her benevolent neutrality and her moral and diplomatic support to the measures which Russia shall deem necessary to guarantee the key to her Empire." This meant that, so far as Germany was concerned, Russia might take possession of territory on the Straits and perhaps even of Constantinople. The possession of this "key," which Russia would virtually have acquired by the Treaty of San Stefano in 1878 and which Bismarck now promised in 1887, meant much more than the mere lock and chain against the English fleet for which Saburov had stipulated in 1881. Bismarck was willing to concede even this "key" in order to lessen the likelihood of a coalition between Russia and France. He may also, no doubt, have counted upon the fact that England would still have something to say if Russia tried to oust the Sultan from his capital. This so-called "Re-insurance Treaty" of June 18, 1887, was to be in force three years.[33] It outlasted Bismarck's own tenure of office, but was not renewed by his successor, Caprivi. During the three years it was in force it did not wholly prevent the beginning of a *rapprochement* between France and Russia which eventually devel-

---

[33] For the text of the treaty and the negotiations leading up to it see G.P., V, 211-268; and Goriainov, in *Amer. Hist. Rev.*, XXIII, 330-349 Jan., 1918). Taube, *La Politique Russe d'Avant-Guerre* (Paris, 1928), 74-84.

oped into an Alliance, but there is no doubt that it delayed
this coalition which had been Bismarck's worst nightmare.
Such was the success of one set of alliances, establishing
the domination of the Eastern Empires, by which Bismarck
for nearly a score of years conjured away an open clash
between Russia and Austria in the Balkans, preserved
almost unbroken the good relations of Germany with her
powerful neighbors to the south and east, and thereby
lessened the danger from the west. The very existence of
the Alliance of 1881 with Russia and Austria had been preserved with such perfect secrecy that it gave rise to no
suspicions or alarm on the part of France or other Powers.

THE TRIPLE ALLIANCE OF 1882

The formation of the Triple Alliance is commonly attributed to Bismarck. He is pictured as encouraging France
to seize Tunis with the calculation that this "would arouse
such bitterness in Italy that Bismarck could undoubtedly
secure the consent of the Italian Government to an alliance
with Austria and Germany." [34]   It is true that he encouraged France to "pluck the ripe Tunisian fruit" and to engage in other colonial adventures. But he did this mainly in
the hope of winning the friendship of the French by supporting their ambitions, and also of interesting them in
colonial activities which would help them to forget the
defeat of 1870. He hoped they would expend their energies

[34] Seymour, *The Diplomatic Background of the War, 1870-1914*, p. 35.
Cf. also Matter, *Bismarck et son Temps*, III, 445, 512 f.; Hanotaux, *Histoire de la France Contemporaine*, IV, 740; Coolidge, *The Origins of the
Triple Alliance*, 197 ff.   For accounts of the Triple Alliance based on the
new material in *Die Grosse Politik*, and Pribram, see Becker, *Bismarcks
Bündnispolitik* (Berlin, 1923); Rachfahl, *Deutschland und die Weltpolitik,
1871-1914*, I, *Die Bismarck'sche Aera* (Stuttgart 1923), pp. 371-398; Gran-
felt, *Das Dreibundsystem, 1879-1916* (Stockholm, 1924); Lenz, *Deutschland
im Kreis der Grossmächte, 1871-1914* (Berlin, 1925).   The best account of
the Tunis Question is by W. L. Langer, "The European Powers and the
French Occupation of Tunis, 1878-1881," in *Amer. Hist. Rev.*, XXXI, 55-78
251-265 (Oct., 1925; Jan., 1926).

in North Africa and China instead of preparing to regain Alsace-Lorraine. He was quite willing that the French should antagonize the Italians, but he was not calculating to secure the alliance of the latter. It was not with Bismarck that the Triple Alliance originated, but with Italy.

Early in 1882, Italy asked for a treaty of alliance with Germany and Austria. Italy wanted to strengthen her position and to gain support for future ambitions. Italy had come away from the Congress of Berlin "with clean hands," which meant empty hands, though Bismarck had told her that, as far as Germany was concerned, she might take Tripoli any time. She had just received what she regarded as a humiliating slap in the face from the French who had occupied Tunis, the very territory which Italy had not unnaturally been coveting for herself. And she was still afraid "the Prisoner of the Vatican" might attempt to regain his temporal possessions. Italy had everything to gain and little to risk in an alliance with Germany and Austria. This Bismarck fully recognized, and he was not therefore especially eager to incur an Italian liability. Earlier, in 1880, when a treaty with Italy was first suggested to him, his comment was, "You don't need to run after Italy if you want something of her; moreover, her promise will have no value if it is not in her interest to keep it." [35] Of the value of the Italians themselves as Allies, he had no very high opinion. In his private notes, recently published, he refers to "their fickle character," "their childish egoism," and "the restless, arrogant character of Italy's policy, which might easily involve her friends in trouble." [36] He argued the instability of alliances with parliamentary monarchies like Italy and England:

"Not all countries are able to offer the same guarantee that their obligations will be strictly executed, especially in countries in which the legislature exercises more influence

[35] G.P., III, 185.   [36] G.P., III, 185, 198; *cf.* also Pribram, I, 128 ff.

than the dynasty. With England, for instance, there could be no permanent alliance, because in England domestic politics take precedence over foreign affairs. Political parties, which alternate in the government of a country, do not necessarily recognize the obligations of their predecessors, and the monarch is not strong enough by himself to uphold his foreign policy against the party momentarily in power. . . . With us, as in Austria, the case is different. In these two countries, although they also have parliamentary institutions, there exists a sufficiently strong monarchy to be able to carry out its treaty promises under all circumstances." [37]

Nevertheless, Bismarck gradually came to regard with favor Italy's application for an alliance, owing to certain advantages it would have for Germany. But as the German Empire did not touch Italian territory, and was not so directly interested as Austria in a number of troublesome points which would have to be settled, Bismarck suggested that Austria should negotiate the terms of the treaty with Italy. The Italian Ambassador at Berlin was told that "the key to the door which leads to us must be sought in Vienna." [38] Accordingly, the ensuing Austro-Italian negotiations, with occasional suggestions from Bismarck, ultimately resulted in the Triple Alliance Treaty signed at Vienna on May 20, 1882, by Kálnoky, Robilant, and Reuss.[39]

The general purposes of Austria, Italy, and Germany were, according to the preamble, "to augment the guarantees of peace in general, to strengthen the monarchical principle, and by this to insure intact the maintenance of the social and political order in their respective states by agreeing to conclude a treaty which by its essentially conservative and defensive character aimed only to protect them against the dangers which might menace the safety of their states

[37] G.P., III, 207.   [38] G.P. III, 208.
[39] G.P., III, 245-7; Pribram, 24-26.

and the peace of Europe." Though the treaty did not specifically guarantee Alsace-Lorraine to Germany against France, nor Rome to Italy against the papal claims to temporal power, it was hoped by each Power that it would have this effect.

By Art. I, "The High Contracting Powers mutually promise peace and friendship, and will enter into no alliance or engagement directed against any one of their States. They engage to proceed to an exchange of ideas on political and economic questions of a general nature which may arise, and they further promise one another mutual support within the limits of their own interests."

At the negotiations of the Austro-German Alliance of 1879 Andrássy steadily refused to promise Austrian armed support in case of a French attack on Germany, unless France were also joined by Russia; his successor persisted in this refusal in 1882, and hence in Art. II, dealing with a possible French attack, Austria's obligation extended only to Italy, while Germany's and Italy's obligations were mutual: "In case Italy, without direct provocation on her part, should be attacked by France for any reason whatsoever, the two other contracting parties shall be bound to lend help and assistance with all their forces. This same obligation shall devolve upon Italy in case of any aggression without direct provocation by France against Germany."

Art. III provided for the danger of a Franco-Russian coalition: "If one, or two, of the High Contracting Parties, without direct provocation on their part, should chance to be attacked and to be engaged in a war with two or more Great Powers non-signatory to the present treaty, the *casus foederis* will arise simultaneously for all the High Contracting Parties." This virtually extended to Italy the principle agreed upon between Austria and Germany in 1879, except that the addition of the words "without direct provocation" gave the obligation a more restricted and purely defensive character.

According to Art. IV: "In case a Great Power, non-signatory to the present treaty, should threaten the security of the states of one of the High Contracting Parties, and the threatened Party should find itself forced on that account to make war against it, the two others bind themselves to observe towards their Ally a benevolent neutrality. Each of them reserves to itself, in this case, the right to take part in the war if it should see fit to make common cause with its Ally."

Art. V was calculated to secure solidarity of action: "If the peace of one of the High Contracting Parties should chance to be threatened under the circumstances foreseen by the preceding Articles, the High Contracting Parties shall take counsel together in ample time as to the military measures to be taken, with a view to eventual coöperation. They engage henceforth, in all cases of common participation in a war, to conclude neither armistice, nor peace, nor treaty, except by common consent among themselves."

The Treaty of Alliance was for five years, and its contents and its existence were to be kept secret.

The Triple Alliance was expected to bring considerable advantages to each of its members. Italy gained an increase in prestige and power by alliance with the powerful German Empire, and could now be accounted one of the Great Powers. Her royal government, which had shown some signs of tottering before revolutionary agitation, was much strengthened and less likely to be disturbed by papal or French attacks. Moreover, Italy would have less fear of trouble with Austria, who now became her ally instead of her enemy—at least as far as the governments, if not the populations, of the two countries were concerned. The obligations which Italy assumed in return were not heavy. She did not have to assist Austria in a war between Austria and Russia alone. In case of an attack by France upon either Germany or herself, Italy would have the powerful assistance of Germany, and might look forward to a victorious outcome which might give her some increase of territory in the direction of Nice and Savoy or Northern Africa.

Austria's chief benefit from the treaty lay in the hope that in case of an attack from Russia over Balkan questions, she would no longer have to leave a part of her army to guard her southern frontier against the danger of Italian Irredentism. She could throw the whole weight of her forces against Russia or into the Balkans.

Germany hoped the treaty would prevent Italy from allying with France and from thus giving encouragement to the *revanche* party at Paris. In case France should make war, however, the French forces available against the Rhine would be diminished by those which would have to be directed to the Alpine frontier against Italy. If Russia joined France, it would be of great importance to Germany that Austria, no longer in fear for her Italian frontier, would be able to launch the whole strength of the Dual Monarchy against Russia, and thereby relieve the pressure on Germany's eastern front. Even if Italy were unable to provide large fighting forces—both Kálnoky and Bismarck had a very low opinion of Italy's military strength at this time —it was still highly advantageous to Germany and Austria that Italian forces should face west against France, instead of north upon Austria's rear. "Sparing the Austrian forces, rather than winning those of Italy, is our aim," was Bismarck's comment.[40]

The Triple Alliance in its wording and in its origin was essentially defensive in character, and designed primarily to preserve the peace of Europe. This is now clear from the detailed negotiations concerning its formation, which

[40] G.P., III, 224-225.

have been revealed by Pribram from the Austrian archives, and by the extensive German documents in *Die Grosse Politik*. Its defensive character is now admitted even by French historians who are by no means friendly to Bismarck.[41] Bismarck himself, in a private despatch which he never expected would be made public, referred to it as "our League of Peace." [42] Its peaceful and defensive intent was especially marked in the case of Germany. But it became less so in the case of Italy and Austria, who later wished to use it to support their aggressive intentions. It was, in fact, not long before Italy sought to make use of her new alliance to promote her ambitions in North Africa and elsewhere. Her request for German protection against alleged interference with Italian interests by the French in Morocco caused Bismarck to reply sharply:

> I am not without just irritation over this request of Mancini's, and observe in it a dilettante—confidentially I would even say banausic—ignorance of what is possible and desirable in high diplomacy. There is again manifest in this incident, to put it mildly, that lack of unselfishness which has already so often betrayed the Italians into sending other people into the water for the sake of Italian interests, without wetting even a finger of their own . . . We are ready to stand by Italy's side if she is attacked or even seriously threatened by France. But we cannot hear with indifference the expectation that we should begin trouble with France or place Europe before the possibility of a war of great dimensions, because of vague anxieties about Italy's interests which are not immediate, but which represent hopes for the future in regard to Morocco, or the Red Sea, or Tunis, or Egypt, or other parts of the world.[43]

In 1885, Italy irritated her new allies by seizing Massowah on the Red Sea without notifying them beforehand

[41] *Cf.* Bourgeois et Pagès, p. 197.
[42] "Unsere Friedensliga"; G.P., III, 263; see below at note 45.
[43] Bismarck to Keudell, April 6, 1884; G.P., III. 410.

of her intentions. When the time approached for renewing
the Triple Alliance, Italy complained that she had gained
nothing as a result of the treaty. Bismarck replied bluntly,
but truly, that the Alliance was made to secure the peace
of Europe and not to win new conquests for its members.
When Italy hinted that she wanted promises of wider support given her as the price of her renewal, Bismarck at first
told her flatly that she could renew it as it stood without
modifications, or she could leave it and drop out. But
later, in 1887, when Franco-German relations were strained,
and Italy intimated that she would shift to the side of
France if her desires were not heeded, Bismarck changed
his mind. He was willing to recognize Italian ambitions
in North Africa and even put pressure upon Austria to
accept the principle that Italy had the right to share with
Austria in the decision of the future fate of the Balkans,
the Ottoman coasts, and the islands in the Adriatic and
Aegean Seas.[44]

Austrian policy in the Balkans, after 1906, similarly
attempted to make use of the Alliance for aggressive rather
than peaceful purposes. But the details of this later perver-
sion of the originally defensive character of the Triple
Alliance cannot be discussed here. They do not alter the
fact that Bismarck in no sense intended to use the Triple
Alliance for aggressive action by Germany against France.
For him it always remained, as it had been in its origin,
a defensive treaty. Unfortunately it was not easy to convince the French of this. As its terms were secret, the
French not unnaturally suspected that it constituted a
menace to themselves. This suspicion was strengthened by

[44] Arts. I-IV of the separate Italo-German renewal treaty of Feb.
20, 1887; and Art. I of the Austro-Italian renewal treaty of the same date,
which was embodied as the famous "Art. VII" of the last renewal treaty
of Dec. 5, 1912. *Cf.* Pribram I, 44 ff. 103, and *passim;* G.P., IV, 179-260.
For the text of these articles and the other concessions eventually made
to Italy, see Arts. VI-XI of the 1912 renewal treaty in the Appendix below.

the rapid increase in German and Italian armaments in the 1880's, and by Bismarck's rather defiant tone during the Boulanger period. It was this secrecy as to the terms of the Triple Alliance, and the exaggerated suspicions to which it gave rise, which contributed so much toward the embitterment of Franco-German relations and to the formation of the Franco-Russian Alliance in the early 1890's.

THE RUMANIAN ALLIANCE OF 1883

Even the Triple Alliance did not complete the circle of treaties by which Bismarck wished to assure the peace of Europe. In the summer of 1883 King Carol, the Hohenzollern ruler of Rumania, visited Germany. Bismarck took the occasion to sound Austria, "whether it would not be desirable and possible to extend our League of Peace [Friedensliga] with Italy to the East, and thereby lead in firm paths the policy of Rumania, and eventually also that of Serbia and the Porte. Except for Russia and France, there is no state in all Europe today which is not interested in the maintenance of peace. The firm pivot for the crystallization of any such scheme would always be our own permanent Dual Alliance." [45] As Austria responded favorably, Bismarck had two long interviews with the Rumanian premier, whom he found "more declamatory than businesslike." M. Bratianu was very eager for the kudos which would come from an alliance with the Great Powers. He was loud in his denunciation of Russian intrigues in Austria as well as in Rumania and Bulgaria. At the prospect of Austro-German backing, his chauvinistic imagination began to build castles in the air in which the Italian conquest of Nice, Savoy, and Corsica should be but the prelude to Rumania's acquisition of the Danubian Delta and Bessarabia. He had to be brought down to earth by energetic reminders from Bismarck and Kálnoky that the proposal

[45] Bismarck to Prince Reuss at Vienna, Aug. 19, 1883; G.P., III, 263

under discussion was to secure peace, not conquests; the
Contracting Powers ought mutually to promise that they
would refrain from all acts of provocation which might disturb the peace; if, contrary to their efforts, any war should
break out, it would be time enough later to discuss the division of the spoils.

M. Bratianu thereupon bridled his imagination and on
October 30, 1883, signed the purely defensive kind of an
alliance which Bismarck had in mind. The Austro-Rumanian Treaty, which formed the basis of Rumania's adherence
to the Triple Alliance "Treaty of Peace," provided in substance that if Rumania or Austria were attacked without
provocation on their part [by Russia], the two Contracting
Powers would mutually assist one another against the aggressor. Russia was not named in the text of the treaty
owing to Emperor William's wish on this point, and to the
danger of adding fuel to Pan-Slav agitation in case the
Treaty should leak out later through some indiscretion.
But the negotiations show clearly that Russia was the state
which the Contracting Powers had in mind. Germany, by
an agreement signed on the same day, undertook the same
obligations respectively toward Austria and Rumania that
they had taken toward one another. The treaty was to be
secret and to endure for five years with an automatic extension for three years more if not denounced by any of the
parties. In 1889 Italy, like Germany, adhered to the Austro-Rumanian treaty, and the Quadruple Agreement was
usually renewed from time to time (with slight modifications). The last renewal took place on February 5, 1913,
when it was extended to July 8, 1920.[46]

46 G.P., III, 269-282; Pribram, I, 29-34, 69-77, 85-90, 107-111, 209, 245 f.
In this connection it may be mentioned that Austria had signed a secret
treaty with Serbia on June 28, 1881, which virtually placed Serbia under
Austria's protection and domination during the reign of the pro-Austrian
ruler, Milan Obrenovitch, i.e., until 1889, thus temporarily bringing still

THE BREAKDOWN OF THE WIRE TO RUSSIA IN 1890

Thus, in the period 1871-1890, the peace of Europe was secured by the domination of the Eastern Empires and by the system of genuinely defensive alliances which Bismarck had built up, though during the last three years the system was somewhat less secure. No Power cared to risk a war against Germany's overwhelming military force, supported and insured as it was by the secret alliances which had brought Austria, Russia, Italy, Rumania, and even England more or less into coöperation with Germany. France in her painful isolation did not dare to undertake a war of *revanche*. England, though ready to coöperate with the Triple Alliance in the Mediterranean, did not care to depart from her traditional no-alliance policy.[47] She still preferred to enjoy the Balance of Power between any European coalitions which might arise. No one yet threatened that proud supremacy of the seas, so vital to her commerce and her imperial relations with her colonies.

But the dismissal of Bismarck in March, 1890, brought a change, and opened the way for the formation of an alliance between Russia and France. Even during the three preceding years, in spite of the Re-insurance Treaty, friction had increased between Germany and Russia, owing to complications in Bulgaria, and to the German newspaper campaign against Russian securities. But until Bismarck's dismissal, the loyalty of M. Giers, the Russian Minister of Foreign Affairs, to the German alliance, and Tsar Alexander's antipathy to France had prevented a Franco-Russian

---

another state within the circle of the Triple Alliance Powers; Pribram, I, 18 ff.

[47] For England's failure to respond to Bismarck's feelers for an Anglo-German understanding or alliance in 1887 and in 1889, see G.P., IV 376 ff. The importance of these feelers has been exaggerated by Hammann. *Der Missverstandne Bismarck*, pp. 20 f., 59, and by Eckardstein, *Lebenserinnerungen*, II, 282; III, 1 ff.

coalition which had always been Bismarck's greatest night-mare.[48]

In December, 1889, well in advance of its expiration, Giers considered whether the Re-insurance Treaty of 1887 ought to be renewed by Russia and, if so, in what form. On the whole, it seemed more useful for Russian interests in the Balkans and for the preservation of peace than an alliance with France. The latter would endanger peace by encouraging French chauvinists and by embittering relations between France and Germany. In accordance with this policy, Count Schuvalov had an intimate conversation with Bismarck on February 10, 1890, in which both favored the renewal of the treaty. "It is a document that defines clearly the policy which we are following and which, in my judgment, ought not to be changed," said Bismarck.[49]

But the conflict of temperament and policy which had been developing between the aged German Chancellor and his imperious young master was nearing the explosion which took place on March 17. With Bismarck out of office Schuvalov did not know what to do. He reported that what was passing at Berlin was more than strange, and that one was forced to ask oneself whether the young Emperor was in a normal state. On the night of March 21, the Ambassador was awakened by a messenger from Emperor William who requested him to come to His Majesty at eight o'clock in the morning. Scarcely had he arrived when the Emperor received him with great kindness and cordiality saying,

[48] In December, 1886, Giers said to the German Chargé d'Affaires in St. Petersburg: "Il n'y a pas de politique raisonable à faire avec ces gens-là [en France]"; and a week later, "Comment peuvent-ils être assez bêtes, ces Français, pour se figurer que l'Empereur Alexandre marcherait avec les Clemenceaus contre son oncle! C'est une alliance qui ferait horreur à l'Empereur, qui n'ira pas tirer les marrons du feu pour le Commune"; and again on October 20, 1887, "Les Français sont le plus infecte des peuples, le gouvernement français est mauvais, bête; le gâchis à Paris est complet"; G.P., VI, 107, 108, 118.

[49] Goriainov, p. 341; G.P., VII, 1 ff.

"Sit down and listen to me. You know how much I love
and respect your sovereign. Your Emperor has been too
good to me for me to do otherwise than to inform him
personally of the situation created by the events which have
just taken place. . . . I beg you to tell His Majesty that
on my part I am entirely disposed to renew our agreement,
that my foreign policy remains and will remain the same
as it was in the time of my grandfather." [50]   After having
read Schuvalov's despatch the Tsar wrote on it, "Nothing
more satisfactory could be looked for. We shall see by the
sequel whether deeds correspond to words." [51]

But there then emerged the malign and super-suspicious
influence of Baron Holstein. He and another counsellor in
the German Foreign Office drew up a long memoir of fine-
spun arguments against the renewal; with these they won
over the Kaiser and the new Chancellor, Caprivi. It was
decided at Berlin on March 27 to drop the negotiations for
renewal, because the terms of the Re-insurance Treaty were
regarded as contrary to the spirit, if not the letter, of the
Triple Alliance, and also because, "if the treaty became
known, either by a deliberate or accidental indiscretion, it
would endanger the Triple Alliance and be calculated to
turn England away from us." Schweinitz, the German
Ambassador at St. Petersburg, was hastily summoned back
to Berlin for a consultation. He did not think it likely
that Russia would deliberately divulge the treaty; but he
recognized the "possibility of indiscretions from some other
source," [52] by which probably he meant no other than Bismarck himself. When Schweinitz returned to St. Petersburg next day, and reported Germany's negative decision,
the Tsar was content, but his Foreign Minister, Giers, was
"in some consternation." Already old and feeble, Giers
feared that under his successors the Russian militarists and

[50] Goriainov, p. 343; cf. G.P., VII, 21.   [51] Goriainov, p 344.
[52] G.P., VII, 11.

Pan-Slavs might get the upper hand and threaten peaceful relations between Germany and Russia. He hoped by a treaty to bind his successors. Six weeks later he again brought up the subject and urged the renewal of the treaty. He was willing to make any changes Germany wanted, or even to have merely an exchange of notes, or at any rate some kind of a written agreement between the two countries. Since a further refusal on Germany's part might tend to drive Russia into the arms of France, Schweinitz advised "some kind of a written agreement which, even if it became known, could not be used against us." Just after this advice reached Berlin, Bismarck gave an interview to a Russian journalist, which alarmed the German Foreign Office,[53] and made them fear that even if the Tsar were discreet, the irritated ex-Chancellor might let the dangerous cat out of the bag. The leading Foreign Office officials— Marschall, Holstein, Kiderlen, and Raschdau—all hastened to write memorials against a renewal of the Re-insurance Treaty or anything resembling it; and the Kaiser and Caprivi accepted their view. Schweinitz was told positively to drop the whole matter. Thus fell one of the main props of Bismarck's balance between Russia and Austria. Russia was left isolated and more ready to listen to the solicitous voice of the republican radicals on the Seine.

Historians have generally exaggerated the non-renewal of the Re-insurance Treaty as a factor in the formation of the Franco-Russian Alliance. This is due partly to Bismarck himself. Esteemed by the German people as a demigod, but neglected by the young Emperor and the new Court, the lonely and morose old man at Friedrichsruh filled the columns of the *Hamburger Nachrichten* with ill-natured articles justifying his own successful policies and bitterly criticizing anonymously those of his successor: "Least of all is it Germany's business to support Austria's

[53] G.P., VII, 23, 35.

ambitions in the Balkans." [54] "By following the path
upon which she has entered, Germany is in danger of
gradually becoming dependent upon Austria, and in the
end she may have to pay with her blood and treasure for
the Balkan policy of Vienna." [55]

This was bad taste on Bismarck's part, and it was very
embarrassing to William II and Caprivi. They winced at
his criticisms and descended to his rancorous level by an
act of petty-minded folly. When Bismarck made a tri-
umphal progress to Vienna in 1892 to attend the marriage
of his son, Count Herbert, to Countess Hoyos, Caprivi
ordered the German Ambassador in Vienna not to attend
the wedding and, if possible, to prevent Bismarck's reception by Emperor Francis Joseph. Bismarck in revenge
reproached Caprivi in the *Neue Freie Presse* with having
lost for Germany the friendship of Russia. "The wire
which connected us with Russia is torn down." He implied
that the Tsar was therefore turning toward France and that
Caprivi was responsible for the danger to Germany of the
new coalition which he himself had always skilfully averted.
The implication was strengthened by Caprivi's apparently
self-incriminating statement in the Reichstag six months
later (November 23, 1892): "We exerted all our care to
keep the wire up; only we did not want it to draw us out
of those connections which bind us with Austria-Hungary
and Italy." The implication was finally accepted as a
certainty when Bismarck virtually revealed in the *Hamburger Nachrichten* (four years later) the existence of the
Re-insurance Treaty of 1887, closing with the blunt statement, "So came Kronstadt with the Marseillaise and the
first drawing together of the absolutist Tsardom and the
French Republic, brought about, in our opinion, exclusively

---

[54] *Hamburger Nachrichten,* April 26, 1890: Hofmann, *Fürst Bismarck,*
1890-1898, I, 256

[55] January 24, 1892; Hofmann, *Fürst Bismarck,* 1890-1898, II, 5

by the mistakes of the Caprivi policy." [56] The accuracy of
Bismarck's charge seemed to be finally confirmed by a curt
official note a few days later,[57] denouncing his revelation
as a "violation of the most confidential secrets of state which
constituted a blow at the grave interests of the Empire."

So the world accepted the idea that the Franco-Russian
Alliance was the result of Caprivi's stupidity in not continuing Bismarck's juggling feat of "keeping five balls in
the air at once." But if one looks more closely at the
documents now in hand, one can see that historians have
been misled by the apparent conjunction of events in 1890-
1891 and by Bismarck's propaganda. The Franco-Russian
Entente did not result simply from Caprivi's failure to
renew the Re-insurance Treaty. It was due to a number
of other factors. One of these was the growth of German
industry, commerce, naval ambition, and colonial expansion which started Germany on "The New Course" to
Constantinople and Bagdad, thereby antagonizing Russia.
Emperor William's desire for a naval base led to the so-
called Heligoland Treaty of July, 1890, which made Russia
suspect—incorrectly—that Germany would draw closer to
England. A second factor was the growth of Pan-Slavism
and of Russia's determination to dominate the Balkans.
This antagonized Austria and made it impossible for Berlin
to continue Bismarck's policy of maintaining a delicate
equipoise between Vienna and St. Petersburg. William II
had eventually to choose between Russia and Austria, and
he chose Austria; whether he chose rightly is another question; but the choice having been made, Russia became
perforce the enemy of the Central Powers. Therefore,
according to a well-informed German writer, the mistake of
Bismarck's successors was not in letting down the wire
between Berlin and St. Petersburg—that was perhaps inevitable anyway; the mistake was in failing to conciliate

[56] Hofmann, *Fürst Bismarck*, 1890-98, II, 373.
[57] *Reichsanzeiger*, Oct. 27, 1896.

and win England by playing off England against her natural Russian and French rivals, and by coming to a reasonable understanding with England in regard to naval and colonial questions.[58]   A third factor which made for the Franco-Russian Alliance, was the persistence of the *revanche* idea and the slow consolidation of power in the French Republic which followed the bursting of the Boulanger bubble. France had at last sufficiently settled down so that the Tsar was willing to overcome his repugnance to an alliance with the Revolutionary Government which had never forgiven Germany for the cruel wound inflicted in 1871.

FRANCO-GERMAN RELATIONS, 1871-1890

In the bitter years after the Franco-Prussian War, France sat alone among the Powers of Europe, like a wall-flower at a dance, watching Germany revolve with many partners. France was condemned to isolation by her own military weakness after defeat, by the methods which Bismarck adopted to keep her friendless, and by the instability of her Republican form of government which was regarded askance by the old monarchs of Europe. She had to suffer the humiliation and the inevitable friction of German armies on her soil until the billion dollar indemnity was paid. It was not until the War Scare of 1875 that France found for the first time that she had honest neighbors who, if they did not take her to their hearts as partners, were at least not willing to sit idly by with hands crossed and see her menaced or crushed. Tsar Alexander II of Russia gallantly informed General Le Flô, the French Ambassador at St. Petersburg, that "the interests of our two countries are common; you would know this very quickly and you would know it from us if, as I refuse to believe, you should be some day seriously menaced." [59]   Queen Victoria likewise

[58] Hammann, *Der Missverstandne Bismarck, passim.*
[59] Bourgeois et Pagès, p. 168.

let it be known that in this matter she was of one opinion
with the Tsar. But neither of these two Great Powers was
yet ready to enter into any closer relations with the French
Republic. Alexander II, with a natural antipathy to republican institutions, preferred the monarchical solidarity represented by the League of the Three Emperors, and his
attention was engaged in the Eastern 'Question where German friendship was of greater value than French support.
Similarly, the English acquisition of the Suez Canal and the
resulting occupation of Egypt gave rise to a situation which
made close Anglo-French relations virtually impossible for
a quarter of a century.

Bismarck, however, in the ten years 1875-1885, made
many efforts to win French good-will and induce the French
to accept without reserve the settlement of 1871. He
wanted to make them forgive and forget the loss of Alsace-
Lorraine, so that Germany would not have to fear a war
of revenge. In the interests of better relations between the
two countries he was willing to receive a visit from Gam-
betta, who was regarded as the chief exponent of *revanche*
in France until his death in 1882.[60] When St. Vallier succeeded Gontaut-Biron as French Ambassador at Berlin
early in 1878, Bismarck overwhelmed him with marks of
attention and kindness, and there was talk of "a new era"
in the relations of France and Germany. At the Congress
of Berlin, and on many subsequent occasions, he assured
France of his readiness to give her diplomatic support if she
wished to protect her Algerian frontier by taking Tunis.
As he said to St. Vallier:

> "The Tunisian pear is ripe and it is time for you to pick
> it. The insolence of the Bey has been like an August sun
> to this African fruit; which might easily spoil meanwhile, or
> be stolen by someone else, if you leave it longer upon the
> tree. I don't know whether this tempts you or what you wish

[60] G.P., III, 387.

to do, but I want to repeat to you what I said in July to M. Waddington, 'It is my desire to give you evidences of good-will in questions which touch you and where there are no German interests opposed to yours.' This is, in fact, only right, for I appreciate the efforts which you and he have made to calm the feelings and restore security and confidence between our two countries. . . . I believe that the French people, though they are now giving evidence of great good sense, need satisfactions for their pride, and I desire sincerely to see them obtain those which they can find in the Mediterranean basin which is their natural sphere of expansion. The more success they have in this direction, the less they will be inclined to indulge against us the complaints and sorrows whose legitimacy I will not discuss, but the removal of which is not in our power." [61]

On later occasions Bismarck encouraged the French in the same way to an extension of their colonial power in other parts of Africa and in China. The recent publication of his private memoranda leaves no doubt that he hoped that, if France would turn her attention to colonial activities outside Europe, she would be more likely to forget Alsace-Lorraine. In the Madrid Conference on the Morocco question, he instructed the German representative to "go hand in hand with France who, because of her neighboring Algerian possessions, has rightly founded interests in Morocco," and for this attitude he received the genuine thanks of the French Ambassador.[62] In his instructions for the German Ambassador at Paris on July 16, 1881, he wrote:

"There is a wide field in the Mediterranean in which we can leave to the French a wholly free hand. It is not out of the question to hope that French policy in the end will come to see that a friendly German Empire with 45,000,000 inhabitants is more desirable and a stronger figure among

61 St. Vallier to Waddington, Jan. 5, 1879; Bourgeois et Pagès, p. 365 f.
62 G.P., III, 396 ff.

French assets than a million Alsace-Lorrainers. France can be certain that we shall never oppose her justifiable policy of expansion in the Mediterranean and there is reason to believe that Russia also will take the same attitude as Germany." [63]

This instruction represents Bismarck's sincere purpose of trying to secure a genuine reconciliation with France in the half dozen years following the Congress of Berlin. Similarly he refused to give any support to the family of Abd-el-Kader, the heroic Algerian chieftain who had carried on such a troublesome war of self-defense against French efforts at conquest and colonization in North Africa.[64] He refused to take notice of ebullitions of French chauvinism. Some French newspapers, the League of Patriots, and fire-eaters like Paul Déroulède still kept up a violent agitation against Germany. But Bismarck ordered his Ambassadors and the German Press to ignore them as far as possible. "It is best that matters of this kind be left in dead silence." [65]

In his irritation at England's dilatory action in regard to Southwest Africa and in his desire for a sincere *rapprochement* with France, he was willing to coöperate with the French in a conference on Egypt and other African colonial questions. By the fall of 1884, there was even talk of Franco-German naval coöperation which might grow into an alliance. But the French were suspicious of Bismarck's "Machiavellian motives." They suspected that he wished to embroil them with England.[66] The acceptance of the loss of Alsace and Lorraine as final and unquestioned was just what the French Ambassador always expressly refused:

"A nation, as regards the dismemberments which it has suffered, unless it courts with indifference the fate of Poland,

[63] G.P., III, 401.   [64] G.P., III, 406.
[65] Instruction of September 16, 1882; G.P., III, 404.
[66] G.P., III, 421 ff.; Bourgeois et Pagès, pp. 190-211.

ought never to pardon anything, never forget anything [*ne doit jamais rien pardonner, jamais rien oublier*]. I have never said a word to the German Chancellor which could encourage him in any illusions as to us. . . . To work for peace for the present and to reserve the future [*pacifier le présent, réserver l'avenir*], such is the program which I have always had before my eyes. . . . At the beginning of our discussions I specified with Count Hatzfeldt and with the Chancellor himself that neither Alsace nor Lorraine should ever be a question between us, that here was a domain reserved on both sides where we ought to be forbidden to penetrate, because we could never meet in good agreement on it. I shall never speak of Alsace, I have said; and on your part, if you sincerely desire an understanding with us on various points, avoid drawing the sword over our wound, because the French nation will not remain in control of her feelings." [67]

This attitude of proud irreconcilability, asserted by the French Ambassador in 1884, sums up admirably one of the fundamental reasons for the failure of the olive branches which Bismarck had been holding out. Another reason was the underlying suspicion and distrust with which each side received the suggestions of the other. The result was that the period of relative friendliness which had characterized Franco-German relations in the decade 1875-1885 came to an end and was succeeded by the tense relations of the Boulanger period.

General Boulanger, who became Minister of War in the Freycinet Cabinet in January, 1886, speedily became for the French masses the symbol of military revival and the hope of *revanche*. For fifteen long and bitter years they had borne their isolation and humiliation. Now they listened eagerly to the man on horseback who declared in chauvinistic speeches and in his organ *La France Militaire*:

[67] Baron Courcel to Jules Ferry, December 3, 1884; Bourgeois et Pagès, p. 387; *cf.* also pp. 205 ff.

"We remember that they are waiting for us in Alsace and Lorraine." [68] For the next fifteen months French Cabinets rose and fell, but public opinion always demanded that Boulanger be included among the Ministers. During this period he aimed to increase and strengthen the French army by every means. Lumber was purchased for new barracks, increased quantities of picric acid were imported from Germany for the manufacture of explosives, and French regular troops were gradually brought back from China and Africa. The Cabinet, though divided, was finally persuaded by Boulanger to approve a trial mobilization of part of the army for the fall of 1887. When a more cool-headed and responsible French statesman, like Rouvier, had the courage to constitute a Cabinet without Boulanger, in May, 1887, this only increased still further the General's popularity, and with it the peril to the internal and external peace of the country. He appeared before the ecstatic crowds on the Paris boulevards. By repeatedly standing for election to the Chamber of Deputies in the provinces, he gradually began to secure a national plebiscite in his favor. There were thousands who looked forward to the overthrow of the Republic which had been too yielding and conciliatory toward Germany and who hoped for a strong dictatorship under *"le brav' général."* French chauvinism was further stirred by the fiery speeches of Paul Déroulède, by the activities of the League of Patriots, and by the intemperate editorials of the greater part of the French Press. All these manifestations of French nationalism were duly reported to Bismarck at length by the German Military Attaché in Paris.[69]

The German Ambassador, Count Münster, however, sent moderate and more quieting reports as to conditions in France, though he admitted that there was an extraordi-

[68] Report of the German Military Attaché in Paris; G.P., VI, 133.
[69] G.P., VI, 127 ff.

nary outburst of *revanche* feeling among the people. He
believed, nevertheless, that it was artificially stimulated,
and that at bottom the French people really did not want
la guerre sainte, however much they might talk about it in
the newspapers and public meetings. The republicans in
the provinces, in contrast to Paris, were decidedly peaceful,
and Boulanger was not nearly so dangerous as people believed. He could hardly establish a dictatorship on account
of the jealousy of other generals and of the solidity of republican feeling. Whatever the masses thought, the French
Government really wanted peace, because they were afraid
of Germany. Financially also France was too poor to wage
war, and military service was unpopular. The Ambassador
was so convinced that there was no real danger of a Bou-
langist *coup d'état* or an attack upon Germany, that he took
the unusual step of writing his views in a personal letter to
Emperor William I.

Bismarck, however, was not at all convinced of the accuracy of Münster's diagnosis of the French situation. He
covered Münster's reports with question marks and doubts.
He scolded him for writing a letter direct to the Emperor,
which Münster thereupon agreed should not be delivered.
Bismarck's distrust of France rested partly on his knowledge of French history and of the events of the Second
Empire when Napoleon III had talked peace and yet had
entered upon one war after another. It arose also from his
futile efforts to come to a better understanding with France
during the half dozen years before the rise of Boulanger.
Still another reason for his distrust of the French were the
rumors in September, 1886, that Russian agents in Paris
had been putting out feelers toward a Franco-Russian alliance.[70] He instantly made inquiries at St. Petersburg to
learn if the rumors had any foundation. In the negotiations a little later for the Re-insurance Treaty with Russia,

70 G.P., VI, 93 ff.

he made surprisingly large concessions to Russian ambitions toward Constantinople, with the hope of holding Tsar Alexander III away from France and in firm friendship with Germany.[71]

A further reason why Bismarck was unwilling to accept Münster's optimistic views on France was the fact that he was preparing to lay before the Reichstag the Army Bill of 1887, which would considerably increase the size of the German army. French chauvinism was one of the best vote-getters possible for the bill. If Münster was correct, half the argument for the increase of the German army was gone. So Bismarck took the view of the military attaché instead of the ambassador at Paris. The German armament bill passed and thereby increased the suspicion and distrust in France and Russia, which always accompanied the growth of German armaments. New military expenditures on a wide scale were then made in France and Russia, and a still further increase was proposed in Germany in the following year. So great was the suspense and war-talk on both sides of the Rhine that there developed in the spring of 1888 another war scare not unlike that of 1875. On January 11, 1888, Bismarck made the famous speech in the Reichstag in which, while increasing Germany's armaments, he still insisted that Germany had no intention of provoking a war with France or with Russia.

In spite of "incidents" like the German arrest of Schnaebele,[72] which sharpened bitter feelings in both coun-

[71] G.P., V, 211 ff.

[72] Schnaebele, who had been accused of complicity in an espionage case at Strasbourg, was a French police officer near the Alsatian border. On April 20, 1887 he was arrested upon German soil while at an interview with a German police agent concerning border questions. The French Press made a great outcry that he had been enticed over the border in order that he might be seized. There is no proof of this. When Bismarck was finally convinced that Schnaebele crossed the border for an official interview upon the invitation of a German customs officer, he at once ordered his release; G.P., VI, 182-192. C. Grant Robertson, *Bismarck*, p. 460, is incorrect in concluding that the Schnaebele incident was delib-

tries, cooler counsels prevailed at Paris. Boulanger's credit sank more rapidly than it had risen, and Franco-German tension became less strained. But it was during this period that the first steps took place which may be regarded as the beginnings of Franco-Russian *rapprochement,* which later was extended to include England and thus formed ultimately the Triple Entente. The domination of the Eastern Empires was coming to an end.

erately planned to provoke the French into a serious indiscretion in order to assist the passage of the German Army Bill by the Reichstag. The dates are conclusive. The Army Bill passed on March 11. Bismarck knew nothing about the Schnaebele espionage case until March 12. Schnaebele was not arrested until April 20, and was set free eight days later. For a French view, see Bourgeois et Pagès, pp. 225-229.

CHAPTER III

THE SYSTEM OF SECRET ALLIANCES, 1890-1907; FORMATION OF THE TRIPLE ENTENTE

FRANCO-RUSSIAN RAPPROCHEMENT, 1887-1891

THE Franco-Russian Entente of 1891, which ripened into the Alliance of 1894, was the natural result of the suspicions, the feeling of isolation, and the irritation against Germany which existed in both countries. A *rapprochement* between them, in spite of the fundamental contrast between the republican and absolutist forms of government at Paris and St. Petersburg, was the obvious counterbalance to the Triple Alliance.

Notwithstanding Bismarck's generous promises to Russia in the Alliance of the Three Emperors and the Reinsurance Treaty, Alexander III had been greatly irritated at the election of Ferdinand of Coburg as Prince of Bulgaria. Ferdinand had hesitated to accept the Bulgarian throne, or at least had pretended to hesitate, but had been secretly persuaded into final acceptance, so the Tsar believed, by a treacherous intrigue on Bismarck's part. Though Bismarck had alleged openly that Germany was not interested in Bulgaria and that Russia might have a free hand to do as she pleased there, the German Ambassador at Vienna was supposed to have written a letter to Ferdinand secretly assuring him of Germany's support against Russia in case he accepted the throne of Bulgaria. The letter came into French hands and was conveyed by the French to the Tsar. Though Bismarck assured the Tsar later that the letter was a forgery, there is no doubt that for

a time Alexander III shared some of the French feeling of
bitterness toward Bismarck.[1] He could not reconcile Bismarck's assurances of disinterestedness in Constantinople
and the Balkans with the despatch of German officers to
drill the Turkish army and with the enthusiastic reception
at the German maneuvers given to the Turkish general,
Muktar Pasha. Like the French, he was suspicious and
irritated at the publicly announced renewal of the Triple
Alliance in 1887. As its terms were secret, he not unnaturally suspected that it might contain offensive designs on the
part of Austria and Italy detrimental to Russia's ambitions
in the Eastern Mediterranean. Soon after the renewal of
the Triple Alliance, Crispi, who had become Italian Premier in July, 1887, had ostentatiously visited Vienna, and
then gone on to confer with Bismarck at Friedrichsruh. On
his return journey he informed the *Frankfurter Zeitung*
that Italy wished well to Bulgaria, but "there can be no
doubt that Italy, like every other European state, has every
reason to fear Russia's advances to Constantinople. We
cannot allow the Mediterranean to become a Russian
lake." [2]

To all these grievances was added another. In the summer of 1887, Russia suddenly found that the ruble was falling in value and that there seemed to be a systematic com-
paign in Berlin against Russian securities. This was partly
due to a ukase in May which naturally shook German faith
in Russian credit: it forbade the acquisition or inheritance
of landed property by foreigners in Western Russia, or their
employment as managers of estates. As Germans owned
much land in Russia and were largely employed in the
management of estates, the ukase looked like an unjustifiable expropriation of property. This not unnaturally led to

---

[1] On the so-called "Bulgarian Documents" and their alleged forgery,
see G.P., V. 338-350, and J. V. Fuller, *Bismarck's Diplomacy at its Zenith*,
pp. 205 ff ; 292 ff. [2] Quoted in Robertson, *Bismarck*, p. 460.

a German newspaper campaign against Russian credit.
Though Bismarck may not have inspired these newspaper
attacks, he at least looked upon them with approval as
tending to make the Russians realize how dependent they
were upon German good-will.[3]
The Russians, however, suspected that Bismarck had
inspired this press campaign and were therefore the more
ready to yield to the Pan-Slav desire that Russia should
borrow in Paris. France at the moment was looking for a
field of investment, because commercial conflict with Italy
had shut off the Italian market for French capital.[4] A
group of French bankers was formed at Paris and began
negotiations for a series of Russian loans to be floated in
France. The first, amounting to 500,000,000 francs, was
at last approved by the Governments on both sides and the
bonds were listed on the Paris Bourse in December, 1888.
Naturally Germany looked askance at this proceeding,
which might have eventual political significance. German
newspapers did their best to scare off buyers; but the loan
proved a huge success. Though the sum was a relatively
large one for those days, the 4% bonds issued at 86.45 offered attractive returns and were at once largely oversub-
scribed. The Russians were encouraged the next year to
contract two more loans, one for 700,000,000, and the other
for 1,200,000,000 francs. Both met with equal success.
Thus France set out on the financial path which led further
than she foresaw at the moment, and which inevitably made
thousands of her citizens interested financially and politically in Russia's ambitions. Occasionally saner minds in
France took alarm, and the loans did not succeed so well,
but for the most part Frenchmen were ready to give up an
apparently unlimited amount of savings to invest at good

[3] G.P., V, 330-337; Fuller, p. 202 ff.

[4] Cf. Debidour, *Histoire Diplomatique de l'Europe, 1878-1916* (2nd.
ed., Paris. 1917-1918), I. 130 f.

profits in a country which might become an ally against the common enemy, and which might one day assist in the *revanche* which so many Frenchmen had in their hearts.[5] On the financial ground thus prepared the next step was for France to supply Russia with guns. The Grand Duke Vladimir, Alexander III's brother, on a visit to Paris, was initiated into the reorganization of the army which Freycinet had been carrying out. He was greatly impressed with the new Lebel rifle. Upon request he was given a model of it. Negotiations followed, and ultimately a contract was arranged by which France was to manufacture for Russia half a million rifles similar to the Lebel weapon.[6]

Neither William II nor his Foreign Office advisers supposed that "dropping the Pilot" and abandoning the Reinsurance Treaty would be followed by a Franco-Russian Alliance. But to lessen such a possibility, the Kaiser, with exaggerated views of his own personal influence in diplomacy, proceeded to return to the conciliatory policy toward France which Bismarck had pursued during and after the Congress of Berlin. He attempted to win French good-will by innumerable well-intentioned courtesies, by telegrams of congratulation and condolence, by recognizing the French protectorate over Madagascar, and by diplomatic support

5 Debidour, I, 137, reckons the total borrowings in France by the Russian Government up to 1906 at the enormous sum of 7,903,000,000 francs. These Russian government bonds did not include other vast sums which French private capitalists invested in Russian cotton mills, lumber mills, factories, and other undertakings of all sorts.

6 *Livre Jaune: L'Alliance Franco-Russe*, p. 49. This French Yellow Book, published in 1918, is the authoritative source for the early history of the Franco-Russian Alliance, and renders antiquated the older accounts of Cyon, Hansen, Daudet, Albin, Debidour, Tardieu, and Welschinger. The best recent brief studies are by L. B. Packard, "Russia and the Dual Alliance," in *Amer. Hist. Rev.*, XXV, 391-410, April, 1920; and by W. L. Langer, "The Franco-Russian Alliance," in the *Slavonic Review*, III, 554-575; IV, 83-100, March-June, 1925. See also G.P., VI, 91-124; VII, 191-458; the Belgian documents edited under the direction of B. Schwertfeger by W. Köhler, *Revanche-Idee und Panslawismus*, Berlin, 1919; and, for the later history of the alliance, George Michon, *L'Alliance Franco-Russe, 1891-1917*, Paris, 1927.

in other colonial questions where no German interests were involved. He showed special courtesy to Jules Simon, the head of the French delegation at the Working Men's Conference in Berlin. He invited French artists to participate in a German art exhibition—an invitation which was at first accepted but later refused on account of an outcry in the French Press. He arranged for a visit of his mother, the Empress Frederick, to Paris. But this eventually led to such a hostile demonstration that a serious scandal was narrowly averted by the energy of the French Government and by her departure from Paris on an earlier train than had been intended.[7] It contributed to a new chauvinist outburst and a renewed desire for closer relations with Russia.[8]

With Russia also the Kaiser sought to remain on the old friendly terms. He was profuse in assurances that German policy should suffer no change as a result of Bismarck's dismissal. In August, 1890, he visited the Tsar at Narva and relations seemed cordial between the monarchs as well as between Caprivi and Giers, though the latter failed in his further attempt to get some kind of a written agreement which should replace the Re-insurance Treaty. But in fact the Russians were becoming suspicious that Germany was drawing closer to England. The Treaty of June 14, 1890, by which Germany had given up claims to a great strip of African territory near Zanzibar in return for Heligoland, seemed to point in this direction.[9] If Lord Salisbury had given away a suit of clothes in exchange for a suspender button, as Henry M. Stanley sarcastically de-

---

[7] G.P., VII, 263 ff; Debidour, I, 165-168.

[8] The Russians had at first been alarmed at the Kaiser's efforts at reconciliation with France, and were delighted with the outburst against the Empress Frederick, in which they were suspected by the German Ambassador in Paris of having had a hand. The Tsar took advantage of the favorable opportunity to flatter the French by conferring the Order of St. Andrew upon President Carnot, who returned the compliment by bestowing the Grand Cross of the Legion of Honor upon the Russian Ambassador in Paris. G.P., VII, 196-201.   [9] G.P., VIII, 3-25.

scribed this transaction, there must be a reason, so the Russians argued to themselves. The London *Morning Post* announced that "the period of England's isolation is over." The Kaiser's visit to England in the summer of 1890 seemed a further sign of the way the wind was blowing. His allusion to the Triple Alliance at the opening of the Reichstag May 6, 1890, even though he spoke of it as a guarantee of universal peace, and his new Army Law increasing the German forces by some 18,000 men, were no less disturbing to the Russians than to the French.[10]

THE FRANCO-RUSSIAN ALLIANCE OF 1894.

Such was the situation which at last led the Russians to listen seriously to French feelers for closer relations. In view of the form ultimately given to the Franco-Russian Alliance and later to the Anglo-French military and naval arrangements, it is interesting to note that these first definite negotiations were carried on by the French and Russian military authorities and not by the regular diplomatic representatives. General Boisdeffre, who attended the Russian maneuvers for a fortnight in 1890, talked almost daily with the Russian Minister of War and with Obruchev, the Russian Chief of Staff. The latter had married a French wife and had long been an eager advocate of a Franco-Russian Alliance. Boisdeffre and the Russian generals quickly came to an agreement on the principle that "the two armies would have to act simultaneously in case of an attack from which they both had to fear the consequences." [11] This was a first step toward an Entente Cordiale which, though no written agreements had as yet been signed, was soon regarded by the Russian Ambassador at Paris as being "as solid as granite." [12] It had been solidified

[10] *Cf.* Goriainov, pp. 348-349

[11] Laboulaye, the French Ambassador to Russia, to Ribot, August 24, 1890; *L'Alliance Franco-Russe*, p. 1.

[12] Ribot to Laboulaye, March 9, 1891; *L'Alliance Franco-Russe*, p. 3.

by the Empress Frederick incident and by the growing Franco-Russian suspicion that England was adhering to the Triple Alliance to thwart Russian ambitions in the Eastern Mediterranean. It was just at this time that the Triple Alliance was renewed, in spite of the efforts of the French to detach Italy and the hopes of both French and Russians that Bismarck's dismissal might cause it to weaken and lapse. It had not, however, been renewed without difficulty, owing to Italy's demands for promises of greater support in the maintenance of the *status quo* in North Africa. Austria and Germany had been forced to yield to some extent to Italy's wishes and even to agree to exert themselves to secure England's adhesion to this new stipulation.[13]

The fact that the Triple Alliance had been renewed was published to the world by the Italian Premier, Rudini, in a speech on June 29, 1891. At the same time he also took occasion to refer to Italy's existing agreements with England in such a way as to strengthen Franco-Russian suspicions that England had in some way joined the Triple Alliance. Such a quadruple coalition, even though ostensibly aiming merely at the preservation of the *status quo,* was most annoying to the Russians who wanted to open the Dardanelles, and to the French who had not completed the development of their African colonial empire in the Western Mediterranean.

A few weeks later the French fleet under Admiral Gervais accepted the Tsar's invitation to visit Kronstadt. In addition to their suspicions of the Triple Alliance, Alexander III and Giers had been alarmed by the stiff attitude which the French had adopted in regard to a dispute between Roman Catholic and Greek Orthodox clergy concerning the use of a door in the Church of the Nativity at Beth-

---

[13] Art. IX of the Triple Alliance Treaty of May 6, 1891. *Cf.* Pribram, pp. 66, 208-229; and G.P., VII, 53-106; VIII, 41-72.

lehem.[14] They realized also the importance of making sure
of French friendship if they were to be successful in borrow-
ing more money at Paris.[15] The Kronstadt visit was made
the occasion, especially by the French, for an extraordinary
demonstration of Franco-Russian solidarity. It was to appear to the world as a counter-stroke to the renewal of the
Triple Alliance. The Tsar and Tsarina came aboard the
French flagship, talked to the sailors, showed a thousand
acts of politeness to Admiral Gervais and his officers, and
invited them to Peterhof. Hitherto, in absolutist Russia,
the playing of the Marseillaise had been strictly forbidden,
not only in public places, but even on a piano which might
be heard on the street. But now the prohibition was relaxed—only to be re-imposed again after the departure of
the French fleet—and the news was trumpeted abroad that
the Autocrat of All the Russias had stood bareheaded while
the bands played the marching song of the Sans-culottes
of 1793.[16] It was, however, a stirring moment. "Those of
us who reached manhood in 1890," writes President Poincaré twenty years later, "cannot, even today, recall without
emotion the prodigious effect produced at that time in
France by the demonstration of friendliness by Emperor
Alexander III. It was for Republicans not only a recognition of the Republic by a government whose traditions
and form were furthest removed from us and our institutions; it was for France herself the end of a prolonged isolation and the outward sign of her revival." [17]

The Kronstadt demonstration was received in France
with incredible joy and enthusiasm. The man in the street
believed that an alliance was already assured, that the long
period of isolation was now past, and that France could

---

[14] L'Alliance Franco-Russe, p. 3.   [15] Cf. Langer, pp. 14-17.

[16] Cf. the sarcastic comments of the Belgian minister in St. Petersburg, Schwertfeger, V, 295-300.

[17] Les Origines de la Guerre, p. 55; cf. also Tardieu, France and the
Alliances, pp. 11-14.

now dare to take a stiffer tone toward Germany. It created a new Boulangism without Boulanger. But the French ministry knew that the enthusiasm of the Paris populace was premature. They knew that it takes two to make an alliance or even an entente, and that the ceremonial courtesies of Kronstadt still fell far short of a signed and binding agreement. They therefore hastened to propose an alliance: the two governments should agree to consult with one another in case of any danger, and to mobilize simultaneously the moment any one of the Triple Powers should mobilize; the conditions of their simultaneous mobilization could be worked out by an understanding to be reached by the Russian and French General Staffs.[18]

But Giers, fearful that the French might have aggressive designs for recovering Alsace-Lorraine, wished to make the agreement vague and to extend its application beyond Europe to such places as Africa and China where peace might be threatened. It was only after several weeks that the French were able to secure a written accord in the following form:

"1. In order to define and consecrate the cordial understanding [Entente Cordiale] which unites them, and in their desire to contribute with one accord to the maintenance of peace, which is the object of their sincerest wishes, the two Governments declare that they will confer on every question of a nature to threaten the general peace.

"2. In case this peace should actually be in danger, and especially in case one of the two parties should be threatened by aggression, the two parties agree to come to an understanding on the measures which the realization of that eventuality would make it necessary for both Governments to adopt immediately and simultaneously." [19]

The rather vague and very limited character of this

18 Ribot to Laboulaye, July 24, 1891; *L'Alliance Franco-Russe*, p. 4.
19 Russian formula, confirmed by Ribot, Aug. 27, 1891; *L'Alliance Franco-Russe*, p. 16.

agreement merely obligating the two Governments to take counsel with one another in case of danger, betrayed the divergence of views which still separated Paris and St. Petersburg. France, in constant dread of an attack from across the Rhine and with the secret hope of some day recovering the lost provinces, thought mainly of war with Germany. She did not at this time greatly desire Russian support in North Africa or China, because, as later events showed, she could always come to a compromise agreement with Italy and England in these regions. Nor did the French wish the Russians to open the Dardanelles and control Constantinople. Giers, on the other hand, felt no great hostility to Germany. He and Alexander III were still anxious to maintain the traditional friendship between the two countries. They did not want an alliance directed primarily against the Hohenzollerns and dreaded being drawn into a war against Germany in support of French *revanche.* For Russia the main enemy was England, who blocked the Russian colossus both at the Straits and in the Middle East. But France naturally had no desire to pull these distant chestnuts out of the fire to please her new Russian friends.

Owing to this divergence of interests, as well as to the sickness of Giers and the Tsar's persistent distrust of the French, it was many months before the French were able to give the Entente a more binding and practical form. Upon Giers' visit to Paris in November, 1891, Ribot pointed out to him the danger that Germany might make a sudden surprise attack, which would find Russia and France unprepared. They would not have time to take adequate measures of defense before an irrevocable disaster might overwhelm them, so long as they merely "agreed to come to an understanding." It would be far more valuable and practical to come to an understanding beforehand, in time of peace, as to all the military arrangements which should

come into force instantly in case of sudden war. The Entente ought to be supplemented by a Military Convention
providing that, in case of a sudden German aggression,
Russia and France would instantly mobilize their whole
forces and use them to secure the maximum mutual advantage in accordance with plans which would have been
already agreed upon. Giers not enthusiastic, consented
to lay the idea before the Tsar.[20] Accordingly General
Miribel worked out the basis for such a Military Convention. He estimated in detail the total Triple Alliance
forces (even including the Rumanian) at only 2,810,000
men as against 3,150,000 for the Franco-Russian coalition.
France would throw five-sixths of her forces against Germany. Russia was likewise urged to concentrate her attack
upon Germany rather than upon Austria:

> "The essential thing is to aim at the destruction of the
> principal enemy. The defeat of the others will follow in-
> evitably. In a word, once Germany is vanquished, the
> Franco-Russian armies will impose their wills on Italy and
> Austria." [21]

General Miribel's draft project, after some modifications
to meet the Russian desires, and after long delays caused by
the sickness of Giers and the journeys of the Tsar, finally
took form as the "Draft of a Military Convention." It was
signed by the French and Russian Chiefs of Staff, Boisdeffre
and Obruchev, and approved in principle by the Tsar on
August 17, 1892. But it was not signed by the Ambassador
or Foreign Minister of either country, and therefore could
not yet be regarded as having binding force. There were
two serious political difficulties in the way. The Tsar was
very anxious that absolute secrecy should be preserved, and
that the document should be known only to the President
and Prime Minister of France. "I fear," he said, "that if
they discuss it in the Cabinet, it will have the fatal result

[21] *L'Alliance Franco-Russe*, p. 39.   [21] *Ibid.*, p. 39.

of becoming public, and then, as far as I am concerned, the treaty is nullified." [22]   Another difficulty was the fact that the French Constitution did not permit the President of the Republic to make secret treaties. There was recognized at the very beginning of the negotiations, the "defect of our [French] constitution, which, through fear lest the Executive shall be too strong, has deprived the Head of the State of the essential prerogative of concluding treaties, and consequently deprived our foreign policy of the advantages of secrecy." [23]   These two difficulties, as well as the essential divergence of interests noted above, caused a further delay of a year and a half.

Meanwhile, certain events took place which tended to lessen the Tsar's scruples and his distrust of France, and to increase his readiness to accept at last a binding agreement. A new German Army Law of 1892 increased the German forces by 60,000 men but reduced the term of service in the infantry from three to two years. No settlement had been reached in regard to a Russo-German commercial treaty and a tariff war was being waged between the two countries.[24]   The Siam crisis of July, 1893, which brought France and England closer to war than was realized at the time, showed that the French were ready to take a stiff tone toward England, even in Asia, in a way which Russia liked to see, especially as England seemed to be drawing closer to the Triple Alliance. As a result, Alexander III consented to return the Kronstadt compliments by having the Russian Navy visit Toulon in October, 1893. The Russian officers and men were fêted with extraordinary enthusiasm by the French both at Toulon and Paris. But the Paris Press, at a wise hint from the French Government, refrained from chauvinistic editorials and implica-

[22] *L'Alliance Franco-Russe,* p. 94; *cf.* also pp. 66, 72, 87, 91 ff., 103 ff. 112 ff.

[23] *L'Alliance Franco-Russe,* p. 2; *cf.* also pp. 50, 54, 69, 90 ff., 99 ff., 114. [24] G.P., VII, 389-458.

tions that a Russian alliance would aid in regaining Alsace-Lorraine. The Tsar was favorably impressed with the moderation and strength of the French Government. He accordingly gave his approval to an exchange of official diplomatic notes which was completed on January 4, 1894, and gave binding effect to the Military Convention of August 17, 1892.[25]

As neither the exchange of notes nor the Military Convention signed only by military officers was a formal treaty, neither had to be submitted to the French Parliament for ratification. The terms of the Military Convention, known only to the supreme military officials, did not even have to be divulged to Cabinets which rose and fell so rapidly in France. The text of the Military Convention was kept in an envelope bearing an annotation in President Faure's hand: "The Military Convention is accepted by the letter of M. de Giers giving to the Convention the force of a treaty." M. Viviani carried it under his arm to the Chamber of Deputies when he mounted the tribune to ask for war credits on August 4, 1914. He was prepared to read it if it should be asked for. But as no one demanded it, he prudently kept it in his portfolio.[26] It was never made public until published in a French Yellow Book in 1918. Thus the two difficulties in regard to secrecy and French constitutional requirements were effectively met.

The Military Convention which was given the force of a treaty on January 4, 1894, and thus became the basis of

[25] Montebello to Giers, Dec. 23, 1893; Jan. 4, 1894; *ibid.*, p. 128. "I have received your letter . . . in which you advise me that . . . the draft of the Military Convention . . . may be considered henceforth definitely adopted. . . . The French Government likewise considers the aforesaid Military Convention, the text of which has been approved by both parties, as executory henceforth. In consequence of this agreement, the two Staffs shall have power immediately to deliberate at any time and to communicate to each other all the information which may be useful to them."

[26] Poincaré, *Les Origines de la Guerre*, p. 60.

the very secret Franco-Russian Alliance is so short, simple, and clear that it may be quoted in full:

"France and Russia, animated by a common desire to preserve the peace, and having no other aim than to prepare for the necessities of a defensive war, provoked against either of them by an attack by the forces of the Triple Alliance, have agreed upon the following provisions:

"1. If France is attacked by Germany, or by Italy supported by Germany, Russia shall employ all her available forces to fight Germany.

"If Russia is attacked by Germany, or by Austria supported by Germany, France shall employ all her available forces to fight Germany.

"2. In case the forces of the Triple Alliance or of one of the Powers which compose it should be mobilized, France and Russia, at the first indication of the event, and without a previous agreement being necessary, shall mobilize all their forces immediately and simultaneously, and shall transport them as near to the frontiers as possible.

"3. The forces available which must be employed against Germany shall be for France, 1,300,000 men; for Russia, from 700,000 to 800,000 men. These forces shall begin complete action with all speed, so that Germany will have to fight at the same time in the east and in the west.

"4. The Staffs of the armies of the two countries shall constantly plan in concert in order to prepare for and facilitate the execution of the above measures. They shall communicate to each other in time of peace all the information regarding the armies of the Triple Alliance which is in or shall come into their possession. The ways and means of corresponding in time of war shall be studied and arranged in advance.

"5. France and Russia shall not conclude peace separately.

"6. The present Convention shall have the same duration as the Triple Alliance.

"7. All the clauses enumerated above shall be kept absolutely secret." [27]

The Franco-Russian Alliance of 1894, like the Austro-German Alliance of 1879 and the Triple Alliance of 1882, was in its origin essentially defensive in purpose. This is clear from the preamble to the Treaty itself and from the full account which we now have of the negotiations by which it was concluded.[28] There was originally no intention among responsible authorities of either party that the Alliance should be used for an aggression against Germany or any other Power, or that it should be employed to support dangerous and ambitious policies which might involve a conflict with any of the Triple Alliance Powers or with England. Whatever may have been the hopes inspired by the Alliance in the hearts of Pan-Slavs for realizing Russia's "historic mission" in the Balkans and the Far East, or in French chauvinists for the recovery of Alsace-Lorraine and the extension of French colonial power, the responsible Russian and French Ministers knew better. The French Cabinet did not count upon Russian armed support at Fashoda or in Morocco, nor the Russians upon that of France in the Far East or the Balkans. It was not until much later, in the days of Delcassé, Izvolski, and Poincaré, that the Franco-Russian Alliance was essentially changed in spirit from a defensive to a potentially offensive combination.

To be sure, the Alliance embodied from the outset the militarist doctrine, prevalent since the Napoleonic Wars, that the best military defensive is to wage offensive war. Mobilization by Germany was to be followed by the instant

27 *L'Alliance Franco-Russe*, p. 92.
28 *L'Alliance Franco-Russe, passim.* At one point in the negotiations Alexander III wished to insert a clause that the treaty would be nullified if France provoked a war; but he renounced the idea when General Boisdeffre pointed out that "it was concluded for a defensive war"; *ibid.*, p. 91.

mobilization of the French and Russian armies. Mobilization was expressly understood as being equivalent to war— to the actual opening of hostilities. In the negotiations for the Military Convention in July, 1892,

> "General Obruchev emphasized finally the necessity of the immediate and simultaneous mobilization of the Russian and French armies at the first news received by either of the two countries of a mobilization of the forces of the Triple Alliance. He understands further that this mobilization of France and Russia would be followed immediately by positive results, by acts of war, in a word would be inseparable from an 'aggression.' " [29]

Similarly, General Boisdeffre, in talking with the Tsar the day after the Military Convention had been approved, remarked:

> "The mobilization is the declaration of war. To mobilize is to oblige one's neighbor to do the same. Mobilization involves the carrying out of strategic transportation and concentration. Otherwise, to leave a million men on one's frontier, without doing the same simultaneously, is to deprive oneself of all possibility of moving later; it is placing oneself in the situation of an individual who, with a pistol in his pocket, should let his neighbor put a weapon to his forehead without drawing his own." [To which Alexander III replied], "That is exactly the way I understand it." [30]

This "offensive-defensive" character of the Alliance is further seen in the technical arrangements which were worked out annually later in great detail by the French and Russian General Staffs.[31] On the generally accepted principle that the best form of defensive warfare is to take the

---

[29] *L'Alliance Franco-Russe*, p. 56.   [30] *L'Alliance Franco-Russe*, p. 95 f.
[31] For some of the Franco-Russian military conversations and protocols for the years 1900-1907, see A. Zaiontchkovski, "Relations Franco-Russes avant la Guerre de 1914," in *Les Alliés contre la Russie*, Paris, 1926, pp. 8-43; for the years 1911-1913, M.F.R., 697-718; and L.N., II, 419-437.

offensive against the main enemy force, the French and
Russian Staffs were "perfectly in accord on the point that
the defeat of the German armies continues to be, whatever the circumstances, the first and principal objective
of the allied armies. This is all the more so now [1913]
than formerly, in view of the considerable increase of
the relative military strength of Germany in the Triple
Alliance." [32]

Though the Franco-Russian Alliance aimed primarily
at crushing Germany in case the latter should attempt an
aggression, it did not at first arouse serious suspicions or
antagonism beyond the Rhine. This was partly because its
existence was kept so secret that for months after its establishment the German Ambassador in Paris optimistically
refused to believe in its existence.[33] Even after the open
references to the "Alliance," in speeches in the French
chamber in 1895, or during the visits of Nicholas II to Paris
in 1896 and of President Faure to Russia in 1897, Germany
was not alarmed, because she felt that the Triple Alliance
was still equal in strength to the new combination. She
also believed that England, holding the Balance of Power,
would never join with such long-standing opponents as
France or Russia. The existence of the Franco-Russian
Alliance inspired, however, a new respect in Germany for
her two neighbors, and made her more ready to seek to cooperate with them on innumerable international questions.
In this sense the Franco-Russian Alliance at first tended to

[32] Art. I of the ninth annual conference of French and Russian Staff
officers, Aug., 1913; M.F.R., p. 712; L.N., II, 432.

[33] Cf. G.P., VII, 261-343; IX, 335-425; even as late as December, 1895,
Count Münster was still convinced that "Russia's love [for France] is only
Platonic. Platonic love usually ends in hate"; G.P., IX, 423. Even as
late as December, 1898, after the Fashoda Affair, Count Eulenburg, the
German Ambassador at Vienna and an intimate friend of the Kaiser's,
"felt sure there was no formal alliance", and was convinced that France
could not count on Russia in any Egyptian or other African quarrel;
Rumbold to Salisbury, Dec. 5, 1898; *British Documents on the Origins of
the War, 1914-1918*, I, p. 102.

secure the peace of Europe; also in the sense of the proverb that "one sword holds another in its sheath."

The new Alliance served well its purpose of relieving France and Russia from their isolation. It enabled France to take a stiffer tone toward England, but it did not yet constitute a combination which was strong enough, or which desired, to measure arms with the Triple Alliance. This situation continued for some ten years. Between the putting into force of the Alliance in 1894 and the establishment of the Anglo-French Entente in 1904, the equilibrium between the Triple Alliance and Franco-Russian Alliance was sufficiently well balanced so that neither combination could dare to risk disturbing it by force.

This situation of more or less equilibrium on the Continent even led to a series of temporary diplomatic combinations in which Germany coöperated with Russia and France. In 1894, Germany and France joined hands in preventing England from acquiring a strip of Congo territory for the Cape-to-Cairo Railway.[34]   In 1895, Germany coöperated with France and Russia to compel Japan to restore part of the conquests taken from China.[35]   In 1900, Russia proposed that the same three Powers should try to mediate between England and the Boers. Germany did not wish to antagonize England by such a step, but consented to discuss it. Quite possibly the three Powers might have attempted it, had not France been unwilling to enter into an arrangement with Germany which would have involved a mutual guarantee of territories, and consequently a second renunciation of Alsace-Lorraine.[36]   In this same year also

[34] See below at note 40.
[35] Bourgeois et Pagès, pp. 248-253; G.P., IX, 241-333.
[36] G.P., XV, 406 note, 499-550; XVII, 105, 222 f.; XXIV, 173; Bourgeois et Pagès, pp. 286-289; Sidney Lee, *King Edward VII*, I, 761-773. According to the current Anglo-French version, the Kaiser instigated the mediation proposal, and then sought to lay the odium of it on France and Russia; according to the documents in G.P., the reverse is the fact— Russia originated it, and the French and the Russians then sought to put

German, French, Russian and English troops marched side by side to suppress the Boxer revolt. When the Tsar's proposal for the First Hague Conference—well meant but naïve for those times—took Europe by surprise, Germany and France, and even many of Russia's own officials, joined efforts to restrict the scope of the Conference as much as possible without incurring the odium of seeming to sabotage the Tsar's proposals. Nothing sums up dozens of despatches on this topic better than the confidence which Delcassé is reported to have made to the German Ambassador in Paris:

"Our [French] interests in regard to the Conference are exactly the same as yours. You do not want to limit your power of defense at this moment nor enter upon disarmament proposals; we are in exactly the same position. We both want to spare the Tsar and find a formula for side-stepping this question, but not let ourselves in for anything which would weaken our respective powers of defense. To prevent a complete fiasco, we might possibly make some concessions in regard to arbitration, but these must in no way limit the complete independence of the Great Powers. Besides the Tsar, we must also spare the public opinion of Europe, since this has been aroused by the senseless step of the Russians." [37]

the odium of the proposal on Germany. Certainly the formal proposals were first made to Germany by Russia. Whether Muraviev or the Kaiser was the original Machiavellian instigator of this business can hardly be determined with certainty until the Russian despatches referred to by Lee are published in more complete form and subjected to comparison with those in *Die Grosse Politik*. The recent *British Documents* (I, 235 ff., 247 f.) seem to confirm the German contention that Muraviev first initiated the mediation proposal.

[37] G.P., XV, 186. On this whole conference, where Germany's bluntness caused her to be somewhat unduly blamed for the thwarting of the Tsar's suggestions for the limitations of armaments, see *ibid.*, XV, 141-364; Andrew D. White, *Autobiography*, II, chs. 45-49; F. W. Holls, *The Peace Conference at the Hague*, N. Y., 1900; W. J. Hull, *The Two Hague Conferences*, Boston, 1908; P. Zorn, *Die beiden Haager Friedenskonferenzen*, Stuttgart, 1915; Ch. Meurer, *Die Haager Friedenskonferenz*, 2 vols., München, 1905-07; J. B. Scott, *The Hague Peace Conferences*, 2 vols. Baltimore, 1909; E. J. Dillon, *The Eclipse of Russia*, ch. 14.

Finally, as noted below, the Kaiser frequently mooted a proposal to merge the Triple Alliance and the Franco-Russian Alliance into a grand "Continental League." Such a combination of all five Great Powers, he thought, would not only assure the peace of Europe, but could put a check on England's overweening domination in all colonial matters.

Thus the first years of the Franco-Russian Alliance tended to strengthen rather than endanger the peace of Europe. It established a healthy counter-poise to the Triple Alliance. Neither group was so greatly superior as to be able safely to attack the other, or even to seek to dominate it by threats of force. But during the decade 1894 to 1904, two changes occurred which tended ultimately to destroy this equilibrium. They are of the greatest importance in the development of the system of secret alliances—England's exchange of splendid isolation for an Entente Cordiale with France, and Italy's dubious loyalty toward her Allies.

ENGLAND AT THE PARTING OF THE WAYS, 1890-1898

England's traditional policy, generally speaking, had for centuries been one of "splendid isolation." By keeping her "hands free," she could enjoy the Balance of Power in Europe between the Continental groups and make English influence in either scale decisive. It was only at times when some one Power sought to become overwhelmingly strong, or threatened to endanger British control of the Channel and her maritime supremacy, that England intervened actively and decisively in European politics. In the years following the Franco-Prussian War, England still adhered to her traditional policy. Three times Bismarck sounded her as to an alliance with Germany—in September, 1879, in November, 1887, and in January, 1889,—but in all cases Bismarck's "feelers" came to nothing, partly because Lord

Salisbury feared that he could not get Parliamentary approval for such a policy.[38] England would depart no further from her no-alliance policy than merely to make an entente with Italy and Austria in 1887, in which the three countries expressed their common desire to maintain the peace and *status quo* in the Eastern Mediterranean and Turkey.[39] This agreement did not bind England to any military obligations, but it did confirm her friendly relations with the Triple Alliance. After Bismarck's fall this friendship continued and seemed at first to be strengthened by the Heligoland-Zanzibar Treaty and by the young Kaiser's personal ties and visits to England.

But at about the time of the formation of the Franco-Russian Alliance England appeared to have come to the parting of the ways. Isolation, though splendid, was not always safe or comfortable. Though a match upon the seas for either of the allied groups on the Continent, England was in danger of meeting unpleasant diplomatic defeats, if Germany and France, or Germany and Russia, coalesced against her. Lord Rosebery, in his careless energetic policy, had already had several disagreeable experiences which left a bad taste in the mouth. Without consulting the signatories of the Treaty of 1884, fixing the boundaries of the Congo State, he had signed a treaty giving up to the Congo State territory in the Upper Nile basin in exchange for a strip of Congo territory in the Tanganyika region, across which it was planned to run the British Cape-to-Cairo Railway. France and Germany protested, the latter on the ground that it tended to encircle German East Africa and was contrary to a previous treaty. Rosebery had to

---

[38] G.P., IV, 1-14, 376-419; Lady Cecil, *Life of Robert, Marquis of Salisbury*, II, 364-369; *cf.* also M. Ritter, *Bismarcks Verhältnis zu England und die Politik des Neuen Kurses*, Berlin, 1924; H. Rothfels, *Bismarcks Englische Bündnispolitik*, Berlin, 1924; F. Frahm, "England und Russland in Bismarcks Bündnispolitik," in *Archiv f. Pol. u. Gesch.*, V, Heft 4, 365-431 (1927).   [39] G.P., IV, 261-376; Pribram, pp. 36-42.

withdraw the arrangement, explaining apologetically that he was acting on memoranda left by Lord Salisbury and was unaware of the difficulties.[40] Similarly, in the misunderstandings which arose over the Siamese troubles in 1893, Rosebery found the French assuming a stiff attitude. He bristled up himself, and, on a Sunday, without consulting the Cabinet, sent off a telegram to the English commander at Bangkok which gave Queen Victoria a bad fright. He himself admitted it might have resulted in England's waking up on Monday morning to find herself at war with France.[41]

By her dangerously weak position in Egypt, England was continually exposed to the more or less united opposition of all the Continental Powers. Egypt was like a noose around the British neck, which any Great Power could tighten when it wanted to squeeze a diplomatic concession from the Mistress of the Seas—as France threatened to do in connection with the Siam controversy, and as Germany was felt to have done in connection with railway concessions in Turkey.[42] Such incidents exposed the hollowness of the phrase "splendid isolation." As Lord Grey truly says, speaking of his first Foreign Office experiences in 1892-1895, there was "the constant friction, rising on the slightest provocation to quarrel and hostility, between Great Britain and France or Russia. The ground swell of ill-will never ceased. British interests touched those of France and Russia in many parts of the world; and where interests touch, an atmosphere of ill-will is always dangerous. The blackest suspicion thrives in it, like noxious growth under dark skies in murky air." [43]

[40] G.P., VIII, 428-475; for a somewhat different version, see Viscount Grey, *Twenty-five Years, 1892-1916*, I, 21 f.

[41] G.P., VIII, 103-112; Grey, I, 12-15.

[42] Grey, I, 9-11; G.P., VIII, 143-235, especially 185 ff; and XIV, 451-464; E. M. Earle, *Turkey, the Great Powers, and the Bagdad Railway* (N. Y., 1923), ch. iii.   [43] Grey, II, 11.

Some such considerations as these gradually led English statesmen to the decision that "splendid isolation" was no longer possible. In 1895, Lord Salisbury indicated the changed British attitude by hinting to Germany that the time had come to partition Turkey. Though England had formerly pursued the policy of bolstering up a decrepit Turkish Empire, Salisbury had now at last come to the conclusion that this was a hopeless task. He had been betting on the wrong horse. Turkey might as well be carved up, or at least the slices had better be provisionally assigned in case the Ottoman Empire should finally go to pieces.

The Sultan's misgovernment had steadily weakened Turkey; the Christian populations under Turkish oppression were becoming more and more restless; and the frightful massacres of Armenians, with the more or less tacit approval and connivance of Abdul Hamid, had shocked and roused Europe. Lord Salisbury's proposal was to the effect that in partitioning Turkey, Egypt should go to England, Tripoli to Italy, Salonica to Austria, and Constantinople or the control of the Straits to Russia. Such a partition, based on friendly agreement beforehand and securing a fair share to each of the three Great Powers, might conceivably have gone a long way toward solving the Near Eastern Question, if the great difficulties connected with it could have been overcome.

Unfortunately, Berlin failed to take up Salisbury's suggestion. Marschall and Holstein, who at this time largely determined German policy, were excessively suspicious. They foresaw that France and Italy would be difficult to satisfy. Moreover, what should Germany receive? They feared that an attempt to partition Turkey would give rise to more problems than it settled, and might even involve the Powers in war. They suspected that Salisbury's proposal was intended to sow discord between Russia and the Triple Alliance, so that England would have an opportunity

to fish in troubled waters. Accordingly, when Salisbury
renewed his suggestion directly to the Kaiser a month later
at Cowes, where William was attending the English yachting races, the Kaiser gave a cool reply; he said he believed
it was best to attempt to sustain Turkey, and to force proper
reforms for the protection of the Sultan's Christian subjects. Thereupon Lord Salisbury let the matter drop.[44]

By 1898 the political situation made still more evident
to the British Cabinet the advisability of abandoning the
isolation policy. In Central Africa friction with France
over the Niger boundary was acute; France also was extending her power eastward toward the Upper Nile; and
Major Marchand, leading an exploring expedition toward
the Sudan, had not yet been checked by Kitchener at
Fashoda. In South Africa English friction with the Boers
had been steadily increasing, and was to break out some
months later in the most humiliating and costly war which
England had ever fought. The Kruger Telegram had
shown the lively interest which the Kaiser and his subjects
took in the Boers, and the desirability therefore of putting
an end to any possible support, either secret or open, which
Germany might be inclined to give to the South African
Republics. Finally, in the Far East, Germany had just
secured the lease of a naval base at Kiauchau; Russia was
getting an economic grasp on Manchuria through the extension of the Trans-Siberian Railway; and by the lease of
Port Arthur she would have a foothold which would menace

---

[44] G.P., X, 1-41, 76 f., 111-114. The German documents indicate the
incorrectness of Sir Valentine Chirol's contention (*London Times*, Sept.
11, 13, 1920) that the partition proposal came first from the German and
not from the English side; they also correct many of Eckardstein's legen-
dary assertions in his *Erinnerungen* (I, 207 ff.; II, 284; III, 12 ff.) concerning the Cowes conversations of 1895. *Cf.* also R. J. Sontag, "The
Cowes Interview and the Kruger Telegram", in *Political Science Quarterly*, XL, 217 ff. (June, 1925); and E. N. Johnson and J. D. Bickford,
"The Contemplated Anglo-German Alliance, 1890-1901," in *Political
Science Quarterly*, XLII, 10 ff. (March, 1927).

Peking and seriously jeopardize Britain's naval and commercial predominance in the Far East. The English Press was clamoring to know how the Cabinet would stop Russia.

MR. CHAMBERLAIN'S ALLIANCE PROPOSALS TO GERMANY, 1898-1901

Under these circumstances the British first turned to Russia. On January 19, 1898, they proposed to the Tsar an entente which should put an end to all the long-standing sources of friction between the Bear and the Lion. The idea was to harmonize British and Russian policy in the two decaying empires of China and Turkey, instead of being constantly opposed. What Lord Salisbury secretly suggested to Russia in regard to China and Turkey was "no partition of territory, but only a partition of preponderance" of political influence.[44a] But the Tsar and his shifty ambitious Ministers did not receive the proposal in a way to inspire confidence or to encourage the British to proceed with it. Instead, Russia secured the lease of Port Arthur, and the British made a counter-move by doing likewise in regard to Wei-hai-Wei. Thereupon Mr. Joseph Chamberlain, the British Colonial Secretary, was allowed to try his hand at making an alliance with Germany.

On March 29, 1898, while Lord Salisbury was absent in France for his health, Count Hatzfeldt, the German Ambassador in London, was asked to dinner with Mr. Chamberlain at Alfred Rothschild's house. Chamberlain there declared quite frankly that England had decided to abandon her isolation policy. England and Germany, he admitted, had many petty points of friction in colonial matters, but no great fundamentally opposing interests. He therefore

---

[44a] Salisbury to O'Conor, Jan. 25, 1898; *British Documents on the Origins of the War, 1914-1918* (London, 1927), I, p. 8. The story of this British offer to Russia was first revealed in detail, *ibid.*, pp. 5-41, though the Kaiser got an inkling of it from the Tsar (see below, at note 50).

suggested an Anglo-German defensive alliance.[45] To satisfy Germany's fears that later British Cabinets might not keep the agreement, he was ready to get the treaty publicly approved by Parliament; this, however, "would not prevent the inclusion in the treaty of one or more secret articles," as he remarked confidentially three days later.[46] Finally he hinted that if England did not succeed in making an alliance with Germany, which was the more natural for her, she might turn toward France and Russia. This was said as a hint but not as a threat.

There was no reason to doubt that Chamberlain was sincerely seeking to open negotiations which should lead to an alliance. To have succeeded would have been a great feather in his cap. But other members of the Cabinet, like Lord Salisbury and Balfour, not to mention the Prince of Wales, who were all more Francophil, were less enthusiastic. They were not unwilling to see his efforts fail.

Chamberlain's offer was received in Berlin with the same suspiciousness as the proposed partition of Turkey three years earlier. Count Bülow, who had replaced Marschall as Secretary of State for Foreign Affairs, feared that a publicly announced alliance with England might involve Germany in the risk of being attacked on two fronts—the Russian and the French—where the British navy would be of

---

[45] G.P., XIV, 193-199, 212-216; Eckardstein, I, 292 ff. At a shooting party in January, 1898, the Kaiser had already suggested to the British Military Attaché the desirability of such an alliance, which he said he had been striving after for eight years but had met with no response. At a luncheon at Friedrichshof in August he repeated the suggestion to the British Ambassador. But at a dinner in December he concurred with the Ambassador that "there was certainly no necessity for a formal alliance", because if it became advisable for them to act in common the arrangements could be made in twenty-four hours; *British Documents*, I, pp. 69, 100-105. The editors of the *British Documents* state (p. 101) that these are the only references to the proposals of 1898 for an Anglo-German alliance which they have been able to find in the Foreign Office Archives. This extraordinary fact that the British archives contain no mention of the Chamberlain proposal suggests that this was his own personal venture rather than any official move on the part of the British Cabinet. [46] G.P., XIV, 202.

little assistance to Germany. Moreover, he doubted whether the English Parliament, in view of the bitter public feeling in England since the Kruger Telegram, would ever ratify an Anglo-German alliance. German public opinion would also be against it. He therefore directed Hatzfeldt neither to accept nor reject Chamberlain's offer, but to deal with it in a dilatory fashion. By this means he believed that Germany and England might come to an agreement on some of their outstanding colonial problems, without going so far as to risk a definite alliance.[47]

In this connection the Kaiser took a step which reveals the lack of honesty which he sometimes displayed in his attempts to manage German foreign policy. Without consulting his Ministers, and in spite of the fact that the Chamberlain proposals had been strictly confidential, he wrote to the Tsar on May 30, 1898, saying that England had thrice within the last few weeks asked for an alliance, making enormous offers which opened a brilliant future for Germany, and begging for a quick reply. Before answering the British, the Kaiser added, he wanted to tell "Nicky" of this, since it was a life and death matter. Such an alliance would evidently be directed against Russia. "Now I ask you, as my old and trusted friend, to tell me what you can offer me, and what you will do for me if I refuse the British offers." [48]

This letter was a gross exaggeration, because no "enormous offers" had been made by England. The Kaiser was deliberately attempting by his exaggeration to bid Russia and England up against one another, and to use Chamberlain's offer to sow discord between Russia and England. What he wanted to secure from Nicky was Russian cooperation for bringing France into a Continental League,

[47] G.P., XIV, 199-249; see also pp. 337-344.

[48] M. Semenoff, *Correspondance entre Guillaume II et Nicolas II, 1894-1914* (Paris, 1924), pp. 38-42; *Briefe Wilhelm II an den Zaren 1894-1914* (ed. W. Goetz), Berlin, 1920, p. 309 ff.

which should draw together the Triple and Dual Alliance, and thus make a strong group of the five great European Powers. This idea of a Continental League continually hovered before his imagination for years. By it he hoped to secure the peace of Europe. If Russia could bring the French into such a combination, France would be expected to give up the thought of revenge and the hope of recovering Alsace-Lorraine. This would remove one of the fundamental sources of danger to the peace of Europe. Furthermore, such a Continental League could be effectively used to check England's excessive colonial pretensions in Africa and Asia, and eventually, perhaps, after the growth of the German navy, to place a check on England's supremacy on the seas.[49]

The Tsar, however, did not allow himself to be fooled by the Kaiser into making any commitments. But he replied at once on June 3, 1898:

Dearest Willy,

. . . Three months ago, in the midst of our negotiations with China, England handed us over a memorandum containing many *tempting* proposals trying to induce us to come to a full agreement upon *all the points* in which our interests collided with her's. These proposals were of such a new character, that I must say, we were quite amazed and yet— their very nature seemed suspicious to us; never before had England made such offers to Russia. That showed us clearly that England needed our friendship at that time, to be able to check our development, in a masked way, in the Far East. Without thinking twice over it, their proposals were refused. . . .

It is very difficult for me, if not quite impossible, to answer your question whether *it is* useful *or not* for Germany to accept these often repeated English proposals, as I have not got the slightest knowledge of their value.

[49] G.P., XI, 67-92, XIII, 63, 89; XIV, XIX-XXI, *passim;* and *Willy-Nicky Correspondence, passim.*

You must of course decide what is best and most necessary for your country.

Germany and Russia have lived in peace since old times, as good neighbours, and God grant! that they may continue so, *in close and loyal friendship.* . . .

I thank you once more for writing to me at such a grave moment for you!

God bless you my dearest Willy.

Believe me ever your loving cousin and trusting friend,

Nicky.[50]

This news of "amazing" British offers to Russia, made just before Chamberlain's proposals, made the Kaiser naturally suspect that "perfidious Albion" was trying to play Germany and Russia off against one another, and sow discord between them. It confirmed him in his temperamental suspiciousness of British good faith. So the Chamberlain proposal of March, 1898, was not grasped by Germany, and came to nothing.

The utmost that could be secured was the Anglo-German Convention of August 30, 1898, for the contingent partition of the Portuguese colonies. As Portugal was supposed to be in financial straits and likely to wish to borrow money, Germany and England agreed to consult as to the terms of any loans made, and to divide the Portuguese colonial areas whose tolls were to be pledged as security for the loans. In case Portugal should default on payment, Germany and England would enter upon the administration of the tolls in the areas pledged to each. They agreed jointly to oppose any loans to Portugal by a third Power which

[50] G.P., XIV, 250 f.; Semenoff, p. 42, note, confirming the truth of the Tsar's statement says a British note to Russia of Feb. 12, 1898, formulated the conceptions of the British Cabinet concerning the delimitation of Russian and English spheres of influence both in Turkey and China. Russia was to enjoy freedom of action in Northern, and England in Southern, China; for O'Conor's note of Feb. 12 to Muraviev, see *British Documents,* I, p. 12.

involved pledging the revenue of the Portuguese colonies.[51]

This Convention is important because it aimed to remove one source of rivalry and friction between England and Germany, and became the basis of later negotiations in 1912-1914 for a fair and reasonable agreement for a further contingent rearrangement of colonial possessions. But it also became a source of irritation and suspicion on Germany's part. The Kaiser and Bülow overestimated Portugal's financial embarrassment. They waited in vain for the loan which would bring the expected results from the treaty. Lord Salisbury refused to hinder Portugal from making other loans which did not involve pledging the tolls as agreed in the treaty. In this he was justified by the wording of the treaty, but the Kaiser and his advisers thought it contrary to its spirit. They had expected England would use her influence to prevent Portugal finding any other sources of credit, thus hastening the moment for the contingent partition.

But, instead of this, the Germans soon observed closer relations between Lisbon and London after the visit of King Carlos to Windsor in the spring of 1899. And in fact, upon the outbreak of the Boer War, by the secret Anglo-Portuguese Declaration of October 14, 1899 (often inaccurately called the "Windsor Treaty"), Lord Salisbury renewed with Portugal the old treaty of 1661 by which England promised to defend and protect all the Portuguese colonies. In return, Portugal undertook not to permit the transporting of munitions of war for the Boers into the Transvaal, and not to issue any formal declaration of neutrality, inasmuch as that would hinder the supplying of coal to British warships at Delagoa Bay. Observing this close Anglo-Portuguese friendship and the failure of the Anglo-German treaty to produce the hoped-for results, the

[51] G.P., XIV, 347-355; for the negotiations, see pp. 259-367; Eckardstein, II, 205 ff.; and *British Documents,* I, pp. 44-73.

German Foreign Office naturally suspected the sincerity of England's proffered friendship.[52]

Similarly unfortunate in its effects on the relations of England and Germany was the Yang-tsze Convention of October 16, 1900. It aimed to promote the common interests of the two countries in the Far East by preserving the territorial integrity of China and by keeping her ports open to trade for all countries without distinction; but a misunderstanding as to whether it applied or not to Manchuria, where Germany did not wish to antagonize Russia, ultimately led to friction and distrust on both sides.[53] Disillusionment and disappointment in regard to the Portuguese, Yang-tsze, and Samoa arrangements, as well as the British detention and search of a couple of German steamers bound for South Africa and other sources of friction growing out of the Boer War, were further motives for German coolness toward suggestions for an alliance which Chamberlain continued to make.

Though the German rejection of the Chamberlain proposals was one of the most momentous factors in shaping the fatal course of events in the following years, only a word can be said about them here.[54]

[52] *British Documents*, I, pp. 74-99; G.P., XV, 429; XVII, 17 ff., 34 ff., 85. Brandenburg, p. 133, is incorrect in stating that the so-called Windsor Treaty was signed during the visit of King Carlos in the spring of 1899.

[53] *British Documents*, II, pp. 1-31; G.P., XVI, 197-491; XVII, 85, 103; Eckardstein, II, 201-203, 210-223; O. Franke, *Die Grossmächte in Ostasien* (Hamburg, 1923), pp. 149-177.

[54] The details can easily be found in G.P., XV, 410-426; XVII, 1-118; Eckardstein, *Lebenserinnerungen, passim;* Brandenburg, pp. 114-155; G. P. Gooch, *History of Modern Europe, 1898-1919,* pp. 310-332; and E. Fischer, *Holsteins grosses Nein,* Berlin, 1925. Fischer however fails to note adequately Germany's reasons for distrusting England, and, wise by later events, condemns unduly the German failure to come to an understanding with England. The same criticism may also be made of E. N. Johnson and J. D. Bickford, "The Contemplated Anglo-German Alliance: 1890-1901", in *Political Science Quarterly*, XLII, 1-57 (Mar. 1927). The fact that the new *British Documents* contain practically nothing on the Chamberlain proposals of 1899 indicates that again, as in 1898, he was making a private venture and not representing the official policy of the Cabinet;

In November, 1899, a few weeks after the outbreak of
the Boer War and the consequent anti-English outburst all
over the Continent, the Kaiser and Bülow visited England.
Chamberlain seized upon the occasion for long talks with
both. He suggested closer relations between England,
Germany, and the United States. The detailed notes which
Bülow made of the conversations [55] do not indicate that he
gave Chamberlain much encouragement to think that Germany would abandon the relatively favorable position
which she then enjoyed in exchange for the risk of an alliance with England. Nevertheless a few days later, in a
famous speech at Leicester, the English Colonial Secretary
spoke glowingly of the community of German and British
interests, and publicly proposed an alliance: "At bottom,
the character of the Teutonic race differs very slightly indeed from the character of the Anglo-Saxon race. If the
union between England and America is a powerful factor
in the cause of peace, a new Triple Alliance between the
Teutonic race and the two great branches of the Anglo-
Saxon race will be a still more potent influence in the future
of the world." [56]

But the poisonous effects of the Boer War were already
at work. German, as well as French and Russian, newspapers were attacking England violently. Germans, as
Bülow himself noted, were more stirred up about the Boer
War than the English themselves; the anti-English feeling
in Germany was stronger than the anti-German feeling in
England. In view of this Anglophobia, Bülow did not have
the courage, speaking in the Reichstag on December 11 in
favor of the German Navy Law, to take up sympathetically
Chamberlain's Leicester proposal. On the contrary, he

this tends to justify the German scepticism as to the real possibility of
an Anglo-German Alliance. See also Friedrich Meinecke, *Geschichte des
Deutsch-Englischen Bündnisproblems, 1890-1901*, Berlin, 1927.

[55] G.P., XV, 413-420.
[56] Quoted by Gooch, p. 311.

poured cold water on it, as being quite unnecessary for Germany. It was a rude rebuff to England. Moreover, if it be true, as Chamberlain told Eckardstein,[57] that he had made his Leicester speech at Bülow's own suggestion, and with the expectation that it would find a friendly echo across the North Sea, Bülow's Reichstag speech was a treacherous act greatly resented by Chamberlain. At any rate, the British Foreign Office became more suspicious of the Wilhelmstrasse,—a suspicion which was now beginning to be further fostered by Tirpitz's plans for building up the German navy.

Nevertheless, in 1901, after the Kaiser's much appreciated visit to Osborne at the news that Queen Victoria was dying, Chamberlain again opened negotiations for a defensive alliance between England and Germany, or even between England, Germany and Japan. England still had her hands tied in South Africa where the Boers were resisting with dogged determination. In the Far East, following the suppression of the Boxer Revolt, English friction with Russia had reached an acute stage, because the Tsar's forces would not evacuate Chinese territory. Under these circumstances, a German alliance would have afforded a valuable support to Great Britain. But for this very reason Germany was not at all anxious to commit herself. The negotiations, which were taken over by Lord Lansdowne, dragged on through the year. They were finally dropped in December, 1901, because the British Cabinet felt unable to meet Germany's conditions that the treaty should include the Triple Alliance and that it should be approved by the British Parliament. Whether such approval could have been secured was, in fact, very doubtful. A bitter antagonism had been aroused in both countries by the Boer War and the

---

[57] *Lebenserinnerungen*, II, 107, 111, 124. A current, but inaccurate and misleading English version of this unfortunate Chamberlain-Bülow episode is given by H. H. Asquith, *The Genesis of the War* (N.Y., 1923), pp. 43-49.

Press attacks on both sides which accompanied it. Moreover, the British Cabinet was by no means solid in support of the alliance with Germany. Lord Salisbury had always been sceptical, and finally left on record a strong memorandum against it. Lansdowne and Balfour were not enthusiastic. Chamberlain, except for support from the Duke of Devonshire, had rather been compelled to play a lone hand; and even he, after Bülow's rebuff of his Leicester proposal, did not want to burn his fingers again.[58]

Looking back at the whole series of negotiations, it is possible that some kind of an Anglo-German defensive alliance could have been arranged, if Germany had been more receptive to Chamberlain's offers at the beginning. This would have laid the basis for a better mutual understanding and rendered less painful the popular antagonism caused by the Boer War, in which the German Government's attitude, as distinct from that of the German people and the German Press, was tolerably correct.[59] It would have helped to prevent the mutual suspicions which were nourished by the increase of naval armaments on both sides of the North Sea. It would probably have averted the German fright of 1904 that England was planning "to Copenhagen" the German fleet,[60] as well as the English

58 G.P., XVII, 16-19, 53, 67, 115, 221-224, 297, 316 f. Eckardstein, II, 337 f., 397 ff. According to the Germans, the initiative in reopening these negotiations in March, 1901, came from the British; according to the *British Documents*, II, pp. 60-88, it came from the Germans. For Lord Salisbury's memorandum condemning the inclusion of England in the Triple Alliance, *ibid.*, II, 68 f.

59 The German Government realized from the outset that the cause of the Boers was hopeless, and that Germany was impotent to help them owing to the lack of any adequate German fleet. The German Government had therefore tried to dissuade Kruger from defying England to the point of war. Later, the Kaiser refused to receive Kruger on his mission to Europe, and refused to join in Russian and French mediation projects. (G.P., XV, 367-437, and note 35 above).

60 G.P., XIX, 353-380: "Das erste Deutsch-Englische 'War Scare', Nov.-Dec., 1904," with the quotation (p. 354) from *Vanity Fair* of Nov. 17, 1904 about "the precedent of Copenhagen in 1807." This was just after Sir John Fisher had "purged the navy of obsolete vessels" and carried

panic in 1908-09 at the specter of a German invasion of England.[61] It might even have established a basis of mutual goodwill which would have brought success to the numerous efforts made later for some kind of an agreement to limit the mad competition in Anglo-German naval armaments. And it would have doubtless prevented the formamation of the Triple Entente.

But Holstein, Bülow and the Kaiser miscalculated the situation and let the golden opportunity slip by. They were irritated at what seemed England's unwillingness to afford Germany colonial acquisitions in Samoa and the Portuguese colonies. They were unable, or unwilling, to defy German public opinion by allying with a country which was crushing the Boers. They doubted whether the British Parliament would really sanction such an alliance. Their fundamental miscalculation was their persistent conviction that England would never draw close to her traditional French enemy, and certainly not to her bitter Russian rival. Anglo-Russian antagonism was so axiomatic in the Wilhelmstrasse that Holstein and Bülow were convinced that, even if England did establish a *rapprochement* with France, this would not be dangerous to Germany, since it would undoubtedly lead to the rupture of the Franco-Russian Alliance; an Anglo-Franco-Russian combination seemed impossible. As things stood during the Boer War and the Far Eastern troubles, at the turn of the century, Germany, dominating the Triple Alliance, seemed to stand with hands free between England on one side and the Franco-Russian

out other revolutionary reforms to make the British navy more effective; see his *Memories and Records*, II, 128-153; he himself admits (*ibid.*, I, 22) that in 1908 he urged King Edward to "Copenhagen" the German Navy, while England had seven dreadnoughts and Germany had none. *Cf.* B. E. Schmitt, *England and Germany, 1740-1914*, pp. 178-182, 205-207. For an excellent summary of the broad aspects of Anglo-German relations during the decades after Bismarck, see Friedrich Meinecke, *Geschichte des Deutsch-Englischen Bündnisproblems, 1890-1901*, Berlin, 1927.   [91] *Cf.* the play, "An Englishman's Home."

Alliance on the other. Germany enjoyed, they believed, the advantage of holding the Balance of Power between them. It made her, as Bülow once proudly said, *arbiter mundi*. He saw no reason to abandon lightly her advantage, and to assume instead the risk of defending British possessions all over the world. England needed Germany, he believed, needed her badly, and would probably need her more, rather than less, in the future; therefore Germany could afford to defer assuming the risk of an Anglo-German alliance until English Ministers showed more consideration to Germany's wishes in colonial and other matters.[62] Why should Germany pull the British chestnuts out of the fire? Why allow herself to be shoved forward by the British against the Russians? What could the British Navy do to protect the East Prussian frontier from a Cossack attack? [63]

These are the ideas which occur again and again in the reasoning of Bülow and Holstein, and which were readily accepted by the Kaiser. Though at times he seems to have inclined sincerely to an alliance with England, he was

[62] *Cf.* Bülow to the Kaiser, who was visiting at Osborne, Jan. 21, 1901: "Your Majesty is quite right in feeling that the English must come to us. They have just lost a good deal of hair in Africa; America is uncertain; Japan is not to be depended upon; France is filled with hate; Russia is perfidious; public opinion in all countries is hostile. . . . At present it is beginning gradually to dawn on the mind of the English that they will not be able merely by their own power to hold their World Empire against so many opponents.

"Now the important thing is neither to discourage the English, nor yet allow ourselves to be bound by them prematurely. The English difficulties will increase still further in the coming months, and with them will increase the price which we can demand. We ought not to show England too great eagerness, which would only increase the English demands and diminish our chances of gain; but at the same time we ought to maintain the English in their conviction that we desire the continuance of a powerful England; that we believe in the solidarity of Anglo-German political, cultural, and also commercial, interests; and therefore that we shall in time be ready for this or that agreement with England if we receive proper treatment from the English side. . . . The English threat of an understanding with the Dual Alliance is a spectre invented to frighten us, which the English have used for years"; G.P. XVII, 20 f.   [63] G.P., XVII, 1-129 *passim*; XVIII, 510; XX, 15.

nevertheless, to judge by his letters and marginal notes, obsessed by a strong dislike of most British political leaders, including "Uncle Bertie," which almost amounted to a kind of Anglophobia. Psychoanalysts, perhaps, would say that he suffered from an "anti-English complex" caused partly by a reaction against early maternal influence, and partly by an "inferiority complex"—by an acute realization of Germany's inferiority in naval and colonial power. "Our future upon the Seas," "the trident in our hands," the building of the German navy, and the eager desire for colonies may have been a form of "compensation for the repressed envy with which he regarded England's proud position in the world." [64]

Thus, from a variety of reasons, Holstein, Bülow, and the Kaiser failed to take advantage of the English offers. They held off in the hope of getting better terms—and got nothing. They let slip the golden moments which were never to return. The English, failing finally to arrange an alliance with Germany, turned elsewhere. In 1902 they signed with Japan the well-known alliance which protected their mutual interests in the Far East. In 1904 they signed with France the treaties which were the first step in the formation of the Triple Entente.

ITALY'S DUBIOUS LOYALTY TO HER ALLIES

Italy, like Germany, had been occupied so long establishing her own national unity that she came late into the race for colonial possessions. But if she were to play the part of a Great Power in Europe, and find an outlet for her rapidly increasing population, she felt that she too must

[64] On the curious psychology of "the most brilliant failure in history", as Edward VII called his nephew, see the by no means friendly or sympathetic accounts of Emil Ludwig, *Wilhelm der Zweite* (Berlin, 1925); especially pp. 174-196, 218-265, for the Kaiser's baneful influence on Anglo-German relations; and [F. C. Endres], *Die Tragödie Deutschlands* (Leipzig, 1922; 3rd ed., Stuttgart, 1924), pp. 121-146, with extensive bibliography.

acquire colonies. She had naturally cast her eyes on Tunis. But the French had stepped in ahead of her. She had then sought alliance with Germany and Austria in the hope of getting their support. Bismarck, however, was not at first inclined to allow the Triple Alliance to be exploited for Italy's colonial ambitions. But in 1887, when the Boulanger crisis in France and the Bulgarian situation in the Balkans cast heavy clouds over Europe, Italy was able to extort, as the price of her renewal of the Triple Alliance, new clauses looking toward future acquisitions in North Africa, the Balkans, and the Eastern Mediterranean. As Germany's interests were not identical with those of Austria in the Balkans, and as Austria was unwilling to commit herself in regard to Italy's North African ambitions, it was decided that these matters should be dealt with in separate treaties to be signed by Austria and Italy, and by Germany and Italy, on February 20, 1887, the same day that the Triple Alliance Treaty of 1882 was renewed.

Accordingly, Austria and Italy,

"having in mind only the maintenance, so far as possible, of the *status quo* in the Orient, engage to use their influence to forestall any territorial modification which might be injurious to one or the other. . . . However, if, in the course of events, the maintenance of the *status quo* in the regions of the Balkans or of the Ottoman coasts and islands in the Adriatic and in the Aegean Sea should become impossible, and if, whether in consequence of the action of a third Power or otherwise, Austria-Hungary or Italy should find themselves under the necessity of modifying it by a temporary or permanent occupation on their part, this occupation shall take place only after a previous agreement between the two Powers aforesaid, based on the principle of a reciprocal compensation. . . ." [65]

[65] Art. I of the Austro-Italian Treaty of 1887, which was embodied as "Art. VII" in the Triple Alliance Treaty of 1891 and its subsequent renewals; Pribram, pp. 44, 66, 94, 99 f., 103, and 175-304, *passim*; G.P.,

Germany, on her part, undertook "to use her influence to forestall, on the Ottoman coasts and islands in the Adriatic and Aegean Seas any territorial modification which might be injurious" to Italy. As to North Africa: "If it were to happen that France should make a move to extend her occupation, or even her protectorate or her sovereignty, under any form whatsoever, in the North African territories, whether of the Vilayet of Tripoli or of the Moroccan Empire, and that in consequence thereof Italy, in order to safeguard her position in the Mediterranean, should feel that she must herself take action," Germany promised her armed support, if war should ensue.[66]

In 1891, at the third renewal of the Triple Alliance, Italy made a number of new requests, but the only one which was finally conceded to her was an extension of Germany's obligation to support her in North Africa. Germany and Italy engaged to exert themselves for the maintenance of the *status quo* in Cyrenaica, Tripoli and Tunis. But, "if unfortunately, as a result of a mature examination of the situation, Germany and Italy should both recognize that the maintenance of the *status quo* has become impossible, Germany engages, after a formal and previous agreement, to support Italy in any action in the form of occupation or other taking of guaranty which the latter should undertake in these same regions with a view to an interest of equilibrium and of legitimate compensation." In such an eventuality both Powers would seek to place themselves likewise in agreement with England.[67]

This opened the door, as the Italians hoped, to a possi-

IV, 179-260; VII, 51-123; XI, 267-300; XVIII, 499-647, 681-759; XXI, 351-419; XXX, 493-579; and Crispi, *Memoirs*, III, 301-349.

[66] Arts. I and III of the Italo-German Treaty of 1887, embodied as Arts. VI and X in the Triple Alliance Treaty of 1891 and subsequent renewals.

[67] Art. IX of the Triple Alliance Treaty of 1891 and subsequent renewals.

ble annexation of North African territory. But Germany still hoped to be able to restrain Italy from African adventures which might antagonize England, France or Turkey. She had therefore insisted on the insertion of the phrases "as a result of mature examination" and "after a formal and previous agreement." She also struck out the reference to Morocco, which was in the 1887 treaty and in the first Italian draft of the new clause, in order not to encourage Italy to collide with possible French, English, or Spanish ambitions in that region.

The Italians, however, were bitterly disillusioned in their hopes that these treaty arrangements would speedily enable them to acquire Tripoli. The following years were filled with demands and reproaches toward her allies, which became louder as the Abyssinian adventure went from bad to worse. Crispi complained that he was being browbeaten by France, threatened by Russian intrigues in the Near East and in Abyssinia, and neglected by England—and that for all this Germany and the Triple Alliance were to blame. The French, he said, were dominated by the thought of getting back Alsace-Lorraine, and had warned him to expect no concessions from them as long as Italy remained in the Triple Alliance; on the contrary they would "aim to make life as sour as possible for him." [68]

However, after Crispi had been overthrown as a result of the Abyssinian disaster, his successor, Rudini, began a *rapprochement* with France. By the Franco-Italian Tunis Convention of 1896, Italy at last virtually recognized the French protectorate in Tunis and received in return certain political and commercial privileges. The next year, the Italian Crown Prince, Victor Emmanuel and his Montenegrin bride, visited Paris, and the fêtes in their honor tended to draw the two Latin nations together. Two years later

[68] Crispi's report of a French official statement, Feb., 9, 1896; G.P., XI, 288.

a Franco-Italian commercial treaty put an end to the long
tariff war which had had a ruinous effect on the trade between the two countries and had caused great bitterness.
The *rapprochement* between Paris and Rome was helped
by the new turn which Delcassé gave to Anglo-French relations. After the bitter humiliation of Fashoda, Delcassé
had determined to put an end to the traditional hostility
between France and England. By a convention of March
21, 1899, Delcassé came to an agreement with England in
regard to the delimitation of spheres of influence in the
regions between the Congo and the Upper Nile, and at the
same time quieted Italian apprehensions by indicating that
the French had no aspirations to the east of Tunis, in the
Tripoli region coveted by Italy. This opened the way for
the secret Franco-Italian accord of December, 1900. By an
exchange of notes between Visconti-Venosta and Barrère,
the active French Ambassador at Rome, Italy recognized
French aspirations in Morocco, and France recognized
Italian aspirations in Tripoli.[69]

The growing intimacy between France and Italy was
now emphasized outwardly in every possible manner.
President Loubet bestowed upon Victor Emmanuel the
Grand Cross of the French Legion of Honor. The Italian
fleet visited Toulon and was received with demonstrations
of friendship which recalled the visit of the Russian fleet
at the formation of the Franco-Russian alliance. On December 14, 1901, Prinetti, who was decidedly Francophil,
revealed in the Italian Chamber of Deputies the existence
of the secret Franco-Italian accord made twelve months
before by Visconti-Venosta and Barrère. At the same time
he protested profusely to the German and Austrian ambassadors that Italy was thoroughly loyal to the Triple Alli-

[69] *Livre Jaune: Les Accords franco-italiens de 1900-1902* (Paris, 1920),
pp. 1-4; Pribram, *The Secret Treaties of Austria-Hungary, 1879-1914,* ed.
Coolidge, II, 227, 240-245.

ance, though he admitted it had been an act of disloyalty
on his predecessor's part not to inform Italy's allies at once
of the exchange of notes with France. He tried to excuse it
by alleging that he had supposed Visconti-Venosta had
already notified Germany and Austria of it.[70]
Bülow was worried at Italy's defection. He feared that
Italy might proceed to the annexation of Tripoli, thus antagonizing Turkey and jeopardizing German interests in the
Near East. But publicly he attempted to appear uncon-
cerned, declaring in his famous Reichstag speech of January 8, 1902, that "the Triple Alliance still enjoys the best
of health, and will, as I believe and hope, continue to do so,
like persons who are mistakenly announced as dead but
continue still to live for a good long time." And he added
jauntily, "In a happy marriage the husband must not get
angry right off if his wife innocently takes an extra dance
with another partner. The main thing is that she does not
elope with him; but she will not elope, if she realizes that
she is better off with her husband." This warning to Italy
he emphasized by remarking further that the Triple Alliance was "not a business concern for making gains, but an
insurance company."

Italy, however, did not heed the warning. While carrying on negotiations for the renewal of the Triple Alliance,
she at the same time listened to the wooing of Barrère,
who was determined to secure a promise from Italy that
she would not attack France and would give up any military conventions or other treaty obligations which might
compel her to join in a German aggression against France.[71]
And in fact on June 4, 1902, several weeks before the renewal of the Triple Alliance, Prinetti secretly assured Delcassé that it contained nothing either directly or indirectly
aggressive toward France. Though he stipulated that "this

70 G.P., XVIII, 730 ff.
71 Barrère to Delcassé, May 8, 1902; *Les Accords franco-italiens*, p. 5.

communication is destined to remain secret," Delcassé soon announced its substance in the French Chamber of Deputies.

Delcassé was not yet satisfied. He wanted to get from Prinetti a signed document which would bind Italy to observe strict neutrality in case France should take the initiative in declaring a war to which she had been provoked.[72] Accordingly, by an exchange of notes between Prinetti and Barrère on November 1, 1902, it was mutually agreed:

"In case France [Italy] should be the object of a direct or indirect aggression on the part of one or more Powers, Italy [France] will maintain a strict neutrality.

"The same shall hold' good in case France [Italy], as the result of a direct provocation, should find herself compelled, in defense of her honor or her security, to take the initiative of a declaration of war. In that eventuality, the Government of the Republic [the Royal Government] shall previously communicate its intention to the Royal Government [the Government of the Republic], which will thus be enabled to determine whether there is really a case of direct provocation." [73]

Practically this meant that Italy was now no longer a loyal member of the Triple Alliance. To be sure, Prinetti might soothe his conscience by maintaining that his promise to France merely "defined the character" of Italy's Triple Alliance obligations, and was not directly contrary to them.[74] It is true his promise was not contrary to the *letter* of Italy's obligations to Germany; since, according to Art. II of the Triple Alliance Treaty, Italy was bound to assist Germany only in case Germany was attacked by France "without direct provocation." Italy reserved the

[72] Delcassé to Barrère, June 18, 1902; *Les Accords franco-italiens*, p. 6
[73] Barrère to Delcassé, Nov. 1, 1902; *Les Accords franco-italiens*, 7-9.
[74] This is the aspect of the affair which Barrère gave to Poincaré in 1912, *Les Accords franco-italiens*, 11-14; it was, he said, not "a counter-treaty but a *counterpart* of the Triple Alliance."

right to decide what would constitute "direct provocation. But the interpretation of this phrase might be made as elastic as rubber. When asked by Barrère to define what it meant, Prinetti had cited as examples of "direct provocation" the Schnaebele incident, the Ems telegram, and King William's refusal to receive Benedetti in 1870.[75] This meant that at any time in the future, if some similar incident arose, which France considered a provocation, and which compelled her, "in defense of her honor or her security," to declare war on Germany, Italy would remain neutral. Thus, owing to the inclusion of the phrase "direct provocation," the Franco-Italian accord of 1902 was not exactly contrary to the *letter* of Italy's Triple Alliance obligation; but it was certainly contrary to its spirit and purpose.[76] Italy would no longer help Germany in case of a French attack, which had been one of the original essential purposes of the Triple Alliance. It all depended on how Italy would choose to interpret the essentially indefinite and elastic conception of "direct provocation." Being incapable of precise or judicial definition, this interpretation was likely to depend, as events proved, on what Italy considered her interests at the moment. M. Poincaré shrewdly summed up the real situation when he told Izvolski in December, 1912, that "neither the Triple-Entente nor the Triple Alliance can count on the loyalty of Italy; the Italian Government will employ all its efforts to preserve the peace; and in case of war, it will begin by adopting a waiting attitude and will finally join the camp toward which victory will incline." [77] Henceforth Italy had a foot in both camps and could jump in either direction, though she was

---

[75] *Les Accords franco-italiens,* 7.

[76] Even such a stout champion of France and severe critic of Germany as Pagès admits that Italy's new promise to France was "difficilement conciliable" with her prior obligation to Germany; Bourgeois et Pagès. p. 301, note 1.

[77] *Livre Noir,* I, 365.

not wholly trusted by either her old ally or her new friend.

In the fall of 1903, shortly before Germany was surprised by the conclusion of the Anglo-French Entente which threatened to draw Italy further to the side of these two Mediterranean Powers, she began to fear more seriously that Italy's "extra dance" might develop into an elopement after all. Victor Emmanuel explained to Emperor William that French friendship was important for Italy's commercial relations and for enabling Italy to borrow needed money. Though he was reported to have said of Barrère, "I don't like him, he is a liar and a nasty man," [78] nevertheless he paid a visit a few months later to Paris, which was made the occasion for further demonstrations of Franco-Italian friendship. At about the same time there was a violent renewed outburst of Italian irredentist feeling against Austria, which the Italian Government made little effort to check.[79] In April, 1904, President Loubet returned Victor Emmanuel's visit, going to Naples with the French fleet, and then even going on to Rome, though no French President hitherto had thus snubbed the Pope to honor the King. In the toasts given to Loubet at Naples, the Italians emphasized Franco-Italian friendship, but made no mention of Italy's position in the Triple Alliance. Germany protested against this omission, demanding that if further toasts were exchanged some reference should be made to the Triple Alliance and its peaceful character, in order that the world might not think that Italy had shifted to the side of France. The Italian Minister promised to heed the German protest. But he did not keep his promise. Two more Franco-Italian toasts were exchanged in which the Triple Alliance was passed over in dead silence.[80]

Monts, the German Ambassador at Rome, urged that

[78] G. P., XVIII, 615.   [80] G.P., XX, 37-64.
[79] G. P., XVIII, 616-636.

the way to make Italy return to a more loyal attitude was to take a severe tone toward her. "If we now are polite, friendly, and helpful, the Italians will become altogether intractable. The only motives which appear to be effective here are fear and a feeling of respect." [81] This advice was in accord with Bülow's past warnings to Italy not to let the flirtation with France develop into a permanent *liaison*. But Bülow now decided cordiality was wiser than scolding. He tried to win Italy back by assuring her that Germany had no objections to her taking Tripoli. He also believed it far better that Italy's colonial ambitions should be afforded an outlet in North Africa rather than in Albania and the Adriatic, where she was sure to antagonize Austria. Some months later, as Tittoni expressed contrition and promised "not to do it again," [82] and as the Moroccan cloud was gathering on the horizon, Bülow felt particularly anxious not to offend the Italians, or take a stiff attitude which might drive them further into the arms of France and England. "The façade of the Triple Alliance must be kept as intact as possible," he wrote to the Kaiser, "especially so, because as long as the Italians are still in the Triple Alliance, they will be regarded with distrust on the enemy's side. But in case of complications, we need certainly give ourselves no illusions as to active Italian coöperation. However, it will be a gain, not to be lightly valued, if Italy remains neutral instead of going with France." [83]

In his public utterances, and in the volume defending his policies which he published just before the War, Bülow naturally sought to maintain as far as possible the fiction of Italian loyalty—that is, to give the façade as good an appearance as possible. "Neither at Algeciras, nor during her Tripolitan expedition, nor shortly before this, at the interview of Racconigi, did Italy ever contemplate severing

81 Monts to Bülow, May 6, 1904; G.P., XX, 69.
82 G.P., XX, 81-95.   83 Bülow to the Kaiser, Mar. 5, 1905; G.P.,XX,95.

her connection with us." [84] This has often misled persons into thinking he placed more confidence in Italy after the Franco-Italian agreement of 1900-02 than was really the case. Even such a well-informed scholar as Professor Pribram says: "By the end of 1905, Bülow believed that no danger existed of Italy's alienation from the Triple Alliance." He quotes Bülow as declaring in 1905: "Italy has cast in her lot with the Triple Alliance, not for reasons of mawkish sentimentality, but because she finds it to her advantage to do so. The reasons which originally brought the three great states together are still in existence; nothing has happened to work a change in them." [85] But pre-war declarations of this kind are merely examples of the optimistic Chancellor's usual policy of *"faire bonne mine au mauvais jeu"*—of putting a good face on a bad matter. Privately and in reality he was much worried by Italy's double-dealing.

At the Algeciras Conference, by voting with France and England against Germany, Italy gave another rude shock to the façade of the Triple Alliance, and showed that Bülow had reason to be worried. Speaking in the Chamber of Deputies on March 8, 1906, Sonnino attempted to explain Italy's double policy, saying: "Loyal from our heart to the Triple Alliance, we shall maintain the traditions of intimacy with England and our honest friendship with France." On this the German Emperor commented significantly:

> " 'No one can serve two masters,' it says in the Bible; certainly therefore not three masters! France, England and the Triple Alliance, that is wholly out of the question! It will turn out that Italy stands in the British-French group! We shall do well to reckon with this, and write this 'ally' off as smoke!" [86]

[84] Bülow, *Deutsche Politik,* Berlin, 1913; Eng. trans. *Imperial Germany,* N. Y., 1914, p. 59.
[85] Pribram, pp. 263-4; Pribram-Coolidge, II, 135-6.
[86] G.P., XXI, 353.

THE ANGLO-FRENCH ENTENTE OF 1904

M. Delcassé, who became French Minister of Foreign Affairs in June, 1898, is said to have declared that the first object of his policy would be to secure a *rapprochement* with England. If France were to expand her colonial empire and some day recover Alsace-Lorraine, the age-long hostility with England must be ended. Delcassé therefore took steps toward a reconciliation with "perfidious Albion." He approved a treaty settling a long-standing dispute as to Anglo-French boundaries in the Niger Valley. A few months later, in the face of Kitchener's troops and in defiance of traditional French feelings, he had yielded to the British at Fashoda. On March 21, 1899, he reached an agreement with England delimiting French and English spheres of influence in the region between the Upper Nile and the Congo. He had done what he could to open the way for better Anglo-French relations.

But public opinion in the two countries was still hostile. It was further aggravated by the Boer War. To overcome this was part of the work of Sir Thomas Barclay. Looking at the two countries from a commercial rather than a diplomatic point of view, he secured the approval of Salisbury and Delcassé for a visit to Paris of British Chambers of Commerce in 1900. The banquet of 800 at which he presided proved an encouraging success. This was the year of the great Paris Exposition, and thousands of other British visitors flocked to the French capital. These visits were followed by delegations of French Chambers of Commerce to England, and by a similar exchange of visits by members of Parliament and their wives. With the ground thus prepared, Sir Thomas Barclay began to agitate for the conclusion of an Anglo-French Treaty of Arbitration, which should remove possible causes of friction and place the future of the two countries beyond the dangerous reach of popular emotions. Such a treaty, referring to the Hague Arbitration Tribunal all disputes between the two countries (except those touching vital interests, honor, or independence), was finally signed on October 14, 1903.[87]

Meanwhile, the death of Queen Victoria in 1901, and the retirement of Lord Salisbury in 1902, opened the way for two men who were more enthusiastic than their predecessors for closer relations with France—Edward VII and Lord Lansdowne.

The new King, Edward VII, had spent much of his time as Prince of Wales in Paris or on the Riviera. He spoke French with perfect ease, had formed many warm attachments in France, and had a strong liking for the people as a nation. In the spring of 1903, on his own initiative, he paid to Paris his first formal visit as King, and was delighted by his reception. Though it was not at first enthusiastic, it was respectful, and soon decidedly sympathetic. In one of those tactful speeches, in which he knew how to combine flattering appreciation and hearty personal good-will, thereby winning so many personal friends, he declared to the French:

"It is scarcely necessary to tell you with what sincere pleasure I find myself once more in Paris, to which, as you know, I have paid very frequent visits with ever-increasing pleasure, and for which I feel an attachment fortified by so many happy and ineffaceable memories. The days of hostility between the two countries are, I am certain, happily at an end. I know of no two countries whose prosperity is more interdependent. There may have been misunderstandings and causes of dissension in the past, but that is all happily over and forgotten. The friendship of the two countries is my constant preoccupation, and I count on you all

[87] *Cf.* Sir Thomas Barclay, *Thirty Years of Anglo-French Reminiscences, 1876-1906,* Londo   1914, pp. 175-229, 340-354. *British Documents,* II, 261, 289 ff., 318 f.

who enjoy French hospitality in their magnificent city to aid me to reach this goal." [88]

The warmth of this royal utterance, and his hearty enjoyment of the state banquet at the Élysée, the military review at Vincennes, and the races at Longchamps, all went a long way toward wiping from the French mind the bitter memories of Fashoda and the Boer War. Two months later (July 6-9, 1903) President Loubet paid King Edward a return visit. This was marked on both sides by the greatest cordiality. "France," the French President said to his royal host, "preserves a precious memory of the visit which you paid to Paris. I am sure that it will have the most happy results, and that it will greatly serve to maintain and bind still more closely the relations which exist between our two countries, for their common good and as a guarantee of the peace of the world." In return Edward VII expressed the hope "that the welcome you have received today has convinced you of the true friendship, indeed I will say the affection, which my country feels for France." And upon President Loubet's departure, the King sent a farewell message which found a warm response on both sides of the English Channel: "It is my most ardent wish that the *rapprochement* between the two countries may be lasting."

Delcassé had accompanied President Loubet on this visit and began those conversations with Lord Lansdowne which were to bear fruit eight months later in the famous Anglo-French *Entente Cordiale*. This was signalized by the signing on April 8, 1904, of a series of conventions which settled amicably long-standing disputes concerning the Newfoundland fisheries, Senegambia, Siam, Madagascar, the New Hebrides, and other subjects. The most important convention was that by which France at last gave the English a free hand in Egypt in return for a free hand in Morocco.

[88] Quoted by Gooch, *History of Modern Europe, 1878-1919*, pp. 338-339. *Cf.* also Sidney Lee, *King Edward VII*, II, 221 ff.

Egypt for more than a quarter of a century had been one of the most acute sources of friction between Downing Street and the Quai d'Orsay. It had been the Achilles heel of British foreign policy. All the Great Powers had certain political and financial rights in Egypt which continually hampered England's freedom of action and threatened the efficiency of Egyptian administration. Egyptian finance was now in a flourishing condition. But owing to the international fetters originally imposed under conditions which no longer existed, the Khedive, that is to say, his English advisers, were unable to derive any real profit from the surplus funds. The situation, says Lord Cromer, had become intolerable.[89] It was therefore a great relief to England to obtain a waiver of the financial restrictions and to receive the assurance that "the Government of the French Republic will not obstruct the action of Great Britain in Egypt by asking that a date should be fixed for the British occupation or in any other matter."[90] England's new freedom of action was embodied in a Khedivial Decree which England speedily notified formally to the Powers and to which she secured their assent.[91] Egypt was no longer a vulnerable point in English diplomacy. Within six months, as Kühlmann wrote from Tangiers, "The Egyptian question is dead, but the Moroccan question is very much alive."[92] Morocco, on the other hand, was pregnant with trouble

[89] Cromer, *Modern Egypt*, ch. 48. For Lord Cromer's active influence on the Anglo-French negotiations, see *British Documents*, II, 298 ff., 323, 332 f., 339 f., 354 ff., 364, 400.

[90] Art. I of the convention concerning Egypt and Morocco. For the text of the Anglo-French Conventions see the *British Blue Book* of 1904 (Cd. 1952) and the *French Livre Jaune* of 1904, *Accords conclus le 8 avril, 1904 . . . au sujet du Maroc, de l'Egypte, de Terre Neuve*, etc.; for the secret articles, first revealed in the Paris *Temps*, in 1911, see the *English Blue Book, Treaty Series*, 1911 (Cd. 5969); E. D. Morel, *Morocco in Diplomacy*, London, 1912, p. 234 ff.; *Amer. Jour. of International Law*, VI (1912), supplement, pp. 26 ff; and *British Documents*, II, 374-407.

[91] For the negotiations to secure Germany's assent, see G.P., XX, 121-165.

[92] G.P., XX, 33.

for France and was soon to become a diplomatic nightmare
for all Europe. At the close of the nineteenth century it
was virtually an independent country of some four or five
million inhabitants—Arabs, Berbers, Jews, negroes and
others—under the nominal rule of a Sultan at Fez. But
this rule was a shaky one. There were continual uprisings
from hostile tribes, or from rival claimants to the Umbrella,
which was the symbol of sovereignty in that sunny land.
Arab marauders continually jeopardized the life and property of European traders and travelers. Little satisfaction
could be obtained from the Sultan's government. As a
result of these turbulent conditions, the thirteen Powers,
including the United States, who had once coöperated to
suppress the Barbary Pirates, signed with the Sultan of
Morocco in 1880 the Convention of Madrid. This provided
for the proper protection of foreigners in Morocco and
promised the most-favored-nation treatment to all the Signatory Powers.[93] The two European countries which were
most directly interested in Morocco, because of geographical
propinquity and historic associations, were Spain and
France.

Spain had inherited or conquered during the sixteenth
century a number of settlements on the North coast, between the Straits of Gibraltar on the West, and the French
territory of Algeria on the East. These, however, were
separated from the Moroccan interior by the line of Riff
Mountains, so that Spain did not aspire to acquire any of
the Moroccan *hinterland*. If a partition of Morocco was
to take place, Spain merely wished to be assured of the
Mediterranean coastal strip and of some seaports on the
Atlantic coast opposite the Canary Islands for their protection.

France, though further removed from Morocco geo-
graphically, had in reality a closer and more vital interest

[93] *Amer. Jour. of International Law*, VI (1912), supplement, pp. 18-24.

in the country.   Beginning in 1830, she had gradually built up a great colony in Algeria, or, to speak more correctly, had extended France into Algeria, for Algeria was not a colony in the ordinary sense of the word.   It was divided into departments like France, was represented in the French Chamber of Deputies, and persons born in Algeria enjoyed all the full rights of French citizens.   As the French extended their control southward toward the Sahara, there was no effective natural boundary separating their territories from those of the Sultan of Morocco.   Algeria in consequence was subjected to continual raids from the plundering Moroccan tribesmen.[94]   France could have no peace on the western border of Algeria so long as turbulent conditions continued to prevail in Morocco.   The French, therefore, came to feel that the safety and destiny of Algeria, as well as their aspirations for a great North African Colonial Empire, made it imperative for them to extend their control over Morocco, either by police supervision, or by a protectorate, or by direct annexation.

But Italy, England, and Germany also had political, as well as commercial, interests in Morocco.[95]

[94] The mournful tale of them is to be found in the despatches in the French *Livre Jaune: Affaires du Maroc* (Paris, 1905), *passim.*

[95] Sir Thomas Barclay, well informed, as to the relative commercial interests of the various nations, says: "As it is still currently supposed in both England and France that Germany's brusque entry upon the scene was more or less gratuitous and that she intervened in view of possible interests to come, I may mention as explanatory facts that Germany had considerable interests in Morocco, in some respects greater interests than France. In 1901 the tonnage of ships calling at Moroccan ports was 434,000 for Great Britain, 260,000 for Germany, 239,000 for France, and 198,000 for Spain. At all ports, except Safi, England is an 'easy first', but as between France and Germany the latter is ahead at Casablanca, much ahead at Mazagan, and overwhelmingly ahead at Safi. At Mogador Germany shows a tonnage of 44,000 against France with 24,000. As regards imports into Morocco, Great Britain in 1901 stood first with 24,000,000 f., against France with 10,000,000 f., and Germany and Belgium with 3,000,000 f., each. Spain could only show 600,000 f. Of exports from Morocco, Great Britain received 12,000,000 f., France 6,000,000 f., Spain 5,000,000 f., and Germany 4,000,000 f. Germany's interest,

Italy, being without colonies, cast her eyes covetously toward Morocco, especially after the French had stepped into Tunis ahead of her. But in 1900 France bought off Italy's claims by the secret promise not to oppose Italian aspirations to Tripoli.

England, possessing one of the Pillars of Hercules at Gibraltar, was determined that the other Pillar at Ceuta must never come into the hands of a strong European Power like France; otherwise the English navy and English commerce would lose that vital control of the entrance to the Mediterranean, which Gibraltar had assured to her for two centuries. Ceuta belonged to Spain, but Spain was so weak, especially after the Spanish-American War, that England was content to have her retain it; she had no fear that Spain would ever dispute British control of the Straits. England also coveted Tangier, partly because of her large trade there. If she could not acquire Tangier for herself, she was at least determined not to let it fall into the hands of any other Great Power. England likewise wished to prevent any European Power from establishing a coaling station or naval base on the Atlantic coast of Morocco.

Germany was chiefly interested in preserving and extending her rapidly growing commercial interests in Morocco. Some Germans, including some Foreign Office personages, wanted a German colony in West Morocco which would open new markets for German goods, afford a much needed source for iron ore, and offer a convenient coaling station and naval base for the German fleet in the Atlantic. But the Kaiser was opposed to pressing this, for fear of antagonizing England and France.

By the opening of the twentieth century, it became increasingly evident that the Sultan, in spite of the Madrid

it is seen, was substantial, and among Morocco ports Mazagan and Mogador were places at which Germany was developing a considerable Morocco trade"; Barclay, *Thirty Years Anglo-French Reminiscences*, p. 276.

Convention, was unable to maintain order and protect foreigners properly. As the scramble for colonial possessions became more intense among the Powers, there was danger that one or another of them, probably France, would find reasons for intervening and depriving the Sultan of his independence, or his territories, or both. The future of Morocco therefore became one of the most lively subjects of secret discussion among the diplomats of Europe.

Mr. Joseph Chamberlain broached the question very privately to the German Ambassador on November 3, 1899, suggesting a secret convention: Germany was to renounce all claims to the Mediterranean coasts of Morocco, including Tangier; in return, "England could make Germany the most extensive concessions on the Atlantic coast." [96] Chamberlain, however, wanted the matter kept secret for the present from his Prime Minister, Lord Salisbury. Bülow was interested in the suggestion, and it was discussed behind Lord Salisbury's back by the Kaiser on his visit to England a few weeks later. But the Kaiser, foreshadowing the consistent attitude he adopted in the following years, had no great desire for German territorial acquisitions on the West coast or anywhere else in Morocco. "He himself had never had great interest in this question," he told Eckardstein, "and he had never understood why Germans placed such interest in it." [97] In spite of fresh misgivings aroused everywhere by the French occupation of Moroccan territory at Touat, in the spring of 1900, Chamberlain's suggestion came to nothing, owing in part to Salisbury's reserved and negative attitude. [98]

Bülow did not care to interfere in the Touat affair, "because today this would be equivalent to the possibility of a war with France.[99] He adopted his usual prudent but sphinx-like policy of "wait and see." In spite of recurring

96 G.P., XVII, 297.
97 Eckardstein, II, 93.
98 G.P., XVII, 299-323
99 G.P., XVII, 331.

rumors of possible Anglo-French and Franco-Spanish agreements contemplating a possible partition of Morocco, he maintained this attitude for nearly three years.[100] Then, on March 16, 1904, he received a telegram from the Kaiser, recounting a visit to King Alfonso at Vigo. William II had congratulated the Spanish King upon the rumored Franco-Spanish arrangements for a partition of Morocco, and had declared that Germany wished no territorial acquisitions; Germany wanted only the safeguarding of her commercial interests—"open ports, railway concessions, and the importation of manufactures;" and perhaps by way of compensation the Spanish Island of Fernando Po in the Gulf of Guinea off the German Kamerun coast, for which Germany would pay generously.[101] This declaration of German disinterestedness in Moroccan territory caused some dismay to Bülow and his Foreign Office colleagues, who had been inclined to think Germany might well secure some share of the disintegrating Sherifian Empire. But the Kaiser's declaration tied their hands. In spite of the clamorings of Pan-Germans on the one hand, and of Anglo-French suspicions on the other, the Kaiser's declaration laid down one of the guiding principles of German Moroccan policy in the following years.

Within a few days of the Vigo declaration, one of the Sultan's officials cast into prison a Moroccan in German employ, without giving reasons to the German consul in accordance with custom. The consul protested, but could get no satisfaction and no release for the imprisoned man. German officials suspected that the Sultan was being encouraged in his defiant attitude by the English or the French. They were the more indignant because some months earlier a German citizen (Genthe) had been robbed and murdered in Morocco, and the Sultan had replied

[100] May, 1901, to March, 1904; G.P., XVII, 332-363.
[101] G.P., XVII, 363-5; XX, 268.

evasively to demands for an indemnity to the murdered man's family. Bülow and his German Foreign Office colleagues feared that unless energetic steps were taken, German prestige, and consequently German trade and influence in Morocco, would suffer seriously. Bülow begged the Kaiser to consent to sending a German warship to Tangier to impress upon the Sultan the advisability of giving speedy satisfaction to German demands in these two matters. But the Kaiser was unwilling to sanction such a demonstration.[102] He knew that Anglo-French negotiations concerning Morocco were on the point of being signed, and wisely decided that sending a ship to Tangier just at this moment would arouse suspicion as to the genuineness of his Vigo declaration of Germany's territorial disinterestedness. He believed that,

> "forceful pressure by Germany against Morocco ought to be considered only after our grievances against Morocco have been brought fully with the facts to the knowledge of the three Powers most interested in Morocco [England France and Spain]. It could then be pointed out that remedial measures against the attitude of the Moroccan Government lay in the interests, not of Germany alone, but of all Europeans, and that Germany would gladly have the support and cooperation of the three aforesaid Powers in restoring by proper measures the injured prestige of Europeans in Morocco." [103]

Accordingly, in spite of arguments by Bülow, Lichnowsky, and German officials in Morocco, the Kaiser's decision prevailed and no German naval demonstration took place. But the Kaiser's hope that disorders in Morocco could be dealt with through the friendly coöperation of all the Powers most directly concerned was vain.

At this very moment, Lord Lansdowne and M. Paul

[102] Bülow to the Kaiser, Mar. 30, 1904; G.P., XX, 197-199.
[103] April 3, 1904; G.P., XX, 200.

Cambon, the French Ambassador in London, were signing the famous Anglo-French Convention of April 8, 1904, concerning Egypt and Morocco which has been indicated above. Its "Public Articles" disclaimed, of course, any intention of altering the political status of Morocco, but at the same time "recognized that it appertained particularly to France to preserve order there":

Art. I. [France gives England a free hand in Egypt as indicated above at note 90].

Art. II. The Government of the French Republic declare that they have no intention of altering the political status of Morocco. His Britannic Majesty's Government recognise that it appertains to France, more particularly as a Power whose dominions are coterminous for a great distance with those of Morocco, to preserve order in that country, and to provide assistance for the purpose of all administrative, economic, financial and military reforms which it may require. They declare that they will not obstruct the action taken by France for this purpose, provided that such action shall leave intact the rights which Great Britain enjoys in Morocco in virtue of treaties, conventions and usage. . . .

Art. VIII. The two Governments, inspired by their sincere feeling of friendship for Spain, take into special consideration the interests which that country derives from her geographical position and her territorial possessions on the Moorish coast. . . .

Art. IX. The two Governments agree to afford one another their diplomatic support, in order to obtain the execution of the clauses of the present declaration regarding Egypt and Morocco.

Important "Secret Articles," however, contemplated an eventual partition of Morocco between France and Spain:

Art. II. [England has no present intention of proposing changes in Egypt, but, in case she should consider it desirable to introduce reforms, France] will not refuse to entertain any such proposals, on the understanding that His Britannic Majesty's Government will agree to entertain the suggestions that the Government of the French Republic may have to make to them with a view of introducing similar reforms in Morocco.

Art. III. The two governments agree that a certain extent of Moorish territory adjacent to Melilla, Ceuta, and other *présides* should, whenever the Sultan ceases to exercise authority over it, come within the sphere of influence of Spain and the administration of the coast from Melilla as far as, but not including, the heights on the right bank of the Sebou shall be entrusted to Spain.

Nevertheless, Spain would . . . have to undertake not to alienate the whole, or a part, of the territories placed under her authority or in her sphere of influence.[104]

It is curious to note how casually Viscount Grey and M. Poincaré speak of these secret articles contemplating the partition of Morocco and seek to minimize their importance. Grey says the agreement with France "was all made public except a clause or two of no importance." [105]   It is characteristic of his psychology that when he has to deal with something disagreeable or repugnant, which does not fit in with his conception of things, he rationalizes it into thinking it "of no importance." [106]   M. Poincaré likewise speaks of the secret Moroccan arrangement as destined to remain "temporarily" secret.[107]

Upon the announcement of the public articles, the Spanish professed to be furious: they had not been consulted; they had been treated as *quantité négligeable;* this humilia-

104 See note 90 above.

105 *Twenty-Five Years,* I, 49.

106 So, for instance, in explaining the omission from the report of his speech in Parliament on Aug. 3, 1914, of the last sentence in his 1912 note to Paul Cambon, Grey says, "Perhaps I thought the last sentence unimportant"; *ibid.,* II, 17. Similarly he continually seeks to minimize the political importance of the vital naval and military "conversations" carried on with France in the following years.

107 *Au Service de la France,* I, 107.

tion endangered their dynasty; with clenched fists (prudently kept in his pocket), the Spanish Ambassador declared to Delcassé that "this Anglo-French Convention will have serious consequences and involve unforeseeable complications." [108] But Delcassé speedily bought off Spanish objections by providing that Spain should have her proper share when Morocco was partitioned. By the Franco-Spanish Moroccan Convention of October 3, 1904, in secret articles, Spain gave her approval to the Anglo-French agreement of April 8, 1904, and both France and Spain piously declared that they would remain firmly committed to the integrity of the Moroccan Empire under the sovereignty of the Sultan. But secret articles, which of course were communicated to Lord Lansdowne, frankly contemplated quite the opposite.

In delimiting the spheres of influence, the Spanish were to be given the northern coastal strip on the Mediterranean and the Atlantic, and the French were to have the vast *hinterland*. The boundaries were virtually identical with those which were actually adopted for the French and Spanish protectorates which were arranged by M. Poincaré in 1912.[109]

It has been asserted by a German historian,[110] though without proof, that the German Government in some unofficial way speedily became informed of the secret articles, and saw in them an evidence of the hostile feeling which France had nurtured against her ever since 1870. The assertion has been endorsed by Mr. Gooch [111] and others, but appears to be without foundation. There is no tangible

108 Report of Prince Radolin, German Ambassador at Paris, April 29, 1904; G.P., XX, 169; *cf.* pp. 170-194 for the cautious German attitude during the ensuing Franco-Spanish negotiations.

109 *Cf.* Poincaré, I, 106-118.

110 Veit Valentin, *Deutschlands Aussenpolitik* (Berlin, 1921), p. 54.

111 *Cambridge History of British Foreign Policy,* III, 340; *cf.* also G. Lowes Dickinson, *The International Anarchy,* p. 124.

evidence in *Die Grosse Politik* that Germany was definitely acquainted at this time with the double-faced bargain which Lansdowne and Delcassé had made and in which Spain participated. Had it been definitely known to Germany, it would surely be indicated in the recent German documents, as an evidence of Albion's perfidy and Delcassé's deviltry. It was not necessary, however, for Germany to have been definitely told what had been done. Given the knowledge of French ambitions and interests in Morocco, she could easily surmise the truth. She correctly suspected that there was more to the Anglo-French agreements than met the eye in the published articles. But though not without suspicions as to the fate awaiting Morocco, Bülow and Holstein seem chiefly to have suspected that France and England had made some secret deal in regard to the partition of China,[112] or had entered into some sort of an alliance aimed against Germany.[113]

Who were the originators of the Entente Cordiale and what were their motives? M. Tardieu, who stood close to Delcassé and had good information, says, "The English King was the initiator of the *rapprochement*. He it was who both conceived and facilitated it while many still believed that the moment was premature." [114]   Lord Cromer spoke of it as the "work of that very eminent diplomatist, His Majesty the King, and Lord Lansdowne." [115]   That the main impulse to it came from the side of England and not France grew to be a very general opinion both in England and on the Continent, and it was certainly greeted with more general enthusiasm in England than in France.[116]   Tardieu,

[112] G.P., XIX, 548.
[113] G.P., XX, 16, 27-30, 599-698.
[114] Tardieu, *France and the Alliances*, p. 60.
[115] Speech on receiving the freedom of the City of London, Oct. 28. 1907; *Annual Register*, 1907, p. 242.
[116] *Cf.* J. A. Farrer, *England Under Edward VII*, pp. 89-94. See, however, Lee, *King Edward VII*, II, 216-257, and the recent *British Documents*, II, 253-407, which show that King Edward's influence has com-

however, throughout his volume seems to over-emphasize England's rôle and England's advantages from the Moroccan agreement. There is no doubt that Delcassé, from the moment he took charge of the French Foreign Office in 1898, had worked eagerly for the extension of French influence in Morocco. He had made a treaty with Spain with this in view in 1900, but the treaty was bound to be abortive so long as the greatest Naval Power with large Moroccan interests did not give her consent. Hence, one of his reasons for a *rapprochement* with England. His Minister of Colonies, M. Etienne, and his London Ambassador, Paul Cambon, energetically supported him and were warmly seconded by Lord Lansdowne and Lord Cromer.

As to the motives, those on the English side were primarily somewhat as follows. Having decided to abandon splendid isolation and having failed to receive a satisfactory response from Germany to Chamberlain's alliance feelers, England naturally turned to France. In view of the growing friction between Russia and Japan, ending in the outbreak of war between the two in February, 1904, and the fact that England was allied to Japan, and France to Russia, it was important to establish cordial relations with France to prevent the Russo-Japanese War from involving England and France against one another. England desired to avoid the danger of having the war in the Far East spread to Europe. She perhaps also wanted to forestall the possible renewal of the Triple combination of 1895 (Russia, Germany, France) for concerted pressure against Japan in the Far East.[117] England sincerely desired to wipe off the slate the numerous causes of friction which had so fre-

monly been exaggerated, and that the chief initiative came from Delcassé and the French.

[117] According to the belief of Bernstorff, German Chargé d'Affaires in London, which was at first shared by Bülow and the Kaiser, this was a strong English motive in the *rapprochement* with France; G.P., XX, 14-21; and also 23, 31, 173.

quently brought her to the verge of war with France in the past.[118]   Finally, and perhaps the most important, as Lord Cromer believes, was the desire for freedom of action in Egypt. There is little conclusive evidence that at the outset England planned to isolate Germany or to encourage France to count on England for more than *diplomatic* support, and even this was to be limited to the case of Morocco. On the other hand, there is much evidence that, within a few months, the Anglo-French Entente came to have a far wider significance inimical to the peace of Europe—partly owing to Germany's clumsy and alarming diplomatic gestures.

On the French side the motives were in part somewhat the same. The French were determined to avoid being involved in war on account of the ambitions of her Russian ally in the Far East. They wished to end the long-standing friction with England. They desired freedom of action in Morocco. And they hoped to secure England as a friend, or possibly as an ally, in order to build up a combination of Powers, equal to, or stronger than, the Triple Alliance. France had come painfully to realize that her alliance with Russia was of less value than she had anticipated, at the time of its formation, that it would be. Russia had given her little or no support at Fashoda and on other critical occasions, and now she appeared to be so involved in the Far East as to be of little support to France in case of a Franco-German war. Delcassé had no thought of abandoning the alliance with Russia, but he believed that close relations with England would help to compensate France for the lessened value of the Franco-Russian alliance.

By 1904 Delcassé had thus bought off the Moroccan claims of Italy and England, by promising these countries a free hand in Tripoli and Egypt respectively, and he had

[118] Grey, I, 48 ff., emphasizes this motive.

satisfied Spain with a sphere of influence in northern Morocco. He assumed that he could now proceed leisurely to the "pacific penetration" of the rest of the Sherifian Empire without paying any attention to the natural claims of Germany. He believed that France at last had risen to such a strong diplomatic position, with Russia as an ally and England as a friend, that she could risk ignoring the country which had seized Alsace-Lorraine and long dominated Europe.[119] In this he was mistaken. He was grievously mistaken. As a French critic has well said, "With incredible blindness the Government took precautions with everybody, except the only one of its neighbors whom it had serious cause to fear." [120] And as Mr. Gooch has justly pointed out, "It is regrettable that the British Cabinet did not perceive—or at any rate did not help France to perceive—the wisdom of securing German consent by a *solatium*. Though the Secret Treaties of 1904 reserved no share for Great Britain in the contingent partition of Morocco, and though it has been argued that it was reasonable for the contracting parties to make alternative arrangements in the event of Morocco collapsing from internal weakness, our share in the transaction which suggested double-dealing involves the British Government in partial responsibility for the crises of 1905 and 1911." [121]

THE MOROCCO CRISIS OF 1905

It is commonly believed in France and England that the Kaiser's spectacular visit to Tangier on March 31, 1905, followed by Delcassé's fall on June 6, were the results of a German effort, by a threat of force, at a moment when France's ally lay prostrate in the Far East, to test or break up the newly formed Entente Cordiale and separate Eng-

---

119 Tardieu, *France and the Alliances*, pp. 178-182.
120 R. Millet, *Notre Politique extérieure*, p. 224.
121 Gooch, *Cambridge History of British Foreign Policy*, III, 340.

land from France.[122] But this belief, as the recently published German documents show, is not altogether correct. The misconception has arisen in part from prejudice and ignorance, and in part from the fact that writers have supposed that the Kaiser's Björkö maneuver and Bülow's Morocco moves formed parts of one and the same consistent German policy.

Confronted suddenly with the accomplished fact of an Anglo-French Agreement, in which Germany had not been consulted though German interests were involved, and in which there were good reasons for suspecting that secret clauses lurked behind the public declarations, Bülow and the Kaiser both felt that something must be done. But they differed as to what this should be.

Bülow preferred to adopt a sphinx-like silence, waiting until Delcassé should formally notify Germany of the Moroccan agreement, and offer guarantees for her commercial interests and some equivalent compensations. When Delcassé had continued to ignore Germany for nearly a year, Bülow tried to serve notice on him by forcing the Kaiser to make the spectacular diplomatic gesture at Tangier in March, 1905. This was altogether repugnant to the Kaiser. Nothing shows this more strikingly than a phrase in one of his letters to Bülow:

> Do not forget that you persuaded me *personally, against my will*, to go to Tangier for the sake of the success of your

122 *Cf.* Tardieu, pp. 170 ff; Bourgeois et Pagès, pp. 307 ff.; Viscount Grey reiterates this belief in at least four passages, *Twenty-Five Years*, I, 51, 69, 75, 99; *cf.* also 108 f. So for instance p. 51: "In British minds, certainly in my own, the Anglo-French Agreement was not regarded as more than I have described it. It was the subsequent attempts of Germany to shake or break it that turned it into an Entente. These attempts were not long in coming. The German Emperor made a visit that was like a demonstration at Tangier, and in 1905 the German Government forced the French, by what was practically a challenge, to dismiss M. Delcassé (their Minister for Foreign Affairs who had made the Franco-British Agreement) and to agree to an international conference about Morocco".

Morocco policy. Read through my telegrams prior to the Tangier visit. . . . It was to please you, for the sake of the Fatherland, that I landed, mounted a strange horse in spite of my equestrian disability due to my shrivelled left arm, and might have come within a hair of losing my life—*which was your venture* [*was Ihr Einsatz war*]. I rode among Spanish anarchists *because you wanted it and your policy* was to benefit by it! [123]

Their divergence in views is further indicated by the fact that Bülow did not keep his imperial master fully informed on all phases of the Moroccan affair, which he and Holstein were conducting. The greater part of the documents in *Die Grosse Politik* on the Morocco Crisis bear no marginal notes by the Kaiser, and were apparently not so regularly submitted nor so fully summarized for him as was usually the case. It is also likely that one reason for Bülow's later threat of resignation was his hope that the Kaiser would beseech him to remain, and he would then retain office with a stronger and freer hand.

The Kaiser, on the other hand, wished to avoid antagonizing French susceptibilities. With his "anti-English complex" and his inherited traditional friendship between Hohenzollern and Romanov, he wished to avert the possible danger lurking in the Anglo-French Agreement by realizing his dream of a "Continental League." This flitted frequently before his imagination throughout his reign.[124] It was a method of reviving the Alliance of the Three Emperors so far as was possible after the Tsar had entered into alliance with France. He hoped to use his personal influ-

[123] Kaiser to Bülow, beseeching him not to resign, Aug. 11, 1905; G.P., XIX, 497 f.

[124] *Cf.* G.P., XI, 67-92; XIV, 559 f. marginal note 2, XIX, 303-350; 435-528; and XX, *passim*. According to Kuropatkin's *Diary*, Nov. 17, 1902 (*Krasnyi Arkhiv*, II, 10), the Kaiser at maneuvers in 1896 or 1897 had discussed with General Obruchev how desirable would be a Franco-Russian-German Coalition as a means of dictating to England. Obruchev had mentioned it to President Fàure who thought it "worth being studied".

ence over the weak-willed Tsar to draw Russia into a
defensive alliance with Germany. Russia would then get
her ally France to join it. By thus associating the Triple
and Dual Alliances, he would form a league of the five great
Continental Powers. This would put an end to the danger
to Europe which existed from the antagonism of the two
groups. It would help to assure the peace of the world.
It would also be able to hold in check England's overweening
naval and colonial power. Incidentally, it would increase
his own prestige and influence, because Germany would be
the dominating member of the league. This dream perhaps
was fantastic and impossible of realization, but it formed
the burden of the interesting letters from "Willy" to
"Nicky" during the Russo-Japanese War.[125] At last, for a
brief moment of ecstatic joy in July, 1905, it did seem about
to come true.

(a) THE KAISER'S BJÖRKÖ POLICY

The Kaiser had been cruising in northern waters and
suddenly suggested to the Tsar that they meet on their
yachts at Björkö. The fact that France had just dropped
Delcassé, as we shall see later, and was inclined to accept
Germany's proposal for a Moroccan Conference, seemed to
indicate that France had abandoned hopes of *revanche* and
might at last be brought into more satisfactory relations
with Germany through the Tsar's influence. So the Kaiser
decided to take advantage of the Björkö interview and of

[125] *Cf.* my article, "The Kaiser's Secret Negotiations with the Tsar,
1904-05", in the *Amer. Hist. Rev.*, XXIV, 48-72 (Oct., 1918). This may
now be supplemented by G.P., XIX, *passim* (especially 435-528); A.
Izvolski, *Memoirs*, ch. ii; E. J. Dillon, *The Eclipse of Russia*, chs. xvi-xviii;
H. von Moltke, *Erinnerungen*, p. 325 ff.; Witte, *Memoirs*, pp. 415-430; A.
Savinsky, "Guillaume II et la Russie", in *Rev. des Deux Mondes*, Dec.,
1922, 765-802; the Russian documents in "Russko-germanskii dogovor 1905
goda, zakliuchennyi v Bërke" [Russo-German treaty of 1905, concluded
at Björkö], in *Krasnyi Arkhiv*, V, 5-49 (1924), also in German translation in KSF, II, 453-500 (Nov., 1924); and A. Savinsky, *Recollections
of a Russian Diplomat*, London, 1927. *Cf.* also Taube, pp. 45-84.

the Tsar's difficulties arising from the war with Japan to reopen the negotiations of the preceding autumn with the Tsar and secure his signature to a treaty of alliance. Some months earlier such a treaty had been discussed between them and a draft had been drawn up only to be rejected by Russia for fear of offending France. Now, perhaps, was the time for getting it signed after all.

The *Hohenzollern* steamed into the harbor of Björkö and dramatically dropped anchor along side of the *Polar Star*. "Willy" and "Nicky" exchanged visits. It was a scene which appealed vividly to the Kaiser's histrionic temperament. His exaltation of mind may be judged by a few selections from his autograph letter to Bülow, which covers six printed pages, giving the story of what happened in the cabin of the *Polar Star*:

Wisby, July 25, 1905

My dear Bülow:

By my telegrams you have already learned that the work of *rapprochement* has been crowned and the game won. . . .

And now that it is done, one is surprised and says: How is such a thing possible? For me the answer is very clear! God has ordained and willed it thus; in spite of all man's wit, in scorn of all man's intrigues, He has brought together what belonged together! What Russia rejected in pride last winter, and what she tried in her love of intrigue to turn against us, that now she has most joyfully accepted as a gracious gift after the fearful, stern, and humiliating hand of the Lord has brought her low. I have done so much thinking in the last days that my head has throbbed to be sure that I am acting aright, always to keep in mind the interests of my country no less than those of the Monarchical Idea in general.

Finally, I raised my hands to the Lord above us all and committed myself to Him and prayed Him to lead and guide me as He wished; I was only the tool in His hands and I would do whatsoever He would inspire me to do, though the task be ever so hard. And finally I also uttered the wish of the Old Dessauer at Kesselsdorf, that if He did not wish to help me He should at least not help the other side. Then I felt myself wonderfully strengthened, and the will and purpose became ever firmer and clearer within me: "You will put it through no matter what the cost!" So I looked forward to the interview full of confidence.

And what did I find? A warm, amiable, enthusiastic reception, such as one receives only from a friend who loves one heartily and sincerely. The Tsar threw his arms around me and pressed me to him as though I were his own brother, and he looked at me again and again with eyes that revealed his gratitude and joy. [The Kaiser noted the absence of Lamsdorf, to whom he applied an unprintable epithet.]

The Tsar said he was burning to have a thorough-going discussion. We lighted our cigarettes and were soon *in medias res*. He was uncommonly pleased with our Morocco agreement [for a conference at Algeciras] which would open the way for permanent good relations with France. He heartily approved my hope that from it a lasting understanding, perhaps even an "agreement," with France might blossom forth.

When I pointed out that in spite of egging on by England, France had down-right refused to take up our challenge [in consenting to drop Delcassé] and therefore no longer wanted to fight for Alsace-Lorraine, he said quickly: "Yes, that I saw; it is quite clear that the Alsace-Lorraine question is closed once for all, thank God!" Our talk then turned on England, and it very soon appeared that the Tsar feels a deep personal anger at England and the King. He called Edward VII the greatest "mischief-maker" and the most dangerous and deceptive intriguer in the world. I could only agree with him, adding that I especially had had to suffer from his intrigues in recent years. . . . He has a passion for plotting against every power, of making "a little agreement," whereupon the Tsar interrupted me, striking the table with his fist; "Well, I can only say he shall not get one from me and never in my life against Germany or you, my word of honor upon it!"

[After dinner on the *Hohenzollern* the Kaiser next day, with a draft of the hoped-for treaty in his pocket, visited the *Polar Star*. The conversation again turned on the subject of England's intrigues against Russia in connection with the war with Japan.]

I soon observed how deeply injured the Tsar felt by the attitude of France in the Dogger Bank Affair, and how, at England's behest, Rodjestvenski had been chased out of Cochin-China, virtually into the hands of the Japs: "The French behaved like scoundrels to me; by order of England, my Ally left me in the lurch; and now look at Brest! How they fraternize with the English. . . . What shall I do in this disagreeable situation?"

Now I felt the moment was come! . . . "How would it be, if we, too, should make a 'little agreement?' Last winter we talked about it . . ." "O yes, to be sure, I remember well, but I forget the contents of it. What a pity I haven't got it here." "I have a copy, which I happen to have quite by chance in my pocket."

The Tsar took me by the arm and he drew me out of the dining room into his father's cabin and immediately shut all the doors himself. "Show it to me, please." His dreamy eyes sparkled.

I drew the envelope out of my pocket and unfolded the paper on Alexander III's writing desk in front of the portrait of the Tsar's mother. He read once, twice and a third time, the text which has already been sent you. I prayed God that He would be with us now and incline the young ruler. It was still as death. There was no sound but that of the sea. The sun seemed gay and cheerful in the cozy cabin. Right before me, glistening white lay the *Hohenzollern*, and aloft in the morning breeze, fluttered the imperial flag; on its black cross I was reading the letters, *Gott mit Uns*, when the Tsar's voice near me said: "That is quite excellent. I quite agree!"

My heart beats so loudly that I can hear it; I pull

myself together and say, casually, "Should you like to sign it? It would be a very nice souvenir of our interview." He scanned the paper again, and then he said: "Yes, I will." I opened the ink-well and gave him the pen, and he wrote with a firm hand "Nicolas," then he handed the pen to me and I signed. When I arose he clasped me into his arms deeply moved and said: "I thank God and I thank you; it will be of the most beneficial consequences for my country and yours; you are Russia's only real friend in the whole world. I have felt that through the whole war and I know it." Tears of joy stood in my eyes—to be sure drops of water were trickling down my forehead and back—and I thought of Frederick William III, Queen Louise, Grandpa and Nicholas I. Were they not close by at that moment? Undoubtedly they were looking down from above and were all surely full of joy!

Thus has the morning of July 24, 1905 at Björkö become a turning point in the history of Europe, thanks to the grace of God; and a great relief in the situation for my dear Fatherland which at last will be freed from the frightful Franco-Russian pincers.[126]

The Kaiser's prayerful optimism and emotional fervor were soon given a dash of cold water by Bülow. His Chancellor threatened to resign. His pretext was that the Kaiser had ventured on his own responsibility to modify slightly the draft sent him from the Foreign Office. The Kaiser had added the two words, "in Europe," so that Article II read: "In case one of the two Empires shall be attacked by a European Power, its Ally will aid it in Europe with all its military and naval forces." The Kaiser's added words had the positive advantage for Germany that she assumed no obligations to help the Tsar on the frontier of India or in the Far East, where Russia was most likely to

[126] G.P., XIX, 458-465. The quoted passages are in English in the original, as the Kaiser was evidently giving as nearly as possible the Tsar's exact words. English was the language which "Willy" and "Nicky" regularly used to one another.

come into conflict with England. Bülow's threatened resignation was an unexpected and stunning blow. The Kaiser could not part with him. He offered to get the Tsar to change the treaty back to its original form and made an appeal which Bülow could not refuse:

> You are worth 100,000 times more to me and the Fatherland than all the treaties in the world. . . . No, my friend, stay in office and with me, and we will work further in common together *ad majorem Germaniae gloriam.* . . . After the receipt of this letter, telegraph me, "All right," so that I shall know you will stay. Because the morning after the arrival of your letter of resignation would no longer find your Emperor alive. Think of my poor wife and children! [127]

The Kaiser was soon to suffer a still more stunning blow, which knocked his whole dream into a cocked hat. When the Tsar revealed the treaty to his Minister of Foreign Affairs, Count Lamsdorf "could not believe his eyes or ears." After studying over the problem for most of the night, he explained to the Tsar the serious significance of the document signed in the cabin of the *Polar Star.* He made it clear to his master how contrary the Björkö Treaty was to the spirit of the Franco-Russian Alliance, and how unlikely it was that France could be forced, *volens nolens,* into such a combination with Germany and Russia. Nicky therefore had to write as tactfully as he could to Willy:

> This document, of immense valour, ought to be strengthened, or made clearer, so as to enable all parties concerned to fulfill their duties honestly and frankly. . . .
>
> During your stay at Björkoe I did not have with me the documents signed by my Father, which clearly define the principles of the Franco-Russian Alliance. . . .
>
> The first steps taken with the object of trying to find out whether the French Government could be induced to

[127] G.P., XIX. 497.

join our new treaty showed us that it is a difficult task, and
that it will take a long time to prepare to bring it over of
its free will. . . .

Therefore I think that the coming into force of the Björ-
koe Treaty ought to be put off until we know how the French
will look upon it.[128]

Great was the Kaiser's vexation upon the receipt of this
letter postponing indefinitely the Björkö Treaty.   He
urgently appealed to Nicky to stand by his written agreement, arguing that the treaty did not conflict with the
Franco-Russian Alliance, and that anyway,

Your Ally has notoriously left you in the lurch during
the whole [Russo-Japanese] war, whereas Germany helped
you in every way as far as it could, without infringing the
laws of neutrality.   This puts Russia morally also under obligations to us; *do ut des.*   Meanwhile the indiscretions of
Delcassé have shown the world that, though France is your
Ally, she nevertheless made an agreement with England
and was on the verge of surprising Germany, with British
help, in the middle of peace, while I was doing my best to
help you and your country, her Ally! . . . Our Moroccan
business is regulated to entire satisfaction, so that the air
is free for better understanding between us.   Our treaty is
a very good base to build upon.   We joined hands and
signed before God, who heard our vows!   I therefore think
that the treaty can well come into existence. . . . What is
signed is signed! and God is our testator! [129]

His appeals were unavailing.   The Kaiser's hopes for
a Continental League were permanently dashed to the
ground.[130]

(b) BÜLOW'S MOROCCO POLICY

To return from the Kaiser's attempt to secure a defensive alliance with Russia to his Chancellor's Moroccan

128 Nicky to Willy, Oct. 7, 1905; G.P., XIX, 512.
129 Willy to Nicky, Oct. 12, 1905; G.P., XIX, 513-514.
130 For the details of the fate of the treaty, see G.P., XIX, 515-528.

moves. The latter are the more important, because they
gave rise to the Morocco Crisis of 1905, and led to the
intimate naval and military "conversations" between France
and England, which are of the highest significance in the
development of the system of secret alliances.

At a dinner given in his honor at the German Embassy,
and again a few days later, on March 23, 1904, M. Delcassé
mentioned informally to Prince Radolin the negotiations
for the Anglo-French Agreement which was about to be
signed on April 8. Delcassé indicated the regions it would
deal with—Newfoundland, Egypt, Morocco, Sokoto, and
Siam. As to Morocco, he repeated that "he wished above
all else to maintain the *status quo* as long as possible."
But he said that the weakness of the Sultan's government
endangered commerce in Morocco, and that France felt it
desirable to strengthen the Sultan's position and end the
anarchy. "France does not wish to have any special interests in Morocco," he said, "but it is her task, in the interest of all nations carrying on trade, to put an end as far
as possible to the anarchy in this neighboring state." [131]
This was the first definite knowledge which Bülow received
of the impending Anglo-French Agreement. Aside from
this informal notification and the fact that the Public Articles were soon printed in the newspapers, Germany was not
officially notified of the text, nor formally consulted by
France about this agreement, which threatened seriously to
interfere with German commercial rights and political interests in Morocco. Bülow felt that Germany had been
slighted, and that her prestige as well as her material interests had been injured. To be sure, he at once instructed
the German newspapers to accept the news, without irrita-

[131] Radolin to Bülow, March 23, 1904; G.P., XX, 5-7; *cf.* also 266 ff.,
329 f., 396.   Delcassé to Bihourd, the French Ambassador in Berlin,
March 27, 1904, *Livre Jaune: Affaires du Maroc*, I, 122; *cf.* 167 f., 196 f.,
202 ff.

tion and jealousy, as a new indication of the peaceful situation in the world.[132] And in his much-quoted speech in the Reichstag on April 12, he attempted, as usual, to put a good face on a bad matter by appearing to welcome any agreements between France and England which removed causes of friction. In answer to an interpellation on the subject he cautiously stated that he could hardly say much, because the English and French Ministers had not yet explained it publicly. In a delicate matter of foreign affairs, he added,

> I can only say that we have no reason to suppose that this agreement is directed against any Power whatever. It seems to be an attempt to eliminate the points of difference between France and Great Britain by means of an amicable understanding. From the point of view of German interests we have nothing to complain of, for we do not wish to see strained relations between Great Britain and France, if only because such a state of affairs would imperil the peace of the world, the maintenance of which we sincerely desire. Concerning Morocco, which constitutes the essential point of the agreement, we are interested in this country, as in fact in the rest of the Mediterranean, principally from the economic point of view. . . . We must protect our commercial interests in Morocco, and we shall protect them.[133]

Though Bülow certainly underestimated at first the political significance of the new Anglo-French Entente, he was far from taking it as lightly as one might be led to infer from his Reichstag speech, which was intended to quiet the fears of the German public. In fact, it caused him and his Foreign Office assistants to do a good deal of serious thinking during the following weeks. He and Holstein gradually reached a determination to hold to Germany's rights under the international Morocco Treaty of 1880, and to ignore the Anglo-French Moroccan Convention

[132] G.P., XX, 12 (April 9).   [133] *Affaires du Maroc*, I, 127.

until Delcassé should invite a discussion of it and give
Germany an opportunity to be heard and perhaps get some
equivalent compensations. England and France, they felt,
could not by separate agreement deprive third parties of
their rights in Morocco. France, now given a free hand
in Morocco by England, would try to establish a French
economic monopoly there, as she had done in all her other
colonies. She would "Tunisify" Morocco by "peaceful penetration." So Germany's commercial rights and interests
would be threatened, as the French would get exclusive
trading and financial privileges, and a monopoly of railway
and mining concessions. Furthermore, German prestige
would suffer, if she allowed Morocco to be disposed of by
France and England as if Germany did not exist. Holstein
summed the matter up: "If we let our toes be trodden
upon in Morocco without saying a word, we encourage
others to do the same thing elsewhere." [134]

There were two ways by which Germany might give
expression to her wishes. The first was to tell Delcassé in
a frank and friendly manner that the published Anglo-
French Convention aroused concern in Germany in regard
to her commercial interests, and to ask more fully what
guarantees France would offer for the protection of these
interests. This was the more neighborly way. But it was
not adopted. The second way was to maintain an impassive and sphinx-like silence, neither recognizing nor protesting against the Anglo-French Agreement, but acting as
if it did not exist for Germany, since Germany had not been
officially informed of the text of it. This second plan would
consist in Germany's going step by step with France in
Morocco in the matter of police measures to curb the
anarchy. If France sent warships to Tangier, Germany
could do likewise. In this way, without infringing any

---

[134] Holstein's Memoir of June 3, 1904; G.P., XX, 207-9; cf. also
Bülow to Radolin July 21; G.P., XX, 210-214.

rights, Germany might compel Delcassé to be the first to speak and inquire as to German intentions. The less Germany explained her steps in the newspapers, the more uncertain and uncomfortable the French would become. Then when once Delcassé saw that Germany was in earnest, Germany ought to make concessions and abandon any thought of establishing a foothold in Morocco. This policy was more adventurous and dangerous to the peace of Europe. But it was the one which Bülow and Holstein adopted.[135]

But this sphinx-like waiting policy did not bear fruit as rapidly as had been hoped. Delcassé was evidently becoming increasingly nervous, but he avoided broaching the question. To bring him out of his silence Germany began to encourage the Sultan to resist the police measures which the French at last, in the winter of 1904-05, planned to put into effect. Kühlmann, the German Chargé d'Affaires in Tangier, had already reported that there seemed to be friction between France and England, and that it was not likely that Delcassé could count on more than Platonic support from the British. The Dogger Bank Affair had just occurred and given rise in England to violent indignation against Russia. Kühlmann felt sure that France was in no position to settle the fate of Morocco without Germany's sanction. In fact he believed M. Delcassé to be in the unenviable position of resting one leg on Russia and another on England, and thus to be in danger of falling between two stools as the tension between these two hostile countries tightened. He had also heard that the American Vice-Consul had said to a leading Moor, "Germany has not spoken, and until then, we cannot believe that anything definite has been decided." [136]

During the summer of 1904 the Sultan continued to

[135] G.P., XX, 7-33, 195-234, especially 215 ff.
[136] Kühlmann to Bülow, Nov. 9, 1904; G.P., XX, 232.

answer evasively Bülow's demands in regard to Genthe, a German citizen murdered in Morocco. The German Minister at Tangier, therefore, wanted Germany to assert her prestige by an ultimatum to the Sultan, to be followed, if necessary, by the sending of a warship to Moroccan waters as a diplomatic demonstration. Bülow favored it, but the Kaiser forbade it, and it did not take place.[137] Soon afterwards Germany put aside her grievance over the Genthe murder and began to assume an attitude of friendliness to the Sultan. This was to encourage him to resist the "Tunisification" program which Delcassé was now believed to be preparing to force upon him. This would consist, as was gathered in Tangier from St. René Taillandier, the head of the French Mission, mainly of three points: the reorganization of the Sultan's army by French instructors; the signing by the Sultan of a treaty with the French excluding the political influence of other nations; and the control by France of the Sultan's finances. To Kühlmann this looked very much like the establishment of a virtual protectorate.[138] Germany therefore secretly encouraged the Sultan to resist the imposition of the French program. When he called together a patriotic Assembly of Notables from all Morocco to examine the French demands, Kühlmann approved the measure as "a skilful anti-French move." [139] Then, when the French Press began to demand that the Assembly of Notables be dismissed, Bülow secretly advised the contrary, believing that the proud Moroccan chieftains would declare against the French program. He did not think it likely that the French would go to the point of trying to bluff the Sultan with a threat of war, because the new Rouvier Cabinet did not wish to risk the expenditure

137 G.P., XX, 222-230.
138 Kühlmann to Bülow, Nov. 28, 1904; G.P., XX, 237 ff. For the detailed aims of the Taillandier Mission, see *Affaires du Maroc*, I, 178-184.
139 G.P., XX, 246 ff.

of men and money in a Moroccan campaign, or weaken
France's position toward Germany by transferring troops
to Africa. Bülow, however, had been careful to warn
Kühlmann not to encourage the Sultan to expect that Ger-
many would support him to the point of making war on
France on his behalf.[140]

(c) THE KAISER'S TANGIER VISIT

It was during these rival efforts in Morocco on the part
of Kühlmann and Taillandier to win the ear of the Sultan,
that Bülow suddenly decided to have the Kaiser stop on
his trip from Hamburg to Corfu at Tangier and greet the
Sultan. The original schedule of the Kaiser's trip did not
provide for this, but Bülow had the *Kölnische Zeitung* print
a despatch from Tangier announcing that the Kaiser would
land there on March 31. He then sent the clipping to the
Kaiser, adding, "Your Majesty's visit will embarrass M.
Delcassé, block his plan, and benefit our economic interests
in Morocco." [141] The Kaiser at first agreed, but when he
learned from the newspapers that the Tangier population,
including the English, were planning to exploit his visit
against the French, he wrote Bülow: "Telegraph at once
to Tangier that it is *most* doubtful whether I land, and
that I am only travelling *incognito* as a tourist; therefore,
no audiences, no receptions." Bülow, however, shrewdly
pointed out to him that a public announcement of the visit
had been made, and if it was given up, Delcassé would
spread abroad the idea that it was owing to French representations in Berlin that the visit had been abandoned.
Delcassé would make a diplomatic triumph out of it. So
the Kaiser again agreed, though at Lisbon, and even at the
last moment in the harbor at Tangier, he had further hesitations. But he finally yielded to the advice of those with

[140] G.P., XX, 243.
[141] Bülow to Kaiser, Mar. 20, 1905; G.P., XX, 262.

him, and carried out the program which had been arranged for him.[142]

In spite of the difficulties of landing in a very rough sea and the fright caused to the Kaiser's horse by the din of Arab yelling, music, and the promiscuous discharge of fire-arms, the Kaiser's visit passed off smoothly enough with brilliant Oriental color. At the German Legation he received the members of the German colony and the Diplomatic Corps. To the French representative he said that his visit meant that Germany wanted freedom of trade and equality with others; that he wished to deal directly with the Sultan as a free and equal sovereign of an independent country, and he expected that France would respect his wishes. To the Sultan's Great Uncle and Plenipotentiary, he emphasized the same points, adding that such reforms as were made ought to be in accordance with the Koran and Mohammedan tradition; that European customs ought not to be blindly adopted; and that the Sultan would do well in this matter to heed the advice of his Notables.[143]

Bülow then proposed the calling of an international conference of all the Powers who had signed the Madrid Treaty of 1880.

He thought this the best way of settling the Moroccan question and securing the commercial interests of Germany, as well as of other nations, against the danger of Delcassé's "Tunisification" of the country. Here, he rightly believed, he was on solid ground. He renewed Germany's declaration of territorial disinterestedness, and made it clear that Germany was not seeking any special advantages for herself,

---

[142] G.P., XX, 263 ff. Baron Schoen, who accompanied the Kaiser, gives a good account in his *Memoirs of an Ambassador*, pp. 19-26.

[143] As the speeches were informal, and in the midst of a large and somewhat noisy assemblage, the reports of what he said vary considerably in the accounts of Schoen (G.P., XX, 286), Kühlmann (Schulthess, *Europäischer Geschichtskalender*, 1905, p. 304), and Chérisey, the French representative (*Affaires du Maroc*, I, 205).

but was only acting in the interest of all countries having commercial interests in Morocco.

He felt sure that he would have the support of a majority of the Powers in such a conference. President Roosevelt was sounded and was thought to favor it, as he had always favored an "open door" policy throughout the world.[144] Bülow hoped that Roosevelt's attitude would have a favorable effect on England and strengthen the influence of the London *Times* correspondent at Tangier,[145] who had supported the German point of view. Austria and Italy, he believed, could be counted on as allies. Russia was too much absorbed by the defeats in Manchuria to interpose objections. The Sultan of Morocco himself grasped eagerly at the conference idea, when it was suggested to him, as an easy way of avoiding a virtual French protectorate. France, therefore, would be left in a minority and would have to consent to see her secret agreements with England and Spain replaced by an international settlement. As the whole French Morocco policy had been peculiarly the work of Delcassé, the thwarting of it by the holding of an international conference would probably render his position in France insecure, especially if Germany firmly insisted on a conference. Meanwhile, Bülow continued to maintain toward France his very disconcerting attitude of sphinx-like and impassive silence, still ignoring the Anglo-French Moroccan Agreement of 1904.[146]

As Bülow had calculated, the French in general, and Delcassé in particular, now became very uneasy. They felt that they were being menaced by Germany, but did not understand exactly what she wanted. Some suspected she was looking for a pretext for war, which was certainly not the case, as the recently published German documents

---

[144] G.P., XX, 256 ff. J. B. Bishop, *Roosevelt,* I, 467 ff.
[145] Mr. W. B. Harris, G.P., XX, 261 ff. See also Harris' own memoirs.
[146] G.P., XX, 293 ff.

clearly prove. Within France there was a strong and growing party which felt that Delcassé had been pursuing an
adventurous and dangerous imperialist policy; he was involving the risk of war with the Sultan of Morocco, and
even with Germany, at a time when France was unprepared
from a military point of view and weakened by the defeats
of her Russian ally. This party, which included the French
Ambassador in Berlin,[147] wanted to yield to Germany's proposal for a conference, even though it meant the humiliation and the probable resignation of Delcassé as Minister
of Foreign Affairs. This also was the feeling of M. Rouvier,
the Prime Minister, and eventually of a majority of the
Cabinet.

On April 26, M. Rouvier dined with Prince Radolin at
the German Embassy, and told him with evident emotion
that under no circumstances would he wish to see trouble
between Germany and France; that the French people inclined much more to the German than to the English side,
though there were foolish irresponsible patriots who
preached *revanche*. France and Germany must stand together and preserve the peace of the world. So long as he
was at the head of affairs, this would be his purpose. As
far as Morocco was concerned, he guaranteed that there
would be no change in the *status quo* and no limitation on
the commerce of foreign nations. "It is impossible and it
would be criminal," he concluded, with great emotion, "that
the two countries which are called to come to an understanding and draw closer to one another should quarrel—
and that simply on account of Morocco!" M. Rouvier's
remark had all the more significance from the fact that a
few minutes before the dinner, Prince Radolin had been
informed by a person in M. Rouvier's confidence that "the
Prime Minister by no means identified himself with Delcassé, since he knew that the English navy did not run on

147 *Cf.*   Bihourd's reports, *Affaires du Maroc*, I, 202 ff., 215 f., 240.

wheels" and, therefore, could not protect Paris. From all this Prince Radolin gained the impression that M. Rouvier would not be unwilling to sacrifice his Minister of Foreign Affairs.[148]

(d) DELCASSÉ'S FALL AND ITS CONSEQUENCES

This hint from Rouvier was sufficient to determine Bülow to work henceforth to overthrow the man whom he regarded as dangerous to Germany and to the peace of Europe. Not only did he regard Delcassé as the incarnation of French aggressive imperialism and of the *revanche* spirit, but he believed that so long as he continued at the head of the French Foreign Office, with his intrigues and misrepresentations, there could be no satisfactory relations between the countries on the two sides of the Rhine.[149]

Another party in France, however, made up of a considerable group of newspapers and chauvinists, protested loudly against the German menace. Delcassé counted on them for support, and made a strong fight for his political life. The exciting story of this internal French conflict, as witnessed by the German representative in Paris, may now be followed in detail in the new German documents.[150]

[148] Radolin to Bülow, April 27, 1905; G.P., XX, 344. This telegram, according to a letter of Paléologue's in the Paris *Temps* of March 15, 1922, was deciphered by the French during the war. Its publication by Paléologue gave rise to a lively discussion in 1922, as to whether the German Government had demanded the head of Delcassé, or whether it had been offered to them. Mr. O. S. Hale, of the University of Pennsylvania, in an unpublished study, indicates that there is no truth in the commonly repeated legend, based on an article in *Le Gaulois,* June 17, 1905, that Prince Henckel von Donnersmarck was sent on a special mission by the German Government to demand the resignation of Delcassé. On internal and other evidence Mr. Hale thinks the report in *Le Gaulois* is apocryphal. This confirms the present writer's conclusion that the "Donnersmarck Mission" was a product of French journalistic imagination.

[149] *Cf.* G.P., XX, 393 ff. for a list of half a dozen cases in which Bülow believed Delcassé guilty of misrepresentations and broken promises.

[150] G.P., XX, 344-409. *Cf.* R. Pinon, *France et Allemagne* (Paris, 1913), which is, on the whole, favorable to Germany and critical of Del-

Delcassé insisted on holding out against the German proposal for a conference. He alleged it would put the Sultan under international tutelage, but in reality he feared it would wreck his own program. Moreover, to yield in the face of German pressure would be an intolerable humiliation for France, as well as for himself personally. He declared to his colleagues that Germany was "bluffing," and he wanted to call their bluff even at the risk of war. He would rather resign than yield.

But meanwhile his position was being undermined both at Fez and at Paris. At the end of May the Sultan finally rejected the French demands and adopted the German proposal of inviting the Powers to an international conference. In Paris the German Ambassador maintained a firm and unyielding attitude, and gave the impression that Germany would back up the Sultan with force if necessary.

M. Rouvier was in a most distressing position. He feared that M. Delcassé was leading France to the brink of war. Through a confidential agent he sounded Germany further, and gathered that if he consented to drop Delcassé from the Cabinet, and accepted the idea of a conference, the critical situation would be happily relieved and Germany would not make too great difficulties when the conference met. He therefore finally went to President Loubet, taking M. Delcassé with him, and told the President that he was absolutely opposed to M. Delcassé's policy. He said that

cassé; A. Mevil, *De la paix de Francfort à la conférence d'Algésiras* (Paris, 1909), which takes the opposite point of view. Tardieu *La Conférence d'Algésiras*, as usual, is strongly nationalist. The French Yellow Book, *Affaires du Maroc*, is singularly barren on this important aspect of the Moroccan affair; it contains nothing at all on the critical week of Delcassé's final fall. The material in the recent German documents on Björkö, Delcassé, and the Morocco Crisis of 1905 is summarized by E. Laloy, in *Mercure de France*, CLXXXVI, 594 ff.; CLXXXVII, 564 ff.; CLXXXIX, 293 ff.; CXC, 568 ff.; CXCII, 72 ff. (March-November, 1926); and by R. J. Sontag, in *Amer. Hist. Rev.*, XXXIII, 278-301 (Jan., 1928).

next day he would hold a Cabinet meeting, and would resign, if a majority of his colleagues did not agree with him. Accordingly, on June 6, the Cabinet was forced to choose between M. Rouvier and M. Delcassé. All the Ministers sided with the Prime Minister, according to information conveyed to Radolin. M. Delcassé resigned, and M. Rouvier took over his portfolio.

M. Delcassé's fall did not relieve the tension so much as Rouvier had hoped. There followed many weeks of difficult negotiations before the two countries could find a formula establishing the basis on which the conference should meet. Meanwhile England supported every French argument so strongly, and the English Press launched such a campaign against Germany, that the Moroccan question became almost more of an Anglo-German than a Franco-German conflict. Thanks in part to President Roosevelt's enjoying the confidence of M. Jusserand and Baron Speck von Sternburg at Washington, he was able tactfully and skilfully to secure first a French acceptance of the conference idea, and then the basis on which it should proceed.

When the conference finally met at Algeciras in January, 1906, there still remained the fundamental clash between the Anglo-French and the German positions. France and England pulled every possible political wire to secure decisions which would carry out the intention of the Anglo-French Agreement of 1904 and give France control. Germany pulled with equal energy, but less success, to secure equal rights for all nations and the establishment of a control in Morocco which should be genuinely international and not purely French. In sketching the development of the system of secret alliances, it is unnecessary to go into these Algeciras intrigues. Suffice it to say that Germany won in principle, but France won in practical results. The main importance of the First Morocco Crisis lies in the fact that from the outset it strengthened the ties between

France and England, and led to new secret understandings
between them.

Bülow's Morocco policy seemed to have resulted in a
brilliant diplomatic victory. The Kaiser, who had had no
great share personally in bringing it about nor even full
knowledge of its progress, accepted it with pleasure. He
signalized it, not very tactfully as the French felt, by raising
Bülow to the rank of Prince the day after Delcassé's fall,
and by bestowing a decoration upon Betzold, the secret go-
between in the unofficial negotiations between Rouvier and
Radolin. Bülow had asked that Betzold be given the Order
of the Red Eagle, "Third Class"; the Kaiser ordered it raised
to "Second Class," "because he saved us from war." [151]

Blissfully oblivious of the psychological effect such a
diplomatic humiliation as Delcassé's fall was bound to have
on a proud people like the French, to say nothing of the
impropriety of meddling in the internal politics of a Great
Power, the Kaiser seems sincerely to have regarded Delcassé's departure from the French Foreign Office as really
opening the way, not only for better relations with France,
but even for a new era in the system of alliances. The
French, he believed, had given evidence that they were no
longer minded to pursue the *revanche* policy which Delcassé had personified. "France," he wrote to Bülow from
Björkö, "refused to take up our challenge." And the Tsar
had agreed that it was "quite clear that the Alsace-Lorraine
question is closed once for all, thank God." [152] It opened
the way, he hoped, for the success of his Björkö effort for
a defensive alliance with Russia, in which France would
be included as soon as the Russo-Japanese War was ended.

[151] G.P., XX, 409.
[152] G.P., XIX, 460. A few weeks later the Kaiser appears to have
made a similar remark to Izvolski at Copenhagen; *Memoirs of Alexander
Izvolski*, p. 78; *cf.* also Izvolski's letter in the Paris *Temps*, Sept. 15,
1917, quoted in my *Amer. Hist. Rev.* article on the Björkö meeting, note
48.

He and President Roosevelt had already taken energetic
steps to bring about the peace negotiations which soon took
place at Portsmouth.[153] The Kaiser, therefore, was in a
great hurry to tell Roosevelt of the Björkö meeting, and
directed the following telegram to him:

> The Emperor and I have concluded an agreement to lend
> each other mutual help in case any European power should
> attack one of us, and France is to be cosignatory to it.
> In fact Germany enters the dual-alliance—originally con-
> cluded against it—as third party. It being the leading
> power of the triple-alliance, the latter and the dual-alliance
> —instead of glaring at each other for [no] purpose at all—
> join hands and the peace of Europe is guaranteed. This is
> the fruit of our understanding with France about Morocco,
> the fact, upon which you sent me so kind compliments. I
> am sure, that this grouping of powers is leading to a general
> "détente," will be of great use in enabling you to fulfil the
> great mission of peace, which Providence has entrusted to
> your hands for the good of the world.[154]

In reality, however, Bülow's Morocco policy of 1905 was
one of those victories which are worse than a defeat. In seeking to preserve the independence of the Sultan and the open
door in Morocco by his sphinx-like policy of studied silence,
which gave the impression of a menace, all the more alarming because of its mysteriousness, Bülow had been striving
for the right thing in the wrong way. In trying to frighten

[153] For the Kaiser's initiation and Roosevelt's carrying out of media-
tion between Russia and Japan, see G.P., XIX, 529-630; J. B. Bishop,
Theodore Roosevelt and His Time (N. Y., 1920), I, 374-424; H. C. Lodge,
Correspondence of Theodore Roosevelt and Henry Cabot Lodge (N. Y.,
1925), II, 130-192; and A. Hasenclever, "Theodore Roosevelt und die
Marokkokrisis von 1904-1906," in *Archiv f. Politik und Geschichte*, VI,
Heft 3, 184-245 (1928).

[154] G.P., XIX, 466. The telegram was not sent, because Bülow
objected that the arrangement with the Tsar was strictly secret, and
might leak out prematurely in Washington; but it is highly interesting,
as indicating the Kaiser's interpretation of the Björkö Treaty, and his
close relations with Roosevelt at this time.

Rouvier into ousting his Minister of Foreign Affairs, he had
been egregiously guilty of aiming at the wrong thing in the
wrong way. The incident made a painful impression on
the French. It contributed not a little to the ultimate revival of a new determination on the part of some of her
leading men that they would rather risk war than accept
another such humiliation. M. Poincaré, for instance, in his
public speeches and his writings never tires of referring to
the "brutality" and "odious violence" of Germany's bellicose diplomatic methods. More fatal still for Germany, it
helped rouse the British Government to enter into those
naval and military "conversations" which brought England
into the World War and thus made certain Germany's ultimate catastrophic defeat.

ANGLO-FRENCH MILITARY AND NAVAL "CONVERSATIONS," 1905-1912

As the Franco-Russian Entente of 1891 was followed by
a secret Military Convention, so the Anglo-French Entente
of 1904 was soon supplemented by momentous but very
secret naval and military arrangements, or, as Sir Edward
Grey euphemistically calls them, "conversations." These
lacked, at first, the rigid and binding character of the
Franco-Russian Alliance, but they gradually came to be,
in fact if not in form, a most vital link in the system of
secret alliances. In spite of the meticulous nicety with
which Sir Edward Grey was careful to state that "England's
hands were free," and that "it would be left for Parliament
to decide," he allowed the French to hope confidently that,
in case Germany caused a European war, England would
take the field on the side of the French. He permitted the
English and French Naval and Military Staffs to elaborate
technical arrangements for joint war action, which became
the basis of the strategic plans of both countries. These
came to involve mutual obligations which were virtually as

entangling as a formal alliance. It is always dangerous to allow the military authorities of two countries to develop inter-dependent strategic plans. They come to make arrangements which, by their very nature, necessarily involve obligations which are virtually binding upon the political authorities. Here is where Sir Edward Grey's great responsibility and mistake began. It is therefore important to note in some detail the origin, character, and consequences of these naval and military "conversations." They reach back in part to the time of his predecessor at the Foreign Office, Lord Lansdowne.[155]

In Art. IX of the Anglo-French Convention of 1904, England had promised merely *diplomatic* support to France in connection with Morocco. But after the Kaiser's visit

[155] The secrecy and subleties of diplomatic language in which these conversations were carried on has given rise to a wide literature of apology and accusation. From the English side the most authoritative *apologias* are: Grey, *Twenty-Five Years*, I, 48 ff., 59-118; II, 1 ff., 39 ff., 310 ff.; H. H. Asquith, *The Genesis of the War*, pp. 92-110, 142-216; Lord Haldane, *Before the War, passim;* J. A. Spender, *Life of Sir Henry Campbell-Bannerman*, II, 245-268; C. A. Repington, *The First World War*, ch. i; and W. S. Churchill, *The World Crisis*, I, 1-191. The most noteworthy criticisms of Grey's policy are: Lord Loreburn, *How the War Came, passim;* E. D. Morel, *Ten Years of Secret Diplomacy;* G. P. Gooch, *Camb. Hist. of Brit. Foreign Policy*, III, 338 ff., 438 ff; J. A. Farrer, *England under Edward VII, passim;* G. L. Dickinson, *The International Anarchy, 1904-1914*, pp. 127 ff., 375 ff.; and the indictment, drawn with a lawyer's skill, by J. S. Ewart, *The Roots and Causes of the Wars*, chs. v, xxii.

From the French side, besides the volumes of Pinon, Mévil, and Tardieu mentioned above in note 150, see R. Poincaré, *Les Origines de la Guerre*, p. 72 ff., *Au Service de la France*, I, 146-235, and the criticisms of his policy in the volumes of Fabre-Luce, Judet, Pevet, Victor Margueritte, Morhardt, and Demartial.

From the German side there is abundant material in G.P., XX-XXV, XXVIII-XXXI, *passim; cf.* also H. Herzfeld, "Der deutsche Flottenbau und die englische Politik", in *Archiv. für Politik und Geschichte*, IV, 117 ff. (1926); H. Lutz, *Lord Grey und der Weltkrieg* (Berlin, 1927, English trans., N. Y., 1928); and A. von Tirpitz, *Politische Dokumente: I, Der Aufbau der deutschen Weltmacht* (Stuttgart and Berlin, 1924), *passim.*

American accounts, severely critical of Grey and Poincaré, may be found in H. E. Barnes, *The Genesis of the World War*, ch. viii; and E. F. Henderson, *The Verdict of History: The Case of Sir Edward Grey* (privately printed, 1924).

to Tangier, the English Press and the English Government became obsessed with the idea that Germany was endeavoring to break up the Entente by bullying France. It jarred the sporting spirit of the British to see France menaced because of her new friendship with England, at a moment when France's ally was being so disastrously defeated in the Far East.[156] The English were also irritated by the rapidly growing German navy, as well as by the undercurrent of political and commercial rivalry which had existed for some years in Africa, Turkey, and elsewhere in the world. Level-headed observers in the German Embassy at London, like Count Metternich and Freiherr von Eckardstein, who were not at all blinded by Anglophobia, reported the anti-German feeling in the newspapers and in society as dangerously strong.[157] They found the British Press, in the Morocco question, "more French than the French." They warned the German Government that if war arose over Morocco, "there can be no doubt that England will stand unconditionally and actively on the French side, and go against Germany, even with enthusiasm." [158]

In accord with this public feeling, Lord Lansdowne and M. Paul Cambon entered into discussions for an exchange of notes, by which England should "take a step further," and offer the French something more substantial than mere diplomatic support. Mr. Gooch, on the basis of information supplied to him by the British Foreign Office, implies that the initiative came from France,[159] while M. Poincaré, on

---

[156] Looking back six months later, the German Ambassador in London summed up the situation: "The impression here is that 'Germany has been acting as a bully', and that because we felt ourselves to be the stronger, we wanted to force measures upon the French"; Metternich to Bülow, Dec. 20, 1905; G.P. XX, 689; cf. also, XXI, 46 f.

[157] G.P., XX, 601 ff., 618 ff., 627 ff., 647 ff., 669 ff., 685 ff.

[158] Metternich to Bülow, May 1, 1905; G.P., XX, 607, 618.

[159] "In the middle of May, the French Ambassador complained to Lord Lansdowne of the general attitude of the German Government, which was seeking in all parts of the world to sow discord between France and Great Britain. . . . Lord Lansdowne replied that the moral seemed

the basis of Paul Cambon's reports, implies that it came
from Lord Lansdowne.[160]   From these discussions the
French gathered that Lord Lansdowne was ready to offer
an agreement, veiled from Parliament and the public under
the form of an exchange of notes, to exchange views in
common—an agreement which might lead to a real alliance.[161]   As M. Cambon wrote, later on, in April and September, 1912:

> I know that the British Government does not have the
> right to bind itself without the authorization of Parliament;
> but there is no need of a duplicate agreement, of a treaty
> drawn up and signed [pas besoin d'un accord en partie
> double, de traité signé et paraphré]; we could content our-
> selves with an exchange of declarations. This is what we
> would have done in 1905 with Lord Lansdowne, if the resig-
> nation of M. Delcassé had not cut short our conversations.[162]

to be that each Government should continue to treat the other with the
most absolute mutual confidence, should keep it fully informed of
everything which came to their knowledge, and should, so far as possible, discuss in advance any contingencies by which they might in the
course of events find themselves confronted"; Gooch, *Camb. Hist. of
Brit. For. Policy*, III, 342.

160 "In the month of April, 1905, Lord Lansdowne had appeared
disposed to take one step further, and had proposed to M. Cambon a
general formula for an Entente. . . . "; Poincaré, *Les Origines de la
Guerre* (Paris, 1921), p. 79. That M. Poincaré is correct seems to be indicated by Mr. Spender, who says that on April 25, 1905, Sir Francis Bertie
informed M. Delcassé, on Lord Lansdowne's instructions, that the British Government would join the French in opposing Germany's acquisition
of a port on the coast of Morocco, and hoped to be given a full opportunity to concert with the French Government the measures which might
be taken to prevent it. The French were pleased. A month later, after
further conversations, on May 25, Lord Lansdowne suggested "that the
two Governments should treat one another with the utmost confidence
and discuss all likely contingencies"; J. A. Spender, *Life of Sir Henry
Campbell-Bannerman* II, 248.

161 M. Poincaré says in his recent memoirs (*Au Service de la France*,
I, 187, 221); "The Conservative Government had been able to contemplate
an alliance in 1905." "M. Paul Cambon had written me that at the
time [1905] an agreement of this kind [for an exchange of views in
common] would have been only a beginning on the part of Lord Lansdowne. . . . The forced resignation of M. Delcassé had perhaps made
us lose in 1905 an opportunity for a veritable alliance with England".

162 Paul Cambon to Poincaré, April 18, 1912, *Au Service de la France*,
I, 174.

Would it not be possible [said Cambon to Grey] to return, at least partially, to the proposals of Lord Lansdowne, to bind ourselves, for example, to exchange views in common [de se concerter] in case of menacing complications, and to settle that, in such a hypothesis, we should seek together the means most suited to protect us mutually from the peril of war? In a word, if, faced with this peril, we judge the best method to be an alliance and a military convention, we will employ it.[163]

Now it is interesting to observe how, on the one hand, Lord Lansdowne's proposal encouraged M. Delcassé's hopes and were given an extravagant interpretation by him; and how, on the other, its existence was reported to, or suspected by, the Germans, and then flatly denied by the British.

The Lansdowne-Cambon negotiations seem to have advanced to the point where the notes to be exchanged had already been drawn up and transmitted in written form to M. Delcassé for his final approval.[164] This was just at the moment when the Morocco Crisis was at its height, and he was fighting to persuade his colleagues to reject the German proposal for an international conference. He interpreted the Lansdowne proposal as an assurance of a British alliance and armed support. He used it as an argument to try to persuade President Loubet and the Cabinet to stand by him in refusing the German demands. But, as we have seen, the Rouvier Cabinet and President Loubet declined

163 Paul Cambon to Poincaré, Sept. 21, 1912; *Au Service de la France,* I, 218 f.

164 Both M. Delcassé and M. Chaumié, Minister of Justice at the time, appear to leave no doubt on this point. M. Delcassé, in a letter published in the *Figaro* of March 24, 1922, says: "Le 6 juin je n'avais que depuis quarante-huit heures l'offre anglais de concours". M. Chaumié, in notes on the decisive Cabinet meeting of June 6 made at the time and later published by his colleague in the Ministry of Justice, M. Bienvenu-Martin, in the *Temps* of March 19, 1922, says explicitly: "Ces ouvertures ne sont pas bornées à de simples pourparlers; des notes écrites ont déjà été échangées"

to take the risk of war with Germany, and M. Delcassé resigned.[165]

In October, 1905, the *Matin* published a series of revelations concerning the events of M. Delcassé's overthrow. They included the startling assertion, as coming from Delcassé, that he had been promised by the British Government that, in case of a German attack on France, the English fleet would be mobilized to seize the Kiel Canal and would land 100,000 men in Schleswig-Holstein. The revelations made a sensation at the time, and have remained ever since something of a puzzle to historians, inasmuch as the British have always denied that they made any offer of alliance or armed assistance to France. Mr. Gooch suggests that Delcassé's mistakenly wide interpretation of Britain's attitude may be explained by the probability that King Edward VII, during a visit to Paris, intimated to the French Minister that, in case of need, England would intervene on the French side.[166] One of the editors of *Die Grosse Politik* suggests that the offer came, not from Lord Lansdowne, but from Sir Francis Bertie.[167] This British Ambassador in Paris was certainly strongly pro-French, but it is hardly likely that he would have taken so serious a step without authorization, and there is no convincing evidence that he

[165] On June 7, Flotow, the German Chargé d'Affaires in Paris reported (G.P., XX, 623-5) information coming from the owner of the *Matin* that "a regular offer of an offensive and defensive alliance with an anti-German aim has been made here", but not yet accepted, partly on account of the effect on Russia, and partly because a majority of the Cabinet hoped still for a satisfactory settlement with Germany. On the same day, Flotow was able to sound M. Rouvier through their mutual confidential agent, and the French Premier had declared positively that an Anglo-French alliance was out of the question. It is quite possible that Delcassé, after his fall, may have given Paris newspaper editors a hint of the English proposals—both to justify his own policy, and with the idea that the news would be passed on to Germany and further irritate Anglo-German relations; cf. G.P., XX, 623 note, and 631 note.

[166] Gooch, *l.c.*, p. 343.   Eckardstein, III, 105.

[167] A. Mendelssohn Bartholdy, in *Wissen und Leben*, Feb. 1, 1925, cited by Dickinson, *The International Anarchy*, p. 129, note 1.

did so. Possibly the idea of landing 100,000 men in Holstein came from Sir John Fisher. It was the kind of strategy which he often urged and commended, and accords with his advice to King Edward in 1908: "We should 'Copenhagen' the German Fleet at Kiel à la Nelson." [168] Admiral Fisher's idea may have been handed on to the French by King Edward, or it may have come to them as a result of the direct naval "conversations" which the French and English Staffs were already carrying on in 1905.[169] Sir John Fisher was a very lovable old sea dog, with all the freshness of the salt spray which he loved so well, but he had an indiscreet habit of expressing himself promiscuously.[170] At a dinner in December, 1905, he told Colonel Repington that "he was prepared, on his own responsibility, to order our fleets to go wherever they might be required. He told me that he had seen on paper Lord Lansdowne's assurances to M. Cambon, and that they were quite distinct in their tenor. He had shown them to Sir Edward Grey, and declared that they were part of the engagements taken over from the last Government, and would hold good until denounced." [171] It is not at all unlikely that he conveyed to the French the

---

[168] Cf. Fisher, *Memories and Records,* I, 22, 47 ff., 188, 207, 211, 233; II, 176, 208 ff., 218 f., 225 ff.

[169] Grey, I, 74; II, 2. Sir Alfred Beit and the Kaiser, in an interesting conversation soon after the *Matin* revelations, assumed that the idea came from Fisher; G.P., XX, 694. Fisher, *Memories,* p. 49, in connection with this conversation, says: "The German Emperor did say to Beit that I was dangerous, and that he knew of my ideas as regards the Baltic being Germany's vulnerable spot, and he had heard of my idea for 'Copenhagening' the German Fleet. But this last I much doubt. He only said it because he knew it was what we ought to have done."

[170] For example, upon the news of Tirpitz's dismissal, he addressed him a letter which got into a London newspaper: "Dear old Tirps: Cheer up, old chap! . . . Yours, till Hell freezes, Fisher"; *Memories,* p. 45. To a Russian Grand Duchess, who had written him of a picnic, pleasant except for the gnats biting her ankles, he telegraphed: "I wish to God I had been one of the gnats"; *ibid.,* p. 231. Winston Churchill (*The World Crisis,* pp. 72-79) paints a brilliant picture of Fisher and of his indiscretion in the "Bacon letters affair."

[171] Repington, *First World War,* p. 4.

prospect of British naval support and a British diversion upon the German rear in Holstein or Pomerania.

At any rate, it seems clear that M. Delcassé greatly exaggerated the nature of Lord Lansdowne's offer, whatever assurances he may have received from other high English sources. Perhaps, the wish being father to the thought, he really believed that Lord Lansdowne was holding out the offer of a British alliance. Perhaps he was deliberately overstating its character, in order to persuade his hesitating colleagues to stand firm against Germany. In either case, here was a dangerous example of the way Frenchmen of his character would misinterpret, either unconsciously or deliberately, proposals contemplating something more than mere diplomatic support. It should have been a warning to Sir Edward Grey of the danger of permitting the naval and military "conversations," and of the later exchange of notes with M. Cambon in 1912—the danger of arousing expectations and involving obligations at Paris that England would come in on the side of France in case of a European war.

It is equally interesting to note the German suspicions of an Anglo-French alliance,[172] and the flat denials on the part of the British. On June 16, 1905, Lord Lansdowne told the German Ambassador that "the news that England had offered France an offensive and defensive alliance was completely fictitious [*vollkommen erfunden*]. Since Lord Lansdowne rejected the alliance rumor with the greatest decisiveness and without equivocation, as made out of air," the Ambassador said he would regard the subject as settled. He did not think that Lord Lansdowne, after such a downright declaration, was capable of trying to deceive.[173]

But a few days later, Count Metternich received further

[172] G.P., XX, 494, 615 f., 623 ff., 634 f., 638 ff., 662 ff., and Flotow's report of June 7 (see above, note 165).

[173] Metternich to Bülow, June 16, 1905; G.P., XX, 630. *Cf.* also Gooch, *l.c.*, p. 342 f.

information, apparently coming through confidential sources from M. Rouvier himself, that England had promised naval aid to France. He therefore asked Lord Lansdowne about it, tactfully saying that he did so unofficially, without instructions from Berlin:

> Lord Lansdowne replied that I knew that diplomatic support was assured to the French Government within the corners of the Anglo-French Agreement. This has the natural result that the questions which the Agreement touched would be discussed by the two Governments in friendly fashion, and the most suitable ways and means would be considered to maintain unimpaired the various points of the Agreement. The question of an alliance with France, however, had never been discussed in the English Cabinet, nor had an English alliance ever been offered to the French Government either in recent times or earlier. However, he would not conceal from me that in the eventuality, which he however regarded as wholly out of the question, that Germany should light-heartedly let loose a war against France, one could not foresee how far public opinion in England would drive the Government to the support of France.[174]

Similarly, in October, 1905, Lord Lansdowne's Under Secretary, Sir Thomas Sanderson, felt obliged by the *Matin* revelations to reiterate the denial:

> The English Government has never held out to the French Government the prospect of military aid. A possible rupture between France and Germany has never been even discussed by the Government, and the promise of landing 100,000 men in Schleswig-Holstein belongs to the realm of myth. . . . [Sanderson said] Perhaps French imagination played some part in this. One could well imagine Delcassé had said to his colleagues that he was convinced that England would stand beside France in case of a Franco-German war. This subjective conception, supposing Delcassé had it, was however very different from an English promise or

[174] Metternich to Bülow, June 28, 1905; G.P., XX, 636.

an English offer of assistance. These had never been made, and, as he had said, the eventuality of a war between Germany and France had never even been discussed on the English side.[175]

In view of the seriousness with which the British Government viewed the Morocco Crisis in the early summer of 1905, it is difficult to believe this last statement of Sanderson that "the eventuality of a war between Germany and France had never even been discussed on the English side." Probably these sweeping denials were as correct in letter, and as misleading in spirit, as the similar denials made in Parliament later by Mr. Asquith and Sir Edward Grey after the Grey-Cambon exchange of notes in 1912.

On December 11, 1905, Sir Henry Campbell-Bannerman formed a Cabinet, in which Sir Edward Grey replaced Lord Lansdowne at the Foreign Office.[176] Viscount Grey tells us in his engaging and charmingly written retrospect,[177] no doubt with perfect sincerity, that he accepted the post with reluctance. It brought no joy to him or to his wife, for it meant exile from his home in the country, from his fishing, from his walks in the woods. Perhaps his reluctance may unconsciously have been in part owing to his lack of experience, his inability to speak any foreign language, and also to a sense of inadequacy for the exacting work of the Foreign Office. Perhaps also, in composing his memoirs, his realization of the failure of his long and sincere efforts to preserve the peace of Europe may have led him unconsciously in later years to exaggerate the reluctance with which he took office in 1905. But, as he tells us, he could not justify to his constituents or to his friends a refusal to take up the work. He seemed as well qualified as any one in the Liberal Party.

[175] Metternich to Bülow, Oct. 9, 1905; G.P., XX, 663.
[176] Spender, *Life of Sir Henry Campbell-Bannerman*, II, 188 ff. 245 ff.
[177] *Twenty-Five Years*, I. 59-66.

One of the first tasks which claimed his attention was to quiet the fears of the French. The Algeciras Conference was about to meet. Germany was thought to be pursuing a threatening policy, and the French were nervous to know whether the new Liberal Government would sustain the assurances of Lord Lansdowne, or go even further. On January 10 and 15, 1906, Cambon asked Grey the pressing question whether the British Government "would be prepared to render France armed assistance," in case of German aggression, and whether it would sanction the continuation of the naval and military conversations. Grey replied that he could not at the moment make any promises, as the Ministers were all dispersed, taking part in the elections. He could only state as his personal opinion, adopting the attitude of Lord Lansdowne, that if France were to be attacked by Germany in consequence of a question arising out of the Morocco Agreement, public opinion in England would be strongly moved in favor of France. As to the naval and military conversations which had been going on, the former had been direct between the French and English Naval Staffs. They were already on a satisfactory basis, having been conducted on the English side by Sir John Fisher. But the plans for military coöperation were less satisfactory, being at the moment in the hands of an unofficial intermediary. Between January 10 and 15, however, Sir Edward Grey had managed to see the Secretary for War, Mr. Haldane, at an election meeting in Northumberland. Mr. Haldane had authorized Grey to say that these military communications might now proceed directly and officially between General Grierson and the French Military Attaché, but it must be understood that these communications did not commit either Government.[178]

The story of the new turn now given to the military

[178] Grey to Bertie, British Ambassador in Paris, Jan. 10, 15, 1906; Grey, I. 70-74.

conversations has been interestingly told by the intermediary in question, Colonel Repington, the military correspondent of the London *Times*.[179] Although Anglo-German tension was relaxed at the moment and there seemed to be a prospect of better relations between the two countries,[180] Colonel Repington wrote an alarm article in the *Times* of December 27, which gave a warning of what he supposed to be Germany's threatening intentions. Next day, in response to it, he received a visit from Major Huguet, the French Military Attaché, dined with him, and was told that the French Embassy people were greatly worried about the general situation. Sir Edward Grey, who had just taken over the Foreign Office, had not renewed the assurances given by Lord Lansdowne, and M. Cambon was at the moment absent in France. Major Huguet said he knew the British navy was ready, and he trusted it, but he did not know what it would do to coöperate in case of trouble. The French Army also was ready, but he feared the Germans might attack suddenly, probably through Belgium. He therefore wanted the British to stiffen the Belgians, if war came. Colonel Repington at once reported this by letter to Sir Edward Grey. A couple of days later he discussed the whole situation at dinner with Sir John Fisher, who said he had perfect confidence in the navy and was prepared to order it to go wherever it might be required. On New Year's Day Repington received the reply from Grey: "I am interested to hear of your conversation with the French Military Attaché. I can only say that I have not receded from anything Lord Lansdowne said to the French, and have no hesitation in affirming it." [181] Colonel Repington then dined with General Grierson, Head of the Operations Bureau, who told him that, on the assumption

179 Repington, *The First World War*, ch. i.
180 Metternich to Bülow, Dec., 4, 20, 1905; G.P., XX, 681, 685.
181 Repington, p. 4.

that Germany violated Belgium, England could put two divisions into Namur by the thirteenth day of mobilization, and the Field Army, such as it then was, into Antwerp by the thirty-second day. After getting the approval of various officials, including Sir George Clark, Secretary of the Imperial Defense Committee, Colonel Repington saw Major Huguet again, and gave him a short list of questions to be submitted to the French General Staff. Major Huguet hurried to France and soon brought back a set of interesting and satisfactory answers which he was able to show to Colonel Repington on January 12.[182] With the authorization of Haldane and Grey these then became the basis for official discussions direct between the French and British military authorities through Major Huguet and General Grierson.

Sir Edward Grey returned to London on January 26 and found M. Cambon anxiously waiting for a more definite statement as to whether France could count upon British assistance. After talking further with Haldane and the Prime Minister, but without accepting the latter's suggestion that the statement to be made to Cambon should be approved in a meeting of the whole Cabinet, Grey gave Cambon his momentous answer on January 31. The long summary of it which he sent to Bertie in Paris shows clearly enough its double character. With one hand he held out what he withdrew with the other. He encouraged the French to expect aid, if needed; but he made no promises of armed support and reserved liberty of action. He told M. Cambon encouragingly that since their last interviews on January 10 and 15,

A good deal of progress has been made. Our military and naval authorities had been in communication with the French, and I assumed that all preparations were ready, so

[182] Repington's questions and the French replies, printed *ibid.*, pp. 6-10.

that, if a crisis arose, no time would have been lost for want of a formal engagement. . . . I had taken an opportunity of expressing to Count Metternich my personal opinion, which I understood Lord Lansdowne had also expressed to him [Cambon] as a personal opinion, that, in the event of an attack upon France by Germany arising out of our Morocco Agreement, public feeling in England would be so strong that no British Government could remain neutral.[183]

Sir Edward Grey also pointed out to M. Cambon the possible disadvantages to France of making a more formal statement of Anglo-French relations: at present, under the Agreement of 1904, France had an absolutely free hand in Morocco, with the promise of English diplomatic support; but, if England extended her promise beyond this, and made a formal alliance which might involve her in war, he was sure the British Cabinet would say that England must from time to time be consulted with regard to French policy in Morocco, and, if need be, be free to ask for alterations in French policy to avoid war. Was not the present situation so satisfactory that it was better not to alter it by a more formal engagement?

M. Cambon was not convinced by this. He pointed out that if the Conference broke up, and Germany placed herself behind the Sultan, "war might arise so suddenly that the need for action would be a question not of days, but of minutes, and that, if it was necessary for the British Government to consult, and to wait for manifestations of English public opinion, it might be too late to be of use." [184]

To M. Cambon's request for "some form of assurance which might be given in conversation," Grey replied that he could give no such formal assurance,

[183] Grey to Bertie, Jan. 31, 1906; Grey, I, 76. For Grey's conversation with Metternich, here referred to, see Grey, I, 80, and G.P., XXI, 45-51; and for Lansdowne's statement to Metternich, which Grey now adopted as his own, see above at note 174.

[184] Grey to Bertie, Jan. 31, 1906; Grey. I, 77.

without submitting it to the Cabinet and getting their authority, and that were I to submit the question to the Cabinet I was not sure ·that they would say that this was too
serious a matter to be dealt with by a verbal engagement
but must be put in writing. As far as their good disposition
towards France was concerned, I should have no hesitation
in submitting such a question to the present Cabinet. Some
of those in the Cabinet who were most attached to peace
were those also who were the best friends of France; but,
though I had no doubt about the good disposition of the
Cabinet, I did think there would be difficulties in putting
such an undertaking in writing. It could not be given unconditionally, and it would be difficult to describe the conditions. It amounted, in fact, to this; that, if any change
was made, it must be to change the "Entente" into a defensive alliance. That was a great and formal change, and I
again submitted to M. Cambon as to whether the force of
circumstances bringing England and France together was
not stronger than any assurance in words which could be
given at this moment. I said that it might be that the pressure of circumstances—the activity of Germany, for instance
—might eventually transform the "Entente" into a defensive
alliance between ourselves and France, but I did not think
that the pressure of circumstances was so great as to dem-
onstrate the necessity of such a change yet. I also told him
that, should such a defensive alliance be formed, it was too
serious a matter to be kept secret from Parliament. The
Government could conclude it without the assent of Parliament, but it would have to be published afterwards. No
British Government could commit the country to such a
serious thing and keep the engagement secret.[185]

When M. Cambon, in summing up, dwelt upon Grey's
expression of personal opinion that "in the event of an
attack by Germany upon France, no British Government
could remain neutral," Grey was careful to point out that
"a personal opinion was not a thing upon which, in so seri-

[185] Grey to Bertie, Jan. 31, 1906; Grey, I, 77-78.

ous a matter, a policy could be founded," and added: "Much would depend as to the manner in which the war broke out between Germany and France. I did not think people in England would be prepared to fight to put France in possession of Morocco. They would say that France should wait for opportunities and be content to take time, and that it was unreasonable to hurry matters to the point of war. But if, on the other hand, it appeared that the war was forced upon France by Germany to break up the Anglo-French 'Entente,' public opinion would undoubtedly be very strong on the side of France. . . . If the French Government desired it, it would be possible at any time to reopen the conversation. Events might change, but, as things were at present, I did not think it necessary to press the question of a defensive alliance." [186]

This long and critical interview, which we have tried to summarize without bias or essential omissions, is significant for several reasons. In the first place, it reveals Sir Edward Grey's very strong sympathy with France, his evident desire to go as far as possible in giving her diplomatic support, but at the same time his unwillingness to make any formal engagement, written or verbal, which might bind England to go to war. Such an engagement must be sanctioned by Parliament, but it was very unlikely that Parliament would assent. Moreover, it would greatly increase the irritation between England and Germany. He gave France as much encouragement as he could, without going to the point where he thought he ought to inform the Cabinet and Parliament. He was satisfied in his own mind that he had avoided changing the Entente into a formal alliance. As he wrote to his wife next day, in a letter which she was never to read on account of the carriage accident which caused her sudden and tragic death: "I had tremendously difficult talk and work yesterday, and

[186] Grey to Bertie, Jan. 31, 1906; Grey, I, 78-79.

very important. I do not know that I did well, but I did honestly." [187]

In the second place, Sir Edward approved and confirmed the official military and naval conversations between the British and French Staffs. He assumed, as he told M. Cambon, "that all preparations are ready." As will be indicated further on, Haldane at once set very actively to work to reorganize the British Army and prepare for its coöperation with the French. These preparations continued right down to the outbreak of war in 1914, and inevitably came to involve England in increasingly binding obligations of honor to support France in case of a European war arising out of any question whatsoever—not merely one arising out of the Morocco question—provided that France did not appear to be the active aggressor. Probably Sir Edward Grey did not at the time see the full implications and danger of these "conversations." But his Prime Minister saw them. For we know that Sir Henry Campbell-Bannerman wrote to Lord Ripon on February 2, a couple of days after Grey's talk with Cambon: "Cambon appears satisfied. But I do not like the stress laid upon joint preparations. It comes very close to an honorable undertaking, and it will be known on both sides of the Rhine. But let us hope for the best." [188] He showed a true prophetic instinct, but it was submerged and lost to sight under the secret activities of the military authorities and the Foreign Secretary's strange silence or ignorance in regard to them for the next five years. It was not until 1912 that circumstances caused the military and naval "conversations" to be revealed to the whole Cabinet, and not until Grey's speech

[187] Grey, I, 79.

[188] Spender, *Life of Sir Henry Campbell-Bannerman*, II, 257. In spite of his just misgivings, the Prime Minister appears, however, to have acquiesced in the military conversations, provided they "were not talked about" and "should not commit either Government", if we are to believe the statements of Haldane (*Before the War*, p. 162), and Repington. (p. 13).

on August 3, 1914, that Parliament and the British public had any inkling of them.

In the third place, neither Sir Edward Grey's statement to M. Cambon, nor his approval of the naval and military conversations, was made with the knowledge and sanction of the Cabinet. The Prime Minister had written him on January 21: "Would you like the answer to the French to be confirmed by a Cabinet before it is given?" He suggested the 30th, the 31st, or the 1st of February. Viscount Grey in his memoirs says he has no recollection or record of any answer to this question.[189] His only explanations of why no Cabinet sanction was given are rather feeble: the Ministers were dispersed seeing to the elections, and the earliest date suggested by the Prime Minister was January 30, and "the French had been kept long enough waiting for a reply." [190] But, as his interview with Cambon did not take place until the 31st, this is hardly a satisfactory explanation. Moreover, a Cabinet meeting was actually held on this very day.[191] It would have therefore been perfectly easy for him to have pursued the proper course of consulting the Cabinet before talking with Cambon, or at least of informing his colleagues immediately afterwards of what he had said to the French and of the naval and military conversations which were already going on. But he did not do so. Why? One can only conjecture as to this strange aspect of his psychology. Possibly he felt that his talks with Campbell-Bannerman and Haldane after reaching London gave sufficient sanction. Possibly he considered that he was merely continuing Lord Lansdowne's policy, and that a continuation of policy in a matter like foreign affairs, which is not ordinarily supposed to be radically altered by change in parties, did not need to be brought before a new Cabinet. Perhaps he feared that the more

[189] Grey, I, 84.
[190] Grey. I. 84.   [191] Loreburn. *How the War Came,* p. 80 f.

cautious and pacifically inclined members of the Cabinet, like Mr. Morley and Lord Loreburn, and even the Prime Minister himself, would not be willing to go as far as he himself did in encouraging the French and in making joint military preparations. Throughout his memoirs and in his dealings with the Germans, as revealed in the new German documents, one finds that Sir Edward Grey had a very strong undercurrent of sympathy with the French and a correspondingly strong suspicion of Germany's intentions. Probably therefore he preferred to be free to give Cambon his personal friendly views, in a way that he might not have been able to do, if a Cabinet had discussed the subject and adopted a formal statement of policy which would have tied his hands.

At any rate he concealed the matter from the majority of his colleagues in a way which seems hardly to accord with the seeming honesty and frankness of his memoirs. He entered upon that slippery path of thinking that he could encourage the French with joint military preparations, and yet keep his "hands free"—a fatal double policy which he pursued for eight years. After the War, with more experience and with a realization of the seriousness of the criticisms of men like Lord Loreburn, he admits in his memoirs, rather sadly and regretfully, "I think there should have been a Cabinet." [192]   In this he is right.

Lord Haldane has left an account of these secret preparations for military coöperation with France. He has told how, in the midst of the General Election of January, 1906, he "at once went to London, summoned the heads of the British General Staff, and saw the French Military Attaché, Colonel Huguet, a man of sense and ability. I became aware at once that there was a new army problem. It was,

---

[192] Grey, I, 84, and again, p. 96: "I have always regretted that the military conversations were not brought before the Cabinet at once: this would have avoided unnecessary suspicion."

how to mobilize and concentrate at a place of assembly to be opposite the Belgian frontier, a force calculated as adequate (with the assistance of Russian pressure in the East) to make up for the inadequacy of the French armies for their great task of defending the entire French frontier from Dunkirk down to Belfort, or even farther south, if Italy should join the Triple Alliance in an attack." [193] He began therefore at once to organize a British expeditionary force which should coöperate with the French to solve this problem. Impressed with the importance of high morale and quality in modern warfare, he believed that even a small force, if sufficiently long and closely trained, added to French and Russian troops, would be able to defeat any German attempt to invade and dismember France. A close investigation showed that it was not possible under the existing conditions to put in the field more than about 80,000 men, and these only after an interval of over two months.[194] The French naturally pointed out that so slow-moving a machine would be of little use to them; they might be destroyed before it arrived. In their interests, therefore, Haldane had to make "a complete revolution in the organization of the British Army." He accomplished this by the end of 1910. He made it possible "rapidly to mobilize, not only 100,000, but 160,000 men; to transport them, with the aid of the navy, to a place of concentration which had been settled between the Staffs of France and Britain; and to have them at their appointed place within twelve days." [195]

In view of Lord Haldane's own statements of how he saw Colonel Huguet, personally authorized the direct negotiations between the French and British Staffs represented by Huguet and Grierson, and at once reorganized the British

193 Haldane, *Before the War*, p. 30; see also pp. 28-35 and 156-182.
194 Haldane, p. 32. If Haldane is correct, General Grierson's assurances to Repington, referred to above at note 182, appear to have been unduly optimistic.   195 Haldane, p. 33.

Army for coöperation with the French, a sinister light is
thrown on the obliquity of the British secret preparations
and the denials of their existence, by a statement which
Lord Haldane himself made to the German Ambassador in
London. It was occasioned by a French deputy who had
inconsiderately interpellated M. Clemenceau as to the
existence of an Anglo-French military convention. M.
Clemenceau had replied evasively, seeming to admit a naval,
but not a military, convention. This had naturally roused
German fears and suspicions, especially in view of Sir John
Fisher's sweeping reorganization of the British Navy, his
beginning of the building of dreadnoughts,[196] and the
threatening speech of one of the civil Lords of the
Admiralty, Mr. Arthur Lee, that the British Fleet would
know how to strike the first blow before the other party had
read the news in the papers. When questioned by Count
Metternich in regard to Clemenceau's declaration, Lord
Haldane made a sweeping denial which it is difficult to
reconcile with the facts. Taken in conjunction with the
secret Anglo-French "conversations" and preparations which
had been going on for more than a year, it made an impression in Berlin which may be seen from the Kaiser's marginal
notes. According to Count Metternich's report:

> Mr. Haldane replied most definitely that a military con-
> vention between France and England did not exist, and had
> not existed; and also that no preparations had been made
> for the conclusion of one. Whether non-committal con-
> versations between English and French military persons had
> taken place or not, he did not know [Kaiser: "Impudence!
> He, the Minister of a Parliamentary country, not supposed
> to know that! He lies!"]. At any rate, no English officer
> has been authorized by the English Government [Kaiser:
> "Indeed! He did it himself!"] to prepare military arrange-
> ments with a French military person for the eventuality of

196 Fisher, *Memories and Records,* II, 65 ff., 128-153.

war. It was possible that a General Staff Officer of one country might have expressed himself to the General Staff Officer of another country as to war-like eventualities. He, the Minister of War, however, knew nothing of this [Kaiser: "Magnificent lies!"].[197]

In the course of these Anglo-French joint military preparations, British and French Staff Officers thoroughly reconnoitered the ground upon which their armies were to fight in Belgium and in France. Sir Henry Wilson, Director of Military Operations, spent his holidays going all over it on his bicycle. The whole wall of his London office was covered by a gigantic map of Belgium, indicating the practicable roads which armies might follow. "He was deeply in the secrets of the French General Staff. For years he had been laboring with one object, that, if war came, we should act immediately on the side of France. He was sure that war would come sooner or later." [198]

Not only the French, but the Russians also, soon came to count upon Haldane's Expeditionary Force as a certain and essential part of their strategic plans in case of a war against Germany. This is significantly indicated, at least as early as 1911, in the secret report, since published by the Bolshevists, of the annual conference between the heads of the French and Russian Staffs. In August, 1911, at Krasnoe Selo, General Dubail was able to assure his Russian colleagues, as a matter of course, "that the French army would concentrate as quickly as the German army, and that from the twelfth day it would be in a position to take the offensive against Germany, *with the aid of the English army on its left wing*," that is, on the Belgian frontier.[199]

[197] Metternich to Bülow, Jan. 31, 1907; G.P., XXI, 469. On German fears and suspicions of British naval and military intentions, 1904 to 1907, see G.P., XIX, 351-380, "The First German-English War Scare"; XX, 599-698; XXI, 421-521; and Tirpitz, *Politische Dokumente: Der Aufbau der deutschen Weltmacht*, 14 ff.   [198] Churchill, *The World Crisis*, p. 53.

[199] Protocol of the seventh annual Franco-Russian Military Conference, Aug., 31, 1911; L.N., II, 421; M.F.R., p. 698. As early as the annual

THE ANGLO-RUSSIAN ENTENTE OF 1907

An Anglo-Russian Entente, settling the long-standing sources of friction between the two countries in the Middle East, was an obvious complement to the Anglo-French Entente. It appears to have been discussed between King Edward VII and M. Izvolski during the Russo-Japanese War, and to have been warmly received by him and some of the Russian Liberals, though not by the Tsar and the Russian reactionaries and militarists.[200]

Izvolski, though occupying at the time the comparatively unimportant diplomatic post at Copenhagen, was already ambitiously counting upon promotion to a more important position, either as ambassador at one of the great capitals of Europe, or as Russian Minister of Foreign Affairs. He was naturally flattered to be made the recipient by King Edward of a proposal of such far-reaching possibilities. Henceforth he made it one of the cardinal aims of his policy. He saw that Russia was greatly weakened by her war with Japan (which he declares he had tried to avert), and that the Franco-Russian Alliance had conse-

conference of 1908, the Anglo-French connection had become so close that the French officers persuaded the Russians to agree to mobilize all their forces even in case of a German mobilization *against England*. A. Zaiontchkovski, *Les Alliés contre la Russie* (Paris, 1926), pp. 20-21.

[200] *The Memoirs of Alexander Iswolsky* (London, 1920), pp. 20, 35, 81 ff.; Ph. Crozier, "L'Autriche et l'Avant-guerre", in *Revue de France*, April 1, 1921, pp. 275-277. According to Witte (Georges Louis, *Carnets*, Paris, 1926, II, 63 f.; Dillon, *Eclipse of Russia*, pp. 350-353; Witte, *Memoirs*, pp. 432-434), Edward VII sent to him, Witte, on his way back from Portsmouth, N. H., in Sept., 1905, the draft of an Anglo-Russian accord. This may be the basis for "Nicky's" letter to "Willy" of Nov. 10/23, 1905 (G.P., XIX, 523): "England is trying hard to get us round for an understanding about Asiatic frontier questions and this directly after the renewed Anglo-Japanese alliance! I have not the slightest wish to open negotiations with her, and so it will drop of itself". Sidney Lee, *King Edward VII*, II, 308 f., mentions only an invitation from Edward VII to Witte to visit England, but says nothing of the draft of an Anglo-Russian accord. For King Edward's urging upon Izvolski an Anglo-Russian Entente in a conversation at Copenhagen in April, 1904, see *ibid.*, II, 284 ff.

quently lost weight in the balance as compared with the Triple Alliance. Both Russia and the Franco-Russian combination needed the strengthening which would come from closer relations with the greatest sea-power in the world.

Izvolski believed that Russia was subject to two serious dangers. One was a possible renewal of trouble with Japan, who had made humiliating demands at Portsmouth and was suspected of preparing for a new struggle in the Far East.[201] Russia needed long years of peace to recover from the effects of the war, and the only method to assure it was to make certain that the Japanese would remain quiet. The best way to accomplish this was to come to an understanding with them by a virtual partition of interests in Manchuria by a secret treaty, though publicly both were pledged to an observance of the "open door." The natural bridge between Russia and Japan was England, Japan's ally since 1902. A *rapprochement* with England would facilitate a sincere reconciliation with Japan, fortify Russia's position as an ally of France, and give a new and more solid basis to the somewhat weakened Franco-Russian Alliance.

The other danger for Russia was that trouble might develop with England as a result of the long-standing conflict of interests in the Near and Middle East. Men still remembered the Crimean War, the strained situation when the British Fleet threatened the Dardanelles in 1878, and the Pendjeh incident which nearly led to war between the two countries in 1885. More recently the Dogger Bank Affair and other incidents of the Russo-Japanese War had inflamed popular feeling in both countries. But a conflict with England would throw Russia into the arms of Germany, and this would endanger the Franco-Russian Alliance which was the foundation rock of Russian policy, in spite of the disappointments which both allies had suffered in connection with it. On the other hand, if Russia could

[201] G.P., XXV, 25, 28, 53 ff., 233 f.

wipe the slate clean of her rivalries and quarrels with Great Britain, this would greatly strengthen her own international position. It would allow her to return to an active forward policy in the Balkans after being checkmated in the Far East. It would also be welcomed by France, who would be glad to see her ally and her new friend on better terms with one another. An Anglo-Russian Entente and a reconciliation with Japan might tend toward the formation of a quadruple combination which would quite outmatch the Triple Alliance and could hold in check Austrian ambitions in the Balkans and German ambitions in Turkey. This therefore was the program which Izvolski determined to carry out upon taking up his new position of Russian Minister of Foreign Affairs in May, 1906.

King Edward and Sir Edward Grey were also favorable to an understanding with Russia. The first Morocco crisis and the growing German navy had filled them with suspicions of Germany's intentions and with the desire to remove the danger of Russian enmity in case of possible trouble with Germany. Sir Charles Hardinge was another ardent advocate of a *rapprochement* with Russia. He had been British Ambassador at St. Petersburg since 1904, but was recalled in the fall of 1905 to become Permanent Under Secretary in place of Sir Thomas Sanderson. He took pains to explain in St. Petersburg and London that his recall would afford him an opportunity to work with further success for close Anglo-Russian relations.[202] Henceforth he was to exert a strong pro-Russian influence on Sir Edward Grey in the direction of creating the group of Powers which came to be known as the Triple Entente. In this he was actively seconded by Sir Arthur Nicolson who went to St. Petersburg in his place.[203]

Within a few months after Izvolski took over the Foreign Office from Count Lamsdorf, the Anglo-Russian nego-

[202] G.P., XXV, 3, 10.   [203] Grey. I, 155 ff.

tiations were well under way. In passing through Berlin on October 29, 1906, Izvolski admitted that, owing to fears of Japan's aggressive intentions, he was compelled to seek an understanding with England concerning Tibet, Afghanistan, and Persia.[204] Grey and Nicolson worked out draft proposals.[205] These provided for the partition of Persia into spheres of influence. This idea at first met with no approval in St. Petersburg. Russian imperialists demanded that Persia come entirely under Russian influence, and that Russia must build a trans-Persian railway and press on to the Persian Gulf. But Izvolski believed such an aggressive policy was impossible of realization and likely to lead to a conflict with England. So the English proposal for a partition of Persia into English and Russian spheres of influence was adopted.[206] In March, 1907, the visit of a Russian fleet to Portsmouth foreshadowed the coming Anglo-Russian agreement. Upon King Edward's invitation, a deputation of Russian officers and sailors visited London, were entertained as guests at the Admiralty, and given a special show in their honor at the Hippodrome. After a banquet in the evening, there was a gala performance for them at the Alhambra, attended by the First Lord of the Admiralty, Sir John Fisher, and Sir Edward Grey. "It has certainly never happened before," commented the German Ambassador, "that an English Minister of Foreign Affairs has gone to a variety theatre to greet foreign guests." [207]

But, as in the case of the Franco-Russian negotiations two decades earlier, the divergence in political ideals on the Seine and the Neva had delayed an understanding, so now the divergence between English liberalism and Russian autocracy hampered the conclusion of a settlement. The

---

[204] G.P., XX, 39 ff.; XXV, 233 f.

[205] Grey to Nicolson, Nov. 6, 1906; Grey, I, 156.

[206] Russian Ministerial Council of Feb. 1/14, 1907; Siebert-Schreiner, p. 474 ff.

[207] Metternich to Tschirschky, Mar. 28, 1907; G.P., XXV, 32 note.

Russian reactionaries and militarists, and also the Tsar, were at first opposed to a *rapprochement* with England. Izvolski later told Sir Edward Grey that he eventually had great difficulty in getting it accepted.[208] In England likewise the criticism in the Liberal Press of Russian pogroms, the oppressive character of Tsarist absolutism, the suspension of the Duma, and the misunderstanding and friction caused by Sir Henry Campbell-Bannerman's phrase, "La Duma est morte; vive la Duma!", did not facilitate the work of Grey, Hardinge and Nicolson.[209] Nevertheless, the gulf was eventually bridged, owing apparently more to the eagerness and pressure of the British, rather than the Russian, Foreign Office.[210]

Another cause of delay was the English desire that Russia should come to a satisfactory reconciliation with Japan. Grey held it important that the Russo-Japanese and Anglo-Russian negotiations should proceed simultaneously and be concluded practically *pari passu*.[211] As it happened, the Russian agreement with Japan was finally signed on July 30, 1907, a month before that with England. It included a mutual declaration to respect the *status quo* and the rights of one another in the Far East, and a recognition of the independence and territorial integrity of China and the principle of the "open door." [212] These laudable clauses were made known to Germany, but there were evidently secret supplementary clauses, because the secret Russo-Japanese Treaty of 1910 speaks of the demarcation of

208 Grey, I, 177. *Cf.* also Grey to Nicolson, Nov. 6, 1906 (Grey, I, 156): "Of course, I understand M. Izvolski's difficulty with the military party"; and G.P., XXV, 40 ff.

209 Grey, I, 149 ff.; G.P., XXV, 21 ff.

210 This, at any rate was the impression of German observers; *cf* G.P., XXV, 5, 21, 27, 54, 67.

211 Grey to Nicolson, April 1, 1907; Grey, I, 158.

212 See the text in A. M. Pooley, *The Secret Memoirs of Count Tadasu Hayashi* (London, 1915), pp. 224-238, 327-328. *Cf.* also G.P., XXII, 67; and XXV, 53-64.

spheres of interest in Manchuria "as defined in the supplementary article to the Secret Treaty of 1907." [213]   And in reality an astonished and disillusioned world, which had counted upon Russo-Japanese rivalry to see to it that the "open door" was preserved in Manchuria, soon discovered that the two empires which had so recently engaged in deadly struggle, had found it convenient to pool their interests in exploiting Manchuria to the practical exclusion of third parties.   In various underhand ways, and in virtual defiance of their public declarations in favor of the principle of equal commercial opportunities for all, they practically partitioned Manchuria between themselves.[214]   The Russo-Japanese Treaty of July 30, 1907 had been preceded by an agreement [215] settling commercial and fishery questions arising out of the Treaty of Portsmouth between the two countries, and also by a treaty between Japan and France, providing for their mutual interests in the Far East.[216] These treaties of Japan with Russia and France, together with her alliance with England, renewed in 1905, established a basis for friendly coöperation in the Far East on the part of the three Western Powers who were soon to form the so-called Triple Entente.   Germany felt diplomatically isolated.   She put out some feelers to President Roosevelt for an Entente with the United States for the preservation of China and of their mutual interests in the Far East.   But these feelers were not successful.[217]

Finally, on August 31, 1907, there was signed the Anglo-Russian Agreement dealing with the Middle East—Tibet,

213 Siebert-Schreiner, p. 17.

214 *Ibid.*, pp. 8-43. G.P., XXXII, *passim.*   T. F. Millard, *America and the Far Eastern Question* (New York, 1909), chs. xv-xx.   S. K. Hornbeck, *Contemporary Politics in the Far East* (New York, 1916), ch. xv. O. Franke, *Die Grossmächte in Ostasien* (Hamburg, 1923), pp. 308-343; Tyler Dennett, *Americans in Eastern Asia* (New York, 1922).

215 July 28, 1907; *cf.* Pooley, *l.c.*, pp. 229 ff.

216 June 10, 1907; *ibid.*, pp. 212-223, 325-6; and G.P., XXV, 53 ff, 67 ff.   217 G.P., XXV, 67-99.

Afghanistan, and Persia.[218] Both contracting Powers recognized the territorial integrity of Tibet under the suzerainty of China, and agreed not to interfere with the
country's internal concerns or attempt to secure special
concessions there. The land of the Lamas was to remain
a barrier between the Russian bear and the British lion in
India.

As to Afghanistan, in return for an English promise not
to occupy or annex it so long as the Ameer fulfilled his obligations, Russia declared the country to be outside her
sphere of influence; she withdrew her diplomatic agents
from Herat and agreed to deal with the Ameer only through
the British authorities. Afghanistan therefore was no
longer to be a field for Russian intrigue against India, and
the English were freed from a great bugbear that had worried them for a century.

Persia was by far the most important subject of the
Agreement. Though the preamble piously declared that the
two Great Powers mutually agreed to respect the "integrity" and "independence" of Persia, the Agreement went on
to divide Persia into three regions: the northern and
largest region, bordering on Russia and comprising the
richest and most populous parts of Persia, was to be a Russian sphere of influence, in which Great Britain would not
seek for herself, or any third Power, any concessions of a
political or commercial nature. The southern region,
largely barren desert but containing roads leading to India,
was in like manner to be a British sphere, in which Russia
would seek no concessions. Between these two lay a central neutral region, including the head of the Persian Gulf,
in which neither Great Power was to seek concessions except in agreement with the other. In all this the Shah was
not consulted in the least. A cartoon in *Punch* hit off the

218 For the text see *British Foreign and State Papers,* vol. 100,
pp. 555 ff.

arrangement aptly enough: the British lion and the Russian bear are seen mauling between them an unhappy Persian cat; the lion is saying to the bear, "Look here! *You* can play with his head, and *I* can play with his tail, and we can *both* stroke the small of his back"; while the poor cat moans, "I don't remember having been consulted about this." [219]

In his memoirs Viscount Grey argues, but unconvincingly, that England had the better of the bargain: "What we gained by it was real—what Russia gained was apparent." [220] In fact, the reverse was true. Though England gained peace of mind in regard to the Indian frontier, she also lost much. She lost her independence of action in Persia. Hitherto she had been free to protest and object to the encroachments of the Russian imperialist steamroller crushing southward upon defenseless Persia. Henceforth she found herself involved as an accomplice in the destruction of the financial and political independence of the Shah's empire. Sir Edward Grey soon found himself drawn along in the wake of Russian aggression and intrigue, in a way most embarrassing to him when questioned on the subject in the House of Commons. He protested frequently against the activities of Russian agents in Persia. He even hinted he would resign. "Persia," he says, "tried my patience more than any other subject." [221] Russian unscrupulousness and double-dealing in the Middle East continued to be a recurrent source of annoyance to him almost up to the outbreak of the World War. One of President Poincaré's objects in visiting St. Petersburg in July, 1914, was to smooth this discord in the harmony of the Triple

[219] "The Harmless Necessary Cat," *Punch*, CXXXIII, 245, Oct. 2, 1907.   [220] Grey, I, 155.

[221] Grey, I, 164. *Cf.* Siebert-Schreiner, p. 550 (where Grey's irritation and talk of resignation were due to Russia's "Potsdam agreements" in 1910-11), and p. 615 (where they were due to Russian action in Persia).

Entente.[222]   But Grey was helpless to make his protests effective, because his distrust of Germany made him unwilling to take a really stiff attitude to Russia, or to recede from the Agreement of 1907, lest he should thereby endanger the solidarity of the Triple Entente. The Russians were quite aware of this, and took advantage of it. Sazonov put the situation in a nutshell in a significant letter to the Russian Minister in Teheran:

> The London Cabinet looks upon the Anglo-Russian Convention of 1907 as being important for the Asiatic interests of England; but this Convention possesses a still greater importance for England from the viewpoint of the policy which is being pursued by England in Europe. . . . The English, engaged in the pursuit of political aims of vital importance in Europe, may, in case of necessity, be prepared to sacrifice certain interests in Asia in order to keep a Convention alive which is of such importance to them. This is a circumstance which we can, of course, exploit for ourselves, as, for instance, in Persian affairs.[223]

Though the Anglo-Russian Convention was all made public, included no obligations of military or diplomatic support, and did not at once lead to a closely knit diplomatic partnership, it did nevertheless complete the circle for a closer political coöperation between Rusisa, France and England. The Press of these countries began to talk of the new "Triple Entente."

222 Poincaré, *Les Origines de la Guerre*, p. 201 f. *Cf.* K.D., 52.

223 Oct. 8, 1910; Siebert-Schreiner, p. 99. The dismal and disgraceful story of how Russia did this may be read in Siebert-Schreiner, pp. 49-141, and in the engaging personal narrative of the blunt financial American adviser who tried—in vain—to rescue the Persian cat from the deadly grasp of the Russian bear: W. Morgan Shuster, *The Strangling of Persia* (New York, 1913).

CHAPTER IV

THE SYSTEM OF SECRET ALLIANCES, 1907-1914: TRIPLE ALLIANCE AND TRIPLE ENTENTE IN OPPOSITION

BETWEEN the years 1907 and 1914 there was an increasing crystallization of opposition between the two groups into which the six Great Powers of Europe had now become divided. During the first four years it developed slowly; then, with the French occupation of Fez, the German threat at Agadir, the Italian seizure of Tripoli, Anglo-German naval rivalry, the failure of the Haldane Mission, and the Balkan Wars, it proceeded more rapidly. It was reflected in Morocco, Mesopotamia, the Balkans, and in many other matters, ranging all the way from European armaments to Chinese loans. In the case of the Balkans, it was so fundamental and so closely bound up with the immediate causes of the World War, that a separate chapter on "Balkan Problems," following the present one, will be devoted to some aspects of it in that troubled region. But to give a full account of this crystallizing opposition in all its complicated and disputed phases would go far beyond the limits of this volume. Fortunately, it has been excellently summed up by others.[1] No attempt therefore is here made

[1] Bernadotte E. Schmitt, "Triple Alliance and Triple Entente, 1902-1914" in *Amer. Hist. Rev.*, XXIX, 449-473 (April, 1924); G. P. Gooch, *History of Modern Europe, 1878-1918* (New York, 1923), chs. xi-xvi; E. Brandenburg, *Von Bismarck zum Weltkriege* (Berlin, 1924), chs. xi-xvii, of which the second edition (1926) is now available in an English translation; G. L. Dickinson, *The International Anarchy, 1904-1914* (London, 1926); and many others. Professor C. R. Beazley also is said to be preparing a considerable work on the diplomatic situation preceding the War.

to give any detailed account of this period. The aim has been rather to indicate, in the light of the new German documents, M. Poincaré's *Memoirs*, and other recently published material, the more important factors which increased this crystallizing opposition and gave it the fatal turn which it took in 1914.

This opposition of Triple Alliance and Triple Entente was accompanied and accentuated by four sets of tendencies.

(1) Both systems of alliance tended to be deformed from their originally defensive character. They tended to become widened in scope to cover policies involving offensive military action. For example, Germany felt compelled to back up Austria, if her ally became involved in war with Russia by her efforts at self-preservation from the "Greater Serbia" danger—in a way which Bismarck would hardly have tolerated. In precisely the same way, France under M. Poincaré felt compelled to back up Russia, if her ally became involved in war with Austria and Germany by her efforts to safeguard her Balkan ambitions—in a way which M. Poincaré's predecessors would hardly have permitted.

(2) Germany tried to strengthen the Triple Alliance, and, similarly, M. Poincaré tried to tighten up and strengthen the Triple Entente. But the latter was more successful than the former. The Triple Alliance, in spite of its renewal in 1907 and in 1912, tended to become relatively weaker. It was weakened by Austria's internal troubles and Balkan complications, by the deep-seated distrust between Austria and Italy, and by Italy's *sacro egoismo,* which often made her oppose her allies, especially Austria, in diplomatic questions and caused her allies to doubt her loyalty in case of war. The Triple Entente, on the other hand, became relatively stronger, because its members were not divided from one another by any such sharp conflicts of interest as between Austria and Italy, and because England, France, and Russia were able to make in-

creasingly close arrangements for military and naval coöperation.

(3) Although the Triple Alliance and Triple Entente—and especially the latter—were tightened up and strengthened, there still remained more occasions of friction, distrust, and suspicion within each diplomatic group than is commonly supposed. This will be seen also in the next chapter on "Balkan Problems." There was in fact by no means so much harmony and mutual confidence within the Triple Alliance as was usually assumed by writers a few years ago—nor was there so much within the Triple Entente as has been assumed by "revisionist" writers more recently. Italy's "extra dance" with France after 1902, and with Russia after Racconigi in 1909, were the most notable examples of this kind of domestic unfaithfulness within a diplomatic group, and continued to be a source of uncertainty and worry on all sides. But Italy's case was merely an example of what the Triple Entente feared might happen within its own circle. France, for instance, was much worried whenever England entered into confidential negotiations with Germany, as in the Haldane Mission or in the Bagdad Railway question; or when Russia made with Germany the Potsdam Agreements of 1910-1911, or seemed inclined to undertake diplomatic maneuvers in the Balkans without first fully informing her French ally, as happened on several occasions. Sir Edward Grey was worried lest the Entente with Russia concerning the Middle East would break down, if he did not give her the diplomatic support which M. Sazonov desired at critical moments, as in the Liman von Sanders affair—and in July, 1914. When he made friendly arrangements with Germany in regard to the Bagdad Railway and the Portuguese colonies, he thought it prudent to counter-balance them, as it were, by consenting to the desire of his two Entente friends that he should enter into negotiations for an Anglo-Russian naval con-

vention. Germany also found herself frequently embarrassed by the "stupidities" in which Austria indulged in the Balkans, against Germany's better judgment or without her approval. Within each group therefore special efforts were continually being made to lessen the friction and suspicion, and to increase the harmony, solidarity, and security of the group. This was done by making concessions to the selfish aims or special interests of the fellow members, or by giving "blank cheques" to one's ally in the shape of assurances of "complete fulfilment of the obligations of the alliance," even in matters which might easily develop into a European war. The acquiescence or encouragement which M. Poincaré gave to Russia, and which Germany gave to Austria, is to be explained in large part by this desire to preserve the solidarity of the group, rather than by any desire for a war to recover Alsace-Lorraine in the one case, or to gain the hegemony of Europe in the other. But it had the effect of encouraging Russia and Austria along the slippery Balkan path which eventually led to the yawning chasm of 1914.

(4) In both groups of Powers there was a rapid increase of military and naval armaments. This caused increasing suspicions, fears, and newspaper recriminations in the opposite camp. This in turn led to more armaments; and so to the vicious circle of ever growing war preparations and mutual fears and suspicions. In 1907, before the opposition had crystallized clearly, the Triple Alliance and Triple Entente, in Professor Schmitt's happy phrase, "had stood side by side; in 1914 they stood face to face."

GERMAN FEAR OF "ENCIRCLEMENT" AFTER 1907

Germany at first gave an outward appearance of accepting the Anglo-Russian Convention of 1907 with equanimity. Even before its conclusion, Count Bülow, in his Reichstag speech of April 30, 1907, had referred to the negotiations with quiet optimism. Afterwards, when the Anglo-Russian Convention was published, he instructed the German Press to be moderate and practical in its comments, and to accept the Convention for what it professed to be—a settlement of Anglo-Russian differences and not a combination inimical to German interests.

But in reality Germany felt very uneasy. She feared that the clauses in regard to Tibet, Afghanistan, and Persia were not merely an end in themselves, but rather a means to an end—the formation of a diplomatic combination on the part of England, France, and Russia. This Triple Entente would outmatch the Triple Alliance in diplomatic strength because Italy, owing to her hatred and jealousy of Austria in the Balkans and her desire to stand well with France and England, would vote with them, rather than with her own allies, as she had done at Algeciras. The Triple Entente Powers would also outmatch the Triple Alliance in economic resources and in military and naval strength. They would therefore feel able to block Germany's construction of the Bagdad Railway, obstruct her industry and commerce, and thwart her colonial ambitions, wherever these came into competition with their own. Moreover, in the most inflammable subjects, like Alsace-Lorraine, Morocco, the Middle East, and naval competition, one or other of the Entente Powers stood in direct opposition to Germany. The Balkans also might easily prove another highly inflammable subject. If Russia's reconciliation with England should prove (as it turned out to be the case) the preliminary to a Russian effort to revive her old aggressive Balkan policy, and to recover in the Near East the prestige which she had lost in the Far East, the ally of France would almost inevitably come into conflict with the ally of Germany. If a crisis should arise over any of these questions, Germany, supported by Austria and perhaps by Italy, would be likely to find herself faced by the Triple Entente and its superior

strength.   Germany would either have to back down or
fight.   Neither prospect, under the circumstances, was
attractive.

These were the considerations which preyed upon the
minds of the Germans and created a nervous *malaise* which
finally took form in the conviction that they were being
"encircled."   Though Russia and England had protested
abundantly that the Anglo-Russian Convention was in no
way directed against Germany and had no ulterior purposes,
their words did not carry conviction at Berlin, and their
attitude in regard to the Bagdad Railway seemed to indicate a collective determination to obstruct one of Germany's
dearest projects.

In 1902 Germany secured from Turkey the concession
for the Bagdad Railway.   This was to extend the rail connection from the eastern terminus of the Anatolian Railway at Konia, already in German hands, all the way via
Bagdad to the Persian Gulf.   The next year the Deutsche
Bank made arrangements with the Ottoman Bank for
financing the construction of the line.   Germany desired and
invited the participation of foreign capital in the costly
enterprise.   But she soon met with opposition, instead
of coöperation, on the part of Russia, France, and England.[2]

Russia, on various political, economic, and strategic
grounds, had been opposed from the outset to the whole
German railway project.   Moreover, since she had no surplus capital for investment, there was never any serious
question of her financial participation in it.   Her policy
was to obstruct a scheme to which she had many objections
and in which she was unable to take a part.

In France, the bankers, for the most part, favored par-

[2] *Cf.* G.P., XVII, 371-517; XXV, 177-280; and the excellent account
in E. M. Earle, *Turkey, the Great Powers, and the Bagdad Railway*
(New York, 1923), chs. iv-viii, with bibliographical notes. These are now
supplemented to some extent by the *British Documents*, II, 174-196.

ticipation, both because they already had large investments in Turkey, and because this looked like another good business proposition. The French Government, however, favorable at first, then hesitating, finally declared its opposition to the investment of French capital in the German undertaking. M. Delcassé even went to the point of preventing Bagdad Railway bonds from being quoted on the Paris Bourse.[3] This hostile attitude of the French Government was partly owing to the vigorous representations made by French commercial interests, clericals, and politicians, and partly also, if we are to believe M. Izvolski, to French desire to support the policy of their Russian ally.[4]

In England Mr. Balfour and Lord Lansdowne had stated at first, on April 7, 1903, that the British Government approved the bankers' negotiations for the participation of British capital in the construction of the Bagdad Railway. But at once an outcry was raised in the British Press and in Parliament against the Government's favorable attitude: the railway would injure British vested interests in Mesopotamia and the Persian Gulf; it would increase the influence of the Germans in Turkey at British expense and bring them too close to India; it would rouse suspicions in Russia as to British intentions; and, in any case, the English ought not to participate, unless they did so on equal terms and to the same extent as the Germans. So Mr. Balfour was forced to announce in the House of Commons on April 23 his repudiation of the approval which he had given on April 7.[5] Henceforth the British also were inclined to obstruct the railway in various indirect ways. They long refused to consent to the raising of the Turkish tariff from eight to

[3] G.P., XXV, 195; Earle, p. 147 ff.

[4] G.P., XXV, 231. Russian influence was also suspected of causing England's change of attitude from one of favor to one of opposition; G.P., XVII, 443.

[5] *Parliamentary Debates, House of Commons* (1903), CXX, 1247-8, 1358, 1361, 1354-7, 1371-4; CXXI, 271 f.; G.P., XVII, 431 ff.; Earle, p. 176 ff.

eleven per cent. Their ostensible reason was that the burden of the increase would largely fall on themselves, because they had the largest share of the trade with Turkey.
But the practical result was that it made it more difficult
for the Turkish Government to finance the kilometric and
income guarantees which the Bagdad Railway agreement
called for, and which seemed necessary for its construction.

In spite of this policy of opposition and non-participa-
tion on the part of the three Entente Powers, the Germans
managed to push rapidly the building of the first 200-kilo-
meter section from Konia to Eregli. Within something
over a year, on the Sultan's birthday, October 25, 1904, they
were able to open this first section to traffic with pompous
ceremonies and justifiable self-congratulation. But here
construction came to a sudden stop, and the rail ends were
left sticking out into space. The next 200-kilometer section,
reaching toward the Taurus Mountains, involved innumerable engineering difficulties and a far greater expenditure per kilometer of construction. The Turkish Government could not arrange the financing of additional bonds to
meet the guarantees for this section without an increase in
her customs revenues. Yet it was impossible for Turkey to
raise her tariff, as she desired to do, because by existing
treaties she could not do so without the consent of the Great
Powers; and Russia, France, and England for a long time
refused to give their consent.[6] By their refusal they practically blocked the further construction for the next few
years.

In the course of 1905 and the following year Germany
attempted some negotiations in a renewed effort to secure

6 G.P., XXII, 329-400; Earle, p. 95 f. They finally gave their consent in September, 1906, to become effective in July, 1907, but attached
numerous conditions which made it difficult to divert any of the increased revenue to the payment of railway guarantees. One condition
was that three-fourths of the increased revenue must go to Macedonian
reform.

the financial participation and political coöperation of the French and the British in the building of the Bagdad Railway. After Delcassé's fall there was talk of a deal with M. Rouvier, by which Germany's Moroccan claims should be abandoned in exchange for French support to the Bagdad Railway. But the talk came to nothing.[7] In the summer of 1906 some members of the new Liberal Government in England, including Grey and Haldane, were believed to desire a Bagdad settlement with Germany. But Sir Edward Grey, in the spirit of the Entente with France, insisted that if England participated, France also must participate.[8] The English Press also demanded that, either the whole Bagdad Railway ought to be internationalized, or, if Germany controlled the railway as far as Bagdad, then England ought to control the section from Bagdad down to the Persian Gulf.[9] But no practical arrangement could be found for satisfying these English demands. Similarly, long German negotiations with Izvolski, contemplating German abstention from activity in Persia if Russia would withdraw her opposition to the Bagdad Railway, reached no definite conclusion.[10]

Three months after the signature of the Anglo-Russian Convention of 1907 the Kaiser visited Windsor and was cordially received. He took advantage of the occasion to reopen the Bagdad Railway discussion with Lord Haldane and Sir Edward Grey. He found that the former, as Minister of War, was anxious that the British should control the section from Bagdad to the Persian Gulf, as a "gate," to protect India from the possibility of troops coming down the new railway. The Kaiser at once declared, "I will give you the gate," and telegraphed to Bülow to this effect.[11] A lively exchange of views followed for a few hours in

---

[7] G.P., XX, 356, 395 f., 431; XXV, 180 f., 194 ff.; Earle, p. 169 ff.
[8] G.P., XXV, 226.   [9] G.P., XXV, 240 ff.   [10] G.P., XXV, 103-175.
[11] G.P., XXV, 261 ff.; Haldane, *Before the War*, p. 48 ff.

Windsor, London and Berlin. The British "recognized that
the object of the commercial development of Mesopotamia
was one that should not be opposed." But they desired
"that the quickest route between West and East should not
be under the exclusive control of a virtually foreign company, which would be in a position to affect seriously commercial relations between England and India, or to sanction
its use for strategic purposes in hostility to British interests"; they "could not, however, discuss this question à
deux, but only à quatre, for the various interests, strategical, political and commercial, affect France and Russia as
well." [12] Sir Edward Grey's insistence that France and
Russia must be associated with England in the discussions
proved a fatal obstacle to reaching any satisfactory agreement on the Kaiser's proposal. Lord Haldane laid the
blame for this on the German Foreign Office, which he
thinks did not approve of the Kaiser's move. And there is
some truth in this view.[13] But it is also true that Sir
Edward Grey's insistence on conversations à quatre was a
main cause of the Kaiser's offer of the "gate" remaining
abortive. Germany objected that, since France had no
special interests in Mesopotamia and the Persian Gulf, and
since Russia's interests related largely to Persia, she could
satisfy these two countries in separate negotiations. But if
the whole Bagdad Railway question was to be dealt with in
conversations à quatre, Germany would inevitably be in a
minority of one to three. Germany therefore could not be
expected to negotiate at such a disadvantage and subject
her interests to the united opposition of the other three.[14]
Sir Edward.Grey's insistence on the solidarity of England,
France and Russia, in this matter of the Bagdad Railway

12 Note of a private conversation between Sir Edward Grey and
Mr. Haldane on Nov. 14, 1907, given by the latter to the Kaiser; G.P.,
XXV, 263.
13 Cf. Bülow to Schoen, Nov. 14, 1907; ibid., 261.
14 G.P., XXIV, 77, 83; XXV, 264 ff.

in the fall of 1907, foreshadowed the solidarity of the Triple Entente in wider fields later. It also put an end to any important further discussions of the Bagdad question until Russia deserted her friends in making with Germany the "Potsdam Agreements" of 1910-1911.

ANGLO-GERMAN NAVAL RIVALRY, 1904-1908

The German suspicion that England was aiming to limit Germany's freedom of action also arose in connection with the Second Hague Peace Conference and the naval discussions at the beginning of the period of *Dreadnought* construction and rivalry. The British navy had just been reorganized and strengthened by Sir John Fisher, while the German navy was just beginning to grow in power. The proposal to discuss the limitation of armaments, urged by England, looked like a scheme to arrest naval development. It seemed to prevent Germany from catching up in strength at a moment when England still enjoyed a marked naval superiority. Nor could Germany, with Austria weakened by internal difficulties and Italy an ally of doubtful loyalty, consent to limit her army. There was the danger of a war on two fronts, when Russia should have recovered from her war with Japan and revived her active Balkan policy. So Germany insisted that the limitation of armaments should not be one of the subjects included in the call for the Conference. When the subject was nevertheless raised in the course of the Conference by England and the United States, Germany's opposition to it was, to be sure, largely but tacitly shared by France and Russia. But these two countries left it to the German delegates to voice the opposition and thereby incur the odium of wrecking the proposals.

No doubt Germany made a great mistake. Though limitation of armaments is a most difficult problem, as the long and sterile efforts of the League of Nations and the failure of President Coolidge's Conference have abundantly shown.

it is possible that, had Germany taken a different attitude in 1907, the other European Powers might have followed her, and a beginning might have been made to check the fatal increase in rival armies and navies. At any rate Germany could not have been branded as the country which was most responsible for thwarting an effort to lessen a progressive danger which was one of the main causes of the World War.[15]

By the irony of history it was during the Hague Peace Conference that Anglo-German naval rivalry reached a new and hitherto unequalled stage of mutual suspicion and bitterness. By the Navy Laws of 1898 and 1900 Admiral von Tirpitz and the Kaiser laid the foundations for a strong German navy. Their motives were many and mixed. They wished to give expression to the greatness of the New Germany by creating a fleet which should be comparable to her growing commerce and colonial interests and afford them protection. They desired preservation from the danger of being blockaded from food and raw materials in case of war. But above all, they wanted to have a naval force which could be used to back up German diplomatic arguments in the struggle for colonial and commercial advantages. The Kaiser's marginal notes are filled with the idea that other countries, and particularly England, paid little or no heed to Germany's legitimate desires, simply because Germany had no force to back up her demands. If Germany had a navy, even a much smaller one than that of England, the British would be willing to make diplomatic concessions rather than take the risk of a naval conflict. This was Tirpitz's fundamental notion when he speaks of the new German navy as a "risk navy." He had no thought

15 On the Second Hague Conference, see G.P., XXIII, 99-397, and the writings of A. P. Higgins, F. W. Holls, J. B. Scott, A. H. Fried, O. Nippold, P. Zorn, L. Renault, and E. Lémonon. The Reichstag Investigating Committee is soon to publish an important work on Germany's influence at the Second Hague Peace Conference.

of attacking England in any near future. That would be
folly for many years to come. But a respectable German
sea force would compel England to make concessions in the
colonial world rather than take the "risk" of a naval struggle. For this it was not necessary for Germany to build a
fleet fully equal to that of England; some proportion like
2:3 or 10:16 would suffice.[16]

But in fact Admiral Tirpitz completely misconceived the
psychological effect which his creation of even a "risk navy"
would have on the British mind and policy. Though it
may have contributed to induce the British to make various proposals for limiting naval competition and to enter
into various diplomatic negotiations, it did not intimidate
them or cause them to make important concessions. On the
contrary, it rather created an atmosphere of suspicion and
antagonism which was altogether unfavorable for friendly
diplomatic agreements concerning the Bagdad Railway and
other matters. Every increase in the German navy, instead
of frightening the British into making concessions, tended
to stiffen their opposition and their determination to maintain the wide margin of British naval superiority deemed
vital to the safety and very existence of the British Empire.

So, for instance, in 1904, as the English observed the
new-born German navy, still in its infancy but already
showing signs of robust growth, they began a wide-sweeping
rearrangement and reorganization of the British Fleet.
They proceeded to create a strong force in the North Sea
and make it ready for instant action against Germany.
Sir John Fisher, with his characteristically energetic policy
of "Ruthless, Relentless, and Remorseless!" [17] "brought
home some 160 ships from abroad which could neither fight
nor run away," [18] and effected other revolutionary changes,

---

[16] *Cf.* Tirpitz, *Der Aufbau der deutschen Weltmacht* (Berlin, 1926),
passim.

[17] Fisher, *Memories and Records*, II. 135.   [18] Fisher, II. 65 f., 139 ff.

so that, as he himself said, "We shall be thirty per cent. more fit to fight and we shall be ready for instant war!" [19] The next year he laid the keels for the first *Dreadnoughts*. These were to be far superior to anything afloat and give the British navy a strength which no country could menace. But their introduction more than doubled the cost of capital ship construction. Furthermore, they rendered relatively less important the older and smaller types of vessel which had hitherto constituted England's naval superiority. It enabled Tirpitz to follow England's example, and be only a little behind her in the race in the construction of this new type of vessel, which neither country had possessed hitherto; whereas in the older types of vessel Germany was hopelessly behind. To express the same thing in figures: England had authorized the laying down by 1908 of 12, and Germany of 9 Dreadnoughts; whereas the ratio between England and Germany in vessels of the older pre-Dreadnought type was 63:26. Tirpitz also believed that Germany, where sailors were conscripted instead being paid wages for voluntary enlistment, and where cost of ship construction was relatively low, could stand longer and more easily than England the heavy strain of naval expenditure. With this double advantage on Germany's part, as it seemed to him, he was always skeptical about the sincerity and motives of British proposals for restriction of naval construction. He was steadily opposed to any serious limitation on his own program, by which he believed the German navy could gradually approach nearer in strength to the British navy, though it might never actually equal it. It would have to pass through the "danger zone" of inferiority, during which England might possibly attack and destroy it in a "preventive" war. But he did not think this danger great, especially if German diplomacy avoided irritating England in other fields. Once safely

[19] Fisher, *Memories and Records*, II, 134.

through the "danger zone," after a dozen years, Germany would have a very respectable "risk navy." Germany could stand the financial strain; in the long run England could not. So all Germany had to do was to push construction.

Thus, by a third Navy Law in 1906, Tirpitz secured the authorization of six new capital ships; and by the law of 1908, reducing the replacement period from 25 to 20 years, he provided for the early replacement of old obsolete vessels by new ships, not of the same size as the discarded ones, but of the new Dreadnought type. This law of 1908 fixed the construction of new and replacement ships of the Dreadnought type at the rate of four a year from 1908 to 1911, and two a year from 1912 to 1917. Meanwhile the German Navy League was clamoring for a big German navy. The Press on both sides of the North Sea was whipping up national passion, and the rumors of the Kaiser's ill-considered letter to Lord Tweedmouth added fuel to the flame. All this led to the British "war-scare" of 1908, and to further futile negotiations for some kind of a naval understanding.[20]

Sir Henry Campbell-Bannerman, in a speech on December 21, 1905, setting forth the platform of the new Liberal Government, had lamented the great expenditures on armaments: "A policy of huge armaments keeps alive and stimulates and feeds the belief that force is the best, if not the only, solution of international differences. It is a policy that tends to inflame old sores and to create new sores. . . . We want relief from the pressure of excessive taxation, and

[20] On Anglo-German naval relations 1904-1908, see Fisher, I, ch. xii; II, chs. ix, x; Churchill, pp. 19-41; Hurd and Castle, *German Sea-Power* (New York, 1913); Schmitt, *England and Germany, 1740-1914* (Princeton, 1916), 173-187, and, in more detail, from the German side, G.P., XIX, 351-380; XXIII, 27-53; XXIV, 3-210; Tirpitz, *Der Aufbau der deutschen Weltmacht*, 1-162; Bülow, *Imperial Germany* (Berlin, 1913); Haller, *Die Aera Bülow* (Berlin, 1922); Brandenburg, ch. xi; Herzfeld, "Der deutsche Flottenbau und die englische Politik," in *Archiv f. Politik u. Geschichte*, IV, 1926, 115-146, and Admiral Karl Galster, *England, Deutsche Flotte, und Weltkrieg* (Kiel, 1925).

at the same time we want money for our own domestic needs
at home, which have been too long starved and neglected
owing to the demands on the taxpayer for military purposes
abroad. How are these desirable things to be secured if in
time of peace our armaments are maintained on a war
footing?" [21] In the course of the next three years, the
English made many proposals for reducing naval expenditure and thereby lessening the growing friction with Germany. It was proposed that the subject should be discussed
at the Hague Peace Conference; [22] that Sir John Fisher
should have a talk with Admiral Tirpitz; or that there
should be a mutual inspection of shipyards and communication of naval programs.[23] It was informally intimated that,
if Germany was uneasy at England's "insurance policy" of
closer relations with France and Russia, the best way to
dissipate this uneasiness and revive the former cordial
Anglo-German relations would be for Germany to retard
her naval program, or come to some understanding for an
agreed-upon ratio between the English and German
navies.[24]

But England could never get a satisfactory answer from
Germany to any of these proposals. Being made after Sir
John Fisher had so greatly strengthened the Home Fleet in
the North Sea and begun to build Dreadnoughts, these proposals looked to the German mind like an intimation from
the Supreme Naval Power that it desired naval competition
to cease at the moment of its own greatest preponderance.
Coinciding also with Lord Haldane's organization of the

[21] The London *Times*, Dec. 22, 1905; *cf*. also Spender, *Life of Sir
Henry Campbell-Bannerman*, II, 208, 327-332.

[22] G.P. XXIII, 25-253 *passim; cf*. also Campbell-Bannerman's cordial and conciliatory article, "The Hague Conference and the Limitation of Armaments", in the first number of the London *Nation*, Mar. 2,
1907; Campbell-Bannerman's views, however, were severely criticized in
the Paris *Temps* of March 4; the French, at bottom, had no more sympathy with disarmament proposals than the Germans.

[23] G.P., XXIII, 39 ff., 52.   [24] G.P., XXIV, 99 ff.

British Expeditionary Force and with England's closer diplomatic relations with France and Russia, they looked like a concerted plan on the part of these three Powers to put pressure on Germany. Any yielding to such pressure was sharply resented as inconsistent with Germany's dignity as a Great Power. As Bülow wrote privately to Bavaria and some of the other German Governments on June 25, 1908, after President Fallières's visit to London and King Edward's famous meeting with the Tsar at Reval: "Agreements which aim at a limitation of our defensive power are not acceptable for discussion by us under any circumstances. A Power which should demand such an agreement from us should be clear in its mind that such a demand would mean war." [25] By the Kaiser especially, the British proposals were indignantly repudiated as unjustifiable attempts to interfere with his sovereign right and duty to take all measures necessary for the dignity and defense of the German Empire. Commenting upon Count Metternich's report of July 16, 1908, of an informal luncheon discussion with Sir Edward Grey and Lloyd George, in which it had been intimated that a naval discussion would improve diplomatic relations, the Kaiser wrote:

> Count Metternich must be informed that good relations with England at the price of the building of the German navy are *not* desired by me. If England intends graciously to extend us her hand only with the intimation that we must limit our fleet, this is a groundless impertinence, which involves a heavy insult to the German people and their Kaiser, which must be rejected *a limine* by the Ambassador. . . . France and Russia might with equal reason then demand a limitation of our land armaments. The German Fleet is not built *against* anyone, and also not *against* England! But

25 G.P., XXV, 478. For other German intimations that any attempt to put pressure on Germany to limit her navy would be answered by declaration of war, see G.P., XXIV, 53, 103, 127.

according to *our* need! That is stated quite clearly in the Navy Law, and for 11 years has remained unchanged! This law will be carried out to the last iota; whether it suits the British or not, is no matter! If they want war, they can begin it; we do not fear it! [26]

The Kaiser's fears that England was trying to put a check upon Germany's navy, and "encircle" her in other ways, were increased by the numerous visits and interviews which Edward VII had with French and Russian rulers and ministers in the summer of 1908. In May President Fallières was very cordially received in London and given a dinner at the Foreign Office to which the only person invited, outside a French and English group, was the Russian Ambassador—a distinction which seemed to embarrass good Count Benckendorff.[27] The French Press made the most of the visit, and Tardieu in the *Temps* expressed the hope that Anglo-French relations were taking a firmer form, provided England made fundamental changes in her military system —a hint at the universal military service which Lord Roberts and others were now beginning urgently to advocate in public speeches. In June, King Edward's visit to the Tsar at Reval seemed more than a mere act of family courtesy, since he was accompanied by Admiral Fisher, Sir John French, and Sir Charles Hardinge, who had long talks with Izvolski and the Russian Premier, Stolypin. Hardinge told Izvolski that England had no hostile feelings toward Germany and was anxious to maintain the most friendly relations with her, but that "owing to the unnecessarily large increase in the German naval program, a deep distrust in England of Germany's future intentions had been created." This distrust was likely to increase with the progress

[26] G.P., XXIV, 104
[27] G.P., XXIV, 63. On President Fallières's visit, the French Press, and Delcassé's talks with Asquith, Grey, and Sir Charles Hardinge on his "private visit" to London a month later, see G.P., XXIV, pp. 57-78; and Sidney Lee, *King Edward VII,* II, 584 ff.

of time, the realization of the German program, and the heavier taxation entailed by England's necessary naval counter-measures. "In seven or eight years' time a critical situation might arise, in which Russia, if strong in Europe, might be the arbiter of peace, and have much more influence in securing the peace of the world than at any Hague Conference. For this reason it was absolutely necessary that England and Russia should maintain towards each other the same cordial and friendly relations as now exist between England and France." [28] Izvolski got the impression that the English wanted Russia to build up her army and navy as much as possible as a future check to Germany.

Sir John Fisher relates that he sat several times next Stolypin and Izvolski, and urged them to build up the Russian army on the Western frontier against Germany: "Stolypin said to me, 'What do you think we need most?' He fancied I should answer, 'So many battleships, so many cruisers, etc., etc.,' but instead I said, 'Your Western Frontier is denuded of troops and your magazines are depleted. Fill them up and then talk of Fleets!' Please see enclosure from Kuropatkin's secret report: 'The foundation of Russia's safety is her Western boundary!' " [29]

---

[28] Grey, I, 203. Viscount Grey prints Hardinge's report on the Reval conversations (I, 202-209), and calls it (p. 196) "the real, full, authentic confidential record of what took place"; but he indicates on p. 209 that sundry details concerning Macedonian reforms, Persia, and Crete are omitted. For Hardinge's complete report, see B.D., V, 232-246. Cf. Izvolski's account of the Reval meeting in his despatch to Benckendorff in London, June 18, 1908 (Siebert-Schreiner, p. 478), according to which Hardinge said: "If Germany should continue to increase her naval armaments at the same accelerated pace, in six or seven years a most alarming and strained situation might arise in Europe. For this reason we in the interest of peace and the preservation of the Balance of Power, desire that Russia shall be as strong as possible on land and on sea." Izvolski added, "Sir Charles reiterated this idea more than once, whereby he apparently wished to have it understood that he is expressing not his own personal opinion, but the decided political conviction of the London Cabinet." For German uneasiness as to the Reval meeting, see G.P., XXV, 441-494.

[29] Fisher to Lord Esher, Sept. 8, 1908; Fisher, *Memories*, p. 186 f.

Aside from this renewal of Anglo-Russian cordial relations and English encouragement to Russia to build up her armaments again—which she soon proceeded to do—the Reval interview actually dealt mainly with the question of Macedonian reforms, Persia, Crete, the Sanjak railway project, and the attitude of the Russian Press. There was no attempt to build up a closer Anglo-Russian combination against Germany, and Izvolski was profuse in his assurances that it was in no way unfriendly to Germany. But the Kaiser was not convinced, and Reval marks a cooling off in Anglo-German relations. It also made him more positive in his refusal to discuss with England any limitation of his naval program, when Hardinge broached the subject directly to him at the time of King Edward's brief visit to Kronberg on August 11, 1908. There was a heated discussion. Hardinge, according to the Kaiser's lively account in dialogue form, complained that Germany was building Dreadnoughts so rapidly that in a few years she would be as strong as England in these capital ships. The Kaiser said this was "absolute nonsense," sent for a copy of *Nauticus,* an almanac of detailed naval statistics of all nations which Hardinge appeared never to have heard of, and showed him his errors. When Hardinge persisted that the competitive naval construction must cease, the Kaiser used his regular argument that Germany was not building in competition with England, but only for her own needs as laid down in Tirpitz's Navy Laws. When Hardinge still insisted, "You must stop or build slower," the Kaiser looked him sharp in the eye and replied, "Then we shall fight, for it is a question of national honor and dignity." Hardinge turned red, and, seeing he was on dangerous ground, begged the Kaiser's pardon, asked him to forget words said in private conversation, and changed the subject. In conversation later in the day with the Kaiser, Hardinge was as affable and friendly as could be, and was not a little surprised to be decorated with the Order of the Red Eagle, First Class.[30]   The English Cabinet, whose views Hardinge had been representing, were determined to preserve England's supremacy of the seas and keep ahead of Germany in Dreadnought construction.   But they foresaw the bitterness which would be engendered between the two countries by further naval competition, as well as the terrible financial burden it would impose on England.   They therefore sincerely desired and tried to come to some sort of understanding with Germany on the subject.   It was a tragic mistake of Tirpitz and the Kaiser that they should have so flatly refused discussion and thereby pushed England further into the arms of France and Russia, thus strengthening the Triple Entente and helping to crystallize its opposition.

The effect on Germany of England's opposition to the Bagdad Railway, of her efforts to limit the German navy, of the Reval meeting and the apparent consolidation of France, Russia, and England into a Triple Entente, was to produce a conviction that Germany was being "encircled." Germans believed that this encirclement was Edward VII's personal work, and that it aimed at strangling German commercial and colonial expansion, and even at crushing Germany's political and military position.   There is no substantial evidence that there was any deliberate encirclement with such aims on the part of King Edward or the British Government.   Such notions were the product of German imagination, fear, and suspicion.   But there was nevertheless something of a diplomatic encirclement.   Germany was now surrounded by three Great Powers, whose combined strength was supposed to be equal or superior to that of the Triple Alliance, and who were growing increasingly ready to coöperate in defense of their own interests whether

[30] Kaiser to Bülow, Aug. 11-13, 1908; G.P., XXIV, 124-129; cf. also Hardinge's report to Grey of Aug. 16, 1908, printed with other material on the Kronberg visit, in B.D., VI, 173-200.

in Morocco, Mesopotamia, or the Balkans. Though Izvolski hoped that the Triple Entente would give him greater freedom of action in the Near East and Middle East, and though the French counted on it in the same way in Morocco, so far as England was concerned it aimed at the preservation of peace through the establishment of a balance of power. It was insurance against the supposed danger of possible German aggression, and not for any aggression against Germany's existing position in Europe and in the commercial world. But to German eyes it had a more ominous and irritating appearance. This finds expression in extreme form in the Kaiser's marginal notes on reports of the Reval meeting and of English efforts for slowing down German Dreadnought construction. It is also reflected in his indiscreet speech to German officers at Döberitz. His feeling was: "A strong navy; a strong army; and powder dry!" [31]

Bülow on the other hand, with his characteristic policy of putting the best face on an unpleasant situation, believed Germany should scrupulously avoid showing any signs of nervousness and uneasiness. To do so would simply be playing into the hands of Russia and France. While agreeing that Germany must keep herself in the highest possible state of defense, she must do so quietly. He chided the Kaiser as much as he dared for the Döberitz indiscretion,[32] and was inclined to agree with Metternich, the German Ambassador in London, that Germany ought not to close the door to all English suggestions for some arrangement to prevent the evils of Anglo-German naval competition.[33]

He also believed that the consolidation of the Triple Entente made it all the more important that Germany must stand firmly behind her Austrian ally. In a long very confidential circular to the Prussian Ministers in Bavaria

[31] G.P., XXV, 454.
[32] G.P., XXV, p. 466.
[33] G.P., XXVIII, 1-199, *passim.*

and the other leading states in the German Empire, he summed up the situation as optimistically as he honestly could. The Reval meeting, preceded by President Fallières's visit to London, has caused uneasiness in Germany. Grey and Izvolski have given assurances that nothing is being planned against her. Nevertheless it would be a fatal mistake, if, trusting in these assurances, we do not recognize that our freedom of movement may be limited by what has happened. It is Germany's economic and political power, and the fear that she may misuse them, which is driving other states into the Entente against us. "These Ententes and Alliances are therefore in their origin rather of a defensive character. But perhaps they will not hesitate to proceed aggressively against us and hold us down where possible, when they think they have the power to do so." Our ally, Austria-Hungary, is threatened just as we are by this new combination, and especially so, because the passions and intrigues directed against the very existence of the Dual Monarchy arouse in other nations expectations for a successful destructive blow from the outside. The supposedly imminent break-up of Austria-Hungary is a favorite standing theme in the French and other foreign Press. Because of her greater interests in the Balkans, Austria-Hungary is also more exposed than are we to the danger of a conflict with the Entente Powers. Germany and Austria, standing together as a solid block, may be able to withstand all storms. "A loyal coöperation with Austria-Hungary will and must remain in the future also the fundamental basis of German foreign policy." Germany cannot enter into a discussion with other Powers to limit her armaments, but she should avoid as far as possible giving any irritation to others and restrain all jingoistic expressions in the German Press.[34]

There was much shrewd wisdom in this statement.

[34] Bülow's circular, June 25, 1908; G.P., XXV, 474-479.

GERMANY'S RELATIONS WITH FRANCE, 1908-1911

While the naval friction with England continued, and the Young Turk Revolution and Bosnian Crisis led to a new tension with Russia, Germany managed to improve her relations with France in the years from 1908 to 1911.

The Algeciras Conference had not produced very satisfactory conditions in Morocco. The Sultan's brother, Mulai Hafid, had gained a strong following among the chieftains who resented the Franco-Spanish efforts to maintain order. Mulai Hafid finally revolted against his brother's authority. In the disorders which took place a French doctor was murdered, which gave the French occasion to occupy Moroccan territory at Oudjda near the Algerian frontier in the spring of 1907. Further outrages on Europeans led the French to land troops in Casablanca in August, and to place French police in other seaports on the West Coast. The Sultan, losing his authority more and more, was driven from his capital to the coast at Rabat, and finally declared deposed by Mulai Hafid's followers. Bülow and the Kaiser, recognizing that Germany's Morocco policy in the past had consolidated the Anglo-French Entente, refrained from any serious interference with these French measures, though German influence had contributed to the trouble between the rival sultans.[35]

While negotiations were going on concerning the terms under which Abdul Aziz should agree to abdicate in favor of Mulai Hafid, there occurred the Casablanca incident, which for a moment threatened to cause a new flare-up between France and Germany. On September 25, 1908, the German Consul at Casablanca attempted to assist six deserters from the French Foreign Legion to escape on board a German ship. But the deserters were forcibly seized, and

[35] For the details, see the French Yellow Book, *Affaires du Maroc*, III-IV, 1906-1908; and G.P., XXI, 601-689; XXIV, 215-326.

the consular secretary and soldier escorting them were somewhat mishandled by French soldiers. The German Consul
was blamed by France for having exceeded his powers, contrary to international law, in affording protection to persons
within French military jurisdiction. The local French military authorities were accused by Germany of having infringed the inviolability of consular rights. In spite of
some excitement in the French and German Press, good
sense fortunately prevailed in the Foreign Offices at Paris
and Berlin. Both soon agreed to submit the matter to
arbitration, which ultimately resulted in a compromise decision that both sides had been partly in the wrong. Both
Powers were glad to see the incident disposed of in a
conciliatory fashion so that it should not add a new danger
to the peace of Europe which at the moment was threatened
by the uncertain state of affairs growing out of the Turkish
Revolution and the Bosnian Crisis. The Kaiser especially
displayed as much wisdom and energetic influence in favor
of friendly conciliation as he had lacked in dealing with
the English suggestions for a restriction of naval competition. Never in sympathy with the Bülow-Holstein Morocco
policy of the past, he now condemned it sharply, having
come to the conclusion that it was impossible to check the
extension of French political control in Morocco without
resorting to force. On October 4 he informed his Foreign
Office that, so far as still practicable, Germany should withdraw with dignity, and come to an understanding with
France as quickly as possible, in spite of the incident at
Casablanca. A couple of days later, after being painfully
surprised by the Austrian annexation of Bosnia, he wrote
more energetically to Bülow: "In view of these circumstances this wretched Moroccan affair must now be brought
to a conclusion, quickly and definitely. There is nothing
to be made of it; it will be French anyway. So let us get
out of the affair with dignity, so that we may finally have

done with this friction with France, now that great questions are at issue." To which Bülow replied characteristically that he agreed, but must not let the French see this too clearly, or they would never give any compensations for Germany's withdrawal; and he added, "The most desirable thing would be that we should come to an understanding with France and England about Morocco, as well as about other African and Asia Minor questions." [36]

Soon afterwards Germany gave her approval to the terms which the French had drawn up, highly favorable to themselves, as the conditions on which Mulai Hafid was to be Sultan. At the same time Schoen, the German Secretary of State, told Jules Cambon, the French Ambassador in Berlin, that it was time for Germany and France to shake hands on Morocco, and that the Kaiser wished it.[37] This led to negotiations which resulted in the Franco-German Agreement of February 9, 1909. "To facilitate the execution of the Act of Algeciras," France, still professing to respect the independence and integrity of Morocco, promised equality of economic opportunity to the Germans; and Germany, professing to pursue only economic aims, recognized France's special political interests in preserving peace and order, and promised not to interfere with them.[38]

The final negotiations took place very rapidly. This was owing to several reasons. The Bosnian Crisis was becoming dangerously acute as Austria and Serbia armed against one another, so that it was desirable to get the Moroccan question out of the way. In the second place, Bülow had taken up the idea of the German Ambassador in England, in spite of the Kaiser's absolute negative of the preceding summer, of conceding to England a modification of Germany's naval program in return for some politi-

[36] G.P., XXIV, 440 f. On the Casablanca incident itself, cf. ibid., pp. 329-374.
[37] Oct. 28, 1908; G.P., XXIV, 454.   [38] G.P., XXIV. 489.

cal equivalent, such as an exchange of colonial territory, or, better still, an English promise of neutrality in case of a European war.[39]   For success in any such negotiation it was most important to remove all Franco-German friction in Morocco, which had been one of England's original and most persistent reasons for standing by the side of France. It was reported to Bülow that the English Minister in Tangier had had instructions to stir up trouble between the French and Germans, and he felt sure that anti-German propaganda by the English in Paris was likely to continue so long as England had cause to be alarmed over Germany's rapid construction of Dreadnoughts.[40]   To cut the ground from under this propaganda and to remove England's anxiety as to German intentions in Morocco it was highly desirable "to shake hands with France" once and for all in regard to Morocco. A final reason for the speed with which the Franco-German Agreement was concluded lay in the fact that King Edward was to visit Berlin on February 9; Bülow wished to be able to publish the Agreement before his arrival in order to avoid any impression among the public that Edward VII had helped to bring it about.[41]

The Agreement was warmly welcomed in the French Press as putting an end to a long-standing source of irritation between France and Germany, and as assuring to the one the political, and to the other the economic, advantages necessary to each. Grey and Hardinge congratulated Bülow on it, expressing pleasure that a question which had been a constant source of anxiety to England and in which England was bound by the Entente of 1904 to give France diplomatic support was now so happily settled.[42]   The Kaiser hastened to decorate the French Ambassador in Berlin with the Order of the Red Eagle and present him

[39] G.P., XXVIII, 1-87, especially pp. 66, 74.
[40] Bülow to the Kaiser, Dec. 29, 1908; G.P., XXIV, 465.
[41] Bülow to the Kaiser, Feb. 9, 1908; G.P., XXIV, 488.
[42] G.P., XXIV, 491-4.

with an autographed portrait, "because the path I ordered in our Morocco policy has had such a brilliant success in the whole world, and because we owe much to the unselfish and devoted work of Cambon as well as to his loyalty." [43] Schoen instructed the German Minister in Morocco that he was to coöperate fully with the French, prevent all friction, and observe loyally in every way the spirit and purpose of the new convention. Though this Moroccan Agreement of 1909 did not have all the happy results expected from it, it did bring about much more cordial relations between the two countries, until new disorders arose in Morocco in the spring of 1911, which led to the French march to Fez and the German threat at Agadir.

GERMANY'S RELATIONS WITH RUSSIA, 1908-1911

Though the Anglo-Russian Convention of 1907 seemed to Germany an indication that Russia was turning away from the old friendly relations which had united the Hohenzollerns and the Romanovs, it did not at first seriously cloud the relations between the two countries. Izvolski had been profuse in his assurances that the Convention merely aimed to do away with Anglo-Russian friction in the Middle East, and was in no way directed at Germany or inimical to her interests. As Russia's interests seemed deeply centered in Persia, Germany carefully sought to avoid antagonizing her in that quarter. When Persia in 1906 had asked for the establishment of a German Bank at Teheran, with the hope of support against Russian encroachments, Germany had hesitated to heed the request, and informed Izvolski that Germany had no political aims or interests in Persia.[44] In return, early in 1907, Izvolski proposed an agreement by which Russia would withdraw her opposition to the construction of the Bagdad Railway,

---

[43] Kaiser's note, Feb. 11, 1909; G.P., XXVIII, 87.
[44] G.P., XXV, 103-121.

in return for Germany's recognition of Russia's monopoly in political, strategic, and economic matters in Northern Persia.[45] Izvolski carried on negotiations for such a Russo-German agreement during the spring and early summer of 1907, at the same time with his negotiations on the same subject with England, evidently playing off the two countries against one another.[46] But when he had the Anglo-Russian Convention safely in his pocket, he dropped the conversations with Berlin.[47] Russia's objections to the Bagdad Railway would be safeguarded by Sir Edward Grey's policy of insisting that all conversations on the subject must be à quatre, in which the Entente Powers would outnumber Germany three to one. Germany for her part felt sure that Russia's aggressive designs in Persia would inevitably lead to serious friction with England without any German stimulation. Therefore in Bülow's inelegant phrase: *"Il faut les laisser cuire dans leur jus."* [48]

In 1908, however, Germany's relations with Russia began to be less satisfactory. Izvolski wished to recover in the Near East some of the prestige which Russia had lost in her disastrous war in the Far East. He believed that the alliance with France and the Entente with England assured him their benevolent attitude, and that he could proceed to open the Straits for Russian warships. Germany had often declared that she had no objections to this, and Austria could be satisfied by being invited to annex Bosnia and Herzegovina. This was the substance of his "Buchlau Bargain" with the Austrian Foreign Minister, Aehrenthal, which will be described in more detail in the next chapter on Balkan Problems. Aehrenthal, however, acted quickly and made sure at once of his half of the bargain. But

---

[45] Feb. 20, 1907; G.P., XXV, 122 ff.   [46] G.P., XXV, 124-145.

[47] There were, to be sure, some unimportant discussions arising from the conflicts between Hartwig and Richthofen, the overzealous representatives of Russia and Germany at Teheran; G.P., XXV, 147-173.

[48] G.P., XXVII, 735.

Izvolski found that his plan for opening the Straits did not meet with French and English approval, and his consent at Buchlau to having Orthodox Greek Bosnians placed under the Roman Catholic sovereignty of the Hapsburgs was violently denounced by the Pan-Slavs in Russia, as well as by the Serbians, who had coveted Bosnia as part of a future "Greater Serbia." Thereupon Izvolski tried to nullify the Buchlau bargain by insisting that the modification of the Berlin Treaty of 1878, which was involved by the Austrian annexation of Bosnia, should be subjected to revision by a Conference of the Powers. Austria refused. Serbia and Austria began to mobilize against each other.

Though the Kaiser was indignant at the sudden way in which Aehrenthal had annexed Bosnia, Bülow persuaded his master that Germany could not afford to refuse support to her ally's *fait accompli*. Germany was now surrounded by the Entente Powers, and Austria was her only reliable ally. So Germany supported Austria's refusal to accept a Conference, and hastened to propitiate France and England by the Moroccan Agreement of 1909. Meanwhile, by March, 1909, Serbia and Austria seemed on the verge of war. Serbia counted on Russian, and Austria on German, support. Unluckily for Izvolski, Russia's exhaustion and military disorganization after the war with Japan made it out of the question for her to back up by force his demand for a Conference; France was not yet ready to extend the scope of the Franco-Russian alliance to cover Russian ambitions in the Balkans; and England gave Russia little support.

To avert an actual clash of arms between Austria and Serbia, Germany then proposed a solution to extricate Izvolski from the *cul-de-sac* into which he had strayed, and demanded a yes or no answer in regard to it; if Russia rejected it, Germany would let the Austro-Serbian quarrel take its course. and the outcome under the circumstances would certainly not have been in Serbia's favor. Izvolski thereupon accepted the German solution, and the Bosnian Crisis was ended.[49]

The outcome of the Bosnian Crisis was a diplomatic victory for Austria and Germany, and a corresponding humiliation for Russia and Serbia, with all the feeling of soreness which such humiliations leave behind. Izvolski never forgave Aehrenthal for his quick action in annexing Bosnia without further consultation and in refusing a Conference. He claimed that in both these matters Aehrenthal had broken his word and was no gentleman. Aehrenthal denied the truth of the allegations and threatened to publish the documents, whereupon Izvolski begged Germany to prevent the publication; upon Germany's advice, Aehrenthal refrained from carrying out his threat.

This personal feud between Izvolski and Aehrenthal had been transferred to the pages of the English *Fortnightly Review*, where the recriminations further embittered the two men. Count Berchtold, then Austrian Ambassador in St. Petersburg, became involved, because Dr. Dillon had found material for one of the *Fortnightly* articles at Berchtold's castle at Buchlau. So for nearly a year it was virtually impossible for Izvolski and Berchtold to carry on diplomatic intercourse with one another. In the meantime Izvolski succeeded in making a secret agreement with Italy at Racconigi,[50] by which, among other things, Italy promised to regard with benevolence Russia's interest in the Straits in return for Russia's similar promise in regard to Italy's interests in Tripoli. Izvolski was thus getting Italy's consent to what he had failed to secure by the Buchlau bargain, and Italy was taking another "extra dance" outside the circle of her own Triple Alliance partners.

It was not until early in 1910 that Izvolski and Aehrenthal again took up "normal diplomatic" relations. Rumors

[49] For the details, see below, ch. v.
[50] Oct. 24, 1909; see below, ch. v.

of their *rapprochement*, and even of a secret agreement between them, caused terror: at Belgrade it was feared that Russia was about to abandon Serbia to Austria's tender mercies; and at Constantinople it was feared that the partition of Turkey was being contemplated.[51] Even at Berlin there were fears that Izvolski, aided and abetted by France and England, was trying to make a secret agreement with Austria in order to drive another wedge into the Triple Alliance and sow discord between Berlin and Vienna.[52] For weeks Izvolski tried to pin Aehrenthal down to signing an agreement which would put Austria on record in favor of the *status quo* in the Balkans and which could be confirmed by being communicated to all the Great Powers. Izvolski wished publicly to tie Austria's hands in the Balkans, until Russia should have reorganized her army and navy and tightened up the Triple Entente to a more active support than France and England had given Russia during the Bosnian crisis. Aehrenthal, however, though ready to sign a private agreement with Russia, saw no need to communicate it to the Powers. After misunderstandings and recriminations, Izvolski finally published some of the correspondence without asking Aehrenthal's consent, an unfriendly act which still further accentuated the personal feud between them.[53] Meanwhile Izvolski went ahead with other maneuvers for securing Russia's ambitions in regard to the Straits and for forming a Balkan league under Russian patronage.[54]

The Bosnian Crisis had less disastrous effects upon the relations between Russia and Germany than upon those between Russia and Austria just described. Germany's

[51] Despatches from Russia's representatives at Constantinople and Belgrade, Feb. 2 and 4, 1910; Siebert-Schreiner, p. 285.

[52] G.P., XXVII, 438 ff.

[53] On this whole episode of an Austro-Russian "rapprochement", see Siebert-Schreiner, pp. 282-300. G.P., XXVII, 435-555.

[54] See below, ch. v.

intervention to end the crisis was, to be sure, soon exaggerated by Izvolski and Sir Arthur Nicolson, into a "brutal ultimatum" and denounced by the Pan-Slavs.[55] But though the Pan-Slav Press reserved its bitterest shafts for Germany and not Austria, the Russian Foreign Office, knowing the truth about Germany's intervention, manifested less resentment against Berlin than against Vienna. This was indicated in many ways. While Izvolski and Berchtold were not on speaking terms for months, the genial Pourtalès remained on the most cordial personal relations with the Russian Foreign Minister, partly because Izvolski found he could pour out into the German Ambassador's ear all his complaints about Aehrenthal's conduct.[56] Similarly, when the Tsar went to Racconigi in October, 1909, he ostentatiously avoided Austrian soil, although his obvious path lay across it; [57] but with the German Emperor, the Tsar had cordial meetings near Finland [58] and at Kiel.[59]

In September Izvolski passed through Berlin. Though travelling *incognito,* he made a point of dining with Bethmann-Hollweg and becoming acquainted with the new German Chancellor. They had a frank and friendly discussion of the general political situation, past, present, and future, in which Izvolski poured out his usual complaints about Aehrenthal "in a passionate and excited fashion, as if he had come directly from a duel with Aehrenthal"; [60] Izvolski hoped that Germany would restrain Aehrenthal from further reckless aggression in the Balkans, and assured Bethmann that Russia was far from pursuing any policy hostile to Germany. Both men agreed that the Press, especially the Russian Press, had done great harm.[61] This friendly relation was aided by Germany's continued policy of care-

---

[55] G.P., XXVI, 738 ff., 783 ff.   [56] G.P., XXVI, 810 ff.
[57] G.P., XXVII, 403 ff., 425; Siebert-Schreiner, pp. 148, 152.
[58] G.P., XXVI, 817-836.   [59] G.P., XXVI, 849 f.
[60] G.P., XXVI, 854.
[61] Bethmann's memorandum, Sept. 15, 1909; G.P., XXVI, 852-855.

fully refraining from all political interference in Persia,[62] where revolution and disorders were causing a sharp conflict of interests between Russia and England [63]—a situation which Germany regarded with perfect complacency. Germany's non-interference with Russia's "strangling" of Persia was ultimately rewarded by Russian concessions in regard to the Bagdad Railway embodied in the Potsdam Agreements. But before these are described a word may be said about Bülow's resignation and the new men who entered the German and Russian Foreign Offices in 1909 and 1910—the men who in July, 1914, were to have in their hands the fate of the world.

When Herr von Bethmann-Hollweg replaced Count Bülow at the Wilhelmstrasse in July, 1909, and Kiderlen-Wächter became Secretary of State a little later, Germany's international position seemed considerably improved. Count Bülow in his volume on *Imperial Germany* has pictured with characteristic optimism and excessive self-complacency the favorable position in which he left the country at his resignation. But the new Chancellor, reviewing the situation of 1909 in his *Reflections on the World War,* shows that the tasks which he inherited from Bülow were by no means light and easy.

The Moroccan Treaty of February 9, 1909, with France and the diplomatic triumph of Austria in the Bosnian Crisis had brought a feeling of relief at Berlin. The Triple Entente seemed definitely weakened and the danger of "encirclement" less alarming. On June 3, 1909, at a secret meeting attended by Tirpitz, Bethmann, Moltke, and Metternich, who had come over from London for it, Bülow declared that not for twenty years had Germany been so respected and feared in the world. The one dark cloud on

[62] G.P., XXVII, 721-824.
[63] *Cf.* Siebert-Schreiner, 49 ff.; Grey, I, 147-165; W. M. Shuster, *The Strangling of Persia* (New York, 1912).

the horizon was the Anglo-German situation; this looked like a thunder-storm; therefore he had called this meeting to consider it.[64] In April the Kaiser had severely scolded Metternich, among other things, for telling England that Germany intended no new naval program in the future; now it appeared that Tirpitz and the Kaiser were contemplating a supplementary navy law in 1912. Metternich replied that he had been expressly authorized by the Kaiser to speak as he had done, and that it was a pity he had not been told sooner, if Tirpitz now had it in mind to ask in 1912 for a further increase of the navy. He closed the letter with words which are as noble a tribute to his own character, as they are a condemnation of the Kaiser and his Admiral: "I am well aware that my attitude in the naval question, in which I have followed my duty in reporting repeatedly that this is the question which chiefly poisons our relations with England, does not meet the approval of His Majesty, and also that the Secretary of the Navy attacks my attitude in his talks with His Majesty. Naturally it is not pleasant for the head of the Navy that our building program and our relations to England depend on one another. But I should be falsifying history, if I reported otherwise than I do, and I cannot sell my convictions, even for the favor of my Sovereign. Also I am doubtful whether smooth and pleasant despatches, up to the point when we suddenly find ourselves face to face with war with England, would be a service to His Majesty." [65]

In the meeting of June 3, Bülow defended his Ambassador against the unmerited criticisms of Tirpitz and the Kaiser: "The first duty of His Majesty's representative abroad is to report the truth and picture conditions as they really are. He, Bülow, would always stand behind an Ambassador who did that, heedless of whether the unvar-

---

[64] Protocol of the meeting of June 3, 1909; G.P., XXVIII, 168-176.
[65] Metternich to Bülow, June 2, 1909; G.P., XXVIII, 167.

nished truth was pleasant or not to hear. It does no good to scold the barometer because it points to bad weather." [66]

In the course of the discussion Bethmann, Minister of the Interior, suggested that an agreement with England might be reached on the basis of Germany "slowing down" naval construction from four to three ships annually, if England would make concrete political offers in return. But Tirpitz blocked the path at every turn, refusing even the 4:3 ratio for British and German capital ships to which he had previously assented, and revealing a sly *reservatio mentalis:* if Germany slowed down from four to three new ships a year from 1909 to 1912, she might counterbalance this loss by speeding up from two to three in the following years, so that Germany's total number of Dreadnoughts would be the same around 1915 in either case. Though accepting in principle Bethmann's suggestion for slowing down, Tirpitz declined to fix or work out any formula to accomplish it, until the English had made concrete proposals. And in general he was in favor of "quietly waiting." This was very discouraging to Metternich and Bülow, and probably had much to do with Bülow's resignation on June 26, which was accepted by the Kaiser on July 14.

The ostensible reason for Bülow's resignation was the refusal of the Blue-Black-Bloc (the Conservative-Clerical coalition) on June 24 to vote the new finance bill, including a heavy inheritance tax, made necessary by the insatiable demands of new armaments. This gave Bülow a good excuse to retire from office. It was a motive which looked perfectly obvious to the public and has generally been accepted as the reason for his abandoning the Chancellorship after ten years of weary work. But as one reads his long struggle to defend Metternich's view in favor of naval limitation against Tirpitz's stubborn and slippery evasion

[66] G.P., XXVIII, 168 f.

of all worth-while concessions, and especially as one reads the protocol of the secret meeting of June 3, 1909, and the documents connected with it, one gets the impression that one of Bülow's main reasons for resigning was the opposition of Tirpitz and the Kaiser to the efforts for a reasonable naval agreement with England. Like Metternich, Bülow would no longer sell his convictions even for his Sovereign's favor. This reason, however, involving internal friction within the Government, the Kaiser's political influence, and relations with England, was one of which no hint must be given to the public. So the world has been left to believe that he parted from the Kaiser mainly for two reasons: first, because his finance bill was voted down in the Reichstag; and second, because the Kaiser was displeased with his inadequate defense of His Majesty in the *Daily Telegraph* affair some months earlier. But if Bülow's resignation was motivated, as suggested, by the naval question, then nothing in the exercise of his Chancellorship became him like the manner of his leaving it.

Bülow's "resignation with brilliants" was accepted on July 14. He received the Order of the Black Eagle, the highest distinction of the kind in the gift of the Kaiser. He had earned it, for no German Chancellor had so difficult a personal position, and yet acquitted himself so brilliantly. Easy-going, *débonnaire*, good-natured, and with an ever-ready wit, he had known how to handle Reichstag majorities no less cleverly than he had handled the All Highest. With something of Tirpitz's shrewd patience in evading commitments, but lacking the Admiral's powerful determination, clearness of purpose, and absolute self-reliance, Bülow had preferred to gain his ends by gentler methods, by his clever dialectical skill, and by his occasional withholding of the full truth or more often by obscuring it with his witty subtlety. He knew also how to humor, flatter, and disarm his opponents (enemies he had few or none), and the literary turn of his speeches and despatches makes them delightful reading. But his flippant habit of darkening counsel by amusing metaphors and his assumed optimism silenced healthy criticism and resulted in his piloting the ship of state into dangerous currents at the moment when he handed over the helm to Bethmann. He (and Holstein) were mainly responsible for the failure to grasp Chamberlain's proffered hand at the turn of the century, and for the other policies which led to the formation of the Triple Entente. The real hollowness of his achievement, which he painted *couleur de rose* in *Imperial Germany*, was revealed in the catastrophe of 1914. His reputation has exceeded his deserts. He will go down in history as a Chancellor of lost opportunities.

Some months before his resignation, Bülow had called to Berlin from the obscurity of Bucharest a man whom many regard as the best horse in the German stable since Bismarck's day. Herr von Kiderlen-Wächter certainly had something of the Iron Chancellor's forceful dominating energy and direct methods, but he lacked the readiness to see an opponent's point of view, and as far as possible meet it, which had been one of the secrets of Bismarck's diplomatic success. With his light-hearted Swabian warmth of temperament and levity of conversation, Kiderlen lacked also the moral force which gave Bismarck such a hold on the old Emperor and the German people. In his highly diverting daily letters to the beautiful blond whom he first met when he was forty and she thirty-eight, who never became his wife, but who often lived in his house, Kiderlen has left a fascinating record of personal devotion and of public affairs. Indiscreet, but not uninteresting, are the nicknames which he used to designate even the great ones of this world: "Eel" (Bülow, who was slippery); "Earthworm" (Bethmann, whom the Kaiser could tread upon); "Poor Beauty Boy" (a pun upon Schoen, whom Kiderlen replaced as Secretary of State in 1910); "Hippopotamus" (Marschall von Bieberstein); "The Sudden One" ("Der Plötzliche," *i.e.*, the Kaiser); and "Uncle *motu proprio*" (the Pope).[67] Kiderlen was a career diplomat with excellent training and opportunities for observation. Entering the Foreign Office in 1879 as a specialist in commercial matters, he had served as Embassy Secretary at St. Petersburg, Paris, and Constantinople (1881-1888), and then for ten years accompanied the Kaiser on his journeys as reporter for the Foreign Office. But some of his indiscreet witticisms were brought to the ears of the Kaiser, probably by a jealous Admiral, and the imperial displeasure was visited upon him by his being "exiled" to Bucharest.[68] As German Minister there from 1900 to 1910, he did much to cement the relations between Rumania and the Triple Alliance. In spite of the Kaiser's displeasure, Kiderlen's ability was recognized as so indispensable that his advice was often sought by Bülow. In the winter of 1908-1909, during Schoen's sickness, Kiderlen was at Berlin as Acting-Secretary of State. It was he, rather than Bülow, who brought about the Morocco Agreement of 1909 and the final settlement of the Bosnian Crisis. A year after Bülow's resignation, when Bethmann needed a strong and skilful diplomat at his elbow, Kiderlen was at last brought back from Bucharest for good, and given the office of Secretary of State, made vacant by Schoen's appointment as Ambassador to Paris (June, 1910). For two years and a half, until his sudden death at the very end of 1912, Kiderlen was Bethmann's *spiritus rector* at the Foreign Office, casting his influence in favor of keeping Austria in check, of good relations with Russia, of a naval understanding with England, and of the abandonment of all

---

[67] E. Jäckh, *Kiderlen-Wächter, der Staatsmann und Mensch* (2 vols., Berlin, 1925), *passim*. This delightful biography is largely made up of selections from Kiderlen's letters to Hedwig Kypke.

[68] E. Jäckh, I, 100 f.

claims in Morocco in return for compensations in the French Congo.[69]

Herr von Bethmann-Hollweg, who took over Bülow's difficult inheritance, lacked his predecessor's brilliance, but inspired more general confidence by his diligence, sincerity, and upright nobility of character, for which he was esteemed by all who knew him at home and abroad. "Somewhat idealistic and weak, but a suitable person," was Kiderlen's comment on hearing that out of the various candidates the Kaiser had picked an old friend of his youth.[70]   Trained as a jurist, Bethmann had risen by ability and hard work in the civil administration to the position of Imperial Secretary of State for the Interior, with which he was far better acquainted than with Foreign Affairs.   But he at once applied himself very diligently to getting personally well acquainted with all Germany's ambassadors and foreign ministers, and studied the Foreign Office despatches so assiduously that his subordinates feared he would lose himself in the details.   With the Kaiser Bethmann kept on intimate and friendly terms.

When both were in Berlin, they rode or walked almost daily together, discussing all political questions, in which the Kaiser had much wisdom as well as many prejudices. Bethmann was something of an idealist.   He ardently desired peace in Europe.   Therefore at heart he was opposed to greatly increased armaments.   He hoped for an understanding with England on the naval question, and believed it could be reached—Germany slowing down her rate of naval construction, and England in return making political concessions in connection with the Bagdad Railway and perhaps even some kind of agreement to be neutral.   The English were convinced of his sincerity in this purpose. Sir Edward Grey declared in 1912, after the Haldane Mission, that any possible differences between Germany and

[69] Jäckh, II, 79-232.   [70] Jäckh, II, 32.

England would never assume dangerous proportions, "so long as German policy was directed by the Chancellor"; upon which the Kaiser commented indignantly, "This shows that Grey has no idea who is really Master here and that I rule. He prescribes to me who my Minister shall be if I am to make an agreement with England." [71]

Bethmann's disinclination for increased armaments and his wish to make naval concessions brought him into conflict with the Kaiser, and he twice offered his resignation. But the Kaiser would not accept it because he had such confidence in Bethmann's character, and because he knew how highly he was esteemed abroad as an influence for peace. One may argue that Bethmann, for his own honor and conscience, ought to have insisted on his resignation being accepted, when he could not persuade the Kaiser to follow his advice rather than that of Tirpitz; that he ought to have put loyalty to his own conscience above personal loyalty to the Kaiser. But as he wrote rather pathetically to Kiderlen at New Year's, 1912: "Really this whole policy [of increased taxation for larger armaments] is such that I cannot join in it. That you know. But I ask myself ever and again whether I should not make the situation still more dangerous, if I should leave now, and then probably be not the only one." [72]   Thus, it was really loyalty to his country, rather than mere personal loyalty to the Kaiser, that made him compromise with his own conscience and remain in office as the spokesman of part at least of the measures demanded by the army and navy and approved by the Kaiser. It was the misfortune of Bethmann and of Germany that he never had a wholly free hand to carry out the policies which he favored. He continually had to contend against the influence of the army and navy officials who had direct access to the Emperor at any time, whereas

[71] Metternich to Bethmann, Mar. 17, 1912; G.P., XXXI, 182 f.
[72] Jäckh, II, 174.

Germany's ambassadors and Foreign Office secretaries could usually present their views only through the medium of the "civilian Chancellor."

In the Russian Foreign Office also a change took place. In September, 1910, Izvolski finally secured for himself the Russian Embassy in Paris and the generous salary attached to it. Ever since the fiasco of his effort to open the Straits by the Buchlau bargain and the humiliating outcome of the Bosnian Crisis, he had been the target of Pan-Slav attacks at home. He was also criticized by level-headed men like Kokovtsev and Krivoshein, the Ministers of Finance and Agriculture, who felt that he had brought Russia into a perilous situation in antagonizing Austria and Germany while the Russian army and navy were still a negligible quantity. Izvolski would have been glad to escape this fire of criticism at once by exchanging the Russian Foreign Office for the Paris Embassy. But he did not like to resign immediately after the Bosnian Crisis; this would be too patent an evidence of his own failure or the Tsar's displeasure. Nor had the Tsar any suitable person to put in his place. So Izvolski remained Minister of Foreign Affairs for a year and a half after the Bosnian Crisis, but spent many months abroad. During his absence in April and May, 1909, Charykov was in charge at the Singer's Bridge. When Charykov went as Ambassador to Constantinople in June, Sazonov took his place as Izvolski's chief assistant at the Foreign Office.[73]

M. Sergei Dimitrijevitch Sazonov, who became Russian Minister of Foreign Affairs upon Izvolski's transfer to Paris in September, 1910, was by nature of a mercurial and emotional temperament. In his youth it is said that he intended becoming a monk, but gave it up on account of his bad

---

[73] On Izvolski and his critics in Russia from March, 1909, to Sept., 1910, see the despatches of Hintze and Pourtalès, in G.P., XXVI, 737 ff., 777 ff., 801 ff., 855 ff.; XXVII, 521 ff; and Sazonov, *Fateful Years*, ch. i.

health and entered the diplomatic service.   Slim and rather small of stature, with a nervous and abrupt manner, he always gave an impression of being frail in body and change-able in mind.   In June, 1904, he became Counsellor to the Embassy in London, where he remained three years and acquired a friendly attitude toward England.   In 1907, he was transferred to the Vatican, a pleasant but unimportant post which he filled for two years.   In June, 1909, he re-turned to St. Petersburg as Assistant Minister of Foreign Affairs under Izvolski.   His selection to succeed Izvolski in 1910 was, therefore, not unnatural.   His appointment was recommended by Izvolski, who thought there was no one else better fitted for the office.

In Russian domestic politics, Sazonov was conservative, solidly in favor of the retention of old Russian institutions and little in sympathy with the constitutional movement brought about by the Russo-Japanese War.   In foreign pol-itics, he was an ardent patriot.   His lips trembled with emotion as he once remarked that he could not survive a second defeat such as Russia had suffered in her unfortunate war with Japan.[74]   The German Ambassador at St. Peters-burg described him as "filled with glowing patriotism bor-dering on chauvinism.   When he talks of past events in which he thinks Russia has suffered injustice, his face as-sumes an almost fanatical expression.   Nevertheless, dis-cussion with him is much easier and pleasanter than with Izvolski, because he always observes form, remains master of himself, and does not emphasize personal matters." [75]

Toward Germany Sazonov was favorably inclined per-sonally.   His grandmother was German and he had many personal relations with Germany.   When he talked with Bethmann, he preferred to use German rather than French.

[74] Mühlberg, German Ambassador in Rome, to Bülow June 11, 1909; G.P., XXVI, 809.

[75] Pourtalès to Bethmann, Aug. 23, 1910; *ibid.*, 867.

He had much sympathy with the large group at the Tsar's court who wished to see restored the old cordial relations between Germany and Russia, who looked to Berlin rather than to Paris and London, and whose shibboleth was monarchical solidarity rather than constitutional democracy. To this group belonged Baron Fredericks, the venerable, influential, and universally respected Master of the Tsar's Household; Kokovtsev, Minister of Finance; Krivoshein, Minister of Agriculture; to a certain extent Stolypin, the Premier; Witte, who was out of office, but still influential; and a large number of "Baltic Germans" who by their ability had acquired a great number of civil and military offices in the Tsar's empire. But Sazonov also believed, like so many Pan-Slavs, that Bismarck had done Russia a great injustice at the Congress of Berlin, as had Bülow in the Bosnian Crisis. Nevertheless, he wanted to coöperate with Germany and reëstablish mutual confidence. He therefore welcomed the visit which the Tsar was to pay the Kaiser at Potsdam in November, 1910.

Sazonov, like Bethmann, was sincerely desirous of peace. But, as will appear in more detail in the next chapter, he was very nervous at any advance of Austrian or German influence in the Balkans which might endanger Russia's historic mission of acquiring control of the Bosphorus and the Dardanelles and even of Constantinople. He was also very sensitive to the criticism of the Pan-Slav Press. It is true that hardly ten per cent of the Russian people could read at all, and a still smaller proportion paid any attention to newspapers, so that there was in Russia no general "public opinion" in the Western sense of the word. Nevertheless Russian newspapers did exercise a much stronger influence on Russian foreign policy than is usually supposed, both through their criticisms of ministers at home and through their attacks on statesmen abroad. With the Russian Revolution of 1905, the establishment of the Duma,

and the formation of the Entente with the two great de-
mocracies of the West, a majority of the Russian Press had
become "liberal" in domestic matters, and strongly Anglophil and Francophil in foreign politics. It attacked Germany as the stronghold of absolutism and reaction, and as
the instigator and protector of Austrian aggressions in the
Balkans. It demanded that Russian Foreign Ministers
should extend protection and help to the Slavs of the Balkans in their struggle to emancipate themselves from the
Turkish and Hapsburg yoke. It had therefore been very
bitter in condemning Izvolski's Buchlau bargain, which had
placed Orthodox Greek Serbs under Austrian rule. It attacked Germany no less than Austria as the enemy of the
Slav cause. It was this Pan-Slav Press of which Sazonov,
timid by nature and none too secure in his official position,
was in constant fear during the next four years. It drove
him at times into a stronger support of Serbia and a sharper
antagonism to Austria and Germany than he personally
favored himself. It partly accounts for the changeableness
and instability of his policies, which worried France and
England as well as Germany. Pourtalès, the shrewd German Ambassador at St. Petersburg frequently noted how
Sazonov's attitude seemed to shift, now one way and now
another, in accordance with the rise and fall of the wave
of Pan-Slav Press criticism and the militarist influence of
the Grand Duke Nicholas and his bellicose circle. In fact,
between 1908 and 1914, there was no single topic which was
so frequently a subject of complaint and discussion between
representatives of Germany and Russia as the malign influence of the Pan-Slav and Pan-German Press in stirring up
bad blood between the two countries. After the Bosnian
Crisis, for instance, "Willy" wrote to "Nicky":

> A few weeks ago, when affairs threatened to become
> dangerous, your wise and courageous decision secured peace
> among the nations. I was most gratified that by my co-

operation you were able to fulfil your task. I
very naturally expected that you and I would win universal applause, for I ventured to think that we have earned
the gratitude of all well-meaning people. But to my regret
and astonishment I observe that a great many blame us
both instead. Especially the press has behaved in the
basest way against me. By some papers I am credited with
being the author of annexation and am accused amongst
other rot and nonsense of having humiliated Russia by my
proposal. Of course you know better. Yet the fact must be
taken note of that the papers mostly create public opinion.
Some of the papers err through their ignorance and lack of
correct information; they can scarcely see farther than their
nose's length. But more dangerous and at the same time
loathesome is that part of the press which writes what it is
paid for. The scoundrels who do such dirty work, are in no
fear of starving. They will always incite the hostility of
one nation against the other and when at last, by their
hellish devices, they have brought about the much desired
collision, they sit down and watch the fight which they or-
ganized, resting well assured that the profit will be theirs,
no matter what the issue may be. In this way in 99 cases
out of a hundred, what is vulgarly called "public opinion"
is a mere forgery.[76]

To this the Tsar replied: "Everything you write about
the Press, as you know from our previous conversations, I
agree with completely. It is one of the curses of modern
times." [77]

In his discussions with the German Ambassador at St.
Petersburg concerning the Press, Sazonov sometimes argued
that what the Russian Press said was of little or no importance; that the German Government and the German Press
made a mistake in paying so much attention to it; that it
represented the views only of a small group of uninfluential
Russian fanatics. But at other times the Russian Foreign

[76] May 8, 1909; G.P., XXVI, 786 f.   [77] G.P., XXVI, 788 note

Minister contradicted himself by using an exactly opposite line of argument: he must do this or he could not do that, because he had to have regard for public opinion and what the newspapers would say. His opponents might force him from office if in the interests of the peace of Europe he made too great concessions to Germany or failed adequately to safeguard Russia's national ambitions and to protect the Balkan Slavs. When he took this line he was much nearer the real facts of the situation. Pourtalès recognized this, and frequently urged the German Government not to make Sazonov's position unnecessarily difficult and embarrassing.

But it would be a mistake to think that Sazonov was wholly innocent of all connection with the Press which he genuinely feared. On the contrary, the Russian Foreign Office stood in close touch with *Novoe Vremia* and other papers which were most chauvinist and critical in tone. Sazonov (or his subordinates) often furnished the information and arguments which these papers were to use against Germany. He thus stirred them up to a nationalist campaign, behind which he would take refuge as a justification of the policy which he was "compelled by public opinion" to adopt. In critical negotiations with Germany, as in the Potsdam Agreements and the Liman von Sanders affair, important secrets often "leaked" from the Russian Foreign Office to the representatives of the Russian (and also of the French and English) Press in St. Petersburg; when matters thus got into the newspapers, they raised questions of prestige which made it more difficult for both Governments to make concessions toward a reasonable compromise settlement.[78]

There were also journalists outside Russia who wrote in the Pan-Slav cause, and who exercised an influence on

[78] For a few of Pourtalès's more important accounts of the Russian Press and Sazonov's relations with it, see G.P., XXVII, 844 f., 851 ff., 885, 890 ff., 924 ff.; XXXVIII, 226, 253 ff., 269, 293 ff., 300 f.; XXXIX, 540-589, *passim. Cf.* also *Journal Intime de Alexis Souvorine*, Paris, 1927.

Sazonov while at the same time receiving funds from the Russian Foreign Office. Of these the most important was Wesselitzki, the London correspondent of the *Novoe Vremia*. He had been given subsidies and the use of a summer villa at St. Petersburg when Izvolski was Minister of Foreign Affairs. "These expenditures were not in vain," wrote Izvolski in 1911, when urging that his successors at the Russian Foreign Office should continue to subsidize Wesselitzki.[79] As president of the Foreign Press Association in London, and in his frequent visits to foreign capitals, as well as in the materials which he contributed to the *Novoe Vremia*, Wesselitzki took every opportunity to sow discord between Russia and Germany and to tighten up the bonds between the members of the Triple Entente. Complaints of his mischievous activities and of the articles which he wrote under the pseudonym "Argus," appear frequently in the recently published German documents.[80]

After this brief digression on Bethmann and Sazonov, and the forces which influenced their policies, we may now return to an account of their negotiations in 1910-1911.

Izvolski's departure to Paris in September, 1910, left Sazonov and the Tsar free to carry out their desire of establishing more cordial relations with Germany. Though the Kaiser was still suspicious and much irritated at what he regarded as Russia's unfriendly Anglophil attitude since 1907, Bethmann and Kiderlen were ready to meet the Russians more than half way on their visit to Potsdam in November, 1910. Kiderlen hoped to clear up misunderstandings and so to lessen the opposition which had grown

[79] Izvolski to Neratov, Nov. 23, 1911; M.F.R., p. 138; Stieve, I. 181. For a detailed statement of the "reptile funds" distributed to Russian newspapers in 1914, with names and amounts, totalling nearly a million rubles, see I. I. Tobolin, "Reptilnyi Fond, 1914-1916", in *Krasnyi Arkhiv*, X, 332-338 (1925).

[80] *Cf.* especially G.P., XXV, 442 ff., and the index references, *ibid.*, p. 701; also XXVII, 440, 447 ff., 501 ff.

up between the Triple Entente and Triple Alliance. Neither
Germany nor Russia were to be expected to modify in any
way their respective alliances. But he was ready to assure
Russia that Germany was neither bound nor inclined to
support any new Austrian ambitions in the Balkans. Nor
was Germany pursuing any political aims of her own in
the Near East; she regarded the Badgad Railway primarily
as an economic enterprise; and she merely wanted to see
Turkey maintained intact, in the interests of peace and
the *status quo*. There were many subjects in which Russian and German interests ran parallel, and it would be
desirable to discuss them confidentially but frankly, and
thus put an end to mutual recriminations and restore the
friendly contact which had been lost under Izvolski's management of Russian foreign policy.[81]

These views met with a warm response from the new
Russian Minister. Sazonov declared that the Bosnian
Crisis belonged to the past and would not influence Russian
policy in the future. Russia no longer had any expansionist
policy. Her single task was her own internal consolidation.
Russia's agreement of 1907 aimed purely to put an end to
friction in the Middle East. If England pursued an anti-
German policy, she would not find Russia on her side.
Russia and Germany were neighbors and ought to live on
good terms.[82]

As to Persia, the Germans again declared that they had
no political aims in that troubled country, but wanted the
"open door" for their commerce, which was handicapped
by the Russian tariff charged upon goods in transit and by

[81] Kiderlen's memorandum, Oct. 30, 1910. G.P., XXVII, 832-834.
Also Bethmann's private letter to Aehrenthal of Nov. 14, in which the
German Chancellor frankly informed Aehrenthal of the Potsdam conversations, and especially of the fact that he had felt able to assure
Sazonov "that Austria-Hungary is not contemplating any kind of expansion
policy in the Balkans", and that Germany had never bound herself
to support any such Austrian plans (*ibid.*, 850).

[82] Bethmann to Kaiser Nov. 1, 1910; G.P., XXVII, 835-837.

lack of good communications. Sazonov replied that the
anarchical conditions in Northern Persia made it impossible for Russia to withdraw her troops. But if Germany
would withdraw from all railway and telegraph projects in
the Russian sphere in Persia, Russia would withdraw all
discriminating tariffs and other obstacles to the importation of German goods into Persia. To open up the country
Russia proposed to extend her railway system from the
Caucasus via Tabriz and Teheran to the western frontier
of Persia at Khanikin; and the Germans could then build a
line to connect Khanikin and the Bagdad Railway. Bethmann understood that "Russia would no longer lay any
obstacles in the way of the construction of the Bagdad Railway as far as Bagdad." In his report to the Tsar on the
Potsdam meeting, Sazonov said "the question of the Bagdad
Railway was not raised"; though he admitted that he told
Bethmann that "if other interested Powers were to participate in this line, Russia could not remain empty-handed
and would then want to have the Khanikin-Bagdad
section." [83]

In his audience with the Kaiser Sazonov had been impressed with the Kaiser's irritation against England's naval
policy, his fears of a "preventive attack," and his hope that
the German fleet would soon have assumed proportions
which would make England afraid to incur this risk. He
had also tried to draw the Kaiser's attention to the danger
to Russia, with her twenty million Mohammedan subjects,
arising from the Pan-Islam propaganda.

The Potsdam conversations were cordial and frank on
both sides. Bethmann and Sazonov each got a very favorable impression of the other. An excellent start was made
in removing suspicions and in bringing the two countries

---

[83] Bethmann to Pourtalès, Nov. 8, 1910; G.P., XXVII, 840 ff.; Sazonov's report to the Tsar, Nov. 4/17, 1910; *Krasnyi Arkhiv*, III, 5-8; L.N.,
II, 331-334.

back into the old paths from which they had strayed as a result of Izvolski's active Entente policy and unsuccessful Balkan ambitions. As the substance of the conversations had not been confirmed in writing, Bethmann drew up for Sazonov's approval a statement in general terms as the basis of a reference which he wished to make on the subject in his coming Reichstag speech. He also drafted nine paragraphs which he hoped Sazonov would sign, with such modifications as he saw fit, as a more precise written formulation of the Potsdam conversations.[84]

But Sazonov caused difficulties. On returning home, he seems to have feared criticism from the Pan-Slav Press. He had therefore, without consulting Germany, given an interview to the *Novoe Vremia*. This paper then published an account exaggerating the points conceded by Germany and minimizing those conceded by Russia. Sazonov explained apologetically to Pourtalès that he wished to turn aside the possible wrath of this section of the Russian Press.[85] To Pourtalès he gave also his full approval of the statement which was to be the basis of Bethmann's Reichstag speech. One sentence of this hinted at a point to which Kiderlen attached the greatest importance: "The result of the last interview I might sum up as a renewed assurance that both Governments will not enter into any sort of combination which could have an aggressive tendency against the other." [86] But neither to the Tsar, nor to the Press, nor apparently to the Ambassadors of France

---

[84] G.P., XXVII, 846 ff.   [85] G.P., XXVII, 844 f., 851 ff.

[86] G.P., XXVII, 849, 855. One may note an interesting difference between Bethmann, the sincere seeker for a business-like agreement on economic questions like commerce in Persia and the Bagdad Railway, and Kiderlen, the more subtle politician concerned in the play of the system of alliances. To Bethmann, "the only essential things in the Potsdam conversations are the Persian and the Bagdad Railway questions" (*ibid.*, 842), But for Kiderlen, "the assurance of Russia concerning her relation to England is for me the alpha and omega of the whole agreement" (*ibid.*, 862).

and England, did Sazonov say a word of this general political understanding by which Russia promised not to support
any policy hostile to Germany which England or France
might undertake. He doubtless feared it might cause irritation in London and Paris. Therefore he gave evasive or
dilatory replies to Pourtalès's efforts to get him to sign a
written statement, such as the nine paragraphs which Bethmann had drafted, in which were precisely formulated the
points relating to general policy as well as the specific
agreements concerning Persia and the Bagdad Railway.
He suggested that the two sets of points be dealt with in
separate documents, and finally preferred not to sign any
statement at all on general policy, asserting that the verbal
promises of ministers, and especially of the Kaiser and the
Tsar, were much more valuable than any exchange of
written notes.[87]

Meanwhile Bethmann's Reichstag speech of December
10, 1910, summing up the Potsdam interview as a renewed
assurance that Germany and Russia would not enter into
any hostile combinations one against the other, had fallen
like a bomb in Paris and London,[88] where Sazonov had
allowed the impression to prevail that Persia and the
Bagdad Railway were the only important questions discussed. The newly appointed English Ambassador in St.
Petersburg, Sir George Buchanan, now hastened to present
his credentials to the Tsar. He emphasized England's
earnest wish to see the Anglo-Russian understanding maintained and consolidated, and expressed his anxiety concerning Sazonov's negotiations with Germany. Whereupon
the Tsar, always inclined to agree with whoever had his
ear at the moment, assured Buchanan that Russia "would
conclude no arrangement with Germany without first submitting it to His Majesty's Government." [89]

---

87 G.P., XXVII, 879 ff.   88 G.P., XXVII, 888 ff.; XXIX, 61 f.
89 Buchanan, *My Mission to Russia*, I, 93; *cf.* Sazonov, *Fateful Years*
ch. ii.

Pourtalès, shrewdly suspecting that English pressure explained Sazonov's evasive attitude, decided it was useless to press further for a signed statement on general policy. He therefore accepted with apparent grace and trust Sazonov's suggestion that merely verbal promises sufficed concerning general policy, and that the details of the Persian question could be left to a written agreement. Sazonov was much relieved in his mind at this.[90]

Accordingly, in the course of the next six months, a Russo-German agreement on the Middle East was gradually worked out. The negotiations were delayed by England's constant efforts to limit the entrance of German influence into Persia, and to secure control or participation in the section of the railway from Bagdad down to the Persian Gulf. There was also some recrimination over the publication in the London *Evening Times* of the secret draft treaty under discussion, the Russians and Germans each suspecting the other of being responsible for the "leak." But the Agadir Crisis caused Germany to make concessions and the agreement was finally signed on August 19, 1911. Germany disclaimed economic concessions (railways, roads, navigation, and telegraphs) in the Russian sphere in Persia; there were provisions for an eventual Russian railway in Persia from Teheran to the western border at Khanikin, and for linking this by a German branch line to the Bagdad Railway; and most important for Germany—Russia would no longer place obstacles in the way of the construction of the Bagdad Railway or in the participation of foreign capital.[91]

The Potsdam conversations in no way troubled the solidarity of the Triple Alliance, because Germany had kept

[90] G.P., XXVII, 875-883.

[91] *Krasnyi Arkhiv,* III (1923), 10-13; G.P., XXVII, 957 f.; for the negotiations, *ibid.,* 905-963; Siebert-Schreiner, pp. 501-576; the Izvolski-Sazonov correspondence, *passim,* in M.F.R., L.N., and Stieve; and Earle, ch. x.

Austria promptly informed of all her steps, and because
Austria had no special interests in the Middle East. But
the serenity of the Triple Entente was considerably ruffled
by Sazonov's separate negotiations with Germany in a field
where England and France had very active interests. M.
Pichon, the French Minister of Foreign Affairs, was severely
criticized in the Chamber of Deputies and in the Press for
not safeguarding French interests and the solidarity of the
Entente. Prominent men like M. Hanotaux in France, and
Mr. Lloyd George in England, asked whether Sazonov's
conduct was not leading to a dissolution of the Triple Entente. No little irritation was felt in Paris and London
at Sazonov's independent course of action and departure
from the Anglo-French standpoint that all Bagdad Railway
negotiations ought to be à quatre.[92]

In the end, however, Russia's withdrawal of opposition
to Germany's cherished desire of pushing the Bagdad Railway to completion opened the way for Germany's successful negotiations with Turkey and with England for
further mutually advantageous arrangements. Germany
acquired docks at Alexandretta and a branch line from there
northward by which railway materials could be more easily
imported for extending construction east of the Taurus
Mountains. The Powers consented to an increase of the
Turkish tariff from 11% to 15%, which would provide
funds for paying the railway guarantees. England was
given two of the seats on the Board of Directors of the
Bagdad Railway Company, assured a dominant position in
the navigation rights and oil resources of southern Mesopotamia, and largely relieved of her fears that the Bagdad
Railway would be a German menace to the safety of India.
The negotiations for all these arrangements were protracted

[92] Cf. G.P., XXVII, 855, 887 ff.; XXIX, 61 ff.; Siebert-Schreiner,
pp. 527 ff.; Earle, p. 241 ff.; Sazonov, p. 34 f.; and Stieve and Montgelas,
Russland und der Weltkonflikt, p. 39 f.

over three years, but had been successfully concluded on June 15, 1914, two weeks before the Sarajevo assassination; the agreements lacked only the final signatures at the moment they were tossed to the winds by the outbreak of the World War.[93]

The Potsdam conversations and agreements of 1910-1911 are another indication of the fact that questions of economic imperialism are far easier for Governments to handle successfully than questions affecting prestige, alliances, or armaments; in fact the former may sometimes serve as a convenient bridge to the latter.

While Germany was thus on the way toward better relations with Russia in the summer of 1911, her relations with the two other members of the Triple Entente were suddenly made much worse by a new Morocco crisis.

THE AGADIR CRISIS, 1911

The Franco-German Morocco Agreement of 1909 was at first lived up to loyally by both parties. Pichon and Bethmann both made cordial public statements to that effect in the fall of 1909. But gradually friction developed again. The Mannesmann Brothers had acquired from Mulai Hafid certain mining rights not recognized by the French, which conflicted with the claims of the international "Union des Mines Marocaines." The Franco-German consortium for the development of the Cameroon-Congo trade had finally to be given up, on account of the protests of the French nationalists that the Germans were getting the greater advantage, and the Germans were then left seriously embarrassed. The disorders in the country gave the French a pretext for a steady extension of their police and military control, and Mulai Hafid was forced by an ultimatum to accept a loan which brought him more

[93] On the Bagdad Railway negotiations between 1911 and 1914, see G.P., XXXI, 71-377; XXXVII, 141-470; Earle, pp. 244-274.

completely under French domination. It gradually became
clearer and clearer that with this extension of French influence the equality of economic opportunity contemplated
in the 1909 Agreement, and the idea of an independent
Sultan at the head of a well-regulated government, were
both fictions in contradiction with the actual trend of
events. Nevertheless the fictions served as a basis for
friendly relations between France and Germany for two
years.[94]

The military and financial methods of the French had
not endeared them to the Moroccan chieftains. The latter
resented Mulai Hafid's subservience to the French and the
continual encroachments upon their own national independence. The native discontent came to a head in March,
1911, after Colonel Mangin's public execution of a couple
of Moroccan soldiers caught in the act of deserting. A revolt broke out in Fez. Alarming reports were sent out by
the French that the lives of Europeans in Fez were in
danger. On April 5, Jules Cambon, the French Ambassador
in Berlin, informed Germany that the murder of Captain
Marchand and the other disorders in Morocco would probably make it necessary for the French to occupy Rabat and
send a punitive expedition into the Shawia district as well
as a military force to rescue the Europeans in Fez. He
added that this action was only due to extreme necessity,
to preserve the sovereignty of the Sultan, and would be
exercised in accordance with the spirit of the Algeciras Act.
Kiderlen, who mainly directed Germany's policy in the
Agadir affair, replied that he understood perfectly the
anxiety of the French Government as to the fate of the

[94] On Moroccan affairs after 1909 see French Yellow Book, *Affaires
du Maroc*, V, VI; the German White Book of 1910, *Denkschrift und
Aktenstücke über deutsche Bergwerksinteressen in Marokko;* G.P., XXIX,
1-70; P. Albin, *Le Coup d'Agadir* (Paris, 1912); A. Tardieu, *Le Mystère
d'Agadir* (Paris, 1912); J. Caillaux, *Agadir, Ma Politique Extérieure*
(Paris, 1919).

Europeans in Fez, but that the French occupation of a
second port like Rabat, in addition to Casablanca, would be
likely to excite rather than allay the passions of the natives; it might also arouse public feeling in Germany and
look like a further step toward the elimination of the Algeciras Agreement. He hoped that the French would delay
military occupation as long as possible, and that Moroccan
affairs could be satisfactorily arranged between Germany
and France—a hint at compensations for Germany which
Cambon clearly understood.[95] A little later Cambon reaffirmed that France would respect the Act of Algeciras and
withdraw the troops as soon as order had been restored
at Fez.

Kiderlen did not give an approval nor lodge a formal protest, but pointed out warningly that in cases like Fez it
was easier to occupy a city than to withdraw again; and
if French troops remained in Fez, so that the Sultan reigned
only under cover of French bayonets, Germany could no
longer regard him as the independent sovereign contemplated by the Algeciras Act; this and the Agreement of 1909
would fall to the ground, and Germany would reassume
complete liberty of action.[96] The Kaiser, on the other hand,
when he heard the news of massacres in Fez and the flight
of Mulai Hafid into the French Consulate, said the French
ought to send a large force; Germany had no reason to
hinder it, as it would divert French troops and military
expenditure from Germany's western frontier; if the French
infringed the Algeciras Agreement, let other Powers, like

[95] *Affaires du Maroc,* VI, 179 f., 185, 189 ff; Caillaux, *Agadir,* 257 ff.;
G.P., XXIX, 78 ff.

[96] Kiderlen's note of April 28; G.P., XXIX, 97 f.; *Affaires du Maroc,*
VI, 247 f. The English at first had somewhat the same feeling; Sir
Arthur Nicolson, said the Russian Ambassador in London, "did not
conceal from me the fact that the Morocco question is disquieting the
London Cabinet. . . . The experience of all European States, beginning
with England, shows that it is easier to occupy a city than to withdraw
again" (Benckendorff to Neratov. May 9, 1911; Siebert-Schreiner, p. 581).

Spain, protest; the Foreign Office ought to check the clamor that warships should be sent to Morocco.[97]

How far the French reports of disorders represented a genuine fear that their authority and European lives were endangered, and how far they were exaggerated as a pretext for securing a stronger grasp on the country, it is difficult to say. That they had been steadily extending their political grip on Morocco, and intended eventually to reduce it to a French protectorate, there is no doubt. Kiderlen likened it to the spread of oil upon water.[98] When the Russian Ambassador in Paris asked M. Cruppi, the French Minister of Foreign Affairs, how long the French would remain in Fez, the Minister answered evasively.[99] And Caillaux, who became Prime Minister in June 1911, has declared: "Our problem was nothing less than to regain all the ground lost since 1905, and to repair the consequences of the serious diplomatic check which we had suffered." [100]

In 1905, it will be remembered, Delcassé had been forced from office; but Delcassé was now back in the Cabinet again, just as the French were preparing to occupy Rabat and march to Fez. To be sure, he had only the naval portfolio, and the Prime Minister, Monis, had assured the German Ambassador that, "he had taken Delcassé into his cabinet on account of his notable work in the navy, and because his great technical knowledge was indispensable. Delcassé has firmly promised not to mix in foreign policy; anyway, his views today differ from those of some years ago." [101] But it was natural that, with his restless energy and memory of the past, Delcassé was suspected by the German Press of having a hand in the Moroccan policy, and later events

[97] Kaiser to Bethmann, April 22; XXIX, 89.
[98] G.P., XXIX, p. 169 f.
[99] Izvolski to Neratov, May 24, 1911; L.N., I, 107.
[100] Caillaux, *Agadir*, p. 29.
[101] Schoen to Bethmann, March 4, 1911; G.P., XXIX, 74 note.

proved he had remained as determined an opponent of Germany as ever.[102] He told Izvolski that "his entrance into the Cabinet indicated the special care which would be devoted to France's military forces. His first task was the creation of a strong navy, and the efforts for the army would be redoubled. Although he had no intention of overstepping his office and arousing distrust in Germany," he was anxious to tighten up the relations with Russia. "According to general opinion, he will inevitably influence the activity of M. Cruppi, as the latter is very little versed in foreign affairs." [103]

Germany's intentions were a puzzle to the French at the time, and have remained something of a mystery, but they are now clear from a long memorandum which Kiderlen drew up on May 3 (greatly condensed):

> Three years have shown that the independence of Morocco, as contemplated in Algeciras Act, cannot be maintained in the face of native rebellion and imperialistic pressure from France and Spain. Sooner or later Morocco will inevitably be absorbed by these two neighbors. It is unlikely that a walled city like Fez can be captured by the natives and the revolt seems to be on the ebb. But the French fear for its safety and are preparing to send an expedition. This they have a right to do, and one must await the development of events. But if they march to Fez, it is hardly likely that they will withdraw; even if French public opinion approved withdrawal, it would be regarded by the natives as a sign of weakness. This would lead to new uprisings and new French military expeditions. The course of events shows that the provisions of the Act of Algeciras cannot be carried out. A Sultan who can only assert his authority with the aid of French bayonets can-

---

102 "In some of the German papers, Delcassé is regarded as the true originator of French Moroccan policy" (Russian Chargé d'Affaires at Berlin to Sazonov, April 28, 1911; Siebert-Schreiner, p. 580).

103 Izvolski to Sazonov, March 3 and 14, 1911; M.F.R., pp. 41, 43; L.N., I, 45, 48; Stieve I, 38, 41.

not maintain the independence which was the purpose of
the Algeciras Act. Germany must recognize these facts and
readjust her policy in accordance with them. After the
French have been in Fez a while, we shall ask in a friendly
way when they expect to withdraw. When they say that
they cannot withdraw, we shall say that we understand this
perfectly, but we cannot longer regard the Sultan as a sovereign independent ruler as provided by the Act of Algeciras;
and since this is a dead letter, the Signatory Powers regain
their freedom of action. It will do no good to protest
against the French absorption of Morocco. We must therefore secure an object which will make the French ready to
give us compensations. Just as the French protect their
subjects in Fez, we can do the same for ours at Mogador
and Agadir by peacefully stationing ships there. We can
then await developments and see if the French will offer us
suitable compensations. If we get these, it will make up for
past failures and have a good effect on the coming elections
to the Reichstag.[104]

The Kaiser was persuaded to approve this policy, though
he ought to have foreseen that the *modus operandi* was
dangerously analogous to that of Bülow and Holstein in
1905. He then departed for England to attend the unveil-
ing of a memorial to Queen Victoria. Here he was cordially
received, and got the impression that the English regarded
the French Morocco action with regret. Sir Ernest Cassel
and Prince Louis of Battenberg hinted that they hoped that
German policy would not differentiate itself from that of
England. But the Kaiser and Bethmann saw no reason for
taking the hint, because Germany had not been consulted
by England about Morocco in 1904, nor by Russia at
Reval.[105]

[104] G.P. XXIX, 101-108.
[105] Bethmann's memorandum, May 23; *ibid.*, p. 120 f. Sir Edward
Grey, however, reminded the German Ambassador on May 22, that in
Moroccan questions England was bound by her agreement of 1904 to
support France (*ibid.*, p. 119; Siebert-Schreiner, p. 583).

At the outset Kiderlen's program bade fair to work excellently. As the Pan-German Press began to demand compensations or the partition of Morocco, and the German Government maintained an ominous silence as to how it would use its freedom of action, the French began to be worried. Izvolski reported that so far as he was able to judge, "the Berlin Cabinet has chosen a very advantageous and skilful position: without protesting as yet against the French manner of action, it reserves the power of announcing at any moment that the Algeciras Act has been infringed—in this way German diplomacy dominates the situation and can, not only according to the development of events on the spot, but also according to the general trend of her domestic or foreign policy, suddenly render the Moroccan question more acute. . . . Sir Francis Bertie is personally convinced that Germany is only awaiting a suitable moment to declare the Act of Algeciras non-existent and then occupy one or two ports (including Mogador) on the Atlantic coast of Morocco." [106] A fortnight after the French military expedition occupied Fez, the Spanish troops landed at Larache. The French in turn denounced this action as a blow to the Algeciras Act and as endangering the international situation.[107]

By the middle of June the French intimated that they were ready to talk of a compensation for Germany; Cambon hinted at it very guardedly on June 11, when speaking of Morocco as a ripe fruit which must inevitably fall to France; [108] and Cruppi in Paris mentioned it in connection with a Congo-Cameroon railway project, but Kiderlen regarded this as a mere bagatelle. He wanted the whole French Congo! [109] But he did not want to ask for it until

[106] Izvolski to Sazonov, May 11, 1911; M.F.R., p. 88; L.N., I, 104; Stieve, I, 98 f.
[107] G.P., XXIX, 140 ff.; *Affaires du Maroc,* VI, 332 ff.
[108] G.P., XXIX, 124, 177 note; *Affaires du Maroc,* VI, 349 f.
[109] G.P., XXIX, 149 ff.

the appearance of a German ship at Agadir had frightened
the French into coming forward with a very generous offer
in return for Germany's abandoning Morocco to them
completely.[110]

When therefore Cambon came to Kissingen to broach
the subject with him on June 20, Kiderlen took an attitude of reserve.   When Cambon intimated that France
would be willing to make concessions in the Congo, but that
there was no use talking further if Germany wanted part of
Morocco, Kiderlen agreed completely.   When Cambon left
Kissingen for Paris to see how much his Government would
offer, Kiderlen's last words were, "Bring us back something
from Paris." [111]   As several days passed without any French
offer being made, and as the Kaiser was about to start on
his northern cruise, Kiderlen went to Kiel to report on the
situation and get a renewal of his consent to send warships
to Morocco.   On June 26 Kiderlen's laconic telegram,
"Ships granted," indicated that he had secured the Kaiser's
approval.   Accordingly, the gunboat *Panther*, returning
from southern Africa, was ordered to drop anchor at Agadir
on July 1.[112]

On Saturday afternoon, July 1, as the *Panther* steamed
into Agadir, Germany notified France and the other Powers
that German business houses, alarmed at the fermentation
among the natives caused by recent events, had asked for
protection for their life and property in southern Morocco;
the German Government had therefore sent a warship to
Agadir, which would withdraw as soon as affairs in Morocco
had calmed down.[113]   It was true that German firms had
petitioned the Foreign Office to protect their interests in
southern Morocco,[114] but it is clear Kiderlen was using this

---

110 Zimmermann's memorandum, June 12, and Kiderlen's comments;
ibid., 142 ff., 177 ff., 184 ff.; also Jäckh, II, 123 ff.

111 *Affaires du Maroc*, VI, 372 ff.; G.P., XXIX, 142 note.

112 G.P., XXIX, 152 f.   114 G.P., XXIX, 153 note.

113 G.P., XXIX, 153 ff.

merely as a pretext. His real motive was to bring the French to the point of making a generous offer of Congo territory, and to emphasize to the Powers that the Algeciras Act had broken down.

On July 9, Cambon came again to see Kiderlen. He was deeply depressed and disturbed at the Agadir action, of which Germany had given no preliminary notice, whereas France had given ample notification of her march to Fez. The interview was long and difficult, and punctuated by silences. Each wanted the other to make proposals. Finally the words "Congo" and "Togo" were mentioned. But neither speaker would commit himself further, each declaring that he must get further information and instructions.[115] This delay and diplomatic fencing drew from the Kaiser the impatient comment:

> After four weeks! This is a cursed comedy! Nothing accomplished! What the devil is to be done now? This is a sheer farce, negotiating and negotiating and never getting any further! While we are losing precious time, the British and the Russians are stiffening up the frightened French and dictating to them what they at the most can condescend to allow us.[116]

Kiderlen was now in a very difficult position. When Cambon came to see him again on July 15, and spoke only of insignificant compensations, he decided to beat about the bush no longer. He took a map, pointed to the French Congo, and said Germany ought to have the whole of it. Cambon nearly fell over backward in astonishment. He declared that no French Government could ever give up a whole colony, but that part of it might be surrendered, if Germany gave up Togo and some of the Cameroons. From this interview Kiderlen received the impression that "to

115 *Affaires du Maroc*, VI, 403 f.; Caillaux, 278 ff; G.P., XXIX, 173 ff.; Jäckh. II, 123 ff.   116 G.P., XXIX, 177 f.

get a satisfactory result it would be necessary to take a very strong stand." [117] The whole matter was telegraphed to the Kaiser, who was still on his northern cruise. He was more dissatisfied than ever, and also alarmed at Kiderlen's attitude. He ordered positively that no steps involving threats to France should be taken in his absence. Realizing that it would be easier for the French Government to cede Congo territory to Germany, if Germany gave in exchange some small African territories of her own, he authorized Kiderlen to proceed with Cambon on this basis.[118] At the same time Treutler, the Foreign Office Minister who accompanied the Kaiser, telegraphed to Kiderlen: "As you know, it would be very difficult to get His Majesty's consent to steps which he assumes might lead to war." [119] Kiderlen was now ready to resign, because of the Kaiser's attitude, and because he himself believed the way to make the French yield was to make them feel that their refusal might mean war. But Bethmann persuaded him to stay in office and continue to negotiate on the basis indicated by the Kaiser.[120]

It was at this moment, when the Kiderlen-Cambon negotiations seemed to be making little progress, that England intervened. Many weeks before the *Panther* went to Agadir, Sir Edward Grey had feared that Germany meant to seek her compensation in West Morocco and establish the naval base on the Atlantic coast. To this England had been resolutely opposed for years; it had been one of her main motives for supporting France in Morocco. The *Panther* seemed to confirm Grey's fears. Therefore on July 4 he warned Germany that "a new situation has been created by the despatch of a German ship to Agadir; future developments might affect British interests more directly than they had hitherto been affected; and, therefore, we

[117] G.P., XXIX, 184 ff.
[118] Treutler to Bethmann, July 17; G.P., XXIX, 187 f.
[119] G.P., XXIX, 188.
[120] G.P., XXIX, 189 ff.; Jäckh, II, 128-134.

could not recognize any new arrangement which was come
to without us." [121]   Grey would have been less disturbed
in his mind if he had known that Germany's real objective
was the Congo and not a naval base on the Atlantic coast
of Morocco. Kiderlen made a mistake in not reassuring him
on this point. But Kiderlen, Bethmann and the Kaiser
had all been bent on carrying the discussion of compensations directly with France alone, and had intimated politely
that intervention by others was not desired.[122]   They hoped
to get more from France if others were not admitted to the
discussion. Grey waited for more than two weeks for Germany to make some reply to his statement of July 4 that
England wanted to be consulted in regard to any Moroccan
settlement; but Germany remained silent. Grey was
ready to accept a Franco-German settlement based on an
exchange of French Congo territory for German African
possessions, provided the terms of the settlement were acceptable to the French, and provided the Germans abandoned all intentions of having a foothold on the Moroccan
coast. He had welcomed the suggestion of finding a solution
in the French Congo.[123]   But when Kiderlen demanded the
whole Congo, the French told Grey that the German demands were unacceptable, reminded him of England's obligations under the Moroccan Agreement of 1904, and suggested that he take the initiative in calling another conference of the Powers to deal with the question.[124]

This hint that the Franco-German direct negotiations were
likely to break down revived Grey's fears that the Germans
would stay at Agadir. He therefore asked the German
Ambassador to come to him, and told him informally that
he understood that "there was danger that the negotiations

[121] G.P., XXIX, 167; Grey, I, 214. On the same day Grey told Paul
Cambon that the Moroccan question ought to be discussed *à quatre*—by
France, Spain, Germany, and England (*Affaires du Maroc*, VI, 392 ff.)
[122] G.P., XXIX, 155 ff.   [123] Grey, I, 223 f.
[124] De Selves to Paul Cambon, July 20; *Affaires du Maroc*, VI, 418 f.

would end without success, and then the question would come up: What is Germany doing in Agadir and its hinterland?" This was a question, he said, which involved English interests. So long as there had been a prospect that France and Germany might reach a settlement by exchanging colonial territory in Central Africa, he had kept aside; but as this now seemed unlikely, and as serious British interests were involved, he wished to suggest privately that it was time for England also to be heard—time for a discussion à trois—between France, Germany, and England. Grey was wise in wishing to find out Germany's real purpose and deal with it by the usual secret diplomatic methods without the noisy and embarrassing interference of the Press everywhere. But Metternich had no instructions to tell him that Germany wanted compensations in the Congo and not a naval port at Agadir. Grey therefore evidently came to the conclusion it was time to give Germany an unmistakable public warning, even though involving all the dangers of newspaper excitement and questions of "prestige." That very same evening without giving Metternich time to get new instructions from Berlin, Grey allowed Lloyd George to announce to the world that England demanded that she be consulted. In this famous Mansion House speech of July 21, Lloyd George said:

But I am also bound to say this—that I believe it is essential in the highest interests, not merely of this country, but of the world, that Britain should at all hazards maintain her prestige amongst the Great Powers of the world. Her potent influence has many a time been in the past, and may yet be in the future, invaluable to the cause of human liberty. It has more than once in the past redeemed continental nations, who are sometimes too apt to forget that service, from overwhelming disaster, and even from national extinction. I would make great sacrifices to preserve peace. I conceive that nothing would justify a disturbance of in-

ternational good-will except questions of the gravest national moment. But if a situation were to be forced upon
us in which peace could only be preserved by the surrender
of the great and beneficent position Britain has won by centuries of heroism and achievement, by allowing Britain to
be treated, where her interests were vitally affected, as if
she were of no account in the Cabinet of nations, then I say
emphatically that peace at that price would be a humiliation
intolerable for a great country like ours to endure.[125]

This speech caused an explosion of wrath in Germany,
where it was interpreted as a threat, and where it was felt
that England was interfering in Franco-German negotiations which were none of her business. It made all the more
effect that it was delivered, not by Grey himself, who was
regarded as being unduly anti-German, but by the Chancellor of the Exchequer who had the reputation of being
a man of peace and generally favorable to Germany. When
he spoke out in this way he was regarded as having been
selected by the Government in order to make the warning
all the more emphatic. Both the Prime Minister and Sir
Edward Grey had been consulted, and approved Lloyd
George's action. Winston Churchill, the Home Secretary,
was enthusiastic for it.[126] But he makes plain that he
knew it was playing dangerously with fire. It greatly increased the already existing tension between England and
Germany growing out of the naval competition. It might
indeed have easily led to war, had not the Kaiser and
Bethmann been determined not to allow the Moroccan
affair to cause a European conflict. It did, however, produce two results which ultimately contributed to a peaceful
solution of the Moroccan question. It led Germany to
inform England at once that she had no intention of estab-

---

[125] Grey, I, 216.
[126] Asquith, *Genesis of the War*, p. 148; Churchill, I, 46 ff. Grey (I,
217) says he did not instigate it, but welcomed it.

lishing herself on the Atlantic coast of Morocco, which had been Grey's great cause of alarm. And it also caused Germany to moderate somewhat her demand on France. After four months of protracted and difficult negotiations, Kiderlen and Cambon were able to sign the agreement of November 4, 1911. By this Germany virtually acknowledged that the French might establish their desired protectorate over Morocco; in return France ceded more than 100,000 square miles of the French Congo, giving the Germans two much-needed river outlets to the Congo for the export of their Cameroon products; to give the appearance of an exchange of territories and make it easier for the French Government to justify the agreement to French public opinion, Germany ceded to France the "duck's bill," a small tract of valueless Cameroon territory east of Lake Chad. That the agreement represented a tolerably equitable compromise is evidenced by the fact that it met bitter criticism and opposition from the nationalists and colonial enthusiasts in both countries.[127]

As between England and Germany, the Agadir Crisis not only increased the friction between the two governments at the time, but it seems to have deepened Grey's suspicions of Germany's warlike inclinations. This is evident from his observations on the subject in his memoirs,[128] where he implies (quite contrary to facts) that "the Agadir Crisis was intended to end either in the diplomatic humiliation of France or in war;" and adds: "The militarists in Germany were bitterly disappointed over Agadir, and when the next crisis came we found them with the reins in their hands." [129] His feeling at the time was significantly expressed in his statement to the Russian Ambassador in London: "In the event of a war between Germany and

127 On these later negotiations and the Moroccan Convention of November 4, 1911, see G.P., XXIX, 293-454; *Affaires du Maroc*, VI. 423-635; and D.D.F., 3me Série, I, *passim*, especially No. 160.

128 Grey, I, 210-239.   129 Grey, I, 231, 233.

France, England would have to participate. If this war should involve Russia [the Ambassador had just assured him that it would], Austria would be dragged in too, for, although she has not the slightest desire to interfere in this matter, she will be compelled by force of circumstances to do so. There is no doubt that in such an event the situation in Albania will become aggravated. Consequently, it would no longer be a duel between France and Germany—it would be a general war." [130]   Grey added, however, that he did not believe Emperor William wanted war. Two weeks earlier the Russian Ambassador had reported: "There is no use concealing the fact—one step further, and a war between England and Germany would have broken out as a result of the Franco-German dispute, although independent of it."

Between England and France the Agadir Crisis, like the Morocco Crisis of 1905, led to a tightening of the bonds between the two. France was grateful for Lloyd George's speech, and for the indications that England would not only give her the diplomatic support promised in the agreement of 1904, but also the military support contemplated in the military and naval "conversations" which had been going on between the two countries since 1906. On July 20, after Kiderlen's demand for the whole Congo and the day before Lloyd George's Mansion House speech, there took place at the French Ministry of War a Conference between General Wilson, the Head of the Department for Military Operations of the English General Staff, and General Dubail, the French Chief of Staff. It was "to determine the new conditions for the participation of an English army in the operations of the French armies in the North-East in case of a war with Germany." [131]   The protocol of the Conference

---

[130] Benckendorff to Neratov, August 16, 1911; Siebert-Schreiner, p. 598.

[131] French General Staff History, *Les Armées Françaises dans la Grande Guerre* (Paris, 1925), I, 49.

took care, as usual, to state that these "conversations, devoid of all official character, cannot bind either Government in any way," and aimed merely "to foresee the indispensable preparatory measures." But six weeks later, General Dubail stated to the Russians, as if there were no doubt in the matter, that the French army was ready to take the offensive against Germany "with the aid of the English army on its left wing." [132]

Russia, having just established more friendly relations with Germany as a result of the Potsdam agreements, did not wish to endanger these by too active a support of France in the Agadir affair. At the beginning, when requested by her ally to make representations at Berlin, Russia had done so in a perfunctory way, but without exerting any real pressure.[133] Later during the long Franco-German negotiations for a Congo-Cameroon exchange of territories, Izvolski himself says he worked "with all his strength" to moderate the French and urged them to yield to many of the German demands.[134] This is confirmed by Caillaux,[135] and by the French Ambassador in Russia, M. Georges Louis, who reported that Russia would honor her signature on the alliance, but that Russian public opinion would hardly understand a Franco-Russian war occasioned by a colonial question like Morocco. And when M. Louis pointed out to the Tsar that Morocco was as much of a vital interest to France, as the Caucasus and the control of the Black Sea to Russia, Nicholas II replied: "Keep in view the avoidance of a conflict. You know our preparations are not complete." [136] Russia did not at this time want to be

132 Protocol of the Franco-Russian Military Conference of August 31, 1911; M.F.R., p. 698; L.N., II, 421.
133 G.P., XXIX, 112, 117, 158 f., 168 ff.
134 Izvolski to Neratov, Sept. 14, 1911; M.F.R., p. 114; L.N., I, 132 f.; Stieve, I, 146.
135 Caillaux, *Agadir*, p. 142 ff.
136 Louis to De Selves, Sept. 7, 1911; Judet, *Georges Louis*, 156 f.; *cf.*, however, Poincaré, I, 294 ff.

drawn into a war over Morocco any more than France had
wished hitherto to be drawn in over Balkan questions.
Russia needed to build up her army and navy much further
before risking a European War. But the very fact of this
lukewarm support by Russia of French colonial interests,
and by France of Russia's Balkan ambitions, became an
added spur to Izvolski to tighten up the Franco-Russian
Alliance after 1911. And in this he was soon aided by M.
Poincaré, who became Minister of Foreign Affairs in France
early in 1912.

Another effect of the Agadir Crisis and the consequent
strengthening of the French grip on Morocco and the Western Mediterranean was Italy's decision that the time had
come for her to seize Tripoli. This so weakened Turkey
that Serbia and Bulgaria hastened to take steps toward
the formation of a Balkan League, with Russia's assistance,
which led to the Balkan Wars. These in turn further
embittered the relations between Serbia and Austria, and
so contributed to one of the main causes of the World War.

THE HALDANE MISSION, 1912

In 1908, as has been indicated above, Tirpitz had secured
the adoption by the Reichstag of a naval program providing for the construction of four capital ships annually from
1908 to 1911, and for two annually from 1912 to 1917.
The English had become greatly alarmed, both for their
actual safety and for the disastrous effect upon Anglo-
German relations. They had therefore made efforts to call
a halt, or come to some understanding, but these had failed
owing to the Kaiser's decisive opposition, culminating in
his interview with Sir Charles Hardinge at Cronberg in
August, 1908.

During the following months English alarm steadily
increased, and frightened imaginations pictured a German
invasion of England. Further antagonism between the two

countries was caused by the unfortunate *Daily Telegraph* affair. The Kaiser had allowed an English friend to summarize a confidential talk in which the Kaiser refuted the idea that he was hostile to England. The English were "mad, mad as March hares," he had said, to suspect the German navy, which was simply to protect German commerce and not to attack England. The Kaiser was the friend of England. He wished to restrain the German people, whose prevailing sentiment was not friendly to England. But the English suspicions and Press attacks made his task of preserving peace difficult. As proof of his friendly attitude in the past, he recalled that during the Boer War he had refused to join France and Russia in putting pressure on England in favor of the Boers; on the contrary, he had even sent Queen Victoria a plan of campaign for use against the Boers. The Kaiser sent the manuscript of this summary to Bülow at his summer home at Nordeney on the shore of the North Sea, and Bülow, without studying it, sent it to the Foreign Office for examination and comment. But here an official, supposing that it had received Bülow's approval, allowed it to go out, and it was published in the London *Daily Telegraph* on October 28, 1908.[137]

The Kaiser had hoped the article would disarm England's suspicions and improve the relations between the two countries. It had precisely the opposite effect. It caused a storm of newspaper attacks on both sides of the North Sea, many of which were directed against himself personally. The English doubted his sincerity; they ridiculed and resented the idea that any advice of his had helped them win the Boer War; but they noted as ominous his admission that the prevailing sentiment in Germany was unfriendly

---

[137] Reprinted in G.P., XXIV, 170-174; for the details of this incredible mistake and the storm which the article raised in both Germany and England, see *ibid.*, pp. 167-210.

to England. In Germany, the Liberals and Socialists protested bitterly against his ill-considered act and the dangers of his personal rule. Bülow tendered his resignation, but withdrew it after the Kaiser promised in the future not to talk politics without his Chancellor's advice. But in the great Reichstag debate growing out of this affair, the Kaiser felt that Bülow did not adequately defend his sovereign's position. He no longer regarded his Chancellor with the same favor and confidence.

Count Metternich, the German Ambassador in England, was greatly distressed at seeing the two countries drifting into mutual misunderstandings and recriminations which one day might lead to war. English public opinion was demanding that the Cabinet should assure the "Two Power Standard" (that the English navy should be as strong as the combined navies of any other two Powers), and that if Germany built four Dreadnoughts annually, England should build eight. Lord Roberts began to tour the country trying to arouse England to the creation of a huge army and the adoption of the continental system of universal military service, naming Germany as the enemy of the future. A year ago, reported Metternich, these speeches would have been regarded as so exaggerated that they would have made no impression; today they are taken more seriously. The fundamental cause of all this alarm and agitation, Metternich believed, was the rapid increase of the German navy. He therefore suggested the desirability of slowing down Germany's program of construction from four to three ships annually, and of trying to come to some understanding with England.[138]

Bülow personally was in favor of the suggestion. To facilitate an understanding with England he hastened to make the Morocco settlement of 1909, which he hoped

[138] Metternich to Bülow, Nov. 22, 27; Dec. 11, 20, 29, 1908; Jan. 1, 14, 20; G.P., XXVIII, 23-75.

would remove one of the political causes of England's distrust. He sent Metternich's despatches to Tirpitz for comment.

But the Admiral disagreed fundamentally with the wise Ambassador's diagnosis of the English situation. Tirpitz received part of his information about England from the German naval attachés, whose reports often sound like an echo of their master's voice and wishes. Tirpitz insisted that the fundamental cause of British alarm and agitation was not the German navy, but German industrial and commercial competition. The British were now getting accustomed to the idea of a respectable German navy, but what troubled them was the fact that Germany, like Holland in the seventeenth century, was everywhere taking their trade and capturing their markets. It would do little good to slow down the naval program; and, anyway, it was fixed by law and could not be altered. To alter it as a result of the English clamor would be an intolerable humiliation for Germany and encourage the navy propaganda in England. Therefore Germany ought to go ahead with the creation of the "risk navy," and trust to passing safely through the "danger zone" without a British attack. He also rejected Bülow's suggestion that it would be wiser to spend more money on naval defense—coast fortifications, torpedo-boats, and submarines—to which England would have no objection, rather than on so many Dreadnoughts, which Metternich believed were the main sources of irritation and alarm in London. He finally threatened to resign, if Bülow insisted.[139]

So Bülow, weakened in favor with the Kaiser after the *Daily Telegraph* affair, gave way before Tirpitz, and virtually abandoned Metternich's suggestion for the time being. He let slip the opportunity of taking the initiative afforded by King Edward VII's visit to Berlin in February, 1909,

[139] Tirpitz to Bülow, Jan. 4, 1909; G.P., XXVIII, 51-55.

when Lord Crewe touched upon the question of naval competition.

As Metternich had forecast, the British agitation continued, and under its influence Mr. McKenna, First Lord of the Admiralty, proposed that for three years England should lay down six Dreadnoughts a year against Germany's four. A considerable number in the Cabinet and in Parliament thought that four British ships would still be enough to maintain a safe margin of British superiority. To overcome their objections and carry his bill, Mr. McKenna exaggerated the rate of speed at which the German ships were being completed. He alleged that Germany was exceeding the "normal rate" by secretly assembling materials beforehand, so that she might have 13 completed as early as 1911, instead of in 1912, as contemplated in the German navy law and as Metternich had expressly assured Grey beforehand was the actual intention.[140] Thus, Germany might have 13 Dreadnoughts to England's 16 in 1911, and an even more dangerous proportion in the following years. These statements of the First Lord of the Admiralty crystallized the general feeling of uneasiness into a first-class "navy scare." The public believed that Germany was trying to steal a march on England, and now clamored for eight ships, instead of the six which Mr. McKenna had asked for. "We want eight and we won't wait," was the popular cry. In the end, eight were voted, four at once, and four contingent upon Germany's continuing to build according to her program.

The effect on Anglo-German relations was deplorable. The Kaiser boiled with indignation at McKenna's "lies," and blamed Metternich for letting the wool be pulled over his eyes and for not taking a stiffer tone to Grey.[141] He was particularly displeased that Metternich had given the Eng-

---

140 Metternich to Bülow, Mar. 3, 10, 17, 1909; G.P., XXVIII, 93-112.
141 Cf. Kaiser's comments, G.P., XXVIII, 99, 102, 105, 113, 126.

lish to understand that Germany did not intend further to increase her program in the future—"a colossal personal concession, given right out of hand without getting the slightest thing from England in return, except untold lies, slanders, suspicions, and incivilities." [142]

Although Mr. McKenna later admitted his statements to have been incorrect,[143] they had done their damage in further increasing Anglo-German antagonism. In view of the offer implied in the English plan for four contingent ships, Bülow called a special meeting which was attended by Tirpitz, Bethmann, Moltke, and Metternich who came over from London. But the conditions demanded by Tirpitz and the Kaiser were such that there was no prospect of success in opening a negotiation.[144] Three weeks later Bülow was defeated in the Reichstag on his finance bill and resigned. Shortly afterwards the British voted to lay down the keels of the four contingent ships.

In this domestic conflict between Metternich and Bülow on one side, and Tirpitz and the Kaiser on the other, there is no doubt that wisdom lay with the former. Though it is true, as Tirpitz maintained, that commercial and industrial competition caused Anglo-German antagonism, it is much more true, as Metternich believed, that the naval question was the fundamental cause, and that the British were determined, cost what it might, to maintain the naval superiority which was vital for their commerce and for the very existence of the Empire. Metternich was quite right when he observed: "The services of Tirpitz in the development of our navy are unquestioned and great. But it is again evident that military, technical, and organizing ability are not necessarily united with correct political judgment. His judgment in regard to England is in such contradiction

[142] Kaiser to Bülow, April 3, 1909; G.P., XXVIII, 145.

[143] G.P., XXVIII, 391-395.

[144] Proctocol of meeting, June 3, 1909; G.P., XXVIII, 168 ff.; cf. above, 256 ff.

to the actual facts, that it almost seems as if he closed his eyes to them." [145]

Bethmann-Hollweg, who succeeded Bülow as Chancellor, agreed with Metternich as to the need for coming to a naval agreement with England. He believed that Germany could not be expected to have her 1908 program modified by a formal Reichstag amendment, but she might "retard the rate" of construction, by laying down less than the authorized four Dreadnoughts annually; he hoped that in return England might make concessions in regard to colonial questions and the Bagdad Railway and perhaps give some kind of neutrality promise. With this in view he opened negotiations with the British Ambassador, Sir Edward Goschen, in August, 1909, but they came to nothing.[146] In the course of the next two years he took up this idea several times, as well as various minor proposals to mitigate naval rivalry and suspicions, such as a mutual visiting of navy yards and exchange of information by naval attachés. But he had no success.[147] Finally, in the fall of 1911, after the heat of the Agadir Crisis had somewhat cooled down, the idea was taken in hand more definitely by two business men.

Albert Ballin, the head of the Hamburg-American Line, believed that the rapid building of the German navy was the main cause of Anglo-German antagonism and might some day lead to war. He considered this naval rivalry a far more serious threat to the peace of Europe than the Franco-Russian alliance. He was also on intimate and very friendly terms with Tirpitz and the Kaiser, as well as with Bethmann. He was aware that the German Government intended to lay a new navy law before the Reichstag in the spring of 1912, and he wished to bring about some

[145] Metternich to Bülow, Nov. 27, 1908; G.P., XXVIII, 19.

[146] G.P., XXVIII, 201-278.

[147] G.P., XXVIII, 281-423; cf. Grey to Goschen, May 5 and Oct. 26, 1910 (Grey, I. 244-247).

understanding with England before this made matters worse. His friend, Sir Ernest Cassel, was a rich and influential London banker. Born in Germany, Cassel had emigrated to England as a boy, and had at heart the interests of the land of his birth no less than of his adopted country. Like Ballin in Germany, he enjoyed in England a social and political position of great influence without holding any office in the Government. He had become an intimate friend of Edward VII, both as his banker and political adviser. He carried great weight among English business men in the "City," as well as in English political circles. Ever since July, 1909, Ballin and Cassel had been consulting together how to bring about an understanding between Germany and England.[148] In the winter of 1911-12, while the Berlin and London Foreign Offices were discussing possible colonial agreements,[149] and the English were becoming worried over rumors of an imminent new German Navy Law,[150] Ballin saw Cassel, who thereupon got into touch with Sir Edward Grey. This paved the way for the Haldane Mission. On January 29, 1912, Cassel came to Berlin with a memorandum [151] which had been approved by Sir Edward Grey, Winston Churchill, and Lloyd

[148] G.P., XXVIII, 205 ff.; Huldermann, *Albert Ballin,* 216 ff.

[149] G.P., XXXI, 71-94.

[150] G.P., XXVIII, 3-67.

[151] The full details of the Haldane Mission can now be followed in G.P., XXXI, 95-251; Tirpitz, *Erinnerungen,* p. 185 ff.; *Der Aufbau der deutschen Weltmacht,* pp. 197-338 (including many documents most of which were later published in G.P.); "Warum kam eine Flottenverständigung mit England nicht zur Stande?", in *Suddeutsche Monatshefte,* 23. Jahrgang (Nov., 1925), pp. 95-155, including polemical articles by Fritz Kern, Hans Hollmann and others, for and against the Tirpitz publication of documents; Bethmann-Hollweg, *Betrachtungen,* I, 48 ff.; Huldermann, *Albert Ballin,* pp. 235-270; E. Jäckh, *Kiderlen-Wächter,* II, 155 ff.; Siebert-Schreiner, pp. 613-639; Haldane, *Before the War,* pp. 55-72; Churchill, *The World Crisis, 1911-1914,* pp. 94-115; Asquith, *Genesis of the War,* 153-160; Grey, I, 240-248; Poincaré, I, 163-188. The subject is excellently summarized by B. E. Schmitt, in an article in *The Crusades and Other Historical Essays presented to Dana C. Munro* (N. Y., 1928), pp. 245-288.

George. This memorandum was to serve as a basis for opening official negotiations, and ran as follows:

1. Fundamental. Naval superiority recognized as essential to Great Britain. Present German naval program and expenditure not to be increased, but if possible retarded and reduced.

2. England sincerely desires not to interfere with German Colonial expansion. To give effect to this she is prepared forthwith to discuss whatever the German aspirations in that direction may be. England will be glad to know that there is a field or special points where she can help Germany.

3. Proposals for reciprocal assurances debarring either power from joining in aggressive designs or combinations against the other would be welcome.[152]

Sir Ernest Cassel showed this memorandum to the German Chancellor, who replied in writing that he welcomed this step taken by the British Government, and was in full accord with the memorandum, except that the new 1912 German naval estimates had already been arranged. He added that he and the Kaiser would be greatly pleased if Sir Edward Grey would visit Berlin, as the most effectual way of bringing the negotiations rapidly forward. He also gave Cassel a sketch of the proposed new Supplementary Navy Law, which indicated the creation of a third and new Naval Squadron to be formed from five existing reserve ships and three new ships; these three new ships, to be constructed during the next six years represented an augmentation of the 1908 program by three capital ships; that is, whereas by the 1908 program two capital ships were to be laid down annually between 1912 and 1917, by the new proposal three ships would be laid down in 1912, 1914, and 1916.[153] Cassel returned with this, and replied on Grey's behalf that if the German naval expenditure could be so

[152] G.P., XXXI, 98.   [153] G.P., XXXI, 99 note.

arranged, by a modification of the German rate of construction or otherwise, as to render unnecessary any serious
increase of British naval expenditure, "British Government
will be prepared at once to pursue negotiations, on the
understanding that the point of naval expenditure is open
to discussion and that there is a fair prospect of settling
it favorably." [154] If this understanding was acceptable, a
British Minister would come to Berlin. Bethmann replied
that it was acceptable, provided England gave adequate
guarantees of a friendly orientation of her general policy.
"The agreement would have to give expression to a statement that both Powers agreed to participate in no plans,
combinations or warlike engagements directed against
either Power." [155]

Sir Edward Grey himself was unwilling to accept the
cordial invitation to Berlin. His reasons, according to his
memoirs of a dozen years later, were his fears that "the
visit might arouse suspicion and distrust at Paris"; that
the whole plan might be "one of those petty unofficial
manoeuvres that could be avowed or disavowed at Berlin
as best might suit German convenience"; and that he "had
no great hope that anything would come of it." [156] Probably
at the time his strongest motives were his deep distrust of
Germany, and his fear of alarming France and so weakening the Entente. He decided not to go to Berlin himself,
but arranged that Lord Haldane, the Minister of War,
should go in his place. He desired that Haldane's visit
"should be private and informal, so that, if nothing came
of it, there should be no sensation and little disappointment
to the public." [157] In 1910, when Bethmann was trying to
secure an understanding with England, Grey had written
to the British Ambassador in Berlin: "The mutual arrest

[154] Cassel to Ballin, Feb. 3, 1912; Churchill, p. 98; G.P., XXXI, 102.
[155] G.P., XXXI, 103 f.   [157] Grey, I, 242 f.
[156] Grey, I, 241 ff.

or decrease of naval expenditure is *the* test of whether an understanding is worth anything," and that in Bethmann's overtures "the naval question was not sufficiently prominent." [158] He apparently did not think that there was any better chance of German naval reduction in 1912. He seems to have been convinced that the Kaiser had taken the initiative,[159] and then, if he had gone to Berlin and the negotiations had come to nothing, the German Government would have tried to put the blame upon him, Grey. But above all, Grey was determined not to endanger in the slightest degree the Entente with France. He had been told by Winston Churchill that the Admiralty was contemplating bringing home the Mediterranean ships, in order to meet the new Third Squadron which Tirpitz wanted; and that this meant relying on France in the Mediterranean (as was later actually arranged), so that certainly no change in the Entente would be possible, even if Grey desired it.[160] To allay French fears Grey at once informed the French Ambassador of the projected negotiations and assured him that he would do nothing with Germany that would tie his hands.[161] His statement to Paul Cambon shows what a restricted conception he had of the Haldane Mission: Haldane was "to find out whether Germany's recent overture was serious or not. He was also to attempt to gather information about the Bagdad Railway. But there is no question of entering upon negotiations. We desire only to

[158] Grey to Goschen, May 5, 1910; Grey, I, 245.

[159] Grey gave Paul Cambon the impression that the initiative had not come from England but from the Kaiser (Poincaré, I, 165, 168), and Churchill said the same to the German naval attaché, (G.P., XXXI, 104). But the Kaiser denied this at once in a marginal note, saying that he knew nothing of the proposal until Sir Ernest Cassel came to him with Grey's offer (*ibid.*, p. 122). The fact seems to be that the initiative came from Ballin and Cassel, and that only after the latter had talked with Grey, did the Kaiser suggest that the best way to facilitate the negotiations would be for Grey to come to Berlin.

[160] Jan. 31, 1912; Churchill, p. 97.

[161] Grey, I, 242.

learn the intentions of the German Government and to
inquire about its plans for a naval program." [162]   This
attitude on Sir Edward Grey's part in itself foredoomed the
Haldane Mission to failure.

Two other circumstances were hardly calculated to
facilitate it. On February 7, the day of Lord Haldane's
arrival in Berlin, the Kaiser in his speech at the opening
of the Reichstag had announced in general terms that projects for the increase of the army and navy would be introduced later in the session. To this Winston Churchill
immediately replied in a defiant speech at Glasgow, char-
acterizing the German Navy as a "luxury": "The British
Navy is to us a necessity and, from some points of view,
the German Navy is to them more in the nature of a
luxury. . . . We shall make it clear that other naval
Powers, instead of overtaking us by additional efforts, will
only be more outdistanced in consequence of the measures
which we ourselves shall take." The speech offended Mr.
John Morley and some of the other more pacific members
of the British Cabinet, who sincerely hoped for an understanding with Bethmann, and it created no little indignation
in Germany.[163]

In spite of these inauspicious circumstances Lord Haldane's reception at Berlin was most cordial and aroused
considerable optimism, both in his own mind and especially
in that of the Kaiser. His first interview on February
8 was with Bethmann at the British Embassy. He got the
impression, which he always retained, that the Chancellor
was as sincerely desirous of avoiding war as he was himself.
Next day he lunched with Tirpitz and the Kaiser, and had
a long and friendly discussion. He emphasized England's

[162] Poincaré, I, 166. Haldane himself while in Berlin, also made a
point of visiting the French Embassy and informing Jules Cambon that,
even if a naval accord were reached, it would respect the existing ratio
and not disturb the Entente (Poincaré, I, 167; G.P., XXXI, 126).

[163] Cf. Churchill, 99-101; and G.P., XXXI, 55, 62, 126.

necessity of having a fleet large enough to protect her commerce and vital supply of food and raw materials. He admitted that Germany was free to build as she pleased, but so was England, and England would probably lay down two keels to every one which Germany added to her program. After a long discussion between him and Tirpitz about the Two Power Standard and naval ratios, in regard to which they could find no mutually satisfactory basis, the Kaiser proposed that it would be better to avoid for the moment discussing shipbuilding programs; instead of attempting to define ratios between the two navies, it would be better to have the agreement deal with the political question of general policy and colonial matters; after this was concluded and published, the Kaiser would have Tirpitz tell the Reichstag that the new political agreement with England had entirely altered the situation, and the three extra ships which the new navy law proposed to lay down in 1912, 1914, and 1916, would not be asked for until 1913, 1916, and 1919. Haldane tactfully assented to his suggestion and it was agreed that next day he should try to work out with Bethmann some formula of political agreement.[164]

In a long final interview on February 10, 1912, Bethmann proposed the following formula for a political agreement:

I. The High Contracting Powers assure each other mutually of their desire for peace and friendship.

II. They will not, either of them, make any combination, or join in any combination, which is directed against the other. They expressly declare that they are not bound by any such combination.

III. If either of the High Contracting Parties becomes entangled in a war with one or more other Powers, the other of the High Contracting Parties will at least observe toward

164 Kaiser to Bethmann, Feb. 9; and Tirpitz's memorandum; G.P., XXXI, 112 ff.; 225 ff.; Haldane, *Before the War*, p. 57 ff.; Bethmann, *Betrachtungen*, I, 50 ff.; Tirpitz, *Memoirs*, I, 218 ff.

the Power so entangled a benevolent neutrality, and use its utmost endeavor for the localisation of the conflict.

IV. The duty of neutrality which arises from the preceding Article has no application in so far as it may not be reconcilable with existing agreements which the High Contracting Powers have already made. The making of new agreements which make it impossible for either of the Contracting Parties to observe neutrality toward the other beyond what is provided by the preceding limitation is excluded in conformity with the provision contained in Article II.[165]

Haldane objected to Article III as being too wide-reaching. It would preclude England from coming to the assistance of France should Germany attack her and aim at getting possession of such ports as Dunkirk, Calais and Boulogne. This England could never tolerate, because it was essential to her island security that these ports should remain in the friendly hand of France. Suppose, he said, that England were to attack Denmark, to seize a naval station, or for some other object disagreeable to Germany, Germany must have a free hand. Similarly, if Germany fell upon France "with her tremendous army corps," England could not bind herself to remain neutral. Furthermore, such a formula might also hamper England in discharging her existing treaty obligations to Belgium, Portugal and Japan. Lord Haldane therefore proposed to modify Articles II and III so that they would read:

II. They will not either of them make or prepare to make *any unprovoked attack* upon the other, or join in any combination or design against the other *for purposes of aggression,* or become party to any plan or naval or military enterprise alone or in combination with any other power directed to such an end.

[165] Haldane, p. 64; G.P., XXXI, 116 ff. Kiderlen was not present at any of the conversations with Haldane, but he assisted Bethmann in drawing up this formula.

III. If either of the High Contracting Parties becomes entangled in a war with one or more other powers, *in which it cannot be said to be the aggressor,* the other of the High Contracting Parties will at least observe towards the power so entangled a benevolent neutrality and use its utmost endeavor for the localisation of the conflict.[166]

In his eagerness to secure an agreement Bethmann bit at this bait, without committing himself to accept it. Later, however, Germany argued, and with good reason, that the words "unprovoked" and "aggressor" were too uncertain in interpretation. In the complex situations which lead to war, it is always difficult to tell which side is really the aggressor. To make neutrality dependent on this uncertainty of interpretation would be robbing the agreement of all its value. Suppose Germany were drawn into a war with Russia and France, England's neutrality would then depend on whether or not she judged that Germany had "provoked" the war.

On colonial questions it was much easier for Haldane and Bethmann to come to a tentative agreement, which, however, was not to be regarded as binding upon either. In disposing of the Portuguese colonies Germany was to get Angola, and England Timor. Germany might buy the Belgian Congo, in return for giving a right of way to a Cape-to-Cairo Railway. England would cede Zanzibar and Pemba, in return for a satisfactory arrangement concerning the Bagdad Railway, such as 51% control of the section from Bagdad to Basra near the Persian Gulf.[167]

In regard to naval rivalry, Haldane agreed that the new Navy Law, having been publicly announced by the Kaiser, would have to be brought before the Reichstag, but he doubted very much whether the British Cabinet would regard as satisfactory the slight postponement in construc-

[166] G.P., XXXI, 118 f. Italics are by the present author.
[167] G.P., XXXI, 119 f.

tion which the Kaiser had mentioned the day before. England would be compelled to take counter-measures, and English public opinion would not be likely to sanction any "political agreement" between the countries at a moment when both were increasing naval expenditures.

After all these points had been noted down for further discussion by the London and Berlin Governments, Lord Haldane returned to England, carrying in his pocket the draft of the proposed German Navy Law. This had been confidentially given to him by the Kaiser, with permission to show it privately to his colleagues, although its contents was still unknown to the Reichstag and the German public. As it was a bulky document requiring technical knowledge, Haldane had not attempted to study it in Berlin. When he handed it over to Winston Churchill and the Admiralty for examination, they believed that it would entail very serious naval expenditures on the part of both England and Germany. The British therefore drew up and forwarded to Berlin a memorandum calling attention not merely to the three new capital ships contemplated, but to the great increase in personnel and expenditure by which Germany was proposing to provide for her new Third Squadron. To meet it England would have to lay down two keels to one for every capital ship added to the German Navy above the existing law; and she would make a further concentration of the Fleet in Home Waters, all involving £18,500,000 spread over the next six years. Public opinion would hardly regard these serious measures and counter-measures as appropriate to the coincident reëstablishment of cordial relations.[168] In other words, as Metternich bluntly reported, the "political agreement" was in danger of being shipwrecked on the Navy Law. To save the former, Germany must abandon or greatly modify the latter. In fact Grey told him flatly a few days later that it would be

[168] G.P., XXXI. 134 f.

impossible to sign any political agreement at the moment
when both countries were making increased naval expenditures, because public opinion would regard this as inconsistent.[169]

At Berlin this memorandum made a bad impression.
Grey seemed to have damped all hopes of an understanding. He had abandoned the basis of discussion agreed to
by Haldane at Berlin, shifting it away from the neutrality
agreement, and giving priority to a criticism of the Navy
Law and naval details, some of which (like the question of
increase of personnel) had not been mentioned at all by
Haldane. Even in colonial matters Grey seemed to be
withdrawing what he had held out at first, and to be
making difficulties: he had discovered that the Dutch had
a prior right to purchase Timor; that England could hardly
give up Zanzibar and Pemba without receiving some German territory in return; and that the suggested Bagdad
Railway concession was insignificant and unsatisfactory.[170]

The Kaiser was especially indignant at the change in
England's attitude. He was willing to proceed with negotiations on the basis of Haldane's conversations at Berlin,
but not on the new basis which Grey was taking in London.
A memorandum to this effect was drawn up for Metternich,
but was held back by Bethmann for several days. In spite
of everything, he and Kiderlen were still making a valiant
struggle to satisfy Grey. They were trying to persuade
Tirpitz and the Kaiser to abandon the three extra capital
ships and postpone still further the publication of the
Navy Law.[171] But the Kaiser was impatient to have the
Navy Law laid before the Reichstag, inasmuch as it had
already been announced in his speech, and been in English

[169] Metternich to Bethmann, Feb. 22, 24, 29; G.P., XXXI, 128-145.
[170] G.P., XXXI, 137-154.
[171] G.P., XXXI, 148-153; Tirpitz, *Der Aufbau der deutschen Weltmacht,* 290 ff., 306 ff.

hands for more than a fortnight. At Bethmann's insistence
it had been withheld from publication hitherto, in order
not to jeopardize the negotiations with England. Finally,
on March 5, the Kaiser telegraphed to Bethmann that the
memorandum for Metternich must be delivered to Grey
on the morning of March 6, so that the Navy Law could
then be laid before the Reichstag in the evening. He also
took the unusual step of telegraphing himself directly to
Metternich: it appeared that England had abandoned the
basis agreed upon by Haldane; the Kaiser would stick to it
and to the Navy Law except for a partial postponement of
capital ships; but navy personnel was not to be a subject
of discussion with England; if England withdrew her ships
from the Mediterranean to the North Sea, this would be
regarded as a threat of war and would be replied to by an
increased Navy Law and by possible mobilization.[172]

Bethmann now sent in his resignation: he could no
longer assume responsibility for such a policy or for such a
direct dictation by the Kaiser to Germany's Ambassadors,
without previous consultation with the Chancellor. The
Kaiser hastened back to Berlin, persuaded Bethmann to
remain in office, and agreed to a further postponement of
the Navy Law and the continuance of the negotiations with
England. Thereupon Tirpitz in turn threatened to resign,
if the Navy Law were dropped altogether.[173] After a sharp
domestic conflict between the two Ministers, the Admiral
virtually triumphed over the civilian Chancellor. It was
decided that no reduction in the Navy Law should be made
beyond the minor matter of retarding the date for the capital ships, which Tirpitz had already grudgingly conceded.

Meanwhile Bethmann had been continuing his negotiations with England,[174] but they never had any chance of

172 G.P., XXXI, 156.
173 *Ibid.*, 157 note; Tirpitz, pp. 317-325.
174 G.P., XXXI, 159-210.

success as far as a neutrality agreement or naval limitation was concerned. They were virtually abandoned as hopeless on March 29, when Grey informed Metternich that the English Cabinet had finally decided definitely against Bethmann's original neutrality formula. Grey offered instead another much more restricted formula, which Germany rejected as not giving any satisfactory security against war with England.[175] Already, on March 18, Winston Churchill had laid before Parliament the British Navy Estimates, providing for two keels to every additional German one, and for the other greatly increased naval expenditures which he had threatened as England's reply to the expected German Navy Law. The Atlantic fleet would be moved from Gibraltar to Home Waters and replaced at Gibraltar by the Mediterranean ships which had hitherto had their base at Malta. He indicated, however, that if Germany made no increase, neither would England; the two navies would then stand in the same ratio to each other as before, and both countries would be spared enormous expenditures.[176] He did not make this proposal officially to Germany, however. On April 14 the German Navy Law was finally laid before the Reichstag, and accepted by it, unmodified, on May 14.[177]

The Haldane Mission failed primarily from two causes: England's unwillingness to make any political agreement concerning neutrality which would in any way limit her freedom to aid France; and Germany's unwillingness to make any worth-while reductions in the Supplementary Navy Law which would satisfy England. Each country was seeking a concession which dominant ministers in the other were determined not to make. Only in the third group of subjects under consideration—colonial matters and the

---

[175] G.P., XXXI, 210 ff.
[176] G.P., XXXI, 193-201; Churchill, 107 ff.
[177] Tirpitz, 334 ff.

Bagdad Railway—was it possible to continue successful negotiations; in this less difficult field of economic imperialism mutually satisfactory agreements were gradually worked out, and were complete for signature on the eve of the World War.[178] Thus, the Haldane Mission, like the Potsdam negotiations with Russia in 1910, resulted in removing some causes of friction, but they both failed in one of their main objects—the securing of some written agreement which would lessen Germany's political isolation and loosen the bonds of the Triple Entente.

THE TIGHTENING OF THE TRIPLE ENTENTE, 1912

Germany's overthrow of M. Delcassé in 1905, and her sudden sending of the *Panther* to Agadir, were regarded by the French as "brutal acts"—as exhibitions of the German habit of thumping the green table with the mailed fist to secure diplomatic victories. On both occasions they had been frightened by what they feared were German threats of war if they did not yield. In both cases therefore they had been forced to make what they felt to be humiliating concessions, because they were not prepared to take up the German challenge. Or as M. Poincaré puts it: "Germany's policy continued to be dominated by the arrogant spirit which since the war of 1870 had led to the Franco-German incidents of 1875 and 1887, and which between 1905 and 1911 had constantly poisoned affairs in Morocco. After the insult of Tangiers came the threat of Agadir. Instead of being stung into action by these repeated provocations, France, in her desire for peace," [179] agreed to the Algeciras Conference, and to territorial concessions in the Congo in exchange for liberty of action in Morocco. These acts of Germany, as well as her ultimatum to Russia in the Bosnian Crisis and the Kaiser's bellicose gestures, had

---

[178] G.P., XXXI, 255-305; XXXVII, 1-470.
[179] *Foreign Affairs* (N.Y.), Oct., 1925, 7.

gradually aroused in a group of French politicians a new national spirit. They had revived the desire for *revanche* and the recovery of Alsace-Lorraine. They had created the feeling that France had suffered long enough from the German menace from across the Rhine. There had grown up the determination that in the future, if Germany made a new threat of force, it would be better to risk war than accept a new humiliation. This new national spirit, determination, and self-confidence was greatly increased by the friendship of England and the growing conviction that in case of a conflict with Germany, England would not only stand behind France with her fleet, but would send English troops to strengthen the left wing of the French army in northern France. This would give a good prospect of victory, and the fruits of victory would be the recovery of the lost provices and the end of the nightmare of the German menace. Most of these French leaders, like the mass of the French people, did not want war; but if Germany's desire for the "hegemony of Europe" and her attempt again to use the mailed fist to force a diplomatic triumph brought on another international crisis, it would be better to fight than to back down. As they had little doubt that Germany would attempt some new aggression, this would make war "inevitable." France must therefore prepare for it by increasing her own army and navy at home, and by tightening her relations with her ally on the other side of Germany and with her friend across the Channel.

This new national feeling was personified in M. Raymond Poincaré and the little group of men with whom he was closely associated. Not only was he the embodiment of the *réveil national*. By his determination, firmness, and ability, he did more than any other man to strengthen and to stimulate it. It found expression in the overthrow of the Caillaux Ministry, which was accused of having been too yielding to Germany in the Agadir Crisis, and in the formation, on January 13, 1912, of the "Great Ministry" or "National Ministry," in which M. Poincaré was Prime Minister and Minister of Foreign Affairs, M. Millerand Minister of War, and M. Delcassé Naval Minister. In announcing its program, M. Poincaré declared that its first task would be to unite all groups of Republicans by a single national feeling, to organize the new protectorate in Morocco, and to maintain courteous and frank relations with Germany; and, he added,

> As always, we intend to remain loyal to our alliances and our friendships—we shall make it our duty to unite, like twin convergent forces, the financial strength which is such a help for France, with her military and naval strength. However profoundly pacific our country may be, it is not master of all eventualities and it intends to live up to its duties. The army and the navy will be the object of our attentive solicitude.[180]

Born at Bar-le-Duc in Lorraine, M. Raymond Poincaré was ten years old when the German armies overran France in 1870, and took his home from his country. Son of a distinguished meteorologist, brother of a distinguished physicist, and related to a distinguished mathematician, M. Poincaré himself soon showed an ability at the bar which brought him into the Chamber of Deputies at the early age of twenty-seven, and into the Cabinet as Minister of Education six years later in 1893. Later he was Vice-President of the Chamber and twice Minister of Finance, before taking the Premiership and Foreign Affairs portfolio in 1912. No one since Bismarck's day has equalled him in sheer ability. His length of public service, his extraordinary vitality and endurance, his capacity for mastering and remembering detail, his clearness of purpose and determination to achieve it, have all combined to make him one of

[180] Poincaré, I, 24; G.P., XXXI, 379.

the most remarkable of modern statesmen. All these native qualities, united with his dialectical skill and legal training, enabled him easily to vanquish his opponents in the Chamber of Deputies and to dominate his colleagues or subordinates in the Cabinet. One may not always approve of his aims, but one must admire the skill and ability with which he has achieved them. He knew precisely what he wanted, and he set about to secure it with singular directness and determination. The simplicity and brevity of his despatches are a refreshing contrast to the usual diplomatic circumlocutions and verbiage. His natural timidity was more than compensated by his bold energy. Such was the man who mainly directed and controlled French foreign policy from 1912 to 1914. In his memoirs he frequently denies that he pursued a personal policy as Minister of Foreign Affairs, or exceeded his constitutional position after he became President of the Republic in February, 1913, by imposing his wishes on the Ministers of Foreign Affairs who succeeded him. But with his ability, energy, and strong personality, it was inevitable that he should be the guiding spirit. In spite of his denials, we believe that he exercised a strong influence in the direction of an aggressive and dangerous policy, which was not a reflection of the wishes of the great majority of the truly peace-loving French people from 1912 to 1914, and which they would not have approved, had they been fully aware of it and the catastrophe to which it was leading.[181]

The man who coöperated most closely with M. Poincaré in his task of tightening the Triple Entente was the Russian Ambassador at Paris. It now is clear that Izvolski was vain, self-important, inclined to intrigue, and not always trustworthy. Consequently his reports must be

[181] Next to the revelation of his character and aims in his own Memoirs (see above, ch. i, at notes 45-47), the best-informed and most fair-minded account of M. Poincaré in English is the biography by Sisley Huddleston, *Poincaré*.

taken *cum grano salis*.[182] Nevertheless, his characteriza-
tions of M. Poincaré in the following quotations seem to be
substantially accurate. He describes the new Minister of
Foreign Affairs as "a very strong personality"; a man whose
sensitive *amour propre* must be "taken into account"; one
who "while often displaying useless rudeness and breaking
windows without reason, has never given me cause to doubt
his veracity"; "a passionate character and one who goes
in a straight-line," whose "energy and decision" it is important to have wholly on Russia's side and turn to advantage.[183] After his election to the Presidency, M. Poincaré
told Izvolski that he would still "have full opportunity to
influence directly the foreign policy of France, and that he
would not fail to take advantage of it to insure intact the
policy founded on a close alliance with Russia. In his
opinion it is of the highest importance for the French Government to prepare French opinion in advance to take part
in a war which might break out over the Balkan question.
For this reason the French Government requests us not to
undertake any personal action of a nature to provoke such
a war without an exchange of views beforehand with
France." [184] Thenceforth, to the World War, the Russians
found him "an ardent and convinced partisan of a close
union between France and Russia and of a constant
exchange of views between the two allies on all the most
important questions of international policy"; [185] and in

---

[182] M. Poincaré has much to say on this score (e.g., I, 294 ff., 317 ff.;
II, 335 ff.; III, 90 ff.). He has even said that he had so little confidence in
Izvolski that in August, 1912, he "made energetic representations about him
to M. Kokovtsev, President of the Russian Council, asking for his recall"
(*Foreign Affairs* (N.Y.), Oct. 1925, p. 10). If this is true, and if he had
so little confidence in Izvolski before the War as he indicates in his
post-war memoirs, it is a pity he did not make his energetic representations
to the Tsar and to Izvolski's official superior, M. Sazonov, and really
secure his recall. Probably he feared that to do so might antagonize
Sazonov and weaken the Alliance.

[183] L.N., I, 203, 216, 266, 281 f.   [184] L.N., II, 14 f.

[185] L.N., II, 360. Kokovtsev had the same impression (*ibid.*, II, 393).

general, in a view of the Balkan situation, a man who would never fail Russia in case of a war with Germany.[186]

One of the first tasks which occupied M. Poincaré's attention, after forming his "National Ministry," was the cementing of closer relations with England. The Haldane Mission and the possibility of an Anglo-German *rapprochement* caused him some uneasiness, in spite of Sir Edward Grey's assurances. He therefore welcomed a curious step taken by Sir Francis Bertie, the English Ambassador at Paris. Although Grey was making no concessions which would satisfy Germany, Bertie feared that in the future he might change his mind under the influence of men like Lord Loreburn, Harcourt, and the other members of the Cabinet who were more eager for an understanding with Germany, and who might make trouble if they learned of the Anglo-French military and naval "conversations" which had been going on for six years but of which they had not been informed. Bertie therefore quite privately and unofficially suggested to Poincaré that he would do well to point out firmly to Grey the dangers involved in any neutrality agreement with Germany. Taking the hint, but not revealing where it came from, Poincaré sent an energetic despatch to Paul Cambon to this effect. Cambon presented the substance of it to Grey on March 29.[187] This was the very day on which the British Cabinet finally decided to give its negative answer to Bethmann's neutrality formula, and buried the hopes which had centered in the Haldane Mission.[188] It is not clear whether Cambon's interview came before or after the Cabinet meeting, nor whether it had any decisive effect on England's action. That Poincaré may have boasted later to Izvolski of having wrecked the

[186] L.N., I, 326, 346 ff.; II, 10, 15, 345, 570.

[187] Poincaré, I, 170-178.

[188] G.P., XXXI, 210 ff. Germany suspected that Grey's negative attitude was partly caused by French pressure (*ibid.,* 144, 476 ff., 489 ff.).

Haldane Mission is quite possible.[189]   But in view of Sir
Edward Grey's evident determination from the outset not
to concede any neutrality agreement which would limit his
freedom in taking sides with France in case of a Franco-
German war, and in view of the fact that even before March
29 the Haldane negotiations had virtually broken down, it
seems very doubtful whether Poincaré's intervention had
the decisive effect which Izvolski implies. Of course, it may
be that Poincaré made earlier representations to Grey on
the subject than those which he gives in his memoirs. Grey
in his memoirs says nothing of this intervention on Poincaré's part. On this point, as on so many others, we must
await a full publication from the English archives to learn
the precise truth.

The Haldane Mission, however, impelled Poincaré to
try to secure from England a binding statement in writing.
Winston Churchill's plan to withdraw British ships from the
Mediterranean for a stronger concentration against Germany in the North Sea, foreshadowed in his speech of March
18, 1912,[190] aroused a lively discussion in the British and
French Press. It was urged that the time had come for
naval coöperation between the two countries. If England
withdrew her naval forces from the Mediterranean and
protected the north coast of France against the possibility
of a German attack, France could withdraw her fleet from

    [189] Izvolski to Sazonov, Dec. 5, 1912 (M.F.R., p. 609; L.N., I, 365 f.;
Stieve, II, 377): "In my conversation with Poincaré and Paléologue I have
been able to learn *in a very confidential way* that, *à propos* of the famous
trip of Lord Haldane to Berlin, . . . Poincaré told the British Government that so long as France and England had no written agreement of a
general political character, the signing of such an agreement between
Germany and England would at once put an end to the existing Anglo-
French relations. His protest had the expected effect and the London
Cabinet rejected the German proposition." Poincaré made these confidences to Izvolski in December, 1912, if correctly reported, just at the
time he was trying to convince Russia of the strength and solidarity
of the Triple Entente and to persuade Sazonov in consequence to take a
stiffer attitude in support of Serbia.
    [190] Churchill, pp. 97, 111 ff.; G.P., XXXI, 147 f., 156, 198, 218.

Brest and look after British interests, as well as her own, in the Mediterranean. In connection with this discussion, many British newspapers urged that the Anglo-French Entente should be definitely extended to a regular defensive alliance. "The only alternative to the constant menace of war is a new system of precise alliances." [191] This also was the feeling of M. Poincaré. Upon instructions from him, Paul Cambon spoke to Sir Arthur Nicolson about the need of strengthening the Entente Cordiale through a written agreement:

> "You see there is a cause of weakness in M. Poincaré's situation. More than anyone else, he is a partisan of the Entente with England, but to the important politicians, to his colleagues in the Cabinet, to the leaders of French public opinion who question him, he cannot give them to understand that there exist between us other bonds than those of sympathy. This is enough between two Governments sure of their reciprocal intentions. It is not enough for public opinion. The enemies of England in France (they are few but they exist) proclaim that our relations with you offer no security. I have, therefore, asked myself if we could not find together a formula which would permit us to reassure uneasy and doubting spirits. I know that the British Government does not have the right to bind itself without the authorization of Parliament, but there is no need of an agreement in duplicate, of a treaty drawn up and signed; we could content ourselves with an exchange of declarations. This is what we would have done in 1905 with Lord Lansdowne, if the resignation of M. Delcassé had not cut our conversation short." [192]

Sir Arthur Nicolson was personally favorable to making such an agreement, which, according to M. Poincaré, would

[191] *London Daily Express* of May 27, 1912; see also summaries of the British and French Press concerning the desirability of changing the Entente Cordiale into a regular alliance in G.P., XXXI, 475-556; Siebert-Schreiner, pp. 640-646.

[192] Cambon to Poincaré, April 18, 1912; Poincaré, I, 173 f.

have been a step further in the transformation of the
Entente into an alliance.[193]   But Sir Edward Grey, who had
already been severely criticized in Parliament for sub-
serviency in following in the wake of the French and Russian imperialism in Morocco and Persia, did not feel like
taking such a momentous step without the knowledge of
the whole Cabinet.   The majority of them were still unin-
formed even of the military "conversations" which had been
going on since 1906.   Cambon's suggestion, therefore, remained for the moment without results.   Meanwhile M.
Poincaré strengthened the Triple Entente and the naval
position of France in the Mediterranean by a Naval Convention with Russia.[194]

In May, 1912, Winston Churchill, accompanied by Mr.
Asquith, visited Malta to confer with General Kitchener
as to the situation in Egypt and the British position in the
Mediterranean.   Upon his return he announced more definitely in Parliament, on July 22, the Admiralty plan for
withdrawing ships from the Mediterranean for concentration in the North Sea.   At the same time he proposed to
the French Military Attaché a draft plan for the coöperation
of the British and French fleets.   But the French hesitated
to accept it, because its cautious preamble stated that it
was not to affect the liberty of action of either party; this
robbed it of its value in the eyes of the French.[195]

But Grey and Churchill did not want to tie their own
hands by any binding written obligation.   Even a naval
arrangement, by which England withdrew her Mediterranean fleet to the North Sea, while the French shifted
their Brest fleet to Toulon, was in danger of creating an
obligation on England's part to protect the northern

[193] Poincaré, I, 174.   France and England kept Russia in the dark
about this; denials were made by Nicolson to Benckendorff in London,
and by Poincaré to Izvolski in Paris; Siebert-Schreiner, pp. 641-644.

[194] See below, at notes 205-207.

[195] Poincaré, I, 215-219.

coasts of France, as Grey had gathered in conversations with Cambon in July.[196]

Churchill also was well aware of this danger. Like Mr. Campbell-Bannerman in 1906,[197] and like Mr. Asquith in 1911,[198] he perceived that the French would be encouraged to count upon British assistance; this would virtually create an obligation and thus limit England's freedom of action. As he pointed out to Grey: "Freedom will be sensibly impaired if the French can say that they had denuded their Atlantic seaboard and concentrated in the Mediterranean on the faith of naval engagements made with us. [He did not think that such a statement by the French would be true, because such a distribution of the fleets was the best policy for both Governments anyway.] Consider how tremendous would be the weapon which France would possess to compel our intervention if she could say, 'On the advice of and by arrangement with your naval authorities, we left our northern coasts defenseless.' Everyone must feel, who knows the facts, that we have the obligation of an alliance without its advantages, and above all without its precise definitions." [199]

While these Anglo-French negotiations were going on but before a decision had been reached, it was announced prematurely, through an inadvertence on the part of one of M. Delcassé's subordinates, that the Brest fleet was to be transferred to the Mediterranean. This news, says M. Poincaré, caused great excitement, and was interpreted by the Press as a sign that an Anglo-French naval agreement had been definitely concluded.[200] This incident gave a new

---

[196] Poincaré, I, 218.   [197] See above, ch. iii, at note 188.

[198] *Cf.* Asquith to Grey, Sept. 5, 1911 (Grey, I, 92): "Conversations such as that between Gen. Joffre and Col. Fairholme seem to me rather dangerous; especially the part which refers to possible British assistance. The French ought not to be encouraged, in present circumstances, to make their plans on any assumptions of this kind."

[199] Churchill to Grey, Aug. 23, 1912, Churchill, p. 112.

[200] Poincaré, I, 217.

impulse to the negotiations. Poincaré again instructed
Cambon to ask Grey for a written agreement. Grey finally
consented to give one. But before taking such an important
step he rightly believed that it should be known to and
approved by the whole Cabinet, and all its members were
at last informed of the Anglo-French "conversations" which
had been going on since 1906. He also insisted that it should
not take the shape of a formal diplomatic document, but
merely of a personal correspondence between himself and
M. Cambon.[201] Accordingly, on November 22, he handed
M. Cambon a letter which had been approved by the Cabinet, and received one in similar terms from him in exchange
next day. Grey's cautiously expressed letter was as follows:

FOREIGN OFFICE,

My dear Ambassador,   November 22, 1912.

From time to time in recent years the French and British
naval and military experts have consulted together. It has
always been understood that such consultation does not restrict the freedom of either Government to decide at any
future time whether or not to assist the other by armed
force. We have agreed that consultation between experts is
not, and ought not to be regarded as, an engagement that
commits either Government to action in a contingency that
has not arisen and may never arise. The disposition, for instance, of the French and British fleets respectively at the
present moment is not based upon an engagement to cooperate in war.

You have, however, pointed out that, if either Government
had grave reason to expect an unprovoked attack by a third
Power, it might become essential to know whether it could
in that event depend upon the armed assistance of the other.

I agree that, if either Government had grave reason to expect an unprovoked attack by a third Power, or something
that threatened the general peace, it should immediately discuss with the other whether both Governments should act

[201] Poincaré, I, 219 ff.; Grey, I, 93 ff.

together to prevent aggression and to preserve peace, and, if so, what measures they would be prepared to take in common. If these measures involved action, the plans of the General Staffs would at once be taken into consideration, and the Governments would then decide what effect should be given to them.

Yours, &c.

E. GREY.[202]

These Grey-Cambon letters fixed the relations between the French and British Cabinets, so far as any written statements were concerned, down to the outbreak of the War. Sir Edward Grey continued to cherish the illusion that he still had his "hands free"; and this was true as far as the wording of the letters went. But as Mr. Campbell-Bannerman and Mr. Asquith had pointed out, the military conversations were dangerous in the encouragement they gave to the French; and as Winston Churchill warned, the new arrangement of the British and French navies, which took place in the fall of 1912, tied England to France more closely still. It created for England an inescapable moral obligation to protect the coast of France in case of a war between France and Germany—that is, to participate on the French side no matter how the war arose. To be sure, Poincaré was aware that Grey had carefully stated that if there was reason to expect "an unprovoked attack," the two Governments would "discuss" whether they would act together. He knew that Grey would have to reckon with a strong pacific group within the British Cabinet and among the British people; with them it would make a great difference how the war arose. Hence he was very careful, as will appear in connection with the crisis of July, 1914, to make it appear that Austria and Germany were the aggressors. The French military authorities also, in drawing up "Plan XVII" (which in a modified form was the plan of

[202] Grey, I, 94 f.

campaign used by the French in 1914), were aware that they could not count with certainty upon the coöperation of the British army; but they had no doubt that they could depend upon the British navy:

> On the sea, however, we can count without risk upon the effective support of the British fleet. On land, an understanding established between the General Staffs of the two countries has provided for the employment on our extreme left of an English army comprising . . . 120,000 men. [But this support remains doubtful.] We should therefore act prudently in not taking into consideration these English forces in our plan of operations." [203]

This, however, did not mean that General Joffre did not expect English military aid, but merely that the French mobilization plan should not be made absolutely dependent upon British military coöperation. The further details of "Plan XVII" show that not only was the British Expeditionary Force expected, but elaborate provisions were made for its transportation and concentration on the Belgian frontier.[204]

Significant from the political point of view is this French conviction that they could count on the British navy, for this would involve British participation in the war, with all advantages to France and Russia which would accrue from England's great naval superiority in the way of blockading Germany and shutting her off from food and war materials, to say nothing of the great moral effect of having the British Empire actively engaged on the side of the Franco-Russian Alliance.

Closely connected with these Anglo-French naval arrangements was the Franco-Russian Naval Convention of July 16, 1912. Russia wished to have absolutely undis-

---

[203] Basis of "Plan XVII"; French General Staff History, *Les Armées françaises dans la Grande Guerre,* I, 19.

[204] *Les Armées françaises dans la Grande Guerre,* I, 47 ff.

puted naval domination of the Black Sea. She had also long wished to control the Straits and Constantinople. A first step in this direction would be to secure a free passage for her warships through the Bosphorus and the Dardanelles. Izvolski had several times attempted to gain this but without success.[205] Italy's naval activity and closing of the Dardanelles during the Tripolitan War again made Russia acutely sensitive to the importance of the Straits Question. She believed that her French ally could and ought to aid the Russian fleet to retain its supremacy in the Black Sea, by hindering the Austrian or Italian naval forces from passing the Straits. In case of a European War this would safeguard the left flank of the Russian army; this in turn would be of advantage to the Triple Entente in the other theatres of war. Russia also wished to be able to transfer some of her Baltic fleet to augment her Black Sea fleet, and to have a possible naval base in the Mediterranean. This could be provided if the French would develop the port of Bizerta in Northern Africa and allow the Russians to use it. Such were some of the considerations which made the Russians desire a closer naval agreement with France. The French, on their part, were glad to meet all Russian wishes as far as possible, in order to strengthen the solidarity of action between the two countries.[206]

The Franco-Russian Military Convention of 1894 contained nothing concerning the coöperation of the navies of the two countries. This was owing to the relatively late establishment of Naval Staffs as distinct from the Army Staffs, the French Naval Staff not being formed until 1902,

---

[205] See below, ch. v, *passim.*

[206] *Cf. L'Alliance Franco-Russe,* pp. 133-139; Poincaré, II, 112-114; V. Egoriev and E. Schvede, "La Convention Navale de 1912," in *Les Alliés contre la Russie* (Paris, 1926), pp. 54-64 (containing new material from the Russian archives); Izvolski correspondence, July 18, Aug. 2, 5, 6, 10, 14, 17, 18; and Sazonov's report to the Tsar of Aug. 17, 1912 (M.F.R., pp. 229-256; L.N., I, 296-309; II, 338 f., 527-534; Stieve, II, 194-228); G.P., XXXI, 520-546.

and the Russian not until 1908. But by 1911 both countries recognized the desirability of extending their alliance by a Naval Convention analogous to the Military Convention. In the spring of 1912, upon the initiation of the Russians, negotiations to secure this took place in Paris between army and navy officers of both countries. They resulted in the secret Naval Convention signed on July 16 by Admirals Aubert and Lieven and by the Naval Ministers, Delcassé and Grigorovitch, and confirmed by an exchange of notes between Sazonov and Poincaré a month later, upon the latter's visit to Russia. It declared: "The naval forces of France and Russia will coöperate in all the eventualities in which the alliance contemplates and stipulates the combined action of the land armies." It also provided in time of peace for the preparation of this coöperation by means of conferences at regular intervals between the Naval Staffs of the two countries. The protocols of these subsequent conferences are not given in the *French Yellow Book,* but their substance has recently been revealed from the Russian archives. They dealt with the development of Bizerta as a naval base for the French and Russian fleets, for its connection with Sebastopol by wireless telegraph and for secret naval codes. In general it was agreed that naval domination was to be secured by France in the Mediterranean, by England in the North Sea, and by Russia in the Baltic and Black Seas.

When Poincaré visited Russia in August, 1912, one of his main topics of conversation with Sazonov was the closer coöperation of the naval forces of the Triple Entente. He confided to Sazonov, according to the latter's report to the Tsar, that "although there does not exist between France and England any written treaty, the Army and Navy Staffs of the two countries have nevertheless been in close contact. This constant exchange of views has resulted in the conclusion between the French and English Governments of a verbal agreement, by virtue of which England has declared herself ready to aid France with her military and naval forces in case of an attack by Germany." [207] He begged Sazonov to "preserve the most absolute secrecy in regard to the information," and not give the English themselves any reason to suspect that he had been told of it. He also urged Sazonov to take advantage of his coming visit to England to discuss the question of a possible Anglo-Russian naval agreement, which would thus complete the naval coöperation of the three Triple Entente Powers in case of a conflict with Germany.[208]

Sazonov followed Poincaré's suggestion. On his visit to Balmoral in September, he informed Grey of the substance of the new Franco-Russian Naval Convention, saying that the French would endeavor to safeguard Russian interests in the southern theater of war by preventing the Austrian fleet from penetrating into the Black Sea; he then asked whether England would perform the same service for Russia in the North by keeping the German fleet out of the Baltic. According to Sazonov's report to the Tsar, Grey declared that, if the contemplated conditions arose, England would make every effort to strike the most crippling blow at German naval power:

> On the question of military operations he said that negotiations had already taken place between the competent authorities concerned, but in these discussions the conclusion had been reached that while the British fleet could easily penetrate into the Baltic, its stay there would be very risky. Assuming Germany to succeed in laying hands on Denmark and closing the exit from the Baltic, the British fleet would be caught in a mouse-trap. Accordingly, Great Britain would have to confine her operations to the North Sea.

[207] Sazonov's report to the Tsar of Aug. 17, 1912; M.F.R., p. 256; L.N., II, 339. [208] *Ibid.*

On his own initiative Grey then gave me a confirmation
of what I already knew through Poincaré—an agreement exists between France and Great Britain, under which in the
event of war with Germany Great Britain has accepted the
obligation of bringing assistance to France not only on the
sea but on land, by landing troops on the Continent.

The King touched on the same question in one of his
conversations with me, and expressed himself even more
strongly than his Minister. When I mentioned, letting him
see my agitation, that Germany is trying to place her naval
forces on a par with Britain's, His Majesty cried out that
any conflict would have disastrous results not only for the
German navy but for Germany's overseas trade, for he said,
"We shall sink every single German merchant ship we shall
get hold of."

These words appeared to me to give expression not only
to His Majesty's personal feelings but also to the public
feeling predominant in Great Britain in regard to Germany.[209]

Whether Sazonov correctly reported what Poincaré and
Grey had said to him is very doubtful.[210] But the fact that
he made such statements to the Tsar shows how much the
French and the Russians—and especially the Russians—
were encouraged by the existence of the Anglo-French military and naval "conversations" and inclined to interpret
them as a promise of British support in case of a general
European War. This Naval Convention also gave rise to
evasive statements on the part of the Entente Powers which
naturally increased Germany's suspicions of their aggressive intentions. By some "leak" in the French or Russian
Foreign Office, the French Press soon indicated the existence
of the Franco-Russian Naval Convention. This led to
inquiries by Germany. At St. Petersburg Kokovtsev denied that any such convention had been signed, but natu-

209 *Krasnyi Arkhiv*, III, 18; L.N., II, 347 f.; Stieve, II, 290 f.
210 *Cf.* Grey, I, 286-289.

rally refused to confirm his denial by a public statement, "because every word of it would be twisted around and the outcry would be all the greater." [211] Other Russian and French officials gave evasive answers to the effect that no agreement had been signed, but that since France and Russia were allies, their military and naval staffs must from time to time consult together.[212] Similarly, after the Grey-Cambon exchange of letters, Mr. Asquith and Sir Edward Grey continued to deny solemnly in Parliament that England had any secret agreements which bound her to participate in a continental war, although, as we have seen, this is what the French and Russians confidently counted upon. Inasmuch as the German Government by the spring of 1914 had in some secret way become informed [213] of the Grey-Cambon letters all these denials caused uneasiness in Germany. This was especially the case in connection with the negotiations for an Anglo-Russian naval convention just before the War.

The Grey-Cambon letters, following the consistent diplomatic support which England had given France throughout the Morocco crises, established a very satisfactory basis of mutual confidence between the French and British Governments. This confidence and harmony was strengthened by many factors: by the common distrust of Germany; by the cordial personal relations between Sir Edward Grey and Paul Cambon; by the fact that England had no aggressive aims which conflicted with French interests; and by the care with which M. Poincaré sought to consult Sir Edward Grey's wishes and as far as possible conform French policy to them. There was in fact more harmony and mutual confidence between France and England, though

[211] G.P., XXXI, 523 f., 528.

[212] G.P., XXXI, 523 ff.; L'Alliance Franco-Russe, 138; Poincaré, II, 114.

[213] G.P., XXXI, 544 note; Grey, I, 286. Presumably the information came through Siebert, a secretary in the Russian Embassy in London, see ch. i. note 68.

they were only "friends," than between France and Russia
who were allies. It was a striking example of the fact that
a well established friendship is better than an alliance.
Many writers, however, especially the "revisionists" and
critics of Poincaré, have argued that there was a complete
unity also between Paris and St. Petersburg; that Poincaré
and Izvolski worked harmoniously hand in hand, though
they are not agreed as to whether the Frenchman was the
tool of the Russian, or *vice versa*. Their arguments rest
largely on the Izvolski correspondence and their conviction
that Izvolski and Poincaré were both working for war, the
one to get Constantinople and the Straits, the other to recover Alsace-Lorraine. But we believe that a closer examination of the Izvolski correspondence, of M. Sazonov's
character and methods, and of M. Poincaré's memoirs
would show that there was by no means that perfect unity
between the two allies which has often been assumed.

As has been pointed out in the second chapter, the
Franco-Russian Alliance in its origin was essentially defensive in its wording and purpose. For nearly twenty
years it remained so. It was not interpreted to cover Russian ambitions in the Balkans and the Far East, nor French
ambitions in North Africa and the lost provinces on the
Rhine. Russia had given France only lukewarm support
in 1905, at Algeciras, and in the Agadir Crisis. France's
negative attitude had been one of the reasons for Izvolski's
failure to open the Straits after the Buchlau bargain; and
again in 1911 France refused to be "nailed down" to support another of Izvolski's efforts to open the Straits in the
Charikov affair.[214] But in 1912, under the Premiership of
M. Poincaré, the character of the alliance began to be
changed. France began to support more actively Russia's
aggressive policies in the Balkans, and assured her that
France would give her armed support if they involved

[214] For the details, see below, ch. v.

Russia in war with Austria and Germany. One of the first signs and causes of this change is to be found in connection with the intrigues against M. Georges Louis.[215]

M. Georges Louis, a trained diplomat, served as Political Director in the French Foreign Office from 1904 to 1909, and then as Ambassador to Russia until his recall in February, 1913. He had used his influence to restrict the application of the Franco-Russian Alliance to its originally defensive character. He favored the Anglo-French policy of maintaining the integrity of the Ottoman Empire in contrast to Russia's designs upon it. He feared Russia's Balkan ambitions might involve France in war, and he was suspicious of the aims and intrigues of Izvolski. In the fall of 1911, when temporarily filling again the vacant office of Political Director at Paris, he had thwarted Izvolski's efforts to "nail France down" to a written agreement to support a plan for opening the Straits to Russian warships.[216] He had thereby incurred the displeasure of Izvolski and Sazonov. They also complained that as Ambassador he did not transmit accurately to Paris the views of the Russian Minister of Foreign Affairs. If this was true, it was certainly not wholly the Ambassador's fault, but was in part owing to M. Sazonov's lack of frankness in stating his views, and also to the fact that he often shifted them suddenly. He had, for instance, drawn up and shown to Georges Louis a *questionnaire* on February 14, 1912. This raised a whole

[215] This unsavory affair has been dealt with at great length by M. Ernest Judet, *Georges Louis* (Paris, 1925) and by M. Poincaré, I, 294 ff., 333 ff.; II, 32 ff.; Judet, championing the cause and memory of his friend, bases his account in considerable part on official despatches contained among Georges Louis's papers and on his *Carnets* (2 vols., Paris, 1926), which is made up of Georges Louis's notes of conversations with prominent persons. M. Poincaré's reply to Judet's stinging attack is largely based on official despatches which he has been able to select from his own papers or from the French archives. In the following paragraphs only a bare summary of the facts can be given.

[216] See below, for the details, ch. v. at notes 114-126; also Judet, pp. 131-167; Poincaré, I. 333-347.

series of fundamental questions about the Balkans growing
out of Italy's Tripolitan War, and seemed to indicate that
Sazonov was contemplating some important action to which
he wished to secure French assent. "These are the most
serious questions which Russia can raise for her ally," Louis
wrote to Poincaré next day.[217] But Sazonov then apparently changed his mind suddenly; to Louis's repeated efforts
to induce him to discuss the *questionnaire* and the intentions which lay back of it, Sazonov only answered evasively.
On many other occasions, as in the case of the Potsdam negotiations, Sazonov took important steps or consulted with
Germany without first informing Georges Louis; this lack
of regard for Franco-Russian solidarity was very irritating
to Poincaré. It was his great aim to have the Triple Entente present a solid diplomatic front to the Triple Alliance.

M. Sazonov also nourished a personal grievance against
Georges Louis. This arose from the curious fact, which one
would hardly have expected between two allies, that Sazonov's agents had discovered how to decipher the French
secret diplomatic code, and were spying upon the telegrams
between Georges Louis and the French Government. M.
Louis suspected this and repeatedly warned Poincaré that
the cipher ought to be changed more frequently. In April,
1912, in one of Georges Louis's deciphered telegrams, Sazonov thought he discovered that Louis had accused him of
being dilatory in regard to a Chinese loan.[218] Thereupon
he instructed Izvolski to try to get Georges Louis recalled
and have someone else sent as French Ambassador to St.
Petersburg. Izvolski readily undertook the task, though it
was a very delicate and embarrassing one. Poincaré at

217 Judet, p. 174; *cf.* Poincaré, II, 24 ff.
218 Judet, p. 85. In reality Louis had referred to the dilatoriness of
the "ministry" before Sazonov became Minister of Foreign Affairs, but
Sazonov's agent had made the mistake of deciphering "minister" instead
of "ministry" and Sazonov had taken this to be a personal reference to
himself.

once complied with the request. On May 8, 1912, he had
M. Paléologue, the new Political Director, telegraph to
Georges Louis:

> With as much surprise as regret, the President of the
> Council has been officially notified that the Russian Gov-
> ernment wishes to see France represented by an Ambassador
> who displays more activity in his political functions and
> social relations. . . .
>
> The diplomatic problems which are at present being
> discussed between Paris and St. Petersburg are too serious
> for our efforts to be paralyzed soon by the fact that M.
> Sazonov declares that he does not feel in touch with
> you. . . .
>
> M. Poincaré therefore invokes your patriotism to resign
> your Embassy, with the intention of finding another place
> for you as soon as possible. I am forced to recognize, as
> well as he, the imperative necessity of providing for your re-
> placement.[219]

On receipt of this Georges Louis was at first dum-
founded. Then, suspecting that Sazonov and Izvolski were
intriguing against him, and being assured by Kokovtsev,
the President of the Russian Council, that the Russian
Government knew nothing of any request for his recall, he
telegraphed to Poincaré begging him to delay his decision,
and hurried to Paris to lay his suspicions before Poincaré
in person. One of the most influential members of the
Cabinet, M. Léon Bourgeois, opposed yielding to Izvolski's
request for the Ambassador's dismissal, and other friends
rallied to his support. Meanwhile, something of the affair
had leaked out, and several newspapers raised an uproar
against Izvolski's unwarranted interference in French affairs. The incident threatened to become a scandal, seriously troubling Franco-Russian relations. So Poincaré
found it more prudent to issue a sweeping denial that any

[219] Judet, p. 28 f.

request had been made to him for Georges Louis's recall, and the Ambassador was allowed to return to his post until the outcry had died down and a more suitable occasion should occur for his removal.[220]

This Georges Louis incident is important because it increased Poincaré's distrust of Izvolski, and made him all the more anxious to get into closer relations with Sazonov and so keep a more solid hold on the policies of France's ally. To secure Sazonov's confidence and loyal coöperation in maintaining solidarity of action on the part of the two Allied Powers was M. Poincaré's great aim henceforth. He sought to accomplish this in many ways: by visiting Russia in August, 1912, and in July, 1914; by reiterating that France was ready to support Russia in case of war; by backing up Russia's Balkan policies much more actively; by arranging French loans for Russian military preparations against Germany; by strengthening France's own armaments; and by the ultimate removal of Georges Louis.

By his visit to Russia in August, 1912, M. Poincaré did much to strengthen the bonds between the two allied countries. He sought to counteract the effect of the Tsar's recent meeting with the Kaiser at Port Baltic, and make sure that Russia made no further separate arrangements with Germany after the fashion of the Potsdam Agreements.[221] He also wished to clear up and smooth out the Georges Louis incident. He discussed with Sazonov, Kokovtsev, and the Tsar all the chief matters in which France and Russia had common interests—Asia Minor, the Chinese loan, the Turco-Italian War, the recent Naval Convention, the prospect of English coöperation, and the preparations made by the French and Russian Staffs for

---

[220] Judet, pp. 83-130; Poincaré, I, 333 ff.

[221] On the meeting of the Tsar and the Kaiser at Port Baltic, see Poincaré, I, 310 ff.; 379 ff.; Sazonov, *Fateful Years* (N. Y., 1928), p. 43 ff.; and G.P., XXXI, 427-454.

military action in case of war with Germany. He particularly urged Russia to develop her strategic railways to the West to facilitate the rapid concentration of the Russian forces against Germany. On all these points there was substantial harmony. But on one question, the most important one of all, Poincaré discovered another alarming evidence of Sazonov's lack of frankness: he had not revealed the terms of the secret Balkan League which had been drawn up with Russian assistance during the preceding winter. This had been signed on March 13, 1912, but Sazonov had given no hint of its contents and the fact that it was likely to lead to war in the Balkans. When he now read it to his French guest, Poincaré shrewdly perceived its dangerous character and exclaimed: *"C'est un instrument de guerre."* [222] He justly protested to Sazonov at having been kept so long in the dark about a matter which might involve Russia, and consequently France in war. He urged that each should keep the other fully informed as to his intentions. He defined the alliance in its originally defensive form, but immediately added words which encouraged Sazonov to believe that in a crisis Russia could count upon France. As Sazonov reported, among other things, to the Tsar:

> After having confirmed our reciprocal intention of observing with vigilance events in the Balkans, and of exchanging continuously our news and views on the subject, we agreed anew with M. Poincaré to set up a common action to prevent by diplomatic means an aggravation of the situation so soon as any complication should arise and according to circumstances.
>
> M. Poincaré considered it his duty to emphasize the point that public opinion in France would not permit the Government of the Republic to decide on a military action for the

[222] So he told Izvolski; M.F.R., p. 273; L.N., I, 324; Stieve, II, 250. See also below, ch. v.

sake of purely Balkan questions if Germany did not take part and if she did not provoke on her own initiative the application of the *casus foederis*. In this latter case we could certainly count on France for the exact and complete fulfilment of her obligations toward us.

On my part I declared to the French Minister that, while always being ready to range ourselves on the side of France in the cases contemplated by our alliance, we also could not justify to Russian public opinion taking an active part in the military operations provoked by colonial questions outside Europe, so long as the vital interests of France in Europe were not touched. . . . I am very glad to have had the occasion for making the acquaintance of M. Poincaré and of entering into personal relations with him, all the more so, because the exchange of views which I have had with him has left me with the impression that in his person Russia possesses a sure and faithful friend endowed with exceptional political ability, and with an inflexible determination. In case of a crisis in international relations, it would be very desirable that our ally should have as her head, if not M. Poincaré himself, at least a personality possessing the same decision and as free from the fear of responsibility as the present French Prime Minister.[223]

Faced with the *fait accompli* of the Balkan League and the potential dangers involved in it, Poincaré took steps with the other Powers to try to prevent the Balkan States from actually going to war. But they came too late. The Balkan Wars of 1912-1913 increased the delicacy and the importance of Franco-Russian relations, and also of relations between the Triple Entente and Triple Alliance. During the first weeks of the Balkan Wars his policy remained the same as on his visit to Russia; restraint of Sazonov from rash steps through insistence on a preliminary exchange of views, coupled, however, with assurances of

[223] Sazonov's report to the Tsar, Aug. 17, 1912; M.F.R., p. 255 ff.; L.N., II, 338 ff.; Stieve, II, 219 ff.; and (in part) Siebert-Schreiner, pp. 652-655. *Cf.* also Poincaré, II, 99-169, especially 114 ff.; and below, ch. v.

complete loyalty to the obligations of the alliance; subordination of Russia's Balkan interests to the greater question of the preservation of peace between the Great Powers; the establishment of complete solidarity of purpose and action on the part of the Triple Entente Powers, coupled, however, with a willingness to coöperate with the Triple Alliance so long as the latter did not make excessive claims. But as the War proceeded and the Balkan allies won their great victories, there was some change, or rather shift of emphasis, in his guidance of French policy. This change, however, was not nearly as great as many of his critics have asserted, nor as considerable as Izvolski was inclined to represent in his despatches to St. Petersburg.

Poincaré found that Sazonov's purposes were not always clear and easy to reckon with. Sazonov did not always exchange views and come to a prior understanding with France. He had been dilatory or non-committal in replying to French proposals. At the beginning of the War he had rejoiced with the Pan-Slavs at the astonishing military successes of the Balkan States over Turkey. But the overwhelming victories of Kirk Kilissé and Lulé Burgas, and the rapid advance of Ferdinand's troops toward Constantinople, was an unpleasant damper on his enthusiasm. A Bulgarian occupation of the Turkish capital threatened to thwart indefinitely Russia's own historic hopes in that quarter. Even if the Powers who had political and financial interests there should refuse to permit the Bulgarians to have the city, they might take advantage of the opportunity to carry out Sir Edward Grey's idea of an internationalization of the Straits. Accordingly, even while the battle of Lulé Burgas was still in progress, Sazonov had urged the Bulgarians to recognize "the necessity for prudence and to halt in time," endeavoring to bribe them to listen to reason by promises of future diplomatic support. At the same time he informed France and England that he would greatly welcome intervention at Sofia and Belgrade in favor of mediation to restrain the victorious Slavs—in the war which Russia had helped to cause by her part in the formation of the Balkan League.[224] Three days later, in spite of the fact that Poincaré had already taken the initiative in the direction desired by Russia, and without any warning or prior consultation, Sazonov presented all the Powers with a complete program for immediate intervention: the maintenance of the Sultan in Constantinople with a defense zone including Thrace and Adrianople; an autonomous Albania; compensations to Rumania for remaining neutral; Serbian access to the Adriatic; and free transit for Austrian goods through the new Serbian territory.[225]

Except for Serbian access to the Adriatic, this whole program was in the nature of concessions to the Triple Alliance. As compared with Constantinople, Sazonov cared very slightly for "the little Slav sisters" or for the solidarity of the Triple Entente. Without giving Poincaré time to recover from his astonishment at the proposed concessions, Sazonov sent him the further startling news that if the Bulgarians occupied Constantinople the whole Russian Black Sea Fleet would "appear before the Turkish capital." [226] The Russian Admiralty plans went further: "For the protection of our Embassy and our interests in general, it will naturally be necessary to land, and in order not to weaken the navy crews, the despatch of some troop divisions with machine guns is desired. . . . The occupation of the Bosphorus one would not extend very far, but it would then be easier to remain there forever. If we have the Bosphorus tight in hand, the troublesome Straits Question is already half settled. If a favorable opportunity for such an advance

[224] Sazonov to Benckendorff and Izvolski, Oct. 31, 1912; *Krasnyi Arkhiv*, XVI, 19; Siebert-Schreiner, p. 381 f.; Stieve, II, 326.

[225] Sazonov's circular, Nov. 2; M.F.R., p. 293; L.N., II, 565; Stieve, II, 328.

[226] Sazonov to Izvolski, Nov. 4; L.N., I, 339; Stieve, II, 331.

cannot be found, then it must be artificially created; because, if it is impossible to get possession of the whole Straits, we should at least have an eye to the enormous political advantage which the Bosphorus has." [227]

French public opinion, however, had been reassured by the Balkan victories and began to take a new interest in Russia's Balkan policies. A public declaration by Poincaré of French loyalty to Russia had aroused great enthusiasm. "Nothing succeeds like success," Izvolski reported; "under the influence of recent events one notices here a marked change in feeling in favor of the Balkan States and the Russian point of view"; and he added that he would do all he could to strengthen this new attitude, especially by influencing the Press, but for this he needed more money at his disposal.[228] Poincaré was not enthusiastic for Sazonov's program of intervention which would antagonize Bulgaria and Serbia. He was impressed by the new weight and influence which the Balkan victories had given to the Slav cause and to the Triple Entente in the Balance of Power in Europe. He also suspected that Austria, backed by Germany, might take advantage of the situation to attempt territorial aggrandizements, and this he was determined to prevent, not only in the interests of Russia and Serbia, but of France and the prestige of the Triple Entente. He was more concerned over what Austria might do, than at Sazonov's anxiety about Constantinople. As Izvolski reported on November 7: "Whereas France up to the present has declared that local, so to speak, purely Balkan events could not induce her to take any active measures, the French Government now appears to admit that an acquisition of territory on the part of Austria in the Balkans would affect the general European equilibrium and consequently also the

---

[227] Admiralty Staff Report, Nov. 2, 1912; *Krasnyi Arkhiv*, VI, 52.

[228] Izvolski to Sazonov, Oct. 28, M.F.R., p. 292; L.N., II, 564; Stieve, II, 320. On Izvolski's activities in bribing the French Press, see below, ch. V, note 117.

special interests of France. . . . Poincaré is perfectly conscious of the fact that France may thus become involved
in a warlike action. For the present, of course, he submits
this question merely for our consideration, but in a conversation with me Paléologue plainly admitted that the
proposed agreement might lead to some kind of active
step." [229]

Serbia's occupation of Northern Albania and desire for
a port on the Adriatic soon became a dangerously acute
question. Austria threatened to use force if necessary to
prevent this, and had the support of both her allies. Sazonov naturally favored the Serbian demand, but not to the
point of making war. He was secretly inclined to find some
compromise proposal, such as giving Serbia a railway outlet
on the Adriatic, but not part of Northern Albania to which
Austria and Italy particularly objected. When he inquired
what would be the attitude of France if an active intervention by Austria could not be avoided, Poincaré replied,
according to Izvolski:

> It is for Russia to take the initiative in a question in
> which she is the most interested party. France's task is
> to lend her the most effective support. If the French Gov-
> ernment should take the initiative it would risk falling short
> of, or overstepping, the intentions of its ally. . . . In short,
> added M. Poincaré, if Russia goes to war, France will do
> the same, for we all know that Germany will stand behind
> Austria in this question.[230]

This statement, which has been much quoted by Poincaré's critics as showing the triumphant influence exerted
on him by the intriguing Izvolski, is severely criticized by
Poincaré in his memoirs as being inaccurate. As a matter
of fact, he was again insisting that he did not wish to make
promises until Sazonov had taken the initiative in saying

[229] M.F.R., p. 296; L.N., I, 342; Stieve, II, 336.
[230] Izvolski to Sazonov, Nov. 17, M.F.R., p. 300; L.N., I, 346; Stieve,
II, 346. Cf. however, Poincaré, II, 336 ff.

clearly what he wanted. Then France would be able to make her views known. As to war, he again defined the obligations of the alliance in the same terms he had used to Sazonov in August: France would go to war if the particular case of the *casus foederis* provided in the Alliance were fulfilled, namely, "if Russia is attacked by Germany or by Austria supported by Germany." Until then he would keep his hands free. A couple of days later he took care to warn Georges Louis of Izvolski's misrepresentations and asked him to correct any false impressions which they may have caused. Izvolski's report is therefore undoubtedly inaccurate as a representation of Poincaré's words; but it is accurate as a representation of what Sazonov was being told by his Russian Ambassador in Paris were Poincaré's views. And it indicates that Poincaré was now ready to consider seriously the question of war arising out of Balkan problems in which Russia was interested. In 1912, however, Russia was not prepared for war; none of the Great Powers wanted it, and the Serbian question was referred for settlement to the London Conference of Ambassadors.

With a person of Izvolski's intriguing, ambitious, and not wholly trustworthy character as Russian Ambassador at Paris, it was all the more important that France should have at St. Petersburg a man of Georges Louis's views, who was on his guard against the danger of Russia's ambitions in regard to the Straits. But on February 17, 1913, Georges Louis was suddenly notified of his definite dismissal and replacement by M. Delcassé. M. Poincaré had just become President of the Republic and the responsibility for the change in the French Embassy at St. Petersburg could be technically placed upon the shoulders of the Briand Cabinet in which M. Jonnart succeeded Poincaré as Minister of Foreign Affairs.[231] After being thus "politically assassi-

[231] Judet, pp. 205-234; Poincaré, II, 70; *Foreign Affairs* (N. Y.), IV, 11, Oct., 1925.

nated," as his friends called his dismissal, Georges Louis's diplomatic career was ruined. No new place was found for him. He died in 1917 in the midst of the War which it had been his aim to avert. Doubtless there is some truth in Poincaré's explanation that Louis's frail health and his lack of intimate relations with Sazonov and influential circles at St. Petersburg made it desirable in the interests of allied solidarity that he should be replaced by someone who would coöperate more cordially with Sazonov and his Balkan policies. The fact that he was succeeded by Delcassé, and then by Paléologue, who were both strongly in favor of strengthening the bonds of the alliance by giving Russia strong support, did make for harmony between the Cabinets of Paris and St. Petersburg. It did tend thereby to tighten the Triple Entente, but it also encouraged Sazonov in his support of Serbia and his stiff attitude to Austria and Germany which was one of the main causes of war in 1914.

THE RENEWAL AND WEAKNESS OF THE TRIPLE ALLIANCE, 1912

Bismarck, who regarded the Austro-German Alliance of 1879 as strictly defensive, had refused to permit military agreements between the German and Austrian Staffs, for fear that they might hamper the political freedom of action of the civilian authorities. This Alliance, therefore, as well as the Triple Alliance, had long remained without being supplemented by any such definite military convention, stating the number of troops which each ally was bound to furnish in case of war, as in the case of the Franco-Russian Military Convention in 1894.[232] Nor for many years were

---

[232] Two minor exceptions to this general statement were the convention of 1888 providing for the service of Italian troops on the Rhine frontier in case of a Franco-German war (cf., G.P., VI, 247), and a convention of 1900 providing for naval coöperation by the Triple Alliance in case of war with France and Russia (Pribram, I, 241). See also W. Foerster, "Die deutsch-italienische Militärkonvention," in KSF, V, 395-416, May, 1927.

there any regular periodical conferences between the Staffs of the Triple Alliance Powers, with written protocols fixing in detail the coöperation of their armies, as in the case of the annual conferences between the French and Russian Staffs from 1900 onwards.[233] But in January, 1909, when the Bosnian Crisis began to look alarming, Moltke and Conrad, the Chiefs of Staff of the German and Austrian armies did enter into a correspondence concerning possible military coöperation.[234] It was carried on with the knowledge and approval of the civilian authorities of the two countries, and was continued intermittently during the following years. It was also supplemented by personal meetings between the two generals at visits during military maneuvers and other occasions. One Austrian writer sees in this correspondence a "military convention" which transformed the Austro-German Alliance from its originally defensive character into an offensive agreement. He even makes it the "key" to the whole question of responsibility for the war.[235] But nowhere did Moltke and Conrad, or any other persons in authority, ever refer to this exchange of views as a "military convention." On the contrary, it was more in the nature of a general discussion of the political situation, and an exchange of information as to the plan of campaign which each intended to put into operation, if war should be declared by the civilian authorities. Conrad was trying to persuade Moltke to make Germany's mobilization plan provide for as many troops as possible against Russia, so as to lessen the number which the Tsar would have available against Austria. Moltke, in turn, wanted to have Conrad plan to use few troops in Serbia, and send as many as possible into Galicia against Russia, in order to

[233] For summaries of the earlier Franco-Russian military conferences, see *Les Alliés contre la Russie*, pp. 8-39; and for the protocols of those in 1911, 1912, and 1913, see M.F.R., pp. 697-718; and L.N., II, 419-437.

[234] Conrad, I, 379-406; II, 54-62.

[235] H. Kanner, *Der Schlüssel zur Kriegsschuldfrage*, Munich, 1926.

relieve the pressure on Germany's eastern frontier, while
the bulk of the German forces were being thrown against
France. Their arrangements with one another were hardly
as definite or as binding as those which were being made
by the French and Russian Staffs. Though some of the
Moltke-Conrad letters were shown to the civilian authorities, they did not legally modify the terms of the Alliance.
This remained fixed in writing, and its interpretation and
application rested with the civilian, and not the military,
authorities.

On the other hand, it is undoubtedly true that this
Moltke-Conrad correspondence tended to foster the conviction at Vienna, that if Austria attacked Serbia, she could
count on a threat of German mobilization to bluff Russia
into remaining inactive; or upon German support, if Russia
made war. In this sense it did tend to give the Alliance
a potentially offensive, rather than defensive, character.
Another result of their correspondence was the fact that
Moltke and Conrad made mobilization plans which were
dependent for success on one another, and, as in all such
cases, this enabled the military authorities in a time of crisis
to exert pressure on the civilian authorities in favor of war.
To what extent this was actually the case in July, 1914, will
be discussed later in the second volume. In the years before the final crisis, the personal friendship and mutual confidence between Moltke and Conrad had been one of the
factors in strengthening the bonds between these two
allies.

Italy was the element of weakness in the Triple Alliance.
Ever since the Algeciras Conference Germany had regarded
her loyalty with doubt. Conrad was so convinced not only
of her probable disloyalty to her treaty obligations, but of
her positive hostility, that he speaks of her as Austria's
"principal opponent." He made plans for mobilization
against her, and even wanted a "preventive war" against

her.[236] Italy's war with Turkey for the possession of Tripoli had further displeased her allies, not only because they had not been fully consulted beforehand, but because it embarrassed them to have their nominal ally attack the Turks, whose friendship and good-will they were trying to cultivate. To be sure, the events of the war and Italy's establishment as a sea-power in the Mediterranean had led to a decided coolness in her relations with France. But these had improved again by the summer of 1912 so that Poincaré and Sazonov both agreed that it was best to keep Italy as a "dead weight" in the Triple Alliance, where she would be useful to both France and Russia.[237]

Though the Triple Alliance was to run until 1914, the question of its renewal had already begun to be discussed in the summer of 1911. Italy favored its early renewal as a means of placating her allies on the eve of her Tripolitan adventure. Germany favored it, being always glad of anything which might make for better relations between her two allies, and thus help to counter-balance the growing strength and solidarity of the Triple Entente. Aehrenthal at first was not opposed to it.[238] But Conrad and the military officers were so incensed at Italy's insults and treacheries that they saw no use in trying to keep her even as a nominal ally. General Auffenberg related with childish indignation to the German Ambassador in Vienna evidences of Italian animosity which he had just seen in the Southern Tyrol: every day or two a patrol had to be detailed to clean up the insulting epithets scribbled on a war memorial; he had seen cigarette boxes in which all the Austrian territory from Fiume to the Brenner Pass was marked as belonging to Italy; irredentist propaganda even took the form of calling the horses and mules by the names of Austrian

[236] For the period 1907-1912, *cf.* Conrad, I, 110, 128, 141, 173, 224, 272.

[237] Sazonov's report to the Tsar, Aug. 17, 1912; L.N., II, 340.

[238] G.P., XXX, 495-510.

cities like Trent and Trieste! "In case of a war Italy would explode against us like a keg of powder," he added, declaring that the best thing for Austria to do would be to crush the irredentist hopes by war, and then Austria would be freer to deal with Serbia or meet a Russian attack.[239] Aehrenthal, however, had Francis Joseph on his side, and secured the dismissal of Conrad because the latter was urging war with Italy and friendship with Russia. The Tripolitan War delayed the negotiations for the renewal of the Triple Alliance. It was finally renewed, however, on December 5, 1912, without modification, being extended for six years from July 8, 1914.[240] A couple of weeks later, Italy notified Germany that, in view of the existing political conditions, frankness compelled her to say that she would be unable to carry out her agreement of 1888 for sending troops to coöperate with a German army on the Rhine.[241]

THE EFFECTS OF THE BALKAN WARS

The outbreak of the Balkan Wars and the consequent intensification of the conflict of interests between all the Powers, great and small, affected the system of alliances in several ways.

It increased the internal friction within the Triple Alliance and Triple Entente. A study of the daily and even hourly interchange of telegrams which went on between the members of each group during the succession of crises and kaleidoscopic changes which took place in the Balkans during 1912 and 1913 shows, for instance, that Germany was constantly irritated by the selfish policies and rash acts of her Austrian ally. She was irritated because Austrian policies sometimes ran counter to her own views on Balkan affairs, and sometimes because they might endanger the

[239] Tschirschky to Bethmann, Nov. 18, 1911; *ibid.*, 514 ff.
[240] Tschirschky to Bethmann, 568; Pribram, I, 268-298.
[241] G.P., XXX, 574-579; Pribram, I, 299.

peace of Europe. For example, Germany had no great desire for the creation of an autonomous Albania. The Kaiser did not think that the country was capable of governing itself, and he thought it very doubtful whether any European prince could be found who could succeed in the difficult task.[242] In spite of this, however, Germany consented to support Austria's wishes (and also Italy's) for the creation of an autonomous Albania which should exclude Serbia from access to the Adriatic. Similar clashes of interest existed between France and her ally. France desired the maintenance of the integrity of the Ottoman Empire, in which she had large financial interests, and wanted the right to construct railways in northern Asia Minor, which would strengthen and develop Turkey. Russia opposed these railways because they might aid Turkey to move troops more easily to prevent the Russian advance south of the Caucasus. An interesting example of this internal conflict within each group is seen in the intrigues in regard to the disposal of Kavala at the close of the Balkan Wars. Austria and Russia, for various reasons to be explained in the next chapter, wanted to give Kavala to the Bulgarians; their allies, Germany and France, instead of agreeing with them respectively, were in favor of letting the Greeks keep it. The Greeks kept it.

This internal friction, however, was more than counterbalanced by the feeling in each group that it must do everything possible to preserve unity and solidarity among its members. Allies must stand together and support one another's policies, consenting to policies which were unpalatable, or even consenting to acts which might involve dangers to the peace of Europe. In this way Austria was often a liability, rather than an asset, to Germany, as was also Russia to France. Sometimes the dominant member exerted successfully a restraining influence on her ally in favor

[242] G.P., XXXVI, 127-745, *passim.*

of moderation and the preservation of the peace, as in the case of Germany's veto on Austria's contemplated intervention against Serbia in July, 1913, or France's unwillingness to approve Sazonov's proposed measures for exerting pressure on Turkey in connection with Liman von Sanders affair.[243]

In the recently published German documents and in Conrad's memoirs one finds many cases indicating that Germany encouraged Austria to take steps against Serbia for putting an end to the "Greater Serbia" danger in the belief that it threatened the existence of the Dual Monarchy and consequently of Germany's only remaining reliable ally.[244] They occur in official despatches from the German Foreign Office to the German Ambassador in Vienna, in the correspondence and interviews between Moltke and Conrad, and occasionally in the meetings between the German Kaiser and Franz Ferdinand. On the other hand, however, one finds as many, if not more, cases of an exactly opposite kind, in which German officials, especially the Kaiser, urged Austria to come to some arrangement with Serbia and warned her against using force.[245] On the whole, we believe we are justified in saying that Germany's influence was in favor of moderation and peace rather than the contrary—until the provocation of the Sarajevo assassination.

[243] See below, ch. v.

[244] G.P., XXVI, *passim* (Bosnian Crisis); XXX, 253; XXXIII, 274 ff., 330, 373 f.; XXXIV, 34 ff.; XXXVI, 386 ff.; XXXIX, 325 ff. (Konopischt Meeting). Conrad, I, 95 f., 106 ff., 129 ff., 202 f., 369 ff.; II, 54 ff.; III, 38 f., 143 ff., 294, 328, 368 f., 424 ff., 469 f., 474, 609 ff., 667 ff. *Cf.* also W. Schüssler, *Oesterreich und das deutsche Schicksal* (Leipzig, 1925), pp. 8 ff., 177 ff.; and H. Kanner, *Der Schlüssel zur Kriegsschuldfrage* (Munich, 1926), *passim.*

[245] G.P., XXXIII, 42, 80, 92 ff., 116, 150, 295 ff., 355 ff., 371 ff., 426 ff., 478 f.; XXXIV, 444 ff., 455 ff., 538 ff., 619 ff., 674 ff., 820 ff.; XXXV, 52 ff., 66 ff., 122 ff., 319 ff. (Kavala affair and non-revision of the Treaty of Bucharest); XXXVI, 27 ff.; XXXVIII, 335, 342 ff. Conrad, I, 156, 165; III, 78 ff., 143 ff., 164 ff., 318, 404, 410, 417, 429 ff., 448, 597 f., 627 f., 632, 644 f., 729. *Cf.* also H. Friedjung, *Das Zeitalter des Imperialismus* (Berlin, 1919-1922), III, *passim.*

To what extent France in the same way gave dangerous encouragement or exercised wise moderation on Russia, it is difficult to say. The evidence furnished by Sazonov's correspondence with Izvolski and Benckendorff, his reports to the Tsar, and other Russian material on the one hand, is often contradicted, on the other, by Poincaré's memoirs and by the *French Yellow Book* on Balkan Affairs. But it must be remembered that this *Yellow Book* is very far from complete, the documents in it evidently being selected to support the view that M. Poincaré's policy was always in the interests of the peace of Europe. On this question, no wholly satisfactory answer can be given until the French make a full publication of their pre-War documents, similar to that already made by Germany and to that in course of publication by England.

One effect of the Balkan Wars, which was most serious to the peace of Europe and to the crystallization of opposition between the Triple Alliance and the Triple Entente, was the intensification of the general movement for an increase of armaments on the part of all the Continental Powers. We have already noted above the antagonism between England and Germany caused by the rapid construction of Dreadnoughts and the failure of the Haldane Mission. At the same time that Germany passed the Naval Bill of 1912 she made a considerable increase in her army. In 1913 a new Army Law provided for a much larger increase to take place in the following years. Before France was aware of this German Army Law of 1913, Poincaré and the little group associated with him had already decided to bring in a bill greatly increasing the strength of the French army. Convinced that sooner or later a war was "inevitable," they persuaded the French Chamber of Deputies to vote the law extending the French term of active military training from two to three years, and the liability for service in the reserve from the age of forty-five to forty-eight. According to the opinion of Colonel Buat, who was one of the ablest French experts and officially in charge of one section of the French General Staff, France would have in 1914 a slightly larger army than Germany in the first weeks of a war.[246] The idea that Germany was overwhelmingly superior in numbers in her invasion of Belgium and France in 1914 is a myth. In Russia also strenuous efforts were being made to organize and train a greater number of her vast population. The increases in Austria and Italy were relatively slight. We refrain at this point from giving any figures as to the relative size of armies and military expenditures because such figures are apt to be extremely misleading. Figures comparing English and German naval expenditures have no significance unless allowance is made for the cheaper costs of construction in Germany and the system of obligatory service instead of voluntary enlistment. Similarly the size and strength of armies is not indicated merely by the numbers of troops, but depends in large part upon efficiency of equipment, rapidity of mobilization, and other technical matters which would require long comment if trustworthy and really just bases of comparison are to be made. By the spring of 1914 all these armaments in progress of preparation had raised in both Triple Alliance and Triple Entente a growing uneasiness and suspicion. Everywhere thoughtful observers were alarmed at the situation, but little was accomplished to alleviate it. Colonel House went to Europe with the hope of doing something about it, and wrote to President Wilson, a month before the assassination of the Austrian Archduke:

> The situation is extraordinary. It is militarism run stark mad. Unless someone acting for you can bring about a different understanding, there is some day to be an awful cataclysm. No one in Europe can do it. There is too much

[246] E. Buat, *L'armée allemande pendant la guerre de 1914-1918*, Paris, 1920; Montgelas, *Leitfaden*, 81-87.

hatred, too many jealousies. Whenever England consents, France and Russia will close in on Germany and Austria. England does not want Germany wholly crushed, for she would then have to reckon alone with her ancient enemy, Russia; but if Germany insists upon an ever-increasing navy, then England will have no choice. The best chance for peace is an understanding between England and Germany in regard to naval armaments and yet there is some disadvantage to us by these two getting too close.[247]

One beneficial consequence of the Balkan crisis was the increased effort sincerely made to establish a "Concert of Europe," which should counteract the opposition between the Triple Alliance and Triple Entente. This was the aim of the London Conference of Ambassadors, and it succeeded in its task of finding peaceful solutions of most difficult problems. Possibly if such another conference could have been arranged in July, 1914, it also might have averted the catastrophe. In this matter of the Concert of Europe each statesman was continually torn between two conflicting purposes. On the one hand, he wished to preserve and strengthen the solidarity of the group which he represented —Triple Alliance or Triple Entente as the case might happen to be. He therefore aimed to reach a prior agreement within his own group which would safeguard the prestige and interests of the other two members and thus of the group as a whole; and then to try to impose the acceptance of this prearranged agreement upon the members of the opposing group. This of course tended to accentuate the crystallization of opposition between Triple Alliance and Triple Entente, and if carried too far, as in 1914, would precipitate war. At the same time, on the other hand, most of the statesmen of Europe were aiming at an altogether different purpose. In the interests of peace, they were

---

[247] Charles Seymour, *The Intimate Papers of Colonel House* (Boston and New York, 1926), I, 249; *cf.* also G.P., XXXIX, 107-117.

genuinely trying to maintain the Concert of Europe, that is, to have all six Great Powers arrive at collective action and common views in a conciliatory spirit and by means of compromises. This often involved sacrificing to some extent the interests of his own country, or at least those of his ally. In Balkan questions Austria and Russia had the greatest interests and were therefore the countries most frequently expected to make sacrifices. England, whose interests were least, and who was not bound by any formal alliance, could most easily afford to serve as a medium in smoothing out opposition between the others. It is not here possible to review in detail the extent to which each of the leading statesmen of Europe pursued each of these two opposite purposes. As one reads the complicated diplomatic negotiations of the years immediately preceding the War one gets the impression, beyond all doubt, that Sir Edward Grey was the man who most sincerely and tirelessly placed the Concert of Europe above the interests of any single Power or group. Next to him in support of the Concert of Europe would come Bethmann-Hollweg and the German Secretary of State, Kiderlen-Wächter; but Kiderlen died in December, 1912, and after that the German Chancellor was less able to make his influence prevail over that of Tirpitz and the Kaiser. In France, M. Poincaré was more interested in the solidarity of the Triple Entente, than in the Concert of Europe; but in order to preserve the confidence and friendship of England, which was one of his primary aims, he also frequently took the lead in steps for initiating or upholding collective action by the Powers. Sazonov and Izvolski cared less for the Concert of Europe, and Count Berchtold least of all.

It was while Europe was thus divided into two opposed groups that a new danger arose from the assassination of the Austrian Archduke and a new intensification of Balkan problems.

CHAPTER V

BALKAN PROBLEMS, 1907-1914

THE Balkan situation was one of the most important factors in causing the World War. It sharpened the antagonism between the Triple Alliance and the Triple Entente, stimulated a general increase in armaments, and led to the assassination of the Austrian Archduke with its catastrophic consequences. It was an old and complicated question which had troubled the peace of Europe for a century and a half. No attempt can be made here to trace its development, which has been ably dealt with by many writers.[1] It arose from many elements. The progressive disintegration of the Ottoman Empire, caused by external as well as internal causes, produced a continual unrest in the Near East. This was increased by Russia's persistent desire to acquire increased influence in the Balkan Peninsula and to realize her age-long dream for control of the waterways to the Mediterranean. The Hapsburgs, sitting astride the Danube for centuries, were trying to preserve authority over subject peoples, many of whom had become fired with nationalism and a desire to break away and unite with their brothers living in the independent States bordering on Austria-Hungary. The ambitions of Serbia, Bulgaria, Rumania and Greece to extend their territories to include all peoples of their own nationality brought them into constant conflict with Turkey, Austria-Hungary or

[1] For a very useful list of works on the Balkans see R. J. Kerner, *Slavic Europe: A Selected Bibliography in the Western European Languages* (Cambridge, Mass., 1918), especially Nos. 737-842, 3121-3144, 3592-4186, 4357-4411, 4490-4518.

one another. The antagonism between Austria-Hungary and Serbia was increased by the Austrian annexation of Bosnia and Herzegovina, the creation of Albania, and the Serb agitation for national unity at Austria's expense. To understand how the World War had its beginnings in this corner of Europe, it will be convenient to review some of the Balkan problems between 1908 and 1914.

THE BEGINNINGS OF AUSTRO-SERBIAN ANTAGONISM [2]

Serbian national poets and historians love to recall to their people the heroic days of Stephen Dushan in the fourteenth century, when the great Greek Orthodox Serbian Empire stretched from the Danube nearly to the Gulf of Corinth, and from the Aegean to the Adriatic. From those far-off days to the decades immediately preceding the World War, when Serbian nationalists began to dream of again extending their boundaries to include "Old Serbia" and even more territory, the Serbian people suffered long

[2] In addition to the works cited by Kerner, as indicated in the preceding footnote, the more important recent books from the Austrian point of view are: H. Friedjung, *Das Zeitalter des Imperialismus, 1884-1914* (3 vols. Berlin, 1919-22); F. F. G. Kleinwächter, *Der Untergang der österreichisch-ungarischen Monarchie* (Leipzig, 1920); L. Mandl, *Die Habsburger und die serbische Frage* (Vienna, 1918); Theodor von Sosnosky, *Die Balkanpolitik Oesterreich-Ungarns seit 1866* (2 vols. Stuttgart, 1913-1919); J. Redlich, *Oesterreichische Regierung und Verwaltung im Weltkrieg* (New Haven), 1925; H. Delbrück, "Serbien, Oesterreich und Russland," in *Deutschland und die Schuldfrage* (ed. W. Ziegler, Berlin, 1923; pp. 95-112); and the works of Burian, Conrad, Hoyos, Musulin, Pribram, and Szilassy. Above all, Oe.—U.A., I-VIII, *passim*.

From the Serb and Croat point of view: H. Wendel, *Der Kampf der Südslawen um Freiheit und Einheit* (Frankfort, 1925), written in a somewhat lyrical vein, but containing a valuable bibliography (pp. 757-773) including numerous Slavic works; R. W. Seton-Watson, *Sarajevo: A Study in the Origins of the Great War* (London, 1926), giving the best account in English of the Jugoslav Movement; L. von Südland [Pilar], *Die Südslawische Frage und der Weltkrieg* (Vienna, 1918); Goricar and Stowe, *The Inside Story of Austro-German Intrigue* (New York, 1920); and the works of Cvijitch, Jevtitch, Markovitch, and Stanojevitch.

From a more general point of view: *Die Grosse Politik, passim;* H. Wickham Steed, *Through Thirty Years, 1892-1922* (2 vols. London, 1924); and the works of Bogitchevitch, Brandenburg, Kanner, and Valentin.

years of oppression and hardship. First came the Turks.
On Vidov-Dan, 1389, an army of Serbs, Albanians and
Croats was terribly crushed at Kossovo, and submerged
under the Turkish flood. But from the field of battle
there rose up a Serb hero who penetrated to the victorious
Sultan's tent and there slew him, as the hateful oppressor
of the Slav peoples. So the anniversary of Kossovo became a great day in the Serb calendar: Vidov-Dan was a
day of sorrow for the national defeat of 1389, but a day of
rejoicing for the assassination of the cruel foreign oppressor.[3] For more than four centuries after Kossovo the
greater part of the Serb people lived and suffered under
Turkish rule. Some Serbs, for obvious reasons of convenience, abandoned Greek Orthodoxy for Mohammedanism,
especially in Bosnia, and remained Moslems ever afterwards.

Austria was the European Power which first brought
to the Serbs some relief, and caused the Turkish flood to
recede. It was Prince Eugene, with his Hapsburg army,
who recaptured Belgrade in 1717 and helped arouse in the
Serbs a longing for independence from Turkish misrule.
When Hapsburg troops had to retreat twenty years later,
many Serb peasants followed on the soldiers' heels to escape servitude under the Sultan. They settled north of
the Danube in the southern fringe of the Hapsburg lands.
There they lived and multiplied and were joined by other
fugitives from south of the Danube. At first these Serb
settlers were well treated by their new rulers, and were
appreciated as good soldiers to defend the country against
the Turks. But in the later eighteenth century Roman
Catholic propaganda and economic oppression by feudal
Magyar landlords made existence so bitter for the Serb
settlers that many preferred to escape back to their brothers

[3] Vidov-Dan, St. Vitus's Day, June 15/28, 1914, the day of the Archduke's assassination, was the 525th anniversary of the Battle of Kossovo.

of the South. As between Magyar exploitation and Turkish misrule, the latter was the lesser of two evils. So began an antagonism, which persisted ever afterwards, and was aggravated in 1867 when Emperor Francis Joseph withdrew the special privileges which had long been enjoyed by the Serbs of the "Military Frontiers."[4] Nevertheless, common enmity to the Turks generally tended to preserve a political friendship between the ruling authorities at Vienna and Belgrade.

In the year 1878, to be sure, Austria "occupied" the provinces of Bosnia and Herzegovina, which were largely inhabited by peasants of Serb blood and were coveted by the new Kingdom of Serbia; but the pill was coated by the fact that, at the Congress of Berlin, Austria secured for Serbia the valuable Pirot and Nish districts, which Russia would have assigned to her own protégé, Bulgaria. Political friendship between the Austrian and Serbian Governments, though not between the peoples of the two countries, was again secured by the secret Austro-Serbian Treaty of 1881, signed for ten years, in which both States promised to pursue a mutually friendly policy, and not to tolerate within the territory of one any intrigues against the other.[5] In the year following, a tariff agreement admitted Austrian manufactured articles into Serbia at half the tariff rates asked of other countries, and in return special advantages were given to Serbian pigs and prunes imported into Austria-Hungary. In 1885 it was the support of Austria which saved the Serbian army from destruction after its fatal defeat by the Bulgarians at Slivnitza. King Milan, both off and on the throne, squandered much of his money and spent much of his bizarre existence in Vienna. And so,

[4] Cf. Michael Pupin, *From Immigrant to Inventor* (New York, 1923), ch. i.

[5] Pribram, I, 18; also his article, "Milan IV von Serbien und die Geheimverträge Oesterreich-Ungarns mit Serbien, 1887-1889," in *Historische Blätter*, I, 1922.

in spite of Russian intrigues from within, Serbian policy, generally speaking, continued to be Austrophile until the great assassinations of 1903.

It was the misfortune of the Serbian people that, at the beginning of the movement for national independence in the days of Napoleon, there arose not one, but two, national leaders. Instead of one great man dominating the movement, and establishing a single strong dynasty, there were two rivals: Kara George and Milosh Obrenovitch. Ever since the assassination of the former in the interests of the latter, in 1817, the unhappy country was torn by the feuds of these rival families, and by a series of palace revolutions and violent changes of dynasty. These culminated in 1903. On the night of June 11, a band of conspirators, consisting mainly of Serbian army officers, entered the royal palace at Belgrade, dragged King Alexander Obrenovitch and his unpopular wife from their hiding place, and brutally murdered them.[6] Belgrade rejoiced; the church bells were rung; the city was decorated with flags; and the Legislature unanimously thanked the assassins for their work. Though he may not have been directly privy to the plot, Peter Karageorgevitch, grandson of the man murdered nearly a century before, profited by it, and he ascended the throne as Peter I. This hideous crime, "brutal but not unprovoked," and the favors shown to those who were responsible for it, outraged the sense of decency in the crowned heads of Europe, most of whom soon withdrew their representatives from Belgrade as a sign of their disapproval. Great Britain did not renew diplomatic relations for three years.

---

[6] For a recent vivid account of this deed, see the article of Dragisha Vasitch, in *Knjizhevna Republika*, summarized in *The Living Age*, Jan. 3, 1925; and the detailed contemporary narrative of Pomiankowski, the Austrian Military Attaché, in the Berlin *8-Uhr-Abendblatt*, Nos. 46-50, Feb. 23-28, 1928; for its importance in internal Serbian politics, see below, Vol. II, ch. ii.

Though frowned on at first by Europe, the new reign marked a notable revival in Serbian life. A freer, more democratic, spirit prevailed. A patriotic national movement developed, which expressed itself in new economic activity, in newspapers and literature, and in the spread of the "Greater Serbia" idea. Peter I was personally popular, devoted to the interests of his country, and noted for his soldierly qualities of loyalty and simplicity. The fact that he had fought for the Serbian cause in the revolt of Herzegovina gave him an added popularity far beyond the bounds of his own kingdom; it made him "our King" to the Serbs beyond the Danube and the Drin. Many a Bosnian peasant is said to have made a pilgrimage to Belgrade, merely to hang about the streets till he could catch a near view of the new sovereign and future "liberator." He was to lead Serbian "Piedmont" in the movements for reuniting all races of Serb blood—Serbs, Bosniaks, Slovenes, Croats, and Dalmatians—into a "Greater Serbia," as the House of Savoy had led in the unification of Italy half a century earlier. His marriage with Princess Zorka, daughter of Nicholas of Montenegro, seemed to forecast close relations between these two Slav states. Many of his years of exile had been passed in Russia. His brother, Prince Arsene, had served as an officer in a crack regiment of Russian Guards. His two Montenegrin sisters-in-law married Russian Grand Dukes. These facts all seemed to suggest a Russophile orientation in Serbian policy with the accession of Peter I in 1903. And such proved to be the case. It was actively hastened also both by encouragement from the Pan-Slav elements in Russia, and by the irritating attitude adopted by Austria-Hungary.

Austrian ministers soon observed with dismay this growth of Serbian nationalism and pro-Russian feeling. If unchecked, it threatened the integrity of the Hapsburg lands. It meant that the Kingdom of Serbia would act as a dangerous magnet, tending to draw away Austria's Serb subjects to form the "Greater Serbia." If the decaying Turkish Empire should ever fall to pieces, if nationalist revolts should break out in Austria-Hungary in some crisis, such as the death of Emperor Francis Joseph, or if war should be declared in the Balkans or in Europe, Serbia would be likely to try to annex territories inhabited largely by Serbs. Probably Pan-Slav interests would lead Russia to support the Serbians. If Serbia secured Bosnia, her next step would be to attempt to unite the Croats, the Dalmatians, the Slovenes, and the Serbs in the Banat in southern Hungary. This would encourage the other subject nationalities under Hapsburg rule—the Rumanians, Czechs and Slovaks—to break away. This would spell *Finis Austriae*.[7]

In view of the danger to the Dual Monarchy from its subject nationalities, Austrian officials began to adopt measures to stifle this growing movement in Serbia for political and economic independence from Hapsburg influence. Serbia, having no direct outlet to the sea, had been virtually dependent upon Austria-Hungary for a market for her agricultural products. To strengthen herself, Serbia began in 1905 to negotiate with Bulgaria for a customs-union; but Austria interfered. In 1906, when the Austro-Serbian tariff treaty expired, feeling in both countries ran so high that it was not renewed, especially as the Magyar landlords found that Serbian products came into competition with their own. As a consequence, a bitter tariff war— the so-called "Pig War"—ensued. But instead of crushing Serbia economically, Austria only caused the Serbians to seek other markets, especially in Germany; and at home the Serbians began to erect slaughter houses and factories of their own. Germany easily managed to supply the Serbian peasants with goods which had formerly come from Austria. This displacement of Austrian by German goods

[7] *Cf.* Conrad, I, 13-28.

caused not a little hard feeling between Vienna and Berlin which persisted for years.[8] Austria's attempt at economic intimidation, far from compelling Serbia to return to an Austrophile policy, had just the opposite effect; it embittered Peter I's Ministers, and drove them more than ever into the open arms of Russia. It made them realize more clearly Serbia's need for a direct economic outlet to the sea, such as a railway connection with a port on the Adriatic in Albania or Montenegro, or on the Aegean at Salonica.[9] They welcomed negotiations for a railway crossing Serbia from the Danube to the Adriatic which was urged on their behalf by Russia in the spring of 1908, as a counter-measure to Austria's project for a railway from Bosnia through the Sanjak of Novi Bazar to Salonica.[10] The outbreak of the Young Turk Revolution in the summer hastened the negotiations, but led them to a fiasco in the most unexpected manner. It brought to a crisis the question, often discussed since 1876, and several times conditionally assented to by Russia, of Austria's "annexation" of the "occupied" provinces of Bosnia and Herzegovina. This in turn was closely connected with Russia's much-desired aim of opening the Bosphorus and the Dardanelles to the passage of Russian ships of war.

[8] Stanojevitch, *Die Ermordung der Erzherzogs Franz Ferdinand* (Frankfort, 1923), p. 38; Conrad (III, 407), in 1913, spoke of, "Deutschland, welches in gierigem Egoismus die Monarchie aus Serbien und überhaupt vom Balkan kommerziell zu verdrängen trachtet." The figures for Germany's displacement of Austria in Serbia in the years 1905, 1906, 1907, are significant: imports from Germany, in millions of dinars, 6.2, 9.7, 20.3; exports to Germany, 2.1, 19, 32; imports from Austria-Hungary 33.3, 22.2, 25.5; exports to Austria-Hungary 64.7, 30, 12; *Statesman's Year Book.*

[9] *Cf.* Dr. Baernreither, "Unsere Handelsbeziehungen zu Serbien," in *Oest. Rundschau,* XXIX, 1 ff., 1911; and "Aehrenthal und Milovanovitch" in *Deutsche Revue,* Jan., 1922. Dr. Baernreither was an enlightened Austrian enjoying the confidence of the Archduke Franz Ferdinand, who disapproved of Aehrenthal's policy and wished to make reasonable economic concessions to Serbia; see the selections from his diaries published by Josef Redlich, in *Foreign Affairs* (N. Y.), VI, 645-657, July, 1928

[10] G P., XXV. 281-382.

RUSSIA AND THE STRAITS

In the course of the nineteenth century, especially after the events of 1878, Russia had come to regard the closure of the Dardanelles against foreign warships by the Sultan as a valuable protection and asset for Russia. As Count Kapnist remarked in May, 1897: "Russia needs this gate-keeper [portier] in Turkish clothes for the Dardanelles, which under no circumstances ought to be opened. The Black Sea is a Russian *mare clausum.*" [11] This remained one of the corner-stones of Russian policy down to the World War. Russia did not desire any modification of the treaties which excluded warships of the other Great Powers from ingress into the Black Sea.

But the treaties which excluded Russian war vessels from passing inward or outward through the Straits of the Bosphorus and Dardanelles were quite a different matter. These were humiliating restrictions. They were inconsistent with Russia's prestige as a Great Power. They were contrary to her ambitions since Peter the Great's day for the control of a free outlet to the Mediterranean. They were a serious and positive handicap when she was engaged in war,

[11] G.P., XII, 285. On the earlier history of the closure of the Straits, see above, ch. ii, note 27; on the later history, E. A. Adamov, *Konstantinopol i Prolivy* [Russia and the Straits], 2 vols., Moskva, 1925-26; E. A. Adamov, *Razdel Aziatskoe Turtsii* [Partition of Asiatic Turkey], Moskva, 1924; I. M. Zakher, "Konstantinopol i Prolivy" in *Krasnyi Arkhiv*, VI, 48-76; VII, 32-54 (1924); A. Popov, "Pervaia Balkanskaia Voina" [First Balkan War], *ibid.*, XV, 1-29; XVI, 3-24 (1926); M. N. Pokrovski, *Drei Konferenzen*, Berlin, 1920; B. Shatzky: "La question de Constantinople et des Détroits," in *Rev. d'Hist. de la Guerre Mondiale*, IV, 289-309; V, 19-43 (Oct., 1926; Jan., 1927); G.P., X, 1-41, 70 f., 109-114; XI, 99-106; XII, 47-87; XIV, 531-563; XVII, 34, 84, 102; XVIII, 409-446; XIX, 229-244; and XXII, XXVI, XXVII, XXX-XXXIX, *passim; Livre Jaune: L'Alliance Franco-Russe,* p. 19 ff.; *Affaires Balkaniques,* M.F.R., L.N., Stieve, and Conrad, *passim;* a good brief account by G. Frantz, "Die Meerengenfrage in der Vorkriegspolitik Russland," in *Deutsche Rundschau,* LIII, 142-160 (Feb., 1927); P. Mohr, "Konstantinopel und die Meerengenfrage," in *Meereskunde,* Heft 178 (1927); and the references below in the present chapter.

as in the case of the Russo-Japanese War, because they prevented her from freely using her Black Sea Fleet where it might be most needed. Furthermore, they prevented the augmentation of this Black Sea Fleet for war against Turkey by any other means except naval construction on Russia's southern shores; it could not be increased by construction on the Baltic, or by the purchase of warships in England, as the Tsar sorrowfully observed in January, 1914.[12]

So the opening of the Straits to Russian warships became one of the first aims of Russian ministers in the decades immediately preceding the World War. This was quite distinct from two other aims which are often confused with it, but which were really different and would have involved even more serious European complications; one was the forcible seizure of Turkish territory along the heights of the Bosphorus; the other was the acquisition of control over Constantinople itself. To be sure, Russian warships once in the Straits would be in an easy position to accomplish either of the two other aims. But, generally speaking, the temerity of Russian ministers, though considerable, did not usually go to the point of planning to seize Constantinople itself. This city, they were inclined to admit, must remain in the hands of the Sultan so long as the Ottoman Empire survived; to try to seize it would meet with too great opposition from the Great Powers, not to mention Bulgaria and Greece. Constantinople, however, must in no case be allowed to fall under the control of any other Power —neither under Bulgaria during the Balkan Wars, nor under Germany through the appointment of General Liman von

[12] M. W. Rodzjanko, *Erinnerungen,* p. 90 (Berlin, 1927). For England's persistent opposition to Russia's sending a couple of torpedo boats even though under a commercial flag, into the Black Sea in 1902, and also to Russia's sending any of her Black Sea Fleet out of the *mare clausum* during the Russo-Japanese War, see G.P., XVIII, 407-446; XIX, 229-244; and B.D., IV, 44-60.

Sanders to the command of a Turkish army corps in the Sultan's capital, as will be seen later.

Occasionally, however, ambitious Russian ministers seriously considered in secret the project for a sudden descent with a landing force to seize in time of peace the heights of the Bosphorus in the neighborhood of Constantinople. One of these occasions was in the winter of 1896-97. A word may be said of it, because it is the forerunner of several similar projects later, and because it typifies the confusion of authority and purposes which existed in the higher spheres at St. Petersburg.

To M. Nelidov, the Russian Ambassador at Constantinople, the frightful Armenian massacres caused a revulsion of feeling in Europe against the Sultan and anarchic conditions in his capital which seemed likely to afford Russia a good opportunity to make a bold *coup de main* to seize the heights of the Bosphorus above Constantinople. In the latter part of 1896 Nelidov came up to St. Petersburg to set forth his plan. Nicholas II at once approved it, even though it threatened, as Witte pointed out, a general European War. Nevertheless it was seriously considered in a special secret ministerial council and was favored by Vannovskii and Tyrtov, Ministers of War and Marine, and by Durnovo, President of the Council. Nelidov's plan was to despatch suddenly 30,000 troops on warships and transports from Odessa to the Upper Bosphorus and land them to seize control of the Straits, before England or any of the other Great Powers could prevent the filibustering expedition. Europe would be faced with a *fait accompli*. Nelidov was to return to his post at Constantinople; when he judged that the situation in the Sultan's capital had reached the proper critical point, the signal for the sudden descent of the Russian landing force was to be given by a harmless sounding telegram, "Long without news." But when the plan was further studied by the military and naval authorities, it appeared that, even with the most secret precautions, it would be almost impossible to concentrate and despatch a sufficiently large number of troops and transports without attracting the attention and opposition of England. Moreover, Count Witte and Pobiedonostev were opposed to it on economic, political and moral grounds, and cast the weight of their personal influence against the rash project, so that it was ultimately abandoned by the Tsar. But that Nelidov's plan was seriously considered, and was even thought by Witte to have been on the point of being carried out, is significant of the aims of Russian diplomats and of the readiness with which the weak-willed Nicholas II at first assented to it.[13]

THE BALKAN QUESTION "PUT ON ICE," 1897-1907

Soon after the abandonment of Nelidov's project, Emperor Francis Joseph visited Nicholas II at St. Petersburg. Friendly conversations took place which resulted in an important Austro-Russian Balkan agreement. It was at this time that Russia was embarking more actively on her

13 Nelidov's project of 1896-97, first hinted at anonymously by E. J. Dillon, and then by several memoir writers, has recently been confirmed by documents published by the Bolshevists. See E. J. Dillon, *The Eclipse of Russia* (N. Y., 1918), pp. 231-244; S. I. Witte, *Memoirs* (Garden City, 1921), pp. 186-189; Baron Rosen, *Forty Years of Diplomacy* (N. Y., 1922), I, ch. xiv; M. Pokrovski, "Russko-germanskie otnosheniia" [Russo-German relations], in *Krasnyi Arkhiv*, I, ch. i (1922), part of which is publishd in German translation, "Lange ohne Nachricht," in KSF, IV, 175-181 (Mar., 1926); G. N. Trubetzkoi, *Russland als Grossmacht* (Stuttgart, 1913), pp. 161-162. Sazonov refers to it in his report to the Tsar of Nov. 23/Dec. 6, 1913, in L.N., II, 367. That Germany got wind of Nelidov's plan is evident from G.P., XII, 67-69. Probably one reason that Russia did not dare to carry out Nelidov's plan was the fear of offending her French ally; for nine hundred years France had had large interests in the Eastern Mediterranean which she did not care to see jeopardized by a too active advance even of her own ally. Hanotaux, who had served as secretary at the French embassy in Constantinople, had often said to the German Ambassador at Paris: "La question des détroits nous touche de trop près' et j'espére toujours que la Russie n'y touchera pas, car cela pourrait devenir trop gros pour nous!" (Münster to Holstein. April 25, 1896; G.P., XII, 51).

policy of economic and political penetration in the Far East, and wished to be freed from possible complications in the Balkans. In case her aggressive attitude in Manchuria should lead to trouble with China or Japan, it was important that her Balkan rear should not be endangered from the side of Austria, or otherwise. In the spring of 1897, therefore, consequent upon Francis Joseph's visit, the Austrian and Russian foreign ministers exchanged friendly notes declaring in favor of the *status quo* in the Balkans, and asserting their intentions to pursue "a policy of perfect harmony." Austria reserved her claims to Bosnia and Herzegovina, and expressed herself in favor of an independent Albania. The status of Constantinople and the Straits, "having an eminently European character," was not to be modified by any separate Austro-Russian arrangements.[14] By this agreement the Balkan question was said to be "put on ice," and for a decade the tension between the rival aims of Russia and Austria was in fact somewhat relieved.

But it would be a mistake to assume, as most writers do, that Russia had abandoned, even temporarily, the consideration of her ambitions in the Near East while pressing her imperialist policy in the Far East. This misconception arose largely from the inspired Russian Press and from misinformed persons who believed that the Russian Bear had shifted his appetite completely to the plains of Manchuria. In reality, though the Tsar and his ministers talked of "Port Arthur," they were at the same time thinking of "Constantinople." Of this there are several indications.

[14] Notes of Goluchowski and Muraviev of May 8 and 17, 1897; Pribram, pp. 78-82; G.P., XII, 273-305. For further efforts to extend Austro-Russian Harmony in the Balkans by the Mürzsteg Program, the Neutrality Declaration of 1904, and the Macedonian reform plans of 1904-1907, see Pribram, p. 98; G.P., XVIII, 85-405; XXII, 3-8, 19-522; and *British Documents*, I, 281 f., 295-305.

In 1899, Muraviev, the Russian Minister of Foreign Affairs, uneasy at the rapid growth of German activity in Turkey and the beneficial effect which it might have upon the Sick Man's health, spoke bluntly to the German Ambassador about Russia's "exclusive claim to Constantinople"; and added, "Already the Tsar's Government must now have a watchful eye that no other Power assumes a dominating position on the Bosphorus." [15] He then tried to bluff Germany into signing a written agreement guaranteeing the Bosphorus to Russia; he threatened that he would come to an understanding with England, if Germany refused. But Bülow preferred to adhere to Germany's traditional policy of declaring that Germany did not oppose Russia's aspirations at the Straits (because he felt sure that England would still do so); but he was unwilling to put anything into writing, for fear that Russia might reveal it to England, and thus endanger Anglo-German good relations.[16]

In 1900 Muraviev drew up a long secret memorandum, for discussion by the army and navy authorities, in which he urged the preparation of measures by which Russia might at any given moment take possession of the shores of the Bosphorus; and the Sultan must be prevented from doing anything which would strengthen his position on the Straits.[17]

On March 1, 1903, General Kuropatkin, the Minister of War, noted in his diary:

> I told Witte that our Tsar has grandiose plans in his head: to capture Manchuria for Russia, and to annex Korea. He is dreaming also of bringing Tibet under his dominion.

[15] G.P., XIV, 550.

[16] G.P., XIV, 531-563; especially No. 4022.

[17] M. Pokrovski, "Tsarskaia diplomatiia o zadachakh Rossii na Vostoke v 1900 g." [Imperial diplomacy concerning Russia's aims in the East in 1900], in *Krasnyi Arkhiv*, XVIII (1926), pp. 3-29, especially pp. 9-11 and 17.

He desires to take Persia, and to seize not only the Bosphorus but also the Dardanelles.[18]

In the spring of 1904, Izvolski, who had just been transferred from Tokio to Copenhagen, was already contemplating a revolution in Russian diplomacy: the abandonment of the long-standing Asiatic conflict with England in favor of an entente which he hoped would enable Russia to open the Straits for her own war vessels. In one of his first conversations with King Edward VII at Copenhagen (which in view of Sir Edward Goschen's presence was something more than a purely private and personal talk), Izvolski set forth his views about Russia's necessities for a free passage of the Straits. King Edward replied that the closure of the Straits was not "absolute and eternal," but that for the moment British public opinion was so absolutely opposed to any opening of the Straits that he could not and would not at present do anything in defiance of it.[19]

Similarly, in the later negotiations for the Anglo-Russian Agreement of 1907, at least so far as they were carried on by Benckendorff, the Russian Ambassador in London, Izvolski again tried to carry out his fond hope of opening the Straits. He did this by offering the concession, unusual for Russian diplomacy, that England and the other Powers might send their vessels of war through the Dardanelles, but not into the Black Sea.[20] Russia would thus

[18] *Krasnyi Arkhiv*, II, 31 (1923). Six weeks earlier he had written in his diary (Jan. 5/18; *ibid.*, p. 20): "I emphasized [to the Tsar] the necessity of shifting our main attention from the Far East to the West. The Tsar formulated it something like this: not to take our eyes off the East, but to pay the greatest attention to the West."

[19] Ph. Crozier, "L'Autriche et l'Avant-guerre," in *Revue de France*, April 1, 1921, p. 276; *cf.* also Izvolski, *Memoirs* (London, 1920), pp. 20, 81 ff.; Lee, *King Edward VII*, II, 283 ff.; and G.P., XIX, 177 ff., 188.

[20] The proposal "which Count Benckendorff had discussed with me at the time of the Anglo-Russian Convention . . . had been that, while Russia should have egress from the Black Sea through the Straits, other

retain her *mare clausum,* while Russia and England would
share equally in the favorable position which their fleets
would have for exercising control over Constantinople and
the Dardanelles. But Sir Edward Grey, in view of British
public opinion and the fact that other Powers had a right
to be consulted in any modification of the Straits treaties,
did not want any mention to be made of the Bosphorus
and the Dardanelles in the Anglo-Russian Convention
which dealt primarily with the Middle East. So Izvolski
failed to induce England to abandon her traditional attitude. Thereupon Izvolski decided to turn to Baron Aehrenthal and seek a solution of the Straits Question through
coöperation with Austria.

THE BUCHLAU BARGAIN OF SEPTEMBER, 1908

In 1906 the direction of Foreign Affairs in Russia and in
Austria passed into the hands respectively of two men who
represented more aggressive and ambitious policies than
their predecessors. At St. Petersburg, Alexander Izvolski,
shrewd, subtle, proud, belonging to the Russian rural nobility but supposed to be a great admirer of British Liberalism, wished to win back for Russia in the Balkans the
prestige which she had recently lost in her disastrous ad-

Powers should have liberty to send their vessels of war into the Straits
without going into the Black Sea;" Grey to Nicolson, Oct. 14, 1908;
Grey, I, 179. Izvolski also says there had been negotiations with England twice concerning the Straits, "une fois par l'intermédiaire de Benckendorff, et la seconde fois par mon intermédiaire, lors de mon séjour à
Londres, en automne 1908;" L.N., I, 148; Stieve, I, 163; M.F.R., p. 122.
And Hintze, Emperor William's personal representative in Russia, gathered from Sir Arthur Nicolson that the Straits question had been discussed in connection with the Anglo-Russian Convention negotiations
(G.P., XXII, 80-81, note; XXVI, 127, 218-219, note). We may therefore reject as untrue both Viscount Grey's later statement that "the
question of the Straits was not mixed up with those Anglo-Russian negotiations about Persia" (Grey, I, 159), and Izvolski's "particular assurance" to Aehrenthal in September, 1907, "that he had not spoken of the
question to the English" (G.P., XXII, 80-81); for Benckendorff's equally
untrue denial, see G.P., XXV, 306.

venture in the Far East. At Vienna, Baron Aehrenthal, energetic, ambitious, the courtier-aristocrat, wished to free Austria from the excessive dependence on Germany which had characterized his predecessor's policy. He wished to strengthen the Dual Monarchy in the Balkans, by putting an end to the Serbian danger which he believed threatened to disrupt the Hapsburg Empire.

Here were two political adventurers, equally ready to fish in troubled waters to satisfy their ambitions, even to the extent of upsetting international treaties and endangering the peace of Europe. On Aehrenthal has usually fallen the odium for the Bosnian "Annexation Crisis" of 1908-09, but recently published Russian and German documents indicate that Izvolski had quite as much to do with the initiation of this plan for modifying the Treaty of Berlin as did Aehrenthal.

A few days after signing the Convention of 1907 with England and thus relieving Russia from the danger of complications in the Middle East, Izvolski visited Vienna. He was decorated with the Grand Cross of the Order of St. Stephen, received in audience by Francis Joseph, and had a long conversation with Aehrenthal. He hinted very confidentially that he intended to solve the Straits Question in the manner desired by Russia, which was true; and he particularly assured Austria that he had not spoken of the question to the English; which was untrue.[21] He went on to tell Aehrenthal:

> Russia has lost Manchuria with Port Arthur and thereby the access to the sea in the East. The main point for Russia's military and naval expansion of power lies henceforth in the Black Sea. From there Russia must gain an access to the Mediterranean.[22]

21 G.P., XXII, 76, 79 ff., and preceding note.
22 G.P., XXII, 83 f.

Aehrenthal thanked him for his confidence, but, following Bismarck's earlier advice to take a reserved attitude
until Russia should show her hand and declare more definitely her intentions, gave a dilatory and non-committal
reply. He merely remarked that it was a difficult problem,
and that if the Straits Question were really opened up,
Austria would want to define her attitude, adding:

> I beg you to inform me in good time before the moment
> comes for putting the Russian plans into action, precisely
> as I should feel myself under obligations to inform the Rus-
> sian Government in case Austria-Hungary should ever in-
> tend to annex Bosnia and Herzegovina.[23]

Shortly afterwards Aehrenthal told Conrad, the Austrian Chief of Staff, that Russia, having limited her policy
in Asia, "will now take up again her Western Balkan policy
and demand freedom of the Straits for Russian vessels, but
not for others"; and the two discussed the annexation of
Bosnia and Herzegovina as possible compensation for conceding the freedom of the Straits to Russia.[24] Here then
at Vienna, in September, 1907, in the confidential conversation of Izvolski and Aehrenthal, was foreshadowed the
bargain which was struck between them at Buchlau just a
year later.

Izvolski apparently did not proceed immediately with
his plans, possibly because of Aehrenthal's reserved attitude
and because of England's known opposition to them. But a
few months later, after Aehrenthal had "thrown a bomb
between his legs" [25] by his statement in the Delegations of

---

23 G.P., XXII, 81, 84.   24 Conrad, I, 513 f., 528, 530.

25 "C'est une bombe qu'il m'a jetée entre les jambes," said Izvolski
to the German Ambassador in St. Petersburg, referring to Aehrenthal's
announcement of the Sanjak railway project; G.P., XXV, 313. Izvolski
at once countered with a Danube-Adriatic railway project which would
cut Austria's projected line at right angles, and greatly benefit Serbia
by giving her direct access to the sea. On these rival railway projects
see G.P., XXV, 281-382; Schwertfeger, Zur Europäischen Politik, III,

Austria's desire for a railway from Sarajevo to Mitrovitza, to connect up with the Macedonian and Greek railways, Izvolski took up again Nelidov's idea of accomplishing Russia's historic mission by force rather than by diplomacy. In a secret Ministerial Conference of February 3, 1908, he pointed out that if Russia continued the passive defensive policy of 1897 of leaving the Balkan Question on ice, Russia "runs the risk of losing all at once the fruits of her century-long efforts, ceasing to play the rôle of a Great Power, and falling into the position of a second-rate State to which no one pays attention." After calling attention to the situation in the Caucasus, Persia, and the Balkans, and also to Russia's recent *rapprochement* with England, he suggested that joint Anglo-Russian military action in Turkey "offered an extremely attractive prospect, which might lead to dazzling results and to the realization of Russia's historic mission in the Near East." But this would involve the whole Turkish and Near Eastern Question. He, therefore, sought the advice of the other Ministers as to how far they could back up an active aggressive policy.

In reply General Palitsyn, Chief of the General Staff, said he had urged three months earlier the use of force in the Caucasus, but that now the situation no longer demanded it; he called attention to Russia's military unpreparedness. General Polivanov, of the War Ministry, agreed with him that "Russia lacks artillery, machine guns, uniforms. The restoration of order, of complete order in the army and fortresses, will take stupendous sums and much time." The Minister of Marine confessed that the Black Sea Fleet was not ready for war, needing sailors, coal, ammunition, guns, and mines. M. Kokovtsev, the Finance Minister, complained that neither he nor the whole Council had been kept informed of Izvolski's warlike and expensive

64-72; Conrad, I, 555; G. Giolitti, *Memoirs of My Life* (London 1923), pp. 207-211.

plans; he was energetically opposed to military action in Persia and to pulling chestnuts out of the fire for Foreign Powers; such a policy would not be understood in Russia, "and it is also not clear whom we should be defending in Persia." As to the Balkans, the question was still more serious; he would limit Russia's action to the possible protection of Bulgaria in case of a Turco-Bulgarian war. Meanwhile money must be raised by every means for reorganizing the army and navy and making adequate military preparations.

Izvolski therefore again emphasized the unfavorable consequences of a strictly defensive policy. But Premier Stolypin summed up the discussion by declaring that Izvolski must not count on support for an aggressive and adventurous policy at present. Otherwise a new revolution might break out in Russia and endanger the dynasty. "But after some years, when we have secured complete quiet, Russia can speak again as in the past."

At present she must limit herself to what could be accomplished by the diplomatic skill of the Minister of Foreign Affairs. In approving this policy of avoiding war for the present, and preparing for the future, Nicholas II noted in pencil: "God helps those who help themselves." [26]

Unable to get unanimous Russian backing for active military measures, Izvolski then turned again to Aehrenthal and Austria, to secure by diplomacy a more modest part of Russia's Historic Mission—the opening of the Straits for the Russian warships of the future. A year before he had tried to win England's consent to this as part of the Anglo-Russian Entente, but without success.

Count Aehrenthal on his side had been secretly consider-

---

[26] Protocol of the Ministerial Council of Jan. 21/Feb. 3, 1908; printed by M. Pokrovski, *Drei Konferenzen* (Berlin, 1920), pp. 17-31; and in part by Adamov, *Konstantinopol i Prolivy*, I, 8 ff.; *cf.* also Polivanov's diary [in Russian], quoted by G. Frantz, *Russland auf dem Wege zur Katastrophe* (Berlin, 1926), pp. 7-10.

ing for some months the desirability of converting the occupation of Bosnia and Herzegovina into full ownership, both on account of administrative difficulties and of the growing danger of the "Greater Serbia" propaganda.

The administration of Bosnia was in the hands of a military governor (*Landeschef*), but his authority was restricted at every point by a civilian assistant (*Ziviladlatus*) on the spot, who represented the supreme authority of the Austro-Hungarian Joint Minister of Finance in Vienna. By the Dual Compact in 1867 the Hapsburg Monarchy could acquire no territory except by the common consent of both halves of the Monarchy. This was one of the reasons why, in 1878, Bosnia and Herzegovina had been merely "occupied" jointly by Austria-Hungary, instead of being directly annexed to Austria. It was also the reason the administration of the provinces had been placed under the Austro-Hungarian Joint Minister of Finance. This Minister, however, occupied with other matters and far away in Vienna, was often out of touch with the exact situation in Bosnia and Herzegovina. In consequence he often sent orders to his representatives there, which conflicted with the views of the military governor on the spot. The result was frequent friction between the *Landeschef* and the *Ziviladlatus*.

Though the Hapsburgs had done much, during the period of occupation, for the material improvement of Bosnia and Herzegovina, by building roads, establishing schools, and enforcing order, there was also much in their administration which could be justly criticized, and they had failed to win the loyalty of all the inhabitants. The Mohammedans, and most of the Roman Catholic elements in the population, were fairly well disposed, but the great majority of the Greek Orthodox Serbs were persistently hostile.

With the outbreak of the Turkish Revolution, the administrative and revolutionary dangers threatened to be-come more serious. The Young Turks, who had announced the calling of a democratic parliament for the whole Turkish Empire, might demand that representatives from Bosnia should sit in it. They might even seek to nullify the Austrian occupation which had existed since 1878. Moreover, if war should break out between Austria and Turkey, would it be the duty of the Bosnians to fight on the side of their "sovereign," the Sultan, or on the side of the actual Austrian rulers of the district? The situation offered an excellent opportunity for anti-Austrian agitation, and the "Greater Serbia" propaganda made the most of it. By annexing Bosnia and Herzegovina, Aehrenthal hoped to put an end once and for all to any doubts that the provinces were to belong to Austria-Hungary.[27]

The sudden Young Turk Revolution of 1908, and the vista of uncertain possibilities which it opened, seemed to both Izvolski and Aehrenthal to offer a favorable opportunity for a mutually advantageous bargain at Turkey's expense. Russia might settle the "Straits Question," by securing the right to send Russian warships through the Bosphorus and the Dardanelles; and Austria might strengthen her position in Bosnia and Herzegovina, by converting the occupation which she had enjoyed for thirty years into a direct annexation. This was the substance of an *aide-memoire* which Izvolski sent to Aehrenthal on July 2, 1908,[28] in connection with the negotiations concerning the Sanjak and the Danube-Adriatic railway projects. Aehrenthal was delighted with Izvolski's proposal, which fell in so nicely with his own plans. In order to arrange the details

[27] Conrad, I, 13-28, 87-109; 170-4; 518-524, 527-9, 540-3, 557; G.P., XXVI, 1-22; Freiherr von Musulin, *Das Haus am Ballplatz* (Munich, 1924), p. 163 ff.; Brandenburg, pp. 261-269 (Eng. trans., pp. 305-314); Stephan, Count Burián, *Austria in Dissolution* (N. Y., 1925), pp. 265-310.
[28] Conrad, I, 107 f.; printed, with Aehrenthal's reply of Aug. 27, in G.P., XXVI, 190-195.

of the bargain, he invited the Russian Minister of Foreign Affairs to a meeting at Count Berchtold's castle at Buchlau in Moravia.

As the conversations between Izvolski and Aehrenthal at Buchlau on September 15, 1908, took place without witnesses or definite agreements in writing drawn up on the spot, conflicting versions arose a few weeks later, when the bargain did not turn out as had been anticipated. Izvolski declared that he had been tricked and misrepresented. But the facts can be stated with considerably certainty, on the basis of what each Minister stated privately to third parties within a few days.[29] Izvolski assented to the Austrian annexation of Bosnia and Herzegovina, and Aehrenthal to the opening of the Straits to Russian ships of war. Aehrenthal also promised to abandon his Sanjak railway project and all intentions of extending Austrian influence toward Salonica, and to withdraw the Austrian military garrisons from the Sanjak of Novi Bazar. As these changes modified important terms of the Treaty of Berlin, Izvolski thought that they would have to be confirmed by a Conference of the Powers which had signed the Treaty. To this Aehrenthal apparently did not object at the time. Less important points discussed and agreed upon were the abolition of Austria's rights over the Montenegrin coast, the annexation of Crete to Greece, and acquiescence in the independence of Bulgaria, if Prince Ferdinand should finally decide to proclaim himself full sovereign. The one important matter which was not made definite, and gave rise to endless and bitter controversy, was the date at which these changes were to be made and published. Aehrenthal claims to have told Izvolski explicitly that the annexation of Bosnia would have to be made prior to the meeting of the Austro-Hungarian Delegations, which was fixed for October 8, when he would have to make a public state-

[29] G.P., XXVI, 25-64.

ment.[30] Izvolski, however, got the impression that the Austrian Minister would merely lay the annexation plan before the Delegations for consideration, not that he would inform them of it as a *fait accompli*. He seems to have anticipated that this bargain would meet with some serious difficulties, and he evidently did not expect that Aehrenthal would take any definite steps until the substance of the Buchlau conversations had been confirmed in writing. Later, after the annexation, he complained bitterly that Aehrenthal was "no gentleman," and had "broken faith" in proceeding so speedily with the annexation.[31]

Possibly at Buchlau Aehrenthal had not made up his mind exactly as to his procedure. But by September 26 he had evidently decided to act quickly, for he sent Bülow a long private letter informing him of the Buchlau agreement and justifying his own part in it, but not indicating any date for the annexation.[32] On September 29 personal letters

[30] Tschirschky, German Ambassador at Vienna to Bülow, Nov. 2, 1908; G.P., XXVI, 31 note, 234. See also G.P., XXVI, 35 ff., 186 ff., 228 ff., 307 ff., 837; and note 61 below. H. Friedjung, *Zeitalter des Imperialismus,* II, 226 ff.; Th. von Sosnosky, *Die Balkanpolitik Oesterreich-Ungarns seit 1866,* II, 167 ff.; L. Molden, *Alois Graf Aehrenthal,* p. 59 ff.; and Eduard Ritter von Steinitz, "Iswolski und die Besprechungen in Buchlau," in KSF, V, 1151-1179, Dec., 1927; also Count Berchtold, "Russia, Austria and the World War," in *Contemporary Review,* CXXXIII, 422 ff., April, 1928.

[31] For his first expectations see G.P., XXVI, 35 ff., 55 ff.; for his later complaints, G.P., XXVI, 118 ff., 135 f., 147 ff., 180 ff., 206 ff., 235 ff., 396 ff.; and below, note 75. See also Ph. Crozier, "L'Autriche et l'Avant-guerre," in *Revue de France,* April 15, 1921, pp. 566-574; and the anonymous articles in the *Fortnightly Review* for Sept. and Nov., 1909, "Baron Aehrenthal and M. Iswolski: Diplomatic Enigmas" and "M. Iswolski and Count von Aehrenthal: A Rectification," the first inspired by Izvolski, and the second inspired by Aehrenthal and written by Mr. E. J. Dillon after a visit with Count Berchtold at Buchlau—a fact which soon gave rise to an unpleasant scene between Berchtold and Izvolski (*cf.* G.P., XXVII, 442-446; J. von Szilassy, *Der Untergang der Donau-Monarchie,* 194 ff.); Georges Louis, *Carnets,* I, 66-69, 115.

[32] G.P., XXVI, 35-39. Two days later Aehrenthal told the German Ambassador in Vienna that "circumstances might compel him to begin even in the very immediate future with the accomplishment" of his annexation plans; the circumstances to which he referred were the propagandist agitation of the Serbians and the probability that Prince Ferdi-

from Emperor Francis Joseph, to be presented on October 5 to the rulers of the leading states, were sent to the Austrian ambassadors abroad. The letters announced that he would proclaim the annexation of Bosnia and Herzegovina on October 7.[33]

Meanwhile Izvolski, not expecting that Aehrenthal would act so precipitately with a *fait accompli,* started on a leisurely tour to sound the Powers on the Buchlau bargain and to secure their consent thereto. On September 26, at Berchtesgaden, he saw Schoen, the German Secretary of State for Foreign Affairs, and emphasized the difficulties which Serbia was likely to make, adding that he thought a European Congress would be necessary to sanction the new arrangements. Schoen listened, and indicated that perhaps Germany would expect some services in return for consenting to the opening of the Straits. On September 29 and 30, at Desio, Izvolski took Tittoni into the secret. This was the first definite information that the Italian Minister had had of the impending changes, and his feelings were hurt. He straightway begged urgently at Vienna for a postponement of the annexation, but his prayer fell on deaf ears, and was overtaken by the course of events. Though indignant at Aehrenthal's Balkan plans and silence in regard to them, Tittoni was willing enough to satisfy Izvolski's ambitions in regard to the Straits in return for a favorable attitude on Russia's part toward Italy's eventual seizure of Tripolis. In the communiqué issued to the press on the Desio interview and in Tittoni's speech in Parliament on December 4, 1908, emphasis was laid on the complete har-

nand of Bulgaria was about to proclaim his independence of Turkey; *ibid.,* 43 f.

[33] G.P., XXVI, 97-101; for Francis Joseph's letter to Nicholas II, see *Krasnyi Arkhiv,* X, 42-43 (1925) and KSF, IV, 238-240 (April, 1926). Since Ferdinand of Bulgaria proclaimed his independence on Oct. 5, Aehrenthal hurriedly notified Turkey of the Bosnian annexation on Oct. 6, one day earlier than the date announced in the Emperor's letters (G.P., XXVI, 112).

mony of Russo-Italian views—which was set down in a formal written agreement at Racconigi thirteen months later, in October, 1909.[34]

From Desio Izvolski started for France. At Meaux, just before his train reached Paris, he bought a newspaper and was startled at the indications that Aehrenthal and Prince Ferdinand of Bulgaria appeared about to put into immediate effect part of the plans which had been discussed at Buchlau.[35] The news was confirmed by a letter from Aehrenthal which was handed to him upon his arrival at Paris.

THE BOSNIAN CRISIS OF 1908-1909

In Serbia the news caused great indignation and excitement. Newspaper "extras" bitterly denounced the infringement of the Treaty of Berlin and demanded preparations for a life and death struggle against Austria. Only thus could the Powers be aroused to support Serbia.[36] Serbian Ministers assumed that war was inevitable. The Skupshtina was hurriedly called together; credits were voted for war; preparations for mobilization were made; armed irregular bands, the famous "Comitadjis," were formed; and the "National Defense" (Narodna Odbrana) society was estab-

[34] G.P., XXVI, 43, 55-64; XXVII, 319 ff., 399 ff. Writing on Nov. 4, 1909, Izvolski speaks of this identity of Russo-Italian views on Balkan questions between himself and Tittoni as having been formulated "nearly two years ago"; ibid., p. 424; Siebert-Schreiner, p. 151. This Desio interview and earlier negotiations concerning the Sanjak railway project may explain Giolitti's curious mistake (Memoirs of My Life, London, 1923, pp. 202-204) in giving 1907, instead of 1909, as the date of the Racconigi bargain.

[35] Crozier, op. cit., p. 571. The Austrian Ambassador at Paris, hearing that President Fallières would be out of town on Oct. 5, decided to present Francis Joseph's letter to him on Oct. 3 under strict secrecy, but Pichon at once telegraphed the news to the French ambassadors abroad and something of it leaked out to the French papers (Crozier p. 567 f.; G.P., XXVI, 101 f.).

[36] Report of Austrian Chargé d'Affaires in Belgrade, 9 P.M., October 5, 1908; Conrad, I, 113; G.P., XXVI, 247 ff.

lished by leading citizens to prevent the annexation.[37] Prince George Karageorgevitch hastened to Russia to beg help from the Tsar, and was soon followed by Pashitch, the powerful leader of the pro-Russian Radicals. Milovano-vitch, the Serbian Premier and Minister of Foreign Affairs, started on a tour of the European capitals to secure assis- tance in preventing Aehrenthal from taking sovereign pos- session of the two provinces, which were regarded as the very heart of the hoped-for future South Slav Kingdom.

But while Serbian Ministers protested loudly in one breath against the wicked infraction of the Treaty, in the next they suggested "autonomy" for Bosnia and Herze- govina, and "territorial compensations" for their own Kingdom.[38] They urged the partition of the Sanjak between Serbia and Montenegro. This would connect these two Slav countries by a common boundary and form a barrier against further penetration by Austria to the South; it was part of the region through which the projected Danube-Adriatic railway would run, giving Serbia direct access to the sea, and cutting off Aehrenthal's projected railway to Salonica at right angles. What would the Powers do for Serbia? And in particular what would Russia, the Protectress of the Slavs, do?

Izvolski was now in great embarrassment. He feared that Aehrenthal was about to secure the advantages of Aus- tria's half of the Buchlau bargain, before he had gotten French and English consent to Russia's half. Therefore he did not want the Serbians to stir up trouble until he had the Straits safely in his pocket. So he told the Serbians to keep quiet for the moment, and wait for a conference of the Powers:

[37] Stanojevitch, 47; for further details, see below, Vol. II, ch. ii, "The Assassination Plot."

[38] Reports of Vesnitch from Paris, Oct. 5; of Milovanovitch from London, Oct. 29; and of Pashitch from St. Petersburg Nov. 25, 1908; Bogitchevitch, 147 ff. (French edition, 1925, p. 171 ff.); G.P., XXVI, 252 ff.

You Serbians surely cannot be thinking of driving Austria-Hungary out of Bosnia and Herzegovina by force of
arms. And we Russians, on the other hand, cannot wage
war on Austria on account of these provinces. . . . I have
foreseen this step of Austria-Hungary's, and it did not surprise me. For that reason I made our acceptance of it dependent upon her renunciation of her rights to the Sanjak of
Novi Bazar; and then will follow the revision or alteration
of the Treaty of Berlin, which we shall demand; upon this
occasion Serbia, too, will be able to present her wishes as
regards the rectification of her frontiers. . . . I do not understand your state of agitation. In reality you lose nothing, but gain something—our support. I trust that the
Serb people in Bosnia and Herzegovina will continue as
hitherto their cultural activity for their own renaissance,
and, awake as they are, it will never be possible to dena-
tionalize them.[39]

But Izvolski soon found that in Paris he could get no
effective backing for his projected opening of the Straits.
M. Pichon was "sympathetic" but non-committal, wishing
first to know what England's attitude would be.[40]   On
crossing the Channel, Izvolski discovered, to his great
chagrin, that England was still opposed to it, in spite of the
more intimate relations which he expected from the Entente
of 1907. Sir Edward Grey tactfully told him that a request
for opening the Straits was "fair and reasonable," and not
objectionable "in principle," provided they were opened "on
terms of perfect equality to all," i.e., including the English. But Grey was absolutely opposed to Izvolski's project,
which consisted in opening the Straits to Russian warships,
while leaving them still closed against war vessels of the
other Great Powers. Any such purely one-sided modification of existing treaties, exclusively for the benefit of the
Russians, would give them in time of war "the advantage
of having the whole of the Black Sea as an inviolable harbor,

[39] Report of Vesnitch, Serbian Minister in Paris, of conversation with
Izvolski, Oct. 5, 1908; Bogitchevitch, 151-154; and in the same strain
Prince Urusov to Simitch at Vienna, Oct. 10; ibid., 154-156.
[40] L.N., I, 145 f.; G.P., XXVI, 133-136.

from which cruisers and commerce destroyers could issue, and retire at will from pursuit by a belligerent." Any modification of the existing treaties closing the Straits to warships "must be one which would contain such an element of reciprocity as would, in the event of war, place belligerents on an equal footing." [41] This, of course, was not at all what Izvolski intended. Like Saburov thirty years earlier he wanted to have the door to Constantinople and the Black Sea bolted from the inside, so that Russia, and no one else, could open and lock it at pleasure. In vain he tried to frighten Grey into accepting his proposal by hinting that a refusal might break up the Anglo-Russian Entente. "M. Izvolski went on to say that the present was a most critical moment. It might either consolidate and strengthen the good relations between England and Russia, or it might upset them altogether. His own position was at stake, for he was entirely bound up with the policy of a good understanding with England, which he had advocated against all opposition." [42]

Izvolski now began to lose all hope of securing the opening of the Straits to Russian warships after all. If he could not secure his half of the Buchlau bargain, perhaps it would still be possible to thwart Aehrenthal, by insisting that the annexation question be laid before a Conference of the Signatory Powers. Unless he succeeded in this, he would have to confess to a humiliating diplomatic defeat and a severe loss of personal prestige. Already the Pan-Slavs in Russia had begun to criticize him angrily and bitterly for being outwitted by Aehrenthal, for allowing Prince Ferdinand to assert his independence unaided instead of receiving it from the hands of the Tsar, and especially for having sacrificed the Orthodox Slavs of Bosnia to the Romanist

[41] Grey's memorandum to Izvolski, Oct. 14, 1908; M.F.R., p. 530; L.N., II, 458.

[42] Grey to Nicolson, Oct. 14, 1908; Grey, I, 178. *Cf.* also G.P., **XXVI**, 140, 144, 149 ff., 157 ff., 173 ff., 195 f.

sovereignty of the Hapsburgs. Even one of his own ambassadors did not hesitate to denounce the folly of his superior
for raising the Straits Question and for his leisurely tour of
Europe after Buchlau instead of returning to Russia; the
whole affair might cause Izvolski's fall from office:

> M. Izvolski is undoubtedly very intelligent and highly
> cultivated, but unfortunately he is weighed down by exces-
> sive irritability and pride. An unfavorable newspaper ar-
> ticle costs him his night's rest. In his combinations he is
> too subtle and tricky, so that he often does not see the
> forest for the trees and what is simplest. All his arrange-
> ments aim only at the enhancement of his personal prestige.
> His eventual successor will be M. Charykov.[43]

Izvolski, therefore, in view of his weakened position at
home and his failure at Paris and London, began to pre-
tend to the Serbians, in spite of what he had just said to
M. Vesnitch in Paris, that he had never approved Austria's
annexation of Bosnia. While still in London he "did not
conceal his vexation at Austria, and protested most energetically against the affirmation that he had given his approval
to the annexation." He declared that he would do everything to protect Serbian interests and secure compensation
for them.[44] Stopping at Berlin on his way home from
Paris and London, he denounced Austria in still stronger
terms to Milovanovitch: "He condemned Austria-Hungary, which has entirely lost the confidence of Russia and
of the Western Powers; he expressed the conviction and
the hope that her action in this affair would be avenged
upon her in a sanguinary manner." But in Berlin he found
that Germany was firm in supporting her Austrian ally's
refusal to submit the annexation to a Conference unless its

[43] Remarks of Muraviev at Rome, as reported by Monts to Bülow,
Oct. 25, 1908; G.P., XXVI, 220. On the feeling in St. Petersburg, *ibid.*,
pp. 124-129, 169-173, 199, 235-239, 265 ff.

[44] Report of Gruitch from London, October 13, 1908; Bogitchevitch,
157-161.

decisions, including recognition of the annexation, were agreed upon beforehand. In the face of this opposition, he now feared that he might not be able to thwart Austria, by insisting on a Conference, without endangering the peace of Europe. For such a conflict he knew that Russia was wholly unprepared. Therefore, he told the Serbians to avoid war for the present, but intimated to them, that, even if the annexation was allowed to stand, it need not be regarded as a final settlement:

> His [Izvolski's] policy was directed toward a goal, which, after liquidation of all Russian questions outside of Europe, would lead Russia on to her European objectives; Serbia was an important factor in this policy as a center of the Southern Slavs. Bosnia was, in the opinion of Russia and Western Europe, now more certainly assured to Serbia than ever, even if the Annexation should be recognized; Serbia must take the first steps toward the realization of her national tasks in the direction of the Sanjak and Bosnia. For the present a conflict must be avoided, as the ground had not yet been prepared either militarily or diplomatically. If Serbia brought on a war, Russia would have to abandon her, and she would be vanquished, although this would be a very severe blow, not only for the Russian national sentiment, but also for Russian interests and future plans.[45]

In the course of the next four months Izvolski's embarrassment increased. But he continued to encourage the Serbians with the hope that the Annexation Question would be submitted to a Conference of the Powers for revision, and he tried by every means to accomplish this. But it became evident that he would not be successful.[46]

Meanwhile, excitement in Serbia, as well as among the

[45] Report of Milovanovitch from Berlin, Oct. 25, 1908; *ibid.*, 161-163. On Izvolski's interviews with Bülow in Berlin, see G.P., XXVI, 201-212.
[46] G.P., XXVI, 247-363; Siebert-Schreiner, pp. 229-272.

Slavs in Bosnia and Croatia, continued to increase. Demonstrations of defiance against the Hapsburgs became more frequent. Austria, on her side, redoubled her repressive measures and made wholesale arrests of agitators and suspected traitors. In a notorious treason trial some of her officials even resorted to the use of documents said to have been forged in the Austrian Embassy at Belgrade, which the Austrian historian, Friedjung, unfortunately for his reputation, made the mistake of accepting as genuine.[47]

The situation in Bosnia and Serbia became so threatening for Austria, that in December, 1908, Conrad, the Chief of Staff, was permitted to carry out "brown mobilization," a supposedly inconspicuous measure, by which Austrian troops were pushed up toward the Serbian frontier without disturbing the normal peace traffic on the railways.[48] This threatened a local conflict between Austria and Serbia, which might easily develop into a general European war. Russia, however, wished to avoid any armed conflict at this time, since she was as yet wholly unprepared for a general European war, and would be unable to give Serbia armed support. Neither could she count on her ally, for France was not at all inclined to be dragged into a war with Germany over a Balkan dispute. So Russia was forced to continue to beg the Serbians to submit for the present, and to trust in the future. Guchkov, a leading member of the Russian Duma, told the Serbian Minister in St. Petersburg:

> When our armament shall have been completely carried out, then we shall have our reckoning with Austria-Hungary. Do not begin any war now, for this would be your

[47] J. Goricar and L. B. Stowe, *The Inside Story of Austro-German Intrigue* (New York, 1920), pp. 28-48; H. Wickham Steed, *Through Thirty Years* (London, 1924), I, 308-316; T. G. Masaryk, *Der Agramer Hochverratsprozess und die Annexion von Bosnia und Herzegovina*, Vienna, 1909; R. W. Seton-Watson, *The Southern Slav Question and the Hapsburg Monarchy* (London, 1911).

[48] Conrad, I, 120.

suicide; conceal your purposes, and make ready; the days of your joy will come.[49]

Izvolski himself was reported as saying:

Serbia will be condemned to a pitiful existence until the moment for the downfall of Austria arrives. The Annexation has brought this moment nearer, and when it comes, Russia will unroll and solve the Serbian question. Izvolski sees that the conflict with Germandom is inevitable, but Russia's policy must be purely Slavophile.[50]

A few days later Kosutitch noted that these were also the views of Nicholas II:

The Tsar said the Serbian sky is overcast with black clouds by this blow. The situation is frightful, because Russia is unprepared for war, and a Russian defeat would be the ruin of Slavdom. The Tsar has the feeling that a conflict with Germandom is inevitable in the future, and that one must prepare for this.[51]

As the situation on the Serbian frontier became increasingly threatening, and as the Powers, in spite of a lively interchange of despatches,[52] could come to no solution, Germany finally made a proposal for preserving the peace of Europe, by helping Izvolski to extricate himself from his embarrassment, while at the same time satisfying Austria.

GERMANY'S SOLUTION OF THE CRISIS

It is often said that Germany instigated Aehrenthal's annexation program in the interests of the Bagdad Railway and German imperialism. There is no truth in any such statement. As a matter of fact, Germany had not even been given a timely and definite warning by her ally of the

[49] Report of Kosutitch, Mar. 3, 1909; *Deutschland Schuldig?*, p. 112
[50] March 10, 1909; *ibid.*, 114.
[51] Mar. 19., 1909; *ibid.*, 114; Bogitchevitch, 150-151.
[52] G.P., XXVI, 385-770. Siebert-Schreiner, pp. 229-272.

step she was contemplating, and consequently had no opportunity to interpose a restraint until it was too late.[53]

When Aehrenthal wrote Bülow on September 26 of the Buchlau bargain, the German authorities were scattered at various summer resorts. Bülow was at his villa at Norderney on the North Sea coast; Schoen, the Secretary of State for Foreign Affairs, was at Berchtesgaden in the Bavarian Tyrol; and the Kaiser was at Rominten in East Prussia. Aehrenthal's letter of September 26 wandered first to Norderney, and then, after a delay, to Rominten, so that the Kaiser did not learn of Austria's intentions until the very day of annexation. He was highly indignant, not only that he had been kept so long in ignorance, but also at Austria's action itself. He regarded it as an unjustifiable attack on Turkey, which would be disastrous to German influence in Constantinople, threaten the Bagdad Railway, and sow suspicion in England against the Central Powers. "Vienna will be charged with duplicity and not unjustly. She has duped us in a most unheard-of fashion." "My personal feelings as an ally have been most seriously wounded." Such were some of the Kaiser's marginal comments. He feared that this was the beginning of the partition of Turkey, and might lead to a European war. "If the Sultan in his necessity declares war, and hoists in Constantinople the green flag of the Holy War, I should not blame him." "With a policy of this kind Austria will drive us into a dangerous opposition to Russia." He was afraid that if

[53] Aehrenthal had preferred to face even his ally with a *fait accompli.* At the end of August, he had twice assured Germany he had no intention of annexing Bosnia and Herzegovina (G.P., XXVI, 20-22). On Sept. 5, he hinted to Schoen of the bargain he was planning with Izvolski (*ibid.,* p. 26 f.); but the first definite information was his letter to Bülow of Sept. 26 (*ibid.,* p. 35), which did not reach the Kaiser at Rominten until Oct. 6 (*ibid.,* 53, note). The Austrian Ambassador in Paris presented Emperor Francis Joseph's letter concerning the annexation on Oct. 3; thus the President of France was officially informed three days before the German Emperor,—a fact which greatly incensed the Kaiser (*ibid.,* 53, 102).

Germany did not take a stand against the Annexation, everyone would believe that it had taken place with his approval.[54]   His Ambassador at Constantinople, Baron Marschall, favored disavowing it, even at the risk of forfeiting the alliance with Austria.[55]

Bülow, however, differed from his master. Convinced that Germany must support Austria in the Balkans, lest otherwise the Triple Alliance would be weakened, he believed that Germany must uphold Austria in the step which she had taken. If Germany assumed a negative or hesitating attitude in this question, Austria would never forgive her. Though Germany had a right to be indignant with Austria for not consulting her earlier, it would do no good to protest now. Anyway, Russia appeared to have given her consent. The Kaiser finally accepted Bülow's point of view; but he regretted that "Aehrenthal's frightful stupidity has brought us into this dilemma, so that we are not able to support and protect our friends, the Turks, when our ally has outraged them." Bülow thereupon informed Vienna, that, "In case difficulties or complications arise, our ally can count upon us," and that Austria was to judge of what must be done in the Serbian question.[56]   But the Kaiser's feeling of irritation remained; he may have had the shrewd political instinct to realize that in thus giving a blank cheque to Austria, he was assuming a risky liability, and creating a dangerous precedent.

After proclaiming the Annexation of Bosnia and Herzegovina, Aehrenthal entered into negotiations with the Young Turks to satisfy their claims. They, like the Serbians, had at first made a loud outcry against the nullification of the clauses of the Treaty of Berlin. They assembled troops and attempted to boycott Austrian goods. But they gradually became convinced that none of the

---

54 G.P., XXVI, 39, 43, 45, 53, 102, 112.
55 G.P., XXVI, 99-103.   56 G.P., XXVI, 106, 160 ff.

European Powers would actually go to the length of giving them armed support. In view of Germany's strong stand behind Austria, the Young Turks finally decided, on February 26, 1909, to accept the Austrian offer of £T2,500,000 "for the loss of crown property," as a solace for abandoning their nominal sovereignty over the annexed provinces.[57]

Turkey's acceptance of Aehrenthal's *fait accompli* did not settle the question, however. It only increased the embitterment of the Serbians. Hitherto they had comforted themselves with the hope that Turkish claims, supported by the Entente Powers, could be used as a basis for forcing Austria to submit the Annexation to a Conference of the Powers, at which Serbia could at least secure "autonomy" for the provinces and "compensation" for herself. These hopes, too, were shattered, as Austria firmly refused to make concessions.

In the weeks following Austria's settlement with Turkey, the Great Powers telegraphed urgently back and forth in an attempt to reconcile Izvolski's promise to the Serbians that a Conference should be held, and Aehrenthal's steady refusal to submit the Annexation to revision. No solution was reached, until Germany finally made a proposal which eventually relieved the situation. To avert the possibility of an outbreak of hostilities on the Austro-Serbian frontier, which seemed imminent, and to bridge the gulf between Izvolski and Aehrenthal, Germany, on March 14, confidentially proffered mediation to Russia: Germany would request Austria to invite the Powers to give their formal sanction by an exchange of notes to the Austro-Turkish agreement, involving the nullification of Article 25 of the Treaty of Berlin, provided Russia promised beforehand to give her sanction, when invited by Austria to do so.[58]

This proposal had a threefold advantage: it secured to Austria a recognition by the Powers of the change in the

[57] G.P., XXVI, 415-488.   [58] G.P., XXVI, 669 ff.

status of Bosnia and Herzegovina and deprived Serbia of
legal grounds and hopes that the *fait accompli* would be
overturned; it satisfied the Entente demand that no change
in a treaty is valid unless formally recognized by all who
signed it; and, finally, by omitting any reference to a Conference, which might still meet to consider other Balkan
questions which had been raised, it avoided humiliating
Russia by a direct rejection of the Conference idea which
Izvolski had been steadily demanding for months.   It let
Izvolski easily out of the embarrassing blind alley into
which he had strayed.   Izvolski appreciated the proposal
and was inclined to accept it.[59]   He "recognized the conciliatory spirit . . . of this effort of Germany to bring about
a relaxation of the tension." [60]   But he still hesitated to
give a definite answer, as he continued to cling to the hope
of a Conference and the avoidance of another diplomatic
defeat.   His inclination to accept the German proposal,
however, was stimulated by the fact that a Russian Ministerial Council on March 17 decided that Russia was totally
unprepared to support Serbia by force of arms, and also
by a hint from Aehrenthal that Austria might publish the
documents relating to the Buchlau bargain and thus prove
the untruthfulness of the assertions which Izvolski had been
spreading everywhere about the origin of the Bosnian affair.
Izvolski instantly begged Bülow to dissuade Aehrenthal
from any such publication, and Germany accordingly did
so, suggesting to Austria that it was better to keep this
trump in one's hand as long as possible.[61]

[59] Pourtalès to Bülow, Mar. 16, 18, 20; G.P., XXVI, 673-692.

[60] Izvolski to the Russian Ambassadors in London and Paris, March
17, 1909; Siebert-Schreiner, p. 254.

[61] G.P., XXVI, 668; *cf.* also pp. 230, 234-246, 308, 668-671, 825.   In
order to hide his own mistakes and misrepresentations, Izvolski apparently
did not tell the Tsar the frank truth about the Buchlau bargain; this is
indicated by the contents of the Tsar's letters to William II and Francis
Joseph (Semenoff, *Correspondance entre Guillaume II et Nicolas II*,
pp. 230-251; Zaionchkovski, "Vokrug anneksii Bosnii i Gertsegoviny" in

Aehrenthal was willing to accept the German mediation proposal, provided Serbia made a formal declaration admitting that the annexation of Bosnia had not infringed her rights and promising in the future to give up her attitude of opposition and protest.

Meanwhile an internal struggle was going on in Austria itself as to peace or war with Serbia. Conrad, the Austrian Chief of Staff, was again urging that the Hapsburg Monarchy should seize this favorable moment for the "inevitable" war with Serbia. By a "preventive war" now, "the dangerous little viper" could be crushed and rendered harmless for the future. Russia and Italy, he urged, were not sufficiently prepared to fight. Rumania was still loyal, and Turkey was satisfied. France and England might disapprove, but would not intervene. No such favorable moment for the reckoning with Serbia and averting the "Greater Serbia" danger was likely ever to recur, because, in the future, Russia and Italy would have reorganized and increased their armies. Austria might then have to reckon with a war on three fronts. Aehrenthal and Franz Ferdinand, on the other hand, had been inclined to peace, but Bülow feared they might at any time yield to Conrad's arguments. On March 15 Aehrenthal did, in fact, advise Francis Joseph to approve the calling up of more troops and their secret transportation toward the Serbian frontier.[62] The situation was therefore critical. To prevent an Austro-Serbian outbreak, Bülow believed it was necessary to press his mediation proposal and secure a definite answer from Izvolski. On March 21, he sent instructions to this effect to the German Ambassador at St. Petersburg:

Krasnyi Arkhiv, X, 41-53, partly translated in *Die Kriegsschuldfrage*, IV, 238-250, April, 1926), and also by the fact that Izvolski removed the Buchlau papers from the Russian archives (statement of Zinoviev, a Foreign Office secretary, to the French Ambassador, Aug. 26, 1912; Georges Louis, *Carnets*, II, 30). See also below, note 66.

62 Conrad, I. 138-157.

Say to M. Izvolski that we learn with satisfaction that
he recognizes the friendly spirit of our proposal and seems
inclined to accept it . . . and that we expect an answer—
yes or no; we must regard any evasive, conditional or un-
clear answer as a refusal. We should then draw back and
let things take their course. The responsibility for further
events would then fall exclusively on M. Izvolski, after
we had made a last sincere effort to help him clear up the
situation in a way which he could accept.[63]

By this Izvolski understood that he was "placed before
the following alternatives: either an immediate regulation
of the annexation question by an exchange of notes, or the
invasion of Serbia." [64] He consulted the Tsar and next
day gave the formal affirmative answer desired. The Tsar
had already telegraphed the Kaiser that he was heartily
pleased that Germany's proposal had made a peaceful compromise possible.[65]

Such were the events which soon became distorted into
the legend that Germany had threatened Russia with force
and humiliated her with an ultimatum. The legend was
exploited in the Russian Press, spread in England by Sir
Arthur Nicolson, and used by Izvolski as a means of saving
his face before his critics in Russia.[66] But it was not an
ultimatum. It was an attempt on Germany's part to bridge

[63] Bülow to Pourtalès, Mar. 21, 1909; G.P., XXVI, 693 ff. Though
Bülow signed this note, it was Kiderlen-Wächter, who composed it and
gave it its friendly but decisive tone; see E. Jäckh, *Kiderlen-Wächter, der
Staatsmann und Mensch* (Berlin, 1925), II, 26-29.

[64] Izvolski to the Russian Ambassadors in London and Paris, March
23, 1909; Siebert-Schreiner, 259 ff.

[65] Tsar to Kaiser, Mar. 22, 1909; G.P., XXVI, 700.

[66] For the long controversy which arose over the nature of Germany's
action, see G.P., XXVI, 693 note, and 777-855 *passim*. Bülow proposed to
publish the documents to set the matter in its true light and counteract
the legend of a German threat of force. The proposal was favored by
Charykov, the Acting Minister during Izvolski's absence; but it was
abandoned upon Izvolski's return, on account of his opposition to making
documents public which would have shown how he and the Pan-Slav
Press misrepresented things (*ibid.*, pp. 788-793, 796-801, 811, 814).

the gulf between Russia and Austria and prevent outbreak of war between Serbia and Austria. Sir Edward Grey had meanwhile come forward with a similar mediation formula and told Austria in language almost identical with that of Bülow to Russia, that, "if this fails, he would draw back and let things take their course." [67]

After Russia had accepted Germany's proposal, England, France and Italy soon followed suit. Upon Austria's invitation the Powers accordingly exchanged notes, giving a belated sanction to the unilateral action by which Aehrenthal had presumed to nullify the solemn clause of a European treaty.

Before the news of Russia's yielding had reached Vienna, or in spite of it, the war party had gotten the upper hand. A Ministerial Council of March 29 finally decided to order "Yellow Mobilization" or "Mobilization B" (Balkans). This involved the full mobilization of five of the total fifteen army corps which at that time composed the Austro-Hungarian army. It was thus a "partial mobilization" for the case of a war against Serbia and Montenegro only, but was complete for the five corps involved. Conrad left the Council with the conviction that now, at last, the reckoning with Serbia, which he had so often urged, was about to begin.[68]

Serbia, however, finally heeded the warnings she had been receiving from Russia, to avoid war for the present and to trust to the future. She decided at the eleventh hour to yield to the advice of the Powers. On March 31, 1909, she made at Vienna the formal declaration which had been agreed upon by Aehrenthal and Sir Fairfax Cartwright, the English Ambassador at Vienna, in the following terms:

[67] Metternich to Bülow, Mar. 22, 1909; G.P., XXVI, 701.
[68] Conrad, I, 162; for the technical mobilization measures, I, 116 ff., 160, 640 ff.

Serbia recognizes that she has not been affected in her rights by the *fait accompli* created in Bosnia, and that consequently she will conform to the decisions that the Powers may take in regard to Article 25 of the Treaty of Berlin. In deference to the advice of the Great Powers, Serbia undertakes to renounce the attitude of protest and opposition which she has adopted since last autumn with regard to the Annexation. She undertakes, moreover, to modify the direction of her present policy toward Austria-Hungary, and to live in future on good neighborly terms with the latter.

In conformity with these declarations and with confidence in the peaceful intentions of Austria-Hungary, Serbia will replace her army, as far as concerns its organization and the location and number of the troops, to the state in which it was in the spring of 1908. She will disarm and disband the volunteers and irregular forces and prevent the formation of new irregular corps on her territory.[69]

Within the next few weeks the Serbian and Austrian armies were demobilized and the Annexation Crisis was relieved. But, as will be seen later, the Serbians, encouraged by Russia, did not live up to the promises which they had been forced to give, and Conrad repeatedly complained later that Germany had prevented Austria in 1909 from settling the Serbian danger in the only permanently satisfactory way, viz., by the use of force.

THE CONSEQUENCES OF THE BOSNIAN CRISIS

We have dealt in some detail with these events, because the effects of the Annexation Crisis continued to be felt long afterwards,[70] and are to be counted among the causes of the War of 1914. In 1909, to be sure, Aehrenthal seemed

[69] G.P., XXVI, 731; *cf. Austrian Red Book* of 1914, no. 7.
[70] For interesting contemporary comment on the immediate effects of the Bosnian Crisis, see G.P., XXVI, 773-871.

to have achieved a diplomatic victory as brilliant for Austria, as it was humiliating for Russia and Serbia. He was congratulated on his success from all sides, and was rewarded with the title of Count. It was, however, one of those pyrrhic victories, which seem brilliant at the moment, but which bring more misfortune than success, if looked at from a longer perspective. Aehrenthal had, indeed, secured a clearer legal title to Bosnia. He had shown that the Hapsburg Monarchy was still able to pursue a vigorous and independent policy of its own, and gain the prestige which comes with a successful diplomatic move. But, on the other hand, he had caused Europe to distrust the methods of Austrian diplomacy, and incurred the odium of an unjustifiable breach of a solemn treaty. This fact was hardly obscured by the exchange of notes with which the Powers ultimately sanctioned his illegal nullification of treaty stipulations. He had also forced from Serbia a humiliating declaration, which he hoped would put an end to the "Greater Serbia" propaganda. But such a humiliation of one nation by another is hardly ever statesmanlike or really successful in achieving its aim. On the contrary, it usually leaves a bitter sting, which is likely to give trouble later. Serbia did not, in fact, live up to her promise to live on good neighborly terms with Austria. She allowed her soil to be the hearth from which a subversive agitation was spread, encouraging disloyalty and treason among the Bosnians and other Slav subjects of the Hapsburg Monarchy. Aehrenthal was soon to find that he had failed in the main purpose for which he had undertaken Annexation—the strengthening of the Austrian hold on Bosnia and Herzegovina. He had achieved a momentary success at the cost of future difficulties. "I hope our action will succeed," he had said to the German Ambassador at the beginning of the crisis; "if not, I am naturally done for, but in that case, at least, we shall have met defeat with honor;

otherwise we should have continued to sink miserably step by step." [71]

Germany, likewise, incurred some of the suspicion and odium which fell upon her ally. This distrust and antagonism was to be found, however, much more among the Entente Powers, particularly in Russia and England, than, as one might have expected, in Serbia.[72] Though Germany had not actually had definite foreknowledge of Aehrenthal's Annexation step, nor encouraged him to take it, the Powers —and many historians—were hardly convinced by Germany's assertions, at the time and later, as to the real facts. They naturally suspected, from the way in which Berlin firmly supported Vienna during the whole crisis, that Germany was Austria's accomplice from the outset and thoroughly approved of her action.[73] Germany's effort to find a solution, which would sanction Austria's *fait accompli,* and at the same time offer Izvolski a line of retreat from a position which Russians more sensible than he realized was untenable, was twisted into a "threat of force" or "ultimatum." It was represented as a brutal German attempt

---

[71] Brandenburg, p. 287.

[72] Stanojevitch, pp. 36-42, shows that the Serbians felt no particular animus against Germany during the following years. This was owing in part to the greatly increased trade relations between the two countries during and after the "Pig War." It may have been also owing partly to Serbia's realization that Germany often used her influence to restrain Austria from an aggressive Balkan policy. Though Izvolski's bitter hatred was mainly directed against Aehrenthal, that of the Russian people, led by the Pan-Slav Press, was henceforth directed more against Germany; see Pourtalès' reports, Mar.-Sept. 1909; G.P., XXVI, 777-858. The English Government's attitude was colored by the strongly Russophil attitude of Sir Arthur Nicolson, British Ambassador to Russia, who was soon to become permanent Under-Secretary in the British Foreign Office and to exert a strong pro-Russian influence on Sir Edward Grey; *cf.* Grey, I, 182, 304 ff.; and G. P., XXVI, 732, note; 738 ff., 866.

[73] "We have to deal with an action which permits of no contradiction, which has been agreed upon between Vienna and Berlin," telegraphed Izvolski to the Russian ambassadors in London and Paris on Mar. 23, 1909, in reporting the last stage of the crisis; Siebert Schreiner, p. 260.

to humiliate Russia and drive a wedge into the Triple
Entente by forcing Russia to abandon the Entente with
England in favor of some new agreement between the three
Eastern Emperors. It was set down as a new evidence of
the brutality of Germany's diplomatic methods. Unfortunately for Germany, confirmation seemed to be given to
this feeling by Emperor William's vainglorious and tactless
speech, when on a visit to Vienna in 1910, he proclaimed to
the world that he had stood by his ally "in shining armor."

The effect of the whole episode on the third partner in
the Triple Alliance was thoroughly unfortunate for the
Central Powers. Italy had not been fully consulted beforehand by her ally, nor had she been able to take any important part in the solution of the crisis. Italian pride had
been offended, and Italian ambitions seemed threatened by
Austria's further grip upon the Balkan Peninsula. The
latent emotional hatred of Austria in Italian hearts was
rekindled by a feeling of military and naval inferiority at
the sight of Austrian troops dominating the frontiers, the
fortifications of Pola, and the contemplated construction of
Austrian Dreadnoughts. The tradition of Venetian domination in the Adriatic seemed threatened by Aehrenthal's
more aggressive policies. Hitherto Italian hopes had been
protected by the *status quo* principle of *quieta non movere,*
but Austria's action looked like an alarming departure from
it. To these fears were added the perennial irredentist
friction, the fact that Austria was the only Power which had
not answered the invitation for the International Exposition planned for 1911, and the bitter memories revived by
the semi-centennial celebrations of the Wars of 1859. This
bitter feeling found vent in a passionate and loudly applauded oration by ex-Premier Fortis: "There is only one
Power with whom Italy sees a possibility of conflict, and
that, I regret to say, is our ally. The Government must
invite the nation to new sacrifices to adjust our military

forces to the needs of the situation." Italy's doubts of the value of the Triple Alliance to herself were increased. She was quite ready a few months later to sign with Russia the secret agreement of Racconigi. This aimed at Russo-Italian diplomatic coöperation against Austria in the Near East, and marked another mile-stone in Italy's shift from the Triple Alliance to the Triple Entente.[74]

It was in Russia, however, that the Bosnian Crisis had the most serious effects. The Pan-Slav Press was excited to a long and violent campaign against Germany, the burden whereof was that a war between Slavdom and Teutondom was "inevitable," and that Russia must consequently hasten to make preparations for it. And, in fact, it was shortly after this that Russia undertook the sweeping reorganization and increase of her army and navy which was still in progress in 1914. To Izvolski, personally, this diplomatic defeat, which he had to some extent brought upon himself, was the most bitter experience of his life. It affected his behavior all the rest of his days, filling him with a desire for revenge and for the recovery of lost personal prestige. The bitterness which he felt is hardly conveyed in the formal despatch in which he announced to his Ambassadors in Paris and London that he had been forced to accept the German solution of the crisis. The storm of criticism to which he was subjected by the Pan-Slav elements in Russia was one of the reasons which forced him to give up his position of Minister of Foreign Affairs in September, 1910, and take in exchange the Russian Ambassadorship in Paris.[75] There he was henceforth in a position to devote his untiring energy and wily intrigues to knitting together more closely Russia's bonds with France and England. He now realized that only by their support and by increased arma-

[74] G.P., XXVI, 793 ff., 819 ff.; XXVII, 397-431.
[75] G.P., XXVI, 777-793, 796-817, 823-828, 834-840, 853-858, 971; see also *supra,* notes 31, 61, 66.

ments could he avert another such diplomatic defeat, or, if
need be, risk a decision by war. His efforts to accomplish
these aims can be traced in detail in recently published
documents,[76] as has been briefly indicated in the preceding
chapter.

The prevailing feeling among Russian diplomats, after
the Annexation Crisis, was characteristically expressed by
the Russian Ambassador in Paris:

> Foreseeing the further development of the European
> situation, many newspapers come to the conclusion that pre-
> cisely as Germany and Austria have now achieved a bril-
> liant victory, so must the two Western Powers, together
> with Russia, now pay their attention to the systematic
> development of their forces in order to be able, once they
> are in a position not to fear a challenge of the Triple Al-
> liance—and in this case Italy would separate herself from
> the Triple Alliance—to set up on their part demands which
> would restore the political balance which has now been dis-
> placed in favor of Germany and Austria. . . . All these
> circumstances show how necessary it is for us to bind our-
> selves still more closely to France and England in order
> to oppose in common the further penetration of Germany
> and Austria in the Balkans.
>
> Such an opposition need not, under all circumstances,
> lead to an armed conflict with the Triple Alliance. Just as
> Austria, supported by Germany, concentrated her fighting
> forces and threatened Serbia without listening to the just
> demands of Europe, so might we, too, in agreement with
> France and England, after our military strength will have
> been re-established, force Austria-Hungary in a favorable
> moment to give up her Balkan plans and to restore to the
> now subjugated Serbians their freedom of action. The ex-
> perience of the last crisis has proved that if military meas-

[76] G.P., XXVII-XXXVII; Siebert-Schreiner; M.F.R.; L.N.; Stieve;
and in the works of Barnes, Bogitchevitch, Brandenburg, Churchill, Ewart,
Fabre-Luce, Gooch, Grey, Judet, Montgelas, Poincaré, Schmitt, Stieve, and
Valentin.

ures are already prepared in times of peace, diplomatic questions may all the easier be solved by threats and the exercise of strong pressure. The art of diplomacy consists in selecting the favorable moment, and in utilizing a favorable general situation, so that, conscious of one's own strength, one may hold out to the end. Thus we shall undoubtedly be able to weaken the unfavorable impression which the failure of our policy has now produced and in this way we will gradually succeed in liberating the kindred Balkan States from the Austro-German influence.[77]

To the Serbians Izvolski continued to give secret encouragement, urging them to prepare for a happier future in which they could count upon Russian support to achieve their Jugo-Slav ambitions. He never really accepted the annexation of Bosnia and Herzegovina as a final settlement, but regarded it, and encouraged the Serbians to regard it, as a Serbian Alsace-Lorraine. For the liberation of these provinces all Serbs, both in Serbia and Austria-Hungary, should continue to make secret preparations. This was the policy which inspired his secret negotiations with Italy and Bulgaria in October and December, 1909, and which ultimately led to the formation of the Balkan League of 1912. All of these contemplated the possibility of changes in the Balkans which might ultimately lead to that triumph of Slavdom over Germandom which the Tsar and his Ministers had assured the Serbians was "inevitable." [78] These encouraging assurances from Russia for the future realization of the "Greater Serbia" ambitions partly explain Serbia's failure to keep the promises made to Austria at the close of the Bosnian Crisis. That Serbia from the very outset had no serious intention of living up to her new promises, but intended merely to shift the basis and

[77] Nelidov to Izvolski, Mar. 19/Apr. 1, 1909; Siebert-Schreiner, 266-268. Nelidov, of course, depended on his dispatches from Izvolski for his version of the Bosnian Crisis.

[78] See above, at notes 49-51.

method of her secret underground campaign against Austria, is seen from the following illuminating document, drawn up only a few days after the promises of March 31 were solemnly made:

Instructions of the Royal Serbian Government of April 17, 1909, to the Serbian Minister in Vienna concerning the continuation of the Great Serbia propaganda in Austria-Hungary.

The Royal Serbian Government, whose foreign policy embraces the interests of all Serbdom, trusting in the support of England, France and Russia, is firmly determined to await the moment when Serbia can with the best prospects of success proceed to the realization of her legitimate interests in the Balkans and in the whole Slavic South. Till then the Royal Government wishes to maintain with Vienna merely purely routine and scrupulously correct relations, without any political agreement of any kind. For this reason the Government will undertake no step to promote a renewal of the commercial treaty with the Monarchy; for this reason also, it must establish its national activity in the territory of the Hapsburg Crown Lands on new bases.

[The Instructions then warn the officials of the Serbian Legation and consulates in Austria-Hungary that, henceforth, in contrast to the past, they must refrain from all active and personal participation in national Serbian propaganda, and must wipe out all traces of such activities of the Serbian Ministry of Foreign Affairs, so that all correspondence which had been carried on hitherto with political agents in Austria-Hungary should definitely cease. After April 28th, the Serbian Legation and consulates in Austria-Hungary were no longer to be furnished with funds for these purposes, except 250,000 dinars in connection with the Agram treason trial, and 4,000 dinars for "influencing" the Austro-Hungarian Press. Funds for obtaining military information will no longer be needed by the Serbian Legation in Vienna, because henceforth the necessary sums for this will be placed at the disposal of the Serbian Ministry of War and its agents. The Instructions then go on to explain the secret new basis on which the "Greater Serbia" propaganda is henceforth to be carried on.]

In order that the foreign policy of the Royal Government, which embraces the whole of Serbdom, may remain intact, in spite of the above mentioned renunciation of all direct activity in Austria-Hungary, the Royal Government has placed its national propaganda in the Slavic South under the Pan-Slav national propaganda; its organization will receive its definite form in fraternal Russia July 1 of this year. Through a backing of this kind, the support of the all-powerful Government of the Russian Empire will be assured for our aspirations in decisive questions. This organization will be provided with considerable means. A new focus [of agitation] is being projected in the fraternal Czech Kingdom, around which can rally all those who wish to seek, or must seek, the salvation of their national individuality in the triumph of the Pan-Slav idea.

So far as a revolutionary propaganda appears necessary it is to be cared for henceforth from St. Petersburg and from golden Prague. We shall also promote this activity through connections which in the future it will also be the business of the General Staff to maintain.[79]

That Serbia counted confidently on Russian assistance in seizing Bosnia and Herzegovina by force in the future is further indicated by a secret circular emanating from the executive committee of a Pan-Slav Conference in St. Petersburg a few weeks later. It is addressed to the Slav organizations in the Balkans and in summary is as follows: Russia is on the point of reorganizing her army and reforming her internal administration. Until this double work of consolidation is completed, the Slav peoples must have patience and continue to trust in Russia. The Serb delegates at the Slav Conference in St. Petersburg and Moscow have been able

[79] Quoted by Conrad, I, 181. For a summary of this or a similar document, see G.P., XXVI, 776 f.

to convince themselves on the spot that all classes of Russian society are inspired with the desire to have Russia able to take up energetically her mission as the Protectress of the Slav world. Serbia and Montenegro must hold themselves ready to complete their union by the occupation of Novi Bazar and to invade Bosnia and Herzegovina. Bulgaria must be ready to seize the territories promised to her in the Treaty of St. Stefano and extend herself to the gates of Constantinople. The Young Turk régime cannot last much longer and the liquidation of Turkey is much nearer than one might suppose. This will be the moment for Russia, in union with the other Slav peoples, to realize Slav ideals and prevent Austria and Germany from exploiting Turkey to their own advantage. Meanwhile all Slav peoples must unite in solidarity and work especially to increase their economic strength. They must shut out German commerce and industry from their territories by a radical boycott. As for the money needed by the Slavs of the Balkans for their military preparations, Russia will furnish this directly or procure it with the help of France and England. Certainly within two or three years at the most, the time will come when the Slav World under Russian leadership must strike the great blow.[80]

[80] Brockdorff-Rantzau, German Chargé d'Affaires in Vienna to Bethmann, July 25, 1909; G.P., XXVI, 844 f. For Russian efforts to provide financial aid, both directly and by means of loans from France, to provide the Balkan states with munitions of war, see L.N., I, 283 ff.; II, 155 ff, 233 f., 242 f., 262 f.; Stieve, Nos. 280, 283, 317, 346, 1070, 1082, 1101, 1169, 1201, 1205, 1217-8, 1223-4, 1233-5, 1245-1250, 1322, 1328, 1330, 1335, 1346, 1348, 1356, 1363, 1365, 1374; Siebert-Schreiner pp. 312, 339 ff., 451 ff.; Poincaré, II, 33, 49 ff.

French investments, including both Government loans and private banking investments, in the Balkan states (not including Turkey) rose from 920 million francs in 1902 to 3,130 million in 1914, an increase of 242%; her investments in Russia rose from 6,900 million in 1902 to 11,300 in 1914, an increase of 63%; while French total foreign investments, even including her own colonies, rose from 20,860 million in 1902 to 38,230 in 1914, an increase of only 83%; figures for 1902 from *Bulletin de Statistique et de Législation Comparée*, Oct. 1902; figures for 1914 from H. G. Moulton *The French Debt Problem* (N. Y., 1925), p. 20. As French

It was this encouragement to Serbia, secretly on the part of the Russian Government and more or less openly by the Pan-Slav Press, which helped to stimulate the violent nationalist agitation among the Serbs both in Serbia and Bosnia and also among the Croats. It helped further to unsettle the unbalanced minds of pro-Serb youths who carried out a series of attempts to assassinate Austrian officials which finally culminated in the tragic assassination of the Austrian Archduke at Sarajevo and thus led directly to the World War. Austrian Ministers were more or less aware of this encouragement and suspected that Russia rather than Serbia was the root of the Austro-Serbian antagonism.

From the formal and external point of view, however, Austro-Serbian relations appeared to be improved after Serbia's declaration of March 31, 1909, that she would henceforth live on proper friendly terms with the Dual Monarchy. Austrian and Serbian troops were demobilized on both sides of the frontier. Serbian propagandist agitation against the Dual Monarchy ceased to be open and public, but it did not become less dangerous because it was secretly taken over by Serbian military officers and driven underground. The Austro-Serbian antagonism remained almost as keen as before on both sides of the frontier. While the "Narodna Odbrana," and later the "Black Hand," carried on the secret subversive work of Serbian agitation, the Austrian authorities on their part did their full share in keeping the wound open, and in stirring Serb hatred by wholesale arrests of suspected agitators in Austria-Hungary. The further story of this antagonism and of the Archduke's assassination will be taken up later.

foreign loans were very closely connected with French foreign policy, these figures give some indication of the rapid increase of French political interest in the Balkans; they help explain the fact that M. Poincaré was often more pro-Serbian than M. Sazonov himself, and very determined in 1914 to see that Serbia received Entente support against Austria.

The three years from 1909 to 1912—from the end of the Annexation Crisis to the completion of the Balkan League —were free from acute conflicts over Balkan problems (except for the effects of Italy's Tripolitàn War against Turkey). During these years Austria was busy consolidating her position in the newly annexed provinces. She had renounced her project for an extension of her railway system from Bosnia down the Vardar Valley to Salonica, and had withdrawn her military garrisons from the Sanjak of Novi Bazar, as a concession to Serbian and Montenegrin (and Russo-Italian) desires.

In Germany, Bülow resigned as Chancellor in July, 1909, for reasons which have already been indicated above, and was succeeded by Bethmann-Hollweg, an old personal friend of William II's university days at Bonn.

The new Chancellor lacked diplomatic experience and was devoid of the highest qualities of statesmanship. He possessed none of the happy literary facility and cleverness of speech, by which Bülow had been able to gloss over the mistakes of his neglected opportunities and to represent Germany's situation in a more rosy light than was warranted by the facts.[81] But Bethmann possessed much native shrewdness, a high sense of honor and honesty, and a sincere desire to preserve the peace of Europe. During the Tsar's visit to Potsdam in November, 1910, he assured Sazonov, the new Russian Minister of Foreign Affairs, that if Austria should pursue expansionist plans, which he believed would not be the case, Germany was neither "bound

---

[81] This literary facility and optimism, which characterized Bülow's Reichstag speeches, is also reflected in his *Deutsche Politik* (1913, revised ed., 1916), intended as a defense of his administration. The best and severest indictment of it is by J. Haller, *Die Aera Bülow* (Berlin, 1922). Bethmann's more simple honesty and lack of *finesse* is seen in his *Betrachtungen zum Weltkriege* (2 vols., Berlin, 1919-1921). Severe criticisms of his policy are to be found in the writings of Tirpitz and in H. von Liebig. *Die Politik von Bethmann Hollwegs* (3rd ed.. Munich, 1919).

nor inclined to support her." Sazonov on his side declared that he desired the maintenance of Turkey, and sought to give the impression that Russia's interests were again being directed toward Asia and the Far East. On this understanding, mutually advantageous arrangements were then agreed upon in regard to Persia and the Bagdad Railway. Bethmann's reserved attitude toward Austria, which was in accord with the originally defensive character of the Austro-German treaty of 1879 and Bismarckian traditions, coincided with the views of the German Ambassador at Vienna, who, a year after the Annexation Crisis, wrote:

> Germany is not a Balkan Power. During the past year, for reasons of higher policy, we threw the weight of our political influence into the scales in favor of Austria. In my opinion we should do well to prevent, as far as possible, a repetition of this procedure. For the future, we ought to preserve a free hand for ourselves, and allow ourselves to be drawn as little as possible into Balkan questions, so that we shall be able at the psychological moment to choose our policy freely or to use it as profitably as possible.[82]

Henceforth, until July, 1914, Germany, while still assuring Austria of her readiness to fulfil her obligations as an ally, repeatedly exercised a restraining influence on Austria, especially during the Balkan Wars, in the interests of the peace of Europe. This was so much the case that Vienna officials, notably the Austrian Chief of Staff, often felt exasperated at the lack of support from Berlin in Balkan affairs. In spite of the generally good understanding between the heads of the German and Austrian army staffs, Moltke and Conrad, there was more friction between the two allies than has generally been supposed. Occasionally, Bethmann felt it necessary to renew promises to support policies which Austria deemed essential for her vital

[82] Tschirschky to Zimmermann, May 1, 1910; G.P., XXVII, 537.

interests in the Balkans, because he would otherwise have caused such dissatisfaction at the Ballplatz as to have seriously weakened the alliance which still remained the corner-stone of German foreign policy. But much more often his instructions to the German Ambassador in Vienna were in the direction of holding back Austria from taking action against Serbia, from antagonizing Russia, and from other reckless measures. Sometimes Austria heeded the advice, and sometimes she did not. But to represent Germany as exercising a complete control over her ally, as so many writers have done, is altogether incorrect. It was not until after the World War began and Austria exhibited such military weakness and failure that Germany gradually assumed that complete control over her ally's destiny which popular opinion ordinarily attributes to her.[83]

THE RACCONIGI BARGAIN OF OCTOBER, 1909

While Germany was thus working, on the whole, to restrain Austria and lessen the tension in the Balkans, Russia was actively preparing for the "inevitable" conflict between Slavdom and Germandom, which would bring about the final realization of Russia's historic mission in regard to Constantinople and the Straits, and incidentally the realization of Serbia's ambition for a "Greater Serbia" at Austria's expense. With this in view, Izvolski arranged that the Tsar should visit Victor Emmanuel at the castle of Racconigi, south of Turin, in October, 1909. He indi-

[83] On Austro-German relations, 1909-1914, see G.P., XXVII-XXXVII, *passim;* Pribram, pp. 268-298; Brandenburg, pp. 315 ff., 337 ff., 362 ff. For some examples of Germany's restraint upon Austria or non-support of her policies, see for instance, Conrad's comments in regard to Serbia (III, 77, 78, 164-9, 258, 404, 595-8), Albania (III, 63-64, 77, 108, 136, 268-9, 323, 586), Rumania (429-432, 671), Montenegro (III, 166-7, 318-9), Turkey (III, 27, 644-5), the preservation of peace (78-81, 102, 239), and in general (III, 407, 410, 417, 421, 429, 627-8, 632, 729). For the interesting but opposing views of Jagow and Lichnowsky in July, 1914, in regard to the Austro-German alliance, see K.D., 62, 72.

cated his resentment over the Annexation by ostentatiously making a wide detour to avoid stepping on Austrian soil, and the fact was widely commented upon in the Press everywhere.[84]   The important secret Russo-Italian agreement signed here by Izvolski and Tittoni begins with the usual pious wish for the preservation of the *status quo* in the Balkans, but goes on to state that, if this should prove impossible, as both Powers expected, they would agree to support the principle of nationality in the development of the Balkan states.   The important clauses were the 4th and 5th:

4. If Russia and Italy wish to make agreements concerning the European East with a Third Power, beyond those which exist at present, each will do it only with the participation of the other.

5. Italy and Russia engage themselves to regard with benevolence, the one Russia's interests in the question of the Straits, the other Italian interests in Tripoli and Cyrenaica.[85]

These clauses ran so counter to Izvolski's and Tittoni's solemn public and private assurances that they were kept even more closely secret than was the case with most secret treaties.   Izvolski does not appear to have informed the Russian Ambassadors in Paris and London of their exact nature at once.[86]   He did not even tell M. Poincaré until after the outbreak of the Balkan War three years later, and even then he merely read the text aloud on the promise that the French Premier would not reveal it to the Cabinet

[84] *Cf.* G.P., XXVII, 403 ff., 425; Siebert-Schreiner, pp. 148, 152. For the earlier negotiations between Izvolski and Tittoni, see above at note 34.

[85] M.F.R., p. 298; L.N., I, 358; Stieve, II, 363; KSF., IV, 415-417 (June, 1926).

[86] Siebert-Schreiner, pp. 146-177, contains many telegrams concerning the Racconigi meeting, but they do not reveal the essential character of the agreement until Italy seized Tripoli in 1911; then the London Ambassador was told of the 5th clause (p. 158), and Izvolski reminded Tittoni "not to forget Italy's obligations in regard to our claims to the Turkish Straits" (p. 161).

or even his closest collaborators. M. Poincaré nevertheless at once informed his colleagues of its contents, though he "did not read them the text of the agreement, because it had not been handed to him." [87]

M. Tittoni similarly was careful that no inkling of it should reach Germany or Austria though they were Italy's allies. With characteristic duplicity, at the same time he was promising to make no agreements concerning the Balkans without Russia's participation, Tittoni was actually negotiating an agreement with Austria on the very subject. He had begun the negotiations in the preceding June, by proposing to Austria "an agreement that neither of the two states without the knowledge of the other should make an agreement concerning the Balkans with a third state." [88] A week before the Racconigi meeting Tittoni wished to add more definitely that Italy and Austria should "agree not to conclude agreements with Russia without the participation of one another." [89] Then he signed the Racconigi agreements. A few days later, nevertheless, Italy signed an agreement with Austria, behind Russia's back and in total disregard of the Racconigi promise, embodying essentially the proposals which Tittoni had been negotiating since June.[90] To such deceit toward both Russia and Austria did Italian ambitions for Balkan and African territory lead M. Tittoni and the Italian Government! Racconigi betrays the same morality on Italy's part as in the agreements with France in 1902.

Notwithstanding the extreme secrecy in which Izvolski and Tittoni wrapped their arrangement, rumors and suspicions of what they had done were widespread. By Italy and the Entente Powers, the meeting of Nicholas II and Victor Emmanuel was hailed with enthusiasm. The British

87 Poincaré, II, 365.   88 G.P., XXVII, 319.   89 G.P., XXVII, 334.
90 Austro-Italian Agreement of Nov. 30, 1909, defining "Art. VII" of the Triple Alliance Treaty; Pribram, 99 f., G.P., XXVII, 336

Under-Secretary, Sir Charles Hardinge, expressed to the Russian Chargé d'Affaires his "intense satisfaction," saying it "was most opportune and of great importance not only to Russia, England and France, but even more so to Italy. . . . He [Hardinge] shares the opinion of a part of the European Press regarding the strange position which Italy has assumed in respect to the grouping of the Powers. Chiefly in the event of complications in the Near East, Italy would either have to be untrue to her ally or act counter to her own national interests. These words confirm the deep impression made on Government circles here [in London] by the meeting at Racconigi; they seem to incline to the belief that Italy in the future will stand closer to the Entente than to the Triple Alliance." [91] Germany, Austria and Turkey were correspondingly alarmed, but they were given the solemn but lying assurance that nothing had been agreed except the laudable desire of Italy and Russia to preserve the *status quo* in the Balkans and to allow the Balkan states their normal and peaceful development.[92]

The Racconigi Agreement, which contemplated the possible partition of Turkey and the satisfying of Russia's ambitions in regard to the Straits, also served admirably another of Izvolski's purposes—that of tending to draw Italy away from the side of the Triple Alliance to that of the Triple Entente, or at least of neutralizing Italy as a "deadweight" in the Triple Alliance.[93] It played henceforth an important part in Izvolski's Balkan policy no less than in Tittoni's African ambitions. It was further consolidated by the very intimate relations between the two when they were later Ambassadors in Paris together, in close touch with M. Poincaré.[94]

[91] Siebert-Schreiner, p. 148 f.
[92] Siebert-Schreiner, pp. 149-152. G.P., XXVII, 409-431, *passim.*
[93] G.P., XXVII, 411, 421.
[94] *Cf.* M.F.R., L.N., and Stieve, *passim;* Judet, *Georges Louis,* p. 150 ff. 173; Poincaré, I, 32 ff., 336 ff.; II, 363 ff.

Along with his Racconigi policy, Izvolski undertook to consolidate the Balkan States into a solid block under Russian guidance and protection. Hitherto the greatest obstacle to harmonious action by the mutually jealous Balkan Powers had been the fact that Serbia, Bulgaria, and Greece all made claims to the greater part of Macedonia, which was still in constant ferment under Turkish misrule. This obstacle could be overcome if Serbia abandoned some of her claim to Macedonia in favor of Bulgaria, and was promised compensation out of territories belonging to the Hapsburg Monarchy, when this should finally be disrupted, either by the death of the aged Emperor Francis Joseph,[95] or by the disintegrating influence of the restless nationalities under Hapsburg rule. Accordingly, in the summer and fall of 1909 Izvolski endeavored to bring about a *rapprochement* between Serbia and Bulgaria in the common interests of Slavdom, but Balkan jealousies and suspicions were too strong to permit success to these first efforts, and the negotiations came to a standstill.[96]

At Constantinople an active newly-arrived Russian Ambassador, Charykov, appeared to be working for an entente or league between Turkey and the Balkan States, which might greatly increase Russia's influence in the Balkans and form a barrier to "the advance of Germanism." [97]   But Charykov had little chance of success with the Turks, who were suspicious of Bulgaria, Serbia, and Greece, all of whom coveted Turkish territory. With Bulgaria, however, Russia opened negotiations for a secret military convention, extending the scope of the secret treaty of 1902 by which Russia undertook to protect Bulgaria against attack by

---

[95] As contemplated by Delcassé in his letter of 1899, urging the indefinite prolongation of the Franco-Russian Alliance; *Livre Jaune, L'Alliance Franco-Russe*, p. 131.

[96] *Cf.* Siebert-Schreiner, pp. 273-281; G.P., XXVII, 157-174; and the telegrams of the Serbian Minister, Milovanovitch, in *Deutschland Schuldig?* (Berlin, 1919), pp. 115-119.   [97] G.P., XXVII, 159 ff., 170 ff.

Rumania. Izvolski's new proposal to King Ferdinand provided for mutual aid in certain contingencies in case of wars against Turkey and Austria, and promised the utmost possible Russian support to secure for Bulgaria the great gains in territory once contemplated in the Treaty of San Stefano of 1878. Article V of the proposed military convention declared,

> The realization of the high ideals of the Slav peoples upon the Balkan Peninsula, so near to Russia's heart, is possible only after a favorable outcome of Russia's struggle with Germany and Austria-Hungary.[98]

The negotiations did not ultimately result in the signing of the proposed military convention,[99] but they are indicative of Russian efforts, successful later, for forming a Balkan bloc which it was hoped would help the Triple Entente to triumph over the Triple Alliance.

Russia's Racconigi Agreement with Italy and negotiations with Bulgaria and Serbia did not mean, however, that she intended any immediate warlike solution of the Balkan problem. They were merely part of that "preparation for the future," which was Russia's policy until she had finished reorganizing her army and navy, and had succeeded in winning more definite assurances from France and England for support of her Balkan ambitions. During 1910, partly through the influence of Germany, a certain ostensible *rapprochement* had been brought about between Russia and Austria which for the moment relieved the tension be-

---

[98] Proposed Russo-Bulgarian Military Convention of Dec., 1909; Bogitchevitch, 115-121; Laloy, *Les Documents Secrets Publiés par les Bolcheviks* (Paris, 1919), pp. 52-58.

[99] V. Radoslavov, "Der russisch-bulgarische Vertragsentwurf von 1909," in KSF, IV, 272 f., May, 1926. The negotiations were continued in 1910 during the visit of Ferdinand of Bulgaria to St. Petersburg (*cf.* G.P., XXVII, 176, 183, notes). They are apparently referred to by Neratov in a telegram to Sofia of Nov. 23/Dec. 6, 1911 (*Krasnyi Arkhiv*, IX, p. 11, 1925), when he speaks of "our confidential proposal to Bulgaria in 1910."

tween these two Great Powers over the Balkan Problem.[100]
But this understanding was merely temporary, and in-
tended, at any rate by Russia, merely as a stop-gap until
Sukhomlinov's army reorganization had produced results
and a new Black Sea Fleet been created. As the Russian
Ambassador in Paris wrote to Izvolski in February, 1910:

> An agreement of this sort, concluded for a certain num-
> ber of years, would leave the Balkan States at perfect
> liberty, both in regard to their internal development as well
> as to their mutual relations, which they might develop in
> every possible way. At the same time Russia would be
> placed in a position which would enable her to develop her
> military forces in all security and to prepare herself for
> those events which cannot be avoided. In the meantime
> the further evolution of the Ottoman Empire would be
> clearer—the problems would mature, and we should be able
> to meet the events that are to be foreseen much better
> equipped than otherwise.[101]

Similarly M. Nekliudov relates that in 1911, when he
was received by the Tsar before taking up his post at
Sofia, Nicholas II said to him, "after an intentional pause,
stepping backwards and fixing me with a penetrating stare:
'Listen to me, Nekliudov; do not for one instant lose sight
of the fact that we cannot go to war. I do not wish for
war; as a rule I shall do all in my power to preserve for
my people the benefits of peace. But at this moment, of
all moments, everything which might lead to war must be
avoided. It would be out of the question for us to face
a war for five or six years—in fact till 1917. . . . Though
if the most vital interests and the honour of Russia were
at stake, we might, if it were absolutely necessary, accept
a challenge in 1915; but not a moment sooner—in any
circumstances or under any pretext whatsoever.' " [102]

100 *Cf.* Siebert-Schreiner, pp. 282-303; G.P., XXVII, 433-517.
101 Nelidov to Izvolski, Feb. 3, 1910; Siebert-Schreiner, p. 283.
102 Nekliudov, *Diplomatic Reminiscences,* p. 5.

As Mr. Lowes Dickinson justly observes: "Had this remark been the Kaiser's instead of the Tsar's, all our war-historians would have been citing it as a definite proof of the guilt, and the sole guilt of Germany. I do not cite it as a proof of the guilt, still less the sole guilt, of Russia. I cite it as one more illustration of the state of mind of all ministers and all princes—'The war will come. We don't want it; but we must be ready. And when it comes . . . !' " [103]

IZVOLSKI'S EFFORT TO OPEN THE STRAITS IN 1911

Izvolski had made two futile and unfortunate efforts to realize his ambition of opening the Straits to Russian war-ships. The first was made during the negotiations for the Anglo-Russian Convention of 1907, and the second in the Buchlau Bargain of 1908. Both had failed on account of opposition from Sir Edward Grey and lack of support from the French. But in the fall of 1911, Izvolski believed that the European situation invited a more successful effort. The French march to Fez, and the resulting Agadir Crisis, had drawn closer the ties between the Entente Powers, particularly the bonds between France and England. Germany, having roused England to the verge of war in defense of France and the Morocco Agreement, had been compelled to accept a settlement, which was on the point of being signed, by which she abandoned all claims in Morocco in exchange for portions of the French Congo. Russia had not given France any such active and effective diplomatic support as had Sir Edward Grey and Mr. Lloyd George. On the contrary, Izvolski had worked "with all his strength" to moderate France and urged her to give in to many of the German demands.[104] M. Neratov, who had charge of the

[103] Dickinson, p. 303 f.
[104] Izvolski to Neratov, Sept. 1/14, 1911; M.F.R., p. 114; L.N. I, 133; Stieve, I, 146. Neratov's telegram to Izvolski of 18/31 Oct. (Stieve, I,

Russian Foreign Office during Sazonov's long illness, gave
repeated warnings that "Russian public opinion would
hardly understand a [Franco-German] war occasioned by
colonial questions." The Tsar took the same attitude.
Even when M. Georges Louis, the French Ambassador in
St. Petersburg, pointed out to him that North Africa was
as much of a "vital interest" to France as the Caucasus to
Russia, Nicholas II had replied, "Keep in view the avoidance of a conflict. You know that our preparations are not
complete." [105] Yet in spite of this indifference to the very
vital interests of the French, Izvolski flattered himself that
he could coax from them a promise of support in the question of the Straits, as a *quid pro quo* for accepting without
objections the Franco-German Morocco settlement. When
he learned from Tittoni in September, 1911, that Italy,
stirred by the establishment of the French protectorate in
Morocco, and taking advantage of the various secret promises made to her by the different Powers, was about to seize
Tripoli, he believed that the favorable moment had come
to cash in his part of the Racconigi Bargain.

Russia's raising of the Straits Question in 1911 has
usually been explained as the unauthorized act of M.
Charykov, the Russian Ambassador at Constantinople—
"The Charykov kite," Mr. Gooch calls it [106]—intended to
be merely a feeler to see how the wind was blowing in regard
to the question. The fact that Charykov's action was soon
disavowed by the Russian Foreign Office has given color to

170) shows that he also, though more guardedly, advised France to yield
to German demands.

[105] Georges Louis to M. de Selves, Sept. 7, 1911; Judet, *Georges
Louis*, p. 156 f.

[106] *History of Modern Europe, 1878-1919*, p. 488. Mr. Gooch attributes the initiation of the affair to Sazonov, but Sazonov was absent from
the Foreign Office from early July to mid-December, 1911, because of ill
health, leaving the direction of affairs to Izvolski in Paris and Neratov
in St. Petersburg. In September he was at Davos recovering from an
operation; *cf.* M.F.R., pp. 66, 113 f.; Stieve, I, 72, 136, 147.

this view; but the truth is the whole affair originated with Izvolski, while Charykov was made the scapegoat, and recalled when it failed. This seems to be the conclusion to be drawn from the more recent material available on this interesting incident.[107]

On learning of Italy's intended action, Izvolski immediately wrote to Neratov on September 26, recalling the Racconigi secret agreement, rejoicing in the embarrassment which Italy would cause for Germany and the Triple Alliance, and urging that the moment had come "to draw the greatest possible advantages for our own interests from the approaching events." Now was the time, while Turkey was weakened by war with Italy, to force the Young Turks to settle such questions as the railways in Asia Minor, the Turco-Persian boundary, and above all the question of the Straits.

Izvolski at once saw Tittoni at Paris, "to remind him of the conditions on which we promised on our side to recognize Italy's freedom to action in Tripoli," and to beg him that "Italy, at the moment when she was proceeding to carry out her program in Tripoli, should give us assurances in return that she would not forget in the future to fulfill the parallel obligations undertaken by her in regard to our rights to the Turkish Straits." Tittoni answered affirmatively and promised Izvolski precise written assurances.[108] Having written to Neratov initiating a revival of

[107] M.F.R., pp. 114-145, 530-538; L.N., I, 134-179; II, 458-470; Stieve, I, 150-200; II, 20-27. Siebert-Schreiner, pp. 161, 319-330. G.P., XXX, 201-255. E. A. Adamov, *Konstantinopol i Prolivy*, p. 14 ff. Bogitchevitch, p. 167. E. Judet, *Georges Louis* (Paris, 1925), pp. 142-167, 245, exaggerates the divergence of views between Izvolski and Georges Louis, while Poincaré, *Au Service de la France*, I, 328-354, makes a skilful brief to beguile the unwary reader into thinking that Izvolski was perfectly satisfied with Georges Louis, and that Poincaré's own policy did not diverge from that of former French Cabinets in the matter of the Straits and the Franco-Russian Alliance.

[108] Izvolski to Neratov, Sept. 13/26, 14/27, 1911; M.F.R., p. 115; L.N., I, 134-138; Stieve, I, 150-152; Siebert-Schreiner, p. 161.

the Straits Question, Izvolski went on a vacation to his family at Tegernsee in Bavaria.

M. Neratov at once fell in with Izvolski's idea. He despatched instructions to Charykov at Constantinople to take advantage of the circumstances of the Turco-Italian War, the Franco-German Moroccan negotiations, and the very feeble character of the new Grand Vizier, to open conversations on the subject of Asia Minor railways, and, if Charykov deemed it wise, on the question of the Straits (and certain other subjects) on the following basis:

> The Imperial Government engages to give the Ottoman Government its effective support for the maintenance of the present régime of the Straits of the Bosphorus and the Dardanelles, extending it also to the territories adjacent. To facilitate the execution of the above clause the Imperial Ottoman Government engages on its side not to oppose the passage of Russian warships through the Straits, on condition that these ships do not stop in the waters of the Straits unless by agreement.[109]

Charykov was also informed that the plan was, first to secure the assent of Turkey, and to reserve the right to make explanations to the Powers concerning this modification of international treaties. Charykov therefore saw the Grand Vizier, Said Pasha, discussed with him all the subjects suggested by Neratov, and handed him a letter containing the proposal for opening the Straits and for settling other questions. He asked for a reply within a week.

Said Pasha did not at all fancy the proposal. He naturally saw that it would place Constantinople at the mercy of a Russian Fleet. The clause referring to Russian support in the Straits and "also the territories adjacent" had an ominous sound. It threatened to reduce Turkey to the posi-

[109] Neratov to Charykov, Sept. 19/Oct. 2, 1911; M.F.R., p. 530 f.; L.N., II, 458 f.

tion of a dependent vassal of the Tsar at a moment when Turkey was helplessly involved in war with Italy. The Grand Vizier therefore resorted to the usual Turkish dilatory tactics in dealing with disagreeable demands. For several weeks he evaded a definite reply, telling Charykov that he was delayed by having to consult other Ministers.[110]

M. Charykov also confided his proposal to the French Ambassador in Constantinople. M. Bompard thought it opportune, but shrewdly suggested the need of getting England's assent, and telegraphed to Paris. The French Government was much alarmed, and at once inquired in St. Petersburg about the meaning of Charykov's confidences to Bompard.[111]

Neratov and Izvolski were now faced with the very delicate task of securing the assent of the Powers to this modification of international treaties concerning the Straits. With Italy and Germany this was easy enough. Italy needed Russia's diplomatic support in putting pressure upon Turkey to cede Tripoli. Tittoni quickly gave to Izvolski a definite promise, written down at Izvolski's own dictation, and guaranteed the Italian Government's approval.[112] Germany also gave her full assent; Bethmann-Hollweg and his Secretary for Foreign Affairs, Kiderlen, shrewdly calculated that England would object anyway, and that there was, therefore, no occasion for Germany to offend Russia needlessly. For Germany to object would simply be pulling the chestnuts out of the fire for the British.[113]

Austria also, influenced by Germany, was ready to give her consent, qualifying it only with a reservation which would protect Austria from an attack by the Russian

---

[110] M.F.R., pp. 531-535; L.N., II, 460-464; *cf.* also G.P., XXX, 203-213.

[111] M.F.R., p. 118 f., 535 f.; L.N., I, 143 f., 464 f.; Stieve, I, 158 f.

[112] M.F.R., pp. 118-537; L.N., I, 142; II, 468; Stieve, I, 157.

[113] G.P., XXX, 206-214, 219 f., 233-240, 251-255; M.F.R., p. 537 f.; L.N., II, 468 f.

Fleet.[114] With France and England, however, the task was much more delicate.

When Izvolski returned from Tegernsee to his post, he found a "very secret" letter from Neratov, telling of Charykov's communications to Said Pasha and Bompard and of the French inquiry, and suggesting to Izvolski that now was the time to nail down the French Government to giving its written promise of assent. He even suggested the very words in which it should be given:

> France engages to consider with benevolence the Russian interests in the question of the Straits of the Bosphorus and the Dardanelles, and not to oppose the realization of the projects which Russia might have in view relative to the Straits and the territories adjacent.[115]

Accordingly, on October 11, M. Izvolski made a long and persuasive plea to M. de Selves, the French Minister of Foreign Affairs,

> not to refuse to formulate in some fashion the French Government's attitude toward the means which we shall sooner or later consider it necessary to take in regard to the Straits and the territories adjacent. . . . In view of M. de Selves' very feeble knowledge in questions of foreign policy, I limited myself to the above mentioned general discussion. I intend to return to the theme a little later and then state our concrete desires.[116]

[114] G.P., XXX, 207-211, 232 ff.; M.F.R., p. 538; L.N., II, 469 f.

[115] Neratov to Izvolski, 22 Sept./5 Oct. 1911; M.F.R., pp. 114, 535; L.N., I, 140; II, 464 f.; Stieve, I, 155. A little later, impatient at French and English hesitation, he became more urgent: "It is desirable to make use of the present political situation in order to induce the French and British Governments to express their views on the question of the Straits, in so far as Russia is concerned, in a concrete form and in writing, independently of any agreements which we shall eventually conclude with Turkey;" Neratov to Benckendorff in London, Oct. 20/Nov. 2, 1911; Siebert-Schreiner, p. 326. On 14/27 Oct. he wrote in the same strain to Izvolski in Paris; M.F.R., p. 125; L.N., I, 153; Stieve, I, 169 f.

[116] Izvolski to Neratov, Sept. 28/Oct. 11, 1911; M.F.R., p. 119 ff.; L.N., I, 144 ff.; Stieve, I, 160 ff.

Next day M. Izvolski again complained of M. de Selves' ignorance. "The misfortune is that M. de Selves is very little informed on all these questions, and at the same time is wholly absorbed with the Morocco and Congo question." He also added a word on the desirability of bribing French newspapers:

> It is very important to take care that we have here "a good Press." In this matter, however, I lack unfortunately the chief weapon, because my requests to be provided with special funds for the Press have resulted in nothing. I shall naturally do all I can; but this [Straits question] is precisely one of those questions in which public opinion, as a result of old traditions, is rather predisposed against us. An example of how advantageous it can be to hand out money for the Press here is shown in the Tripoli Affair. I know that Tittoni has worked the principal French papers in a very thorough fashion and with a very generous hand. The results are evident.[117]

Though M. Justin de Selves was in fact probably not well informed on the Balkan Problem, his "encyclopaedic ignorance" has been exaggerated. He was cautious, sincere, and honest, and did not want to be precipitated into a rash promise which might encourage France's ally to risky Balkan adventures or which might displease the friend of France across the English Channel. He therefore quickly got into touch with Downing Street. He learned from Paul Cambon that news had reached London, by way of Italy, that Charykov had made an official request at Constantinople, and that England took the same stand as in 1908: England was ready to see the Straits opened, provided they were opened to the warships of all nations alike, but not if

[117] Izvolski to Neratov, Sept. 29/Oct. 12, 1911; M.F.R., p. 121; L.N., I, 148 f.; Stieve, I, 163. For interesting but exaggerated accounts of the bribery of the French Press see *Hinter den Kulissen des französischen Journalismus; Von einem Pariser Chefredakteur* (Berlin, 1925), and Poincaré, III, 97-114.

they were opened only to Russia, thus converting the Black Sea into a potential Russian naval fortress.[118] Sir Arthur Nicolson "doubted whether the moment was well chosen." Sir Edward Grey would go no further than to confirm his declarations of 1908. The Russian Ambassador in London, though he "had convinced himself how highly Sir Edward values the Entente and how firmly determined he is to preserve it and avoid anything which might endanger its existence," soon had to confess sadly that "it is always difficult to induce the British Government to assume engagements on principle for future eventualities." [119]   Further interviews merely made it clearer that it was impossible to persuade Sir Edward Grey to alter his attitude.

On November 4, Izvolski finally sought "to nail France down" to a written promise, while de Selves was in a pleasant mood of relief at the conclusion of long negotiations with Germany, and before the inexperienced Minister should have time to get advice from England or elsewhere about the problem of the Straits:

> In view of the signing of the Franco-German Agreement, it seemed to me indispensable, immediately and without waiting for our official acceptance of it, to nail down [120] the results of my conversations with de Selves concerning the Straits and North China. I therefore wrote M. de Selves a letter on November 4, in which I expressed, approximately in the form you proposed to me in your last letters to me,[121] our confidence in the assent of France to our wishes in these questions. . . . I hope to receive from de Selves an unconditional confirmation of the contents of this letter, the text of which I shall send you by Thursday's courier.

[118] P. Cambon to de Selves [early in Oct.]; L.N., I, 149 f.; Stieve, I, 164 f.

[119] Benckendorff to Neratov, Oct. 10/23, and Oct. 26/Nov. 8, 1911; Siebert-Schreiner, pp. 321, 327.

[120] Russian *zakriepit* "to nail down," "clinch," or "rivet."

[121] See above, note 115.

I have preferred quick procedure rather than more formal negotiations chiefly in order not to give de Selves a chance to discuss our demands with England or perhaps with the other Powers.[122]

In his letter to M. de Selves, Izvolski complimented him on the Morocco settlement "to which Russia would give her full and complete agreement," and coaxingly "expressed his firm hope that at the moment at which France, the friend and ally of Russia, is proceeding to establish her position in North Africa on a new and firm foundation, the French Government, to which the Imperial Cabinet has unceasingly given its most sincere diplomatic support, is ready on its side to assure us that it recognizes our liberty of action in the Straits as well as in North China, and will not deny its assent to the measures which we might be put in a position to take for the safe-guarding of our interests and strengthening of our position there." Even to M. de Selves these honeyed words must have seemed hypocritical, since Russia's diplomatic support in the Agadir Affair had been *nil* and whatever success France had secured in the negotiations with Germany had been chiefly due to British support and to M. Caillaux's efforts. M. Izvolski was arriving after the event and claiming a reward which he had done nothing to earn,—a reward which threatened to suck France into the wake of Russia's risky Balkan course and to displease England.

M. de Selves, however, was not to be taken in so easily. His suspicions of the Russian Ambassador are indicated by the fact that he inquired at St. Petersburg whether Izvolski had written the letter on his own initiative or upon instructions from Neratov.[123]   He was shrewd enough to

122 Izvolski to Neratov, Oct. 24/Nov. 6, 1911; M.F.R., p. 123; L.N., I, 154; Stieve, I, 171 f.   On Nov. 9, he again pointed out the advantage of "eliminating conferences between Paris and London."

123 Neratov to Izvolski, Oct. 29/Nov. 11, 1911; M.F.R. p. 125; L.N., I, 162; Stieve, I, 177 f.

consult Sir Edward Grey again, and learned that England
had no intention of approving a Russian guarantee of "the
status quo of the Straits and the territories adjacent,"
which went far beyond Izvolski's proposal of 1908. Grey
gave Russia "a dilatory reply." He approved the non-
committal reply which de Selves proposed to make ver-
bally to M. Izvolski as "very wise and conceived in the
same spirit of courtesy and prudence as that which he
[Grey] has made to the Russian Ambassador." [124] De
Selves therefore avoided committing himself to Izvolski.
In explaining to Neratov his failure to "nail France down,"
Izvolski several times laid it to M. de Selves' "unfortunate
ignorance" and his preoccupation in defending the Mo-
roccan Agreement against attacks in the Chamber of
Deputies.[125] Perhaps M. de Selves was wiser than M.
Izvolski supposed.

Fortunately for France, M. de Selves was able to hand
over to M. Georges Louis the delicate task of framing an
answer to Izvolski's letter of November 4. M. Louis had
been French Ambassador to St. Petersburg, but at this
moment was temporarily filling a vacancy in the French
Foreign Office.

Thoroughly acquainted by experience with the question
and with M. Izvolski's shifty methods, M. Louis cautiously
raised objections to the looseness of the phrase concerning
Russia's "liberty of action in the Straits." M. Izvolski
made elaborate explanations, and was willing to change it.
After long discussions M. Louis drew up a polite but non-
committal formula, which formed the basis of the answer
which M. de Selves finally handed to M. Izvolski on January 4, 1912:

[124] Daeschner, Chargé d'Affaires in London, to de Selves, Nov.
14, 1911; Judet, p. 163. For Grey's own courteous but non-committal
replies to Benckendorff, see Siebert-Schreiner, pp. 321-329.
[125] Izvolski to Neratov, Nov. 8, 23, and Dec. 7.

In a general way I am happy to confirm to Your Excellency the declarations of the French Government on the occasion of the events of 1908, relative to the satisfactions which the Russian Government may be led to seek in the question of the Straits of the Bosphorus and the Dardanelles. The French Government remains disposed to exchange views with the Russian Government, if new circumstances render necessary an examination of the question of the Straits.[126]

While Sir Edward Grey and M. de Selves, by polite but dilatory answers, were saving themselves from being nailed down in advance to definite support of an indefinite program, events had been taking place at Constantinople which also contributed to Izvolski's chagrin. After Charykov had tried in vain for weeks to secure an answer from the Grand Vizier, Said Pasha, he turned to the Turkish Minister of Foreign Affairs. On November 27, he officially presented to Hassim Bey a note embodying Russia's request for opening the Straits and settling other points. Hassim Bey was furious. He feared that Russian warships in the Bosphorus would mean Russian domination at Constantinople, the establishment of a Russian protectorate over the Turkish Empire, or even the beginning of its final dismemberment. Russia had destroyed the independence of Persia and was preparing the same fate for Turkey.

In his peril and perplexity, Hassim Bey hurried to inform his good friend the German Ambassador. "The great blow has just been struck us," were his first words to Baron Marschall. He then proceeded to tell of Charykov's demands, and to pour out all his fears and indignation against Russia, and against the Triple Entente which he suspected (quite wrongly) was standing behind Russia. Beside the danger from Russian warships before the walls of Constantinople, Charykov's proposal in regard to railways in North-

---

[126] M.F.R., p. 536; L.N., II, 466; Stieve, II. 22. *Cf.* also Judet, pp. 164-9, and Poincaré, I, 341-7.

ern Asia Minor meant that railways which were for the strategic defense of Turkey against Russia would be put into the hands of Russia and her ally France! Baron Marschall sympathized with him completely. He, too, saw shattered at a blow all his own efforts of twenty years in strengthening German influence in Turkey, in trying to save the Ottoman Empire from disintegration, and in building the Bagdad Railway. He foresaw that an acceptance of Russia's demands would be interpreted by the Balkan States as indubitable evidence of the great superiority of the Triple Entente over the Triple Aliance. The Balkan States would be quick to line up on the side of the former, because superior strength was the unfailing argument which determined their political allegiance. He pleaded at great length with the German Foreign Office to aid Turkey in resisting Russia. When he was told that Germany would not oppose the opening of the Straits because there was little doubt that England would oppose it, and that Germany would only be playing England's game and offending Russia needlessly, Baron Marschall sent in his resignation. Later, however, he was persuaded to withdraw it, when it soon appeared that the German Foreign Office had quite correctly surmised England's attitude.[127]

Rumors of Charykov's negotiations had meanwhile leaked out and caused no less indignation among the Young Turks and in the Turkish Press than Hassim Bey had expressed to Baron Marschall. On December 6, the *Jeni Gazette,* though it usually inclined to favor England, published a leading article to the effect that, "The Russians want to degrade the great and glorious Turkish Empire into a province standing under a Russian protectorate, but the Ottomans will never tolerate this." Hassim Bey was further encouraged to resist Charykov's demands on learning that Sir Edward Grey had told the Turkish Ambassador in

127 Marschall to Bethmann, Dec. 1 to 15, 1911; G.P., XXX, 212-245.

London that "Russia's step seems to me out of place at this moment," and that the assent of all the Signatory Powers would be necessary.[128]

As a result of the attitude of England, France and Turkey, it began to be clear that Izvolski's idea could not be realized at the moment. Accordingly, M. Sazonov, who had just come to Paris after his long rest at Davos, gave an interview to Stéphane Lauzanne:

> There is no "Dardanelles Question" such as is printed every day a little everywhere. A "question" in the diplomatic sense of the word presupposes in effect a demand formulated by a Government, as well as diplomatic steps [*démarches*] or negotiations. But Russia demands nothing, has undertaken no negotiations, nor attempted any diplomatic step.[129]

How little truth there was in Sazonov's disavowal, the reader of the preceding pages may judge for himself. On December 15, Charykov was now instructed to tell Hassim Bey that since Russia's proposals had been prematurely divulged, and not by Russia's fault, it was impossible to continue the negotiations. Sazonov sent a telegram to Russian Ambassadors abroad trying to give the impression that Charykov had exceeded his instructions in extending private conversations into official negotiations. In March, 1912, Charykov was recalled and replaced at Constantinople by M. Giers. So ended Izvolski's third effort to open the Straits.

Izvolski still entertained some forlorn hopes that he might use de Selves' answer of January 4, 1912, as a basis for securing future French assent to his favorite project. M. Poincaré [130] would have us believe that the Russian

128 Marschall to Bethmann, Dec. 6, 1911; G.P., XXX, 218.

129 Paris, *Matin*, Dec. 9, 1911; G.P., XXX, 233 ff., 245 ff. In passing through Berlin two days later Sazonov told Bethmann that the interview was authentic; G.P., XXX, 234, 239.

130 Poincaré, I, 344 ff.

Ambassador was "entirely satisfied" with the attitude of France. But he gives this impression by quoting merely three sentences out of a letter of Izvolski to Neratov; the whole tenor of the rest of the letter, however, indicates that Izvolski was really sadly disappointed, was trying to put the best face on his failure, and was merely advising Neratov to accept the French answer because there was no present prospect of getting a more satisfactory one. As a matter of fact, Izvolski was almost as bitterly disappointed over this fiasco as over that of 1908, only he could not voice aloud his dissatisfaction at France and England, who were chiefly to blame, as he had done after 1908 against Austria; France and England were fellow members of the Triple Entente, whereas Austria belonged to the rival group. He seems to have come to the conclusion after this that there were only two ways to open the Straits; either by pouncing upon them in time of peace, or as the result of a general European war. On several occasions between 1912 and 1914 Russian Ministerial Councils seriously considered the first alternative only to abandon it as impractical. So there was left only the second alternative, a general European war. To prepare for this Izvolski worked persistently and consistently during the two following years, and, when at last it suddenly burst forth, was said to have claimed exultingly: *"C'est ma guerre!"*

RUSSIA AND THE BALKAN LEAGUE

Five centuries of Turkish oppression, combined with the rising tide of nationalism in the nineteenth century, had inspired the Christian peoples of the Balkans with a passion for national unity and independence. By the year 1911, owing to the progressive decay of the Ottoman Empire, long steps had already been made toward the realization of their ardent hopes. Greece, Serbia, Bulgaria and Rumania had been constituted into independent kingdoms

But there were thousands of Greeks, Serbs, Bulgarians and Rumanians, not to mention Macedonians and Albanians, still living under the foreign rule of Turkey or Austria. They, too, longed to be liberated and united with their brothers in the independent kingdoms. The supposedly democratic revolution in Turkey, and Austria's annexation of Bosnia and Herzegovina in 1908, for a moment seemed to indicate that these two States were showing signs of rejuvenation and that the day of Slav liberation was likely to be delayed. But the impractical ideals of the Young Turks and their foolish disregard of traditional rights and prejudices only resulted in antagonizing more completely the non-Turkish elements, and in weakening still further the decaying Empire which Abdul Hamid's skill and ruthless methods had managed to preserve. The Tripolitan War gave it another staggering blow, and led directly to the formation of the Balkan League, which finally drove the Turks almost completely from Europe. This natural ambition of the Balkan States, to liberate and annex their brothers under alien rule, was the main cause of the Balkan League, but it is doubtful whether it could have been formed except for the very active part taken by MM. Hartwig and Nekliudov, the Russian Ministers at Belgrade and Sofia.

During the early months of the Tripolitan War various Russian representatives were pursuing three quite different Balkan policies—a striking example of lack of unity and discipline in the Russian diplomatic service. They all wanted to take advantage of Turkey's difficulties with Italy to strengthen Russia's position in the Balkans and in Europe, but they had altogether different ideas of how this must be done. Izvolski, with the coöperation of Neratov and Charykov, had tried to open the Straits to Russian warships, and had failed. Meanwhile Charykov, on his own initiative, had at the same time been renewing his efforts for the formation of a Balkan League of which Turkey (!) should be a member. He had offered his "good offices" to Said Pasha and Hassim Bey to bring about close relations between Constantinople, Sofia and Belgrade. Such a league might be used to preserve the *status quo* in the Balkans, and to support Russia in a war against Austria. It would reduce Turkey to a kind of vassalage to Russia, because Turkey would be dependent on Russia for protection from the Balkan States.[131] But Charykov's fantastic idea had not the slightest chance of being realized. It was at the antipodes of Russia's traditional policy, which was to push the Balkan States *against* Turkey. It was regarded with suspicion by the Turks. And it was anathema to the Slavs of the Balkans.[132] It ended with Charykov's dis-

---

[131] M.F.R., pp. 531-535; L.N., II, 460-465; G.P., XXVII, 159 ff., 171 ff.; XXX, 205, 218.

[132] Hartwig to Neratov, Oct. 23/Nov. 5, 1911, *Krasnyi Arkhiv*, 1925, VIII, 45 ff.: "The affair of the famous Balkan Federation under the supremacy of the Ottoman Empire is up again. Every time Turkey finds herself in some external troubles, this political combination comes up for consideration . . . among those few remaining European diplomatists, politicians, and publicists who are still wont to believe in Turkey's regeneration. But it is interesting to raise the question: What is the attitude of the Balkan States themselves? . . .

"The passionate sermons about the importance to the Slavs of an alliance with Turkey seem to carry very little conviction with them; under certain conditions, particularly under pressure from Russia, they might not refuse to start on this road, not, however, because they would expect any great benefits from Turkey's friendship, but exclusively for the sake of gaining a respite from the troubles chronically rising in the Balkans, to gain time, and gradually gaining strength, when the favorable moment should arise, to square up accounts with their ancient enemy. The Slavs can have no other point of view on the Federation. . . .

"In my opinion Russia should pursue two clear, quite definite, final aims: (1) to make easier for the Slav nations, called by her into an independent existence, the attainment of their sacred ideals, which means an amicable division amongst them of all Turkish possessions on the Balkan Peninsula; and (2) to accomplish her own century-old problem— the planting of a firm foot on the shores of the Bosphorus at the gates to the 'Russian Lake.' . . .

"The Serbian Government would consider it extremely dangerous to approach the Turks now with any offers of alliance such as Hofmeister Charykov urged upon the Serbian Minister to Turkey. Every favor-

missal in March, 1912, just at the moment a very different kind of Balkan League was actually being signed.

While the policies of Izvolski and Charykov were doomed to failure, a third policy, ardently pursued by Hartwig and Nekliudov in Belgrade and Sofia, ripened into success. They aimed at the formation of a Balkan Slav League under Russian patronage, nominally for the preservation of the *status quo,* but capable of being directed against Turkey or Austria. Active Russian efforts to create such a league had been made from time to time ever since the Young Turk Revolution and the Austrian annexation of Bosnia in 1908.[133] But they had all failed, owing in large part to the inherent hatred and jealousy of Serbia and Bulgaria toward one another, and to the distrust with which the wily King of Bulgaria was regarded by everybody, including even his own ministers. The idea of a Slav Balkan League was galvanized into life again by the news of Italy's war on Turkey in September, 1911.

M. Geshov, the Bulgarian Premier and Minister of Foreign Affairs at the time, has given a dramatic and authentic narrative of his part [134]—how he heard the news of the Tripolitan War at Vichy, hurried home to Sofia via Paris and Vienna, having interviews with de Selves and Aehrenthal, returned to Vienna for secret conferences with King Ferdinand and with Milovanovitch of Serbia, and finally, in a three-hours' talk between stations in a railway compartment outlined a Balkan Agreement to him. It was in the course of this interview, after they had touched upon

seeking step of the Serbians in Constantinople would inevitably arouse distrust in Sofia and injure the prospects of the Serbo-Bulgarian Agreement, which by its political importance will open a new era in the history of the Slavs."

[133] Siebert-Schreiner, pp. 273-281; 304-316; G.P., XXVII, 155-194; Bogitchevitch, 28 ff., 113 ff.

[134] I. E. Guéchoff, *L'Alliance Balkanique,* Paris, 1915, pp. 14-63. This book contains much the same material as I. E. Guéchoff, *La Genèse de la Guerre Mondiale: la Débâcle de l'Alliance Balkanique,* Berne, 1919.

the thorny question of the future division of Macedonia,
that the Serbian Premier exclaimed:

> Ah! Yes! If, at the same time with the liquidation of
> Turkey, the disintegration of Austria could take place, the
> solution would be enormously simplified: Serbia would get
> Bosnia and Herzegovina, as Rumania would get Transyl-
> vania, and we should not have to fear the intervention
> of Rumania in our war with Turkey.[135]

But M. Geshov's narrative tells relatively little of the
part played by Russia in the long and difficult negotiations
which followed. This can now be traced in detail in the
correspondence of Hartwig and Nekliudov with Neratov
at St. Petersburg.[136] These two Russian Ministers at Belgrade and Sofia worked indefatigably to smooth out the
mutual jealousies and suspicions of the Serbian and Bulgarian Ministers toward one another, and to help them in
the almost superhuman task of reaching an agreement as
to the division of spoils to be conquered from Turkey. At
the same time they kept Neratov fully informed of each
step forward in the negotiations. Finally, on March 13,
1912, Serbia and Bulgaria agreed on a Treaty and signed it.

By this Treaty of March 13, 1912, Serbia and Bulgaria
mutually guaranteed each other's territory and independence, and agreed to support one another in case any of the
Great Powers should attempt to acquire by force, even
temporarily, any territory in the Balkans. This protected
Serbia against any attempts of Austria to reoccupy the
Sanjak of Novi Bazar or to seize the parts of Macedonia
and Albania coveted by Serbia. Serbia had hoped in the
early negotiations that the alliance would be primarily
directed against Austria. But Bulgaria had little interest

---

[135] Guéchoff, *L'Alliance Balkanique*, p. 27.

[136] *Krasnyi Arkhiv*, VIII, 1-48; IX, 1-22 (1925). A. Nekludoff, *Diplomatic Reminiscences* (London, 1920), pp. 39 ff., 51 ff., gives only a very
brief account.

in seeing Serbia acquire Bosnia and Herzegovina or other Hapsburg territory. King Ferdinand's eye was directed primarily toward Macedonia, Thrace, and even perhaps Constantinople; he therefore wished the new alliance directed against Turkey. Accordingly, a secret annex provided that if disorders broke out in Turkey and the *status quo* in the Balkans was threatened, Serbia and Bulgaria would enter into an exchange of views for joint military action. If Russia had no objections to their plan of action, the two Balkan Allies would then carry on military operations as agreed; any dispute which might arise was to be referred to the Tsar for arbitration, and his decision was to be binding. A detailed statement set forth the division of the spoils to be acquired in Macedonia from Turkey, and provided among other things that Serbia should lay no claim to territory in the direction of Salonica south of a line from Mt. Golem to Lake Ochrida.[137]

On taking charge of the Foreign Office again at the beginning of 1912, M. Sazonov found the Serbo-Bulgarian Treaty well on the way to completion. Negotiated during his absence, and containing a clause for rigid secrecy, he did not know whether he ought to inform the other members of the Triple Entente of it. Though professing to preserve the *status quo,* and giving Russia a kind of veto on making war (at least so he said), he appears to have realized that it might easily encourage the Balkan States to a war which in turn might involve Russia and her French Ally. For a moment in February, 1912, he apparently thought of engaging France in a full discussion of the new

---

[137] The texts of the Balkan Treaties and Military Conventions are printed by Guéchoff, *L'Alliance Balkanique,* pp. 191-234; by [George Young], *Nationalism and War in the Near East* (London, 1915), pp. 387-428; and by [S. Radev] *La Question Bulgare et les États Balkaniques* (Sofia, 1919), pp. 171 ff., including maps and documents on the later dispute over Macedonia. For a recent keen appreciation of the treaties, see Dickinson, p. 308 ff.

aspect of the Balkan problem. He drew up a *questionnaire* as a basis of discussion: what should France and Russia do in case of an internal Turkish revolution, an Austrian attack on Albania or the Sanjak, or an outbreak of war between Turkey and one of the Balkan states? He showed it to M. Georges Louis. But the French Ambassador was again exceedingly cautious and saw great dangers ahead. "These are the greatest questions," he wrote M. Poincaré, "with which Russia can face her ally." "It would be better for us to consent to discuss them in academic conversations, than to risk being drawn along in Russia's wake by the rapidity of events, without being able to discuss either her action or to set forth our conditions. . . . For M. Sazonov as for M. Izvolski, it is neither in China nor in Persia, but in the Balkans that Russia will direct at present her principal political effort." [138]

Observing M. Georges Louis' extreme reserve, and aware of Izvolski's failure to nail France down to support an opening of the Straits, Sazonov drew back, and contented himself with merely informing France and England of the existence of a Serbo-Bulgarian Treaty, but not of its details and potentially aggressive character.[139] He did not bring up again for discussion his *questionnaire,* and evaded all French efforts to draw him out as to what he had had in mind.[140]

It was not until Poincaré visited St. Petersburg in August, 1912, that he learned for the first time the full text of the Serbo-Bulgarian Treaty, and exclaimed in alarm: *"Mais c'est lá une convention de guerre!,"* exactly the expression which Nekliudov had used when forwarding the document to St. Petersburg. M. Poincaré was indignant

[138] Louis to Poincaré, Feb. 15 and 21, 1912; Judet, *Georges Louis,* p. 174 f.

[139] Sazonov to the Russian Ambassadors in Paris and London, Mar. 30, 1912; Siebert-Schreiner, p. 339.

[140] Poincaré, II, 24-60.

that the details of a treaty, likely to lead to war in the Balkans and arranged under Russia's patronage, had been so long withheld from France by her Ally. As he noted at the time:

> I did not conceal from him [Sazonov] that I could not well explain to myself why these documents had not been communicated to France by Russia. . . . The Treaty contains the germ not only of a war against Turkey, but a war against Austria. It establishes further the hegemony of Russia over the Slav Kingdoms, because Russia is made the arbiter in all questions. I observed to M. Sazonov that this convention did not correspond in any way to the definition of it which had been given to me; that it is, strictly speaking a convention for war, and that it not only reveals mental reservations on the part of the Serbs and Bulgarians, but that it is also to be feared lest their hopes appear to be encouraged by Russia, and that the eventual partition will prove a bait to their covetousness.[141]

Nothing better characterizes the Serbo-Bulgarian Treaty than these words of the French Premier, unless it be what he himself said a week after the outbreak of the Balkan War:

> It is certain that she [Russia] knew all about [the Serbo-Bulgarian Treaty], and, far from protesting against it she saw in this diplomatic document a means of assuring her hegemony in the Balkans. She perceives today that it is too late to wipe out the movement which she has called forth, and, as I said to MM. Sazonov and Izvolski, she is trying to put on the brakes, but it is she who started the motor.[142]

[141] Note by Poincaré of his conversation with Sazonov in August, 1912; *Affaires Balkaniques*, I, 38, 111 ff. Poincaré, II, 114 ff. For Sazonov's report to the Tsar of this same conversation see M.F.R., p. 255 ff.; L.N., II, 338 ff.; see also Judet, 178-203, and Sazonov's recent account in his memoirs, *Fateful Years*, p. 52 ff.

[142] Poincaré to P. Cambon, Oct. 15, 1912; *Affaires Balkaniques*, I, 112.

THE BALKAN DANGER AND THE POWERS IN 1912

Though M. Poincaré, with his characteristic quickness and accuracy of judgment, was quite correct in his view of the dangers latent in the Serbo-Bulgarian Treaty, he and M. Sazonov took no immediate steps to consult with the Powers to avert an outbreak of war in the Balkans. He merely told M. Sazonov that public opinion in France would not allow the French Government to take up arms for Russia over a purely Balkan question—so long as Germany did not intervene. In this latter case, Russia "could certainly count on France for the accomplishment of her exact and entire obligations" as an ally. He confidentially informed Sazonov of the secret Anglo-French "verbal agreement in virtue of which England has declared herself ready to aid France with all her naval and military forces in case of a German attack." He discussed the new Franco-Russian Naval Convention, and urged Sazonov to try to make a similar convention with Sir Edward Grey for the coöperative action of the Russian and English navies. In fact, aside from his brief comment of warning on hearing the terms of the Serbo-Bulgarian Treaty and some discussion of an Austrian peace proposal, virtually all of his conversations during his stay in Russia from August 9th to 16th were devoted to strengthening the bonds of the Triple Entente and securing solidarity of action between France, Russia and England.[143]

After returning to France, though now fully aware of the impending danger of war in the Balkans, M. Poincaré made no proposals to avert it until September 22. Even then he consulted only with the two other members of the Triple Entente, being ever anxious to preserve Entente solidarity and to get concerted agreement to proposals

[143] Sazonov's report to the Tsar, Aug. 17, 1912; M.F.R., 255-262; L.N., II, 338-345; *Affaires Balkaniques*, I, 34-39; Poincaré, II, 99-169.

which could then be notified to the Triple Alliance Powers for their acceptance or rejection.[144]

This tended to sharpen the division of the Great Powers into two hostile groups, whereas Germany, and also Sir Edward Grey and Sazonov, for the most part, took the broader and wiser stand of desiring to have the Powers act collectively and in concert, in order to prevent a possible conflict between the Triple Entente and Triple Alliance.

At times, to be sure, M. Poincaré asserted his solicitude for collective European action. Thus, on August 28, he told the German Chargé d'Affaires that "his policy aimed that the Triple Alliance and Triple Entente should not seek to range themselves on opposite sides, but should work for the establishment of the European Concert." [145] This sounded well. But did his acts correspond to his words? On this same August 28 he telegraphed to London, "It seems to me desirable that an Entente should take place between

[144] M. Poincaré's great insistence on what may be called "Entente Solidarity" is seen on page after page of his own memoirs, in his innumerable public speeches, and in the documents. We give a few examples taken merely from his memoirs within the eight weeks between his visit to Russia and the First Balkan War. On leaving Russia, "the last words spoken to M. Sazonov were to beg him to act with England and with us" (II, 164). The communiqué issued to the Press announced that he and Sazonov "have recognized once more the Entente of the two friendly and allied countries" (II, 164). His reply of August 22 to Berchtold's proposal for preserving peace makes the reservation, "It goes without saying that we shall arrive at an agreement in concert with Russia and England." . . . (II, 176). On Sept. 1, concerning further communications from Berchtold, "I shall examine them with England and Russia;" and he instructed the French Ambassador at Vienna: "Henceforth you can express as your personal opinion that the French Government, firmly attached to the Triple Entente, does not aim at any exclusive interests in the East, and that *the cooperation of all the Powers seems to it necessary for the solution of the Balkan Problem*" (II, 184). It is seldom that M. Poincaré ventures to put into one sentence two such essentially contradictory phrases as "firmly attached to the Triple Entente" and the words which he now italicizes in his *apologia*, but which he did not italicize in 1912. M. Poincaré then asks a rhetorical question which the reader may answer for himself: "Was it possible to take at the beginning of the crisis a more clear and a more pacific position?" (II, 184).

[145] G.P., XXXIII, 79; *cf*. Poincaré, II, 181.

France, England and Russia so that completely harmonious advice can be given at the Sublime Porte." [146]   Two days later he emphasized both at London and St. Petersburg: "It remains understood that the concert of the three [Entente] Powers is necessary for every collective action." [147]

In contrast to Poincaré's policy of "Entente Solidarity," Count Berchtold proposed on August 13 that all the Great Powers enter collectively into a discussion, with a view to securing reforms from Turkey and restraining the Balkan States from disturbing the *status quo*.[148]   Count Berchtold was thus the first of the European diplomatists to propose collective European action in view of the increasing tension between Turkey and the Balkan States, although he had no such definite knowledge of the explosive material hidden in the secret Balkan Treaties as had Sazonov and Poincaré. He acted without first consulting his own Ally, and, at first sight, one is inclined to praise him for taking a statesman-like stand, in favor of preserving peace by the Concert of Europe.[149]   But it appears his proposal was dictated mainly by a desire to "be important," to offset newspaper criticisms of his indolent do-nothing methods, and to seem to take the initiative in the Balkan Problem before Sazonov and Poincaré should announce something from St. Petersburg.[150] Moreover, Berchtold's proposal was so vague, both in its wording and in his own mind, that it did not commend itself

146 *Affaires Balkaniques*, I, 45.

147 *Affaires Balkaniques*, I, 50 f.   In this case, though not always, Sir Edward Grey and M. Sazonov agreed with him in placing "Entente Solidarity" ahead of the "Concert of Europe."

148 *Affaires Balkaniques*, I, 34 ff.; G.P., XXXIII, 47 ff.

149 Fabre-Luce, *La Victoire*, Paris, 1924, p. 165, takes M. Poincaré severely to task for declining "the first part of these proposals" of Berchtold.   Poincaré's reply (II, 160 ff.) to Fabre-Luce is not just; he talks about a different stage in the Berchtold proposals.

150 G.P., XXXIII, 50 f., 61 f., 89 ff., 99.   Kiderlen contemptuously speaks of Berchtold's *Wichtigtuerei* as "stirring up much dust," but as impractical.

to any of the Powers, and was later pushed aside when M. Poincaré took the initiative out of Count Berchtold's hands.

During mid-summer Sazonov had been very optimistic, trusting perhaps too confidently to the power of veto which he says the Balkan Treaty gave him; he thought he could restrain his protégés from a war which he probably wished at this time to avoid. But by September 17, the news of Turkish atrocities and Bulgarian war excitement became so alarming, that he suddenly became frightened. He therefore made a suggestion to all the Powers, "not as a rival but as a supplementary action" to that of Berchtold, that the Powers should advise Turkey to make immediate reforms in Macedonia.[151] As quick action seemed urgent to prevent the Bulgarians taking things into their own hands in Macedonia, Sazonov gave his advice to Turkey immediately, without waiting to hear from his Entente friends. But his proposal had no effective results for several reasons: Sir Edward Grey did not want to put pressure on the Turks; Poincaré did not wish to act except in coöperation with England; and Germany, after past experiences, had little confidence in the success of any reforms by the Turks in Macedonia.[152]

Finally, on September 22, M. Poincaré took the initiative by proposing to England and Russia a formula for restraining the Balkan Powers, which the Triple Entente should agree upon and then present to Germany and Austria for acceptance. Izvolski told him that he feared that this procedure would not receive the assent of Sazonov nor of England, "because it emphasized the division of Europe into two groups." M. Poincaré replied that it could be kept

---

[151] M.F.R., p. 276; L.N., II, 547; Stieve, II, 253; G.P., XXXIII, 106 ff.; *Affaires Balkaniques*, I, 58.

[152] Poincaré, II, 208 ff.; *Affaires Balkaniques*, I, 58 f.; G.P., XXXIII, 106 ff.

secret,[153] and, after some modifications to please England
and Russia, secured an accord with them: the Entente
Powers were to invite Germany and Austria to agree to join
in advising the Balkan States not to disturb the peace, and
warning them that, even if they broke it, they would not
be allowed to make territorial gains. On September 28,
M. Jules Cambon broached the subject to M. Kiderlen-
Wächter at Berlin and found a cordial reception. The only
remaining question seemed to be who should assume the
ungrateful office of making the announcement to the Balkan
States. M. Kiderlen suggested that Russia and Austria
should act in the name of the Great Powers, and his suggestion was adopted. But there were further delays due to
objections raised by Russia and England. On October 7,
the assent of all the Great Powers was finally secured, and
the next day Russia and Austria issued the agreed warning
to the now highly excited Balkan States.[154] It was too late.
On this very day, October 8, Montenegro declared war on
Turkey and was speedily joined by the other Balkan Allies.

THE BALKAN WARS OF 1912-1913

In an outline of Balkan Problems from 1907 to 1914 it
is obviously impossible to enter into all the complicated
kaleidoscopic questions which now arose between the Great
Powers and between the Balkan States themselves. Any
adequate treatment of them would fill a book in itself. The
Balkan Wars therefore must be dealt with very briefly here.

When Bulgaria, Serbia, and Greece joined Montenegro
in war upon Turkey in October, 1912, they quickly astonished themselves and the world by the rapidity and com-

---

[153] Poincaré to P. Cambon, Sept. 22, 1912; *Affaires Balkaniques*, I,
61. In his memoirs (II, 214 ff.) M. Poincaré omits to mention his own
advocacy of concealment, but notes that Sazonov urged that the three
Entente Powers should concert measures in secret.

[154] *Affaires Balkaniques*, I, 63-104; G.P., XXXIII, 133-181; Poincaré,
II, 219-249.

pleteness of their victories. The Greeks occupied Salonica;
the Bulgarians marched victoriously to the defensive forts
outside Constantinople; and the Serbians swept over the
whole upper valley of the Vardar, the Sanjak of Novi Bazar,
and the northern part of Albania. This gave them at last
an outlet on the Adriatic. Only the Turkish fortresses of
Adrianople, Janina, and Scutari held out against the victorious allies.

The Serbians were greatly elated by these conquests
which doubled their territory and seemed to foreshadow
the possibility of the early realization of their "Greater
Serbia" ambitions at Austria's expense. They were actively
encouraged by Hartwig, the Russian Minister at Belgrade.
He was said to have declared to his Rumanian colleague
that Serbia could not possibly renounce her outlet on the
Adriatic; Serbia must be the Slavic advance-post in the
Balkans, and must annex Bosnia, Herzegovina, and the
South Slav districts of Hungary; Rumania, he hinted, had
better look out for her interests in the same way and annex
Transylvania. When this was called to Sazonov's attention,
he denied emphatically that Hartwig could have made such
remarks, but a little later admitted that "Hartwig has great
sympathy for the Slav cause, is of a passionate character,
and perhaps lets himself be carried away occasionally by
his Slavophil sympathies." [155]   But there was little doubt

[155] G.P., XXXIII, 319, 388, 439. Hartwig, in his zeal for the Pan-
Slav cause, very probably made the remarks attributed to him. There
are indications that he often went beyond his instructions and was dangerously indiscreet. Cf. Nekliudov, Diplomatic Reminiscences, pp. 47 ff.
Even Izvolski now complained of "the conviction which is enrooted here
[in Paris], as in London, that Hartwig is acting at Belgrade contrary
to the instructions which he receives. . . . I cannot conceal from you
that Poincaré is firmly convinced that Hartwig, who has known how to
acquire a great influence at Belgrade, is not making any use of it at all
to make the Serbians wise and calm;" Izvolski to Sazonov, Nov. 21,
1912; L.N., I, 351-352. M. Georges Louis had no doubt that Hartwig
was encouraging Serbia against Austria; on Nov. 18 he reported another
remark of Hartwig's on the Balkan victories: "The affair of Turkey
is settled. Now it is the turn of Austria;" Judet, 200-201.

that Russia was energetically supporting the Serbian claim to Northern Albania and ports on the Adriatic. Reports came from St. Petersburg that the Pan-Slav and militarist party of the Grand Dukes was using pressure upon the peace-loving Tsar to resort to war, if necessary, on Serbia's behalf.[156]

To Austria and Italy, as well as to the Albanians themselves, the extraordinary and unexpected victories of the Serbians were most unwelcome. Though the Albanians, numbering less than two million, were still in a relatively primitive state of civilization, and divided into hostile quarreling groups of varying religious affiliations— Roman Catholic, Greek Orthodox, and Mohammedan—they scouted the idea of coming under the rule of the Serbians. They had no mind to exchange the Turkish for a Serbian yoke.[157] Though Albania could not look back to a great historic past, like Greece under Pericles, or like Serbia and Bulgaria in the later Middle Ages, the more intelligent Albanian chieftains now desired an independent, or at least an autonomous, Albanian State. When the Serbian and Greek armies overran their territory and threatened their independence, Ismael Kemal saved the situation by hastily calling an assembly of representative chieftains from all parts of Albania. On November 28, 1912, the national flag, the black double-headed eagle of Scanderbeg on a blood-red ground, was hoisted over Valona, and Albania's independence and neutrality was proclaimed. This was done with the approval of Austria and Italy.

Both Austria and Italy urged the establishment of an Albanian State, though under different forms and for different reasons. Allies, yet rivals, both were in favor of creating Albania as a means of excluding Serbia from the Adri-

[156] G.P., XXXIII, 335 f., 383 ff.

[157] Conrad, II, 157 ff., III, 56 ff., 101 ff.; and M. Edith Durham, *High Albania* (1909), *The Struggle for Scutari* (1914), *and Twenty Years of Balkan Tangle* (1920).

atic, which both aspired to dominate. But both were extremely jealous and suspicious of each other. Both had sought secret support from Russia for the exclusion of the other from all influence in Albania—Austria by Goluchowski's exchange of notes with Muraview in 1897, and Italy by the secret Racconigi Agreement of October, 1909, as has been indicated above. These two jealous Powers differed, however, as to the details of the desired Albanian principality. Austria wanted a completely independent Albania, either under a native chieftain, or under some other ruler whom Austria could more or less control and influence. She hoped to find in a newly created Albania an ally against Serbia on the east and a check upon Italy on the west. Austria therefore desired that the new state be as strong as possible, and that it should include Ipek, Djakovo, Dibra, and Prizren, as well as Scutari and Janina. "An Albania without Scutari, Janina, and Prizren, would be a body without a heart and stomach." [158] An Albania of such size and strength as Austria desired would deprive Serbia of part of the fruits of her unexpected victories, and also tend to check the dangerous "Greater Serbia" movement in the future.

Italy, on the other hand, did not want too strong an Albania, where Italy had political, commercial, and military ambitions. Italy wanted to control the harbor of Valona, build a railway across the mountains to Salonica, and check the northern advance of Greek influence. In possession of Brindisi on one shore of the Adriatic, and in control of the Albanian coast on the other, Italy aspired virtually to close up the Adriatic into an Italian lake. Italy was satisfied merely to have the Serbians shut out from the coast. Rather than give Albania wide frontiers and a prince who might be under Austrian influence, Italy preferred leaving

[158] Report of an Austrian expert on Albania in January, 1913; Conrad, III, 59.

the region under nominal Turkish suzerainty, with a governor appointed by the Great Powers and assisted by a *gendarmerie* under Swedish, Spanish, Swiss, or Belgian officers. Italy foresaw, as proved to be the case, that a weak Albania under the joint direction of the Great Powers would be far more favorable to Italian interests, than a strong independent Albania under Austrian influence; because in Balkan questions, the grouping of the Great Powers tended to be 4-2 or even 5-1 against Austria—after the Racconigi Agreement Italy inclined more and more to the Entente, and Germany often sided with the Entente when she considered Austria's Balkan policy to be dangerously aggressive.

By the end of November, this Albanian question, together with all the other rivalries and suspicions which had been accentuated by the Balkan War, began seriously to threaten the peace of Europe. Russia, in spite of some wavering on Sazonov's part, inclined to back the Serbians in their actual possession of Northern Albania, and Austria and Italy were determined to support the Albanian chieftains in their opposition to Serbia. Russia began mobilizing part of her forces against Austria. Austria had already made preparations for war against Serbia, and was believed to have mobilized three army corps in Galicia against Russia. On December 7, Conrad, the head of the Austrian militarist group, was reappointed to his old position as Chief of Staff. Russia, however, drew back when the risk of war became imminent. Poincaré, who had warned Russia from a too risky support of Serbia on his visit to Russia, before the Balkan Allies had won their great victories, now encouraged Russia to take a stiff stand. He saw that the new Balkan Alliance was virtually equivalent in strength to a Great Power. With this on the side of Russia, the prospects were highly favorable for French *revanche,* if Austria should attack Russia, and thus involve France and Germany in a general war. He counted on Italy's doubtful loyalty to the Triple Alliance, and he hoped for England's armed support to the Triple Entente, in view of the exchange of notes which had just taken place between Paul Cambon and Sir Edward Grey in London.

Peace between the Great Powers, however, was preserved, thanks largely to efforts of the English and German Governments. Concessions were made on all sides. On December 16, the London Conference of Ambassadors accepted Sir Edward Grey's compromise proposal for an independent Albania whose boundaries were to be determined later.

Like most compromises, this satisfied neither of the two states most directly interested in the fate of the unhappy little country. Serbia felt very bitterly at being deprived of the fruits of her victories and her long hoped-for economic outlet on the Adriatic. Deprived by the Great Powers of territory which she had expected to get in this direction, Serbia quite naturally felt she had a right to ask Bulgaria to revise the terms of the Serbo-Bulgarian Treaty, and to give her some of Macedonia south of the line from Mt. Golem to Lake Ochrida. Bulgaria refused. This eventually led to the second Balkan War, when Bulgaria made her sudden treacherous attack upon Serbia at the end of June, 1913.

Austria also complained bitterly that nearly everything which occurred in connection with Albania in the months following the adoption of Sir Edward Grey's proposal was done in opposition to her wishes and was prejudicial to her interests. This was either because the majority of the Conference took sides against her in favor of Serbia, Russia, and Italy; or because the Serbians and Montenegrins acted in defiance of the decisions of the Powers, by placing *faits accomplis* before the Conference, which the latter was unwilling or unable to remedy. The most notorious and grotesque case of the kind was the way in which King Nicho-

las of Montenegro snapped his fingers in the face of the
Powers and their international fleet and continued the siege
of Scutari, which the Conference had assigned to Albania.
On the other hand, Ipek, Djakova, Dibra, and Prizren were
not included within the boundaries of the new state. This
meant, according to Austria's contention, that something
like half a million Albanians, forming a compact group
within the watershed which constitutes the natural geographical boundary of Albania, were to be left to the mercy
of Serbian and Montenegrin troops. In the south, Greece
demanded that the boundary be drawn in such a way that
the Greek Orthodox Albanians would be assigned to her.
Conrad, the Austrian Chief of Staff, wanted to compel
Greece to abandon these claims on Southern Albania, either
by diplomatic action, or by a joint Austro-Italian show of
force. But here Austria met with opposition from her own
Ally.

Although the Albanian compromise averted the danger
of an immediate war between the Great Powers, it remained
a highly disturbing factor in Balkan politics until it dis-
appeared into relative insignificance at the outbreak of the
World War. It was indirectly the cause of the fratricidal
Serbo-Bulgarian conflict of June, 1913, and it led to a new
Austro-Serbian crisis in the following November.

When Bulgaria suddenly attacked Serbia in the quarrel
over Macedonia, and started the Second Balkan War (June
30-August 10, 1913), she was speedily crushed. Rumania
and Greece seized the favorable opportunity to settle their
grievances against her by joining forces with Serbia. Even
Turkey returned to the attack to recover the Thracian
territory which she had just lost. Attacked on four sides,
and already exhausted by her efforts during the First Balkan War, Bulgaria was quickly forced to beg for peace and
sign the Treaty of Bucharest. This deprived her of a large
part of her recent conquests from Turkey and some of her

own former territory which was ceded to Rumania. It increased the power of her Balkan rivals, and left her isolated and embittered. Henceforth she was eager to gain the support of Austria or Russia—whichever offered her the best prospect of overthrowing the Bucharest Treaty. But she had forfeited the confidence of every one. Russia hesitated to ally with her for fear of antagonizing Serbia, and Austria hesitated similarly for fear of offending Rumania.

Serbia came out of the Balkan Wars greatly increased in power and prestige, and fired with a renewed self-confidence and determination to realize her ambition of a "Greater Serbia." She had nearly doubled her territory, and increased her population from three to nearly four and a half millions. To be sure, the newly acquired districts in Macedonia were predominantly Bulgarian in character, and would therefore present a difficult problem of assimilation and administration as Serbia's first task of the future. But her acquisition of part of Novi Bazar and the upper Vardar valley, and her running frontier with Montenegro, would enable her effectively to bar the progress of Austria toward Salonica. Together these two Slav states partially surrounded the Austrian provinces of Bosnia and Herzegovina. There were soon rumors that Serbia and Montenegro might merge together, as the first step in the formation of "Greater Serbia." The next step would be to take Bosnia, Herzegovina, Dalmatia, and the other South Slav districts belonging to Austria-Hungary.

These dangerous and reckless territorial ambitions, which were taking stronger and stronger hold of all Serbians, even of their greatest leader and Prime Minister, M. Pashitch, are reflected in the remark which he made to his Greek colleague, M. Politis, as they finished dividing up the spoils of the Second Balkan War at the Bucharest Peace Conference: "The first round is won; now we must prepare the second against Austria." [159]　Even more indicative of his megalomania is the statement he made to the Serbian Chargé d'Affaires at Berlin, whom he met a few days later at Marienbad:

> Already in the first Balkan War I could have let it come to an European war, in order to acquire Bosnia and Herzegovina: but, as I feared that we should then be forced to make large concessions to Bulgaria in Macedonia, I wanted first of all to secure the possession of Macedonia for Serbia, and only then to proceed to the acquisition of Bosnia.[160]

It would be a mistake, however, to think that M. Pashitch intended "the second round" against Austria immediately.　Cooler reflection told him that before proceeding to this, it was necessary to consolidate the gains in Macedonia and to make more certain of Russian support. Hence his visit to Russia in January, 1914, to ask for a marriage alliance between the Serbian Crown Prince and the Tsar's daughter, as well as for "120,000 guns and ammunition and some few cannon, especially howitzers." [161] Although M. Pashitch was willing to await the favorable moment, this was not the feeling of many nationalist Serb youths and especially of the Serbian military officers of the secret "Black Hand."　Highly elated by their recent victories, they looked forward with increasing eagerness and impatience to the day, so often promised by Russia, when the great Slav Empire of the north would be ready to help them in the "inevitable" struggle between Slavdom and Germandom, and the final creation of a "Greater Serbia" at the expense of the Hapsburg Empire.[162]

---

[159] Bogitchevitch, 65.　[160] Bogitchevitch, 65.　[161] Bogitchevitch, 175.

[162] On May 6, 1913, Sazonov wrote to Hartwig in Belgrade (*Deutschland Schuldig?* p. 99): "Serbia's Promised Land lies in the territory of the present Austria-Hungary, and not there where she is now making efforts and where the Bulgarians stand in her way.　Under these circumstances it is of vital interest to Serbia to maintain her alliance with Bulgaria on the one hand, and, on the other, to accomplish with steady

In proportion as Serbia was elated and strengthened, Austria felt discouraged and weakened in power and prestige by the results of the Balkan Wars. Though she had taken no part in them, and lost no territory, her position was seriously undermined. Her subject nationalities grew more restless and more accessible to subversive propaganda. Rumania was becoming a less reliable ally, and Serbia a more certain and active enemy. The ever-present friction and distrust between Italy and Austria had been increased, and the danger that Austria might one day have to fight a war upon four fronts—Italian, Serbian, Rumanian and Russian—had become more threatening. Realizing these increased dangers, the militarist party at Vienna again seriously considered whether Austria ought not to deal at once with the Greater Serbia danger.[163]

GERMANY'S WARNING TO AUSTRIA, JULY, 1913

When Bulgaria treacherously attacked Serbia at the end of June, 1913, and began the short but disastrous Second Balkan War,[164] Berchtold at first adopted a reserved "wait

and patient work the necessary degree of preparedness for the inevitable struggle of the future. Time works on the side of Serbia and for the ruin of her enemies, who already show evident signs of decay. Explain all this to the Serbians! I hear from all sides that if ever any voice can have a full effect at Belgrade, it is yours." For the Tsar's long encouraging interview with Pashitch on Jan. 20/Feb. 2, 1914, see *ibid.*, 130-136; and Bogitchevitch, 170-180. For Hartwig's attitude, see above, note 155.

[163] Conrad, III, 11 ff., 74 ff., 98 ff., 238 ff., and especially 303 ff. and 329 ff.

[164] For the oft-repeated assertion that Austria egged Bulgaria on to the attack on Serbia we find no clear and definite confirmation in all the voluminous documents which have now been published. As early as May 6, from reports from Bulgaria and talks with Bulgarian officers, Conrad was convinced that an early war between Serbia and Bulgaria was inevitable, and urged Berchtold to make up his mind to take advantage of it; but Berchtold hesitated (Conrad, III, 302-316). On May 26 Conrad says he heard from the Austrian Military Attaché in Sofia that Berchtold had offered to support Bulgaria, protect her from loss of territory, and loan her money, if Bulgaria would refrain from following in the wake of Russia (Conrad, III, 330); but Conrad's own correspondence and frequent interviews with Berchtold at this time and during the following

and see" attitude, which accorded with his own hesitating nature and the wishes of Germany and Italy.[165] But he did not intend to tolerate any further great increase of Serbian territory, in spite of the moderating counsels of the German Ambassador in Vienna. According to the latter's despatch of July 1, 1913:

> If Russia, in case of decisive Bulgarian victories, should intervene in favor of Serbia, they would oppose it here [Kaiser's marginal comment: "Unbelievable"]. To my question, how this would be done, Count Berchtold thought either by direct steps at St. Petersburg, or perhaps by the occupation of Belgrade [Kaiser: "Totally crazy; that is then war!"].

Interference by Austria-Hungary without Russian provo-

weeks contain nothing which confirms this doubtful report. Neither does *Die Grosse Politik*, unless it be Tschirschky's vague phrase on July 2 that Berchtold "seems to begin to fear the Bulgarian spirits which he called" (G.P., XXXV, 147 note). The editors of the latter declare (G.P., XXXV, 52 note): "The Russian assumption that the Bulgarian Government was egged on to its final intransigence by Austria-Hungary finds no confirmation either in the German documents nor in the Austrian sources." To be sure, the *argumentum ex silentio* is negative and not conclusive. There is no doubt that Berchtold rejoiced at the prospect of the collapse of the Balkan League formed under Russian patronage, though he still suffered from the illusory nightmare that Triple Entente intrigues and Rumanian demands on Bulgaria for territorial compensations might cause its reconstitution (G.P., XXXV, 7, 40, 68 f.). There is also no doubt that Berchtold refused to support the Russian proposal early in June, 1913, that the Great Powers invite the Balkan States to demobilize at once (G.P., XXXV, 26, 41, 240; *Affaires Balkaniques*, II, 209 ff.); that he recognized the "parallelism of Austrian and Bulgarian interests" in their common opposition to a Greater Serbia (G.P., XXXIV, 822; XXXV, 117 f., 320, 329 f., 346 ff.); and also that he was "Bulgarophil" to the extent of trying to bring about a peaceful arrangement between Rumania and Bulgaria without too great territorial concessions on the latter's part (G.P., XXXIV, 577 ff., 843, 873 ff.; XXXV, 17, 56, 61 f., 66 ff., 77, 115 ff.). But that he positively egged Bulgaria on in her suicidal attack on Serbia seems not proven. Had he done so, Germany would have been likely to have known of it, and some allusion would be found to it in the German documents, especially in the frequent uncomplimentary remarks which the Kaiser and his German officials indulged in concerning Berchtold's diplomacy (*cf.* G.P., XXXV, 40, 54, 116, 147 note, 148 note, 365, 378; XXXVI, 28-30, 32).

[165] G.P., XXXV, 7 f., 16 ff., 52 ff., 115.

cation would only be necessary in case Serbia should win decisively and a "Great Serbia" threaten to arise. . . . I called the Minister's attention to the fact that, just as Russian intervention on behalf of Serbia might call forth counter action by Austria-Hungary, just so Austrian interference against Serbia would bring Russia to a counter action. Berchtold observed, "Perhaps." [166]

Two days later Berchtold again expressed his anxieties to the German Ambassador, who reported to Berlin:

Count Berchtold asked me to call on him today. The Minister said he considered it his duty not to leave the German Government in the dark as to the gravity of the position for the Monarchy. The South Slav question, that is to say, undisturbed possession of the provinces inhabited by South Slavs, is a vital question for the Monarchy as well as for the Triple Alliance. The Monarchy's South Slav provinces could not be held if Serbia became too powerful. As to that, all competent opinions here agree. The Monarchy might accordingly possibly be compelled to intervene, in the event of Serbia inflicting a crushing defeat on Bulgaria in conjunction with Rumania and Greece, and annexing tracts of country in excess of the territory of Old Serbia, or something approximating to that. Serbia cannot be left in possession of Monastir, in any case.

To my question, when and how he thought of intervening, the Minister replied that it would no doubt be possible to find the psychological moment. Naturally he could not say anything now as to the method of procedure; that would depend on circumstances. He thought they would have to begin with a diplomatic conversation in Belgrade, which must be supported by military pressure, if it led to no conclusion. Then, if Russia came into the arena, St. Petersburg would become the scene of action.

The Minister again expressed a hope that the Monarchy's difficult position would be understood in Berlin. Far from

[166] Tschirschky to F.O., July 1, 1913; G.P., XXXV, 115 f.

wishing to pursue an adventurous policy, or being bent on conquest, her only object was to safeguard her South Slav possessions, which of course included Trieste. Naturally the most acceptable solution of the question would be a small Serbia, defeated by the enemy, and he would very much prefer this to a possible occupation of Serbia by the Monarchy. But, failing the first alternative, the Monarchy would be compelled to take action, in order to safeguard her possessions. There must be no mistake as to the danger of a Great Serbian "Piedmont," weighing as a military factor, on the borders of the Monarchy.[167]

This telegram arrived at Berlin while Bethmann-Hollweg and Jagow, the German Secretary of State, were absent at Kiel at the Kaiser's annual yachting festival, at which the Italian King and Queen, accompanied by their Minister of Foreign Affairs, San Giuliano, were also present. Zimmermann, the Under-Secretary at Berlin, forwarded the telegram to Kiel, with the moderating German comment:

For the moment there hardly seems to be any ground for special nervousness on Vienna's part, because one can scarcely talk as yet of the danger of a Great Serbia. Our business should be to exercise a quieting influence on Vienna, and see that she keeps us regularly informed of her intentions and takes no decisions before hearing what we have to say.[168]

Meanwhile Berchtold had become increasingly nervous. He feared that Rumania was about to fall upon Bulgaria and so weaken her that Serbia would have a complete victory, and then the Greater Serbia danger would be greater than ever. He therefore telegraphed to the Austrian Am-

[167] Tschirschky to Bethmann, July 3, 1913; G.P., XXXV, 122 ff.; previously published by Count Montgelas in the *Deutsche Allgemeine Zeitung* of March 7, 1920 No. 123, and in his *Leitfaden zur Kriegsschuldfrage* (Berlin, 1923), p. 61 f.

[168] G.P., XXXV, 124; Montgelas, *l. c.*, p. 62. The Kaiser approved Zimmermann's comment and Tschirschky was so informed (G.P., XXXV, 125).

bassadors in Berlin and Rome on July 4, expressing much the same views as in his conversations with the German Ambassador quoted above, and particularly urging that Austria's two allies should "make representations at Bucharest to hold off Rumania from further steps against Bulgaria." [169] Bethmann refused to do this, and made it clear, as he had often done before, that the way to prevent Rumania from falling upon Bulgaria was for Austria to exert energetic pressure at Sofia to induce King Ferdinand to satisfy King Carol's justifiable demands for territorial compensations. For Berchtold's edification Bethmann added the further sapient observations and effective warnings:

> Austria-Hungary from the outset declared that in the present Balkan crisis she is striving after no territorial conquests. She has defined her interest as to the outcome of the Balkan War to the effect that Serbia must not reach the Adriatic, and that a viable Albania must be delivered. The first point she has smoothly accomplished. As to the boundaries of Albania, she has triumphed in the Scutari question, and along with Italy also in the question of the southern boundary of Albania along the coast. The questions still open—the southern boundary on the mainland, the constitution, and the choice of a ruler, etc., will, it is to be hoped, be satisfactorily settled. At any rate the hostilities which have now broken out between Bulgaria and Serbia-Greece in no wise disturb as yet the rule of policy hitherto traced by Austria-Hungary. On the contrary, these hostilities are not undesirable for specifically Austro-Hungarian interests, aside from the further disturbance they cause to trade and travel. It can only benefit the Dual Monarchy, if Bulgaria and Serbia are weak and discordant at the end of the war. Austria gains time thereby to restore the *modus vivendi* with Serbia which under all circumstances is necessary.

[169] G.P., XXXV, 128 f.; Pribram, p. 301, note 424.

How the present hostilities between Bulgaria and Serbia will end, no man knows. But this is certain, that whichever wins, both will be weakened and filled with hatred against one another! Austria-Hungary should not interfere with this result. Even if Serbia should win, it is still a long way to a Great Serbia. For even then, Serbia will not reach the Adriatic, and a few strips of land more or less will not put the fat in the fire. Should Austria-Hungary now try by diplomatic means to chase Serbia out of her newly won territories, she would have no luck, but would certainly rouse deadly hatred in Serbia. Should she try to do this by force of arms, it would mean a European war. Germany's vital interests would thereby be most seriously affected, and I must therefore assume that before Count Berchtold makes any such decisions he will inform us.

I can therefore only express the hope that the people in Vienna will not let themselves be upset by the nightmare of a Great Serbia, but will await further developments from the Serbo-Bulgarian theatre of war. Only insistently can I warn against the idea of wanting to gobble up Serbia, for that would simply weaken Austria.[170]

This speedy and decisive warning from Germany on July 6 effectually deterred Berchtold and Conrad from rashly entering upon any reckless adventure which would have endangered the peace of Europe. We have given the episode in some detail, partly to suggest that Germany might have done the same in July, 1914; partly to illustrate the divergence in views between Berlin and Vienna; and partly to correct false impressions which M. Giolitti has spread concerning this incident, and which have been generally accepted by Entente writers.

Speaking in the Italian Parliament on December 5, 1914, in an attempt to justify Italy's neutrality in the World War by an historical precedent in 1913, M. Giolitti said:

[170] Bethmann to Szögyényi, and Zimmermann to Tschirschky, July 6, 1913; G.P., XXXV, 129 f.

During the Balkan War, on the 9th of August, about a year before the present war broke out, during my absence from Rome, I received from my hon. colleague, Signor di San Giuliano, the following telegram:

"Austria has communicated to us and to Germany her intention of taking action against Serbia, and defines such action as defensive, hoping to bring into operation the *casus foederis* of the Triple Alliance, which, on the contrary, I believe to be inapplicable. (*Sensation.*)

"I am endeavoring to arrange for a combined effort with Germany to prevent such action on the part of Austria, but it may become necessary to state clearly that we do not consider such action, if it should be taken, as defensive, and that, therefore, we do not consider that the *casus foederis* arises.

"Please telegraph to me at Rome if you approve."

I replied:

"If Austria intervenes against Serbia it is clear that a *casus foederis* cannot be established. It is a step which she is taking on her own account, since there is no question of defence, inasmuch as no one is thinking of attacking her. It is necessary that a declaration to this effect should be made to Austria in the most formal manner, and we must hope for action on the part of Germany to dissuade Austria from this most perilous adventure." (*Hear, hear.*)

This course was taken, and our interpretation was upheld and recognised as proper, since our action in no way disturbed our relations with the two Allied Powers. The declaration of neutrality made by the present Government conforms therefore in all respects to the precedents of Italian policy, and conforms also to an interpretation of the Treaty of Alliance which has been already accepted by the Allies.

I wish to recall this, because I think it right that in the eyes of all Europe it should appear that Italy has remained completely loyal to the observance of her pledges. (*Loud applause.*)[171]

[171] *Collected Diplomatic Correspondence* (London, 1915), p. 401.

M. Giolitti repeats his statement in his memoirs, and it
has been blindly copied by Entente writers generally—even
by such a well informed and cautious writer as M. Poincaré.[172] But the statement is incorrect in many respects.

In the first place, Giolitti places the incident on August
9 instead of July 9—that is, at the end instead of at the
beginning of the Second Balkan War; in placing it after
Serbia had made her great gains from Bulgaria and after
Austria was correspondingly dissatisfied with the situation,
he gives his account a more plausible character. In reality
what appears to have happened was this. Berchtold's telegram of July 4, asking for pressure on Rumania and saying
that Austria could not allow Serbia to be greatly increased,[173] reached Rome when Giolitti and San Giuliano
were both absent from the city, San Giuliano being at Kiel.
In the absence of the Prime Minister and the Minister of
Foreign Affairs, the subordinate Foreign Office officials, who
received Berchtold's communication, "got a fright such as
they had never had in their lives"; [174] but they were greatly
relieved when they soon learned from the German Ambassador in Rome of the vigorous warning which Berlin had
at once given Vienna. When San Giuliano returned from
Kiel to Rome, he found the Austrian communication which
had terrified his subordinates, consulted Giolitti by telegraph on July 9, and then replied to the Austrian Ambassador on July 12 (nearly a week after Bethmann had already given his warning to Berchtold), protesting against
any Austrian military action against Serbia, and adding,

172 G. Giolitti, *Memoirs of My Life* (London, 1923), p. 372; Poincaré, III, 231. See, however, G.P., XXXV, 122 note; Pribram, p. 301;
Jagow, *Ursachen,* p. 71, and article in *Deutsche Allgemeine Zeitung,* Feb.
21, 1923; Montgelas, *Leitfaden,* p. 60 ff.; and A. von Wegerer, *Kritische
Bemerkungen zu Kapitel XIII aus Vivianis "Réponse au Kaiser"* (Berlin,
1923), p. 28 ff.

173 G.P., XXXV, 128 ff., 164; Pribram, p. 301, note 424. *Cf.* above,
p. 451.

174 Flotow, German Ambassador in Rome, to Bethmann, July 15,
1913; G.P., XXXV, 165.

"We shall hold you back by the coat-tails, if necessary." [175]

Giolitti is also incorrect in implying that it was Italy, rather than Germany, who deterred Berchtold from taking rash action; [176] it was not San Giuliano's reply of July 12, but Bethmann's prompt warning of July 6, which was of decisive influence at Vienna. Nor is there anything in the documents hitherto published by Germany and Austria which confirms M. Giolitti's assertion that the Triple Alliance *casus foederis* was discussed on this occasion. Nor, finally, is the righteous attitude of the Italian statesmen of December, 1914, quite so admirable and convincing if it be true, as it probably is, that San Giuliano, after his return from Kiel in 1913, confided to the German Ambassador in Rome that he himself, in Berchtold's place, would have followed the path which he feared Berchtold was preparing to follow—action against Serbia, possibly involving a European war.[177]

INTRIGUES OVER KAVALA IN 1913

The Second Balkan War, resulting in the conquest from the Bulgarians of Kavala by the Greeks and of Adrianople by the Turks, led to some very interesting diplomatic intrigues which illumine the methods of pre-War diplomatists. They throw a curious light on the support—or rather lack of support—which allies give one another when their own selfish interests are involved. In fact, the Kavala question caused such an internal split within each diplomatic group,

[175] Merey, Austrian Ambassador in Rome, to Berchtold, July 12, 1913; Pribram, p. 301 f., and note 425.

[176] Giolitti's statement of Dec. 5, 1914, quoted above, that San Giuliano was "endeavoring to arrange for a combined effort with Germany to prevent such action on the part of Austria" etc. *Cf.* similarly Poincaré (III, 321): "A la demande de l'Italie, l'Allemagne retint, en effet, le bras de l'Autriche." It is greatly to be wished that Italy should publish her documents for the pre-War period, as Germany and England are doing, but there seems little prospect of this at present.

[177] Flotow to Bethmann, July 19, 1913; G.P., XXXV. 192 f.

that in the resulting Franco-Russian newspaper recrimina
tions the *Novoe Vremia* demanded a revision of the Franco-
Russian Alliance; [178] and, similarly, the Vienna *Neue Freie
Presse* regretted sorrowfully the hitherto incredible "rift
and serious weaknesses" in the Austro-German Alliance,
"which for more than thirty years had rooted itself in our
consciousness like an oak tree in its soil." [179] While allies
were thus at odds with one another, French and German
ministers were felicitating each other on their successful
coöperation and their hopes of defeating the desires of their
own respective allies, and Sir Edward Grey joyfully observed in this curious inversion of the usual diplomatic
rôles a happy augury for the peace of Europe.[180]

Kavala was a Macedonian walled town and seaport
situated about half-way between Salonica and the Dardanelles. Its tolerably good harbor was the best port available for the Bulgarians on the Aegean. It was near the
center of a rich agricultural region where millions of dollars
worth of the best Turkish tobacco was produced annually.
Aside from Turks and Spanish Jews, its population was predominantly Greek, though the hinterland was predominantly Bulgarian.[181] Greeks and Bulgarians both coveted
it. In the first Balkan War the Bulgarian armies got there
first and occupied it. But in the following war between the
Balkan States, Bulgaria was attacked on all sides and had
to yield it up to the Greeks. On both occasions the usual
unspeakable atrocities were committed.

As to the final fate of Kavala, it soon appeared that the

---

[178] M.F.R., p. 407; L.N., II, 132; Stieve, III, 241; *Affaires Balkaniques,* II, 294 f.; III, 3-7.
[179] Aug. 11, 1913; on these Press feuds, see G.P., XXXV, 368-381.
[180] *Affaires Balkaniques,* II, 294; G.P., XXXV, 368 f.
[181] *Cf.* ethnographic map in *Petermann's Mitteilungen,* 1915, map 44;
Bulgarian Ministry of Foreign Affairs, *La Question Bulgare et les Etats
Balkaniques,* (Sofia, 1919), pp. 78-87, 200-205, 275; *Carnegie Endowment
Report on the Balkan Wars* (Washington, 1914), pp. 78-106, 186-207, 285-
290; G.P., XXXV, 319-383, *passim.*

Great Powers held very divergent views. Austria and Russia, usually diametrically opposed on Balkan matters, were both very anxious to give it to Bulgaria. Berchtold and Sazonov therefore began intrigues in which their methods were precisely analogous and parallel, but in which their objectives were altogether different. Germany and France, on the other hand, were equally insistent that Kavala should go to Greece. England and Italy, less di-rectly interested, were at first inclined to give it to Bulgaria, but both soon acquiesced in letting the Greeks stay in the coveted seaport, because, as Sir Edward Grey observed, "it would be difficult to drive the Greeks out." [182]

Berchtold, by trying to secure Kavala for Bulgaria, hoped to set up a stronger counter-weight to Serbia, now so swollen in size and conceit by her conquests in two Balkan Wars. He hoped also to win King Ferdinand's Government over to the side of the Triple Alliance, thereby frustrate Franco-Russian intrigues at Sofia, and bring about a reconciliation between Bulgaria and Rumania. He was encouraged in these hopes by the fact that the Bulgarian Government, *in extremis* at the end of July, had made posi-tive offers to join the Triple Alliance and Rumania.[183] If this could be brought about, and Bulgaria and Rumania became reconciled, Rumania would then enjoy greater liberty of action, in case of a European war, for directing her main forces against Russia, instead of being compelled to leave them on her own southern frontier for protection against Bulgaria. So Berchtold, at the beginning of the Bucharest negotiations, secretly promised Kavala to the Bulgarians, without informing Germany as a frank and loyal Ally should have done. For this concealment he was

[182] Lichnowsky to Bethmann, Aug. 8, 1913; G.P., XXXV, 368 f.; on the English and Italian attitude see also *ibid.*, pp. 328-332, 339-345, 357, 366.

[183] G.P., XXXV, 329 f., 348.

very properly and severely reproached by Germany when the truth came out a little later.[184]

Sazonov's conceptions and methods were precisely analogous to those of Berchtold. He calculated, by giving Kavala to Bulgaria, to win her definitely to the side of the Triple Entente, checkmate suspected Austrian intrigues at Sofia, and bring about a reconciliation between Bulgaria and Serbia; then, in case of a European war, Serbia need not worry about Macedonia and the Bulgarian frontier, but could turn her main attack against Austria—a possibility of which Berchtold and his Chief of Staff were very much afraid. Furthermore, Sazonov believed that Kavala in Bulgarian hands would be a protection against Greek naval interference with Russia's cherished ambitions in regard to the Dardanelles, especially as the King of Greece was the German Kaiser's brother-in-law. So Sazonov used all his efforts at the Bucharest Peace Conference to get Kavala restored to the Bulgarians. But he did not at once inform his French Ally of the importance which he attached to this policy. He did, however, secure from the Russian treasury, at the suggestion of Izvolski and the French Minister of the Interior, a second sum of 100,000 francs with which to bribe the French Press, stipulating that the money was to be used for propaganda in favor of Russia's Balkan interests as well as in favor of the new law increasing the French army. But the Turks were reported by the Russian financial agent in Paris to be spending much more generously for bribery in the opposite direction—five million francs, with 100,000 to *La Libre Parole* alone. France did not support Sazonov's Kavala policy, and the Franco-Russian newspaper feud, mentioned above, burst forth. Izvolski naturally complained: "This incident is for me personally extremely painful." He bluntly criticized Sazonov for not informing the French Government frankly at the beginning

[184] G.P., XXXV, 320-331, 338 ff., 346 ff., 378.

that the Kavala question was "of first-class importance" for Russia, instead of leaving France to learn this from the Triple Alliance Powers rather than from her own Ally.[185]

Why did Germany and France fail to support their respective allies in this Kavala question?

The Kaiser's philhellenism was strengthened by his annual spring visit to Corfu and the building of the Achilleion. He might also naturally be expected to give political support to his brother-in-law. King Constantine did not hesitate to capitalize his imperial connection as far as possible. On July 31, at "Tino's" direction, "Sophy" telegraphed to "Willy," begging him to put in a good word with King Carol of Rumania on behalf of the Greek claims to Kavala. Whereupon the Kaiser telegraphed to King Carol in restrained and considerate terms: "Can you do anything about Kavala? I should regard the question sympathetically. Hearty congratulations and good wishes on your successes.—Wilhelm." [186]

Much more important than these personal considerations, however, was the German Government's hope that German support of Greek claims to Kavala would counteract Gallophil influences at Athens and draw Greece more definitely into the wake of the Triple Alliance, thus securing Greek strategic and diplomatic support in the Eastern Mediterranean and Asia Minor. This at the moment seemed quite possible. Threatened with a deadly struggle with Bulgaria in a Second Balkan War, M. Venizelos had sought German good-will by assuring her that, "Greece would never join the Triple Entente so long as Constantine was King and he was Minister. Greece wants to keep clear of every complication of the Great Powers, but hopes by

---

[185] Sazonov-Izvolski correspondence, July 12 to Aug. 14, 1913; M.F.R., pp. 392-411; L.N., II, 120-135; Stieve, III, 203-244. *Cf.* also *Affaires Balkaniques*, II, 279-295; III, 3-13. The phrases quoted in the last sentence are from Izvolski's letter of Aug. 14.

[186] Aug. 1, 1913; G.P., XXXV, 323.

closer coöperation with Rumania and Turkey to be useful
to the Triple Alliance as a counterweight against the
Slavs." [187] A few days later Theotokis, the Greek Minister
at Berlin, definitely stated that, "Greece was ready to join
the Triple Alliance at any time," in return for support of
her claims to Kavala, certain districts on the South Albanian frontier, and the Aegean Islands.[188] But the German Foreign Office, correctly suspecting that Theotokis had
exceeded his authority, gave him a dilatory answer. Meanwhile the Berlin officials at once loyally informed their
allies at Vienna and Rome of Theotokis' offer and their
doubts concerning it, and asked at Athens for confirmation
of it.

Venizelos replied that Theotokis had in fact exceeded
his instructions, being authorized only to propose an alliance with Rumania, but not one with the Triple Alliance.
Venizelos added that King Constantine at his recent accession had expressed a desire to join the Triple Alliance, but
he himself had opposed alliance with either group, and had
so informed the Triple Entente. Therefore he could not
now change his attitude all at once, without seeming to be
guilty of bad faith. He had told Constantine, however, he
said, that if the King wished to carry out his desire of joining the Triple Alliance, he (Venizelos) was quite ready to
resign; he added generously that he would then do all he
could in Parliament to support the King's new orientation
of Greek policy in favor of the Triple Alliance. Bethmann
and the Kaiser, instead of urging Constantine to take advantage of his Prime Minister's generous gesture, advised

---

[187] Quadt, German Minister at Athens, to Bethmann, June 7, 1913;
G.P., XXXV, 19; cf. also p. 105 f. The Greek Minister at Vienna, Zaimis,
expressed the same idea to Berchtold: Greece was very ready to enter
into good relations with the Triple Alliance Powers, but must avoid
becoming mixed in their affairs; "Ce que nous voulons, c'est de ne pas
être poussé ni par un groupe ni par l'autre" (June 24, ibid., p. 97).

[188] Jagow's memorandum, June 18; G.P., XXXV, 89.

him that Venizelos' resignation at this critical time might be disastrous for Greece, but that he might well negotiate with Rumania. Germany could not endanger her own policy of preserving peace in Europe, as she might do if she should guarantee Greek boundaries and become involved in Balkan complications. But she would welcome joyfully a Greek orientation toward the Triple Alliance, and the question might be advantageously taken up after the close of the present crisis.[189]

Meanwhile, to encourage Greece in her new attitude, Germany decided it was imperative to support the Greek claims to Kavala, even though Austria insisted on taking the opposite line of championing the Bulgarian claims. In the ensuing lively conflict between the Wilhelmstrasse and the Ballplatz, the Berlin authorities pointed out that they could not afford to abandon the Greek claims and run the risk of losing the prospect of Greece joining the Triple Alliance. They feared that otherwise Greece would fall back into the wake of the Triple Entente. Berchtold rejoined that he too, having promised Kavala to Bulgaria, could not stultify himself by reversing his attitude and run the risk of losing the prospect of Bulgarian adherence to the Triple Alliance. He feared that if he did so Franco-Russian intrigues would triumph at Sofia. Berlin also pointed out very properly that the Greek offers had come first, were more dependable and had at once been loyally communicated by Germany to her two allies, while the Bulgarian offers had come afterwards, were very uncertain in view of King Ferdinand's treacherous character, and moreover had been disloyally concealed from Germany by Berchtold.[190]

As to French policy, according to M. Poincaré, who cites the highly selective and relatively meager *French Yellow Book* on the Balkan Wars, "The preoccupation of

[189] G.P., XXXV, 89-97.   [190] G.P., XXXV, 344-355.

France was always the same—to put an end to a war which might become general; she took the side of Greece against Bulgaria, that is in this case of Germany against Russia, solely in the hope of preventing a renewal of hostilities." [191] But in reality, French policy in the Kavala question was dictated also by the traditional policy of France of friendship for Greece, by the French instructors loaned to drill the Greek armies who were supplied with French guns, and by the large investments of French in Greek loans and in the tobacco monopoly in the Kavala region (which the Bulgarians had threatened to confiscate if it came into their possession), all of which tended to make French public opinion philhellenic. But above all, according to Izvolski, it was dictated by "the fear that Germany would gain the upper hand in Athens," that French interests in the Near East would suffer, and that France must get the strategic support of the Greek navy against the rival power of Italy in the Mediterranean.[192]

As to the Balkan States themselves, Greece, Serbia, and Rumania were firm in opposing the Bulgarian claims to Kavala. It looked as if the Bucharest Peace Conference might be broken up, if Bulgaria refused to accept the terms

[191] Poincaré, III, 230. "But who opens the Yellow Books?" he asks (III, 233). The present writer has opened them, and finds that Pichon's despatch to Delcassé of Aug. 9 (*Affaires Balkaniques,* II, 294 f.), which M. Poincaré refers to but refrains from quoting, hints also at quite other motives than the laudable one he mentions. Pichon declares the French attitude "justifiée par notre politique traditionnelle, par le souci de l'équilibre méditerranéen, par les conditions de la guerre entre la Bulgarie et la Grèce, par les victoires et les sacrifices de cette dernière, par l'attitude de l'Allemagne, enfin et surtout par la certitude que j'avais d'une reprise d'hostilités dans l'hypothèse d'une tentative de règlement différent."

[192] See quotation in preceding note. Izvolski to Sazonov, Aug. 2, 5, 12, and 14, 1913; M.F.R., pp. 399-409; L.N., II, 122-135; Stieve, III, 220-224. Jules Cambon to Pichon, Aug. 2 (*Affaires Balkaniques,* II, 281) "quelle que soit l'attitude de la Russie, nous ne saurions, sans péril pour notre influence à Athènes et sans y laisser le champ libre à l'Allemagne, nous départir de l'appui que nous avons donné jusqu'ici aux revendications helléniques."

demanded by the victors. When Austria and Russia realized this, and found that they were not supported by their respective allies, they each tried indirectly to save the situation for Bulgaria. They proposed, separately and in slightly different terms, that the Kavala clauses, or even the whole Bucharest Treaty, should be subject to revision later by the Great Powers. But these proposals, highly offensive to the three Balkan victors, naturally also met with the same negative from Germany and France as in the direct discussion of the Kavala question, the motives being much the same. The revision idea was given the deathblow by the publication of King Carol's telegram to the Kaiser announcing the certainty of peace, "which thanks to You remains a definite one." [193] The Kaiser telegraphed in reply his hearty congratulations. The cautious and considerate Bethmann doubted the advisability of making these telegrams public, for fear of offending Austrian susceptibilities. But the Kaiser insisted, and his Foreign Office Under-Secretary, Zimmermann, thought that their publication, though "hardly agreeable" to Vienna, would have the advantage of checking Berchtold's "zeal for revision." They were therefore published by the Wolff Telegraph Bureau from Bucharest on August 10, 1913, the day the Peace of Bucharest was finally signed, and caused no little irritation in Austria.[194]

THE AUSTRIAN ULTIMATUM TO SERBIA OF OCTOBER 18, 1913

In the summer of 1913, after the First Balkan War and the decision to establish an independent Albania, the Lon-

[193] Aug. 7, 1913; G.P., XXXV, 359.

[194] G.P., XXXV, 359-379. One of the Kaiser's secretaries later tried to smooth Conrad's ruffled feelings by assuring him that the telegrams had been published upon the initiative of King Carol and not of the Kaiser, but this was "not wholly in accord with the historical facts" (G.P., XXXIX, 442). The text of the Bucharest Treaty is printed in *Affaires Balkaniques*, II, 296 ff.

don Conference of Ambassadors agreed to create three commissions which, it was hoped, would help bring into existence an Albanian state capable of life and survival. One
commission was to delimit the southern frontier between
Albania and Greece, another the northern one toward Serbia
and Montenegro, and the third, the Commission of International Control, was to attempt to administer Albania
until the Great Powers could find and agree upon an acceptable Prince for the country.[195]

But there were long delays before the boundary commissions were ready to begin work on the spot. Even when
they finally set forth into the rough mountainous country,
with automobiles which continually broke down and had to
be abandoned for horses or even procedure on foot, there
were more delays and difficulties. In the South, local Greek
officials resorted to all sorts of naïve and futile efforts to
deceive the Commission into thinking that the majority of
the inhabitants spoke Greek and were wildly enthusiastic
for incorporation into Constantine's kingdom. With suspicious regularity processions of peasants came forth from
the villages garbed after the Greek fashion and bellowing
at the top of their lungs, ἕνωσις ἢ θάνατος, "Union or Death."
But the Commission was so convinced that they had been
imported for the occasion, and that strong-arm methods
were being used to keep the Albanians and Mohammedans
shut indoors and silent, that an official protest had to be
made at Athens. In the North, the Serbians were less naïve
and more circumspect, but the members of the Commission
were often stopped or arrested by the Serbian troops. In
both Boundary Commissions the representatives of the six
Great Powers soon tended to divide into three groups corresponding to the political attitude of their superiors in London. The French and Russian delegates took every occasion
to favor the Greeks, Serbians and Montenegrins, while the

[195] G.P., XXXV, 235-315; *Affaires Balkaniques*, II, 209-222.

Austrian and Italian were bent on giving Albania the widest extent possible. Between these two extreme groups, whose bickerings over picayune trifles several times threatened to break up the work of the Commissons altogether, the English and German Commissioners tried to find satisfactory compromises, and at the same time conscientiously reach decisions which accorded with the facts on the spot and the instructions they received from London.[196]

Owing to the delays of the Commissions in fixing the Albanian boundaries and to the mutual enmity of Serbians and Albanians, a frontier conflict broke out. Serbian troops reoccupied Albanian territory. The Albanians, upon this provocation, took revenge by attacking and routing a

[196] For an account, often highly diverting, of these delays and bickerings, see the reports of the German Commissioners in G.P., XXXVI, 129-260. In this boundary matter Germany wanted to preserve the solidarity of the Triple Alliance by supporting all the reasonable desires of her allies, but she did not want to oppose too strongly what Constantine had set his heart upon, for fear of driving him into the arms of the Entente. Germany therefore tried to persuade both sides to be moderate and reasonable. To King Constantine, upon his visit to Berlin on Sept. 6, 1913, the Kaiser pointed out persuasively how great were the gains he had already made: "Janina, Salonica, Kavala, and last not least Crete, all regular basic hellenic Pelita, which it would have taken centuries to acquire. . . . In comparison with all this, a trifling rectification of the Epirus frontier plays absolutely no rôle and is worthless." The Kaiser also pointed to Germany's self-restraint at Nikolsburg in 1866 as an example of the wisdom of moderation after victory, and hinted that, if Constantine refrained from antagonizing Italy in regard to the South Albanian frontier, Rome might eventually concede to him the Aegean Islands, which were of far greater importance (ibid., pp. 144-6). Similarly, in regard to Austria and Italy, the Kaiser noted: "If Austria and Italy are unreasonable toward Greece, we are not to blame! We do not have to join in every folly which they perpetrate. We have already taken over abundantly much at our expense for love of our allies. If the latter just go on making their situation worse in relation to the Triple Entente, we can warn them, but we cannot prevent them. But we do not need to join with them" (G.P., XXXV, 251). Instructions to this effect, in more diplomatic but sufficiently clear language, were sent by Berlin to Vienna and Rome. For Jagow's personal advice to the German delegate on the South Albanian Frontier Commission, see G.P., XXXVI, 160 f. On the general merits of this whole Epirote question, with a full bibliography, see Edith P. Stickney, *South Albania in European Affairs, 1912-1923*, Stanford, 1926.

Serbian detachment. Serbia then mobilized part of her army. The Serbian Press demanded a punitive expedition and the occupation of a considerable part of Albania. It was pointed out that the Scutari and Adrianople incidents had demonstrated the impotency of the Great Powers, who were likely to bow before a *fait accompli* rather than attempt to expel those who were *beati possidentes*. Some of the Powers individually warned Serbia to respect the decisions of the London Conference, but the Conference as a whole could not bring itself to a collective warning, which alone would be effective. Sir Edward Grey's patience threatened to become exhausted. From the point of view of English interests he was indifferent as to whether this or that Balkan village was Turkish, Greek, Serbian, Bulgarian, or Albanian. He conceived of his rôle as that of an honest broker whose Balkan efforts should be directed toward serving the one British interest of preserving the peace of Europe. But he was becoming so wearied with the almost daily complaints and counter-complaints that finally, "he wanted to hear the name 'Albania' as seldom as possible, and one would not be surprised if, yielding to his feeling of irritation, he laid the Albanian flute down on the table and recalled Admiral Burney and the English contingent." [197]

Under these circumstances, and in view of the fact that Serbian troops persisted in remaining in occupation of Albanian territory, Berchtold and the Austrian Chief of Staff, Baron Conrad, again considered what more drastic measures they ought to take.

Conrad again urged that now at last Austria should

[197] Kühlmann, German Chargé d'Affaires in London to Bethmann, Sept. 24, 1913; G.P., XXXVI, 165; on Grey see also pp. 377, 394. On the first part of this paragraph, see *ibid.*, pp. 131-174, 361-382; *Affaires Balkaniques*, III, 46-54; and *Oesterreich-Ungarisches Rotbuch: Diplomatische Aktenstücke betreffend die Ereignisse am Balkan, 13 Aug. bis 6 Nov., 1913* (Vienna, 1914), *passim.*

have her final reckoning with Serbia. He learned from Prince Hohenlohe, who had recently returned from St. Petersburg, that Russia was not likely to interfere, if Austria acted quickly and energetically against Serbia; now was better than later, because Russia was trying to win over Rumania from the side of the Triple Alliance to that of the Triple Entente. This was also the view of Baron Nopsca, who had recently been going about in Rumania disguised as a shepherd. He reported to Conrad that public opinion there was entirely against Austria-Hungary, and that Rumania was falling wholly into Russian and French leading strings. But Berchtold, timid and hesitating, was inclined to be content with gestures and half-measures.[198]

In long Ministerial Councils on October 3 and 13, Austrian officials earnestly discussed what should be done. Three views were represented respectively by Baron Conrad, Count Tisza, and Count Berchtold. Conrad, as usual, insisted that Serbia must be dealt with once and for all, before it was too late, especially as Rumania was falling away from Austria and coming under Russian and French influence. Serbia must either be compelled to accept peaceful incorporation into Austria-Hungary, being given a position somewhat like that of Bavaria or Saxony in the German Empire, and involving "trialism"—a reorganization of the Dual Monarchy into a federal "triple state." Or, if this was not possible, then Conrad favored an ultimatum to Serbia; if no satisfactory reply was forthcoming, he would then urge immediate and energetic war. At its conclusion—he had no doubt but that Austria would be victorious—Austria could annex some parts of Serbia, and could gratify Rumania, Bulgaria and Greece by offering other parts of Serbia to them—the Timok district to Rumania, and Macedonia to Bulgaria and Greece. This would be an effective revision of the Bucharest Treaty very beneficial to Austria.

[198] Conrad, III, 442-447, 453-458.

But above all, no half-measures should be tried, such as a mere occupation of a few Serbian towns as a pledge. The Austrian army, once mobilized, must not be expected to lay down its arms until Serbian territory had been conquered; the morale of the army could not tolerate mobilization without war for a third time [i.e. in addition to 1909 and 1912]. In short, "either the complete incorporation of Serbia by peaceful means—or the use of force." [199]

Count Tisza, the all-powerful Magyar leader, who had become Hungarian Minister-President on June 6, 1913, though recognizing the Serbian danger, was inclined to trust to diplomatic action. He agreed that the London Conference had brought nothing but disillusionment, and therefore favored having Austria-Hungary strike out an independent policy of her own. One could not allow Serbians, Montenegrins, Greeks, and Italians to go on treating Albania as *res nullius*. He was unalterably opposed to the incorporation of more Serbs into the Dual Monarchy either by a peaceful arrangement or by the use of force; it would be impracticable, disadvantageous to the Monarchy itself, and certain to meet with the opposition of Europe. Serbia should be energetically requested to remove her troops from Albanian soil; if this did not suffice, one might send an ultimatum, and inflict a diplomatic, and even, if necessary, a military, defeat. But in no case should Serbian territory be annexed. Tisza hoped that the anti-Austrian Balkan group—Serbia, Montenegro, Rumania, and Greece —could be offset by winning over Turkey and Bulgaria, who were on the point of coming to terms with one another. Such a diplomatic regrouping would reëstablish a favorable Balkan Balance of Power, parallel with the European Balance of Power between the Triple Alliance and Triple Entente. It would also avoid the financial burden of a large increase in the Austro-Hungarian army, to which he himself,

[199] Conrad, III. 442 ff., 461, 465 ff., 724-746.

as Minister-President of Hungary, was opposed. In short, Tisza's program was: restoration of the waning Austrian prestige, by the diplomatic humiliation, but not the territorial partition, of Serbia, and the avoidance of war, if possible. In case Austria had to resort to mobilization, she must still avoid war, if Serbia yielded at the last minute and agreed to pay the costs of mobilization.[200]

In contrast to the clear-cut program of Conrad for military action, and that of Count Tisza for diplomatic action, Count Berchtold, the Minister of Foreign Affairs, had no definite idea of what ought to be done. He was as helpless and incompetent a person as was ever called to fill a responsible position in time of danger. He set forth the *pros* and *cons,* and oscillated timidly and uncertainly between conflicting influences. He hesitated to decide for military action against Serbia for fear that Germany and Italy would not support him. He feared also the danger of Russian interference. He felt the difficulty of persuading Francis Joseph to approve war, and he knew Franz Ferdinand's opposition to it. He was finally inclined to think that some concession to Serbia in regard to the Albanian boundary might be given for the moment, and that military preparations should be made for the future, with the hope that in the meantime the general diplomatic situation might improve.[201]

The result of the discussion was that no definite decision was taken, except the adoption of proposals in regard to finance and a small army increase to be laid before the Delegations the following November. In spite of the fact that the Serbians had burned several villages and massacred Albanians in the neighborhood of Dibra, so that the population was in flight toward the coast,[202] Berchtold contented

[200] Conrad, III, 461, 464-6, 727-730, 735-741. This foreshadows interestingly Tisza's Memoir of 1914, urging a diplomatic shift in the Balkans, as well as his initial attitude in the crisis of July, 1914.

[201] Conrad, III, 463, 466, 724-729, 735.

himself on October 14 with an "amicable request" to Serbia to withdraw her troops from Albania and respect the decisions of the London Conference, within a date which Serbia herself might fix. Sazonov and Pichon also advised Pashitch to withdraw his troops at once, as we learn from Sazonov's report to the Tsar a fortnight later:

> My stay in Paris coincided with the new sharpening of Austro-Serbian relations in consequence of the occupation of several strategic points on Albanian soil by the Serbian troops. In the fear that Austria might give way to the desire to win an easy diplomatic victory in this matter, Pichon and I advised the Serbian Minister [in Paris] to inform his Government that it was preferable to yield to the friendly advice of Russia and France, rather than await threats from Austria. Vesnitch agreed completely, and telegraphed at once in this sense to Belgrade. . . . Pichon promised me to use all his influence to have the Serbian loan admitted to the Paris Bourse.[203]

But the Serbian Prime Minister did not follow this good advice, possibly because he may not have received it in time, or more probably because he was being influenced by the ardent Pan-Slav Russian Minister, Hartwig, and by subterranean pressure from the secret society of Serbian

202 Report of the French Consul in Scutari, Oct. 9; *Affaires Balkaniques*, III, 65. A few weeks later the Boundary Commission observed between Dibra and Prizren that "Nearly all the villages have been wholly or partially burned down by the Serbians. . . . The Serbian outposts here have been pushed some ten kilometres beyond the provisional boundary" (G.P., XXXVI, 241).

203 Sazonov's report to the Tsar, Oct. 24/Nov. 6, 1913; L.N., II, 360; Stieve, III, 328 f. See also Izvolski to Neratov, Oct. 18 (M.F.R., p. 430; L.N., II, 161; Stieve, III, 313), where Izvolski says that the French Government's decision not to withhold the loan any longer was "to make it easier for the Serbian Government to take this step" of withdrawing her troops from Albania. One may doubt, however, whether the furnishing of French money would tend to make Serbia more yielding and pacific. According to Poincaré (III, 306 f.), who says nothing of the French loan, Vesnitch did not send his telegram to Belgrade until Oct. 16.

military officers known as the "Black Hand." [204] On the contrary, Pashitch replied to Austria that the withdrawal of Serbian troops would depend on future conditions in Albania, where the anarchical state of affairs endangered the safety of his own peace-loving subjects. He even asked the London Conference to revise its former decisions, and assign some new strategic positions to Serbia. At the same time, Montenegro, to whom a new loan had just been authorized by the French Government,[205] occupied Albanian territory, and was reported to be on the point of ordering a general mobilization against the people whom the Great Powers were supposed to protect and govern. It was again rumored that Montenegro was about to merge with Serbia toward the formation of a "Greater Serbia." It looked to Vienna as if Serbia, Montenegro, and Greece were seriously intending to reoccupy the unhappy distracted country and present the impotent Powers with a new *fait accompli*.[206]

Meanwhile Berchtold informed Germany of the situation, reiterated that Albania's existence was necessary as a barrier against the Slav advance to the Adriatic, and de-

---

[204] " . . . Finally it is unmistakable that since M. Hartwig's return, opposition [to Austria's requests] has been increasing" (Griesinger, German Minister in Belgrade, to Bethmann, Oct. 17; G.P., XXXVI, 396).

From the German reports (*ibid.*, pp. 397, 399, 415, 417) it appears that Neratov, in charge of the Foreign Office at St. Petersburg during Sazonov's absence, was consulted by Hartwig and endorsed Pashitch's negative reply to Austria. This was in flat contradiction to Sazonov's alleged attitude at Paris. One wonders whether Sazonov quite stated the truth in his report to the Tsar, or whether this is another of the many instances in which Russian ministers pursued divergent policies.

"From conversation with the English Chargé d'Affaires here [in Belgrade], who is usually well informed and can also get his information from the Russian Legation, I gather that the Serbian Government . . . has been forced to attempt to carry through a revision of the frontier, through the influence of the Military Party—through the subterranean activities of the group of officers known here as the '*crna ruka*' ['Black Hand']" (Report of the Austrian Military Attaché in Belgrade, Oct. 18; Conrad III, 475).

[205] Oct.·8; *Affaires Balkaniques*, III, 65.

[206] *Affaires Balkaniques*, III, 66; Conrad, III, 462, 472 f.

clared that further acquiescence would be an abdication on
Austria's part. He therefore expressed "the hope that
Germany, who herself has a great interest in damming back
the Slav flood, would stand morally solid behind Austria
in this matter; because, as far as one could see, it would
only be a question of moral support, since neither Russia
nor France wanted war. One could also therefore hope that
Serbia was only bluffing." [207]

The Berlin Foreign Office assured Berchtold of the moral
support desired, and instructed Germany's diplomatic representatives to back up Austria's efforts in preserving the
life of Albania. It urged that Sir Edward Grey use his
influence, at Belgrade and in the London Conference, to see
that the decisions of the Powers were respected, adding that,
"if the warnings of the Vienna Cabinet at Belgrade remain
unheeded, it is to be feared from the form and content of
Count Berchtold's representations in Berlin that Austria
will go ahead independently." [208]   But Sir Edward Grey was

---

[207] Oct. 15; G.P., XXXVI, 384 ff.

[208] Zimmermann to Lichnowsky, Oct. 16; G.P., XXXVI, 389; cf.
also pp. 384-396. The Kaiser, who was absent from Berlin, was informed
of the steps taken by his Foreign Office, and approved them heartily. But
his approval, and his remarks to Conrad (III, 470) at the Battle of Leipzig
Centennial celebration, that patience has its limits and that Austria must
soon take the sword, did not influence Berchtold in sending his ultimatum
to Serbia, as they were still unknown to him when he sent it. For Dr.
Heinrich Kanner's errors in this connection, see the present writer's comments in the *Amer. Hist. Rev.*, XXXII, 317 ff., 944 ff. (Jan. and July, 1927).
Some weeks earlier the Kaiser had approved of Conrad's idea of the
peaceful incorporation of Serbia into the Dual Monarchy, like Bavaria
in the German Empire, rather than forcible Austrian action, because "it
would be much more advantageous for Germany, if Austria-Hungary were
united with Serbia in one structure, than if she has a South Slav state as
a neighbor who will always fall upon her rear" (Conrad, III, 431). But
after the latest events, upon a report from the German representative at
Vienna that "the solid stand of Germany, of which Berchtold never
doubted, strengthens him in the conviction that Serbia will heed the
eight-day time limit and not go to extremes," the Kaiser noted impul-
sively: "That would be very much to be regretted! Now or never!
One must finally have order and quiet down there!" (G.P., XXXVI.
399).

out of town over the week-end. His Under-Secretary, Sir Eyre Crowe, would take no step without first getting Sir Edward's instructions. Nor was the Under-Secretary's response encouraging: he thought it was merely a question of a few strategic positions in Albania which had been occupied simply *provisionally;* every inch of Albanian territory would of course have to be evacuated, and England would coöperate in this; but he did not think that Grey would favor an immediate demand on Serbia for evacuation, nor one to which a time-limit was attached.[209]

Suddenly, in the middle of the night of October 17-18, Berchtold, gratified at Germany's moral support but without saying anything further to her, and influenced by the latest reports concerning Albania, despatched an ultimatum to Belgrade. It insisted that Serbia respect Albanian territory and withdraw her troops within eight days; "otherwise Austria would be forced, with regret, to have recourse to the proper measures to secure the realization of her demands." [210]

Berchtold's unexpected exhibition of decisive energy took all Europe aback with surprise. To Sazonov it caused much chagrin, because, as he claims to have foreseen would be the case, Austria won an easy diplomatic victory. But he not unjustly complained of Berchtold's "policy of surprises," which her allies were unable to prevent: "As long as Austria asks us beforehand, before taking a momentous decision, he was wholly satisfied, he said. But there is unfortunately no assurance of this, as the last incident shows. Austria is always facing her allies with *faits accomplis;* and they are then compelled to honor their treaty signa-

209 Kühlmann to Bethmann, Oct. 18; G.P., XXXVI, 394.
210 Note to Serbian Government, 12:10 A.M., Oct. 18, 1913; Conrad, III, 473, 747; G.P., XXXVI, 394-402. By diplomatic euphemism it was called a "Note with a time-limit" [befristete Note], as in the case of its fatal successor of July 23, 1914 (as will be indicated below, vol. II, ch. v), but it was in fact essentially an ultimatum.

tures." [211] At Belgrade Pashitch and Hartwig learned of the ultimatum with rage and dismay, especially as it was soon followed by strong warnings from all the Great Powers, now suddenly awakened to the possible danger of serious complications, that Serbia should respect the decisions of the London Conference. Even Rumania added her warning. So Serbia decided at once to yield, and gave orders to her troops to evacuate the occupied Albanian territory. "I do it," said Pashitch, the Serbian Premier, "not under pressure of Austria, but out of regard for the friendly advice of Russia." [212]

These events of 1913 in connection with Albania help to explain Austria's course of action, under much greater provocation, in July, 1914. The decisions of the London Conference had brought her little or nothing, in her own opinion, except disappointments and illusions. Its delays and ineffectiveness in protecting Albanian interests, when defied by the Montenegrins at Scutari and the Serbians at Dibra, explain to some extent why Austria was absolutely unwilling, after the murder of Archduke Franz Ferdinand at Sarajevo, to submit her latest grounds of complaint against Serbia to another Conference of the Powers. "The course of the London Conference was so horrible to recall to memory, that all public opinion would reject the repetition of such a spectacle." [213] On the other hand, when Austria had acted quickly and energetically on her own account, by sending a peremptory ultimatum, Serbia had

[211] Lucius, German Chargé d'Affaires in St. Petersburg, to Bethmann, Oct. 28, 1913; G.P., XXXVI, 420. For Neratov's "complete surprise" and irritation, *ibid.*, 399, 409. *Cf.* also Sazonov's report to the Tsar, Nov. 6, 1913.

[212] Dumaine to Pichon, Oct. 21, 1913; *Affaires Balkaniques*, III, 70. *Cf.* also *ibid.*, III, 67-72; G.P., XXXVI, 401-422; Conrad, III, 474; and Sazonov's report to the Tsar, Oct. 24/Nov. 6, 1913 (L.N., II, 360 f., and Stieve, III, 328 f.).

[213] Bilinski's remark in the Ministerial Council of July 31, 1914; A.R.B., III, 79.

heeded her demands immediately, Russia had not interfered, and the Vienna Foreign Office had accomplished its
immediate purpose.

Another factor in the Balkan situation, which was pregnant with danger for Austria-Hungary and became more
evident after the Balkan Wars, was the change which took
place in Rumania.

THE RUMANIAN RIDDLE

The very secret treaty of 1883, by which Rumania
joined the Triple Alliance Powers, had been renewed at
various times, the last occasion being on February 5, 1913.[214]
During the early years of the treaty, Austria and Germany
had no serious fear that Rumania would ever fail to fulfil
her treaty obligations. King Carol, a Hohenzollern educated in Germany and sympathetic in his whole being with
the German point of view, was universally regarded as an
honest, upright man, whose personal loyalty was trusted
up to his very death in October, 1914. Self-interest likewise
seemed to assure Rumania's loyal adherence to the Triple
Alliance: it guaranteed the little Balkan State against
domination or transgression by Russia in any advance
toward Constantinople, and against attack by Bulgaria or
Turkey for possession of the Dobrudja.

But by 1914 the situation had greatly altered. King
Carol remained as loyal as ever. Sentiment among the
Rumanian people, however, had changed so greatly that

---

214 See above, ch. ii, p. 88 ff.; Pribram, I, 29-34, 69-77, 85-90, 107, 209,
245 f.; G.P., III, 261-282; VII, 149-187; XI, 301-307; XXVIII, 649-680;
XXVII, 195-235; XXX, 581-593. Though the renewal of the Austro-
Rumanian Treaty (to which Germany acceded on Feb. 26 and Italy on
March 5) was signed on Feb. 5, 1913, King Carol delayed for a week
his ratification, giving as his excuse that he feared an impending ministerial crisis "and did not want it signed by various ministers." His more
real reason was that, by delaying ratification and threatening "a new
orientation of Rumanian policy," i.e., away from the Triple Alliance, he
hoped to frighten Austria into a more energetic support of the Rumanian
claims to Silistria against Bulgaria (G.P., XXXIV, 337, 357 ff., 364).

Austria, and to some extent Germany, began to be seriously worried as to whether King Carol's personal prestige would be strong enough to carry his country with him. He was after all a constitutional monarch. Anti-Austrian popular sentiment in a parliamentary democracy might override the monarch's personal preference.

Three factors had contributed toward the development among the Rumanians of a hatred toward Austria, which threatened to undo the alliance: (1) the Magyar policy toward Transylvania, (2) the Austrian policy toward Bulgaria, and (3) the Russo-Serb wooing to win Rumania away from the Triple Alliance to the side of the Triple Entente.

For the first of these factors the Magyar nobility were chiefly to blame. In order to retain the dominant position which they had exercised since the Middle Ages, they had steadily refused, even at the opening of the twentieth century, to grant any really democratic suffrage to the Rumanian and Slav subject peoples in Hungary. The Rumanians in Transylvania were refused a fair number of seats in the Hungarian Chamber of Deputies, and their nationalistic desires in regard to school and language questions had been blindly disregarded. This galling denial of political rights naturally contributed toward the bitterness and irredentist longings which were shared by Rumanians on both sides of the Carpathian Mountains.

The second factor which embittered the people of Rumania, and threatened to transfer Rumania from the side of the Triple Alliance to that of the Triple Entente, was Austria's attitude toward the Bulgaro-Rumanian conflict which arose out of the First Balkan War. By their astonishing victories over Turkey in the first weeks of the war, Bulgaria, Serbia and Greece had occupied wide stretches of territory, which vastly extended their frontiers and greatly increased their prestige, power, and population. Rumania, meanwhile, had maintained a dignified neutrality, remaining at peace with Turkey, while her rivals were growing strong. She alone had gained no new frontiers during the First Balkan War. She alone had liberated and annexed no suppressed nationalities crying to be free. Her people therefore were swept in the spring of 1913 by a new wave of irredentist nationalism and indignation. There was a strong popular demand on the Rumanian Cabinet that something must be done to redress the Balance of Power in the Balkans, which had existed since the Treaty of Berlin in 1878, but which had now been completely upset to Rumania's disadvantage.

Rumanian newspapers bitterly complained of the mistaken policy of folded hands: King Carol should have intervened while the Bulgarian armies were tied up in front of Adrianople and Constantinople and insisted that Bulgaria cede to him the Silistria-Balchik district south of the Dobrudja, as "compensation" for Rumania's benevolent neutrality. Instead of adopting an active selfish policy of this kind, Rumania had pursued a waiting attitude, trusting in the generosity of Bulgaria and in a favorable pressure by the Great Powers to secure her adequate "compensations." But she had been deceived in both hopes. Throughout the early months of the Balkan War, Bulgaria remained obdurate and deaf to Také Jonescu's pleas for "just compensations." And when the question was finally left to the decision of the Great Powers at the St. Petersburg Conference, in March, 1913, Rumania did not get as much as her nationalists thought she had a right to expect.[215]

It was in connection with these negotiations about "compensations" that Rumanian Ministers and public opinion turned more sharply against Austria-Hungary.

[215] *Affaires Balkaniques,* II, 30-35, 40-42, 56, 60 f., 67, 70 f., 74-81, 83-90, 93-109, 130 f., 137, 154 f., 229 f., 236-248, 253, 256, 263, 280; Conrad, III, 26, 33 ff., 39-56, 74 f., 103 f., 113 f., 129-131, 140 ff., 204 ff., 305 ff., 335-339, 365 f., 381 ff.; G.P., XXXIV, 245 ff., 301 ff., 337 ff., 357 ff., 418 ff., 575 ff.; XXXV, 115 ff.; XXXIX, 433 ff.

Austria was suspected (and rightly) of giving slight support
to the demands of her ally against Bulgaria for Silistria
and a strip of territory south of the Dobrudja. King Carol's
Ministers not only demanded this territory, but insisted
that Rumania's prestige obligated Austria to show as much
zeal and energy in securing Silistria for Rumania as in
opposing Serbia's access to the Adriatic. With Germany's
attitude they were satisfied. Although Germany gave them
salutary advice—to leave prestige aside, be content with
moderate compensations, and not to listen to the wooing of
Russia, who would not lift a finger for them as soon as she
had achieved her purpose of breaking up her alliances—
Germany did strongly back up Rumania's claims.[216] But
with Austria they suspected it was otherwise. "People are
especially irritated against Austria-Hungary, because her
support [to Rumania], in comparison with what Russia
gives Bulgaria, is much too weak to lead to any favorable
result. Feeling already runs so high that the King [Carol]
will be compelled in a very short time to come to a grave
decision. The decision will be either for war with Bulgaria, or for peace, but with the summoning of a Russophil
ministry, which would mean that the course of Rumanian
policy, hitherto friendly to the Triple Alliance, would give
way to dependence on the Triple Entente." [217] Austria was
suspected of being "more Bulgarian than the Bulgarians."
When Rumania finally threatened to mobilize against Bulgaria, in order to secure the coveted territory, Austria tried
to hold her back. Prince Fürstenberg, the Austrian Minister at Bucharest, warned King Carol that a Rumanian
attack on Bulgaria would be totally opposed to Austrian
policy; and that if Rumania persisted, Austria might eventually intervene; King Carol should keep on good terms

---

[216] See below, notes 241-244.
[217] Pomiankowski to Conrad, quoting the Rumanian Military Attaché
in Constantinople, Jan. 28, 1913; Conrad, III, 39 f.

with Bulgaria; because, otherwise, he would be playing into the hands of the Russian Pan-Slavs.[218]

This restraint which Austria exercised, or rather tried to exercise, upon King Carol weakened and isolated the King still more among his own people. "King Carol is following Austria's advice for peace in Bulgaria's interests," it was said. The popular pressure became so strong that the King finally had to yield to public opinion. He joined Serbia and Greece in the Second Balkan War against Bulgaria, and secured her coveted "compensations"—a generous slice of Bulgarian territory south of the Dobrudja, stretching from Silistria on the Danube to Constanza on the Black Sea. Rumanian nationalistic aspirations and irredentist ambitions were strongly stirred by this short successful war. As the French proverb says, *"L'appetit vient en mangeant."* As a result, Austria-Hungary now found herself seriously menaced by a "Greater Rumania" movement, which aimed at the ultimate detachment of the Rumanians in Transylvania, just as the "Greater Serbia" propaganda aimed at detaching the Serbs in Bosnia and other parts of the Dual Monarchy. In November, 1913, a Rumanian Minister gave France to understand that the old friendship with Austria was "no longer anything but a shadow; the question of the Rumanians in Transylvania has become the only important one in public opinion, which frankly desires a *rapprochement* with Russia." [219] And in December King Carol himself finally admitted to the Austrian Minister at Bucharest, that public feeling was such that, "to his great regret, he was not in a position to be able to guarantee to fulfil the existing secret treaty between Rumania and the Dual Monarchy." [220]

[218] Conrad, III, 335-338; Jonescu, *Origins of the War.* p. 25; G.P., XXXIV, 843, 873 ff.; XXXIX, 434 ff., 504 f., 512.

[219] *Affaires Balkaniques*, III, 74.

[220] Austrian Military Attaché in Bucharest to Conrad, Dec. 12, 1913; Conrad, III, 496; see also G.P., XXXIX, 464 ff., and Alexander Hoyos,

By his double-faced and futile policy of pretending to support the interests of two opposed states like Rumania and Bulgaria, Berchtold had fallen between two stools. He had lost the confidence and good-will of the one before he had secured that of the other. This "desertion" on Rumania's part was one of the most important facts in Austrian foreign policy in the spring of 1914. The Serbian question has received a great deal more attention from writers, because it ultimately became the occasion of the World War; but, next to it, nothing bothered the heads of the men at the Ballplatz more seriously than this Rumanian question in the months before the War. This brief survey of it will also help to clarify a number of other obscure points, such as the conflicting policies at Vienna, Berchtold's hesitations and mistakes, Austro-German friction, and the Konopischt interview of Emperor William and Franz Ferdinand, about which so many mysterious insinuations have been made.

Russia meanwhile was taking advantage of the situation to win Rumania over to a seat beside the Triple Entente and form a new Balkan group under Russian patronage to replace that which had been broken up by Bulgaria in the Second Balkan War. Though the Tsar ruled over Rumanian populations in Bessarabia, Russian ministers at Bucharest sought to divert Rumanian irredentist ambitions away from Bessarabia to Transylvania. Russia had shrewdly used her influence on the side of Rumania to secure for her the "compensations" in the Treaty of Bucharest.[221] Rumanians noted with gratitude that, in contrast

Der deutsch-englische Gegensatz und sein Einfluss auf die Balkanpolitik Oesterreich-Ungarns (Berlin, 1922), pp. 36 ff.

[221] G.P., XXXIX, 433 ff., 445 ff., 464 ff. *Cf.* also Izvolski to Sazonov, Aug. 1/14, 1913, congratulating him on his Russian policy at Bucharest: "Your diplomatic *chef d'oeuvre* has been the detachment of Rumania from Austria, which I had always dreamed of, but which I had not been able or known how to accomplish;" M.F.R., p. 408; L.N., II, 133; Stieve, III, 243.

to Austria's "perfidious" effort to bring about a revision of the Treaty, Russia had finally joined with Germany in preventing a revision.

Russia's purpose in winning Rumania as part of her preparation for a general European war is well indicated in Sazonov's secret report to the Tsar in December, 1913:

> While repeating my wish for the prolongation as far as possible of the *status quo*, it is also necessary to repeat that the Straits Question can hardly advance a step except by the favor of 'European complications. These complications, to judge by present circumstances, would find us in alliance with France, and in a possible but not at all assured, alliance with England, or at least with her as a benevolent neutral. In the Balkans, in case of European complications, we could count on Serbia, and perhaps on Rumania. From this there results clearly as the task of our diplomacy the creation of conditions for as intimate a *rapprochement* as possible with Rumania. This policy ought to be as persistent as it is circumspect and devoid of rashness. The position of Rumania in the Balkans recalls in many respects that of Italy in Europe. These two powers are subject to megalomania, and, not having strength enough to accomplish their projects openly, are obliged to content themselves with an opportunist policy, observing always on which side lies force, in order that they may range themselves on this side. . . .
>
> Two factors play a great rôle in the instability of the present situation in the Balkans. The first is Austria-Hungary, with the manifest increase of the nationality movement caused by the success of the Serbs and the Rumanians, and the effect of these successes upon their racial brothers within the frontiers of the Hapsburg Monarchy. The second factor is that it is impossible for Bulgaria to resign herself to the painful results of the Treaty of Bucharest.[222]

[222] Secret report of Sazonov to Nicholas II, Nov. 23/Dec. 6, 1913; Adamov, *Konstantinopol i Prolivy,* 74 f.; L.N., II, 371-2; Stieve, III, 382.

Partly as a result of Sazonov's policy, when a new Russian Minister arrived at Bucharest in January, 1914, he found an exceedingly warm welcome in Governmental circles:

> Again and again, sentiments of genuine friendship for Russia have been expressed to me. I found the same welcome in society here. I have spoken to former Ministers, Senators, Deputies, and various leaders of the Rumanian army. . . . To my mind, all this corroborates the fact already pointed out by my predecessor, and also emphasized by my French and English colleagues, that an important and perhaps decisive change in public opinion has been brought about here in favor of Russia. The events of last year which have inspired the Rumanians, and above all their military leaders, with confidence in their own strength, have at the same time also encouraged the efforts of the Irredentists. These are not so much directed against Russia, as toward Transylvania with its three million Rumanians. This latter circumstance also naturally tends to enhance Rumania's sympathy for Russia.[223]

Early in 1914 Russia took further steps to win Rumania. She promoted a Serb-Greek-Rumanian combination, which, while ostensibly aiming at peace and the preservation of the *status quo* in the Balkans, might be used by Russia to solve the Straits Question at a time of "European complications." It also fell in with Russia's policy of supporting Serbia against Austria. In order to bring about such a combination, Sazonov had long interviews with the Serbian and Greek Premiers, M. Pashitch and M. Venizelos, in February, 1914.[224] M. Pashitch also had an encouraging

[223] Poklevski-Koziel, Russian Minister at Bucharest, to Sazonov, Jan. 11/24, 1914; Siebert-Schreiner, p. 436.

[224] Doulcet, Chargé d'Affaires at St. Petersburg, to Doumergue, Feb. 5, 1914; "M. Venizelos has made an excellent impression . . . [Sazonov] has the impression that a very close accord exists between Greece and Serbia against every attack of the Turks; with Rumania the ties are less close, but the visit of M. Venizelos to Bucharest will tend to tighten them;" *Affaires Balkaniques*, III, 112.

and significant talk with the Tsar, of which he has left an
interesting account:

> The audience lasted a full hour. The Tsar received
> me in his cabinet. When I entered, the Tsar was already
> there and at my entrance he came to meet me at the door,
> stretched out his hand without waiting for my greeting and
> invited me to be seated. . . . I set forth the Serbian policy
> which amounts to this, that she desires the maintenance of
> peace in the Balkans, and that new complications be
> avoided, since Serbia needs peace in order to recuperate,
> and in order that she may arm herself afresh for the defense
> of Serbian national interests. I also set forth the difficulties
> which Serbia will have to meet in the pursuit of her peace-
> ful policy. Bulgaria, Turkey, and Austria are dissatisfied:
> Turkey because she lost in the war with the Balkan States;
> Bulgaria because she could not retain or acquire all that
> she wished; and Austria because she lost the prospect of
> an advance to Salonica. . . .
>
> Thereupon the Tsar answered: We have confidence in
> the new Rumanian [Bratianu] Government, that it will at-
> tach itself as closely as possible to Russia. He did not be-
> lieve that matters would be allowed to go so far as to call
> in question the Peace of Bucharest. . . . I took occasion to
> remark that at the time of my stay in Bucharest I had a
> conference with Bratianu, and Bratianu was at that time
> very enthusiastic over the idea of an alliance with Greece
> and Serbia. I also remarked that I intended to return home
> by way of Bucharest in order to see whether Bratianu still
> retained the same willingness and views which he had re-
> vealed to me when I was in Bucharest. The Tsar said that
> would be very good, and that Rumania had three and a half
> million co-nationals in Austria-Hungary and that these de-
> sired union with Rumania. Thereupon, I said to him that
> the Transylvanian Rumanians were better nationalists than
> the Rumanians in Rumania. . . .
>
> I led the conversation around to a discussion of Austria's
> deliveries of arms to Bulgaria, namely that Austria had

furnished arms and munitions out of her magazines and
that Bulgaria had received cannon also. And again the
Tsar added that Germany too was supporting Bulgaria. I
begged him that Russia should likewise aid us, and that out
of her magazines she should deliver to us 120,000 rifles and
munitions and some few cannon, particularly howitzers,
if they could spare them, because the Turks had held up
delivery of our heavy guns when they were in transport
immediately before the war. The Tsar asked me if I had
spoken about the matter to any of the Russian Ministers.
I said, to the Minister of War, Sukhomlinov, and to Sazonov; and the Minister of War had said, it would be all right
if Russian policy permitted it. And here I took occasion
to tell the Tsar how pleased we were that Russia had armed
herself so thoroughly; it gave us a feeling of security and
hope for a better future. The Tsar said that they had done
a great deal, and were still doing much. For that reason
their munition establishments could not assume the task of
manufacturing arms for us. This gave me occasion to say
to the Tsar that immediately upon my return from Tsarskoe
Selo, I would furnish Sazonov with an estimate of what
we needed. He said that was all right, for he would receive Sazonov on the morrow, and would see what we needed.
They would do all they could to lighten the situation for
us. He asked me what we needed. I told him what I had
noted down on the slip I had prepared for Sazonov. . . .

The Tsar inquired how many Serbo-Croats lived in
Austria-Hungary, and what they were now believing and
desiring. I replied about six millions, and told him where
they lived. I also told him of the Slovenes, that they, too,
were gravitating to the Serbo-Croats, and would adopt the
Serbo-Croatian language, owing to the fact that their dialect
is bad and that they have long lost their national independence. Then I told him that just at this time there was a
Slovene stopping at St. Petersburg who was working for
the establishment of a South-Slav Bank, and was trying to
win over the Russian banks to the project. This was quite
agreeable to the Tsar, and he said it was very necessary

that the Russian banks should take a greater interest in the Slavic countries, and that it would be a good thing if Hribar should succeed with his mission.

I then told the Tsar how great a change in sentiment had taken place among the Slavs of Austria-Hungary—how many Starcevitch followers there were who formerly expected salvation from Austria, but now comprehended that this salvation could come to them only from Russia or Serbia, and that they could scarcely await the opportunity to see their desires fulfilled. Then I told him that for every rifle we received, we would have a soldier from these countries to carry it. . . . He asked how many soldiers Serbia could put into the field. Serbia, said the Tsar, had astonished the world when she marched out 400,000 men. I replied: We believe that we can put half a million well clothed and armed soldiers into the field. "That is enough; that is no trifle; one can go a great way with that" [said the Tsar].

Thereupon we discussed the need of fostering the alliance with Greece, for, aside from other considerations, we shall thus safeguard our incoming and outgoing commerce. Furthermore, we must labor to bring about an alliance upon a broader basis with Rumania, and not alone upon the basis of safeguarding the Treaty of Bucharest. . . .

[Pashitch then begged the Tsar to permit a marriage between the Serbian Crown Prince and a Russian Grand Duchess. The Tsar replied smilingly that he had no objections, but followed the principle of allowing his children to choose for themselves.]

Upon my taking leave, the Tsar accompanied me to the door and asked me especially and repeatedly to present greetings to the King, not only from himself, but also from the Tsarina and his family, and wished him good health: "For Serbia we shall do everything; greet the King for me and tell him [in Russian]: For Serbia we shall do everything." [225]

[225] Report of Pashitch of his audience with the Tsar, Feb. 2, 1914; Bogitchevitch, pp. 170-180; *Deutschland Schuldig?*, pp. 130-136.

While thus protesting to the Tsar his desire for peace, M. Pashitch, it is to be noted, asked for "120,000 rifles and munitions and some few cannon"; he spoke of the Slavs in Austria-Hungary "who now comprehend that their salvation can come only from Russia and Serbia, and who can scarcely wait"; and he urged an alliance with Rumania, "not alone upon the basis of safeguarding the Treaty of Bucharest" but with a view to the "three and a half million Transylvanian Rumanians who were better nationalists than the Rumanians in Rumania." Having indicated his real desires to the Tsar, he then set out with Venizelos for the Rumanian capital. Their visit was at once reported to Conrad at Vienna by the Austrian military attaché at Bucharest:

> Premiers Pashitch and Venizelos have spent two days together in Bucharest, highly pleased with their visit, as they both say, and today started together on their return journey to Belgrade and Athens. Their visit is said to concern measures to be taken in case any other State threatens to overthrow by force the terms of the Peace of Bucharest. Pashitch proceeds from the fixed assumption that Turkey and Bulgaria have signed a convention directed against Serbia and Greece, and that its unquestioned existence demands that these two States and Rumania shall join together. The result of the conference here, according to my informant, is a complete agreement of views as to the future attitude of the three States, though Rumania has not entered into any binding engagements. . . . Undoubtedly Russia wants a new Balkan League, and is working in this direction at high pressure.[226]

[226] Hranilovitch to Conrad, Feb. 11, 1914; Conrad, III, 555. That Hranilovitch was substantially correct is seen from the reports of the Russian and French Ministers at Belgrade: Hartwig to Sazonov, Feb. 11/24, 1914 (Siebert-Schreiner, p. 440); and Descos to Doumergue, Feb. H. (*Affaires Balkaniques*, III, p. 113): "M. Patchou [Acting Minister of Foreign Affairs in Serbia] tells me that, according to news from Bucharest, the Bratianu Cabinet will be much more decided and more hostile to

As a further link to bind Russia and Rumania together the Tsar invited the Crown Prince with his wife and son, Prince Carol, to visit Russia. They started on March 27, 1914, and stayed three weeks. One of the objects in view was believed to be the possibility of arranging a marriage between Prince Carol and one of the Tsar's daughters. Such a marriage would obviously strengthen the increasingly close relations between Bucharest and St. Petersburg, and help swing Rumania away from the Triple Alliance into the current of Sazonov's active Balkan policy. Prince Carol, who would ultimately be the ruler of Rumania, had none of King Carol's sympathies for Germany and the Hohenzollerns. He had been educated under the influence of M. Jorga, one of Rumania's strongest nationalist and anti-Austrian leaders.[227] The visit met with such success that in May, Sazonov told the French and English Ambassadors, that, though no marriage was definitely settled, the Tsar's second daughter had declared herself ready for the match.[228]

On June 14, 1914, the Tsar and Tsarina, accompanied by M. Sazonov, returned the visit of the Rumanian Princes. As they stepped ashore from the imperial yacht at Constanza, the sun broke through the clouds after days of heavy rain and added its warmth and brightness to the welcome of the cheering Rumanian populace. King Carol, wearing the uniform of a Russian field marshal, was photographed with his imperial guests, and an enterprising Rumanian Press saw to it that even the most remote villages of Transylvania had full news of the Tsar's visit, with all sorts of exaggerated hopes as to the coöperation of Russia with Rumania. M. Sazonov and M. Bratianu even went on a

Austria than the preceding Ministry, and that Serbia is absolutely sure of Rumania."

[227] Conrad, III, 481 ff., 494 ff., 549 ff., 633 ff.; G.P., XXXIX, 456, 474 ff., 496 501, 566.

[228] Adamov, *Konstantinopol i Prolivy*, I, 357, note 1. The World War put an end to the projected match.

walking tour together to Transylvania. "I did not hear of
this tactless excursion until it was over" writes the Austrian Minister, Count Czernin, "but I shared Berchtold's
surprise at such a proceeding." [229] In the private political
conversations which M. Sazonov had with M. Bratianu,
the Russian Minister gave the impression that important
changes were coming in the European political situation,
and that Rumania would not fare badly "if she understood
the signs of the times and listened to counsels of
wisdom." [230]

M. Bratianu in return assured Sazonov that "Rumania
was not obligated in any way to take part in any war whatever, except where her own individual interests were directly concerned." Not finding this Delphic utterance sufficiently clear, and wishing to press him to a more definite
statement, Sazonov bluntly asked Bratianu the significant
leading question: "What would be Rumania's attitude in
case of an armed conflict between Russia and Austria-
Hungary, if the former were obliged by circumstances to
resort to military action?" Bratianu replied that "the attitude of Rumania in this case would depend on the circumstances which led Russia to resort to military action against
Austria-Hungary, as well as upon what Rumania's interests
demanded at the given moment." From this conversation
Sazonov carried away the comfortable conclusion that,
"Rumania is not bound by any obligation which would force
her to act with Austria and against us under all circumstances, but, in reality, in case of war between us and
Austria-Hungary, Rumania will take the side which will be

[229] Czernin, *In the World War*, p. 112.
[230] P. Lindenberg, *König Karl von Rumänien*, II, 240 ff., 288 ff.
Lindenberg writes with warm feeling for King Carol and with some resentment against Russia. He cites no documents but appears to have
had access to King Carol's papers, as well as the King's own assistance, in
writing the work which was nearly completed when the War broke out.
For accounts of the Constanza meeting as reported to Berlin, see G.P,
XXXIX, 520-529.

strongest and which will be in a position to promise her the greatest gains." [231]

Vienna had been viewing with increasing fears and suspicions the signs of growing intimacy between Bucharest and St. Petersburg, as well as the formation of a Serb-Greek-Rumanian combination, which originated primarily in common hatred of Bulgaria but which might easily be directed against the Dual Monarchy. How was Austria to deal with this danger that Rumania would gravitate to the side of the Triple Entente?

Baron Conrad, while willing to agree with any measures which aimed at winning back Rumania, or making her declare her position more definitely, either for or against Austria, had his staff work out plans for a campaign against Rumania. He advised the building of defensive fortifications on the Rumanian frontier, or better still, a preventive war against Serbia, which would rid Austria once and for all of the Greater Serbia danger and clarify the general political situation.[232] But his advice was not followed, because Emperor Francis Joseph, Archduke Franz Ferdinand, Count Tisza, and the German Emperor were all opposed to any steps which might further antagonize Rumania.[233]

Count Berchtold, like other weak and undecided persons, preferred to wait and see; he hoped Rumania could be won

[231] Sazonov's report to the Tsar, June 11/24, 1914; Adamov, pp. 356-363; L.N., II, 377-384. Sazonov also pointed out to the Tsar how he had successfully flattered Rumania and increased her prestige among the other Balkan States by associating her with the Great Powers in the discussion for keeping the Straits open to commerce during the Tripolitan War. Similarly on July 24, 1914, upon the news of the Austrian ultimatum to Serbia, M. Diamandi, the Rumanian Minister in St. Petersburg, was invited to the important luncheon with M. Sazonov, M. Paléologue and Sir George Buchanan. Such flattery often counts for much in diplomacy, as elsewhere. M. Diamandi has related his version of the Constanza meeting in Revue des Deux Mondes, Jan. 1, 1928, pp. 129-143.

[232] Conrad, III, 404 f., 554, 626, 640-648.

[233] G.P., XXXIX, 333 ff., 358 ff., 511, 515 f.

back by concessions. With this in view, Tisza undertook
negotiations to conciliate the Rumanians in Transylvania;
but, owing to the selfish obstinacy of the Magyars on one
side, and the excessive demands and bitterness of the Rumanians on the other, these negotiations proved futile, and
were abandoned at the end of March, 1914.[234] In the hope
of winning back Rumanian sentiment in favor of Austria,
Berchtold also sent Count Czernin as Minister to Bucharest in October, 1913, in place of Prince Fürstenberg, who
was personally obnoxious to some of the Rumanian Cabinet.
Czernin was expected to be *persona gratissima* at Bucharest.
He was a protégé of Franz Ferdinand, and had written a
pamphlet some years before advocating the rights of the
nationalities oppressed by the Magyars. He had taken
pains to inquire into the wishes of the Transylvanian Rumanians. After reaching Bucharest he made it a point to
express publicly his hopes that the Hungarian Government
would make concessions in the negotiations which Tisza
was then carrying on. He earnestly tried to carry out
Berchtold's instructions to secure better relations between
the two countries who were allies in form, but were becoming enemies in fact. But in a few months Czernin realized
that his mission was hopeless. He found that King Carol
stood almost alone in his sympathy with the Triple Alliance. The treaties which attached his country to Germany
and Austria had been kept so secret that they were known
only to the King himself, to the Premier, M. Bratianu, and
to one or two others. No other Ministers knew of them or
felt bound by them, so that it often happened that Rumanian diplomats abroad worked on the side of the Triple
Entente. So seriously did King Carol feel his own weakness
in the face of Rumanian popular sentiment, that he ad-

[234] Conrad, III, 553, 556, 636. For the views of William II and Franz
Ferdinand at Konopischt on this Rumanian problem, see below, Vol. II,
ch. i; and G.P., XXXIX, 364-370.

mitted to Count Czernin in December, 1913, that "under existing circumstances he would be unable to side with Austria in a war." [235]

So Count Czernin became convinced that Berchtold's optimistic do-nothing policy was folly. Like Conrad, he too came around to thinking something more positive must be done. In March, 1914, he closed one of his pessimistic despatches with the prophetic warning:

> I am in duty bound to call your attention to the fact that we are slipping down an inclined plane here with frightful speed, and there is no time to be lost. It would be an ostrich policy to shut our eyes and let things go on as they are here. For I must most energetically and emphatically repeat, a hundred times if necessary, the Austro-Rumanian Treaty [of Alliance] is a worthless scrap of paper. In case of war, Rumania will not take a stand on the side of the Dual Monarchy. The present situation is the most unfavorable imaginable for us, since it binds us without benefiting us. A passive policy of hesitation, of floating with the current, of *laissez faire, laissez aller,* will not improve this situation. Nothing but a clear-cut positive action on Austria's part, nothing but an iron, unbending determination to compel Rumania to show her colors, can avert at the twelfth hour unfathomable disaster.[236]

Czernin suggested several alternative plans of action which the Dual Monarchy might adopt. One was the cession of Transylvania to Rumania, with the stipulation that the Rumanian Kingdom, thus enlarged, be incorporated into the Hapsburg Empire, similar to Bavaria's position in the German Empire. Czernin thought this plan desirable, but impracticable of realization. As to a preventive war against Serbia, urged by Conrad, Czernin was not one of

---

[235] Conrad, III, 634.

[236] Closing paragraph of a long and remarkable report to Berchtold on the Rumanian situation, March 11, 1914; Conrad, III, 781-789; *cf.* also Czérnin's despatch of April 2; *ibid.,* 633-638.

those who, like Tisza, argued that a war with Serbia was
useless and undesirable because Austria-Hungary was already oversaturated with Slavs; no one, to be sure, wanted
any more Serbs in the Dual Monarchy, he said; but after a
successful war against Serbia, it would be possible to use
Serbian territory to win the good-will of the other Balkan
states; Greece and Bulgaria could be given what they
wanted in Macedonia; Albania could be rounded out to
the east; and Rumania be given the Timok-Njotin district,
a corner in northeast Serbia partly populated by Rumanians.   The point, however, which Czernin particularly
urged, was that the status of the Treaty of Alliance be
cleared up.   In the present situation it was not worth a
scrap of paper to Austria, because King Carol no longer
controlled the situation and would be forced by public opinion to repudiate it or to resign, in case a Russian attack on
Austria should give rise to the *casus foederis*. Austria meanwhile had her hands tied by the treaty, and could not enter
into other diplomatic negotiations which might offend Rumania.   To make Rumania take a stand openly, either for
or against Austria, Czernin therefore suggested a newspaper
"indiscretion" by which the existence of the treaty should
be allowed to leak out; one could then tell by the way the
Rumanian Government denied the accuracy of the newspaper account, and the way public opinion in Rumania
discussed it, what Austria could count upon.   But Berchtold rejected all these suggestions. He merely gave a half-
hearted authorization to Czernin to sound King Carol tactfully as to whether the King would not be willing that the
treaty should be made public. But, as Czernin had foreseen, when he broached the subject, King Carol delicately
evaded it. So Berchtold and his associates were left uncertain whether, in a crisis, the secret treaty with Rumania
would hold or not.

Another suggestion by which Austria might offset the

probable loss of Rumania was that Austria should follow Russia's example, and build up a Balkan League under her own patronage to balance the feared Serb-Greek-Rumanian league under Russian patronage. Bulgaria and Turkey, smarting from recent defeats and eager for support, might be brought together by Austria and be eventually drawn into the Triple Alliance circle to make up for Rumania's "desertion." In other words, Austria might shift the pivot of her Balkan policy from Bucharest to Sofia. Such a Bulgarophil diplomatic program had already been attempted by Berchtold during the Balkan Wars; but it had met with no success and had caused serious differences of opinion between Vienna and Berlin. In the spring of 1914, it was taken up again at Vienna and a long memorandum for its accomplishment had been worked out at the moment that Franz Ferdinand was assassinated at Sarajevo. But there was still the serious difficulty: would Germany consent to this program of her Austrian Ally? Of late Emperor William had become strongly philhellene, supporting Greek claims to the Aegean Islands against Turkish interests.[237] Would he ever consent to abandon a Hohenzollern like King Carol, whom he greatly respected and trusted, and take in his place Ferdinand of Bulgaria, for whom he had a personal aversion and who was universally regarded with distrust? This question of shifting the pivot from Bucharest to Sofia had long been argued without agreement between Berlin and Vienna during and after the Balkan Wars. It also formed the larger part of the fateful memoir and royal missive from Francis Joseph which the Austrian Ambassador handed to William II after lunch at Potsdam on July 5, 1914, as will be related in the second volume, "After Sarajevo."

This Rumanian problem was one of the many points on

[237] Conrad, III, 644, 655 ff., 662. On the Kaiser's philhellenism see above, notes 186-190, in connection with intrigues over Kavala.

which there was a sharp divergence between German and Austrian policy. Though the relations between Bucharest and Vienna had become increasingly strained, Bucharest and Berlin had remained on terms of firm cordiality, and Germany had done much to keep King Carol and his people loyal to the Triple Alliance. These ties had been originally cemented through the kinship of the Hohenzollern rulers. They had been strengthened by the long residence at Bucharest of Kiderlen-Wächter, one of Germany's ablest diplomats since Bismarck's day. Even when Kiderlen was called to Berlin to pilot the Foreign Office in the last months of Bülow and the first years of Bethmann, he continued the close friendly relations which he had established with King Carol and influential Rumanian politicians.[238] Jon Bratianu the Younger, the leader of the so-called Liberal Party, at heart tended more and more to the side of the Triple Entente. He had been educated in France, visited Paris annually, and naturally had Gallic sympathies. These were strengthened by the political calculation as far back as 1909 that the Entente might prove a stronger combination than the Triple Alliance in a general European war, and might therefore be a safer group for Rumania to join.[239] In spite of this, however, he had confidentially assured Kiderlen that "he had inherited from his father the fundamental principle that Rumania's path to Vienna lies through Berlin, and that he had the firm conviction that everything which Berlin advised was for Rumania's genuine best interests." [240] He adhered to this principle and Germany did nothing to forfeit his well-placed confidence.

During the First Balkan War, when Rumania demanded territorial "compensations" from Bulgaria, Germany recognized her demands as justified. Berlin privately urged wise moderation and concessions both at Bucharest and Sofia, in

---

[238] Cf. E. Jäckh, *Kiderlen-Wächter*, I, 179-219; II, 161-237, *passim.*
[239] G.P., XXVII, 200.   [240] G.P., XXVII. p. 223.

order to prevent a Bulgaro-Rumanian war, which would add another Balkan complication and still further threaten the peace of Europe. But at the same time, both before and during the St. Petersburg Conference, Germany exerted her influence strongly in favor of Rumania's claims. She refused all Berchtold's Bulgarophil projects for giving Bulgaria Salonica, Samothrace, or money, as a solace for ceding Silistria to Rumania; she feared that such gifts would be frowned upon by Rumania and increase her distrust of the Triple Alliance—not to mention other objections.[241]

When the Second Balkan War broke out, and Rumanian indignation ran high against Berchtold's suspected Bulgarophilism, Germany refused to join him in putting pressure on Rumania to keep quiet. Berlin regretted his ill-judged effort, believing it would not be successful, and would only deepen Rumanian indignation—as proved to be the case. On the contrary, Germany recognized that Bulgaria's attack on Serbia was the psychological moment for King Carol to make good the claims which Bulgaria had been refusing; Germany could not assume the responsibility of advising Rumania to neglect her vital interests for the sake of Austria's desire to see a strong Bulgaria in Serbia's rear. Resentment would be so great in Bucharest that Rumania would certainly swing over from the Triple Alliance to the Triple Entente. It was a poor policy for Austria to risk losing a faithful ally like King Carol for the hope of getting a treacherous friend like King Ferdinand of Bulgaria. Austria made a mistake in letting herself be so obsessed with the fear of a Greater Serbia and in forgetting that she ruled over Rumanians as well as Slavs. Germany accepted the Rumanian point of view: Austria says that she cannot tolerate a Greater Serbia, but no more can Rumania tolerate a Greater Bulgaria.[242] Berchtold was so

[241] G.P., XXXIV, 444 ff., 456, 459 ff., 520 f., 660 ff., 674 f., 687 ff., 820 ff., 873 ff.   [242] G.P., XXXV, 46 ff., 61 ff., 66 ff.

put out with Germany's solicitude for Rumania's feelings, that he thrice made formal representations in Berlin against it.[243]   But the German Secretary of State, Jagow, while admitting some of his arguments, noted: "Yes, but we do not need by a long shot to join in all Vienna's stupidities."[244]   Accordingly, after King Carol mobilized his army and seized the New Dobrudja by force from Bulgaria, Germany confirmed him in his new territories by helping to prevent the Austrian and Russian efforts to have the Treaty of Bucharest subjected to revision by the Great Powers.

This divergence of views between Berlin and Vienna continued during the months following the Balkan Wars. Bethmann and the Kaiser still placed their hopes on Rumanian loyalty, while Berchtold and his advisers inclined toward closer relations with Bulgaria, since Rumania seemed to be lost.   In the spring of 1914 Rumania's "desertion" seemed more and more probable.   This was partly owing to the active wooing by Russia, and to the propagandist articles by French journalists and professors, who visited and lectured at Bucharest.   It was also partly owing to the Magyar oppression of the Rumanians living in Transylvania and to Austria's suspected Bulgarophilism.   The anti-Austrian demonstrations of the chauvinistic Rumanian "League of Civilization" became louder, and the attacks of the Rumanian Press more virulent.   An anti-Hapsburg play, "Mr. Notary," written by a Transylvanian, was being performed at the National Theatre in Bucharest.   It roused the people to a frenzy.   They marched past the royal palace singing war songs and crying, "Down with Austria" and "Long live Russia."   King Carol genuinely regretted all this.   But he feared to censor "Mr. Notary," lest it serve only to advertise it and make matters worse.[245]   In the

[243] G.P., XXXIV, 820 ff.; XXXV, 66 ff., 115 ff.

[244] G.P., XXXIV, 824.

[245] Despatches of Waldthausen, German Minister at Bucharest, January-April, 1914; G.P., XXXIX, 471-497. These despatches hardly bear

winter he had admitted that, if the anti-Austrian feeling kept up, Rumania would not march with Austria in case of a European war; a treaty of alliance was not enough by itself; it must have popular support. In the spring he confessed that his country was "in a complete paroxysm," and that he was helpless to stem the tide of popular hatred of Austria.[246]

This situation disturbed Berlin considerably. It led the Kaiser to make the Rumanian danger the main subject of his discussions with Franz Ferdinand and the Austrians on his visits to Vienna, Miramar, and Konopischt shortly before the Sarajevo assassination. He hoped that Count Tisza, the Hungarian Premier, would make concessions to the Rumanians in Transylvania. Germany urged that nothing be done like Conrad's plan of fortifying the Carpathian frontier which would certainly be unfavorably interpreted in Bucharest, or like Czernin's schemes for getting the Rumanian treaty made public.[247] But on the whole Germany was inclined to take a less tragic view of the Rumanian situation than Austria, and tried to calm the latter's fears. She hoped that the paroxysm would pass, and that Rumania would swing back to her traditional loyalty, if the Triple Alliance Powers did not show too much uneasiness and nervousness. It might be that in case of a European war King Carol might have difficulty in fulfilling his

out Czernin's reports to Berchtold (April 2, 1914; Conrad, III, 634) that Waldthausen had no real insight into the situation, allowed the wool to be pulled over his eyes, and was nothing more than "a human phonograph," reporting credulously to Berlin whatever he was told by the Rumanian ministers, "who are a hundred times cleverer than he." Czernin, who was not lacking in a sufficiently good opinion of his own astuteness, says of himself: "Bratianu reports to me daily that I am his real friend, that he has never been able to speak with a diplomatic representative so frankly as with me, and all such words. He thinks I am more of a fool than I really am. . . . But I do not trust him around the corner" (*ibid.*, p. 786).

[246] Waldthausen to Bethmann, Dec. 6, 1913, and Mar. 30, 1914; G.P., XXXIX, 466, 481.

[247] G.P., XXXIX, 506, 511, 515 f.

treaty obligations. But even so, it was still a long step
from this to his active participation on the enemy's side,
"quite aside from the fact that complications between the
Great Powers are hardly to be expected in the immediate
future." [248] Rumania's future remained a puzzling riddle,
adding still further to Balkan instability, uncertainties, and
intrigues.

THE LIMAN VON SANDERS AFFAIR

Hitherto we have been considering the Balkan Problems chiefly from the point of view of the rival interests
of Austria and Russia and the nationalist aspirations of the
Balkan States themselves. In the latter part of 1913 the
appointment of the German General Liman von Sanders at
Constantinople caused friction between Russia and Germany, which for several reasons deserves more attention
than it has usually been given. It was the last diplomatic
crisis of importance before July, 1914, and, like the latter,
involved the influence and prestige of these two Great
Powers in the Near East. But it is a good example of how
such a crisis can be settled, if there is sufficient good will
on both sides. Its satisfactory settlement is a proof of the
proposition that war is not "inevitable." We are at last
in fairly full possession of the essential documents relating
to the affair,[249] and are therefore able to follow the inner

[248] Jagow to Waldthausen, April 24, 1914; G.P., XXXIX, 505 f. *Cf.*
also the much more pessimistic views of Vienna as to Rumania, *ibid.*,
pp. 434-515, *passim;* and Conrad, III, 549-563, 633-648, 781-789.

[249] From the Russian side, M.F.R., pp. 629-693 contains a satisfactorily
abundant correspondence between Sazonov and his diplomatic agents—
Giers at Constantinople, Izvolski at Paris, and Benckendorff at London;
only part of this is included in L.N., II, 173-279; Stieve, III, 352-439, IV,
1-28; and Siebert-Schreiner, pp. 678-708. The interesting report to the
Tsar of the conversations of the Russian Premier, Kokovtsev, with Emperor William and Bethmann-Hollweg on the subject is printed in M.F.R.,
pp. 624 ff.; L.N., II, 414 ff.; Stieve, III, 415 ff. For the minutes of the
Secret Ministerial Councils concerning counter-measures to compel Germany and Turkey to abandon the German Military Mission, see Adamov,
Konstantinopol i Prolivy, I, 61-77 (with Sazonov's reports to the Tsar);

workings of Sazonov's mind, with its blunt rudeness of expression, its fickle alternations of pessimism and optimism, its fear of Russian "public opinion," and its dangerous inclination to resort to military measures as a "bluff" to force a diplomatic victory. We are also enabled to get an insight into the domestic cross currents at St. Petersburg, the secret workings of the Triple Entente, and the exceedingly moderate and conciliatory attitude of Germany.

M. Sazonov was highly indignant when he heard in November, 1913, that a German General, Liman von Sanders, was to command Turkish troops at Constantinople. In his mind it was a sly, unjustifiable, and not-to-be-permitted move on Germany's part to gain further power and prestige in the Ottoman Empire and so to thwart Russia in her "historic mission" of securing control of Constantinople and the Straits—regions which he curiously but significantly speaks of as "bordering on our frontier." He instantly telegraphed from Ialta in the Crimea to the Russian Ambassador in Berlin:

> Learning about the agreement of Germany with Turkey relating to the military instructors, I am extremely astonished that this serious question was not touched upon by the [German] Chancellor at the time of my frank and friendly explanations with him. Of itself, a German Military Mission in regions bordering on our frontier could not but

I. Zakher, "Konstantinopol i Prolivy" in *Krasnyi Arkhiv*, VI, 48-76; VII, 32-54, 1924 (with important and significant Russian Admiralty Reports); Pokrovski, *Drei Konferenzen*, pp. 32-45; Stieve, *Iswolski und der Weltkrieg* (Berlin, 1924), pp. 234-266 [English trans., appendix, 11]; Stieve, however, fails to observe the distinction between Old Style and New Style in discussing these councils. See also *Affaires Balkaniques*, III, 81-107, which evidently omits many important telegrams from the German side; *Deutschland Schuldig?* (Berlin, 1919), pp. 159-181; and, most important of all, G.P., XXXVIII, 193-318.

Good brief accounts of the Liman von Sanders affair may be found in Liman von Sanders, *Fünf Jahre Türkei* (Berlin, 1920), pp. 9-30; Montgelas, *The Case for the Central Powers*, 93-95; Brandenburg, pp. 393-395; Dickinson, pp. 348-9; and more fully, R. J. Kerner, in the *Slavonic Review,* VI, 12-27, 344-363, 543-560 (June, Dec.. 1927; March, 1928).

provoke violent irritation in Russian public opinion, and
would certainly be interpreted as an act manifestly hostile
to us. Especially also, the placing of Turkish troops in
Constantinople under a German general must necessarily
arouse suspicion and apprehension among us. Please speak
in this sense to the German Government.[250]

Sazonov's indignation was shared and whetted by M.
Delcassé—though for somewhat different reasons. The
French Ambassador feared it foreshadowed a German "attempt to bring about a seizure of Turkey by the Triple
Alliance Powers, to which the Triple Entente could not shut
its eyes without prejudice to itself." [251] Germany already
enjoyed tremendous economic and political power in Asia
Minor because of the Bagdad Railway, Delcassé argued;
now she would have a fleet in the Eastern Mediterranean
and be getting a naval base and coaling station for it. Italy,
too, would get concessions—the building of a harbor and
railway at Adalia and the establishment of an Italian sphere
of influence in southern Asia Minor. Austria would likewise want something for herself. As far as Italian and
Austrian ambitions in Asia Minor were concerned, Delcassé
was not so far astray; but Germany was opposed to satisfying them, even though they were her allies, fearing that
the other Powers would demand similar "compensations,"
and that this would mean the final carving up of Turkey.
To this surgical operation Germany was strongly opposed

---

[250] Sazonov to Sverbeev, Oct. 28/Nov. 10, 1913; sent also to Giers at
Constantinople; M.F.R., p. 633. *Cf.* G.P., XXXVIII, 206-209.

[251] *Cf.* Delcassé's Tgs. 700, 701, omitted from the French Yellow Book,
but quoted in part by Adamov, p. 59. The first reference to the Liman
von Sanders affair in the French *Affaires Balkaniques* (III, 81) is the
apparently mild and laconic telegram from Delcassé of Nov. 17, 1913:
"The sending of the new German military mission, whose head is to have
the command of the Constantinople Army Corps, is preoccupying M.
Sazonov." For other indications that Delcassé and Pichon *at first* encouraged Sazonov in his attitude of protest, see *ibid.*, pp. 84, 88, 92 f., 96 f.;
G. P., XXXVIII, 211, 224 ff.; and Siebert-Schreiner, p. 678 f.; see also
below, note 294.

at this time, because she feared it might lead to a conflict between the Great Powers; and also because, being tolerably well situated in Asiatic Turkey and enjoying much influence at Constantinople, she wanted to preserve the *status quo* as long as possible, or at least until the Powers could agree upon an amicable and mutually satisfactory basis of division.[252] A few days later Delcassé sent the French Government the gloomy warning: "The falling to pieces of Turkey has already begun, or is about to begin, and Germany will occupy a position guaranteeing to her all the advantages of a partition." [253]

The Liman von Sanders Mission originated with the Young Turk desire to westernize and modernize the administration of the Ottoman Empire. Soon after seizing power they had invited a number of distinguished foreigners to help them: two Frenchmen, M. Laurent, as financial adviser, and M. Baumann, to train the Turkish gendarmerie; a French trained jurisconsult, M. Léon Ostrorog, to assist in judicial reforms; Sir Richard Crawford to reorganize the customs service; Sir William Willcocks to start irrigation works in Mesopotamia; two other Englishmen, Admiral Sir Douglas Gamble and Admiral Limpus were to reorganize and train the navy, while a German General, Von der Goltz, who had already been in Turkish service, was to spend part of his time in training the Turkish army.

Von der Goltz, however, had found his position difficult on account of the lack of unity among the Young Turk officers, their tendency to mix politics with military matters, and their unwise system of promotions. He also complained of the lack of authority in his own hands, and eventually

---

[252] For evidences that Germany was strongly opposed to the partition of Asiatic Turkey, though of course if the Entente Powers forced it, she wanted to have her fair share, see G.P., XXXIV, 207, 219 ff., 229 f., 255 f.; XXXVII, 474 ff.; XXXVIII, 41-48, 54-66, 93 ff., 129, 196-202; Conrad, III, 569 ff.; and Brandenburg, 389 ff. [Eng. trans. p. 456 ff.].

[253] Adamov, I, 59.

abandoned the work.[254]   The old Turkish officers and soldiers, into whom he had tried to infuse Prussian discipline and methods, proved poor material, and made a lamentable exhibition of themselves when Turkey was attacked by the Balkan Allies in the fall of 1912.

On January 2, 1913, during the armistice in the First Balkan War and the pending negotiations in London, the Young Turk Noradunghian confidentially asked Wangenheim, the German Ambassador in Constantinople, to find out for him as quickly as possible the terms on which the French General Eydoux had been engaged to reorganize and train the Greek army.[255]   He was evidently contemplating something of the same kind for Turkey after the overwhelming defeats she had suffered in the past three months.   The assassination of Nazim Pasha and the Cabinet Revolution in Constantinople, following the concessions made by the Turkish delegates in London, delayed whatever plans Noradunghian may have had in mind, but they brought into power Mahmud Shevket Pasha.   With him were a group of patriotic and determined Young Turks, who were bent on energetic reforms in Turkey, with the assistance of European advisers, as the only hope of saving their country from an early and complete dissolution.   As Von der Goltz and his companions had already given the Turks a start in German military methods, it was obvious that Mahmud Shevket should turn to Germany rather than to any other Power for new military instructors.   Accordingly he begged the Kaiser, through the German Military Attaché in Constantinople, for the services of some Prussian officers for the strengthening of Constantinople.   The Kaiser favored the idea, and on April 2 asked his Foreign Office whether it saw any political objections to the plan, adding that the

[254] G.P., V, 182, 186; IX, 3 f., 36 ff., 41, 226; XII, 134, 562, 566 ff.; XXIV, 150; XXV, 490, 527, 541, 612-622; XXVII, 243, 275-284; XXXVIII, 214 f.

[255] G.P., XXXVIII, 193.

matter was not urgent, as it was not desired that the officers should go to Turkey until peace had put an end to the Balkan War. The Foreign Office had no objections.[256]

Long negotiations then began between the Turkish and German military authorities, which finally resulted by November in the signing of a definite contract for a German Military Mission of some forty-two German officers, headed by General Liman von Sanders.

Though it is commonly stated by Entente writers that Germany instigated the Liman von Sanders Mission, there is no indication of this in the German documents; in fact, the weight of evidence is against it, and in favor of the view that it was initiated by the Turks themselves for their own salvation.[257]

More important, however, than the origin of the German

[256] G.P., XXXVIII, 195 f.

[257] On Jan. 28, 1913, the Austrian Military Attaché in Constantinople, after hearing Wangenheim set forth "in his usual lively manner" Turkey's need of a general reorganization, reported to Conrad (III, 40): "As I now learn from a sure Turkish source, this reorganization plan does not originate with Baron Wangenheim, but with the former Turkish Ambassador in Paris, Munir Pasha. The latter put his views down in a memoir which he recommended to his friends and to Mahmud Shevket Pasha." Hilmi Pasha, the Turkish Ambassador in Vienna, correcting Dumaine's assertion to the contrary, assured Tschirschky that "the initiative came exclusively from the Turkish side" (G.P., XXXVIII, 228). Djemal Pasha, who was Minister of Public Works in January, 1913, and then became Military Governor of Constantinople in charge of the Army Corps which he later handed over to General Liman, explains in detail (*Memories of a Turkish Statesman, 1913-1919*, London, pp. 65-70), quoting Mahmud Shevket, how the German Military Mission originated with the latter's determination to strengthen the Turkish army by reorganizing it along the lines which German instructors for thirty years had been trying to introduce. His statements on this point deserve all the more credibility as they coincide very closely with Mahmud Shevket's expression of views to Wangenheim at the time, as now revealed in the German documents (especially G.P., XXXVIII, 198 ff.). Against this unanimous Turkish evidence is only the casual remark of General Liman himself (*Fünf Jahre Türkei*, pp. 12, 25) that the Mission was due to Wangenheim's initiative; but General Liman knew nothing of the whole matter until several months after it had been first broached; he may have gotten this erroneous idea from Wangenheim's zeal in furthering the Mission, or from the German Ambassador's tendency to magnify his own importance.

Military Mission were its aims and potential effects as viewed by the Turks, the Germans, and the Russians.

Mahmud Shevket and the Young Turks, in fear of Russian intrigues south of the Caucasus and in response to pressure for reforms in Armenia, decided in the spring of 1913 to ask for seventeen English inspectors for the Anatolian gendarmerie and civil administration. Grey at first assented, but later cut the number down to five out of regard for Russian and German susceptibilities.[258] At the same time Mahmud Shevket desired that Germany should send new military instructors to Turkey. He believed that it was only through Anglo-German coöperation that Turkey could be regenerated. As he explained to the German Ambassador on April 26, 1913:

> Turkey can only bring about her resurrection if she can count on Germany and England. That these two countries have hitherto been in opposition has been the chief cause of our misfortunes. I must therefore take care that Turkey becomes the ground on which an Anglo-German understanding shall take place. [After discussing the internal reforms needed, he continued.] We have few trained and reliable officials. Here foreign countries must help. I shall therefore turn to the various Cabinets with a request for reformers. For the reorganization of the army I count definitely upon Germany. This is the most important point in my program. The army must be reformed from the bottom up; politics must be driven out of the [Turkish] officer group. For this the activity of the officers of instruction, in the way they have been shoved in here and there into our organization as mere advisers, is not sufficient. Also for the reform of education I count upon the support of the German Government. I shall ask Italy for gendarme officers for Syria, and France for reorganizers for finance and for the postal and telegraph service. Austria's help I would rather not have. On the other hand, I need the Eng-

[258] G.P., XXXVIII, 32-41, 49-54, 58 f., 98.

lish for the different administrative branches in the provinces of North and East Anatolia. . . . The navy also will
be further reformed by the English. On the basis of a
proposal by Admiral Limpus the ships will receive as commanders English officers not in active service.[259]

The German Ambassador listened eagerly to these plans
of the Grand Vizier. He urged Germany to accede to the
request for military instructors. He warmly welcomed
Mahmud Shevket's idea of Anglo-German coöperation for
strengthening Turkey, and let his imagination wander in
happy political vistas of the future: "It opens for us prospects for an understanding with England, or at least the
possibility of coöperation for the maintenance of the
Turkish Empire. On the other hand, if England should
refuse such coöperation with us, she could not ignore the
influence which we should acquire by our controlling position in military matters and in the instruction of the youth.
We should always be in a position through a skilful use of
the German military reformers to control or paralyze possible separate efforts by the British." [260]   But Wangenheim
was such an optimistic enthusiast about the future of
Turkey that his friends said he was "turkified," and he was
so much inclined to exceed his functions and meddle in
Turkish politics that he had sometimes to be called to order
by the Kaiser.[261]   One must therefore take his despatches
with a grain of salt and be on one's guard against accepting
completely his opinions as representing those of his Government.

[259] Wangenheim to Bethmann, April 26, 1913; G.P., XXXVIII, 198 ff.
These views of Mahmud Shevket, set forth on April 26, are the key-note
and first elaboration of the Military Mission plan, and are echoed a
month later in Wangenheim's despatches of May 21 and 29 (see next
paragraph) which Professor Kerner quotes at length (l.c., pp. 15-18).

[260] Wangenheim to Bethmann, May 29, 1913; ibid., p. 59; cf. also
his despatch of May 22 repeating and endorsing Mahmud Shevket's request for a German military mission; ibid., 201 f.

[261] Cf. G.P., XXXIII, 323, 340.

The Kaiser was much more skeptical, and did not altogether endorse Wangenheim's enthusiasm. Commenting on
Mahmud Shevket's plans quoted above, he wrote: "Many
good intentions, but much that is fantastic! In reality
this employment of various European nations for Turkey's
internal affairs is a grand bridge to intrigues and the partition of Turkey! It is not so simple to set bounds to the
Powers and restrict them to their duties! Especially not
the British;" and he feared that a reorganized Turkish
army might "also be used against us or the Bagdad Railway." [262]   However, in spite of these reflections of the
moment, the Kaiser had already approved the idea of German military instructors, and later urged that the slow
arrangements for it be hurried up. On the whole, as he told
the Russians in the fall, he seems to have regarded the
mission as primarily a military, rather than a political,
affair.

The Porte early notified the British Government of the
project,[263] and it was discussed in a general way with the
Tsar and King George upon their visit to Berlin on May
24 to attend the wedding of the Kaiser's daughter to the
Guelf Duke of Brunswick. The Kaiser informed them of
the Turkish request for German officers: "The Tsar as
well as King George were wholly agreed. The King said:
'It is quite natural that they should turn to you for officers
to reorganize their Army. We are asked to send people

[262] G.P., XXXVIII, 201.

[263] Wangenheim to Berlin Foreign Office, May 26, 1913 (*ibid.*, p. 49):
"In the undeveloped conditions here the administration and gendarmerie
need unconditionally the support of the army. Therefore a basic Anglo-
German understanding concerning the work of reform is imperative. The
Porte has informed London that the reorganization of the army and
instruction is to fall to Germany. The English Embassy counsellor said
to me day before yesterday of his own accord: 'Whether Germany and
England want to or not, they will be led by necessity to uphold Turkey.'"
Grey told Lichnowsky on May 30 that he agreed with Germany in wishing to preserve and strengthen Turkey, but thought all the Powers ought
to assist in the reform work (*ibid.*, p. 55 note).

to reorganize their Police and Gendarmerie, which we shall do.' The Tsar also said that it was necessary to fortify the Tchataldja Line very strongly, so that the Bulgarians should not be able to get in [Constantinople]." [264]

Later Sazonov repeatedly objected that the German Government had acted unfairly in concealing everything from Russia about the matter until the news came out in November. He even complained of it to the King of Rumania at the Constanza meeting in June, 1914. This caused the Kaiser to make the pertinent, if not parliamentary, comment: "The old liar! I told it in the spring *personally* to the Tsar; if he did not inform Sazonov, that is not my affair. . . . If the Tsar did not tell him anything of it, he regarded the matter as not important enough to mention and as wholly natural." [265]

However, aside from the undoubted discussion by royalty at the wedding festivities in May, secrecy shrouded the plans for German officers in Turkey while the Balkan Wars (including Turkey) were still going on, and while the details of General Liman's contract were being worked

[264] Kaiser's marginal note, Dec. 3, 1913; *ibid.*, p. 232; *cf.* also to the same effect the Kaiser's statements to Kokovtsev, the Russian Prime Minister, in November, 1913; *ibid.*, 216, 219 comment 2; M.F.R., p. 638; Siebert-Schreiner, p. 676 f. Professor Kerner also mentions this marginal note of Dec. 3 (*l.c.*, p. 18), but later seems to cast doubt upon its trustworthiness, for he speaks of "a vague reference in May, 1913," which the Kaiser "asserts" (p. 25) and "claims" (p. 26) he made to the Tsar and George V. One might doubt the trustworthiness of the Kaiser's memory or sincerity in his notes and statements six months after the event, were it not that this Willy-Nicky-Georgie May conversation is confirmed by Jagow's contemporary despatch to Lichnowsky (May 27; G.P., XXXVIII, 52), and by the fact that the Tsar himself subsequently "admitted that the plan to send a German Military mission to Turkey had been told to him by the Kaiser at the time of the marriage festivities in Berlin" (Pourtalès to Bethmann, Jan. 31, 1914; *ibid.*, 307). What King George replied, when he was asked by Grey about this May conversation, does not appear (*cf.* Siebert-Schreiner, p. 705).

[265] G.P., XXXVIII, 318. For the quite different light in which Sazonov represented this Constanza conversation in his report to the Tsar, *cf.* Adamov, I, 357 f.; L.N., II, 378.

out. Such secrecy was only natural, because their publication might bring upon the Germans "the reproach of taking
sides and cause political difficulties." [266] This secrecy was
nevertheless unfortunate, both for M. Sazonov's personal
feelings and consequently for the friendly relations between
Russia and Germany. It was particularly unfortunate that
no mention of the contract was made to him confidentially,
when he passed through Berlin in October and had a frank
and cordial discussion with the German Chancellor on the
general political situation in Europe. Sazonov not unnaturally felt injured in his feelings by what seemed to him
to be a lack of reciprocal frankness and friendliness on
Bethmann's part. Bethmann on his part was genuinely
innocent of any deliberate *suppressio veri*. He apparently
failed to mention it simply because it did not occur to him.
This explanation accords with his character, with his statement to Kokovtsev later, and with the fact that he had
really known little about the Liman von Sanders arrangements, which had mainly been made through the military
and not the diplomatic channels. [267]

General Liman von Sanders himself knew nothing of
the project until it was proposed to him on June 15. [268]
He was rightly believed to be a much abler man than Von
der Goltz. Never having been to Turkey, he at once began
to read through his predecessor's correspondence to get an
idea of the kind of difficulties he would have to meet. He
had plenty of time for this, as it was still many months
before a contract was signed with Turkey defining his
powers and duties and those of the forty-one subordinate

[266] Jagow to Wangenheim, Aug. 24, 1913; G.P., XXXVIII, 204.

[267] G.P., XXXVIII, 212 ff. Bethmann and the Foreign Office did not
learn the final terms of General Liman's contract until they received a copy
of it on Jan. 8, 1914, from the Prussian Ministry of War (*ibid.*, p. 213
note).

[268] Liman, p. 9 ff. Bethmann was not informed of Liman's selection
until June 30; G.P., XXXVIII, 202 f.

officers who eventually accompanied him. These were details which had to be worked out by the German and Turkish military authorities. In this connection General Liman says, and with truth:

> The work of the members of the Mission was to be strictly military. The wording of the contract shows this clearly. The charge made on many sides, in writings and newspapers, that it was also to have political activity is wholly incorrect.[269]

At the end of November, when the contract was finally ready and signed, General Liman was commanded to an audience with Emperor William. The Kaiser said to him in substance:

> You must not care in the least whether the Young Turks or the Old Turks are in power. You have only to do with the army. Get politics out of the Turkish corps of officers. Dabbling in politics is its greatest mistake. In Constantinople you will meet Admiral Limpus who is at the head of the English Naval Mission. Be on good terms with him. He works for the navy and you for the army. Each of you has his own separate field of work.[270]

On December 14, 1913, he finally arrived at the Turkish capital and was received with martial music and an honorary escort from the Constantinople Fire Department. But already, a month before his arrival, he had become the object of a diplomatic conflict which threatened to involve Russian and German prestige, or even the Triple Entente and the Triple Alliance.

On November 2, 1913, M. Giers, the Russian Ambassador at Constantinople, telegraphed to St. Petersburg announcing the rumor of a coming German Military Mission. According to the friendly explanations of his German colleague, Baron Wangenheim, it was to be like the French

[269] Liman, 11.　　　　[270] Liman, 11.

Military Mission to Greece. But three days later Giers learned that General Liman would also have command of the Turkish Army Corps stationed at Constantinople. This was a new feature to which Russia and France at once, and eventually England, objected. It gave General Liman quite a different position from that of Von der Goltz before him, or from that of the French military instructor in Greece.[271]

On the day the news of the German Military Mission reached St. Petersburg, Sazonov was absent in the Crimea making a report to the Tsar. M. Kokovtsev, the Russian Premier and Minister of Finance, was in France arranging for the five-hundred-million-franc loan for the construction of Russian strategic railways, but he was planning to stop in Berlin on his way home to thank the Kaiser' for decorating him with the Order of the Black Eagle. It was therefore decided that Kokovtsev should take advantage of his visit in Berlin to set forth Russia's objections to the new German Military Mission. His report to the Tsar of his interviews with Bethmann-Hollweg and the Kaiser gives an excellent statement of the Liman von Sanders affair at the moment it became a serious diplomatic question. After mentioning Sazonov's injured feelings at not having been told of the projected Military Mission, Kokovtsev continues [his prolix circumlocutions being somewhat abbreviated]:

> Both the Chancellor and the Emperor left me with the impression that the project was born last Spring, and that

[271] Giers to Sazonov, Tgs. 928, 936, Oct. 20/Nov. 2, and Oct. 23/Nov. 5, 1913; M.F.R., p. 631. Neratov to Sverbeev, Russian Ambassador in Berlin, Tg. 3032, 25 Oct./7 Nov. (M.F.R., p. 632): "Discuss in a friendly way . . . the very undesirable impression which would be made upon us by the placing of divisions and corps in Constantinople under German officers. Acts of this sort, causing unnecessary suspicion, hinder friendly relations with the Berlin Cabinet which are maintained on our side at such serious cost. We should not object to a command, not in the capital but in other parts of Turkey not in our neighborhood."

the Chancellor, according to his affirmation during a completely sincere talk, was scarcely acquainted with it. He had merely learned that the Turkish Government had invited Germany to undertake the instruction of the Turkish army, that this question had been touched upon by the German Emperor in a private talk with Your Majesty in Berlin last May, and that Your Majesty had made no objection in principle, in view of the fact German officers have served as instructors in the Turkish army for more than twenty years; but that afterwards the ultimate arrangements for the organization of a Model Army Corps, under German command in the capital of Turkey, had remained wholly unknown to him and had followed the routine through military departments of the Empire.

In repeated and entirely sincere talks, the Chancellor did not hide from me how particularly painful to him was the possibility of the thought that he had participated in the preparation of a project disagreeable to Russia, and that he had not given a timely notification to our Minister of Foreign Affairs.

"During my four years of office," said Herr von Bethmann-Hollweg, "in the relations between the two Empires which are bound together by traditional ties of friendship and confidence, I have made every effort to avoid every occasion for the smallest misunderstanding, and my honesty guarantees that I shall never lend my hand to an act of disloyalty toward Russia." I have the impression that he was wholly sincere, and I do not think I am mistaken in judgment in saying that the very idea of an army corps at Constantinople under the command of German officers was really not known to him until the last few days just before my arrival, or even in part through my own explanations.

[After admitting the reasonableness of the Germans giving military instruction to the Turks and explaining mildly Russia's objections to Germans exercising command over troops in Constantinople, Kokovtsev summed up] with a demand having the character of an alternative: either give up completely the command over Turkish troops and merely exercise a right of inspection as formerly; or, if that seemed impossible on account of the promises Germany had made to Turkey, concentrate the Model Army Corps, not at Constantinople, but at some other point, e.g. Adrianople or in Asia Minor, but naturally not near our frontier nor in the sphere of interests belonging to France.[272]

The suggestion that General Liman exercise his command, not at Constantinople where his presence might seem to overawe the Ambassadors of the Powers, but at some Turkish provincial town, at first sight seemed a hopeful way out of the objections raised by Russia. Giers, Sverbeev, and Neratov, as well as Kokovtsev, favored this solution. Smyrna and Adrianople were suggested. But at once difficulties arose from the selfish interests of France and Russia themselves. France was strenuously opposed to having General Liman at Smyrna, "where a German command would be very dangerous to French interests." [273] Pichon, however, thought that "at the worst, it might be possible to agree to Adrianople." [274] But the choice of Adrianople, as the Russian Ambassador in Berlin shrewdly pointed out, "would probably cause great excitement in Bulgaria, and still further estrange this country from us [Russians]." [275] Bethmann, on the other hand, in accordance with his conciliatory attitude in the whole affair and his sincere desire to find a solution satisfactory to Russia, was quite ready

[272] Kokovtsev's report to the Tsar, 19 Nov./2 Dec., 1913; M.F.R., 624 ff.; L.N., II, 411 ff. The accuracy of Kokovtsev's report is confirmed by G.P., XXXVIII, 212-217.

[273] Izvolski to Sazonov, Tg. 550, Nov. 12/25; M.F.R., p. 641, but omitted from L.N., and Stieve. Cf. also Izvolski's Tg. 555 (M.F.R., p. 642; L.N., II, 189; Siebert-Schreiner, p. 678): "Pichon has again insisted on the fact that France cannot consent that Germans shall command at Smyrna or Beirut; he has suggested Adrianople to the Porte."

[274] Izvolski's Tg. 550.

[275] Sverbeev's confidential letter to Sazonov, Nov. 8/21; M.F.R., p. 639; Siebert-Schreiner, p. 677.

to consider this. General Liman, therefore, was to be asked
whether it would be possible to change the arrangements
which had been made.[276]   But, as Sverbeev was informed
at the same time, the military authorities in Berlin were
of the opinion that unless the Model Corps was established
at Constantinople, the activity of the German instructors
would be reduced to nil, because the Military Academy and
the General Staff were situated in Constantinople and with
these the German officers would have to be in uninterrupted
relations.   This eventually proved to be General Liman's
opinion after arriving at Constantinople.   But on being
informed of Russia's objections, he "came to the conclusion
that there is no necessity for the General to command the
Army Corps if there are only a sufficient number of troops
to give the military schools an opportunity for practice
exercises.   A German general could command the Army
Corps in Adrianople." [277]   This solution was favored by the
Russian Ambassador in Constantinople, but it was indignantly rejected by the Turks, who resented what they regarded as unwarranted Russian efforts to interfere in
Turkey's internal affairs.[278]

Without waiting to hear General Liman's answer,
Sazonov had hastened to suggest that France and England
better join him in demanding "compensations."   Such a
demand for "some equivalent" was a common enough sec-
ond-line form of attack in diplomacy when a direct effort
at the main objective had failed.   So now M. Sazonov,
after protesting "how difficult it would be for us to permit
our Embassy to remain in a city in which, so to speak,
a German garrison was quartered," suggested to France and

[276] Sverbeev to Sazonov, Tg. 277, Nov. 13/26; M.F.R., p. 643.

[277] Giers to Sazonov, Tg. 1069, Dec. 7/20; Siebert-Schreiner, p. 694.

[278] Giers to Sazonov, Tgs. 1072, 1073, 1078, 1086, Dec. 7/20 to Dec.
11/24, M.F.R., 670-672, and in part in Siebert-Schreiner, p. 695.   Wangenheim's despatches of Dec. 16, 17, 18, 19; G.P., XXXVIII, 259-268; Liman,
p. 14 f.

England that "if it should appear inexpedient to raise further objections in Berlin, a joint step could be taken in Constantinople to point out that the concessions made to Germany raised the question of equivalent compensations for the other Powers." [279] France at first agreed instantly. Pichon "is entirely of your opinion. . . . If the Porte does not renounce the realization of this plan, France will demand extraordinary compensations of a moral and political nature." [280]

Sir Edward Grey, however, did not at first favor Sazonov's suggestion. He diplomatically "conceded in principle" the possibility of compensations, but feared "it might be difficult actually to find such compensations. Pichon's first proposal, that officers of other countries should also receive such posts of command, he deems inpracticable and not in keeping with our [Russian] interests, because our main object, the removal of the Germans from Constantinople, would not thereby be attained. Besides this would mean the first step in the partition of Turkey. . . . Grey thinks it best to continue friendly negotiations with Germany, in order to move her to change her original plan. . . . He believes that Emperor William, as well as the Imperial Chancellor, are seeking a pretext to extricate themselves from this situation." [281] Somewhat ignorant of Balkan problems, he also had a certain distrust of Russian diplomacy on account of Persian affairs and he feared that Sazonov's fickleness of mind might easily lead to some disaster.[282]

Unable to force Germany to yield, and abandoning the

[279] Sazonov to Benckendorff and Izvolski, Tg. 3220, Nov. 12/25; M.F.R., p. 642; Siebert-Schreiner, p. 678. Cf. G.P., XXXVIII, 235 f., 241.

[280] Izvolski to Sazonov, Nov. 13/26; M.F.R., p. 642; L.N., II, 189; Stieve, III, 354.

[281] Benckendorff to Sazonov, Nov. 15/28; M.F.R., p. 644; Siebert-Schreiner, p. 679.

[282] Cf. Sazonov to Benckendorff, Nov. 29/Dec. 12, 1913; Siebert-Schreiner, p. 687.

idea of accepting "compensations," M. Sazonov decided to try to coerce Turkey into annulling or revising the contract by presenting her with something like an ultimatum from the Triple Entente. In order to secure Sir Edward Grey's coöperation in this line of attack, Paul Cambon was instructed to persuade Grey to join "in making the Porte understand the inadmissible consequences which would result from placing the Constantinople Army Corps under a German general. It would, in short, place the Diplomatic Corps which resides in Constantinople under German guardianship. It would be virtually handing over to this Power the key to the Straits. It would make possible military interventions by the German general which might strike directly at the sovereignty of the Sultan. It would destroy the balance among the Powers which is the guarantee for the existence of Turkey. It might eventually bring these Powers into antagonism toward, or even into conflict with, the German Military Mission in case they had to exercise some action or demonstration at Constantinople." If Sir Edward agreed with these views he was to be flattered by being asked to formulate the note which the Entente Powers would present to the. Porte.[283]

Cambon's potent argument, that General Liman's contract would put into German hands "the key to the Straits" —where Admiral Limpus was supposed to assure England's domination—did not fail to have the calculated effect upon Sir Edward Grey. It brought him out of the fogs of the Irish question and galvanized him into an energetic action (which a little later he regretted and reversed). He fell in with the French proposal, and speedily formulated a vigorous "declaration" embodying its arguments and amounting almost to an ultimatum. It warned the Turkish Government that if General Liman retained his command "the other Powers would demand analogous advantages for

283 Pichon to Cambon, Nov. 29; *Affaires Balkaniques,* III, 91 f.

themselves." It was approved by the Prime Minister, M. Asquith, and forwarded to the two other Entente Powers as a basis for identical warnings to be presented by their Ambassadors at Constantinople. In transmitting it to the French Ambassador in Turkey, M. Pichon added, "It is essential that the Ottoman Government can have no doubt as to the absolute agreement which has been established between England, France and Russia on this question." [284]

Sazonov was now assured, as he supposed, of "the absolute agreement" of both France and England. He now suddenly decided to try to use this as a lever at Berlin to bluff Germany into backing down, before the Entente Ambassadors should take action at Constantinople. Such a success at Berlin would be a more signal diplomatic victory and settlement of the affair than one secured in Constantinople. He accordingly telegraphed to Izvolski at Paris to have Bompard delay in presenting the note to Turkey. [285]

At the same time he instructed Sverbeev in Berlin to invite the German Government's attention to the proposed action of the Entente Powers at Constantinople if Germany did not give a satisfactory reply. Jagow, the German Secretary for Foreign Affairs, answered that he could not yet give a definite reply; he had written to General Liman to look into the local conditions in Constantinople; and if he came to an agreement with the Turkish authorities that no technical difficulties prevented the removal of the Model Corps to another center, then the German Government could easily revise General Liman's contract. Next day, December 5, Sazonov was told by the German Ambassador that "notwithstanding the embarrassment of its situation, the German Government was getting on with a possible

[284] Pichon to Bompard at Constantinople, Dec. 3, 1913; *ibid.*, III, 96.

[285] Tgs. 3281 and 3282, indicated in Izvolski's reply Tg. 565, Nov. 21/ Dec. 4; M.F.R., p. 648; this telegram is not included in L.N., Stieve, or Siebert-Schreiner.

settlement of the difficulty which has arisen, but some time would be necessary for this in order not to give the impression of yielding to pressure." Sazonov replied he "was ready to receive the proposal if the German Government did not postpone its decision to a too protracted date." But at the same time he instructed Sverbeev in Berlin to point out Pan-Slav Press criticisms of himself and "the necessity for us [Russians] to be able to remove the plausible reproaches printed as to the perfidy of German policy, and the desirability of winding up this whole incident as quickly as possible. If the German Minister talks about his Government's being unable to settle with the Porte, tell him that we should readily adopt the point of view that the question ought to be deliberated upon, not in Berlin, but in Constantinople, and that we shall take the agreed-upon steps immediately." [286]

Sazonov in fact was in no mood to wait. He concluded that it was impossible to pry Germany into giving an immediate decision, and that his lever had therefore failed. He also heard that the Sultan had issued on December 4 an iradé announcing General Liman's appointment as Member of the War Council and Commander of the Constantinople Corps. He therefore telegraphed to London and Paris on December 7: "We consider it desirable that the three Ambassadors should at once address themselves to the Turkish Government with the following identical note which has been drawn up according to the English proposal." [287]

But M. Sazonov was now chagrined to discover that Sir Edward Grey had meanwhile changed his mind, during the interval in which Sazonov himself had desired a delay in the Entente action at Constantinople. Sazonov now found that the agreement was not so "absolute" as he had

[286] Sazonov to Sverbeev, Nov. 22/Dec. 5, 1913; M.F.R., p. 648.
[287] Tg. 3309; M.F.R., 650; Siebert-Schreiner, p. 681.

supposed. His proposed "note" had a sharper tone than Grey's "declaration."

A misunderstanding also arose as to the form in which the Entente declaration should be presented to the Grand Vizier. Sazonov and Pichon wanted a very strong diplomatic procedure: the simultaneous presentation by the Entente Ambassadors of an identical written note. Sir Edward Grey, however, characteristically desired to treat the Grand Vizier more gently: "In the opinion of Grey the notes ought to be identical, but not presented simultaneously." [288]

Meanwhile also Grey had begun to hear from the German Chargé d'Affaires in London an account of the German Military Mission very different from that which had been pictured to him by Paul Cambon. He was informed by Kühlmann that the arrangement for a German command over the Constantinople Army Corps was simply intended to obviate the inherent weakness in the position of General Liman's predecessor. General Von der Goltz's efforts had been paralyzed by lack of authority and by Turkish inertia which blocked the reforms he tried to introduce. The new plan was to give General Liman a Model Corps over which he would have command, and in which he would therefore enjoy sufficient authority to compel real reforms. The Corps at Constantinople had been chosen as the Model Corps, because that was the seat of the Military School and the General Staff, with which the German instructors would have to be in constant touch. General Liman was simply to have a position in the army analogous to that of the English Admiral Limpus in the navy, against whom no Powers had

---

[288] Etter to Sazonov, Tg. 799, Nov. 19/Dec. 2; M.F.R., p. 646; Siebert-Schreiner, p. 681. *Cf.* Cambon to Pichon, Dec. 2 (*Affaires Balkaniques*, III, 93): "The Prime Minister [Asquith] has approved the proposal of Sir Edward Grey for an action at Constantinople. He thinks this ought not to be collective but identical, and that the Ambassadors could express themselves in about the same terms."

protested. The point about Admiral Limpus made a deep
impression on Grey. He began to see that he might be
getting into a very illogical position if he should demand
that General Liman give up the command of a single
Turkish Army Corps in Constantinople while Admiral
Limpus kept the command over the whole Turkish fleet.
He may well have imagined the poor figure he would cut
in the House of Commons if he were questioned and forced
to defend such an illogical attitude. As the Russian Ambassador ruefully reported a few days later: "Grey did not
know until now the exact details of the contract of the
British Admiral. . . . The position of the British Admiral
really furnishes Germany with an argument which is causing difficulties here. Nicolson has spoken to me about it
several times." [289]

In addition to Kühlmann's arguments, Grey was also
put on his guard against Sazonov's maneuvers by the correct information which he began to get from Sir Louis
Mallet in Constantinople: the importance of continuing
the Anglo-German coöperation in the construction of naval
docks for Turkey at Ismid; Admiral Limpus' declaration
that his powers were really wider than General Liman's;
the fact that he had leased the house in Constantinople
picked out for the German General; and finally Sir Louis
Mallet's warning that out of the Russian demands for
Liman's withdrawal might easily arise a dangerous situation like the French demand for the withdrawal of the
Hohenzollern Candidacy in 1870.[290]

[289] Benckendorff to Sazonov, Tg. Nov. 29/Dec. 12, 1913; M.F.R.,
p. 657; Siebert-Schreiner, p. 688. Cf. also Tg. 813, Dec. 1/14: "I asked
Nicolson, for what reason Grey had changed his original standpoint. He
replied, that meantime details concerning the position of the British Admiral in Constantinople had come to hand from the British Ambassador
in Constantinople, which had deprived Grey of every possibility of agreeing to the draft proposed by you."
[290] G.P., XXXVIII, 232 ff., 240 f., 245 f., 249 ff., 270 ff., 282 f.; and
preceding footnote.

On learning more about the facts of the case, and especially about Admiral Limpus, Grey in fact virtually reversed his attitude. He came to the opinion that Sazonov's projected "note" to Turkey (though based closely on his own and Cambon's proposals) was "premature"; there must not be "any kind of threats at its close"; instead of warning the Sultan of the dangerous consequences of General Liman's appointment, he now suggested a mere "verbal inquiry," politely asking the Turks for information as to the contract made by them with the German General, and the extent of the functions he was to exercise.

M. Sazonov was now much upset in his mind, as may be seen from his telegram to the Russian Ambassador in London on December 12:

> I hear from a very secret source [291] that Grey has explained to the French Ambassador, that he did not wish to go too far in Constantinople, as he is afraid of a change in my attitude, which might lead to a diplomatic failure. I should like to remark, that as to the instructors, it is not a question of a change in our attitude, but of a regrettable change in England's attitude. For Grey will have nothing more to do with a note, which had been based on a telegram of Grey's to the British Ambassador [in St. Petersburg].
>
> Should we be finally obliged to change our attitude in this question, as already in so many others, this is to be attributed only to the lack of confidence in the effectiveness of England's support, and, indeed, this confidence will only be shaken still more by such actions on the part of England. This lack of homogeneity and solidarity between the three Powers of the Entente arouses our serious apprehension, for it constitutes an organic fault of the Triple Entente,

---

[291] This "very secret source" may have been another case of Sazonov's deciphering telegrams sent by the French Government to the French Ambassador in St. Petersburg, similar to the case which contributed to the famous attempted dismissal of M. Georges Louis in May, 1912; *cf.* Judet, *Georges Louis*, pp. 85-88, 99; Poincaré, I, 377 f.

which will always place us at a disadvantage in face of the firm block of the Triple Alliance.

Such a condition of affairs might under certain circumstances entail grave consequences, and most seriously endangers vital interests of every Power of the Triple Entente.[292]

In spite of his irritation and chagrin at Sir Edward Grey's disconcerting change of attitude, Sazonov perceived that there was nothing to be done but accept it. On December 13, therefore, the three Entente Ambassadors at Constantinople made, one after another, their mild "verbal inquiry" as to the nature of General Liman's contract and position, and whether it threatened Turkey's sovereign independence and authority over Constantinople and the Straits. They were given the desired information about the contract, but were told by the Grand Vizier that their other question was Turkey's own private affair. He compared General Liman's position to that of Admiral Limpus, and therefore saw no reason for cancelling or changing the German contract.[293] In view of Sir Edward Grey's attitude there was nothing more to be gained by M. Sazonov through negotiations at Constantinople. Though there was some

[292] Sazonov to Benckendorff, Nov. 29/Dec. 12, 1913; Siebert-Schreiner, p. 687. See M.F.R., p. 657 ff. for Benckendorff's replies. *Cf.* also Buchanan, *My Mission to Russia*, I, 149 f., and the approximately correct surmise of the situation by Kühlmann in London, with the Kaiser's comments (Dec. 12; G.P., XXXVIII, 250): "Apparently an extraordinarily strong pressure is being exercised from the Russian side [Kaiser: 'Rascals!']. The Russian Government is said to have gone so far as to say to Sir Edward Grey that it must regard his attitude in this question as a touchstone for his feelings toward Russia in general [Kaiser: 'Aha']. Because Sir Edward in his policy wants to avoid a break with Russia [Kaiser: 'Ass! He betrays his country's own interests'], he is said to have decided to participate formally in the inquiry in the matter but without showing a strong interest in it himself [Kaiser: 'Then the Grand Vizier can calmly be rude']."

[293] M.F.R., pp. 658-662; Siebert-Schreiner, pp. 688-692; G.P., XXXVIII, 250-268.

talk of altering the status of both General Liman and Admiral Limpus, it came to nothing.

M. Bompard, the French Ambassador at Constantinople did not believe that Russia would ever achieve her purpose by peaceful means; he suggested privately that Russia "should dispatch a warship to the Bosphorus and declare that it would not be withdrawn until the contract with General Liman and his officers had been altered." M. Paléologue, Political Director in the French Foreign Office, thought that "the Turkish batteries would scarcely dare to open fire." And M. Izvolski added that "in the event of our resolving upon an energetic action of this sort, public opinion in France would take our part, since it is susceptible to everything which touches national dignity, and feels most keenly the inadmissibility of German influence in Turkey.[294] M. Sazonov, as will be seen in a moment, was actually contemplating military measures to coerce Turkey. But France and England both intimated that it would be better to await the results of the efforts which the German Government was making to find a solution which would satisfy Russia without seeming to involve the prestige of Turkey or of any of the Great Powers. Though impatient of delay because of the criticisms being levelled against him in the Pan-Slav Press, Sazonov fortunately heeded the advice.

Meanwhile the German Ambassador at Constantinople had been active in trying to find a sensible and peaceful solution of the whole affair. He had urged Turkey to yield and modify Liman's contract. He tried to have the German and Russian military attachés in Constantinople work out an agreement. He finally hurried back to Berlin and there arranged the successful solution. General Liman was ad-

[294] Izvolski to Sazonov, Dec. 19/Jan. 1; M.F.R., p. 602; L.N., II, 222; Stieve, IV, 10; Siebert-Schreiner, p. 701. For pacific assurances by the French to Germany and Germany's impressions thereof, see G.P., XXXVIII, 241, 247, 255, 272, 274 ff., 286 f., 307.

vanced a grade in the Prussian army; by the terms of his contract, this automatically resulted in his advance in the Turkish army to rank of Field Marshal which relieved him of the command of the First Army Corps in Constantinople. He remained Inspector of Turkish troops and Director of the Military School, but did not exercise command over troops in the Turkish capital—the point to which Sazonov had so strenuously objected. This solution, which was satisfactory to Russia, was publicly announced on January 15, 1914.[295] It brought the affair peacefully to an end, without involving the danger of a test of strength between the Triple Entente and the Triple Alliance. As the Russian Ambassador in Berlin wrote to M. Sazonov: "The Berlin Cabinet has actually done everything in its power in order to fulfil our justifiable wishes, and this has not been easy for it, in view of the newspaper campaign directed against the Government." [296]

The whole affair shows how even a serious Russo-German diplomatic crisis could be sensibly and peacefully settled, provided that Germany was willing to make some concessions, and that Russia was restrained by France and England from taking too extreme and hasty steps; and provided also that neither side paid too much attention to the hounding criticisms of its own jingo newspapers and military alarmists. Though Germany had had no intention of suddenly springing a surprise which would embarrass Sazonov, the unfortunate failure of the Tsar in May, and of Bethmann in October, to mention the Military Mission to the Russian Minister of Foreign Affairs gave the latter a natural feeling of grievance. This was accentuated by his fears that the Liman Mission might ultimately block Russia's ambitions in regard to the Straits—a fact which

---

[295] G.P., XXXVIII, 265-302.
[296] Sverbeev to Sazonov, Jan. 3/16, 1914; M.F.R., p. 689; Siebert-Schreiner, p. 707.

is significant of the great importance he attached to Russia's "historic mission"—as is further indicated by his measures of preparedness presently to be described. The effect of the Liman von Sanders affair in Berlin was to strengthen the feeling that though Sazonov was inclined to get excited and even to bluff, it was doubtful whether he would have England's support for his bluff. This was one reason why Germany at first believed it probably safe to support Austria in July, 1914.

M. Sazonov is pictured by many "revisionist" writers as being "converted" in the fall of 1913 to the "Franco-Russian war plot" which MM. Poincaré and Izvolski had been weaving since 1912 by "Balkanizing of the Franco-Russian Alliance." [297] But this picture does too little justice to M. Sazonov's independence of attitude, and gives too much weight to the influence exerted by Izvolski and Poincaré on Russian foreign policy. M. Sazonov often pursued Balkan policies which by no means wholly harmonized with those of Izvolski and still less with those of Poincaré. In the winter and spring of 1914, Russian policy can be more accurately followed in his reports to the Tsar and in the minutes of Russian Councils than in the self-important despatches of the Russian Ambassador in Paris. Izvolski's influence on Russian policy has been exaggerated by Izvolski himself and by writers who take him at his own valuation. M. Poincaré, to be sure, in his recent self-righteous memoirs, goes much too far to the other extreme in attempting utterly to discredit Izvolski. But there seems to be little doubt that in the early months of 1914 Izvolski's influence was somewhat on the wane both in Paris and St. Petersburg. He

[297] Cf. Stieve, *Izvolski and the World War*, pp. 186 ff.; H. E. Barnes, *The Genesis of the World War*, pp. 110 ff., 138 ff.; and note 299 below.

was terribly alarmed by the rumor that he might be superseded by Kokovtsev.

M. Sazonov's real views are well revealed in a long report to the Tsar early in December, 1913.[298]   In this he summed up the general situation after the Balkan Wars, and especially the danger to peace caused by the long failure of Turkey and Greece to come to terms.   In view of Turkey's weakened position, Sazonov concluded that the final dissolution of the Ottoman Empire was not far distant, that all the Powers were calculating the parts which they would appropriate when the final partition took place, and that Russia must therefore decide what attitude she would take in the premises.

An impartial reading of his report, which is too long to quote in full, shows that he did not desire to bring about a European war.   On the contrary, he repeatedly stated that he wished to preserve the *status quo* as long as possible. But the situation in the Balkans was very unstable.   Russia could never permit the Straits to pass into the hands of any other Power, as they had been in danger of doing when the Bulgarians advanced to the outposts of Constantinople in 1912.   Therefore he and the other Russian Ministers must concert plans of preparedness to seize the Straits, in case of European complications which he feared might occur at any moment.   Hence he requested the Tsar to allow him to consult with the other Ministers on these measures of preparedness:

> It is not at all in our direct interest to strive for any increases of territory whatever.   All the needs of our internal development make the task of maintaining peace of first importance.   However, while not abandoning this principal and primary task, we cannot close our eyes to the

[298] Sazonov's report of Nov. 23/Dec. 6, 1913; L.N., II, 363-372; Stieve, III, 374-383 (with the date, Nov. 25/Dec. 8); summarized by Adamov, pp. 70-75; approved by the Tsar at Livadia, Nov. 27/Dec. 10.

dangers of the international situation, dangers the prevention of which does not depend on us alone. That is why we cannot neglect, any more than the other Powers, to raise the question of preserving in advance our rights and interests, if events should demand that we defend them by armed force.

Uncertainty as to the stability and longevity of Turkey raises for us the historic question of the Straits, and a weighing of their importance for us, both from a political and an economic point of view. . . . In case of a change in the *status quo,* Russia cannot permit a solution of the question counter to her interests; in other words, she cannot, under certain circumstances, remain a passive spectator of events. . . .

At present the question of safeguarding the Straits is settled at bottom in a fairly satisfactory manner as regards our direct interests. Turkey is a State neither too strong nor too weak—unable to be a danger to us, but at the same time obliged to give consideration to Russia, which is stronger than she. The very weakness of the Ottoman Empire, and its inability to regenerate itself on the basis of law and civilization, have hitherto been to our advantage, creating among the peoples subjected to the Crescent that aspiration toward Orthodox Russia, which is one of the fundamental bases of our international position in the East and in Europe. . . .

Can we permit the transfer of the Straits into the full possession of another State? To put the question, is to answer it in the negative. The Straits in the possession of a strong State would mean that the economic development of all South Russia would be subjected to it. . . . He who possesses the Straits will not only hold the keys of the Black Sea and the Mediterranean; he will have also the key to the penetration of Asia Minor and the hegemony of the Balkans; consequently, the State which replaces Turkey on the shores of the Straits will probably aspire to follow the paths followed formerly by the Turks. . . .

[Rejecting as unsatisfactory all proposals for neutralizing and demilitarizing the Straits, Sazonov reiterated the need of a detailed program of preparedness.] We must study the measures which can be taken to increase our military and naval strength in the Black Sea. What ought the War and Navy Departments to do to accelerate mobilization, by means of new railways and the development of our means of transport? . . . Is it possible, or not, to determine the task of our army and navy in forcing the Straits and seizing Constantinople, if circumstances should demand it?

Returning to the political aspect of preparedness, one must again repeat that an early dissolution of Turkey could not be desirable for us, and it is necessary to do everything possible, through diplomacy, to postpone such an outcome.

[M. Sazonov then indicated the principal questions to be discussed: (1) the accelerated mobilization of an adequate expeditionary force; (2) the preparation of the lines of communication necessary for this mobilization; (3) the increase of the Black Sea Fleet so that it will surpass the Turkish Fleet, and be able to force the Straits and occupy them temporarily or permanently, if necessary; (4) the increase of naval transports; and (5) the construction of strategic railways in the Caucasus.]

Renewing the wish expressed above for the prolongation as far as possible of the *status quo*,[299] it is also necessary

---

[299] Stieve, *Izvolski and the World War*, p. 189 ff., quoting this paragraph, suppresses the important clause "Renewing . . . *status quo*" as well as other similar phrases, in which Sazonov expresses his desire to preserve peace and the *status quo*. Having suppressed the words which do not fit in with his theories, he says: "this passage is an admission of enormous import," and proceeds with the misleading and unwarranted conclusions: "The kernel lies in the first [!] clause, with the declaration that 'the question of the Straits can hardly be advanced a step except *through European complications*' [italics are Stieve's]. . . . The passage establishes Sazonov's conversion to the idea of world war. Thus at the end of 1913 the Russian Foreign Minister had, as regards the attainment of the specifically Russian aims, completed that fateful change of course which Poincaré on behalf of France had resolutely made as long ago as the end of 1912, when he was ready to attack Austria and Germany. . . . It was this that sealed the doom of Europe," etc. Barnes, p. 139, follows

to repeat that the question of the Straits can hardly be
advanced a step except through European complications.
These complications, to judge from present conditions, would
find us in alliance with France, and in a possible, but not
at all assured, alliance with England, or at least with her
as a benevolent neutral. In the Balkans, in case of European complications, we could count on Serbia, and perhaps
on Rumania. . . .[300]

The Tsar approved Sazonov's report, and the discussion
by various Ministers, as proposed, took place on January
13, 1914. Sazonov also sent a copy of it to M. Grigorovitch,
the Naval Minister, who passed it on to the Admiralty
Staff for examination. The latter naturally endorsed very
heartily Sazonov's proposal for strengthening the Black Sea
Fleet. They urged that only by this means could Russia
make her voice heard in the concert of Europe and in dealings with Turkey, where Russia's influence was already
sadly inadequate. The Admiralty Staff suggested several
measures for the immediate strengthening of the Black
Sea Fleet: speeding up the construction of vessels already
being built; the purchase of Dreadnoughts abroad, and the
prevention of their purchase by Turkey; and the preparation of plans for the combined action of the Baltic and the
Black Sea Fleets against Turkey.[301]

On the basis of these suggestions the Naval Minister
made a long report to the Tsar, endorsing Sazonov's ideas:

> The systematic and successful preparations of operations
> of our fleet for the dominating control on the sea at the
> Constantinople channel and in the waters of the Aegean and
> Mediterranean adjacent to it demand careful and persistent

Stieve in suppressing passages in which Sazonov expresses his desire to
preserve peace and the *status quo*.

[300] For the continuation of Sazonov's report, concerning Rumania,
Serbia, and Austria, see above at note 222.

[301] Report of the Admiralty Staff, Dec. 9/22, 1913; Zakher, "Konstantinopol i Prolivy," in *Krasnyi Arkhiv*, VII, 33 f.

work, not only by the Navy Department, but also by the War Ministry and some others, especially the Ministries of Foreign Affairs, Commerce, Industry, and Finance. This preparedness can be completed only in the course of some years. Therefore the Navy Department wholly agrees with the proposal of the Minister of Foreign Affairs (after the termination of certain preparatory studies) about the necessity of holding a Special Council for the working out of these guiding principles, which result from the idea approved by Your Majesty that Russia cannot allow any Power whatever to establish itself on the Straits of the Bosphorus and the Dardanelles; and that Russia must therefore be ready to take possession of the Straits, in case great European complications should bring up the Eastern Question for a final settlement.[302]

Meanwhile, on January 5, 1914, Sazonov drew up a memorandum for circulation among the other Ministers to serve as a basis for discussion at the Special Council. It summarized the Liman von Sanders negotiations, and went on to declare:

3. Decisions must now be taken to provide for the possible necessity of supporting our demands by measures of compulsion.

4. The measures of compulsion on our part might take the form of the occupation of some point in Asia Minor, e.g. Trebizond or Bayazid, with a declaration that we should stay there until our demands were satisfied.

5. After it had been clearly established what measures of compulsion we should be able to employ, a confidential exchange of views on the subject must be set on foot with the British and French Governments, since measures of compulsion can, necessarily, only be undertaken after we have ascertained whether we can count on corresponding steps on the part of these two Powers.

[302] Grigorovitch's report, approved by the Tsar Dec. 30, 1913/Jan. 13, 1914; *Krasnyi Arkhiv*, VII, 35 ff.

6. In the negotiations with the said Governments, the necessity for extremely cautious and unanimous action on the part of the three Powers must be insisted on, in order, if possible, to prevent the conflict becoming more acute, as a European war might result. At the same time efforts must be made on our part to prepare France and Great Britain for the necessity of pursuing to the end an action once begun in the common interests.

7. Should this point of view be accepted by all three Powers and the negotiations in Berlin not lead to the desired result, an understanding must be arrived at as to an ascending scale in the measures of compulsion:

(a) A rigid financial boycott of Turkey;

(b) Should this method fail to produce the required effect, as in the case of the Adrianople question, the three Powers might withdraw their representatives from Constantinople;

(c) At the same time the Governments of Russia, France, and Great Britain would acquaint the Porte with the date fixed for the fulfilment of their demands, after which the measures of compulsion might begin to be put into force, with the warning that they would not be withdrawn until the demands had been complied with.

8. Should certain preparatory steps of a military nature, such as reinforcements of troops in the Caucasus, be necessary to enable us promptly to put measures of compulsion into effect, it would be desirable to keep these steps as secret as possible. From the political point of view, however, it is clearly necessary that it shall be possible, after issuing a threat, should that become necessary, to take prompt steps to translate the threat into action.[303]

This memorandum indicates clearly Sazonov's desire, "if possible, to prevent the conflict becoming more acute, as a European war might result," but at the same time his

[303] Pokrovski, *Drei Konferenzen,* 32 f.; Stieve, *Izvolski and the World War,* 219 f.

determination to resort to "measures of compulsion" and a threat of force as a bluff to secure a diplomatic victory, and his readiness, if necessary, "to take prompt steps to translate the threat into action"—provided he could feel sure of British and French support. He told the Tsar on January 9 that he believed a firm stand on Russia's part would probably have the desired effect on Germany and Turkey, "but the risk of serious European complications must undoubtedly be kept in view." He was determined that Russia must not accept the Liman von Sanders Mission as a *fait accompli,* because "a yielding would be equivalent to a political defeat and might have altogether ruinous consequences." It would make Germany and her allies more arrogant, and "in France and England there would be strengthened the dangerous conviction that Russia will accept any conditions whatever for the sake of preserving peace. Once such convictions were strengthened in our friend and our ally, the not very close solidarity of the Triple Entente Powers might be finally broken up, and each of them would endeavor to seek security for its interests by making agreements with the Powers of the opposing camp."

Sazonov feared particularly that England and Germany might come to some separate solution of the Liman von Sanders affair by changing the status of Admiral Limpus, and then Russia would be left alone to face Germany. "Russia would be finally left in complete political isolation, because it would hardly be possible to reckon separately even upon France, who also, even without this [possible Anglo-German agreement], is inclined to sacrifice great political interests for the sake of the financial advantages of a settlement. . . . If, however, the replies of France and England [in regard to the use of measures of compulsion] should be regarded as satisfactory, then, reserving all necessary strength and caution for the complications necessity may demand, it would remain for us to defend firmly our interests to the end." [304]

That Sazonov should suspect England's loyalty to Russian interests in the Balkans is not altogether surprising. But that he should also speak thus of France indicates what a strong element of suspiciousness there was in his character, especially in view of the fact that Izvolski had informed him only a few days before that "Poincaré, in the most decisive terms, confirmed Doumergue's declaration . . . that France is firmly determined to act with us in this connection. From Poincaré's words, I have been able to conclude that the expressions of the declaration mentioned have been most carefully weighed by him and his Ministers, and that, in spite of France's love of peace, these words express, with full and deliberate intent, a quiet resolution not to withdraw, under existing circumstances, from those obligations imposed upon her by her alliance with us." [305] It was this suspiciousness which led him to intercept and decipher from time to time the despatches between the French Government and the French Ambassador in St. Petersburg. It was perhaps a realization of this suspiciousness which caused M. Poincaré so frequently to assure Russia that France would support her; these assurances are probably to be interpreted as efforts to strengthen the Franco-Russian alliance and tighten up the Triple Entente, rather than as incitements to bring about a European war by which France might recover Alsace-Lorraine.

On January 13, 1914, just as the Liman von Sanders Affair was about to be given a satisfactory solution, the

[304] Sazonov's report to the Tsar, Dec. 27/Jan. 9; Adamov, pp. 62-64. It is possible that Sazonov used this argument—that Russia was in danger of being politically isolated—in order to persuade the peace-loving Tsar to approve the discussion of plans for preparedness.

[305] Izvolski to Sazonov, Dec. 23/Jan. 5; M.F.R., p. 686; Siebert-Schreiner, p. 704; Stieve, IV, 17. Cf. also Izvolski to Sazonov, Dec. 17/30, 1913, and Jan. 2/15, 1914; M.F.R., pp. 478-481, 674; L.N., II, 218, 229; Stieve, III, 437; IV, 25-28; Siebert-Schreiner, p. 697.

Special Conference, which M. Sazonov had proposed several weeks earlier, finally met under the chairmanship of the Premier and Minister of Finance, M. Kokovtsev. There were present only the most important officials: the Ministers of War (Sukhomlinov), Navy (Grigorovitch), Foreign Affairs (Sazonov), the Chief of Staff (Zhilinski), and a couple of recording secretaries from the Near East Division of the Ministry of Foreign Affairs.[306] M. Sazonov reported that, according to the latest news, General Liman was about to be promoted to the highest rank in the Turkish army and would therefore give up the command of the Army Corps in Constantinople; this seemed good news, but the promotion was not yet an accomplished fact, and one should not therefore be too optimistic.

General Sukhomlinov energetically expressed the opinion that Turkey ought to be persuaded to abandon the German Military Mission altogether, and that all discussion about modifying the terms of its activity was a subordinate matter. Sazonov replied that any advice given in Constantinople would be without result unless accompanied by measures of compulsion such as he had proposed.

M. Kokovtsev, however, wise, peace-loving, and conciliatory, wished to put the brakes on any hasty aggressive action. Before proceeding to discuss measures of compulsion, he begged to lay stress on two matters of primary importance:

> 1. The German Government is looking for a way out of the situation created by Russia's demands. In this connection the Berlin Cabinet points to the necessity, in the interest of a satisfactory solution of the question, of Russia's avoidance of any categorical declaration, of the character of an ultimatum to Germany, as this might compel Ger-

[306] The Minutes of this Conference of Dec. 31/Jan. 13 were published by M. N. Pokrovski in Russian in 1919; in German in 1920 (*Drei Konferenzen*, pp. 32-45); and in English by Stieve, *Izvolski and the World War*, pp. 219-229.

many to adhere still more firmly to her standpoint, since regard must be had to the difficult position of the German Government in the face of public opinion in its own country.

2. The negotiations with the Berlin Cabinet, which have now been going on for two months, should be continued until the Russian Government is convinced that it is impossible to attain in this manner the object indicated.

M. Kokovtsev also pointed out that even the measures of compulsion ought to be taken only "in closest association with the other Powers of the Triple Entente. Before any decision is come to, the Russian Government must know to what extent it will receive the support of France, and whether active participation by Great Britain in the pressure on the Porte can be relied on."

M. Sazonov replied that he contemplated this, and added: "It seems still to be uncertain how far Great Britain would be prepared for energetic action. As regards France, the Russian Government can count on effectual support to the uttermost limit. M. Delcassé has assured the Minister, in the name of the French Foreign Minister, that France would go as far as Russia may wish."

M. Kokovtsev was of the opinion that any measures of compulsion such as the occupation of Asia Minor territory "would inevitably be followed by war with Germany, and put the question: "Is war with Germany desirable, and can Russia wage it?" In reply, Sazonov agreed with Kokovtsev "that in principle a war with Germany would be undesirable;" as to whether Russia could wage it, Sazonov "did not consider himself called upon to decide this." But "the Minister of War and the Chief of Staff declared categorically the complete readiness of Russia for a duel with Germany, not to mention one with Austria. Such a duel is, however, hardly likely; those Powers would be much more likely to have to deal with the Triple Entente." This categorical statement of the Russian militarists disposes of the argument that Russia did not want war in 1914 because they did not think her preparations were sufficiently complete.

M. Kokovtsev, in opposition to all the others, again insisted that an occupation of Trebizond or Bayazid would inevitably lead to intervention by Germany. But Sazonov thought this "would be a very effective measure, and might deter Germany from intervening." His views were shared by the Ministers of War and Navy and by the Chief of Staff. "M. Kokovtsev, who considered that a war at the present moment would be the greatest misfortune for Russia, expressed the opinion that it would be most undesirable to entangle Russia in a European conflict—a view which was shared by the other members of the Conference."

M. Kokovtsev finally summed up the sense of the meeting to the effect that negotiations were to be continued at Berlin to secure General Liman's removal from the command of troops in Constantinople; if it became quite clear that the negotiations would fail, measures of compulsion might be applied, if the Entente Powers were in agreement; but "Should Russia not be assured of the active participation of France and England in common steps with Russia, it does not seem possible to adopt measures of compulsion which might lead to a war with Germany." It was to secure the closer support of England, which was necessary to enable Russia to carry out her ambitions in the Near East, which made Sazonov redouble his efforts in the spring of 1914 to get more definite and binding obligations from Sir Edward Grey in the shape of an Anglo-Russian Naval Convention. Negotiations for this were soon begun, but had to be dropped when news of them leaked out.

From the minutes of this Special Conference one sees clearly that Sazonov sided fully with the militarists in being ready to adopt measures of compulsion to oust General Liman from the command of the Turkish Corps in Constan-

tinople. While not desiring war with Germany and preferring a diplomatic victory, he was nevertheless quite ready
to adopt measures which would probably lead to war with
Germany, provided he was sure of the support of the Entente. He was ready to use a threat of force, and "to
translate the threat into action," if the threat did not prove
to be an effective bluff. This was his attitude in July,
1914, and it led to war. In January, 1914, it did not lead
to war, because Germany made timely conciliatory concessions in the Liman von Sanders Affair, and because M.
Kokovtsev used his influence to prevent any over-hasty
provocative action on Russia's part, like the occupation of
Trebizond or Bayazid. This Conference reveals sharply the
contrast between Kokovtsev's moderate, conciliatory, and
restraining influence on the one hand, and, on the other,
the dangerous policy of military pressure urged by Sazonov
and the military and naval officials. Kokovtsev, as Minister
of Finance, looked at affairs more from a business man's
point of view than from that of a politician. Like Count,
Witte, he had an eye for economic, as well as purely political, considerations. He was not blinded by the diplomatist's shibboleths about Pan-Slav interests, Russia's
"prestige," and her "historic mission." He kept in view the
probable catastrophic effects which a European War would
have upon Russia's commerce, finance, and internal political structure. When he put bluntly the question, "Is a war
with Germany desirable?" the other members of the Conference were forced to agree with him that it was not. It
was therefore an incalculable misfortune for Russia and the
world that, a few days after this Conference, M. Kokovtsev
followed Count Witte into political retirement, and left the
field free to M. Sazonov and the Russian Pan-Slavs and
militarists.[307]

[307] For the intense nationalism of influential men like the President
of the Duma, see M. W. Rodzjanko, *Erinnerungen* (Berlin, 1926; Eng.

M. Kokovtsev's retirement from the Premiership gave rise to a rumor that he might be appointed Russian Ambassador at Paris, and that Izvolski would be transferred to Rome or some other post. This threw Izvolski into a panic. He abjectly besought Sazonov to prevent it:

> A transfer to Rome would involve me in the greatest financial difficulties, since every moving causes great expenditures, and the salary at Rome is 40,000 francs less than here. Dismissal through appointment to the Council of the Empire on the other hand would be for me a direct catastrophe. . . . You know my personal means are very limited, and that I have not yet put my son on his feet nor provided for my daughter. I am compelled to place especial value on my office. [If he lost it, he says, he would have to seek private employment with some bank.] After nearly forty years of diplomatic service, this would be very hard and bitter for me.

Izvolski's plea was effective. A few days later he thanked Sazonov effusively for having "prevented M. N. Kokovtsev's effort to sit himself in my seat." [308]

It is interesting to speculate on how the course of history might have been changed, if Kokovtsev had replaced Izvolski at Paris, or if he had still been able as Premier to exert a restraining influence at St. Petersburg in July,

trans., *The Reign of Rasputin,* London, 1927), *passim.* How strongly Russian diplomacy seems to have been influenced during the Liman von Sanders Affair and the spring of 1914 by the Grand Duke Nicholas, the militarists, and the Pan-Slav Press (which Sazonov apparently often encouraged yet always feared), is indicated in the shrewd and carefully balanced observations of Pourtalès, the German Ambassador in St. Petersburg (G.P., XXXVIII, 253 ff., 269 f., 293 ff.; XXXIX, 540-589, *passim*); Pourtalès, however, was not an alarmist; in fact, after July, 1914, he was criticized for not having been sufficiently so. On this subject in general, see also A. Fischel, *Der Panslawismus bis zum Weltkrieg* (Stuttgart, 1919); E. H. Wilcox, *Russia's Ruin* (New York, 1919); G. Frantz, *Russlands Eintritt in den Weltkrieg* (Berlin, 1924), and *Russland auf dem Wege zur Katastrophe* (Berlin, 1926).

[308] Izvolski to Sazonov, Jan. 30/Feb. 12, and Feb. 12/25, 1914; M.F.R., 488 f.; L.N., II, 238 f.; Stieve, IV, 52, 56.

1914. With his sweet reasonableness, his firm character, and his friendly personal relations with the Kaiser and the Berlin authorities, he might have been able to prevent the over-hasty steps which helped cause the World War. It was Russia's misfortune that she discarded real statesmen like Count Witte and M. Kokovtsev in favor of prestige diplomats like Izvolski and Sazonov.

Although the Liman von Sanders Affair had been happily settled in January, 1914, M. Sazonov, freed from M. Kokovtsev's pacific influence, continued his examination of preparedness plans, and even took up again the discussion of the aggressive project for a sudden seizure of the Straits by an armed landing force, which had been seriously contemplated in 1896 and 1912, but in both cases postponed because of lack of preparations.[309] At another Special Conference on February 21, 1914, presided over by himself, and including military and naval experts and also M. Giers, the active and aggressive Russian Ambassador at Constantinople, Sazonov called attention to his report of December 5, approved by the Tsar,

> that it was necessary to proceed without delay to the preparation of a program, elaborated in every direction, which should aim at the assurance in our favor of the historic question of the Straits. [Though admitting that at the moment political complications in the Balkans were not likely, Sazonov] expressed the firm conviction that should events result in the Straits slipping from Turkey's control, Russia could not permit any other Power to establish itself on their shores. Russia might thus be compelled to seize possession of them, in order then to secure in one shape or another a state of things along the Bosphorus and the Dardanelles corresponding to her interests. The success of this operation would depend in large degree on the rapidity with which it was carried out. . . . [He therefore asked for

[309] On the 1896 project, see above, note 13; and on that of 1912, Zakher, in *Krasnyi Arkhiv*, VI, 50-61, with Admiralty Staff reports.

a technical discussion of measures for expediting the mobilization and transportation of a sufficiently strong landing force; the strengthening of the Black Sea Fleet, so as to be able, jointly with the landing force, to occupy the Straits; and the construction of strategic railways in the Caucasus.]

[With reference to the possibility that Russia's seizure of the Straits might be opposed by Greece and Bulgaria, Sazonov remarked that] in view of their historical enmity and their present conflicting interests, there was a good deal of reason to suppose that, if one of these States came out as our enemy, the other would range itself on our side, so that they would cripple one another. . . . Sazonov said that it could not be assumed that our operations against the Straits could take place without a general European war, and that it was to be assumed that under such circumstances Serbia would direct all her forces against Austria-Hungary. . . . The favorable turn in Rumanian policy and public opinion, now to be observed, justified a certain doubt whether, in the event of our being at war with Austria, Rumania would actually come out against us. . . . In the event of our coming into collision with the Triple Alliance, Germany and Austria would send no troops towards the Straits, and, at the worst, Italy might send landing parties, though it would be dangerous for Italy to expose her frontiers to attack from France.[310]

Thus, according to Sazonov, the diplomatic situation seemed not unfavorable for landing an armed force to seize the Straits, even though it might lead to a collision with the Triple Alliance. But General Zhilinski, the Chief of Staff, "expressed the conviction that the struggle for Constantinople would hardly be possible without a general European war," in which case the troops which it was proposed to send to seize the Straits would be needed on the Western Front against Germany; success there would also

[310] Minutes of the Special Conference of Feb. 8/21, 1914; Pokrovski, *Drei Konferenzen,* p. 46 ff.; Stieve, *Isvolsky and the World War,* p. 232 ff.

mean success in the question of the Straits. M. Giers suggested that the troops for the landing expedition might be
taken from the Caucasus Front; but General Zhilinski and
General Danilov declared that this would be impracticable,
both because they would be needed in the Caucasus in case
of war with Turkey, and because, for technical reasons, they
could not be mobilized quickly. Both these military experts
were agreed that, with a battle proceeding or expected on
the Western Front, the diversion of considerable troops to
the Straits must be regarded as indefensible and impossible:
"The only good strategy is strong strategy. The war on our
Western Front would demand the utmost application of
all the forces of the State, and we could not dispense with
a single army corps to be left behind for special tasks. We
must direct our energies to ensuring success in the most
important theatre of war. With victory in this theatre,
we should secure favorable decisions in all secondary
questions." [311]

In spite of more optimistic arguments by the naval experts in favor of a landing expedition in the Straits, the
Chief of Staff seemed to express the general sense of the
Conference that such an expedition could only take place
during a crisis which would lead to a general European war
and that the troops for it would be needed on the Western
Front against Germany and Austria. Therefore no separate
landing expedition should be attempted for the present.
Nevertheless, everything should be done to prepare for
one. Accordingly, after a long discussion of the technical
details involved, the Conference decided to recommend to

[311] Minutes of the Special Conference of Feb. 8/21, 1914; Pokrovski,
Drei Konferenzen, p. 46 ff.; Stieve, *Isvolsky and the World War,* p. 232 ff.
This strategic point of view, always urged on the Russians by the
French (*cf.* A. Zaiontchkovski, *et al., Les Alliés contre la Russie,* Paris,
1926), and embodied in General Danilov's detailed plan of campaign
drawn up for the Russian General Staff in March, 1914 (printed by
Frantz, *Russlands Eintritt in den Weltkrieg,* pp. 112-162), was of course
the one actually put into operation four months later.

the Tsar a series of preparatory measures. These included increasing the strength and rapidity of mobilization of the expeditionary landing army; the gathering and subsidizing of adequate naval transports provided with sufficient collapsible horse-boxes and small boats for speedy embarkation and disembarkation; the increasing of the Black Sea Fleet by a second squadron of most modern and powerful battle cruisers, if possible, by the purchase of ships abroad; and the building of more strategic railways in the Caucasus, in order to speed up mobilization there, as a necessary part of "the measures required in preparation for our offensive on the Bosphorus." [312] The minutes of this Special Conference were laid before the Tsar on April 5, and received his entire approval.

The Duma also voted 110 million rubles to carry out the naval program for strengthening the Black Sea Fleet during the years 1914-1917.[313] As only 25 millions of this were to be spent in 1914, it would appear that no immediate expedition against Constantinople was intended unless something should occur to threaten the *status quo* and cause a general European war.

From the minutes of this Special Conference it appears that Sazonov contemplated the forcible seizure of the Straits. But the military experts regarded it as impracticable; they wished to reserve the troops for use in the main theatre of war against Germany and Austria. All were agreed, however, that Russia could not allow the Straits to fall into the hands of any other Power. Therefore the fullest preparatory measures must be taken for a landing expedition at the Straits in case European complications should afford an opportunity. This was regarded as probable in the future, but not as immediately imminent.

[312] Pokrovski, pp. 65-67; Stieve, pp. 244-246.
[313] Duma vote of Mar. 17/30, 1914; Zakher, in *Krasnyi Arkhiv*, VII,

SUMMARY

We may now sum up very briefly the main Balkan Problems.

The origin of the trouble lay in the progressive decay of the Ottoman Empire, which was no longer able to maintain control over the Christian subject nationalities. These had become filled with a natural desire for political freedom and national unity. But, owing to the events of past history, considerable sections of these peoples still lived under Turkish or Hapsburg rule, and could not fulfil their nationalistic aspirations except by the further disintegration of Turkey and the partial dismemberment of Austria. Hence the Balkan Wars of 1876-78 and 1912-13. Hence also the antagonism between Austria and Serbia, which grew steadily more acute, because each had a vital interest at stake— Austria to preserve her very existence as a State, Serbia to satisfy twentieth century ideals of political liberty and national unity.

As Turkey declined in power, Russia and Austria became increasingly jealous of each other's influence in the Balkans, Russia wishing to achieve her "historic mission," and Austria to prevent the danger threatening to her from too great Slav power on her southern frontier. Bismarck and the League of the Three Emperors, and later Russia's venture in the Far East, for many years prevented this rivalry from disturbing the peace of Europe. But with the ambitious aims of M. Izvolski and Count Aehrenthal the rivalry became acute through the outcome of the Buchlau Bargain. Aehrenthal succeeded in annexing Bosnia and Herzegovina, while Izvolski failed to open the Straits, because Austria had the support of Germany, but England was unwilling to accept Izvolski's one-sided proposal to open the Straits to Russian warships but not to those of the other Great Powers. Though the Annexation Crisis was settled without war, thanks to the solution proposed by Germany, it increased the antagonism between Austria and Serbia on the one hand, and between Austria and Russia on the other. Henceforth Russia encouraged Serbia to prepare for the future, when, aided by Russia, she could achieve a "Greater Serbia" at Austria's expense. Until Russia was ready, however, Serbia was to wait.

Having made the Racconigi Bargain with Italy, and believing that he could count on the support of the Triple Entente, Izvolski took advantage of the Tripolitan War to make a third diplomatic effort to open the Straits by means of the Charykov negotiations with Turkey. But again he failed largely on account of lack of support from France and direct opposition from England. Henceforth he came to the conclusion that his aim could be achieved only in connection with a general European war, and used all his efforts to strengthen and tighten the Triple Entente for this "inevitable" conflict.

Meanwhile MM. Neratov, Hartwig, and Nekliudov had used the unrest caused in the Balkans by the Tripolitan War to help bring about the Balkan League, its nominal purpose being the preservation of the *status quo,* but its practical effect being an encouragement to the Balkan States to open war on Turkey. Though the Great Powers, especially England and Germany, managed to prevent Europe from being involved in a general conflict, the Balkan Wars resulted in a universal increase of suspicion, hatred, intrigues, and uncertainty, not only among the Great Powers who increased their armaments, but among the Balkan States themselves, and especially in Austria and Serbia. Serbia, greatly embittered at her exclusion by the Powers from a political and economic outlet on the Adriatic, had found some compensation in Macedonia. But this involved Bulgaria's deadly hatred. Serbia therefore tightened her relations with Greece and Rumania under Russian patronage, partly as a protection against Bulgarian revenge and partly with a view to the future struggle as the "Piedmont" of the Balkans, against the hated Hapsburg rule. Though M. Pashitch and the Serbian civil authorities did not want or plan war in 1914, they tolerated an agitation which contributed to a series of assassinations which culminated in the tragedy of Sarajevo. Austria meanwhile became more and more alarmed at the dangers threatening her very existence: the "Greater Serbia" agitation within and without her frontiers, the "desertion" of Rumania, and the closer ties which Russia was establishing with these two countries whose nationalist aspirations could only be satisfied through the dismemberment of Austria-Hungary. Whether Austria *could* have averted the danger from the "Greater Serbia" and "Greater Rumania" irredentist agitation, by giving democratic and reasonably liberal rights to her Slav and Rumanian subjects, or by some form of "trialism," is a hypothetical question to be touched upon later; at any rate she *did* not do so. Instead she chose to see her salvation in a war in which Serbia would be reduced in power by having to cede territory to Bulgaria, Rumania, and Albania. Several times Austria was ready to wage such a war on Serbia, but was held back either by Germany, as in July, 1913, or by concessions on the part of Serbia, as in March, 1909, and October, 1913. But in July, 1914, as will be seen later, Austria welcomed the opportunity for a localized war on Serbia afforded by the assassination of the Austrian Heir to the Throne.

M. Sazonov, though caring little for the Serbs themselves, and leaving them in the lurch in crucial moments, nevertheless encouraged and supported them at other times as an outpost of Slavdom in the Balkans and as an asset in a future war with Austria. Desiring peace, but fearing the power and criticism of the Russian Pan-Slavs and militarists, M. Sazonov was anxious to fulfil Russia's "historic mission." Observing Izvolski's failures to open the Straits by peaceful diplomatic means and his own failure to coerce Germany into an instant modification of General Liman's command at Constantinople, owing in each case chiefly to Sir Edward Grey's attitude, the Russian Foreign Minister came to the conclusion that he could succeed in his Balkan aims only as a result of "European complications." While Izvolski had attempted the more modest task of merely opening the Straits to Russian warships, Sazonov wanted to achieve the wider Pan-Slav "historic mission" of obtaining possession of the Straits and controlling Constantinople. It was because the Liman von Sanders Mission seemed to lessen the likelihood of this that Sazonov was so alarmed by it. Hence his proposal of "measures of compulsion" to force Turkey to abandon it; these, however, were not put into effect, owing to Germany's timely concessions and M. Kokovtsev's restraining influence. Hence also Sazonov's contemplation of a landing force to seize the Straits, which the military experts declared was impracticable at the moment but should be prepared for in case of European complications in the future. During the spring of 1914, together with M. Izvolski and President Poincaré, he worked to tighten the bonds with England by negotiations for an Anglo-Russian Naval Convention, in order that, when the "inevitable" war broke out, the solidarity of the Triple Entente should be more perfect than on former occasions. Consequently, if a new crisis arose, Germany and Austria would have to yield—or fight a war in which the superior forces would be on the side of the Triple Entente. In July, 1914, with the restraining hand of Kokovtsev removed, Sazonov believed that this Entente solidarity was virtually assured, when the murder of the Archduke and the Austrian ultimatum caused the "European complications" by means of which he calculated that Russia could finally achieve her "historic mission."

Turkey and the Balkan States were in unstable equilibrium. An inherent opposition of interests necessarily caused persistent enmity between Greece and Turkey, between Turkey and Russia, and between Austria and Serbia. But Bulgaria and Rumania were pursuing opportunist policies, and were ready to side with whichever group of the Great Powers seemed likely to prove the stronger and offer the greatest gains. No Power ever wants to yield on a matter of prestige, but this Balkan situation made an additional reason why neither France, Russia, Germany nor Austria was at first willing to yield in the Austro-Serbian conflict of July, 1914—it might have a determining effect on the policy of Bulgaria and Rumania. For several years it had been recognized that a strong Balkan bloc would have an influence in a general European war almost equal to that of a Great Power. Hence, in the spring of 1914, Russia was seeking to win Rumania and build up such a bloc including Serbia and Greece, while Austria in turn was preparing to form a counter-bloc with Bulgaria and Turkey. Such was the situation when the shots at Sarajevo precipitated the Austro-Serbian conflict and caused a crisis involving the prestige and power of the Triple Alliance and Triple Entente.

The writer of these lines does not believe that the World War was "inevitable." But he is quite ready to admit that, of all the major conflicts of interest which have been alleged as making it "inevitable," the Balkan problems were those most nearly incapable of a peaceful solution.

APPENDIX

FIFTH TREATY OF THE TRIPLE ALLIANCE

BETWEEN AUSTRIA-HUNGARY, THE GERMAN EMPIRE, AND ITALY

VIENNA, DECEMBER 5, 1912 *

THEIR Majesties the Emperor of Austria, King of Bohemia, etc., and Apostolic King of Hungary, the Emperor of Germany, King of Prussia, and King of Italy, firmly resolved to assure to Their States the continuation of the benefits which the maintenance of the Triple Alliance guarantees to them, from the political point of view as well as from the monarchical and social point of view, and wishing with this object to prolong the duration of this Alliance, concluded on May 20, 1882, renewed a first time by the Treaties of February 20, 1887, a second time by the Treaty of May 6, 1891, and a third time by the Treaty of June 28, 1902, have agreed upon the following Articles:

ARTICLE I. The High Contracting Parties mutually promise peace and friendship, and will enter into no alliance or engagement directed against any one of their States.

They engage to proceed to an exchange of ideas on political and economic questions of a general nature which may arise, and they further promise one another mutual support within the limits of their own interests.

ARTICLE II. In case Italy, without direct provocation on her part, should be attacked by France for any reason whatsoever, the two other Contracting Parties shall be bound to lend help and assistance with all their forces to the Party attacked.

* Pribram, I, p. 101 (Amer. ed. I, p. 245).

This same obligation shall devolve upon Italy in case of any aggression without direct provocation by France against Germany.

Article III.   If one, or two, of the High Contracting Parties, without direct provocation on their part, should chance to be attacked and to be engaged in a war with two or more Great Powers nonsignatory to the present Treaty, the *casus foederis* will arise simultaneously for all the High Contracting Parties.

Article IV.   In case a Great Power nonsignatory to the present Treaty should threaten the security of the states of one of the High Contracting Parties, and the threatened Party should find itself forced on that account to make war against it, the two others bind themselves to observe towards their Ally a benevolent neutrality.   Each of them reserves to itself, in this case, the right to take part in the war, if it should see fit, to make common cause with its Ally.

Article V.   If the peace of one of the High Contracting Parties should chance to be threatened under the circumstances foreseen by the preceding Articles, the High Contracting Parties shall take counsel together in ample time as to the military measures to be taken with a view to eventual cooperation.

They engage, henceforth, in all cases of common participation in a war, to conclude neither armistice, nor peace, nor treaty, except by common agreement among themselves.

Article VI.   Germany and Italy, having in mind only the maintenance, so far as possible, of the territorial status quo in the Orient, engage to use their influence to forestall on the Ottoman coasts and islands in the Adriatic and the Aegean Seas any territorial modification which might be injurious to one or the other of the Powers signatory to the present Treaty.   To this end, they will communicate to one another all information of a nature to enlighten each other mutually concerning their own dispositions, as well as those of other Powers.

Article VII.   Austria-Hungary and Italy, having in mind only the maintenance, so far as possible, of the territorial status quo in the Orient, engage to use their influence to forestall any territorial modification which might be injurious to one or the other of the Powers signatory to the present Treaty. To this end, they shall communicate to one another all information of a nature to enlighten each other mutually concerning their own dispositions, as well as those of other Powers. However, if, in the course of events, the maintenance of the status quo in the regions of the Balkans or of the Ottoman coasts and islands in the Adriatic and in the Aegean Sea should become impossible, and if, whether in consequence of the action of a third Power or otherwise, Austria-Hungary or Italy should find themselves under the necessity of modifying it by a temporary or permanent occupation on their part, this occupation shall take place only after a previous agreement between the two Powers, based upon the principle of a reciprocal compensation for every advantage, territorial or other, which each of them might obtain beyond the present status quo, and giving satisfaction to the interests and well founded claims of the two Parties.

ARTICLE VIII. The stipulations of Articles VI and VII shall apply in no way to the Egyptian question, with regard to which the High Contracting Parties preserve respectively their freedom of action, regard being always paid to the principles upon which the present Treaty rests.

ARTICLE IX. Germany and Italy engage to exert themselves for the maintenance of the territorial status quo in the North African regions on the Mediterranean, to wit, Cyrenaica, Tripolitania, and Tunisia. The Representatives of the two Powers in these regions shall be instructed to put themselves into the closest intimacy of mutual communication and assistance.

If unfortunately, as a result of a mature examination of the situation, Germany and Italy should both recognize that the maintenance of the status quo has become impossible, Germany engages, after a formal and previous agreement, to support Italy in any action in the form of occupation or other taking of guaranty which the latter should undertake in these same regions with a view to an interest of equilibrium and of legitimate compensation.

It is understood that in such an eventuality the two Powers

would seek to place themselves likewise in agreement with England.

ARTICLE X. If it were to happen that France should make a move to extend her occupation, or even her protectorate or her sovereignty, under any form whatsoever, in the North African territories, and that in consequence thereof, Italy, in order to safeguard her position in the Mediterranean, should feel that she must herself undertake action in the said North African territories, or even have recourse to extreme measures in French territory in Europe, the state of war which would thereby ensue between Italy and France would constitute *ipso facto*, on the demand of Italy, and at the common charge of Germany and Italy, the *casus foederis* foreseen by Articles II and V of the present Treaty, as if such an eventuality were expressly contemplated therein.

ARTICLE XI. If the fortunes of any war undertaken in common against France by the two Powers should lead Italy to seek for territorial guaranties with respect to France for the security of the frontiers of the Kingdom and of her maritime position, as well as with a view to stability and to peace, Germany will present no obstacle thereto, and, if need be, and in a measure compatible with circumstances, will apply herself to facilitating the means of attaining such a purpose.

ARTICLE XII. The High Contracting Parties mutually promise secrecy as to the contents of the present Treaty.

ARTICLE XIII. The Signatory Powers reserve the right of subsequently introducing, in the form of a Protocol and of a common agreement, the modifications of which the utility should be demonstrated by circumstances.

ARTICLE XIV. The present Treaty shall remain in force for the space of six years, dating from the expiration of the Treaty now in force; but if it has not been denounced one year in advance by one or another of the High Contracting Parties, it shall remain in force for the same duration of six more years.

ARTICLE XV. The ratifications of the present Treaty shall be exchanged at Vienna within a period of a fortnight, or sooner if may be.

In witness whereof the respective Plenipotentiaries have

signed the present Treaty and have affixed thereto the seal of their arms.

Done at Vienna, in triplicate, the fifth day of the month of December, one thousand nine hundred and twelve.

L. S.	Berchtold
L. S.	von Tschirschky
L. S.	Avarna

SUPPLEMENTARY NOTES

I, 3, note 3. Mr. Gooch's *Recent Revelations of European Diplomacy,* (London, 1927), are brought nearly up to date by supplementary volumes (London, 1928, 1929).

I, 23. Ex-President Poincaré's extraordinary capacity for historical work in addition to all his political activities, and his readiness to reply to his critics, is illustrated in a little book: *Les Responsabilités de la Guerre: Quatorze Questions par René Gerin; Quatorze Réponses par Raymond Poincaré* (Paris, 1930). M. Gerin propounded fourteen shrewd questions to M. Poincaré, begging him to answer them, and promising that, if he did so, he, Gerin, would refrain from making any counter-replies. M. Poincaré accepted the challenge, and set forth his fourteen answers in some one hundred and fifty pages. Though he contributes a little new information, his material is for the most part drawn from his already published memoirs. The weak points in his answers have been thoroughly dissected by G. von Jagow, G. Frantz, A. von Wegerer, and M. Montgelas, in KSF, VIII, 601-665, 705-730, July, August 1930. *Cf.* also the criticism of Poincaré by A. Bach, *Poincaré und der Kriegsausbruch, 1914* (Berlin, 1929); and the volume of Demartial quoted above, p. 6.

I, 47-49. During the past two years many writers have become increasingly aware of the importance of the influence of the Press as one of the causes of the World War, and have devoted monographs to various aspects of the subject. Among the most important of these may be noted: G. Arbouin, *Les Nations d'après leurs Journaux: Petit Essai de Psychologie de la Presse* (Paris, 1917); I. Grüning, *Die russische öffentliche Meinung und ihre Stellung zu den Grossmächten 1878-1914* (Berlin, 1919); R. Ibbeken, *Das aussenpolitische Problem Staat und Wirtschaft in der deutschen Reichspolitik 1880-1914* (Schleswig, 1928); "Irenäus" (pseud. August Stein), *Es War Alles Ganz Anders* (2nd ed., Frankfurt, 1922); A. Jux, *Der Kriegsschrecken des Frühjahrs 1914 in der europäischen Presse* (Berlin, 1929); S. M. von Propper, *Was nicht in die Zeitung kam: Erinnerungen des Chefredakteurs der "Birschewyja Wedomosti"* (Frankfurt, 1929); C. Schoen, *Der "Vorwärts" und die Kriegserklärung* (Berlin, 1929); W. Zimmermann, *Die Englische Presse zum Ausbruch des Weltkrieges* (Charlottenburg, 1928); and in general, O. Groth, *Die Zeitung* (3 vols., Manheim, 1927-30), especially, II, 192-236. See also the present writer's brief account of the pre-war British and German Press in his review of the sixth volume of the *British Documents* in *Current History,* Oct. 1930.

I, 80, note 37. See also Italicus, *Italiens Dreibundpolitik, 1870-1896* (Munich, 1928); the early pages of W. L. Langer's excellent analysis of the general European situation after 1878, *The Franco-Russian Alliance*

(Cambridge, 1929), with an extensive bibliography; the thoughtful survey of B. Molden, "Das deutsch-österreichische Bündnis und der grossdeutsche Gedanke," in KSF, VIII, 312-323, April 1930; and L. D. Steefel's review of recent Bismarck literature in the *Journal of Modern History*, II, 74-95, March 1930.

I, 123, note 36. Later on, to be sure, after England had become the friend of France, the English Foreign Office was inclined to accept the French assertion that the initiative in the discussions for intervention in the Boer War had come from Germany and not from Russia; B.D., III, 411-12, 425-6, 432-3, 436-7; and especially VI, 204-6.

I, 129-141. On the negotiations for an Anglo-German alliance at the turn of the century, see: Lord Newton, *Lord Lansdowne, A Biography* (N. Y. and London, 1929), ch. vi, who concludes that "The failure of the negotiations in 1901 may be described as a turning-point in the history of the world, and will doubtless, provide a subject of endless speculation as to what would have occurred had they ended favorably; but one thing is certain, and that is that William II. would have been almost intolerable as an ally" (p. 208); Willy Becker, *Fürst Bülow und England* (Greifswald, 1929), who lays the blame for failure on Bülow and Holstein (cf. the review by W. Frauendienst in KSF, VIII, 532-9, June 1930); G. Ritter, *Die Legende von der verschmähten englischen Freundschaft* (Freiburg, 1929); the review of both Meinecke and Ritter by O. Becker, in the *Deutsche Literaturzeitung*, 1929, Heft 19, p. 903 ff.; and the article of G. Roloff, "Die Bündnisverhandlungen zwischen Deutschland und England, 1898-1901," in KSF, VII, 1167-1222, Dec., 1929.

I, 152-192. On the Anglo-French Entente of 1904 and the First Morocco Crisis of 1905-06, the full documents from the British side are given in B.D., II and III, "The Anglo-Japanese Alliance and the Franco-British Entente" and "The Testing of the Entente, 1904-06 (London, 1927-28). Excellent accounts are to be found in Lord Newton's *Lord Lansdowne* (N. Y. and London, 1929), chs. x, xiv, and p. 488; in Mr. Harold Nicolson's life of his father, *Lord Carnock* (London, 1930), chs. vi, vii; and especially in the detailed and scholarly volume of Mr. Eugene N. Anderson, *The First Moroccan Crisis, 1904-1906* (Chicago, 1930).

I, 181. For an interesting account of the Dogger Bank Affair, by one who was behind the scenes and perceived Delcassé's effort to turn the affair into a stepping-stone for an Anglo-French-Russian Triple Entente, see Baron Taube, *La Politique Russe d'avant-Guerre* (Paris, 1928), pp. 1-43; and for the documents on the British side of the affair, B.D., IV, 5-41.

I, 209 f. What is said at this point of Sir Edward Grey's reasons for failing to consult and inform the Cabinet concerning the Anglo-French military "conversations" and for his preferring them to any other more definite or written agreement seems to be confirmed by an interesting Memorandum of a Permanent Under-Secretary, Sir T. H. Sanderson. In a Memorandum of Feb. 2, 1906, giving a summary of a conversation which he had just had with M. Paul Cambon concerning the Grey-Cambon "conversations," Sanderson said unofficially and privately to Cambon:

In the first place, in the course of my experience, which was a pretty long one, I knew of no instance of any secret Agreement by the British Government which pledged them further than that if a certain policy agreed upon with another Power were in any way menaced, the two Powers should consult as to the course to be taken. That I thought was the limit to which the Government could properly bind itself without in some way making Parliament aware of the obligations that it was incurring.

Secondly, it was a maxim which had been impressed upon me by several statesmen of great eminence that it was not wise to bring before a Cabinet the question of a course to be pursued in hypothetical cases which had not arisen. A discussion on the subject invariably gave rise to divergences of opinion on questions of principle, whereas in a concrete case unanimity would very likely be secured. [And Grey here noted on the margin: "I am glad this point was so well pointed out to M. Cambon."] M. Cambon observed that this view was a perfectly just one.

Thirdly, I told him that I thought that if the Cabinet were to give a pledge which would morally bind the country to go to war in certain circumstances, and were not to mention this pledge to Parliament, and if at the expiration of some months the country suddenly found itself pledged to war in consequence of this assurance, the case would be one which would justify impeachment, and which might even result in that course unless at the time the feeling of the country were very strongly in favor of the course to which the Government was pledged (B.D., III, 184 f.).

I, 213. The Anglo-Belgian military conversations began on Jan. 18, 1906, upon instructions from General Grierson, between the English Military Attaché, Col. Barnardiston, and the Belgian Chief of Staff, General Ducarne. They had the express sanction of the Foreign Ministers of both countries, as well as of the military authorities. They quickly led to an agreement for the landing of 100,000 British troops on the continent for the defense of Belgium (cf. B.D., III, 186-203; and Carl Hosse, *Die englisch-belgischen Aufmarschpläne gegen Deutschland vor dem Weltkrieg*, Vienna, 1930; Hosse prints for the first time interesting details of the technical railway schedules worked out for the British; he uses photographs of Belgian documents which were taken by the Germans during the war, but restored after the Treaty of Versailles). General Wilson, who succeeded General Grierson as Chief of Military Operations in August, 1910, arranged with Belgium and France for the rapid transport of 160,000 British, who were to take a position on the French left wing. In 1912 there were some doubts for a while about Belgium's readiness to cooperate with the French and British (cf. D.D.F., 3e Série, I, No. 522), and the British Foreign Office, in spite of its obligation to observe Belgian neutrality, appears to have considered the question of marching British troops into the little country, without invitation and even against Belgium's consent, "in order to meet the approach of German troops on the other side" (Harold Nicolson, *Lord Carnock*, London, 1930, p. 399). In 1913 Belgium increased her army and was again ready to enter into close military relations with the French and British at the outbreak of the war. For a good summary of the Anglo-Belgian military conversations, see A. Bach, "Die 'conventions anglo-belges' im Lichte neuer Dokumente," in KSF, VIII, 547-560, June, 1930.

I, 214-222. The negotiations for the Anglo-Russian Entente of 1907 can now be followed in great detail in the fourth volume of the *British Documents*, "The Anglo-Russian Rapprochment, 1903-7" (London, 1929). From them it appears that as early as November, 1903, King Edward had "spoken very earnestly" to Count Benckendorff, the Russian Ambassador, during the latter's visit to Windsor, "His Majesty expressing his desire that an attempt should be made to establish a better understanding between the two Governments" (B.D., IV, 186). For King Edward's conversation with Izvolski on the same subject at Copenhagen in April, 1904, see *ibid.*, p. 188 ff. The impression mentioned by the present writer (I, 218, note 210), that the bridging of the gulf between Russia and England was owing apparently more to the eagerness and pressure of the British, rather than the Russian, Foreign Office, is amply confirmed in the recent British documents (cf. B.D., IV, 183, 188, 195 ff., 232, 237, 400, 410 ff.). A delightful and authoritative account of the long negotiations which led to what came to be known as the "Triple Entente" is to be found in Mr. Harold Nicolson's *Lord Carnock* (London, 1930), chs. viii, ix; he notes (p. 308) that his father, Sir Arthur Nicolson, who conducted the negotiations in St. Petersburg, was requested by Sir Edward Grey to discontinue his habit of using "in official telegrams and despatches the expression 'triple entente' when referring to the joint action of England, France and Russia. The expression is one which is no doubt convenient, but if it appeared in a Parliamentary Bluebook it would be assumed to have some special official meaning and might provoke inconvenient comment or inquiry."

I, 229. The British Government's sudden change of attitude in April, 1903, in refusing to participate in the construction of the Bagdad Railway, is ascribed by Willy Becker, *Fürst Bülow und England* (Greifswald, 1929), to Lansdowne's new policy of an entente with France. But the material in the British documents, private information in my possession, and Lord Newton's *Lord Lansdowne* (N. Y. and London, 1929), p. 253 f., seem to confirm my statement that it was the outcry in the British Press and Parliament which caused the British Government, against Landowne's own better judgment, to make the *volte-face* and to refuse British participation. Possibly also underground Russian influences were at work against British participation, for Russia worked persistently to block or delay the construction of the Bagdad Railway.

I, 230-232. For the details of later British obstruction to the building of the Bagdad Railway during the years 1905-10, so long as Germany did not consent to Grey's conditions that the negotiations must be *à quatre* (that is, include also England's friends, Russia and France) and that Turkey ought not to be burdened with further kilometric guarantees, see the documents in B.D., VI, 91-105, 325-433. The British insistence on negotiations *à quatre* was partly owing to the expectation of being able to get a better bargain from Germany, and partly out of political deference to Russia; but Russia showed small gratitude for this deference when she made a separate bargain without England in the Potsdam Agreements. Besides preventing the Germans from getting Turkish money for the construction of the Bagdad Railway by refusing British consent to an increase of the Turkish customs, (cf. B.D., V, 168 ff., 199, 208 f., 502; and

VI, 325-433 *passim*), other British suggestions for thwarting the Germans were rival railways: an Anglo-Russian line from the Persian Gulf through Persia toward Russia, which "would completely crowd out the Bagdad Railway" and "reduce it to a purely local railway" (B.D., VI, 359); and a British line from Bagdad and the Persian Gulf by way of the Euphrates Valley to Damascus and the Mediterranean; a concession for this was demanded from Turkey (*ibid.*, 371 ff.).

I, 237, note 20. For British fears and suspicions in regard to the German navy in 1907 and 1908, with summaries of the German Press, and with long reports from the British Naval Attaché in Berlin concerning the German navy, see the full details now available in B.D., VI, 1-226. A brief review of these documents, so far as concerns the mischievous influence of the German and British Press, may be found in the present writer's article in *Current History* for Oct., 1930.

Many English officials even believed that Germany was secretly making plans for the invasion of England. One of the most suspicious of these officials was Sir Eyre Crowe. As Senior Clerk in the Foreign Office it fell to him to write the first long comments on the despatches as they came in from Germany's diplomatic representatives abroad. Inevitably his hostile dissection of the reports from Germany greatly influenced Sir Edward Grey and the other officials who next read them, and who generally endorsed with brief comments Crowe's long criticisms. Crowe, whose mother and wife were both German, appears to have been accepted as an infallible authority on Germany. But unfortunately he was prone to accept baseless gossip as gospel truth. For instance, he cites in 1908 three alleged circumstances as evidence that Germany was making plans for the invasion of England. (1) "So great an authority as Moltke regarded the invasion of England as practicable. It is certain that the Great General Staff at Berlin is of the same opinion." (2) "It is only 2 or 3 years ago [in reality *seven* years earlier, in 1901] that Baron von Edelsheim then a captain of that Staff published, with the authorization of his chief, a pamphlet dealing in detail with the measures to be taken for that purpose." (3) "Some 2 or 3 years ago, I think, the Emperor with his own hand made a number of blue pencil corrections or alterations in the designs of 2 new liners [of the Hamburg-American Line], then about to be built, because His Majesty maintained that the designs as submitted to him would not permit of these ships taking their allotted part in the transport of 2 divisions to England" (B.D., VI, 117). The statements in regard to Moltke, the General Staff, and the Emperor are untrue; and Edelsheim was dismissed from the General Staff because he had published his pamphlet *without the approval of his chief*, General von Schlieffen, and because the views expressed in it were *in contradiction* with those of the General Staff. Something has been said above of the malign influence of Herr von Holstein in the Wilhelmstrasse; that of Sir Eyre Crowe in Downing Street deserves further attention.

I, 256-264. For the impressions of Sir Edward Goschen, the British Ambassador in Berlin, in regard to Bülow's resignation, and in regard to his successor, Bethmann-Hollweg, and Kiderlen-Wächter, see B.D., VI, 276 ff.

I, 291. The close relations between the English and French military authorities during the Agadir Crisis are reflected in the confidential report of Aug. 24, 1911, of the British Military Attaché in Paris, Colonel Fairholme, of his conversation with General Joffre:

General Joffre said that he and his Staff have been, and still are, hard at work settling the details of their plans of campaign, which, he stated, will be ready in every particular in a few days' time.

The General went on to discuss the strategical problem.

The one unknown factor is whether the Germans mean to come through Belgium or not. "I wish I knew that," he observed, "and I wish I knew that they intend doing so; it would be better for us." . . .

The new Chief attaches the very greatest importance to the co-operation of a British expeditionary force, which concentrating somewhere between Douai and Cambrai, and falling on the right flank of the German advance, might produce great, and even decisive, results. But it would have to be sent early in the day; its intervention, for instance, on the 18th day of the French mobilization, might not prove a bit too soon. . . .

"In any case," he said, "Germany must pour a large force into Alsace-Lorraine, as, if they allowed us to gain a footing there, the populations of both provinces would rise. *This we know for certain.* And then every possible difficulty would be created for their transport, etc." . . .

I gathered that, if the Germans should advance in force *via* Belgium, the French plan would be to hold them in check on that flank, and to attack vigorously on Alsace and Lorraine. . . .

On my mentioning Italy, the General said very positively, "Italy will make no move. Her interests lie on our side, not on that of Germany and Austria." (B.D., VI, 643 f.)

Harold Nicolson, in the life of his father (*Lord Carnock,* p. 346 ff.) indicates that British preparations for war in the late summer of 1911 were far more advanced than was realized by British public opinion, and that the state of "war preparedness" was not relaxed until September 22, on receipt of news from Berlin that Kiderlen-Wächter was weakening.

I, 293-299. For English comments on the *Daily Telegraph* affair, see B.D., VI, 201-226; and for the English side of the long but futile negotiations for some kind of an agreement to lessen the growing tension over Anglo-German naval rivalry during the years 1909-12, *ibid.,* 227-324, 434-665. The official attitude of the members of the British Foreign Office on them may be well summed up in their "Minutes" on a telegram from Sir Edward Goschen, the British Ambassador in Berlin, to Sir Edward Grey on May 9, 1911 (*ibid.,* 622 f.):

MINUTES.

The German government now at last confess what we suspected from the outset to be the case: they have definitely withdrawn from their promise to submit proposals for a reduction of armaments, on the ground that they consider any such scheme impossible. In view of the repeated public utterances of high German officials, including successive Chancellors, and of the Emperor himself, it is clear that they never did believe that they could put forward such proposals. Their statement to the contrary was used, as was pointed out here at the time, for the purpose of leading H[is] M[ajesty's] G[overnment] on to the conclusion of a general Anglo-German agreement, such as they knew Great Britain was unwilling even to discuss.

They have gone some considerable way in gaining their point. They have induced H[is] M[ajesty's] G[overnment] in the first instance to abandon their original attitude which was that no discussion of a reduction of armaments was of any use if the existing German naval programme was to be carried out in its integrity. The Chancellor on the contrary explained that any negotiation would have to start from the basis of the actual completion of that programme. We abandoned our position, and continued the discussion.

Germany insisted that before a naval understanding could be thought of, there must be a general Anglo-German agreement of a political nature, which would preclude the possibility of war between the two countries in any circumstances. The essential feature of such an agreement was that not only would the two countries refrain from ever attacking the other, but they would undertake each to remain neutral in any war in which the other was engaged. The object of this clearly is to allow Germany to deal with other Powers, such as France and Russia, without any fear of British intervention. . . .

With the view of assuring the success of this negotiation, the German government, being always farsighted in these matters, have for a considerable time carefully laid their plans for leading H[is] M[ajesty's] G[overnment] further on in the same road. The means employed have been those placed at their disposal by the organization of their press bureau, the direct and indirect influence they exercise over the British press, and personal connection, through the Berlin Foreign Office, and through the German ambassador in London, with the leaders of the so-called "pacifist" propaganda in this country. By these means the German gov[ernmen]t have encouraged, if not created, over here an agitation—to which nothing in practice corresponds in Germany—in favour of an Anglo-German understanding as such, of the exact purport of which its promoters and supporters have not the shadowiest notion.

Finally, in order to put still further pressure on H[is] M[ajesty's] G[overnment], they have so played their cards that, if the negotiations come to nothing, they will be able to say,—and they will say it loudly and have it re-echoed throughout Europe—that it is all the fault of H[is] M[ajesty's] G[overnment]. . . .

We are fast drifting back into the position which was summarized in the memorandum of Jan[uary] 1st, 1907. [Cf. B.D., III, 397-420, *App.* A.] Now again, as on former occasions, the German gov[ernmen]t after a period of much unfriendliness on their part, come to woo us with assurances that if we will only do what they wish, it will lead to peace, the end of all friction, and the definite establishment of Anglo-German friendship. This time, if we fall into the same trap, the consequences will be still more serious than before. We shall have to reckon not only with renewed German unfriendliness, and further German demands, passed by the added weight of a strengthened Germany, but we run the imminent risk of practically breaking up the *entente* with France and Russia. . . .

E. A. C[rowe, Senior Clerk, Foreign Office].

The "tempo of construction" proposal has turned out as shadowy as was expected.

Whatever unfavourable comment our failure to conclude an Agreement may expose us to, an agreement which leaves the naval question unsettled would, I believe, command still less support.

W. L[angley, Assistant Under-Secretary of State].

Sir Eyre Crowe's minute is an admirable summary of what has passed and merits the most careful consideration. I entirely agree with his views and am also of his opinion that the object of the German Gov[ernmen]t is to lay on one side the naval agreement and lead us into "a general understanding." We have hitherto resisted, and rightly resisted, going further with Germany as regards an understanding than we have done with France and Russia. I trust that we shall firmly maintain this attitude. . . . A. N[icolson, Permanent under-Secretary of State].

It would be well to have the papers put together, which give the history of the question and will bring out the points of Sir E. Crowe's minute. I remember one occasion on which Count Metternich reproached us because the Prime Minister had stated in Parliament that there could be no question of Germany altering her naval law and had thereby ignored the offer to reduce the "tempo." I am sure I recorded this conversation and it should be included in the collection of papers. [Cf. B.D., VI, 496-7].

The last decision of the Gov[ernmen]t was that an agreement under which Germany undertook not to increase her naval programme might be worth consideration. From the point of view of naval expenditure the German reply is most unsatisfactory. On the other hand the last paragraph apparently makes it easier for us to avoid being entangled in separate political negotiations with Germany to which other Powers are not parties.

We must wait for the full text, which I will circulate to the Cabinet when received.

E. G[rey, Secretary of State].

I, 299-312. On the Haldane Mission itself, see B.D., VI, 666-761. The "Minutes" quoted above help to explain why it was foredoomed to failure.

I, 317-8. Volume VII of *British Documents,* which will deal with Anglo-French relations during the Agadir Crisis and the Haldane Mission, has not yet (June, 1930) been published. But Volume VI, covering Anglo-German naval and political negotiations from 1907 to 1912, confirms my view of the dubiousness of Izvolski's allegation that Poincaré's intervention prevented the success of the Haldane Mission. Long before Poincaré became Prime Minister, it is perfectly clear from numerous letters and "Minutes" that Grey, Nicolson, and Crowe were determined to make no "political understanding" or neutrality agreement with Germany which would in any way limit England's freedom to aid France. As Sir Arthur Nicolson wrote to Lord Hardinge on April 19, 1911:

I sincerely hope that we shall keep clear of any understanding which would tie our hands in any way, or which would in the slightest degree affect our understanding with France and Russia. I hope that our Government now fully realize that the aim of Germany in these negotiations is to smash up, as far as she is able to do, the Triple *Entente* and that her chief object is to isolate France as much as possible (B.D., VI, 621).

After the failure of the Haldane Mission, Nicolson wrote to Goschen: "I need hardly tell you that I feel great relief at the idea that the Formula question is in process of interment; it has always been my dream to be on cordial relations with Germany *without* any definite political understanding, and if, as I hope, the recent conversations have that result no one will be more pleased than I" (B.D., VI, 750). And Grey summed up the Foreign Office view tersely to Nicolson: "Although we cannot bind ourselves under all circumstances to go to war with France against Germany, we shall also certainly not bind ourselves to Germany not to assist France" (BD., VI, 751).

Although Grey was meticulous in keeping the French fully informed of all the negotiations, the French were nevertheless a little nervous (*cf.* B.D., VI, 664, 669 f., 675, 687 f., 690 f., 726 ff.). This nervousness of the French naturally confirmed Grey in his determination not to make any agreement with Germany which might increase French nervousness.

I, 319-20. Mr. Harold Nicolson, in the recent life of his father, draws a very interesting contrast between the attitude of Sir Arthur Nicolson and that of Sir Edward Grey in regard to the Entente with France (*Lord Carnock*, p. 330 ff.; *cf.* also B.D., VI, 739, 747-751). He says:

He [Sir Arthur Nicolson] desired, above all, that the solidarity of the Triple Entente should be patent and proclaimed. He regarded the existing arrangements with France and Russia as possessing all the disadvantages, and none of the benefits, of an alliance. He feared that the Ententes were sufficiently binding to encourage people in St. Petersburg and Paris, but not sufficiently binding to discourage people in Berlin. He considered that in this vital matter the indolent British indulgence in half-measures was not only dangerous but unfair. Unfair to Germany: unfair to France and Russia: unfair, above all, to British public opinion. He urged Sir Edward Grey, in season and out of season, to make it clear to the world exactly where we stood.

The Secretary of State, somewhat naturally, was annoyed by this persistence. It is always irritating for a gentleman in a false position to be assured by other gentlemen that his position is false. And from 1906 onwards Sir Edward Grey's position had been very illogical indeed. His ignorance of Continental psychology had tempted him in the early days of his office to under-estimate the importance which would be attached abroad to "conversations" between General Staffs. His expert knowledge of Ministerial and Parliamentary psychology convinced him, on the other hand, that, once these conversations had been taken seriously by the foreigners, the Cabinet would be extremely annoyed at not having been informed at the time. . . . In wishing to come into the open, to show the solidarity and reliability of the Entente, Nicolson desired solely to avert a European war. Whereas Grey's apprehensions were disturbed by his simultaneous desire to avert a Parliamentary crisis.

I, 342, note 232. See also Graf Waldersee, "Von Deutschlands militärpolitischen Beziehungen zu Italian," in KSF, VII, 636-664, July, 1929.

I, 350. The reference to the myth of Germany's overwhelming superiority in numbers refers of course to the total forces available in Germany, and in France and Belgium at the beginning of the war, and not to the forces actually present in northeast France and Belgium at the moment of the German invasion. Germany had a great military advantage during the first weeks of the war owing to the fact that the French deployed their main forces eastward between Mezières and Belfort instead of northeast to stop a German sweep through Belgium, either because they did not feel sure that the Germans would come through Belgium rapidly, or because of diplomatic policy—the fear that a French deployment toward Belgium might look like a threat to Belgian neutrality—or because of the political and strategic hope of occupying quickly Alsace and Lorraine and so being *beati possidentes* in the peace negotiations at the close of a short war.

I, 357, note 6. On the assassination of King Alexander in 1903, see also D. A. Loncharevich, *Jugoslaviens Entstehung* (Vienna, 1929), pp. 318-323; and, for the hesitation of the Great Powers as to whether they should show their abhorrence of the crime by withdrawing their ministers from Belgrade, B.D., V, 124-148.

I, 360, note 9. For the details on Austria's economic intimidation of Serbia, see B.D., V, 148-167; and Joseph N. Baernreither, *Fragments of a Political Diary,* (edited and introduced by Joseph Redlich, London, 1930), chs. i-v, *passim.*

I, 367, note 20; 369, note 21. In connection with the negotiations for the Anglo-Russian Agreement of 1907 the question of the Straits was several times mentioned (B.D., IV, 254-5, 272, 279-284, 286-7, 289-291, 293-6, 414). The apparent contradiction between the statements of Sir Edward Grey and Izvolski on the one hand, and the contemporary evidence cited in note 20 on the other, is explained by the fact that, though the Straits were considerably discussed, they were not made the subject of formal negotiations for inclusion in the Agreement of 1907. On March 15, 1907, Grey said to Benckendorff, the Russian Ambassador in London:

"I had felt all through these negotiations that good relations with Russia meant that our old policy of closing the Straits against her, and throwing our weight against her at any conference of the Powers, must be abandoned. It was this old policy which, in my opinion, had been the root of the difficulties between the two countries for two generations. And, for us and Russia to settle our difficulties in Asia, and then to find ourselves afterwards in opposition on some other important matter, would be to undo the good which would be done by the present negotiations as to Asiatic frontiers.

I felt, however, that it would be difficult for us to put anything concerning the Straits in the form of an engagement, and it would be necessary for me to speak to the Prime Minister before I could say anything very definite" (B.D., IV, 280).

Four days later, in writing to Sir Arthur Nicolson at St. Petersburg, Grey pointed out some of the difficulties in acceding to Russian desires about the Straits. But Izvolski appears to have overlooked the difficulties and to have jumped eagerly at Grey's statement that the old policy of closing the Straits against Russia would have to be abandoned. Nicolson reported a few days later:

"M. Izvolski said that the conversation [reported from London] constituted to his mind a great evolution in the relations of the two countries, and that though the matter was one which would have to be most carefully considered from all points of view, especially as to the method and moment of advancing further in the question, still he was highly gratified with the tone and tenor of your remarks. . . . I have rarely seen M. Izvolski so contented and satisfied" (B.D., IV, 281-2).

And two days later, in a private letter to Grey, Nicolson repeated: "M. Izvolski is beaming with pleasure over the report which Poklewsky brought to him of your communication to Count Benckendorff in regard to the Bosphorus and the Dardanelles. He quite grasped the sense of your observations and will study the question thoroughly before making an overture; but the fact that the British Government are willing to discuss the question is, he considers, and as he expressed it, a great evolution in our relations and a historical event" (B.D., IV, 283-4). The importance of these conversations lies in the optimism with which Izvolski felt encouraged to proceed to the Buchlau negotiations (without informing England beforehand), and in the pessimistic despair with which he learned on visting England after Buchlau that Grey refused after all to concede opening the Straits to Russian warships alone, according to Izvolski's plan, as I have indicated on pp. 380-1.

I, 368-378. The Buchlau Meeting, and the preliminaries leading up to it, can now be followed in great detail from the Austrian side in Oe.-U.A., I, 1-92. Baron Taube, p. 173 ff., adds some light from the Russian side. But precisely what was said cannot be exactly determined and probably never can be. It had been agreed at Buchlau by Izvolski and Aehrenthal that Izvolski should make a memorandum of their conversations at Buchlau and submit it to Aehrenthal. Unfortunately Izvolski neglected to do this at once. He had not even done it at the time of his return to St. Petersburg six weeks later at the end of October (Oe.-U.A., I, 90, 144, 252). By this time, however, he had learned to his great sorrow that he would be unable, on account of Sir Edward Grey's attitude and on account of domestic criticism in Russia, to pocket his expected share of the Buchlau bargain; his chagrin seems to have warped his recollection of what was said at Buchlau. Aehrenthal also drew up a memorandum of the Buchlau conversations (Oe.-U.A., I, 86-92), but it is not clear that it was strictly contemporary.

I, 378-406. On the long Bosnian Crisis of 1908-09 and its immediate consequences, see Oe.-U.A., I, 92-895; II, 1-285; B.D., V, 366-815; and Harold Nicolson, *Lord Carnock,* chs. x, xi; he points out (p. 311 f.) that it is not true to say that Sir Arthur Nicolson was at the bottom of Izvolski's resistance. And in fact we know that at the end of the crisis Izvolski suddenly capitulated without waiting to hear his advice—much to Nicolson's regret (*cf.* B.D., V, 736-7). Nicolson was also properly and shrewdly skeptical as to Izvolski's account the Buchlau affair; on Jan. 2, 1909, for instance, he wrote confidentially to Grey:

"At the time the preliminary explanations which M. Izvolski gave me did not seem to me to be quite convincing. . . . and it may be that M. Izvolski committed himself a little further than he is willing to admit. His position on the question is a little tangled and hampered by various secret arrangements which seem to be emerging piecemeal into publicity, concluded between Russia and Austria-Hungary; but it would create a painful impression here if it were believed that during M. Izvolski's tenure of office, and after the Sanjak railway incident, *pourparlers* had taken place in respect to the incorporation of Bosnia and Herzegovina" (B.D., V, 547-8).

I, 413-426. On Izvolski's efforts to open the Straits in 1911, see the documents between Nov. 4 and Dec. 30, 1911, listed in D.D.F., 3me Série, I, pp. xxif.

I, 439, note 155. For English complaints of Hartwig's earlier unreliability and aggressive attitude in Persia, see B.D., IV, 199 ff., 403 ff., 420, 425 f., 588 f., 598; and for numerous references to Austria's suspicions of his later Russian intrigues in Belgrade, see the index volume, Oe.-U.A., IX, 53, under "Hartwig."

The Balkan Wars and the other remaining topics in my chapter on "Balkan Problems" are now illustrated in great detail from the Austrian side in Oe.-U.A., IV-VII, *passim;* and from the Serbian side in *Die Auswärtige Politik Serbiens* (edited by M. Bogitchevitch, Berlin, 1929), II, *passim.*

INDEX

Adamov, E. A., i. 361, 372, 415, 481, 487, 498.
Abdul Aziz, Sultan of Morocco, i. 156, 160, 182ff., 246.
Abdul Hamid, Sultan of Turkey, i. 66, 127, 427.
Abyssinia, i., 144.
Adlerberg, General, ii. 301.
Adrianople, i. 338, 439, 466, 512ff., 530.
Ægean Islands, i. 460, 465.
Aehrenthal, Count, i. 251ff., 360, 368ff., 386ff., 394f.; ii. 9, 11, 26.
Afghanistan, i. 217, 220, 227.
Africa, partition of, i. 45, 80ff., 85f., 99, 109, 111, 125, 128, 140, 142ff.; see also Tripoli, Morocco.
Agadir, i. 31, 223, 250, 275, 277ff., 312f., 330.
Agram (Zagreb), ii. 112, 231; treason trial at, i. 400; ii. 55, 92.
Albania, i. 150, 338, 340, 347, 360, 365, 406, 430, 439-444, 451, 463-474; ii. 14, 183f.
Albert, King of Belgium, ii. 541f.
Albin, P., i. 278.
Alexander I, Tsar, i. 55.
Alexander II, Tsar, i. 54ff., 96f.
Alexander III, Tsar, i. 77, 90f., 105ff., 111ff., 174; ii. 280, 480.
Alexander of Battenberg, Prince of Bulgaria, i. 76.
Alexander I, Obrenovitch, i. 357; assassination of, in 1903, ii. 58f., 63, 78f., 86, 142.
Alexander, Prince Regent of Serbia, ii. 59, 143, 145.
Algeciras, i. 150f., 189, 202, 227, 246, 248, 278f., 281f., 312, 330, 344.
Algeria, i. 157, 246.
Alliances and Ententes, in general, i. 34ff., 50ff., 329ff., 346ff.; ii. 380f.; see also Treaties and Conventions; Three Emperors (1872), 53-59; (1881), i. 70f., 105; Austro-

German (1879), i. 34, 68ff., 83, 119, 342ff.; ii. 17; Austro-Serbian (1881), i. 89, 356; Austro-German-Italian (1882), i. 25, 34f., 80ff., 105, 110f, 118ff., 132, 138ff., 215ff., 448ff.; renewals of, i. 106, 111, 142ff., 342ff., 547ff.; Art. VII of, i. 142ff., 408, 548f., ii. 258f.; in opposition to Triple Entente, i. 223ff., 347ff., 397f., 434ff., 509ff.; ii. *passim;* change in character of, i. 224ff., 342ff.; weakness of, i. 224, 243ff., 342ff., 409; ii. 184; text of, i. 547-551; Austro-Rumanian (1883), i. 88f., 426f., 475ff., 494ff.; ii. 17, 191ff., 214ff.; Russo-German (1887, "Reinsurance"), i. 77ff., 90ff., 102, 105, 108f; Franco-Russian (1891-94), 24, 34, 70, 79f., 85ff., 93, 105ff., 132, 139, 167, 176f., 214ff., 316; ii. 279f.; change in character of, i. 224ff., 316, 330ff., 532, and see Triple Entente; text of, i. 118; Anglo-French (1904), ii. 162ff., 179f., 189, 192f.; Russo-German (1905, Björkö), i. 174ff., 190f.; Anglo-Russian (1907), i. 214ff., 251, 367f.; ii. 328, 357, 379; Triple Entente, i. 25, 34f., 148, 219, 222, 276, 302ff., 312ff., 346ff., 397f.; in opposition to Triple Alliance, i. 223ff., 346ff., 434ff., 509ff., 539f.; ii. 191ff., and *passim;* efforts to tighten, i. 312ff., 397f., 434ff., 529ff.; ii. 278ff., and *passim;* Serbo-Bulgarian (1912), i. 430ff.
Alsace-Lorraine, i. 24ff., 51ff., 81, 97, 99ff., 113, 119, 122, 132, 152, 168, 173, 190, 226f., 313f., 532; ii. 283, 367.
Anarchists, ii. 76, 95.
Andrássy, Count Julius, i. 55, 57f., 61ff., 68, 83.
Anglo-German naval rivalry, i. 233ff., 256ff., 293ff.

565

DATE DUE

FEB 13 '73		
MAR 2 '73		
APR 18 '73		
JA 29 '79		
AP 10 '79		
AP 24 '79		
FE 17 '82		
MR 3 '82		
MR 24 '82		
AP 19 '82		
FEB 1 '84		
FE 21 '84		
JAN 22 '87		
FEB 21 '89		